D0382642

# HUMAN RIGHTS: INTERNATIONAL DOCUMENTS

# Human Rights:
## International documents

by

James Avery Joyce
B.Sc.Econ., Ph.D., LL.D., former Staff Member,
United Nations Headquarters and UNESCO

Volume I

1978
SIJTHOFF & NOORDHOFF – ALPHEN AAN DEN RIJN
OCEANA PUBLICATIONS, INC. – DOBBS FERRY, N.Y.

ISBN 90 286 0298 4 (Sijthoff & Noordhoff)
ISBN 0-379-20395-2 (Oceana)



Printed in The Netherlands.

For my learned friend

Peter Benenson

Barrister,

Founder of Amnesty International

ACKNOWLEDGMENTS

The Publisher and Editor respectfully convey their indebtedness to the United Nations, whose publications and other documents in the field of human rights form the major part of these volumes; but, since these pages are numbered consecutively, for reference purposes, throughout the three volumes, the original pagination has, where necessary, been omitted or adjusted accordingly.

TABLE OF CONTENTS

## VOLUME I

## THE MAIN INSTRUMENTS



## VOLUME II

## SELECTED TOPICS

## VOLUME III

## INTERGOVERNMENTAL AND NON-GOVERNMENTAL ORGANISATIONS

# PREFACE

Since the story of human rights is commensurate with the history of mankind on this planet, there is really no place where a documented account of their development can logically begin. Scholars who, at the beginning of this century, were inclined to regard human rights as a branch of modern international law, soon began to push back their enquiries into the politics of the specific national declarations which inspired the American and French revolutions of the late eighteenth century; then further back, through the English Bill of Rights, a century earlier, to the Magna Carta of 1215; finally, stopping somewhere in their European search for origins with Plato and even his Hellenic predecessors. More recently, perhaps, origins have been sought in what Professor Breasted called the 'dawn of conscience' in Ancient Egypt or the already ancient code chiselled on the Stele of Hammurábi in Babylonia. Nowadays, under the impact of the Third World's claims, more and more learned treatises in the field are asking questions about African and Asian folk custom.

But for reasons of time and space, a much simpler task has been imposed on the editor of these three volumes. About the beginning of what can roughly be termed the modern 'movement of human rights' there can be little doubt. It derives its sanction and inspiration from the Universal Declaration, adopted by the United Nations General Assembly on the 10th December, 1948. From that point, our documents proliferate in ever widening circles, and, as the preceding Table of Contents shows, cover practically every subject under the sun.

Who would have thought that within three decades such a treasure house of ideas and concepts would have been assembled and expanded to cover every nation and practically every topic of human intercourse? More important still is the fact of this expanding code of *common standards* having been arrived at through the arduous and often tortuous process of agreement or consensus between some one hundred and fifty sovereign states! But this has indeed happened. And it will go on like this. For the application, in contrast to the formulation, of human rights is only just beginning for most nations and peoples.

Yet, even if the present selection has to cover only thirty years of growth, the problems entailed in selecting from such an *embarras de richesses* can only be solved by adopting some working criteria. In short, starting with the former Universal Declaration and concentrating on the international plane, we can show in Volume I how the main Conventions and other Instruments have emerged from the principles and standards laid down in it. Then we can branch out into its more diversified progeny in Volume II.

So far we are dealing with the United Nations as the main creator, or 'organ', of human rights; but, seeing that the UN is a collectivity of governments, a wide range of activities by governments are recorded in these two volumes. Volume III carries forward the record of inter-governmental action into various functional and regional fields. But, most importantly, this third volume also carries the investigation beyond governments, as such, and explores the ever broadening area of non-governmental action.

It might be questioned, however, why the United Nations documents form so large a part of this collection, when there are other types of documents in existence. The chief reasons for this focussing upon UN texts are four in number: first, because it is probably the most comprehensive documentation to have at one's finger tips; second, it is material that has passed through the crucible of intense public debate and general acceptance; third, it includes a considerable range of different attitudes and positions taken by individual governments; and lastly, in many of these documents — see, for example, Volume II, Chapter 2 on 'Science and Technology' — a considerable number of private sources are cited and commented upon, which cannot be found in official international instruments themselves.

Taken altogether, the documents assembled in these three Volumes will provide the serious researcher not only with the actual texts of specific documents, but, if he resorts to the Index, with a *vade mecum* of ideas, concepts, legal definitions, and draft proposals, which have created, over barely three decades, both an internationally recognised code of State practice and a depository of programmes and developments which have opened a new era in human rights for mankind, or, at least, prepared a guide map for the new Century.

JAMES AVERY JOYCE

Geneva, March 1978

# VOLUME I

## *THE MAIN INSTRUMENTS*

### INTRODUCTION

As the Table of Contents indicates, this Volume consists of the 'basics' on which all the other documents rest. Chapter 1 contains all the International Instruments which have emerged from the Universal Declaration of 1948, up to 1974. Chapter 2 consists of a detailed commentary upon those Instruments, entitled 'UN Action in the Field of Human Rights'. The advantage of this commentary is that it arranges the rights recorded in Chapter 1 under subject headings. Chapter 3 brings up to the end of 1977 the list of rights documents enumerated in Chapters 1 and 2. Chapter 4 includes some short pieces, which do not fall into the longer categories dealt with later in Volume II, but which are of special interest because they are not generally accorded the attention they deserve as topics of major study.

It will be seen from the Secretary General's Foreword in Chapter 1 that all these Instruments (including various Declarations) stem from the Articles of the United Nations Charter that he cites. They are arranged under fourteen headings (listed as A to N). The last ten pages contain a list of the Instruments in order of adoption up to 1971. (This list, as stated above, is supplemented by the further accessions or adoptions up to 1977, set out briefly in our Appendix A).

Although various reports and other documents selected for our second volume fill in the background and other details on some of the most important of the foregoing Instruments, Chapter 2 in this Volume summarises a good deal of useful information, about both the origins and the implementation of those Instruments. It should be explained that the actual publications reproduced in Chapters 1 and 2 are now under revision by the United Nations for republication in 1978 or later; but the most significant of those expected revisions have been added by this compiler in Chapter 3 and at other appropriate points in the present Volume.

There are two Appendices to this Volume. One is a single page summary of the Instruments in force in order of date up to the end of 1977. The other reproduces the Contents pages of the periodical Bulletins published since 1969 by the UN Division of Human Rights. They form a quick ready-reference list showing the titles of all the relevant documents published during this period, covering a decade. Many of the titles so listed refer to documents included *in extenso* or in part in these Volumes.

A final note should be included to draw special attention to the existence of the *Year Book on Human Rights*, which is now published by the United Nations in biennial editions. This is an invaluable handbook, for which, however, there is no space for reproductions in the present Volumes. Each edition contains some three hundred pages on national developments, followed by a detailed summary of UN and international developments. It should be consulted by researchers, if for no other purpose than to examine current data relating to specific countries.

*CHAPTER 1*

# INTERNATIONAL INSTRUMENTS

The following Instruments are contained in a compilation published by the United Nations for the twenty-fifth anniversary of the Universal Declaration in 1973, arranged under some fourteen headings. The full text of each Declaration, Covenant, or Convention is given. The subsequent four years (up to 1977) are dealt with in Chapter 3 of this Volume.

It will be seen that the 'International Bill of Rights' in Section A lays a sure foundation for all that follows. It was well that this collection should begin with the Universal Declaration of 1948, since the Declaration is of unparallelled importance in marking the progress of humanity towards a more stable and rational world order. It is an historical turning point in affirming that, henceforth, the individual is no longer merely an object, but indeed the subject of international law. The two international Covenants and the optional Protocol that follow the Declaration in this first Section are now in force as international law, as will be indicated in the later documents reproduced in Chapter 3.

Certain critics of these basic instruments, which were adopted by the UN General Assembly as long ago as 1966, suggest that, being mainly inspired by Western theories of law and 'colonialist' political ideas, this Bill of Rights is less relevant to the developing countries, who have come more recently into the world arena. For that reason we have stressed in Volume II many of the economic and social implications of human rights, as they affect the developing peoples, but which are less evident in the formal legal Instruments reproduced in this Chapter. More detailed documents are also included in Volume II amplifying the basic texts on decolonisation and racial discrimination, which appear in Sections C and D.

Attention is also drawn to the Conventions, in such Sections as I and J, that relate to the trade union, the employment rights of workers. These are taken up again in Volume III, which considers the ILO as an intergovernmental organisation.

Finally, connoisseurs of human rights will not overlook the somewhat novel International Right of Correction in Section H or the Right to Enjoy Culture in Section N.

1948
1973

Twenty-fifth Anniversary
of the
UNIVERSAL DECLARATION
OF HUMAN RIGHTS

# HUMAN RIGHTS

## A COMPILATION
## OF INTERNATIONAL INSTRUMENTS
## OF THE UNITED NATIONS

UNITED NATIONS
New York, 1973

## NOTE

Symbols of United Nations documents are composed of capital letters combined with figures. Mention of such a symbol indicates a reference to a United Nations document.

ST/HR/1

UNITED NATIONS PUBLICATION

Sales No.: E.73.XIV.2

Price: $U.S. 3.00

(or equivalent in other currencies)

# FOREWORD

On the occasion of the International Year for Human Rights and the International Conference on Human Rights in 1968 the Division of Human Rights of the United Nations Secretariat prepared a compilation of international instruments relating to human rights,[1] which consisted of the texts of conventions, declarations and certain recommendations adopted by the United Nations up to 31 December 1966. It also included a number of instruments adopted by two specialized agencies of the United Nations, the International Labour Organisation and the United Nations Educational, Scientific and Cultural Organization.

The General Assembly in its resolution 2906 (XXVII) of 19 October 1972, recalling that on 10 December 1973 the world community would celebrate the twenty-fifth anniversary of the Universal Declaration of Human Rights, expressed the hope that this anniversary would be celebrated in a manner which would fit the occasion and serve the cause of human rights. This revised edition of the compilation is issued as a contribution to the observance of the anniversary of the Declaration. Instruments adopted up to 31 December 1972 have been included.

Each of these instruments stems from the United Nations Charter, in which the peoples of the United Nations reaffirmed their faith in fundamental human rights, in the dignity and worth of the human person and in the equal rights of men and women, and determined to promote social progress and better standards of life in larger freedom. One of the Purposes of the United Nations, as stated in Article 1 (3) is "To achieve international cooperation in solving international problems of an economic, social, cultural or humanitarian character, and in promoting and encouraging respect for human rights and for fundamental freedoms for all without distinction as to race, sex, language, or religion". Article 1 (4) states that the Organization is "To be a centre for harmonizing the actions of nations in the attainment of these common ends". Chapter IX of the Charter, on international economic and social co-operation, provides in Article 55 that "With a view to the creation of conditions of stability and well-being which are necessary for peaceful and friendly relations among nations based on respect for the principle of equal rights and self-determination of peoples, the United Nations shall promote: . . . c. universal respect for, and observance of, human rights and fundamental freedoms for all without distinction as to race, sex, language, or religion." Article 56 states that "All Members pledge themselves to take joint and separate action in cooperation with the Organization for the achievement of the purposes set forth in Article 55". Article 76 states that "The basic objectives of the trusteeship system, in accordance with the Purposes of the United Nations laid down in Article 1 of the present Charter, shall be: . . . c. to encourage respect for human rights and for fundamental freedoms for all without distinction as to race, sex, language, or religion, and to encourage recognition of the interdependence of the peoples of the world".

Instruments in the present compilation are arranged under the following headings:

A. The International Bill of Human Rights
B. The Proclamation of Teheran
C. The Right of Self-Determination
D. Prevention of Discrimination
E. War Crimes and Crimes against Humanity, including Genocide
F. Slavery, Servitude, Forced Labour and similar Institutions and Practices
G. Nationality, Statelessness, Asylum and Refugees
H. Freedom of Information
I. Freedom of Association
J. Employment Policy
K. Political Rights of Women
L. Marriage and the Family, Childhood and Youth
M. Social Welfare, Progress and Development
N. Right to Enjoy Culture; International Cultural Development and Co-operation

Wherever an international convention has come into force, the date of entry into force is indicated. The compilation also contains a list of the instruments included, arranged by chronological order of adoption.

It is hoped that this compilation will prove to be of value to all those interested in the promotion and protection of human rights and fundamental freedoms, in particular to those taking an active part in the observance of the twenty-fifth anniversary of the Universal Declaration of Human Rights.

---

[1] *Human Rights: A Compilation of International Instruments of the United Nations* (United Nations publication, Sales No.: E.68.XIV.6).

## CONTENTS

---

# A. THE INTERNATIONAL BILL OF HUMAN RIGHTS

## 1. Universal Declaration of Human Rights

**Adopted and proclaimed by General Assembly resolution 217 A (III) of 10 December 1948**

### *Preamble*

*Whereas* recognition of the inherent dignity and of the equal and inalienable rights of all members of the human family is the foundation of freedom, justice and peace in the world,

*Whereas* disregard and contempt for human rights have resulted in barbarous acts which have outraged the conscience of mankind, and the advent of a world in which human beings shall enjoy freedom of speech and belief and freedom from fear and want has been proclaimed as the highest aspiration of the common people,

*Whereas* it is essential, if man is not to be compelled to have recourse, as a last resort, to rebellion against tyranny and oppression, that human rights should be protected by the rule of law,

*Whereas* it is essential to promote the development of friendly relations between nations,

*Whereas* the peoples of the United Nations have in the Charter reaffirmed their faith in fundamental human rights, in the dignity and worth of the human person and in the equal rights of men and women and have determined to promote social progress and better standards of life in larger freedom,

*Whereas* Member States have pledged themselves to achieve, in co-operation with the United Nations, the promotion of universal respect for and observance of human rights and fundamental freedoms,

*Whereas* a common understanding of these rights and freedoms is of the greatest importance for the full realization of this pledge,

*Now, therefore,*

*The General Assembly*

*Proclaims* this Universal Declaration of Human Rights as a common standard of achievement for all peoples and all nations, to the end that every individual and every organ of society, keeping this Declaration constantly in mind, shall strive by teaching and education to promote respect for these rights and freedoms and by progressive measures, national and international to secure their universal and effective recognition and observance, both among the peoples of Member States themselves and among the peoples of territories under their jurisdiction.

### *Article 1*

All human beings are born free and equal in dignity and rights. They are endowed with reason and conscience and should act towards one another in a spirit of brotherhood.

### *Article 2*

Everyone is entitled to all the rights and freedoms set forth in this Declaration, without distinction of any kind, such as race, colour, sex, language, religion, political or other opinion, national or social origin, property, birth or other status.

Furthermore, no distinction shall be made on the basis of the political, jurisdictional or international status of the country or territory to which a person belongs, whether it be independent, trust, non-self-governing or under any other limitation of sovereignty.

### *Article 3*

Everyone has the right to life, liberty and the security of person.

### *Article 4*

No one shall be held in slavery or servitude; slavery and the slave trade shall be prohibited in all their forms.

### *Article 5*

No one shall be subjected to torture or to cruel, inhuman or degrading treatment or punishment.

### *Article 6*

Everyone has the right to recognition everywhere as a person before the law.

### *Article 7*

All are equal before the law and are entitled without any discrimination to equal protection of the law. All are entitled to equal protection against any discrimination in violation of this Declaration and against any incitement to such discrimination.

### *Article 8*

Everyone has the right to an effective remedy by the competent national tribunals for acts violating the fundamental rights granted him by the constitution or by law.

### *Article 9*

No one shall be subjected to arbitrary arrest, detention or exile.

### *Article 10*

Everyone is entitled in full equality to a fair and public hearing by an independent and impartial tribunal, in the determination of his rights and obligations and of any criminal charge against him.

*Article 11*

1. Everyone charged with a penal offence has the right to be presumed innocent until proved guilty according to law in a public trial at which he has had all the guarantees necessary for his defence.

2. No one shall be held guilty of any penal offence on account of any act or omission which did not constitute a penal offence, under national or international law, at the time when it was commited. Nor shall a heavier penalty be imposed than the one that was applicable at the time the penal offence was committed.

*Article 12*

No one shall be subjected to arbitrary interference with his privacy, family, home or correspondence, nor to attacks upon his honour and reputation. Everyone has the right to the protection of the law against such interference or attacks.

*Article 13*

1. Everyone has the right to freedom of movement and residence within the borders of each State.

2. Everyone has the right to leave any country, including his own, and to return to his country.

*Article 14*

1. Everyone has the right to seek and to enjoy in other countries asylum from persecution.

2. This right may not be invoked in the case of prosecutions genuinely arising from non-political crimes or from acts contrary to the purposes and principles of the United Nations.

*Article 15*

1. Everyone has the right to a nationality.

2. No one shall be arbitrarily deprived of his nationality nor denied the right to change his nationality.

*Article 16*

1. Men and women of full age, without any limitation due to race, nationality or religion, have the right to marry and to found a family. They are entitled to equal rights as to marriage, during marriage and at its dissolution.

2. Marriage shall be entered into only with the free and full consent of the intending spouses.

3. The family is the natural and fundamental group unit of society and is entitled to protection by society and the State.

*Article 17*

1. Everyone has the right to own property alone as well as in association with others.

2. No one shall be arbitrarily deprived of his property.

*Article 18*

Everyone has the right to freedom of thought, conscience and religion; this right includes freedom to change his religion or belief, and freedom, either alone or in community with others and in public or private, to manifest his religion or belief in teaching, practice, worship and observance.

*Article 19*

Everyone has the right to freedom of opinion and expression; this right includes freedom to hold opinions without interference and to seek, receive and impart information and ideas through any media and regardless of frontiers.

*Article 20*

1. Everyone has the right to freedom of peaceful assembly and association.

2. No one may be compelled to belong to an association.

*Article 21*

1. Everyone has the right to take part in the government of his country, directly or through freely chosen representatives.

2. Everyone has the right of equal access to public service in his country.

3. The will of the people shall be the basis of the authority of government; this will shall be expressed in periodic and genuine elections which shall be by universal and equal suffrage and shall be held by secret vote or by equivalent free voting procedures.

*Article 22*

Everyone, as a member of society, has the right to social security and is entitled to realization, through national effort and international co-operation and in accordance with the organization and resources of each State, of the economic, social and cultural rights indispensable for his dignity and the free development of his personality.

*Article 23*

1. Everyone has the right to work, to free choice of employment, to just and favourable conditions of work and to protection against unemployment.

2. Everyone, without any discrimination, has the right to equal pay for equal work.

3. Everyone who works has the right to just and favourable remuneration ensuring for himself and his family an existence worthy of human dignity, and supplemented, if necessary, by other means of social protection.

4. Everyone has the right to form and to join trade unions for the protection of his interests.

*Article 24*

Everyone has the right to rest and leisure, including reasonable limitation of working hours and periodic holidays with pay.

*Article 25*

1. Everyone has the right to a standard of living adequate for the health and well-being of himself and of his family, including food, clothing, housing and medical

care and necessary social services, and the right to security in the event of unemployment, sickness, disability, widowhood, old age or other lack of livelihood in circumstances beyond his control.

2. Motherhood and childhood are entitled to special care and assistance. All children, whether born in or out of wedlock, shall enjoy the same social protection.

*Article 26*

1. Everyone has the right to education. Education shall be free, at least in the elementary and fundamental stages. Elementary education shall be compulsory. Technical and professional education shall be made generally available and higher education shall be equally accessible to all on the basis of merit.

2. Education shall be directed to the full development of the human personality and to the strengthening of respect for human rights and fundamental freedoms. It shall promote understanding, tolerance and friendship among all nations, racial or religious groups, and shall further the activities of the United Nations for the maintenance of peace.

3. Parents have a prior right to choose the kind of education that shall be given to their children.

*Article 27*

1. Everyone has the right freely to participate in the cultural life of the community, to enjoy the arts and to share in scientific advancement and its benefits.

2. Everyone has the right to the protection of the moral and material interests resulting from any scientific, literary or artistic production of which he is the author.

*Article 28*

Everyone is entitled to a social and international order in which the rights and freedoms set forth in this Declaration can be fully realized.

*Article 29*

1. Everyone has duties to the community in which alone the free and full development of his personality is possible.

2. In the exercise of his rights and freedoms, everyone shall be subject only to such limitations as are determined by law solely for the purpose of securing due recognition and respect for the rights and freedoms of others and of meeting the just requirements of morality, public order and the general welfare in a democratic society.

3. These rights and freedoms may in no case be exercised contrary to the purposes and principles of the United Nations.

*Article 30*

Nothing in this Declaration may be interpreted as implying for any State, group or person any right to engage in any activity or to perform any act aimed at the destruction of any of the rights and freedoms set forth herein.

## 2. International Covenant on Economic, Social and Cultural Rights

**Adopted and opened for signature, ratification and accession by General Assembly resolution 2200 A (XXI) of 16 December 1966**

***Entry into force*:** Not in force as of 31 December 1972 (see article 27).

PREAMBLE

*The States Parties to the present Covenant,*

*Considering* that, in accordance with the principles proclaimed in the Charter of the United Nations, recognition of the inherent dignity and of the equal and inalienable rights of all members of the human family is the foundation of freedom, justice and peace in the world,

*Recognizing* that these rights derive from the inherent dignity of the human person,

*Recognizing* that, in accordance with the Universal Declaration of Human Rights, the ideal of free human beings enjoying freedom from fear and want can only be achieved if conditions are created whereby everyone may enjoy his economic, social and cultural rights, as well as his civil and political rights,

*Considering* the obligation of States under the Charter of the United Nations to promote universal respect for, and observance of, human rights and freedoms,

*Realizing* that the individual, having duties to other individuals and to the community to which he belongs, is under a responsibility, to strive for the promotion and observance of the rights recognized in the present Covenant,

*Agree* upon the following articles:

PART I

*Article 1*

1. All peoples have the right of self-determination. By virtue of that right they freely determine their political status and freely pursue their economic, social and cultural development.

2. All peoples may, for their own ends, freely dispose of their natural wealth and resources without prejudice to any obligations arising out of international economic co-operation, based upon the principle of mutual benefit, and international law. In no case may a people be deprived of its own means of subsistence.

3. The States Parties to the present Covenant, including those having responsibility for the administration of Non-Self-Governing and Trust Territories, shall promote the realization of the right of self-determination, and shall respect that right, in conformity with the provisions of the Charter of the United Nations.

PART II

*Article 2*

1. Each State Party to the present Covenant undertakes to take steps, individually and through international assistance and co-operation, especially economic and technical, to the maximum of its available resources,

with a view to achieving progressively the full realization of the rights recognized in the present Covenant by all appropriate means, including particularly the adoption of legislative measures.

2. The States Parties to the present Covenant undertake to guarantee that the rights enunciated in the present Covenant will be exercised without discrimination of any kind as to race, colour, sex, language, religion, political or other opinion, national or social origin, property, birth or other status.

3. Developing countries, with due regard to human rights and their national economy, may determine to what extent they would guarantee the economic rights recognized in the present Covenant to non-nationals.

*Article 3*

The States Parties to the present Covenant undertake to ensure the equal right of men and women to the enjoyment of all economic, social and cultural rights set forth in the present Covenant.

*Article 4*

The States Parties to the present Covenant recognize that, in the enjoyment of those rights provided by the State in conformity with the present Covenant, the State may subject such rights only to such limitations as are determined by law only in so far as this may be compatible with the nature of these rights and solely for the purpose of promoting the general welfare in a democratic society.

*Article 5*

1. Nothing in the present Covenant may be interpreted as implying for any State, group or person any right to engage in any activity or to perform any act aimed at the destruction of any of the rights or freedoms recognized herein, or at their limitation to a greater extent than is provided for in the present Covenant.

2. No restriction upon or derogation from any of the fundamental human rights recognized or existing in any country in virtue of law, conventions, regulations or custom shall be admitted on the pretext that the present Covenant does not recognize such rights or that it recognizes them to a lesser extent.

PART III

*Article 6*

1. The States Parties to the present Covenant recognize the right to work, which includes the right of everyone to the opportunity to gain his living by work which he freely chooses or accepts, and will take appropriate steps to safeguard this right.

2. The steps to be taken by a State Party to the present Covenant to achieve the full realization of this right shall include technical and vocational guidance and training programmes, policies and techniques to achieve steady economic, social and cultural development and full and productive employment under conditions safeguarding fundamental political and economic freedoms to the individual.

*Article 7*

The States Parties to the present Covenant recognize the right of everyone to the enjoyment of just and favourable conditions of work which ensure, in particular:

(*a*) Remuneration which provides all workers, as a minimum, with:

(i) Fair wages and equal remuneration for work of equal value without distinction of any kind, in particular women being guaranteed conditions of work not inferior to those enjoyed by men, with equal pay for equal work;

(ii) A decent living for themselves and their families in accordance with the provisions of the present Covenant;

(*b*) Safe and healthy working conditions;

(*c*) Equal opportunity for everyone to be promoted in his employment to an appropriate higher level, subject to no considerations other than those of seniority and competence;

(*d*) Rest, leisure and reasonable limitation of working hours and periodic holidays with pay, as well as remuneration for public holidays.

*Article 8*

1. The States Parties to the present Covenant undertake to ensure:

(*a*) The right of everyone to form trade unions and join the trade union of his choice, subject only to the rules of the organization concerned, for the promotion and protection of his economic and social interests. No restrictions may be placed on the exercise of this right other than those prescribed by law and which are necessary in a democratic society in the interests of national security or public order or for the protection of the rights and freedoms of others;

(*b*) The right of trade unions to establish national federations or confederations and the right of the latter to form or join international trade-union organizations;

(*c*) The right of trade unions to function freely subject to no limitations other than those prescribed by law and which are necessary in a democratic society in the interests of national security or public order or for the protection of the rights and freedoms of others;

(*d*) The right to strike, provided that it is exercised in conformity with the laws of the particular country.

2. This article shall not prevent the imposition of lawful restrictions on the exercise of these rights by members of the armed forces or of the police or of the administration of the State.

3. Nothing in this article shall authorize States Parties to the International Labour Organisation Convention of 1948 concerning Freedom of Association and Protection of the Right to Organize to take legislative measures which would prejudice, or apply the law in such a manner as would prejudice, the guarantees provided for in that Convention.

*Article 9*

The States Parties to the present Covenant recognize the right of everyone to social security, including social insurance.

*Article 10*

The States Parties to the present Covenant recognize that:

1. The widest possible protection and assistance should be accorded to the family, which is the natural and fundamental group unit of society, particularly for its establishment and while it is responsible for the care and education of dependent children. Marriage must be entered into with the free consent of the intending spouses.

2. Special protection should be accorded to mothers during a reasonable period before and after childbirth. During such period working mothers should be accorded paid leave or leave with adequate social security benefits.

3. Special measures of protection and assistance should be taken on behalf of all children and young persons without any discrimination for reasons of parentage or other conditions. Children and young persons should be protected from economic and social exploitation. Their employment in work harmful to their morals or health or dangerous to life or likely to hamper their normal development should be punishable by law. States should also set age limits below which the paid employment of child labour should be prohibited and punishable by law.

*Article 11*

1. The States Parties to the present Covenant recognize the right of everyone to an adequate standard of living for himself and his family, including adequate food, clothing and housing, and to the continuous improvement of living conditions. The States Parties will take appropriate steps to ensure the realization of this right, recognizing to this effect the essential importance of international co-operation based on free consent.

2. The States Parties of the present Covenant, recognizing the fundamental right of everyone to be free from hunger, shall take, individually and through international co-operation, the measures, including specific programmes, which are needed:

(*a*) To improve methods of production, conservation and distribution of food by making full use of technical and scientific knowledge, by disseminating knowledge of the principles of nutrition and by developing or reforming agrarian systems in such a way as to achieve the most efficient development and utilization of natural resources;

(*b*) Taking into account the problems of both food-importing and food-exporting countries, to ensure an equitable distribution of world food supplies in relation to need.

*Article 12*

1. The States Parties to the present Covenant recognize the right of everyone to the enjoyment of the highest attainable standard of physical and mental health.

2. The steps to be taken by the States Parties to the present Covenant to achieve the full realization of this right shall include those necessary for:

(*a*) The provision for the reduction of the stillbirth-rate and of infant mortality and for the healthy development of the child;

(*b*) The improvement of all aspects of environmental and industrial hygiene;

(*c*) The prevention, treatment and control of epidemic, endemic, occupational and other diseases;

(*d*) The creation of conditions which would assure to all medical service and medical attention in the event of sickness.

*Article 13*

1. The States Parties to the present Covenant recognize the right of everyone to education. They agree that education shall be directed to the full development of the human personality and the sense of its dignity, and shall strengthen the respect for human rights and fundamental freedoms. They further agree that education shall enable all persons to participate effectively in a free society, promote understanding, tolerance and friendship among all nations and all racial, ethnic or religious groups, and further the activities of the United Nations for the maintenance of peace.

2. The States Parties to the present Covenant recognize that, with a view to achieving the full realization of this right:

(*a*) Primary education shall be compulsory and available free to all;

(*b*) Secondary education in its different forms, including technical and vocational secondary education, shall be made generally available and accessible to all by every appropriate means, and in particular by the progressive introduction of free education;

(*c*) Higher education shall be made equally accessible to all, on the basis of capacity, by every appropriate means, and in particular by the progressive introduction of free education;

(*d*) Fundamental education shall be encouraged or intensified as far as possible for those persons who have not received or completed the whole period of their primary education;

(*e*) The development of a system of schools at all levels shall be actively pursued, an adequate fellowship system shall be established, and the material conditions of teaching staff shall be continuously improved.

3. The States Parties to the present Covenant undertake to have respect for the liberty of parents and, when applicable, legal guardians to choose for their children schools, other than those established by the public authorities, which conform to such minimum educational standards as may be laid down or approved by the State and to ensure the religious and moral education of their children in conformity with their own convictions.

4. No part of this article shall be construed so as to interfere with the liberty of individuals and bodies to establish and direct educational institutions, subject always to the observance of the principles set forth in paragraph 1 of this article and to the requirement that the education given in such institutions shall conform to such minimum standards as may be laid down by the State.

*Article 14*

Each State Party to the present Covenant which, at the time of becoming a Party, has not been able to secure in its metropolitan territory or other territories under its jurisdiction compulsory primary education, free of charge, undertakes, within two years, to work out and adopt a detailed plan of action for the progressive implementation, within a reasonable number of years, to be fixed in the plan, of the principle of compulsory education free of charge for all.

*Article 15*

1. The States Parties to the present Covenant recognize the right of everyone:

(*a*) To take part in cultural life;

(*b*) To enjoy the benefits of scientific progress and its applications;

(*c*) To benefit from the protection of the moral and material interests resulting from any scientific, literary or artistic production of which he is the author.

2. The steps to be taken by the States Parties to the present Covenant to achieve the full realization of this right shall include those necessary for the conservation, the development and the diffusion of science and culture.

3. The States Parties to the present Covenant undertake to respect the freedom indispensable for scientific research and creative activity.

4. The States Parties to the present Covenant recognize the benefits to be derived from the encouragement and development of international contacts and co-operation in the scientific and cultural fields.

PART IV

*Article 16*

1. The States Parties to the present Covenant undertake to submit in conformity with this part of the Covenant reports on the measures which they have adopted and the progress made in achieving the observance of the rights recognized herein.

2. (*a*) All reports shall be submitted to the Secretary-General of the United Nations, who shall transmit copies to the Economic and Social Council for consideration in accordance with the provisions of the present Covenant;

(*b*) The Secretary-General of the United Nations shall also transmit to the specialized agencies copies of the reports, or any relevant parts therefrom, from States Parties to the present Covenant which are also members of these specialized agencies in so far as these reports, or parts therefrom, relate to any matters which fall within the responsibilities of the said agencies in accordance with their constitutional instruments.

*Article 17*

1. The States Parties to the present Covenant shall furnish their reports in stages, in accordance with a programme to be established by the Economic and Social Council within one year of the entry into force of the present Covenant after consultation with the States Parties and the specialized agencies concerned.

2. Reports may indicate factors and difficulties affecting the degree of fulfilment of obligations under the present Covenant.

3. Where relevant information has previously been furnished to the United Nations or to any specialized agency by any State Party to the present Covenant, it will not be necessary to reproduce that information, but a precise reference to the information so furnished will suffice.

*Article 18*

Pursuant to its responsibilities under the Charter of the United Nations in the field of human rights and fundamental freedoms, the Economic and Social Council may make arrangements with the specialized agencies in respect of their reporting to it on the progress made in achieving the observance of the provisions of the present Covenant falling within the scope of their activities. These reports may include particulars of decisions and recommendations on such implementation adopted by their competent organs.

*Article 19*

The Economic and Social Council may transmit to the Commission on Human Rights for study and general recommendation or, as appropriate, for information the reports concerning human rights submitted by States in accordance with articles 16 and 17, and those concerning human rights submitted by the specialized agencies in accordance with article 18.

*Article 20*

The States Parties to the present Covenant and the specialized agencies concerned may submit comments to the Economic and Social Council on any general recommendation under article 19 or reference to such general recommendation in any report of the Commission on Human Rights or any documentation referred to therein.

*Article 21*

The Economic and Social Council may submit from time to time to the General Assembly reports with recommendations of a general nature and a summary of the information received from the States Parties to the present Covenant and the specialized agencies on the measures taken and the progress made in achieving general observance of the rights recognized in the present Covenant.

*Article 22*

The Economic and Social Council may bring to the attention of other organs of the United Nations, their subsidiary organs and specialized agencies concerned with furnishing technical assistance any matters arising out of the reports referred to in this part of the present Covenant which may assist such bodies in deciding, each within its field of competence, on the advisability of international measures likely to contribute to the effective progressive implementation of the present Covenant.

*Article 23*

The States Parties to the present Covenant agree that international action for the achievement of the rights recognized in the present Covenant includes such methods as the conclusion of conventions, the adoption of recommendations, the furnishing of technical assistance and the holding of regional meetings and technical meetings for the purpose of consultation and study organized in conjunction with the Governments concerned.

*Article 24*

Nothing in the present Covenant shall be interpreted as impairing the provisions of the Charter of the United Nations and of the constitutions of the specialized agencies which define the respective responsibilities of the various organs of the United Nations and of the specialized agencies in regard to the matters dealt with in the present Covenant.

*Article 25*

Nothing in the present Covenant shall be interpreted as impairing the inherent right of all peoples to enjoy and utilize fully and freely their natural wealth and resources.

PART V

*Article 26*

1. The present Covenant is open for signature by any State Member of the United Nations or member of any of its specialized agencies, by any State Party to the Statute of the International Court of Justice, and by any other State which has been invited by the General Assembly of the United Nations to become a party to the present Covenant.

2. The present Covenant is subject to ratification. Instruments of ratification shall be deposited with the Secretary-General of the United Nations.

3. The present Covenant shall be open to accession by any State referred to in paragraph 1 of this article.

4. Accession shall be effected by the deposit of an instrument of accession with the Secretary-General of the United Nations.

5. The Secretary-General of the United Nations shall inform all States which have signed the present Covenant or acceded to it of the deposit of each instrument of ratification or accession.

*Article 27*

1. The present Covenant shall enter into force three months after the date of the deposit with the Secretary-General of the United Nations of the thirty-fifth instrument of ratification or instrument of accession.

2. For each State ratifying the present Covenant or acceding to it after the deposit of the thirty-fifth instrument of ratification or instrument of accession, the present Covenant shall enter into force three months after the date of the deposit of its own instrument of ratification or instrument of accession.

*Article 28*

The provisions of the present Covenant shall extend to all parts of federal States without any limitations or exceptions.

*Article 29*

1. Any State Party to the present Covenant may propose an amendment and file it with the Secretary-General of the United Nations. The Secretary-General shall thereupon communicate any proposed amendments to the States Parties to the present Covenant with a request that they notify him whether they favour a conference of States Parties for the purpose of considering and voting upon the proposals. In the event that at least one third of the State Parties favours such a conference, the Secretary-General shall convene the conference under the auspices of the United Nations. Any amendment adopted by a majority of the States Parties present and voting at the conference shall be submitted to the General Assembly of the United Nations for approval.

2. Amendments shall come into force when they have been approved by the General Assembly of the United Nations and accepted by a two-thirds majority of the States Parties to the present Covenant in accordance with their respective constitutional processes.

3. When amendments come into force they shall be binding on those States Parties which have accepted them, other States Parties still being bound by the provisions of the present Covenant and any earlier amendment which they have accepted.

*Article 30*

Irrespective of the notifications made under article 26, paragraph 5, the Secretary-General of the United Nations shall inform all States referred to in paragraph 1 of the same article of the following particulars:

(*a*) Signatures, ratifications and accessions under article 26;

(*b*) The date of the entry into force of the present Covenant under article 27 and the date of the entry into force of any amendments under article 29.

*Article 31*

1. The present Covenant, of which the Chinese, English, French, Russian and Spanish texts are equally authentic, shall be deposited in the archives of the United Nations.

2. The Secretary-General of the United Nations shall transmit certified copies of the present Covenant to all States referred to in article 26.

## 3. International Covenant on Civil and Political Rights

**Adopted and opened for signature, ratification and accession by General Assembly resolution 2200 A (XXI) of 16 December 1966**

***Entry into force*:** Not in force as of 31 December 1972 (see article 49).

PREAMBLE

*The States Parties to the present Covenant,*

*Considering* that, in accordance with the principles proclaimed in the Charter of the United Nations recognition of the inherent dignity and of the equal and inalienable rights of all members of the human family is the foundation of freedom, justice and peace in the world,

*Recognizing* that these rights derive from the inherent dignity of the human person,

*Recognizing* that, in accordance with the Universal Declaration of Human Rights, the ideal of free human beings enjoying civil and political freedom and freedom from fear and want can only be achieved if conditions are created whereby everyone may enjoy his civil and political rights, as well as his economic, social and cultural rights,

*Considering* the obligation of States under the Charter of the United Nations to promote universal respect for, and observance of, human rights and freedoms,

*Realizing* that the individual, having duties to other individuals and to the community to which he belongs, is under a responsibility to strive for the promotion and observance of the rights recognized in the present Covenant,

*Agree* upon the following articles:

## PART I

### *Article 1*

1. All peoples have the right of self-determination. By virtue of that right they freely determine their political status and freely pursue their economic, social and cultural development.

2. All peoples may, for their own ends, freely dispose of their natural wealth and resources without prejudice to any obligations arising out of international economic co-operation, based upon the principle of mutual benefit, and international law. In no case may a people be deprived of its own means of subsistence.

3. The States Parties to the present Covenant, including those having responsibility for the administration of Non-Self-Governing and Trust Territories, shall promote the realization of the right of self-determination, and shall respect that right, in conformity with the provisions of the Charter of the United Nations.

## PART II

### *Article 2*

1. Each State Party to the present Covenant undertakes to respect and to ensure to all individuals within its territory and subject to its jurisdiction the rights recognized in the present Covenant, without distinction of any kind, such as race, colour, sex, language, religion, political or other opinion, national or social origin, property, birth or other status.

2. Where not already provided for by existing legislative or other measures, each State Party to the present Covenant undertakes to take the necessary steps, in accordance with its constitutional processes and with the provisions of the present Covenant, to adopt such legislative or other measures as may be necessary to give effect to the rights recognized in the present Covenant.

3. Each State Party to the present Covenant undertakes:

(*a*) To ensure that any person whose rights or freedoms as herein recognized are violated shall have an effective remedy, notwithstanding that the violation has been committed by persons acting in an official capacity;

(*b*) To ensure that any person claiming such a remedy shall have his right thereto determined by competent judicial, administrative or legislative authorities, or by any other competent authority provided for by the legal system of the State, and to develop the possibilities of judicial remedy;

(*c*) To ensure that the competent authorities shall enforce such remedies when granted.

### *Article 3*

The States Parties to the present Covenant undertake to ensure the equal right of men and women to the enjoyment of all civil and political rights set forth in the present Covenant.

### *Article 4*

1. In time of public emergency which threatens the life of the nation and the existence of which is officially proclaimed, the States Parties to the present Covenant may take measures derogating from their obligations under the present Covenant to the extent strictly required by the exigencies of the situation, provided that such measures are not inconsistent with their other obligations under international law and do not involve discrimination solely on the ground of race, colour, sex, language, religion or social origin.

2. No derogation from articles 6, 7, 8 (paragraphs 1 and 2), 11, 15, 16 and 18 may be made under this provision.

3. Any State Party to the present Covenant availing itself of the right of derogation shall immediately inform the other States Parties to the present Covenant, through the intermediary of the Secretary-General of the United Nations, of the provisions from which it has derogated and of the reasons by which it was actuated. A further communication shall be made, through the same intermediary, on the date on which it terminates such derogation.

### *Article 5*

1. Nothing in the present Covenant may be interpreted as implying for any State, group or person any right to engage in any activity or perform any act aimed at the destruction of any of the rights and freedoms recognized herein or at their limitation to a greater extent than is provided for in the present Covenant.

2. There shall be no restriction upon or derogation from any of the fundamental human rights recognized or existing in any State Party to the present Covenant pursuant to law, conventions, regulations or custom on the pretext that the present Covenant does not recognize such rights or that it recognizes them to a lesser extent.

## Part III

### *Article 6*

1. Every human being has the inherent right to life. This right shall be protected by law. No one shall be arbitrarily deprived of his life.

2. In countries which have not abolished the death penalty, sentence of death may be imposed only for the most serious crimes in accordance with the law in force at the time of the commission of the crime and not contrary to the provisions of the present Covenant and to the Convention on the Prevention and Punishment of the Crime of Genocide. This penalty can only be carried out pursuant to a final judgement rendered by a competent court.

3. When deprivation of life constitutes the crime of genocide, it is understood that nothing in this article shall authorize any State Party to the present Covenant to derogate in any way from any obligation assumed under the provisions of the Convention on the Prevention and Punishment of the Crime of Genocide.

4. Anyone sentenced to death shall have the right to seek pardon or commutation of the sentence. Amnesty, pardon or commutation of the sentence of death may be granted in all cases.

5. Sentence of death shall not be imposed for crimes committed by persons below eighteen years of age and shall not be carried out on pregnant women.

6. Nothing in this article shall be invoked to delay or to prevent the abolition of capital punishment by any State Party to the present Covenant.

### *Article 7*

No one shall be subjected to torture or to cruel, inhuman or degrading treatment or punishment. In particular, no one shall be subjected without his free consent to medical or scientific experimentation.

### *Article 8*

1. No one shall be held in slavery; slavery and the slave-trade in all their forms shall be prohibited.

2. No one shall be held in servitude.

3. (*a*) No one shall be required to perform forced or compulsory labour;

(*b*) Paragraph 3 (*a*) shall not be held to preclude, in countries where imprisonment with hard labour may be imposed as a punishment for a crime, the performance of hard labour in pursuance of a sentence to such punishment by a competent court;

(*c*) For the purpose of this paragraph the term "forced or compulsory labour" shall not include:

(i) Any work or service, not referred to in subparagraph (*b*), normally required of a person who is under detention in consequence of a lawful order of a court, or of a person during conditional release from such detention;

(ii) Any service of a military character and, in countries where conscientious objection is recognized, any national service required by law of conscientious objectors;

(iii) Any service exacted in cases of emergency or calamity threatening the life or well-being of the community;

(iv) Any work or service which forms part of normal civil obligations.

### *Article 9*

1. Everyone has the right to liberty and security of person. No one shall be subjected to arbitrary arrest or detention. No one shall be deprived of his liberty except on such grounds and in accordance with such procedure as are established by law.

2. Enyone who is arrested shall be informed, at the time of arrest, of the reasons for his arrest and shall be promptly informed of any charges against him.

3. Anyone arrested or detained on a criminal charge shall be brought promptly before a judge or other officer authorized by law to exercise judicial power and shall be entitled to trial within a reasonable time or to release. It shall not be the general rule that persons awaiting trial shall be detained in custody, but release may be subject to guarantees to appear for trial, at any other stage of the judicial proceedings, and, should occasion arise, for execution of the judgement.

4. Anyone who is deprived of his liberty by arrest or detention shall be entitled to take proceedings before a court, in order that that court may decide without delay on the lawfulness of his detention and order his release if the detention is not lawful.

5. Anyone who has been the victim of unlawful arrest or detention shall have an enforceable right to compensation.

### *Article 10*

1. All persons deprived of their liberty shall be treated with humanity and with respect for the inherent dignity of the human person.

2. (*a*) Accused persons shall, save in exceptional circumstances, be segregated from convicted persons and shall be subject to separate treatment appropriate to their status as unconvicted persons;

(*b*) Accused juvenile persons shall be separated from adults and brought as speedily as possible for adjudication.

3. The penitentiary system shall comprise treatment of prisoners the essential aim of which shall be their reformation and social rehabilitation. Juvenile offenders shall be segregated from adults and be accorded treatment appropriate to their age and legal status.

### *Article 11*

No one shall be imprisoned merely on the ground of inability to fulfil a contractual obligation.

### *Article 12*

1. Everyone lawfully within the territory of a State shall, within that territory, have the right to liberty of movement and freedom to choose his residence.

2. Everyone shall be free to leave any country, including his own.

3. The above-mentioned rights shall not be subject to any restrictions except those which are provided by law, are necessary to protect national security, public order (*ordre public*), public health or morals or the rights and freedoms of others, and are consistent with the other rights recognized in the present Covenant.

4. No one shall be arbitrarily deprived of the right to enter his own country.

*Article 13*

An alien lawfully in the territory of a State Party to the present Covenant may be expelled therefrom only in pursuance of a decision reached in accordance with law and shall, except where compelling reasons of national security otherwise require, be allowed to submit the reasons against his expulsion and to have his case reviewed by, and be represented for the purpose before, the competent authority or a person or persons especially designated by the competent authority.

*Article 14*

1. All persons shall be equal before the courts and tribunals. In the determination of any criminal charge against him, or of his rights and obligations in a suit at law, everyone shall be entitled to a fair and public hearing by a competent, independent and impartial tribunal established by law. The Press and the public may be excluded from all or part of a trial for reasons of morals, public order (*ordre public*) or national security in a democratic society, or when the interest of the private lives of the parties so requires, or to the extent strictly necessary in the opinion of the court in special circumstances where publicity would prejudice the interests of justice; but any judgement rendered in a criminal case or in a suit at law shall be made public except where the interest of juvenile persons otherwise requires or the proceedings concern matrimonial disputes or the guardianship of children.

2. Everyone charged with a criminal offence shall have the right to be presumed innocent until proved guilty according to law.

3. In the determination of any criminal charge against him, everyone shall be entitled to the following minimum guarantees, in full equality:

(*a*) To be informed promptly and in detail in a language which he understands of the nature and cause of the charge against him;

(*b*) To have adequate time and facilities for the preparation of his defence and to communicate with counsel of his own choosing;

(*c*) To be tried without undue delay;

(*d*) To be tried in his presence, and to defend himself in person or through legal assistance of his own choosing; to be informed, if he does not have legal assistance, of this right; and to have legal assistance assigned to him, in any case where the interests of justice so require, and without payment by him in any such case if he does not have sufficient means to pay for it;

(*e*) To examine, or have examined, the witnesses against him and to obtain the attendance and examination of witnesses on his behalf under the same conditions as witnesses against him;

(*f*) To have the free assistance of an interpreter if he cannot understand or speak the language used in court;

(*g*) Not to be compelled to testify against himself or to confess guilt.

4. In the case of juvenile persons, the procedure shall be such as will take account of their age and the desirability of promoting their rehabilitation.

5. Everyone convicted of a crime shall have the right to his conviction and sentence being reviewed by a higher tribunal according to law.

6. When a person has by a final decision been convicted of a criminal offence and when subsequently his conviction has been reversed or he has been pardoned on the ground that a new or newly discovered fact shows conclusively that there has been a miscarriage of justice, the person who has suffered punishment as a result of such conviction shall be compensated according to law, unless it is proved that the non-disclosure of the unknown fact in time is wholly or partly attributable to him.

7. No one shall be liable to be tried or punished again for an offence for which he has already been finally convicted or acquitted in accordance with the law and penal procedure of each country.

*Article 15*

1. No one shall be held guilty of any criminal offence on account of any act or omission which did not constitute a criminal offence, under national or international law, at the time when it was committed. Nor shall a heavier penalty be imposed than the one that was applicable at the time when the criminal offence was committed. If, subsequent to the commission of the offence, provision is made by law for the imposition of the lighter penalty, the offender shall benefit thereby.

2. Nothing in this article shall prejudice the trial and punishment of any person for any act or omission which, at the time when it was committed, was criminal according to the general principles of law recognized by the community of nations.

*Article 16*

Everyone shall have the right to recognition everywhere as a person before the law.

*Article 17*

1. No one shall be subjected to arbitrary or unlawful interference with his privacy, family, home or correspondence, nor to unlawful attacks on his honour and reputation.

2. Everyone has the right to the protection of the law against such interference or attacks.

*Article 18*

1. Everyone shall have the right to freedom of thought, conscience and religion. This right shall include freedom to have or to adopt a religion or belief of his choice, and freedom, either individually or in community with others and in public or private, to manifest

his religion or belief in worship, observance, practice and teaching.

2. No one shall be subject to coercion which would impair his freedom to have or to adopt a religion or belief of his choice.

3. Freedom to manifest one's religion or beliefs may be subject only to such limitations as are prescribed by law and are necessary to protect public safety, order, health, or morals or the fundamental rights and freedoms of others.

4. The States Parties to the present Covenant undertake to have respect for the liberty of parents and, when applicable, legal guardians to ensure the religious and moral education of their children in conformity with their own convictions.

*Article 19*

1. Everyone shall have the right to hold opinions without interference.

2. Everyone shall have the right to freedom of expression; this right shall include freedom to seek, receive and impart information and ideas of all kinds, regardless of frontiers, either orally, in writing or in print, in the form of art, or through any other media of his choice.

3. The exercise of the rights provided for in paragraph 2 of this article carries with it special duties and responsibilities. It may therefore be subject to certain restrictions, but these shall only be such as are provided by law and are necessary:

(*a*) For respect of the rights or reputations of others;

(*b*) For the protection of national security or of public order (*ordre public*), or of public health or morals.

*Article 20*

1. Any propaganda for war shall be prohibited by law.

2. Any advocacy of national, racial or religious hatred that constitutes incitement to discrimination, hostility or violence shall be prohibited by law.

*Article 21*

The right of peaceful assembly shall be recognized. No restrictions may be placed on the exercise of this right other than those imposed in conformity with the law and which are necessary in a democratic society in the interests of national security or public safety, public order (*ordre public*), the protection of public health or morals or the protection of the rights and freedoms of others.

*Article 22*

1. Everyone shall have the right to freedom of association with others, including the right to form and join trade unions for the protection of his interests.

2. No restrictions may be placed on the exercise of this right other than those which are prescribed by law and which are necessary in a democratic society in the interests of national security or public safety, public order (*ordre public*), the protection of public health or morals or the protection of the rights and freedoms of others. This article shall not prevent the imposition of lawful restrictions on members of the armed forces and of the police in their exercise of this right.

3. Nothing in this article shall authorize States Parties to the International Labour Organisation Convention of 1948 concerning Freedom of Association and Protection of the Right to Organize to take legislative measures which would prejudice, or to apply the law in such a manner as to prejudice the guarantees provided for in that Convention.

*Article 23*

1. The family is the natural and fundamental group unit of society and is entitled to protection by society and the State.

2. The right of men and women of marriageable age to marry and to found a family shall be recognized.

3. No marriage shall be entered into without the free and full consent of the intending spouses.

4. States Parties to the present Covenant shall take appropriate steps to ensure equality of rights and responsibilities of spouses as to marriage, during marriage and at its dissolution. In the case of dissolution, provision shall be made for the necessary protection of any children.

*Article 24*

1. Every child shall have, without any discrimination as to race, colour, sex, language, religion, national or social origin, property or birth, the right to such measures of protection as are required by his status as a minor, on the part of his family, society and the State.

2. Every child shall be registered immediately after birth and shall have a name.

3. Every child has the right to acquire a nationality.

*Article 25*

Every citizen shall have the right and the opportunity, without any of the distinctions mentioned in article 2 and without unreasonable restrictions:

(*a*) To take part in the conduct of public affairs, directly or through freely chosen representatives;

(*b*) To vote and to be elected at genuine periodic elections which shall be by universal and equal suffrage and shall be held by secret ballot, guaranteeing the free expression of the will of the electors;

(*c*) To have access, on general terms of equality, to public service in his country.

*Article 26*

All persons are equal before the law and are entitled without any discrimination to the equal protection of the law. In this respect, the law shall prohibit any discrimination and guarantee to all persons equal and effective protection against discrimination on any ground such as race, colour, sex, language, religion, political or other opinion, national or social origin, property, birth or other status.

*Article 27*

In those States in which ethnic, religious or linguistic minorities exist, persons belonging to such minorities shall not be denied the right, in community with the other members of their group, to enjoy their own culture, to profess and practice their own religion, or to use their own language.

## PART IV

*Article 28*

1. There shall be established a Human Rights Committee (hereafter referred to in the present Covenant as the Committee). It shall consist of eighteen members and shall carry out the functions hereinafter provided.

2. The Committee shall be composed of nationals of the States Parties to the present Covenant who shall be persons of high moral character and recognized competence in the field of human rights, consideration being given to the usefulness of the participation of some persons having legal experience.

3. The members of the Committee shall be elected and shall serve in their personal capacity.

*Article 29*

1. The members of the Committee shall be elected by secret ballot from a list of persons possessing the qualifications prescribed in article 28 and nominated for the purpose by the States Parties to the present Covenant.

2. Each State Party to the present Covenant may nominate not more than two persons. These persons shall be nationals of the nominating State.

3. A person shall be eligible for renomination.

*Article 30*

1. The initial election shall be held no later than six months after the date of the entry into force of the present Covenant.

2. At least four months before the date of each election to the Committee, other than an election to fill a vacancy declared in accordance with article 34, the Secretary-General of the United Nations shall address a written invitation to the States Parties to the present Covenant to submit their nominations for membership of the Committee within three months.

3. The Secretary-General of the United Nations shall prepare a list in alphabetical order of all the persons thus nominated, with an indication of the States Parties which have nominated them, and shall submit it to the States Parties to the present Covenant no later than one month before the date of each election.

4. Elections of the members of the Committee shall be held at a meeting of the States Parties to the present Covenant convened by the Secretary-General of the United Nations at the Headquarters of the United Nations. At that meeting, for which two thirds of the States Parties to the present Covenant shall constitute a quorum, the persons elected to the Committee shall be those nominees who obtain the largest number of votes and an absolute majority of the votes of the representatives of States Parties present and voting.

*Article 31*

1. The Committee may not include more than one national of the same State.

2. In the election of the Committee, consideration shall be given to equitable geographical distribution of membership and to the representation of the different forms of civilization and of the principal legal systems.

*Article 32*

1. The members of the Committee shall be elected for a term of four years. They shall be eligible for re-election if renominated. However, the terms of nine of the members elected at the first election shall expire at the end of two years; immediately after the first election, the names of these nine members shall be chosen by lot by the Chairman of the meeting referred to in article 30, paragraph 4.

2. Elections at the expiry of office shall be held in accordance with the proceeding articles of this part of the present Covenant.

*Article 33*

1. If, in the unanimous opinion of the other members, a member of the Committee has ceased to carry out his functions for any cause other than absence of a temporary character, the Chairman of the Committee shall notify the Secretary-General of the United Nations, who shall then declare the seat of that member to be vacant.

2. In the event of the death or the resignation of a member of the Committee, the Chairman shall immediately notify the Secretary-General of the United Nations, who shall declare the seat vacant from the date of death or the date on which the resignation takes effect.

*Article 34*

1. When a vacancy is declared in accordance with article 33 and if the term of office of the member to be replaced does not expire within six months of the declaration of the vacancy, the Secretary-General of the United Nations shall notify each of the States Parties to the present Covenant, which may within two months submit nominations in accordance with article 29 for the purpose of filling the vacancy.

2. The Secretary-General of the United Nations shall prepare a list in alphabetical order of the persons thus nominated and shall submit it to the States Parties to the present Covenant. The election to fill the vacancy shall then take place in accordance with the relevant provisions of this part of the present Covenant.

3. A member of the Committee elected to fill a vacancy declared in accordance with article 33 shall hold office for the remainder of the term of the member who vacated the seat on the Committee under the provisions of that article.

*Article 35*

The members of the Committee shall, with the approval of the General Assembly of the United Nations, receive emoluments from United Nations resources on such terms and conditions as the General Assembly may decide, having regard to the importance of the Committee's responsibilities.

*Article 36*

The Secretary-General of the United Nations shall provide the necessary staff and facilities for the effective performance of the functions of the Committee under the present Covenant.

*Article 37*

1. The Secretary-General of the United Nations shall convene the initial meeting of the Committee at the Headquarters of the United Nations.

2. After its initial meeting, the Committee shall meet at such times as shall be provided in its rules of procedure.

3. The Committee shall normally meet at the Headquarters of the United Nations or at the United Nations Office at Geneva.

*Article 38*

Every member of the Committee shall, before taking up his duties, make a solemn declaration in open committee that he will perform his functions impartially and conscientiously.

*Article 39*

1. The Committee shall elect its officers for a term of two years. They may be re-elected.

2. The Committee shall establish its own rules of procedure, but these rules shall provide, *inter alia,* that:

(*a*) Twelve members shall constitute a quorum;

(*b*) Decisions of the Committee shall be made by a majority vote of the members present.

*Article 40*

1. The States Parties to the present Covenant undertake to submit reports on the measures they have adopted which give effect to the rights recognized herein and on the progress made in the enjoyment of those rights:

(*a*) Within one year of the entry into force of the present Covenant for the States Parties concerned;

(*b*) Thereafter whenever the Committee so requests.

2. All reports shall be submitted to the Secretary-General of the United Nations, who shall transmit them to the Committee for consideration. Reports shall indicate the factors and difficulties, if any, affecting the implementation of the present Covenant.

3. The Secretary-General of the United Nations may, after consultation with the Committee, transmit to the specialized agencies concerned copies of such parts of the reports as may fall within their field of competence.

4. The Committee shall study the reports submitted by the States Parties to the present Covenant. It shall transmit its reports, and such general comments as it may consider appropriate, to the States Parties. The Committee may also transmit to the Economic and Social Council these comments along with the copies of the reports it has received from States Parties to the present Covenant.

5. The States Parties to the present Covenant may submit to the Committee observations on any comments that may be made in accordance with paragraph 4 of this article.

*Article 41*

1. A State Party to the present Covenant may at any time declare under this article that it recognizes the competence of the Committee to receive and consider communications to the effect that a State Party claims that another State Party is not fulfilling its obligations under the present Covenant. Communications under this article may be received and considered only if submitted by a State Party which has made a declaration recognizing in regard to itself the competence of the Committee. No communication shall be received by the Committee if it concerns a State Party which has not made such a declaration. Communications received under this article shall be dealt with in accordance with the following procedure:

(*a*) If a State Party to the present Covenant considers that another State Party is not giving effect to the provisions of the present Covenant, it may, by written communication, bring the matter to the attention of that State Party. Within three months after the receipt of the communication the receiving State shall afford the State which sent the communication an explanation or any other statement in writing clarifying the matter, which should include, to the extent possible and pertinent, reference to domestic procedures and remedies taken, pending, or available in the matter.

(*b*) If the matter is not adjusted to the satisfaction of both States Parties concerned within six months after the receipt by the receiving State of the initial communication, either State shall have the right to refer the matter to the Committee, by notice given to the Committee and to the other State.

(*c*) The Committee shall deal with a matter referred to it only after it has ascertained that all available domestic remedies have been invoked and exhausted in the matter, in conformity with the generally recognized principles of international law. This shall not be the rule where the application of the remedies is unreasonably prolonged.

(*d*) The Committee shall hold closed meetings when examining communications under this article.

(*e*) Subject to the provisions of sub-paragraph (*c*), the Committee shall make available its good offices to the States Parties concerned with a view to a friendly solution of the matter on the basis of respect for human rights and fundamental freedoms as recognized in the present Covenant.

(*f*) In any matter referred to it, the Committee may call upon the States Parties concerned, referred to in sub-paragraph (*b*), to supply any relevant information.

(*g*) The States Parties concerned, referred to in sub-paragraph (*b*), shall have the right to be represented when the matter is being considered in the Committee and to make submissions orally and/or in writing.

(*h*) The Committee shall, within twelve months after the date of receipt of notice under sub-paragraph (*b*), submit a report:

(i) If a solution within the terms of sub-paragraph (*e*) is reached, the Committee shall confine its report to a brief statement of the facts and of the solution reached;

(ii) If a solution within the terms of sub-paragraph (*e*) is not reached, the Committee shall confine its report to a brief statement of the facts; the written submissions and record of the oral submissions made by the States Parties concerned shall be attached to the report.

In every matter, the report shall be communicated to the States Parties concerned.

2. The provisions of this article shall come into force when ten States Parties to the present Covenant have made declarations under paragraph 1 of this article. Such declarations shall be deposited by the States Parties with the Secretary-General of the United Nations who shall transmit copies thereof to the other States Parties. A declaration may be withdrawn at any time by notification to the Secretary-General. Such a withdrawal shall not prejudice the consideration of any matter which is the subject of a communication already transmitted under this article; no further communication by any State Party shall be received after the notification of withdrawal of the declaration has been received by the Secretary-General, unless the State Party concerned has made a new declaration.

*Article 42*

1. (*a*) If a matter referred to the Committee in accordance with article 41 is not resolved to the satisfaction of the States Parties concerned, the Committee may, with the prior consent of the States Parties concerned, appoint an *ad hoc* Conciliation Commission (hereinafter referred to as the Commission). The good offices of the Commission shall be made available to the States Parties concerned with a view to an amicable solution of the matter on the basis of respect for the present Covenant;

(*b*) The Commission shall consist of five persons acceptable to the States Parties concerned. If the States Parties concerned fail to reach agreement within three months on all or part of the composition of the Commission, the members of the Commission concerning whom no agreement has been reached shall be elected by secret ballot by a two-thirds majority vote of the Committee from among its members.

2. The members of the Commission shall serve in their personal capacity. They shall not be nationals of the States Parties concerned, or of a State not party to the present Covenant, or of a State Party which has not made a declaration under article 41.

3. The Commission shall elect its own Chairman and adopt its own rules of procedure.

4. The meetings of the Commission shall normally be held at the Headquarters of the United Nations or at the United Nations Office at Geneva. However, they may be held at such other convenient places as the Commission may determine in consultation with the Secretary-General of the United Nations and the States Parties concerned.

5. The secretariat provided in accordance with article 36 shall also service the commissions appointed under this article.

6. The information received and collated by the Committee shall be made available to the Commission and the Commission may call upon the States Parties concerned to supply any other relevant information.

7. When the Commission has fully considered the matter, but in any event not later than twelve months after having been seized of the matter, it shall submit to the Chairman of the Committee a report for communication to the States Parties concerned:

(*a*) If the Commission is unable to complete its consideration of the matter within twelve months, it shall confine its report to a brief statement of the status of its consideration of the matter;

(*b*) If an amicable solution to the matter on the basis of respect for human rights as recognized in the present Covenant is reached, the Commission shall confine its report to a brief statement of the facts and of the solution reached;

(*c*) If a solution within the terms of sub-paragraph (*b*) is not reached, the Commission's report shall embody its findings on all questions of fact relevant to the issues between the States Parties concerned, and its views on the possibilities of an amicable solution of the matter. This report shall also contain the written submissions and a record of the oral submissions made by the States Parties concerned;

(*d*) If the Commission's report is submitted under sub-paragraph (*c*), the States Parties concerned shall, within three months of the receipt of the report, notify the Chairman of the Committee whether or not they accept the contents of the report of the Commission.

8. The provisions of this article are without prejudice to the responsibilities of the Committee under article 41.

9. The States Parties concerned shall share equally all the expenses of the members of the Commission in accordance with estimates to be provided by the Secretary-General of the United Nations.

10. The Secretary-General of the United Nations shall be empowered to pay the expenses of the members of the Commission, if necessary, before reimbursement by the States Parties concerned, in accordance with paragraph 9 of this article.

*Article 43*

The members of the Committee, and of the *ad hoc* conciliation commissions which may be appointed under article 42, shall be entitled to the facilities, privileges and immunities of experts on mission for the United Nations as laid down in the relevant sections of the Convention on the Privileges and Immunities of the United Nations.

*Article 44*

The provisions for the implementation of the present Covenant shall apply without prejudice to the procedures prescribed in the field of human rights by or under the constituent instruments and the conventions of the United Nations and of the specialized agencies and shall not prevent the States Parties to the present Covenant from having recourse to other procedures for settling a dispute in accordance with general or special international agreements in force between them.

*Article 45*

The Committee shall submit to the General Assembly of the United Nations, through the Economic and Social Council, an annual report on its activities.

PART V

*Article 46*

Nothing in the present Covenant shall be interpreted as impairing the provisions of the Charter of the United Nations and of the constitutions of the specialized agencies which define the respective responsibilities of the various organs of the United Nations and of the specialized agencies in regard to the matters dealt within the present Covenant.

*Article 47*

Nothing in the present Covenant shall be interpreted as impairing the inherent right of all peoples to enjoy and utilize fully and freely their natural wealth and resources.

PART VI

*Article 48*

1. The present Covenant is open for signature by any State Member of the United Nations or member of any of its specialized agencies, by any State Party to the Statute of the International Court of Justice, and by any other State which has been invited by the General Assembly of the United Nations to become a party to the present Covenant.

2. The present Covenant is subject to ratification. Instruments of ratification shall be deposited with the Secretary-General of the United Nations.

3. The present Covenant shall be open to accession by any State referred to in paragraph 1 of this article.

4. Accession shall be effected by the deposit of an instrument of accession with the Secretary-General of the United Nations.

5. The Secretary-General of the United Nations shall inform all States which have signed this Covenant or acceded to it of the deposit of each instrument of ratification or accession.

*Article 49*

1. The present Covenant shall enter into force three months after the date of the deposit with the Secretary-General of the United Nations of the thirty-fifth instrument of ratification or instrument of accession.

2. For each State ratifying the present Covenant or acceding to it after the deposit of the thirty-fifth instrument of ratification or instrument of accession, the present Covenant shall enter into force three months after the date of the deposit of its own instrument of ratification or instrument of accession.

*Article 50*

The provisions of the present Covenant shall extend to all parts of federal States without any limitations or exceptions.

*Article 51*

1. Any State Party to the present Covenant may propose an amendment and file it with the Secretary-General of the United Nations. The Secretary-General of the United Nations shall thereupon communicate any proposed amendments to the States Parties to the present Covenant with a request that they notify him whether they favour a conference of States Parties for the purpose of considering and voting upon the proposals. In the event that at least one third of the States Parties favours such a conference, the Secretary-General shall convene the conference under the auspices of the United Nations. Any amendment adopted by a majority of the States Parties present and voting at the conference shall be submitted to the General Assembly of the United Nations for approval.

2. Amendments shall come into force when they have been approved by the General Assembly of the United Nations and accepted by a two-thirds majority of the States Parties to the present Covenant in accordance with their respective constitutional processes.

3. When amendments come into force, they shall be binding on those States Parties which have accepted them, other States Parties still being bound by the provisions of the present Covenant and any earlier amendment which they have accepted.

*Article 52*

Irrespective of the notifications made under article 48, paragraph 5, the Secretary-General of the United Nations shall inform all States referred to in paragraph 1 of the same article of the following particulars:

(*a*) Signatures, ratifications and accessions under article 48;

(*b*) The date of the entry into force of the present Covenant under article 49 and the date of the entry into force of any amendments under article 51.

*Article 53*

1. The present Covenant, of which the Chinese, English, French, Russian and Spanish texts are equally authentic, shall be deposited in the archives of the United Nations.

2. The Secretary-General of the United Nations shall transmit certified copies of the present Covenant to all States referred to in article 48.

## 4. Optional Protocol to the International Covenant on Civil and Political Rights

**Adopted and opened for signature, ratification and accession by General Assembly resolution 2200 A (XXI) of 16 December 1966**

***Entry into force:*** Not in force as of 31 December 1972 (see article 9).

*The States Parties to the present Protocol,*

*Considering* that in order further to achieve the purposes of the Covenant on Civil and Political Rights (hereinafter referred to as the Covenant) and the implementation of its provisions it would be appropriate to enable the Human Rights Committee set up in part IV of the Covenant (hereinafter referred to as the Committee) to receive and consider, as provided in the present Protocol, communications from individuals claiming to be victims of violations of any of the rights set forth in the Covenant.

*Have agreed* as follows:

*Article 1*

A State Party to the Covenant that becomes a party to the present Protocol recognizes the competence of the Committee to receive and consider communications from individuals subject to its jurisdiction who claim to be victims of a violation by that State Party of any of the rights set forth in the Covenant. No communication shall be received by the Committee if it concerns a State Party to the Covenant which is not a party to the present Protocol.

*Article 2*

Subject to the provisions of article 1, individuals who claim that any of their rights enumerated in the Covenant have been violated and who have exhausted all available domestic remedies may submit a written communication to the Committee for consideration.

*Article 3*

The Committee shall consider inadmissible any communication under the present Protocol which is anonymous, or which it considers to be an abuse of the right of submission of such communications or to be incompatible with the provisions of the Covenant.

*Article 4*

1. Subject to the provisions of article 3, the Committee shall bring any communications submitted to it under the present Protocol to the attention of the State Party to the present Protocol alleged to be violating any provision of the Covenant.

2. Within six months, the receiving State shall submit to the Committee written explanations or statements clarifying the matter and the remedy, if any, that may have been taken by that State.

*Article 5*

1. The Committee shall consider communications received under the present Protocol in the light of all written information made available to it by the individual and by the State Party concerned.

2. The Committee shall not consider any communication from an individual unless it has ascertained that:

(*a*) The same matter is not being examined under another procedure of international investigation or settlement,

(*b*) The individual has exhausted all available domestic remedies.

This shall not be the rule where the application of the remedies is unreasonably prolonged.

3. The Committee shall hold closed meetings when examining communications under the present Protocol.

4. The Committee shall forward its views to the State Party concerned and to the individual.

*Article 6*

The Committee shall include in its annual report under article 45 of the Covenant a summary of its activities under the present Protocol.

*Article 7*

Pending the achievement of the objectives of resolution 1514 (XV) adopted by the General Assembly of the United Nations on 14 December 1960 concerning the Declaration on the Granting of Independence to Colonial Countries and Peoples, the provisions of the present Protocol shall in no way limit the right of petition granted to these peoples by the Charter of the United Nations and other international conventions and instruments under the United Nations and its specialized agencies.

*Article 8*

1. The present Protocol is open for signature by any State which has signed the Covenant.

2. The present Protocol is subject to ratification by any State which has ratified or acceded to the Covenant. Instruments of ratification shall be deposited with the Secretary-General of the United Nations.

3. The present Protocol shall be open to accession by any State which has ratified or acceded to the Covenant.

4. Accession shall be effected by the deposit of an instrument of accession with the Secretary-General of the United Nations.

5. The Secretary-General of the United Nations shall inform all States which have signed the present Protocol or acceded to it of the deposit of each instrument of ratification or accession.

*Article 9*

1. Subject to the entry into force of the Covenant, the present Protocol shall enter into force three months after the date of the deposit with the Secretary-General of the United Nations of the tenth instrument of ratification or instrument of accession.

2. For each State ratifying the present Protocol or acceding to it after the deposit of the tenth instrument of ratification or instrument of accession, the present Protocol shall enter into force three months after the date of the deposit of its own instrument of ratification or instrument of accession.

*Article 10*

The provisions of the present Protocol shall extend to all parts of federal States without any limitations or exceptions.

*Article 11*

1. Any State Party to the present Protocol may propose an amendment and file it with the Secretary-Gen-

eral of the United Nations. The Secretary-General shall thereupon communicate any proposed amendments to the States Parties to the present Protocol with a request that they notify him whether they favour a conference of States Parties for the purpose of considering and voting upon the proposal. In the event that at least one third of the States Parties favours such a conference, the Secretary-General shall convene the conference under the auspices of the United Nations. Any amendment adopted by a majority of the States Parties present and voting at the conference shall be submitted to the General Assembly of the United Nations for approval.

2. Amendments shall come into force when they have been approved by the General Assembly of the United Nations and accepted by a two-thirds majority of the States Parties to the present Protocol in accordance with their respective constitutional processes.

3. When amendments come into force, they shall be binding on those States Parties which have accepted them, other States Parties still being bound by the provisions of the present Protocol and any earlier amendment which they have accepted.

*Article 12*

1. Any State Party may denounce the present Protocol at any time by written notification addressed to the Secretary-General of the United Nations. Denunciation shall take effect three months after the date of receipt of the notification by the Secretary-General.

2. Denunciation shall be without prejudice to the continued application of the provisions of the present Protocol to any communication submitted under article 2 before the effective date of denunciation.

*Article 13*

Irrespective of the notifications made under article 8, paragraph 5, of the present Protocol, the Secretary-General of the United Nations shall inform all States referred to in article 48, paragraph 1, of the Covenant of the following particulars:

(*a*) Signatures, ratifications and accessions under article 8;

(*b*) The date of the entry into force of the present Protocol under article 9 and the date of the entry into force of any amendments under article 11;

(*c*) Denunciations under article 12.

*Article 14*

1. The present Protocol, of which the Chinese, English, French, Russian and Spanish texts are equally authentic, shall be deposited in the archives of the United Nations.

2. The Secretary-General of the United Nations shall transmit certified copies of the present Protocol to all States referred to in article 48 of the Covenant.

# B. THE PROCLAMATION OF TEHERAN

## 5. Proclamation of Teheran

**Proclaimed by the International Conference on Human Rights at Teheran on 13 May 1968**

*The International Conference on Human Rights,*

*Having met* at Teheran from April 22 to May 13, 1968 to review the progress made in the twenty years since the adoption of the Universal Declaration of Human Rights and to formulate a programme for the future,

*Having considered* the problems relating to the activities of the United Nations for the promotion and encouragement of respect for human rights and encouragement of respect for human rights and fundamental freedoms,

*Bearing in mind* the resolutions adopted by the Conference,

*Noting* that the observance of the International Year for Human Rights takes place at a time when the world is undergoing a process of unprecedented change,

*Having regard* to the new opportunities made available by the rapid progress of science and technology,

*Believing* that, in an age when conflict and violence prevail in many parts of the world, the fact of human interdependence and the need for human solidarity are more evident than ever before,

*Recognizing* that peace is the universal aspiration of mankind and that peace and justice are indispensable to the full realization of human rights and fundamental freedoms,

*Solemnly proclaims that:*

1. It is imperative that the members of the international community fulfil their solemn obligations to promote and encourage respect for human rights and fundamental freedoms for all without distinctions of any kind such as race, colour, sex, language, religion, political or other opinions;

2. The Universal Declaration of Human Rights states a common understanding of the peoples of the world concerning the inalienable and inviolable rights of all members of the human family and constitutes an obligation for the members of the international community;

3. The International Covenant on Civil and Political Rights, the International Covenant on Economic, Social and Cultural Rights, the Declaration on the Granting of Independence to Colonial Countries and Peoples, the International Convention on the Elimination of All Forms of Racial Discrimination as well as other conventions and declarations in the field of human rights adopted under the auspices of the United Nations, the specialized agencies and the regional intergovernmental organizations, have created new standards and obligations to which States should conform;

4. Since the adoption of the Universal Declaration of Human Rights the United Nations has made substantial progress in defining standards for the enjoyment and protection of human rights and fundamental freedoms. During this period many important international instruments were adopted but much remains to be done in regard to the implementation of those rights and freedoms;

5. The primary aim of the United Nations in the sphere of human rights is the achievement by each individual of the maximum freedom and dignity. For the realization of this objective, the laws of every country should grant each individual, irrespective of race, language, religion or political belief, freedom of expression, of information, of conscience and of religion, as well as the right to participate in the political, economic, cultural and social life of his country;

6. States should reaffirm their determination effectively to enforce the principles enshrined in the Charter of the United Nations and in other international instruments that concern human rights and fundamental freedoms;

7. Gross denials of human rights under the repugnant policy of *apartheid* is a matter of the gravest concern to the international community. This policy of *apartheid,* condemned as a crime against humanity, continues seriously to disturb international peace and security. It is therefore imperative for the international community to use every possible means to eradicate this evil. The struggle against *apartheid* is recognized as legitimate;

8. The peoples of the world must be made fully aware of the evils of racial discrimination and must join in combating them. The implementation of this principle of non-discrimination, embodied in the Charter of the United Nations, the Universal Declaration of Human Rights, and other international instruments in the field of human rights, constitutes a most urgent task of mankind at the international as well as at the national level. All ideologies based on racial superiority and intolerance must be condemned and resisted;

9. Eight years after the General Assembly's Declaration on the Granting of Independence to Colonial Countries and Peoples the problems of colonialism continue to preoccupy the international community. It is a matter of urgency that all Member States should co-operate with the appropriate organs of the United Nations so that effective measures can be taken to ensure that the Declaration is fully implemented;

10. Massive denials of human rights, arising out of aggression or any armed conflct with their tragic consequences, and resulting in untold human misery, engender reactions which could engulf the world in ever growing hostilities. It is the obligation of the international community to co-operate in eradicating such scourges;

11. Gross denials of human rights arising from discrimination on grounds of race, religion, belief or expressions of opinion outrage the conscience of mankind and endanger the foundations of freedom, justice and peace in the world;

12. The widening gap between the economically developed and developing countries impedes the realization of human rights in the international community. The failure of the Development Decade to reach its modest objectives makes it all the more imperative for every nation, according to its capacities, to make the maximum possible effort to close this gap;

13. Since human rights and fundamental freedoms are indivisible, the full realization of civil and political rights without the enjoyment of economic, social and cultural rights, is impossible. The achievement of lasting progress in the implementation of human rights is dependent upon sound and effective national and international policies of economic and social development;

14. The existence of over seven hundred million illiterates throughout the world is an enormous obstacle to all efforts at realizing the aims and purposes of the Charter of the United Nations and the provisions of the Universal Declaration of Human Rights. International action aimed at eradicating illiteracy from the face of the earth and promoting education at all levels requires urgent attention;

15. The discrimination of which women are still victims in various regions of the world must be eliminated. An inferior status for women is contrary to the Charter of the United Nations as well as the provisions of the Universal Declaration of Human Rights. The full implementation of the Declaration on the Elimination of Discrimination against Women is a necessity for the progress of mankind;

16. The protection of the family and of the child remains the concern of the international community. Parents have a basic human right to determine freely and responsibly the number and the spacing of their children;

17. The aspirations of the younger generation for a better world, in which human rights and fundamental freedoms are fully implemented, must be given the highest encouragement. It is imperative that youth participate in shaping the future of mankind;

18. While recent scientific discoveries and technological advances have opened vast prospects for economic, social and cultural progress, such developments may nevertheless endanger the rights and freedoms of individuals and will require continuing attention;

19. Disarmament would release immense human and material resources now devoted to military purposes. These resources should be used for the promotion of human rights and fundamental freedoms. General and complete disarmament is one of the highest aspirations of all peoples;

Therefore,

*The International Conference on Human Rights,*

1. *Affirming* its faith in the principles of the Universal Declaration of Human Rights and other international instruments in this field,

2. *Urges* all peoples and governments to dedicate themselves to the principles enshrined in the Universal Declaration of Human Rights and to redouble their efforts to provide for all human beings a life consonant with freedom and dignity and conducive to physical, mental, social and spiritual welfare.

---

## C. THE RIGHT OF SELF-DETERMINATION

### 6. Declaration on the Granting of Independence to Colonial Countries and Peoples

**(General Assembly resolution 1514 (XV) of 14 December 1960)**

*The General Assembly,*

*Mindful* of the determination proclaimed by the peoples of the world in the Charter of the United Nations to reaffirm faith in fundamental human rights, in the dignity and worth of the human person, in the equal rights of men and women and of nations large and small and to promote social progress and better standards of life in larger freedom,

*Conscious* of the need for the creation of conditions of stability and well-being and peaceful and friendly relations based on respect for the principles of equal rights and self-determination of all peoples, and of universal respect for, and observance of, human rights and fundamental freedoms for all without distinction as to race, sex, language or religion,

*Recognizing* the passionate yearning for freedom in all dependent peoples and the decisive role of such peoples in the attainment of their independence.

*Aware* of the increasing conflicts resulting from the denial of or impediments in the way of the freedom of such peoples, which constitute a serious threat to world peace,

*Considering* the important role of the United Nations in assisting the movement for independence in Trust and Non-Self-Governing Territories,

*Recognizing* that the peoples of the world ardently desire the end of colonialism in all its manifestations,

*Convinced* that the continued existence of colonialism prevents the development of international economic co-operation, impedes the social, cultural and economic development of dependent peoples and militates against the United Nations ideal of universal peace,

*Affirming* that peoples may, for their own ends, freely dispose of their natural wealth and resources without prejudice to any obligations arising out of international economic co-operation, based upon the principle of mutual benefit, and international law,

*Believing* that the process of liberation is irresistible and irreversible and that, in order to avoid serious crises, an end must be put to colonialism and all practices of segregation and discrimination associated therewith,

*Welcoming* the emergence in recent years of a large number of dependent territories into freedom and independence, and recognizing the increasingly powerful trends towards freedom in such territories which have not yet attained independence,

*Convinced* that all peoples have an inalienable right to complete freedom, the exercise of their sovereignty and the integrity of their national territory,

*Solemnly proclaims* the necessity of bringing to a speedy and unconditional end colonialism in all its forms and manifestations;

And to this end

*Declares* that:

1. The subjection of peoples to alien subjugation, domination and exploitation constitutes a denial of fundamental human rights, is contrary to the Charter of the United Nations and is an impediment to the promotion of world peace and co-operation.

2. All peoples have the right to self-determination; by virtue of that right they freely determine their political status and freely pursue their economic, social and cultural development.

3. Inadequacy of political, economic, social or educational preparedness should never serve as a pretext for delaying independence.

4. All armed action or repressive measures of all kinds directed against dependent peoples shall cease in order to enable them to exercise peacefully and freely their right to complete independence, and the integrity of their national territory shall be respected.

5. Immediate steps shall be taken, in Trust and Non-Self-Governing Territories or all other territories which have not yet attained independence, to transfer all powers to the peoples of those territories, without any conditions or reservations, in accordance with their freely expressed will and desire, without any distinction as to race, creed or colour, in order to enable them to enjoy complete independence and freedom.

6. Any attempt aimed at the partial or total disruption of the national unity and the territorial integrity of a country is incompatible with the purposes and principles of the Charter of the United Nations.

7. All States shall observe faithfully and strictly the provisions of the Charter of the United Nations, the Universal Declaration of Human Rights and the present Declaration on the basis of equality, non-interference in the internal affairs of all States, and respect for the sovereign rights of all peoples and their territorial integrity.

### 7. General Assembly resolution 1803 (XVII) of 14 December 1962, "Permanent Sovereignty over Natural Resources"

*The General Assembly,*

*Recalling* its resolutions 523 (VI) of 12 January 1952 and 626 (VII) of 21 December 1952,

*Bearing in mind* its resolution 1314 (XIII) of 12 December 1958, by which it established the Commission on Permanent Sovereignty over Natural Resources and instructed it to conduct a full survey of the status of permanent sovereignty over natural wealth and resources as a basic constituent of the right to self-determination, with recommendations, where necessary, for its strengthening, and decided further that, in the conduct of the full survey of the status of the permanent sovereignty of peoples and nations over their natural wealth and resources, due regard should be paid to the rights and duties of States under international law and to the importance of encouraging international co-operation in the economic development of developing countries,

*Bearing in mind* its resolution 1515 (XV) of 15 December 1960, in which it recommended that the sovereign right of every State to dispose of its wealth and its natural resources should be respected,

*Considering* that any measure in this respect must be based on the recognition of the inalienable right of all States freely to dispose of their natural wealth and resources in accordance with their national interests, and on respect for the economic independence of States,

*Considering* that nothing in paragraph 4 below in any way prejudices the position of any Member State on any aspect of the question of the rights and obligations of successor States and Governments in respect of property acquired before the accession to complete sovereignty of countries formerly under colonial rule,

*Noting* that the subject of succession of States and Governments is being examined as a matter of priority by the International Law Commission,

*Considering* that it is desirable to promote international co-operation for the economic development of developing countries, and that economic and financial agreements between the developed and the developing countries must be based on the principles of equality and of the right of peoples and nations to self-determination,

*Considering* that the provision of economic and technical assistance, loans and increased foreign investment must not be subject to conditions which conflict with the interests of the recipient State,

*Considering* the benefits to be derived from exchanges of technical and scientific information likely to promote the development and use of such resources and wealth, and the important part which the United Nations and other international organizations are called upon to play in that connexion,

*Attaching* particular importance to the question of promoting the economic development of developing countries and securing their economic independence,

*Noting* that the creation and strengthening of the inalienable sovereignty of States over their natural wealth and resources reinforces their economic independence,

*Desiring* that there should be further consideration by the United Nations of the subject of permanent sovereignty over natural resources in the spirit of international co-operation in the field of economic development, particularly that of the developing countries,

I

*Declares* that:

1. The right of peoples and nations to permanent sovereignty over their natural wealth and resources must be exercised in the interest of their national development and of the well-being of the people of the State concerned.

2. The exploration, development and disposition of such resources, as well as the import of the foreign capital required for these purposes, should be in conformity with the rules and conditions which the peoples and nations freely consider to be necessary or desirable with regard to the authorization, restriction or prohibition of such activities.

3. In cases where authorization is granted, the capital imported and the earnings on that capital shall be governed by the terms thereof, by the national legislation in force, and by international law. The profits derived must be shared in the proportions freely agreed upon, in each case, between the investors and the recipient State, due care being taken to ensure that there is no impairment, for any reason, of that State's sovereignty over its natural wealth and resources.

4. Nationalization, expropriation or requisitioning shall be based on grounds or reasons of public utility, security or the national interest which are recognized as overriding purely individual or private interests, both domestic and foreign. In such cases the owner shall be paid appropriate compensation, in accordance with the rules in force in the State taking such measures in the exercise of its sovereignty and in accordance with international law. In any case where the question of compensation gives rise to a controversy, the national jurisdiction of the State taking such measures shall be exhausted. However, upon agreement by sovereign States and other parties concerned, settlement of the dispute should be made through arbitration or international adjudication.

5. The free and beneficial exercise of the sovereignty of peoples and nations over their natural resources must be furthered by the mutual respect of States based on their sovereign equality.

6. International co-operation for the economic development of developing countries, whether in the form of public or private capital investments, exchange of goods and services, technical assistance, or exchange of scientific information, shall be such as to further their independent national development and shall be based upon respect for their sovereignty over their natural wealth and resources.

7. Violation of the rights of peoples and nations to sovereignty over their natural wealth and resources is contrary to the spirit and principles of the Charter of the United Nations and hinders the development of international co-operation and the maintenance of peace.

8. Foreign investment agreements freely entered into by or between sovereign States shall be observed in good faith; States and international organizations shall strictly and conscientiously respect the sovereignty of peoples and nations over their natural wealth and resources in accordance with the Charter and the principles set forth in the present resolution.

. . .

# D. PREVENTION OF DISCRIMINATION

## 8. United Nations Declaration on the Elimination of All Forms of Racial Discrimination

**Proclaimed by the General Assembly of the United Nations on 20 November 1963 (resolution 1904 (XVIII))**

*The General Assembly,*

*Considering* that the Charter of the United Nations is based on the principles of the dignity and equality of all human beings and seeks, among other basic objectives, to achieve international co-operation in promoting and encouraging respect for human rights and fundamental freedoms for all without distinction as to race, sex, language or religion,

*Considering* that the Universal Declaration of Human Rights proclaims that all human beings are born free and equal in dignity and rights and that everyone is entitled to all the rights and freedoms set out in the Declaration, without distinction of any kind, in particular as to race, colour or national origin,

*Considering* that the Universal Declaration of Human Rights proclaims further that all are equal before the law and are entitled without any discrimination to equal protection of the law and that all are entitled to equal protection against any discrimination and against any incitement to such discrimination,

*Considering* that the United Nations has condemned colonialism and all practices of segregation and discrimination associated therewith, and that the Declaration on the granting of independence to colonial countries and peoples proclaims in particular the necessity of bringing colonialism to a speedy and unconditional end,

*Considering* that any doctrine of racial differentiation or superiority is scientifically false, morally condemnable, socially unjust and dangerous, and that there is no justification for racial discrimination either in theory or in practice,

*Taking into account* the other resolutions adopted by the General Assembly and the international instruments adopted by the specialized agencies, in particular the International Labour Organisation and the United Nations Educational, Scientific and Cultural Organization, in the field of discrimination,

*Taking into account* the fact that, although international action and efforts in a number of countries have made it possible to achieve progress in that field, discrimination based on race, colour or ethnic origin in certain areas of the world continues none the less to give cause for serious concern,

*Alarmed* by the manifestations of racial discrimination still in evidence in some areas of the world, some of which are imposed by certain Governments by means of legislative, administrative or other measures, in the form, *inter alia*, of *apartheid* segregation and separation, as well as by the promotion and dissemination of doctrines of racial superiority and expansionism in certain areas,

*Convinced* that all forms of racial discrimination and, still more so, governmental policies based on the prejudice of racial superiority or on racial hatred, besides constituting a violation of fundamental human rights, tend to jeopardize friendly relations among peoples, co-operation between nations and international peace and security,

*Convinced also* that racial discrimination harms not only those who are its objects but also those who practice it,

*Convinced further* that the building of a world society free from all forms of racial segregation and discrimination, factors which create hatred and division among men, is one of the fundamental objectives of the United Nations,

1. *Solemnly affirms* the necessity of speedily eliminating racial discrimination throughout the world, in all its forms and manifestations, and of securing understanding of and respect for the dignity of the human person;

2. *Solemnly affirms* the necessity of adopting national and international measures to that end, including teaching, education and information, in order to secure the universal and effective recognition and observance of the principles set forth below;

3. *Proclaims* this Declaration:

### *Article 1*

Discrimination between human beings on the ground of race, colour or ethnic origin is an offence to human dignity and shall be condemned as a denial of the principles of the Charter of the United Nations, as a violation of the human rights and fundamental freedoms proclaimed in the Universal Declaration of Human Rights, as an obstacle to friendly and peaceful relations among nations and as a fact capable of disturbing peace and security among peoples.

### *Article 2*

1. No State, institution, group or individual shall make any discrimination whatsoever in matters of human rights and fundamental freedoms in the treatmant of persons, groups of persons or institutions on the ground of race, colour or ethnic origin.

2. No State shall encourage, advocate or lend its support, through police action or otherwise, to any discrimination based on race, colour or ethnic origin by any group, institution or individual.

3. Special concrete measures shall be taken in appropriate circumstances in order to secure adequate development or protection of individuals belonging to

certain racial groups with the object of ensuring the full enjoyment by such individuals of human rights and fundamental freedoms. These measures shall in no circumstances have as a consequence the maintenance of unequal or separate rights for different racial groups.

*Article 3*

1. Particular efforts shall be made to prevent discrimination based on race, colour or ethnic origin, especially in the fields of civil rights, access to citizenship, education, religion, employment, occupation and housing.

2. Everyone shall have equal access to any place or facility intended for use by the general public, without distinction as to race, colour or ethnic origin.

*Article 4*

All States shall take effective measures to revise governmental and other public policies and to rescind laws and regulations which have the effect of creating and perpetuating racial discrimination wherever it still exists. They should pass legislation for prohibiting such discrimination and should take all appropriate measures to combat those prejudices which lead to racial discrimination.

*Article 5*

An end shall be put without delay to governmental and other public policies of racial segregation and especially policies of *apartheid*, as well as all forms of racial discrimination and separation resulting from such policies.

*Article 6*

No discrimination by reason of race, colour or ethnic origin shall be admitted in the enjoyment by any person of political and citizenship rights in his country, in particular the right to participate in elections through universal and equal suffrage and to take part in the government. Everyone has the right of equal access to public service in his country.

*Article 7*

1. Everyone has the right to equality before the law and to equal justice under the law. Everyone, without distinction as to race, colour or ethnic origin, has the right to security of person and protection by the State against violence or bodily harm, whether inflicted by government officials or by any individual, group or institution.

2. Everyone shall have the right to an effective remedy and protection against any discrimination he may suffer on the ground of race, colour or ethnic origin with respect to his fundamental rights and freedoms through independent national tribunals competent to deal with such matters.

*Article 8*

All effective steps shall be taken immediately in the fields of teaching, education and information, with a view to eliminating racial discrimination and prejudice and promoting understanding, tolerance and friendship among nations and racial groups, as well as to propagating the purposes and principles of the Charter of the United Nations, of the Universal Declaration of Human Rights, and of the Declaration on the Granting of Independence to Colonial Countries and Peoples.

*Article 9*

1. All propaganda and organizations based on ideas or theories of the superiority of one race or group of persons of one colour or ethnic origin with a view to justifying or promoting racial discrimination in any form shall be severely condemned.

2. All incitement to or acts of violence, whether by individuals or organizations against any race or group of persons of another colour or ethnic origin shall be considered an offence against society and punishable under law.

3. In order to put into effect the purposes and principles of the present Declaration, all States shall take immediate and positive measures, including legislative and other measures, to prosecute and/or outlaw organizations which promote or incite to racial discrimination, or incite to or use violence for purposes of discrimination based on race, colour or ethnic origin.

*Article 10*

The United Nations, the specialized agencies, States and non-governmental organizations shall do all in their power to promote energetic action which, by combining legal and other practical measures, will make possible the abolition of all forms of racial discrimination. They shall, in particular, study the causes of such discrimination with a view to recommending appropriate and effective measures to combat and eliminate it.

*Article 11*

Every State shall promote respect for and observance of human rights and fundamental freedoms in accordance with the Charter of the United Nations and shall fully and faithfully observe the provisions of the present Declaration, the Universal Declaration of Human Rights and the Declaration on the Granting of Independence to Colonial Countries and Peoples.

## 9. International Convention on the Elimination of All Forms of Racial Discrimination

**Adopted and opened for signature and ratification by General Assembly resolution 2106 A (XX) of 21 December 1965**

*Entry into force*: 4 January 1969, in accordance with article 19.

*The States Parties to this Convention,*

*Considering* that the Charter of the United Nations is based on the principles of the dignity and equality inherent in all human beings, and that all Member States have pledged themselves to take joint and separate action, in co-operation with the Organization, for the achievement of one of the purposes of the United

Nations which is to promote and encourage universal respect for and observance of human rights and fundamental freedoms for all, without distinction as to race, sex, language or religion,

*Considering* that the Universal Declaration of Human Rights proclaims that all human beings are born free and equal in indignity and rights and that everyone is entitled to all the rights and freedoms set out therein, without distinction of any kind, in particular as to race, colour or national origin,

*Considering* that all human beings are equal before the law and are entitled to equal protection of the law against any discrimination and against any incitement to discrimination,

*Considering* that the United Nations has condemned colonialism and all practices of segregation and discrimination associated therewith, in whatever form and wherever they exist, and that the Declaration on the Granting of Independence to Colonial Countries and Peoples of 14 December 1960 (General Asssembly resolution 1514 (XV)) has affirmed and solemnly proclaimed the necessity of bringing them to a speedy and unconditional end,

*Considering* that the United Nations Declaration on the Elimination of All Forms of Racial Discrimination of 20 November 1963 (General Assembly resolution 1904 (XVIII)) solemnly affirms the necessity of speedily eliminating racial discrimination throughout the world in all its forms and manifestations and of securing understanding of and respect for the dignity of the human person,

*Convinced* that any doctrine of superiority based on racial differentiation is scientifically false, morally condemnable, socially unjust and dangerous, and that there is no justification for racial discrimination, in theory or in practice, anywhere,

*Reaffirming* that discrimination between human beings on the grounds of race, colour or ethnic origin is an obstacle to friendly and peaceful relations among nations and is capable of disturbing peace and security among peoples and the harmony of persons living side by side even within one and the same State,

*Convinced* that the existence of racial barriers is repugnant to the ideals of any human society,

*Alarmed* by manifestations of racial discrimination still in evidence in some areas of the world and by governmental policies based on racial superiority or hatred, such as policies of *apartheid*, segregation or separation,

*Resolved* to adopt all necessary measures for speedily eliminating racial discrimination in all its forms and manifestations, and to prevent and combat racist doctrines and practices in order to promote understanding between races and to build an international community free from all forms of racial segregation and racial discrimination,

*Bearing in mind* the Convention concerning Discrimination in respect of Employment and Occupation adopted by the International Labour Organisation in 1958, and the Convention against Discrimination in Education adopted by the United Nations Educational, Scientific and Cultural Organization in 1960,

*Desiring* to implement the principles embodied in the United Nations Declaration on the Elimination of All Forms of Racial Discrimination and to secure the earliest adoption of practical measures to that end,

*Have agreed* as follows:

## PART I

### *Article 1*

1. In this Convention, the term "racial discrimination" shall mean any distinction, exclusion, restriction or preference based on race, colour, descent, or national or ethnic origin which has the purpose or effect of nullifying or impairing the recognition, enjoyment or exercise, on an equal footing, of human rights and fundamental freedoms in the political, economic, social, cultural or any other field of public life.

2. This Convention shall not apply to distinctions, exclusions, restrictions or preferences made by a State Party to this Convention between citizens and non-citizens.

3. Nothing in this Convention may be interpreted as affecting in any way the legal provisions of States Parties concerning nationality, citizenship or naturalization, provided that such provisions do not discriminate against any particular nationality.

4. Special measures taken for the sole purpose of securing adequate advancement of certain racial or ethnic groups or individuals requiring such protection as may be necessary in order to ensure such groups or individuals equal enjoyment or exercise of human rights and fundamental freedoms shall not be deemed racial discrimination, provided, however, that such measures do not, as a consequence, lead to the maintenance of separate rights for different racial groups and that they shall not be continued after the objectives for which they were taken have been achieved.

### *Article 2*

1. States Parties condemn racial discrimination and undertake to pursue by all appropriate means and without delay a policy of eliminating racial discrimination in all its forms and promoting understanding among all races, and, to this end:

(*a*) Each State Party undertakes to engage in no act or practice of racial discrimination against persons, groups of persons or institutions and to ensure that all public authorities and public institutions, national and local, shall act in conformity with this obligation;

(*b*) Each State Party undertakes not to sponsor, defend or support racial discrimination by any persons or organizations;

(*c*) Each State Party shall take effective measures to review governmental, national and local policies, and to amend, rescind or nullify any laws and regulations which have the effect of creating or perpetuating racial discrimination wherever it exists;

(*d*) Each State Party shall prohibit and bring to an end, by all appropriate means, including legislation as required by circumstances, racial discrimination by any persons, group or organization;

(*e*) Each State Party undertakes to encourage, where appropriate, integrationist multi-racial organizations and movements and other means of eliminating barriers between races, and to discourage anything which tends to strengthen racial division.

2. States Parties shall, when the circumstances so warrant, take, in the social, economic, cultural and other fields, special and concrete measures to ensure the adequate development and protection of certain racial groups or individuals belonging to them, for the purpose of guaranteeing them the full and equal enjoyment of human rights and fundamental freedoms. These measures shall in no case entail as a consequence the maintenance of unequal or separate rights for different racial groups after the objectives for which they were taken have been achieved.

### *Article 3*

States Parties particularly condemn racial segregation and *apartheid* and undertake to prevent, prohibit and eradicate all practices of this nature in territories under their jurisdiction.

### *Article 4*

States Parties condemn all propaganda and all organizations which are based on ideas or theories of superiority of one race or group of persons of one colour or ethnic origin, or which attempt to justify or promote racial hatred and discrimination in any form, and undertake to adopt immediate and positive measures designed to eradicate all incitement to, or acts of, such discrimination and, to this end, with due regard to the principles embodied in the Universal Declaration of Human Rights and the rights expressly set forth in article 5 of this Convention, *inter alia*:

(*a*) Shall declare an offence punishable by law all dissemination of ideas based on racial superiority or hatred, incitement to racial discrimination, as well as all acts of violence or incitement to such acts against any race or group of persons of another colour or ethnic origin, and also the provision of any assistance to racist activities, including the financing thereof;

(*b*) Shall declare illegal and prohibit organizations, and also organized and all other propaganda activities, which promote and incite racial discrimination, and shall recognize participation in such organizations or activities as an offence punishable by law;

(*c*) Shall not permit public authorities or public institutions, national or local, to promote or incite racial discrimination.

### *Article 5*

In compliance with the fundamental obligations laid down in article 2 of this Convention, States Parties undertake to prohibit and to eliminate racial discrimination in all its forms and to guarantee the right of everyone, without distinction as to race, colour, or national or ethnic origin, to equality before the law, notably in the enjoyment of the following rights:

(*a*) The right to equal treatment before the tribunals and all other organs administering justice;

(*b*) The right to security of person and protection by the State against violence or bodily harm, whether inflicted by government officials or by any individual group or institution;

(*c*) Political rights, in particular the rights to participate in elections—to vote and to stand for election—on the basis of universal and equal suffrage, to take part in the Government as well as in the conduct of public affairs at any level and to have equal access to public service;

(*d*) Other civil rights, in particular:

(i) The right to freedom of movement and residence within the border of the State;

(ii) The right to leave any country, including one's own, and to return to one's country;

(iii) The right to nationality;

(iv) The right to marriage and choice of spouse;

(v) The right to own property alone as well as in association with others;

(vi) The right to inherit;

(vii) The right to freedom of thought, conscience and religion;

(viii) The right to freedom of opinion and expression;

(ix) The right to freedom of peaceful assembly and association;

(*e*) Economic, social and cultural rights, in particular:

(i) The rights to work, to free choice of employment, to just and favourable conditions of work, to protection against unemployment, to equal pay for equal work, to just and favourable remuneration;

(ii) The right to form and join trade unions;

(iii) The right to housing;

(iv) The right to public health, medical care, social security and social services;

(v) The right to education and training;

(vi) The right to equal participation in cultural activities;

(f) The right of access to any place or service intended for use by the general public, such as transport, hotels, restaurants, cafés, theatres and parks.

### *Article 6*

States Parties shall assure to everyone within their jurisdiction effective protection and remedies, through the competent national tribunals and other State institutions, against any acts of racial discrimination which violate his human rights and fundamental freedoms contrary to this Convention, as well as the right to seek from such tribunals just and adequate reparation or satisfaction for any damage suffered as a result of such discrimination.

### *Article 7*

States Parties undertake to adopt immediate and effective measures, particularly in the fields of teaching, education, culture and information, with a view to combating prejudices which lead to racial discrimination and to promoting understanding, tolerance and friendship among nations and racial or ethnical groups, as well as to propagating the purposes and principles of the Charter of the United Nations, the Universal Declaration of Human Rights, the United Nations Declaration on the Elimination of All Forms of Racial Discrimination, and this Convention.

## PART II

### *Article 8*

1. There shall be established a Committee on the Elimination of Racial Discrimination (hereinafter referred to as the Committee) consisting of eighteen experts of high moral standing and acknowledged impartiality elected by States Parties from among their nationals, who shall serve in their personal capacity, consideration being given to equitable geographical distribution and to the representation of the different forms of civilization as well as of the principal legal systems.

2. The members of the Committee shall be elected by secret ballot from a list of persons nominated by the States Parties. Each State Party may nominate one person from among its own nationals.

3. The initial election shall be held six months after the date of the entry into force of this Convention. At least three months before the date of each election the Secretary-General of the United Nations shall address a letter to the States Parties inviting them to submit their nominations within two months. The Secretary-General shall prepare a list in alphabetical order of all persons thus nominated, indicating the States Parties which have nominated them, and shall submit it to the States Parties.

4. Elections of the members of the Committee shall be held at a meeting of States Parties convened by the Secretary-General at United Nations Headquarters. At that meeting, for which two thirds of the States Parties shall constitute a quorum, the persons elected to the Committee shall be those nominees who obtain the largest number of votes and an absolute majority of the votes of the representatives of States Parties present and voting.

5. (*a*) The members of the Committee shall be elected for a term of four years. However, the terms of nine of the members elected at the first election shall expire at the end of two years; immediately after the first election the names of these nine members shall be chosen by lot by the Chairman of the Committee.

(*b*) For the filling of casual vacancies, the State Party whose expert has ceased to function as a member of the Committee shall appoint another expert from among its nationals, subject to the approval of the Committee.

6. States Parties shall be responsible for the expenses of the members of the Committee while they are in performance of Committee duties.

### *Article 9*

1. States Parties undertake to submit to the Secretary-General of the United Nations, for consideration by the Committee, a report on the legislative, judicial, administrative or other measures which they have adopted and which give effect to the provisions of this Convention: (*a*) within one year after the entry into force of the Convention for the State concerned; and (*b*) thereafter every two years and whenever the Committee so requests. The Committee may request further information from the States Parties.

2. The Committee shall report annually, through the Secretary-General, to the General Assembly of the United Nations on its activities and may make suggestions and general recommendations based on the examination of the reports and information received from the States Parties. Such suggestions and general recommendations shall be reported to the General Assembly together with comments, if any, from States Parties.

### *Article 10*

1. The Committee shall adopt its own rules of procedure.

2. The Committee shall elect its officers for a term of two years.

3. The secretariat of the Committee shall be provided by the Secretary-General of the United Nations.

4. The meetings of the Committee shall normally be held at United Nations Headquarters.

### *Article 11*

1. If a State Party considers that another State Party is not giving effect to the provisions of this Convention, it may bring the matter to the attention of the Committee. The Committee shall then transmit the communication to the State Party concerned. Within three months, the receiving State shall submit to the Committee written explanations or statements clarifying the matter and the remedy, if any, that may have been taken by that State.

2. If the matter is not adjusted to the satisfaction of both parties, either by bilateral negotiations or by any other procedure open to them, within six months after the receipt by the receiving State of the initial communication, either State shall have the right to refer the matter again to the Committee by notifying the Committee and also the other State.

3. The Committee shall deal with a matter referred to it in accordance with paragraph 2 of this article after it has ascertained that all available domestic remedies have been invoked and exhausted in the case, in conformity with the generally recognized principles of international law. This shall not be the rule where the application of the remedies is unreasonably prolonged.

4. In any matter referred to it, the Committee may call upon the States Parties concerned to supply any other relevant information.

5. When any matter arising out of this article is being considered by the Committee, the States Parties concerned shall be entitled to send a representative to take part in the proceedings of the Committee, without voting rights, while the matter is under consideration.

### *Article 12*

1. (*a*) After the Committee has obtained and collated all the information it deems necessary, the Chair-

man shall appoint an *ad hoc* Conciliation Commission (herein-after referred to as the Commission) comprising five persons who may or may not be members of the Committee. The members of the Commission shall be appointed with the unanimous consent of the parties to the dispute, and its good offices shall be be made available to the States concerned with a view to an amicable solution of the matter on the basis of respect for this Convention.

(*b*) If the States parties to the dispute fail to reach agreement within three months on all or part of the composition of the Commission, the members of the Commission not agreed upon by the States parties to the dispute shall be elected by secret ballot by a two-thirds majority vote of the Committee from among its own members.

2. The members of the Commission shall serve in their personal capacity. They shall not be nationals of the States parties to the dispute or of a State not Party to this Convention.

3. The Commission shall elect its own Chairman and adopt its own rules of procedure.

4. The meetings of the Commission shall normally be held at United Nations Headquarters or at any other convenient place as determined by the Commission.

5. The secretariat provided in acordance with article 10, paragraph 3, of this Convention shall also service the Commission whenever a dispute among States Parties brings the Commission into being.

6. The States parties to the dispute shall share equally all the expenses of the members of the Commission in accordance with estimates to be provided by the Secretary-General of the United Nations.

7. The Secretary-General shall be empowered to pay the expenses of the members to the Commission, if necessary, before reimbursement by the States parties to the dispute in accordance with paragraph 6 of this article.

8. The information obtained and collated by the Committee shall be made available to the Commission, and the Commission may call upon the States concerned to supply any other relevant information.

*Article 13*

1. When the Commission has fully considered the matter, it shall prepare and submit to the Chairman of the Committee a report embodying its findings on all questions of fact relevant to the issue between the parties and containing such recommendations as it may think proper for the amicable solution of the dispute.

2. The Chairman of the Committee shall communicate the report of the Commission to each of the States parties to the dispute. These States shall, within three months, inform the Chairman of the Committee whether or not they accept the recommendations contained in the report of the Commission.

3. After the period provided for in paragraph 2 of this article, the Chairman of the Committee shall communicate the report of the Commission and the declarations of the States Parties concerned to the other States Parties to this Convention.

*Article 14*

1. A State Party may at any time declare that it recognizes the competence of the Committee to receive and consider communications from individuals or groups of individuals within its jurisdiction claiming to be victims of a violation by that State Party of any of the rights set forth in this Convention. No communication shall be received by the Committee if it concerns a State Party which has not made such a declaration.

2. Any State Party which makes a declaration as provided for in paragraph 1 of this article may establish or indicate a body within its national legal order which shall be competent to receive and consider petitions from individuals and groups of individuals within its jurisdiction who claim to be victims of a violation of any of the rights set forth in this Convention and who have exhausted other available local remedies.

3. A declaration made in accordance with paragraph 1 of this article and the name of any body established or indicated in accordance with paragraph 2 of this article shall be deposited by the State Party concerned with the Secretary-General of the United Nations, who shall transmit copies thereof to the other States Parties. A declaration may be withdrawn at any time by notification to the Secretary-General, but such a withdrawal shall not affect communications pending before the Committee.

4. A register of petitions shall be kept by the body established or indicated in accordance with paragraph 2 of this article, and certified copies of the register shall be filled annually through appropriate channels with the Secretary-General on the understanding that the contents shall not be publicly disclosed.

5. In the event of failure to obtain satisfaction from the body established or indicated in accordance with paragraph 2 of this article, the petitioner shall have the right to communicate the matter to the Committee within six months.

6. (*a*) The Committee shall confidentially bring any communication referred to it to the attention of the State Party alleged to be violating any provision of this Convention, but the identity of the individual or groups of individuals concerned shall not be revealed without his or their express consent. The Committee shall not receive anonymous communications.

(*b*) Within three months, the receiving State shall submit to the Committee written explanations or statements clarifying the matter and the remedy, if any, that may have been taken by that State.

7. (*a*) The Committee shall consider communications in the light of all information made available to it by the State Party concerned and by the petitioner. The Committee shall not consider any communication from a petitioner unless it has ascertained that the petitioner has exhausted all available domestic remedies. However, this shall not be the rule where the application of the remedies is unreasonably prolonged.

(*b*) The Committee shall forward its suggestions and recommendations, if any, to the State Party concerned and to the petitioner.

8. The Committee shall include in its annual report a summary of such communications and, where appropriate, a summary of the explanations and statements of the States Parties concerned and of its own suggestions and recommendations.

9. The Committee shall be competent to exercise the functions provided for in this article only when at least ten States Parties to this Convention are bound by declarations in accordance with paragraph 1 of this article.

*Article 15*

1. Pending the achievement of the objectives of the Declaration on the Granting of Independence to Colonial Countries and Peoples, contained in General Assembly resolution 1514 (XV) of 14 December 1960, the provisions of this Convention shall in no way limit the right of petition granted to these peoples by other international instruments or by the United Nations and its specialized agencies.

2. (*a*) The Committee established under article 8, paragraph 1, of this Convention shall receive copies of the petitions from, and submit expressions of opinion and recommendations on these petitions to, the bodies of the United Nations which deal with matters directly related to the principles and objectives of this Convention in their consideration of petitions from the inhabitants of Trust and Non-Self-Governing Territories and all other territories to which General Assembly resolution 1514 (XV) applies, relating to matters covered by this Convention which are before these bodies.

(*b*) The Committee shall receive from the competent bodies of the United Nations copies of the reports concerning the legislative, judicial, administrative or other measures directly related to the principles and objectives of this Convention applied by the administering Powers within the Territories mentioned in subparagraph (*a*) of this paragraph, and shall express opinions and make recommendations to these bodies.

3. The Committee shall include in its report to the General Assembly a summary of the petitions and reports it has received from United Nations bodies, and the expressions of opinion and recommendations of the Committee relating to the said petitions and reports.

4. The Committee shall request from the Secretary-General of the United Nations all information relevant to the objectives of this Convention and available to him regarding the Territories mentioned in paragraph 2 (*a*) of this article.

*Article 16*

The provisions of this Convention concerning the settlement of disputes or complaints shall be applied without prejudice to other procedures for settling disputes or complaints in the field of discrimination laid down in the constituent instruments of, or in conventions adopted by, the United Nations and its specialized agencies, and shall not prevent the States Parties from having recourse to other procedures for settling a dispute in accordance with general or special international agreements in force between them.

## Part III

*Article 17*

1. This Convention is open for signature by any State Member of the United Nations or member of any of its specialized agencies, by any State Party to the Statute of the International Court of Justice, and by any other State which has been invited by the General Assembly of the United Nations to become a Party to this Convention.

2. This Convention is subject to ratification. Instruments of ratification shall be deposited with the Secretary-General of the United Nations.

*Article 18*

1. This Convention shall be open to accession by any State referred to in article 17, paragraph 1, of the Convention.

2. Accession shall be effected by the deposit of an instrument of accession with the Secretary-General of the United Nations.

*Article 19*

1. This Convention shall enter into force on the thirtieth day after the date of the deposit with the Secretary-General of the United Nations of the twenty-seventh instrument of ratification or instrument of accession.

2. For each State ratifying this Convention or acceding to it after the deposit of the twenty-seventh instrument of ratification or instrument of accession, the Convention shall enter into force on the thirtieth day after the date of the deposit of its own instrument of ratification or instrument of accession.

*Article 20*

1. The Secretary-General of the United Nations shall receive and circulate to all States which are or may become Parties to this Convention reservations made by States at the time of ratification or accession. Any State which objects to the reservation shall, within a period of ninety days from the date of the said communication, notify the Secretary-General that it does not accept it.

2. A reservation incompatible with the object and purpose of this Convention shall not be permitted, nor shall a reservation the effect of which would inhibit the operation of any of the bodies established by this Convention be allowed. A reservation shall be considered incompatible or inhibitive if at least two thirds of the States Parties to this Convention object to it.

3. Reservations may be withdrawn at any time by notification to this effect addressed to the Secretary-General. Such notification shall take effect on the date on which it is received.

*Article 21*

A State Party may denounce this Convention by written notification to the Secretary-General of the

United Nations. Denunciation shall take effect one year after the date of receipt of the notification by the Secretary-General.

*Article 22*

Any dispute between two or more States Parties with respect to the interpretation or application of this Convention, which is not settled by negotiation or by the procedures expressly provided for in this Convention, shall, at the request of any of the parties to the dispute, be referred to the International Court of Justice for decision, unless the disputants agree to another mode of settlement.

*Article 23*

1. A request for the revision of this Convention may be made at any time by any State Party by means of a notification in writing addressed to the Secretary-General of the United Nations.

2. The General Assembly of the United Nations shall decide upon the steps, if any, to be taken in respect of such a request.

*Article 24*

The Secretary-General of the United Nations shall inform all States referred to in article 17, paragraph 1, of this Convention of the following particulars:

(*a*) Signatures, ratifications and accessions under articles 17 and 18;

(*b*) The date of entry into force of this Convention under article 19;

(*c*) Communications and declarations received under articles 14, 20 and 23;

(*d*) Denunciations under article 21.

*Article 25*

1. This Convention, of which the Chinese, English, French, Russian and Spanish texts are equally authentic, shall be deposited in the archives of the United Nations.

2. The Secretary-General of the United Nations shall transmit certified copies of this Convention to all States belonging to any of the categories mentioned in article 17, paragraph 1, of the Convention.

## 10. Discrimination (Employment and Occupation) Convention

**Convention (No. 111) concerning Discrimination in Respect of Employment and Occupation**

**Adopted on 25 June 1958 by the General Conference of the International Labour Organisation at its forty-second session**

***Entry into force*:** 15 June 1960, in accordance with article 8.

*The General Conference of the International Labour Organisation,*

*Having been* convened at Geneva by the Governing Body of the International Labour Office, and having met in its forty-second session on 4 June 1958, and

*Having decided* upon the adoption of certain proposals with regard to discrimination in the field of employment and occupation, which is the fourth item on the agenda of the session, and

*Having determined* that these proposals shall take the form of an international Convention, and

*Considering* that the Declaration of Philadelphia affirms that all human beings, irrespective of race, creed or sex, have the right to pursue both their material well-being and their spiritual development in conditions of freedom and dignity, of economic security and equal opportunity, and

*Considering further* that discrimination constitutes a violation of rights enunciated by the Universal Declaration of Human Rights,

*Adopts* this twenty-fifth day of the year one thousand nine hundred and fifty-eight the following Convention, which may be cited as the Discrimination (Employment and Occupation) Convention, 1958:

*Article 1*

1. For the purpose of this Convention the term "discrimination" includes:

(*a*) Any distinction, exclusion or preference made on the basis of race, colour, sex, religion, political opinion, national extraction or social origin, which has the effect of nullifying or impairing equality of opportunity or treatment in employment or occupation;

(*b*) Such other distinction, exclusion or preference which has the effect of nullifying or impairing equality opportunity or treatment in employment or occupation as may be determined by the Member concerned after consultation with representative employers' and workers' organisations, where such exist, and with other appropriate bodies.

2. Any distinction, exclusion or preference in respect of a particular job based on the inherent requirements thereof shall not be deemed to be discrimination.

3. For the purpose of this Convention the terms "employment" and "occupation" include access to vocational training, access to employment and to particular occupations, and terms and conditions of employment.

*Article 2*

Each Member for which this Convention is in force undertakes to declare and pursue a national policy designed to promote, by methods appropriate to national conditions and practice, equality of opportunity and treatment in respect of employment and occupation, with a view to eliminating any discrimination in respect thereof.

*Article 3*

Each Member for which this Convention is in force undertakes, by methods appropriate to national conditions and practice:

(*a*) To seek the co-operation of employers' and workers' organisations and other appropriate bodies in promoting the acceptance and observance of this policy;

(*b*) To enact such legislation and to promote such educational programmes as may be calculated to secure the acceptance and observance of the policy;

(*c*) To repeal any statutory provisions and modify any administrative instructions or practices which are inconsistent with the policy;

(*d*) To pursue the policy in respect of employment under the direct control of a national authority;

(*e*) To ensure observance of the policy in the activities of vocational guidance, vocational training and placement services under the direction of a national authority;

(*f*) To indicate in its annual reports on the application of the Convention the action taken in pursuance of the policy and the results secured by such action.

*Article 4*

Any measures affecting an individual who is justifiably suspected of, or engaged in, activities prejudicial to the security of the State shall not be deemed to be discrimination, provided that the individual concerned shall have the right to appeal to a competent body established in accordance with national practice.

*Article 5*

1. Special measures of protection or assistance provided in other Conventions or Recommendations adopted by the International Labour Conference shall not be deemed to be discrimination.

2. Any Member may, after consultation with representative employers' and workers' organisations, where such exist, determine that other special measures designed to meet the particular requirements of persons who, for reasons such as sex, age disablement, family responsibilities or social or cultural status, are generally recognised to require special protection or assistance, shall not be deemed to be discrimination.

*Article 6*

Each Member which ratifies this Convention undertakes to apply it to non-metropolitan territories in accordance with the provisions of the Constitution of the International Labour Organisation.

*Article 7*

The formal ratifications of this Convention shall be communicated to the Director-General of the International Labour Office for registration.

*Article 8*

1. This Convention shall be binding only upon those Members of the International Labour Organisation whose ratifications have been registered with the Director-General.

2. It shall come into force twelve months after the date on which the ratifications of two Members have been registered with the Director-General.

3. Thereafter, this Convention shall come into force for any Member twelve months after the date on which its ratification has been registered.

*Article 9*

1. A Member which has ratified this Convention may denounce it after the expiration of ten years from the date on which the Convention first comes into force, by an act communicated to the Director-General of the International Labour Office for registration. Such denunciation shall not take effect until one year after the date on which it is registered.

2. Each Member which has ratified this Convention and which does not, within the year following the expiration of the period of ten years mentioned in the preceding paragraph, exercise the right of denunciation provided for in this Article, will be bound for another period of ten years and, thereafter, may denounce this Convention at the expiration of each period of ten years under the terms provided for in this Article.

*Article 10*

1. The Director-General of the International Labour Office shall notify all Members of the International Labour Organisation of the registration of all ratifications and denunciations communicated to him by the Members of the Organisation.

2. When notifying the Members of the Organisation of the registration of the second ratification communicated to him, the Director-General shall draw the attention of the Members of the Organisation to the date upon which the Convention will come into force.

*Article 11*

The Director-General of the International Labour Office shall communicate to the Secretary-General of the United Nations for registration in accordance with Article 102 of the Charter of the United Nations full particulars of all ratifications and acts of denunciation registered by him in accordance with the provisions of the preceding Articles.

*Article 12*

At such times as it may consider necessary the Governing Body of the International Labour Office shall present to the General Conference a report on the working of this Convention and shall examine the desirability of placing on the agenda of the Conference the question of its revision in whole or in part.

*Article 13*

1. Should the Conference adopt a new Convention revising this Convention in whole or in part, then, unless the new Convention otherwise provides:

(*a*) The ratification by a Member of the new revising Convention shall *ipso jure* involve the immediate denunciation of this Convention, notwithstanding the provisions of Article 9 above, if and when the new revising Convention shall have come into force;

(*b*) As from the date when the new revising Convention comes into force this Convention shall cease to be open to ratification by the Members.

2. This Convention shall in any case remain in force in its actual form and content for those Members which have ratified it but have not ratified the revising Convention.

*Article 14*

The English and French versions of the text of this Convention are equally authoritative.

The foregoing is the authentic text of the Convention duly adopted by the General Conference of the International Labour Organisation during its forty-second session which was held at Geneva and declared closed the twenty-sixth day of June 1958.

IN FAITH WHEREOF we have appended our signatures this fifth day of July 1958.

## 11. Convention against Discrimination in Education

**Adopted by the General Conference of the United Nations Educational, Scientific and Cultural Organization on 14 December 1960**

***Entry into force*:** 22 May 1962, in accordance with article 14.

*The General Conference of the United Nations Educational, Scientific and Cultural Organization*, meeting in Paris from 14 November to 15 December 1960, at its eleventh session,

*Recalling* that the Universal Declaration of Human Rights asserts the principle of non-discrimination and proclaims that every person has the right to education,

*Considering* that discrimination in education is a violation of rights enunciated in that Declaration,

*Considering* that, under the terms of its Constitution, the United Nations Educational, Scientific and Cultural Organization has the purpose of instituting collaboration among the nations with a view to furthering for all universal respect for human rights and equality of educational oportunity,

*Recognizing* that, consequently, the United Nations Educational, Scientific and Cultural Organization, while respecting the diversity of national educational systems, has the duty not only to proscribe any form of discrimination in education but also to promote equality of opportunity and treatment for all in education,

*Having before it* proposals concerning the different aspects of discrimination in education, constituting item 17.1.4 of the agenda of the session,

*Having decided* at its tenth session that this question should be made the subject of an international convention as well as of recommendations to Member States.

*Adopts* this Convention on the fourteenth day of December 1960.

*Article 1*

1. For the purpose of this Convention, the term "discrimination" includes any distinction, exclusion, limitation or preference which, being based on race, colour, sex, language, religion, political or other opinion, national or social origin, economic condition or birth, has the purpose or effect of nullifying or impairing equality of treatment in education and in particular:

(*a*) Of depriving any person or group of persons of access to education of any type or at any level;

(*b*) Of limiting any person or group of persons to education of an inferior standard;

(*c*) Subject to the provisions of article 2 of this Convention, of establishing or maintaining separate educational systems or institutions for persons or groups of persons; or

(*d*) Of inflicting on any person or group of persons conditions which are incompatible with the dignity of man.

2. For the purposes of this Convention, the term "education" refers to all types and levels of education, and includes access to education, the standard and quality of education, and the conditions under which it is given.

*Article 2*

When permitted in a State, the following situations shall not be deemed to constitute discrimination, within the meaning of article 1 of this Convention:

(*a*) The establishment or maintenance of separate educational systems or institutions for pupils of the two sexes, if these systems or institutions offer equivalent access to education, provide a teaching staff with qualifications of the same standard as well as school premises and equipment of the same quality, and afford the opportunity to take the same or equivalent courses of study;

(*b*) The establishment or maintenance, for religious or linguistic reasons, of separate educational systems or institutions offering an education which is in keeping with the wishes of the pupil's parents or legal guardians, if participation in such systems or attendance at such institutions is optional and if the education provided conforms to such standards as may be laid down or approved by the competent authorities, in particular for education of the same level;

(*c*) The establishment or maintenance of private educational institutions, if the object of the institutions is not to secure the exclusion of any group but to provide educational facilities in addition to those provided by the public authorities, if the institutions are conducted in accordance with that object, and if the education provided conforms with such standards as may be laid down or approved by the competent authorities, in particular for education of the same level.

*Article 3*

In order to eliminate and prevent discrimination within the meaning of this Convention, the States Parties thereto undertake:

(*a*) To abrogate any statutory provisions and any administrative instructions and to discontinue any administrative practices which involve discrimination in education;

(*b*) To ensure, by legislation where necessary, that there is no discrimination in the admission of pupils to educational institutions;

(*c*) Not to allow any differences of treatment by the public authorities between nationals, except on the basis of merit or need, in the matter of school fees and the grant of scholarships or other forms of assistance to pupils and necessary permits and facilities for the pursuit of studies in foreign countries;

(*d*) Not to allow, in any form of assistance granted by the public authorities to educational institutions, any restrictions or preference based solely on the ground that pupils belong to a particular group;

(*e*) To give foreign nationals resident within their territory the same access to education as that given to their own nationals.

*Article 4*

The States Parties to this Convention undertake furthermore to formulate, develop and apply a national policy which, by methods appropriate to the circumstances and to national usage, will tend to promote equality of opportunity and of treatment in the matter of education and in particular:

(*a*) To make primary education free and compulsory; make secondary education in its different forms generally available and accessible to all; make higher education equally accessible to all on the basis of individual capacity; assure compliance by all with the obligation to attend school prescribed by law;

(*b*) To ensure that the standards of education are equivalent in all public education institutions of the same level, and that the conditions relating to the quality of the education provided are also equivalent;

(*c*) To encourage and intensify by appropriate methods the education of persons who have not received any primary education or who have not completed the entire primary education course and the continuation of their education on the basis of individual capacity;

(*d*) To provide training for the teaching profession without discrimination.

*Article 5*

1. The States Parties to this Convention agree that:

(*a*) Education shall be directed to the full development of the human personality and to the strengthening of respect for human rights and fundamental freedoms; it shall promote understanding, tolerance and friendship among all nations, racial or religious groups, and shall further the activities of the United Nations for the maintenance of peace;

(*b*) It is essential to respect the liberty of parents and, where applicable, of legal guardians, firstly to choose for their children institutions other than those maintained by the public authorities but conforming to such minimum educational standards as may be laid down or approved by the competent authorities and, secondly, to ensure in a manner consistent with the procedures followed in the State for the application of its legislation, the religious and moral education of the children in conformity with their own convictions; and no person or group of persons should be compelled to receive religious instruction inconsistent with his or their conviction;

(*c*) It is essential to recognize the right of members of national minorities to carry on their own educational activities, including the maintenance of schools and, depending on the educational policy of each State, the use or the teaching of their own language, provided however:

(i) That this right is not exercised in a manner which prevents the members of these minorities from understanding the culture and language of the community as a whole and from participating in its activities, or which prejudices national sovereignty;

(ii) That the standard of education is not lower than the general standard laid down or approved by the competent authorities; and

(iii) That attendance at such schools is optional.

2. The States Parties to this Convention undertake to take all necessary measures to ensure the application of the principles enunciated in paragraph 1 of this article.

*Article 6*

In the application of this Convention, the States Parties to it undertake to pay the greatest attention to any recommendations hereafter adopted by the General Conference of the United Nations Educational, Scientific and Cultural Organization defining the measures to be taken against the different forms of discrimination in education and for the purpose of ensuring equality of opportunity and treatment in education.

*Article 7*

The States Parties to this Convention shall in their periodic reports submitted to the General Conference of the United Nations Educational, Scientific and Cultural Organization on dates and in a manner to be determined by it, give information on the legislative and administrative provisions which they have adopted and other action which they have taken for the application of this Convention, including that taken for the formulation and the development of the national policy defined in article 4 as well as the results achieved and the obstacles encountered in the application of that policy.

*Article 8*

Any dispute which may arise between any two or more States Parties to this Convention concerning the interpretation or application of this Convention, which is not settled by negotiations shall at the request of the parties to the dispute be referred, failing other means of settling the dispute, to the International Court of Justice for decision.

*Article 9*

Reservations to this Convention shall not be permitted.

*Article 10*

This Convention shall not have the effect of diminishing the rights which individuals or groups may enjoy by virtue of agreements concluded between two or more States, where such rights are not contrary to the letter or spirit of this Convention.

*Article 11*

This Convention is drawn up in English, French, Russian and Spanish, the four texts being equally authoritative.

*Article 12*

1. This Convention shall be subject to ratification or acceptance by States Members of the United Nations Educational, Scientific and Cultural Organization in accordance with their respective constitutional procedures.

2. The instruments of ratification or acceptance shall be deposited with the Director-General of the United Nations Educational, Scientific and Cultural Organization.

*Article 13*

1. This Convention shall be open to accession by all States not Members of the United Nations Educational, Scientific and Cultural Organization which are invited to do so by the Executive Board of the Organization.

2. Accession shall be effected by the deposit of an instrument of accession with the Director-General of the United Nations Educational, Scientific and Cultural Organization.

*Article 14*

This Convention shall enter into force three months after the date of the deposit of the third instrument of ratification, acceptance or accession, but only with respect to those States which have deposited their respective instruments on or before that date. It shall enter into force with respect to any other State three months after the deposit of its instrument of ratification, acceptance or accession.

*Article 15*

The States Parties to this Convention recognize that the Convention is applicable not only to their metropolitan territory but also to all non-self-governing, trust, colonial and other territories for the international relations of which they are responsible; they undertake to consult, if necessary, the governments or other competent authorities of these territories on or before ratification, acceptance or accession with a view to securing the application of the Convention to those territories, and to notify the Director-General of the United Nations Educational, Scientific and Cultural Organization of the territories to which it is accordingly applied, the notification to take effect three months after the date of its receipt.

*Article 16*

1. Each State Party to this Convention may denounce the Convention on its own behalf or on behalf of any territory for whose international relations it is responsible.

2. The denunciation shall be notified by an instrument in writing, deposited with the Director-General of the United Nations Educational, Scientific and Cultural Organization.

3. The denunciation shall take effect twelve months after the receipt of the instrument of denunciation.

*Article 17*

The Director-General of the United Nations Educational, Scientific and Cultural Organization shall inform the States Members of the Organization, the States not members of the Organization which are referred to in article 13, as well as the United Nations, of the deposit of all the instruments of ratification, acceptance and accession provided for in articles 12 and 13, and of notifications and denunciations provided for in articles 15 and 16 respectively.

*Article 18*

1. This Convention may be revised by the General Conference of the United Nations Educational, Scientific and Cultural Organization. Any such revision shall, however, bind only the States which shall become Parties to the revising convention.

2. If the General Conference should adopt a new convention revising this Convention in whole or in part, then, unless the new convention otherwise provides, this Convention shall cease to be open to ratification, acceptance or accession as from the date on which the new revising convention enters into force.

*Article 19*

In conformity with Article 102 of the Charter of the United Nations, this Convention shall be registered with the Secretariat of the United Nations at the request of the Director-General of the United Nations Educational, Scientific and Cultural Organization.

DONE in Paris, this fifteenth day of December 1960, in two authentic copies bearing the signatures of the President of the eleventh session of the General Conference and of the Director-General of the United Nations Educational, Scientific and Cultural Organization, which shall be deposited in the archives of the United Nations Educational, Scientific and Cultural Organization, and certified true copies of which shall be delivered to all the States referred to in articles 12 and 13 as well as to the United Nations.

The foregoing is the authentic text of the Convention duly adopted by the General Conference of the United Nations Educational, Scientific and Cultural Organization during its eleventh session, which was held in Paris and declared closed the fifteenth day of December 1960.

IN FAITH WHEREOF we have appended our signatures this fifteenth day of December 1960.

## 12. Protocol Instituting a Conciliation and Good Offices Commission to be responsible for seeking a settlement of any disputes which may arise between States Parties to the Convention against Discrimination in Education

**Adopted by the General Conference of the United Nations Educational, Scientific and Cultural Organization on 10 December 1962**

***Entry into force*:** 24 October 1968, in accordance with article 24.

*The General Conference of the United Nations Educational, Scientific and Cultural Organization*, meeting in Paris from 9 November to 12 December 1962, at its twelfth session,

*Having adopted*, at its eleventh session, the Convention against Discrimination in Education,

*Desirous* of facilitating the implementation of that Convention, and

*Considering* that it is important, for this purpose, to institute a Conciliation and Good Offices Commission to be responsible for seeking the amicable settlement of any disputes which may arise between States Parties to the Convention, concerning its application or interpretation,

*Adopts* this Protocol on the tenth day of December 1962.

*Article 1*

There shall be established under the auspices of the United Nations Educational, Scientific and Cultural Organization a Conciliation and Good Offices Commission, hereinafter referred to as the Commission, to be responsible for seeking the amicable settlement of disputes between States Parties to the Convention against Discrimination in Education, hereinafter referred to as the Convention, concerning the application or interpretation of the Convention.

*Article 2*

1. The Commission shall consist of eleven members who shall be persons of high moral standing and acknowledged impartiality and shall be elected by the General Conference of the United Nations Educational, Scientific and Cultural Organization, hereinafter referred to as the General Conference.

2. The members of the Commission shall serve in their personal capacity.

*Article 3*

1. The members of the Commission shall be elected from a list of persons nominated for the purpose by the States Parties to this Protocol. Each State shall, after consulting its National Commission for UNESCO, nominate not more than four persons. These persons must be nationals of States Parties to this Protocol.

2. At least four months before the date of each election to the Commission, the Director-General of the United Nations Educational, Scientific and Cultural Organization, hereinafter referred to as the Director-General, shall invite the States Parties to the present Protocol to send within two months, their nominations of the persons referred to in paragraph 1 of this article. He shall prepare a list in alphabetical order of the persons thus nominated and shall submit it, at least one month before the election, to the Executive Board of the United Nations Educational, Scientific and Cultural Organization, hereinafter referred to as the Executive Board, and to the States Parties to the Convention. The Executive Board shall transmit the aforementioned list, with such suggestions as it may consider useful, to the General Conference, which shall carry out the election of members of the Commission in conformity with the procedure it normally follows in elections of two or more persons.

*Article 4*

1. The Commission may not include more than one national of the same State.

2. In the election of members of the Commission, the General Conference shall endeavour to include persons of recognized competence in the field of education and persons having judicial experience or legal experience particularly of an international character. It shall also give consideration to equitable geographical distribution of membership and to the representation of the different forms of civilization as well as of the principal legal systems.

*Article 5*

The members of the Commission shall be elected for a term of six years. They shall be eligible for re-election if renominated. The terms of four of the members elected at the first election shall, however, expire at the end of two years, and the terms of three other members at the end of four years. Immediately after the first election, the names of these members shall be chosen by lot by the President of the General Conference.

*Article 6*

1. In the event of the death or resignation of a member of the Commission, the Chairman shall immediately notify the Director-General, who shall declare the seat vacant from the date of death or the date on which the resignation takes effect.

2. If, in the unanimous opinion of the other members, a member of the Commission has ceased to carry out his functions for any cause other than absence of a temporary character or is unable to continue the discharge of his duties, the Chairman of the Commission shall notify the Director-General and shall thereupon declare the seat of such member to be vacant.

3. The Director-General shall inform the Member States of the United Nations Educational, Scientific and Cultural Organization, and any States not members of the Organization which have become Parties to this Protocol under the provisions of article 23, of any vacancies which have occurred in accordance with paragraphs 1 and 2 of this article.

4. In each of the cases provided for by paragraphs 1 and 2 of this article, the General Conference shall arrange for the replacement of the member whose seat has fallen vacant, for the unexpired portion of his term of office.

*Article 7*

Subject to the provisions of article 6, a member of the Commission shall remain in office until his successor takes up his duties.

*Article 8*

1. If the Commission does not include a member of the nationality of a State which is party to a dispute referred to it under the provisions of article 12 or article 13, that State, or if there is more than one, each of those States, may choose a person to sit on the Commission as a member *ad hoc*.

2. The States thus choosing a member *ad hoc* shall have regard to the qualities required of members of the Commission by virtue of article 2, paragraph 1, and

article 4, paragraphs 1 and 2. Any member *ad hoc* thus chosen shall be of the nationality of the State which chooses him or of a State Party to the Protocol, and shall serve in a personal capacity.

3. Should there be several States Parties to the dispute having the same interest they shall, for the purpose of choosing members *ad hoc*, be reckoned as one party only. The manner in which this provision shall be applied shall be determined by the Rules of Procedure of the Commission referred to in article 11.

*Article 9*

Members of the Commission and members *ad hoc* chosen under the provisions of article 8 shall receive travel and *per diem* allowances in respect of the periods during which they are engaged on the work of the Commission from the resources of the United Nations Educational, Scientific and Cultural Organization on terms laid down by the Executive Board.

*Article 10*

The Secretariat of the Commission shall be provided by the Director-General.

*Article 11*

1. The Commission shall elect its Chairman and Vice-Chairman for a period of two years. They may be re-elected.

2. The Commission shall establish its own Rules of Procedure, but these rules shall provide, *inter alia*, that:

(*a*) Two-thirds of the members, including the members *ad hoc*, if any, shall constitute a quorum.

(*b*) Decisions of the Commission shall be made by a majority vote of the members and members *ad hoc* present; if the votes are equally divided, the Chairman shall have a casting vote.

(*c*) If a State refers a matter to the Commission under article 12 or article 13:

(i) Such State, the State complained against, and any State Party to this Protocol whose national is concerned in such matter may make submissions in writing to the Commission;

(ii) Such State and the State complained against shall have the right to be represented at the hearings of the matter and to make submissions orally.

3. The Commission, on the occasion when it first proposes to establish its Rules of Procedure, shall send them in draft form to the States then Parties to the Protocol who may communicate any observation and suggestion they may wish to make within three months. The Commission shall re-examine its Rules of Procedure if at any time so requested by any State Party to the Protocol.

*Article 12*

1. If a State Party to this Protocol considers that another State Party is not giving effect to a provision of the Convention, it may, by written communication, bring the matter to the attention of that State. Within three months after the receipt of the communication, the receiving State shall afford the complaining State an explanation or statement in writing concerning the matter, which should include, to the extent possible and pertinent, references to procedures and remedies taken, or pending, or available in the matter.

2. If the matter is not adjusted to the satisfaction of both parties, either by bilateral negotiations or by any other procedure open to them, within six months after the receipt by the receiving State of the initial communication, either State shall have the right to refer the matter to the Commission, by notice given to the Director-General and to the other State.

3. The provisions of the preceding paragraphs shall not affect the rights of States Parties to have recourse, in accordance with general or special international agreements in force between them, to other procedures for settling disputes including that of referring disputes by mutual consent to the Permanent Court of Arbitration at The Hague.

*Article 13*

From the beginning of the sixth year after the entry into force of this Protocol, the Commission may also be made responsible for seeking the settlement of any dispute concerning the application or interpretation of the Convention arising between States which are Parties to the Convention but are not, or are not all, Parties to this Protocol, if the said States agree to submit such dispute to the Commission. The conditions to be fulfilled by the said States in reaching agreement shall be laid down by the Commission's Rules of Procedure.

*Article 14*

The Commission shall deal with a matter referred to it under article 12 or article 13 of this Protocol only after it has ascertained that all available domestic remedies have been invoked and exhausted in the case, in conformity with the generally recognized principles of international law.

*Article 15*

Except in cases where new elements have been submitted to it, the Commission shall not consider matters it has already dealt with.

*Article 16*

In any matter referred to it, the Commission may call upon the States concerned to supply any relevant information.

*Article 17*

1. Subject to the provisions of article 14, the Commission, after obtaining all the information it thinks necessary, shall ascertain the facts, and make available its good offices to the States concerned with a view to an amicable solution of the matter on the basis of respect for the Convention.

2. The Commission shall in every case, and in no event later than eighteen months after the date of receipt by the Director-General of the notice under article 12, paragraph 2, draw up a report in accordance with the provisions of paragraph 3 below which will be sent

to the States concerned and then communicated to the Director-General for publication. When an advisory opinion is requested of the International Court of Justice, in accordance with article 18, the time-limit shall be extended appropriately.

3. If a solution within the terms of paragraph 1 of this article is reached, the Commission shall confine its report to a brief statement of the facts and of the solution reached. If such a solution is not reached, the Commission shall draw up a report on the facts and indicate the recommendations which it made with a view to conciliation. If the report does not represent in whole or in part the unanimous opinion of the members of the Commission, any member of the Commission shall be entitled to attach to it a separate opinion. The written and oral submissions made by the parties to the case in accordance with article 11, paragraph 2 (*c*), shall be attached to the report.

*Article 18*

The Commission may recommend to the Executive Board, or to the General Conference if the recommendation is made within two months before the opening of one of its sessions, that the International Court of Justice be requested to give an advisory opinion on any legal question connected with a matter laid before the Commission.

*Article 19*

The Commission shall submit to the General Conference at each of its regular sessions a report on its activities, which shall be transmitted to the General Conference by the Executive Board.

*Article 20*

1. The Director-General shall convene the first meeting of the Commission at the Headquarters of the United Nations Educational, Scientific and Cultural Organization within three months after its nomination by the General Conference.

2. Subsequent meetings of the Commissions shall be convened when necessary by the Chairman of the Commission to whom, as well as to all other members of the Commission, the Director-General shall transmit all matters referred to the Commission in accordance with the provisions of this Protocol.

3. Notwithstanding paragraph 2 of this article, when at least one-third of the members of the Commission consider that the Commission should examine a matter in accordance with the provisions of this Protocol, the Chairman shall on their so requiring convene a meeting of the Commission for that purpose.

*Article 21*

The present Protocol is drawn up in English, French, Russian and Spanish, all four texts being equally authentic.

*Article 22*

1. This Protocol shall be subject to ratification or acceptance by States Members of the United Nations Educational, Scientific and Cultural Organization which are Parties to the Convention.

2. The instruments of ratification or acceptance shall be deposited with the Director-General.

*Article 23*

1. This Protocol shall be open to accession by all States not Members of the United Nations Educational, Scientific and Cultural Organization which are Parties to the Convention.

2. Accession shall be effected by the deposit of an instrument of accession with the Director-General.

*Article 24*

This Protocol shall enter into force three months after the date of the deposit of the fifteenth instrument of ratification, acceptance or accession, but only with respect to those States which have deposited their respective instruments on or before that date. It shall enter into force with respect to any other State three months after the deposit of its instrument of ratification, acceptance or accession.

*Article 25*

Any State may, at the time of ratification, acceptance or accession or at any subsequent date, declare, by notification to the Director-General, that it agrees, with respect to any other State assuming the same obligation, to refer to the International Court of Justice, after the drafting of the report provided for in article 17, paragraph 3, any dispute covered by this Protocol on which no amicable solution has been reached in accordance with article 17, paragraph 1.

*Article 26*

1. Each State Party to this Protocol may denounce it.

2. The denunciation shall be notified by an instrument in writing, deposited with the Director-General.

3. Denunciation of the Convention shall automatically entail denunciation of this Protocol.

4. The denunciation shall take effect twelve months after the receipt of the instrument of denunciation. The State denouncing the Protocol shall, however, remain bound by its provisions in respect of any cases concerning it which have been referred to the Commission before the end of the time-limit stipulated in this paragraph.

*Article 27*

The Director-General shall inform the States Members of the United Nations Educational, Scientific and Cultural Organization, the States not Members of the Organization which are referred to in article 23, as well as the United Nations, of the deposit of all the instruments of ratification, acceptance and accession provided for in articles 22 and 23, and of the notifications and denunciations provided for in articles 25 and 26 respectively.

*Article 28*

In conformity with article 102 of the Charter of the United Nations, this Protocol shall be registered with the Secretariat of the United Nations at the request of the Director-General.

DONE in Paris, this eighteenth day of December 1962, in two authentic copies bearing the signatures of the President of the twelfth session of the General Conference and of the Director-General of the United Nations Educational, Scientific and Cultural Organization, which shall be deposited in the archives of the United Nations Educational, Scientific and Cultural Organization, and certified true copies of which shall be delivered to all the States referred to in articles 12 and 13 of the Convention against Discrimination in Education as well as to the United Nations.

The foregoing is the authentic text of the Protocol duly adopted by the General Conference of the United Nations Educational, Scientific and Cultural Organization during its twelfth session, which was held in Paris and declared closed the twelfth day of December 1962.

IN FAITH WHEREOF we have appended our signatures this eighteenth day of December 1962.

## 13. Equal Remuneration Convention

**Convention (No. 100) concerning Equal Remuneration for Men and Women Workers for Work of Equal Value**

**Adopted on 29 June 1951 by the General Conference of the International Labour Organisation at its thirty-fourth session**

***Entry into force*:** 23 May 1953, in accordance with article 6.

*The General Conference of the International Labour Organisation,*

*Having been convened* at Geneva by the Governing Body of the International Labour Office, and having met in its thirty-fourth session on 6 June 1951, and

*Having decided* upon the adoption of certain proposals with regard to the principle of equal remuneration for men and women workers for work of equal value, which is the seventh item on the agenda of the session, and

*Having determined* that these proposals shall take the form of an international Convention,

*Adopts* this twenty-ninth day of June of the year one thousand nine hundred and fifty-one the following Convention, which may be cited as the Equal Remuneration Convention, 1951:

*Article 1*

For the purpose of this Convention:

(*a*) The term "remuneration" includes the ordinary, basic or minimum wage or salary and any additional emoluments whatsoever payable directly or indirectly, whether in cash or in kind, by the employed to the worker and arising out of the workers' employment;

(*b*) The term "equal remuneration for men and women workers for work of equal value", refers to rates of remuneration established without discrimination based on sex.

*Article 2*

1. Each Member shall, by means appropriate to the methods in operation for determining rates of remuneration, promote and, in so far as is consistent with such methods, ensure the application to all workers of the principle of equal remuneration for men and women workers for work of equal value,

2. This principle may be applied by means of:

(*a*) National laws or regulations;

(*b*) Legally established or recognised machinery for wage determination;

(*c*) Collective agreements between employers and workers; or

(*d*) A combination of these various means.

*Article 3*

1. Where such action will assist in giving effect to the provisions of this Convention, measures shall be taken to promote objective appraisal of jobs on the basis of the work to be performed.

2. The methods to be followed in this appraisal may be decided upon by the authorities responsible for the determination of rates of remuneration, or, where such rates are determined by collective agreements, by the parties thereto.

3. Differential rates between workers, which correspond, without regard to sex, to differences as determined by such objective appraisal, in the work to be performed, shall not be considered as being contrary to the principle of equal remuneration for men and women workers for work of equal value.

*Article 4*

Each Member shall co-operate as appropriate with the employers' and workers' organisations concerned for the purpose of giving effect to the provisions of this Convention.

*Article 5*

The formal ratification of this Convention shall be communicated to the Director-General of the International Labour Office for registration.

*Article 6*

1. This Convention shall be binding only upon those Members of the International Labour Organisation whose ratifications have been registered with the Director-General.

2. It shall come into force twelve months after the date on which the ratifications of two Members have been registered with the Director-General.

3. Thereafter, this Convention shall come into force for any Member twelve months after the date on which its ratification has been registered.

*Article 7*

1. Declarations communicated to the Director-General of the International Labour Office in accordance with paragraph 2 of article 35 of the Constitution of the International Labour Organisation shall indicate:

(*a*) The territories in respect of which the Member concerned undertakes that the provisions of the Convention shall be applied without modification;

(*b*) The territories in respect of which it undertakes that the provisions of the Convention shall be applied subject to modifications, together with details of the said modifications;

(*c*) The territories in respect of which the Convention is inapplicable and in such cases the grounds on which it is inapplicable;

(*d*) The territories in respect of which it reserves its decisions pending further consideration of the position.

2. The undertakings referred to in subparagraphs (*a*) and (*b*) or paragraph 1 of this article shall be deemed to be an integral part of the ratification and shall have the force of ratification.

3. Any Member may at any time by a subsequent declaration cancel in whole or in part any reservation made in its original declaration by virtue of subparagraphs (*b*), (*c*) or (*d*) of paragraph 1 of this article.

4. Any Member may, at any time at which the Convention is subject to denunciation in accordance with the provisions of article 9, communicate to the Director-General a declaration modifying in any other respect the terms of any former declaration and stating the present position in respect of such territories as it may specify.

*Article 8*

1. Declarations communicated to the Director-General of the International Labour Office in accordance with paragraphs 4 or 5 of article 35 of the Constitution of the International Labour Organisation shall indicate whether the provisions of the Convention will be applied in the territory concerned without modification or subject to modification; when the declaration indicates that the provisions of the Convention will be applied subject to modification, it shall give details of the said modifications.

2. The Member, Members or international authority concerned may at any time by a subsequent declaration renounce in whole or in part the right to have recourse to any modification indicated in any former declaration.

3. The Member, Members or international authority concerned may, at any time at which this Convention is subject to denunciation in accordance with the provisions of article 9, communicate to the Director-General a declaration modifying in any other respect the terms of any former declaration and stating the present position in respect of the application of the Convention.

*Article 9*

1. A Member which has ratified this Convention may denounce it after the expiration of ten years from the date on which the Convention first comes into force, by an act communicated to the Director-General of the International Labour Office for registration. Such denunciation shall not take effect until one year after the date on which it is registered.

2. Each Member which has ratified this Convention and which does not, within the year following the expiration of the period of ten years mentioned in the preceding paragraph, exercise the right of denunciation provided for in this article, will be bound for another period of ten years and, thereafter, may denounce this Convention at the expiration of each period of ten years under the terms provided for in this article.

*Article 10*

1. The Director-General of the International Labour Office shall notify all Members of the International Labour Organisation of the registration of all ratifications, declarations and denunciations communicated to him by the Members of the Organisation.

2. When notifying the Members of the Organisation of the registration of the second ratification communicated to him, the Director-General shall draw the attention of the Members of the Organisation to the date upon which the Convention will come into force.

*Article 11*

The Director-General of the International Labour Office shall communicate to the Secretary-General of the United Nations for registration in accordance with Article 102 of the Charter of the United Nations full particulars of all ratifications, declarations and acts of denunciation registered by him in accordance with the provisions of the preceding articles.

*Article 12*

At such times as it may consider necessary, the Governing Body of the International Labour Office shall present to the General Conference a report on the working of this Convention and shall examine the desirability of placing on the agenda of the Conference the question of its revision in whole or in part.

*Article 13*

1. Should the Conference adopt a new Convention revising this Convention in whole or in part, then, unless the new Convention otherwise provides:

(*a*) The ratification by a Member of the new revising Convention shall *ipso jure* involve the immediate denunciation of this Convention, notwithstanding the provisions of article 9 above, if and when the new revising Convention shall have come into force;

(*b*) As from the date when the new revising Convention comes into force this Convention shall cease to be open to ratification by the Members.

2. This Convention shall in any case remain in force in its actual form and content for those Members which have ratified it but have not ratified the revising Convention.

*Article 14*

The English and French versions of the text of this Convention are equally authoritative.

The foregoing is the authentic text of the Convention duly adopted by the General Conference of the International Labour Organisation during its thirty-fourth session which was held at Geneva and declared closed the twenty-ninth day of June 1951.

IN FAITH WHEREOF we have appended our signatures this second day of August 1951.

## 14. Declaration on the Elimination of Discrimination against Women

**Proclaimed by the General Assembly of the United Nations on 7 November 1967 (resolution 2263 (XXII))**

*The General Assembly,*

*Considering* that the peoples of the United Nations have, in the Charter, reaffirmed their faith in fundamental human rights, in the dignity and worth of the human person and in the equal rights of men and women,

*Considering* that the Universal Declaration on Human Rights asserts the principle of non-discrimination and proclaims that all human beings are born free and equal in dignity and rights and that everyone is entitled to all the rights and freedoms set forth therein without distinction of any kind, including any distinction as to sex,

*Taking into account* the resolutions, declarations, conventions and recommendations of the United Nations and the specialized agencies designed to eliminate all forms of discrimination and to promote equal rights for men and women,

*Concerned* that, despite the Charter of the United Nations, the Universal Declaration of Human Rights, the International Covenants on Human Rights and other instruments of the United Nations and the specialized agencies and despite the progress made in the matter of equality of rights, there continues to exist considerable discrimination against women,

*Considering* that discrimination against women is incompatible with human dignity and with the welfare of the family and of society, prevents their participation, on equal terms with men, in the political, social, economic and cultural life of their countries and is an obstacle to the full development of the potentialities of women in the service of their countries and of humanity,

*Bearing in mind*, the great contribution made by women to social, political, economic and cultural life and the part they play in the family and particularly in the rearing of children,

*Convinced* that the full and complete development of a country, the welfare of the world and the cause of peace require the maximum participation of women as well as men in all fields,

*Considering* that it is necessary to ensure the universal recognition in law and in fact of the principle of equality of men and women,

*Solemnly proclaims* this Declaration:

### *Article 1*

Discrimination against women, denying or limiting as it does their equality of rights with men, is fundamentally unjust and constitutes an offence against human dignity.

### *Article 2*

All appropriate measures shall be taken to abolish existing laws, customs, regulations and practices which are discriminatory against women, and to establish adequate legal protection for equal rights of men and women, in particular:

(*a*) The principle of equality of rights shall be embodied in the constitution or otherwise guaranteed by law;

(*b*) The international instruments of the United Nations and the specialized agencies relating to the elimination of discrimination against women shall be ratified or acceded to and fully implemented as soon as practicable.

### *Article 3*

All appropriate measures shall be taken to educate public opinion and to direct national aspirations towards the eradication of prejudice and the abolition of customary and all other practices which are based on the idea of the inferiority of women.

### *Article 4*

All appropriate measures shall be taken to ensure to women on equal terms with men, without any discrimination:

(*a*) The right to vote in all elections and be eligible for election to all publicly elected bodies;

(*b*) The right to vote in all public referenda;

(*c*) The right to hold public office and to exercise all public functions.

Such rights shall be guaranteed by legislation.

### *Article 5*

Women shall have the same rights as men to acquire, change or retain their nationality. Marriage to an alien shall not automatically affect the nationality of the wife either by rendering her stateless or by forcing upon her the nationality of her husband.

### *Article 6*

1. Without prejudice to the safeguarding of the unity and the harmony of the family, which remains the basic unit of any society, all appropriate measures, particularly legislative measures, shall be taken to ensure to women, married or unmarried, equal rights with men in the field of civil law, and in particular:

(*a*) The right to acquire, administer, enjoy, dispose of and inherit property, including property acquired during marriage;

(*b*) The right to equality in legal capacity and the exercise thereof;

(*c*) The same rights as men with regard to the law on the movement of persons.

2. All appropriate measures shall be taken to ensure the principle of equality of status of the husband and wife, and in particular:

(*a*) Women shall have the same right as men to free choice of a spouse and to enter into marriage only with their free and full consent;

(*b*) Women shall have equal rights with men during marriage and at its dissolution. In all cases the interest of the children shall be paramount;

(*c*) Parents shall have equal rights and duties in matters relating to their children. In all cases the interest of the children shall be paramount.

3. Child marriage and the betrothal of young girls before puberty shall be prohibited, and effective action, including legislation, shall be taken to specify a minimum age for marriage and to make the registration of marriages in an official registry compulsory.

*Article 7*

All provisions of penal codes which constitute discrimination against women shall be repealed.

*Article 8*

All appropriate measures, including legislation, shall be taken to combat all forms of traffic in women and exploitation of prostitution of women.

*Article 9*

All appropriate measures shall be taken to ensure to girls and women, married or unmarried, equal rights with men in education at all levels, and in particular:

(*a*) Equal conditions of access to, and study in, educational institutions of all types, including universities and vocational, technical and professional schools;

(*b*) The same choice of curricula, the same examinations, teaching staff with qualifications of the same standard, and school premises and equipment of the same quality, whether the institutions are co-educational or not;

(*c*) Equal opportunities to benefit from scholarships and other study grants;

(*d*) Equal opportunities for access to programmes of continuing education, including adult literacy programmes;

(*e*) Access to educational information to help in ensuring the health and well-being of families.

*Article 10*

1. All appropriate measures shall be taken to ensure to women, married or unmarried, equal rights with men in the field of economic and social life, and in particular:

(*a*) The right, without discrimination on grounds of marital status or any other grounds, to receive vocational training, to work, to free choice of profession and employment, and to professional and vocational advancement;

(*b*) The right to equal remuneration with men and to equality of treatment in respect of work of equal value;

(*c*) The right to leave with pay, retirement privileges and provision for security in respect of unemployment, sickness, old age or other incapacity to work;

(*d*) The right to receive family allowancces on equal terms with men.

2. In order to prevent discrimination against women on account of marriage or maternity and to ensure their effective right to work, measures shall be taken to prevent their dismissal in the event of marriage or maternity and to provide paid maternity leave, with the guarantee of returning to former employment, and to provide the necessary social services, including child-care facilities.

3. Measures taken to protect women in certain types of work, for reasons inherent in their physical nature, shall not be regarded as discriminatory.

*Article 11*

1. The principle of equality of rights of men and women demands implementation in all States in accordance with the principles of the Charter of the United Nations and of the Universal Declaration of Human Rights.

2. Governments, non-governmental organizations and individuals are urged, therefore, to do all in their power to promote the implementation of the principles contained in this Declaration.

# E. WAR CRIMES AND CRIMES AGAINST HUMANITY, INCLUDING GENOCIDE

## 15. Convention on the Prevention and Punishment of the Crime of Genocide

**Approved and proposed for signature and ratification or accession by General Assembly resolution 260 A (III) of 9 December 1948**

***Entry into force*****:** 12 January 1951, in accordance with article XIII.

*The Contracting Parties,*

*Having considered* the declaration made by the General Assembly of the United Nations in its resolution 96 (I) dated 11 December 1946 that genocide is a crime under international law, contrary to the spirit and aims of the United Nations and condemned by the civilized world,

*Recognizing* that at all periods of history genocide has inflicted great losses on humanity, and

*Being convinced* that, in order to liberate mankind from such an odious scourge, international co-operation is required,

*Hereby agree as hereinafter provided*:

### *Article I*

The Contracting Parties confirm that genocide, whether committed in time of peace or in time of war, is a crime under international law which they undertake to prevent and to punish.

### *Article II*

In the present Convention, genocide means any of the following acts committed with intent to destroy, in whole or in part, a national, ethnical, racial or religious group, as such:

(*a*) Killing members of the group;

(*b*) Causing serious bodily or mental harm to members of the group;

(*c*) Deliberately inflicting on the group conditions of life calculated to bring about its physical destruction in whole or in part;

(*d*) Imposing measures intended to prevent births within the group;

(*e*) Forcibly transferring children of the group to another group.

### *Article III*

The following acts shall be punishable:

(*a*) Genocide;

(*b*) Conspiracy to commit genocide;

(*c*) Direct and public incitement to commit genocide;

(*d*) Attempt to commit genocide;

(*e*) Complicity in genocide.

### *Article IV*

Persons committing genocide or any of the other acts enumerated in article III shall be punished, whether they are constitutionally responsible rulers, public officials or private individuals.

### *Articie V*

The Contracting Parties undertake to enact, in accordance with their respective Constitutions, the necessary legislation to give effect to the provisions of the present Convention and, in particular, to provide effective penalties for persons guilty of genocide or any of the other acts enumerated in article III.

### *Article VI*

Persons charged with genocide or any of the other acts enumerated in article III shall be tried by a competent tribunal of the State in the territory of which the act was committed, or by such international penal tribunal as may have jurisdiction with respect to those Contracting Parties which shall have accepted its jurisdiction.

### *Article VII*

Genocide and the other acts enumerated in article III shall not be considered as political crimes for the purpose of extradition.

The Contracting Parties pledge themselves in such cases to grant extradition in accordance with their laws and treaties in force.

### *Article VIII*

Any Contracting Party may call upon the competent organs of the United Nations to take such action under the Charter of the United Nations as they consider appropriate for the prevention and suppression of acts of genocide or any of the other acts enumerated in article III.

### *Article IX*

Disputes between the Contracting Parties relating to the interpretation, application or fulfilment of the present Convention, including those relating to the responsibility of a State for genocide or for any of the other acts enumerated in article III, shall be submitted to the International Court of Justice at the request of any of the parties to the dispute.

*Article X*

The present Convention, of which the Chinese, English, French, Russian and Spanish texts are equally authentic, shall bear the date of 9 December 1948.

*Article XI*

The present Convention shall be open until 31 December 1949 for signature on behalf of any Member of the United Nations and of any non-member State to which an invitation to sign has been addressed by the General Assembly.

The present Convention shall be ratified, and the instruments of ratification shall be deposited with the Secretary-General of the United Nations.

After 1 January 1950, the present Convention may be acceded to on behalf of any Member of the United Nations and of any non-member State which has received an invitation as aforesaid.

Instruments of accession shall be deposited with the Secretary-General of the United Nations.

*Article XII*

Any Contracting Party may at any time, by notification addressed to the Secretary-General of the United Nations, extend the application of the present Convention to all or any of the territories for the conduct of whose foreign relations that Contracting Party is responsible.

*Article XIII*

On the day when the first twenty instruments of ratification or accession have been deposited, the Secretary-General shall draw up a *procès-verbal* and transmit a copy thereof to each Member of the United Nations and to each of the non-member States contemplated in article XI.

The present Convention shall come into force on the ninetieth day following the date of deposit of the twentieth instrument of ratification or accession.

Any ratification or accession effected, subsequent to the latter date shall become effective on the ninetieth day following the deposit of the instrument of ratification or accession.

*Article XIV*

The present Convention shall remain in effect for a period of ten years as from the date of its coming into force.

It shall thereafter remain in force for successive periods of five years for such Contracting Parties as have not denounced it at least six months before the expiration of the current period.

Denunciation shall be effected by a written notification addressed to the Secretary-General of the United Nations.

*Article XV*

If, as a result of denunciations, the number of Parties to the present Convention should become less than sixteen, the Convention shall cease to be in force as from the date on which the last of these denunciations shall become effective.

*Article XVI*

A request for the revision of the present Convention may be made at any time by any Contracting Party by means of a notification in writing addressed to the Secretary-General.

The General Assembly shall decide upon the steps, if any, to be taken in respect of such request.

*Article XVII*

The Secretary-General of the United Nations shall notify all Members of the United Nations and the non-member States contemplated in article XI of the following:

(*a*) Signatures, ratifications and accessions received in accordance with article XI;

(*b*) Notifications received in accordance with article XII;

(*c*) The date upon which the present Convention comes into force in accordance with article XIII;

(*d*) Denunciations received in accordance with article XIV;

(*e*) The abrogation of the Convention in accordance with article XV;

(*f*) Notifications received in accordance with article XVI.

*Article XVIII*

The original of the present Convention shall be deposited in the archives of the United Nations.

A certified copy of the Convention shall be transmitted to each Member of the United Nations and to each of the non-member States contemplated in article XI.

*Article XIX*

The present Convention shall be registered by the Secretary-General of the United Nations on the date of its coming into force.

## 16. Convention on the Non-Applicability of Statutory Limitations to War Crimes and Crimes against Humanity

**Adopted and opened for signature, ratification and accession by General Assembly resolution 2391 (XXIII) of 26 November 1968**

***Entry into force*:** 11 November 1970, in accordance with article VIII.

*Preamble*

*The States Parties to the present Convention,*

*Recalling* resolutions of the General Assembly of the United Nations 3 (I) of 13 February 1946 and 170 (II) of 31 October 1947 on the extradition and punishment of war criminals, resolution 95 (I) of 11 December 1946 affirming the principles of international law recognized by the Charter of the International

Military Tribunal, Nürnberg, and the judgement of the Tribunal, and resolutions 2184 (XXI) of 12 December 1966 and 2202 (XXI) of 16 December 1966 which expressly condemned as crimes against humanity the violation of the economic and political rights of the indigenous population on the one hand and the policies of *apartheid* on the other,

*Recalling* resolutions of the Economic and Social Council of the United Nations 1074 D (XXXIX) of 28 July 1965 and 1158 (XLI) of 5 August 1966 on the punishment of war criminals and of persons who have committed crimes against humanity,

*Noting* that none of the solemn declarations, instruments or conventions relating to the prosecution and punishment of war crimes and crimes against humanity made provision for a period of limitation,

*Considering* that war crimes and crimes against humanity are among the gravest crimes in international law,

*Convinced* that the effective punishment of war crimes and crimes against humanity is an important element in the prevention of such crimes, the protection of human rights and fundamental freedoms, the encouragement of confidence, the furtherance of co-operation among peoples and the promotion of international peace and security,

*Noting* that the application to war crimes and crimes against humanity of the rules of municipal law relating to the period of limitation for ordinary crimes is a matter of serious concern to world public opinion, since it prevents the prosecution and punishment of persons responsible for those crimes,

*Recognizing* that it is necessary and timely to affirm in international law, through this Convention, the principle that there is no period of limitation for war crimes and crimes against humanity, and to secure its universal application,

*Have agreed* as follows:

### *Article I*

No statutory limitation shall apply to the following crimes, irrespective of the date of their commission:

(*a*) War crimes as they are defined in the Charter of the International Military Tribunal, Nürnberg, of 8 August 1945 and confirmed by resolutions 3 (I) of 13 February 1946 and 95 (I) of 11 December 1946 of the General Assembly of the United Nations, particularly the "grave breaches" enumerated in the Geneva Conventions of 12 August 1949 for the protection of war victims;

(*b*) Crimes against humanity whether committed in time of war or in time of peace as they are defined in the Charter of the International Military Tribunal, Nürnberg, of 8 August 1945 and confirmed by resolutions 3 (I) of 13 February 1946 and 95 (I) of 11 December 1946 of the General Assembly of the United Nations, eviction by armed attack or occupation and inhuman acts resulting from the policy of *apartheid*, and the crime of genocide as defined in the 1948 Convention on the Prevention and Punishment of the Crime of Genocide, even if such acts do not constitute a violation of the domestic law of the country in which they were committed.

### *Article II*

If any of the crimes mentioned in article I is committed, the provisions of this Convention shall apply to representatives of the State authority and private individuals who, as principals or accomplices, participate in or who directly incite others to the commission of any of those crimes, or who conspire to commit them, irrespective of the degree of completion, and to representatives of the State authority who tolerate their commission.

### *Article III*

The States Parties to the present Convention undertake to adopt all necessary domestic measures, legislative or otherwise, with a view to making possible the extradition, in accordance with international law, of the persons referred to in article II of this Convention.

### *Article IV*

The States Parties to the present Convention undertake to adopt, in accordance with their respective constitutional processes, any legislative or other measures necessary to ensure that statutory or other limitations shall not apply to the prosecution and punishment of the crimes referred to in articles I and II of this Convention and that, where they exist, such limitations shall be abolished.

### *Article V*

This Convention shall, until 31 December 1969, be open for signature by any State Member of the United Nations or member of any of its specialized agencies or of the International Atomic Energy Agency, by any State Party to the Statute of the International Court of Justice, and by any other State which has been invited by the General Assembly of the United Nations to become a Party to this Convention.

### *Article VI*

This Convention is subject to ratification. Instruments of ratification shall be deposited with the Secretary-General of the United Nations.

### *Article VII*

This Convention shall be open to accession by any State referred to in article V. Instruments of accession shall be deposited with the Secretary-General of the United Nations.

### *Article VIII*

1. This Convention shall enter into force on the ninetieth day after the date of the deposit with the Secretary-General of the United Nations of the tenth instrument of ratification or accession.

2. For each State ratifying this Convention or acceding to it after the deposit of the tenth instrument of ratification or accession, the Convention shall enter into force on the ninetieth day after the date of the deposit of its own instrument of ratification or accession.

*Article IX*

1. After the expiry of a period of ten years from the date on which this Convention enters into force, a request for the revision of the Convention may be made at any time by any Contracting Party by means of a notification in writing addressed to the Secretary-General of the United Nations.

2. The General Assembly of the United Nations shall decide upon the steps, if any, to be taken in respect of such a request.

*Article X*

1. This Convention shall be deposited with the Secretary-General of the United Nations.

2. The Secretary-General of the United Nations shall transmit certified copies of this Convention to all States referred to in article V.

3. The Secretary-General of the United Nations shall inform all States referred to in article V of the following particulars:

(*a*) Signatures of this Convention, and instruments of ratification and accession deposited under articles V, VI and VII;

(*b*) The date of entry into force of this Convention in accordance with article VIII;

(*c*) Communications received under article IX.

*Article XI*

This Convention, of which the Chinese, English, French, Russian and Spanish texts are equally authentic, shall bear the date of 26 November 1968.

In witness whereof the undersigned, being duly authorized for that purpose, have signed this Convention.

# F. SLAVERY, SERVITUDE, FORCED LABOUR AND SIMILAR INSTITUTIONS AND PRACTICES

## 17. Slavery Convention

**Signed at Geneva on 25 September 1926**

***Entry into force*:** 7 July 1955, the date on which the amendments to the Convention, as set forth in the Annex to the Protocol signed at the Headquarters of the United Nations on 7 December 1953, entered into force in accordance with article III of the Protocol.

*Whereas* the signatories of the General Act of the Brussels Conference of 1889-90 declared that they were equally animated by the firm intention of putting an end to the traffic in African slaves,

*Whereas* the signatories of the Convention of Saint-Germain-en-Laye of 1919, to revise the General Act of Berlin of 1885, and the General Act and Declaration of Brussels of 1890, affirmed their intention of securing the complete suppression of slavery in all its forms and of the slave trade by land and sea,

*Taking into consideration* the report of the Temporary Slavery Commission appointed by the Council of the League of Nations on June 12th, 1924,

*Desiring* to complete and extend the work accomplished under the Brussels Act and to find a means of giving practical effect throughout the world to such intentions as were expressed in regard to slave trade and slavery by the signatories of the Convention of Saint-Germain-en-Laye, and recognising that it is necessary to conclude to that end more detailed arrangements than are contained in that Convention,

*Considering*, moreover, that it is necessary to prevent forced labour from developing into conditions analogous to slavery,

*Have decided* to conclude a Convention and have accordingly appointed as their Plenipotentiaries [*names omitted*]

. . . *have agreed* as follows:

### *Article 1*

For the purpose of the present Convention, the following definitions are agreed upon:

(1) Slavery is the status or condition of a person over whom any or all of the powers attaching to the right of ownership are exercised.

(2) The slave trade includes all acts involved in the capture, acquisition or disposal of a person with intent to reduce him to slavery; all acts involved in the acquisition of a slave with a view to selling or exchanging him; all acts of disposal by sale or exchange of a slave acquired with a view to being sold or exchanged, and, in general, every act of trade or transport in slaves.

### *Article 2*

The High Contracting Parties undertake, each in respect of the territories placed under its sovereignty, jurisdiction, protection, suzerainty or tutelage, so far as they have not already taken the necessary steps:

(*a*) To prevent and suppress the slave trade;

(*b*) To bring about, progressively and as soon as possible, the complete abolition of slavery in all its forms.

### *Article 3*

The High Contracting Parties undertake to adopt all appropriate measures with a view to preventing and suppressing the embarkation, disembarkation and transport of slaves in their territorial waters and upon all vessels flying their respective flags.

The High Contracting Parties undertake to negotiate as soon as possible a general Convention with regard to the slave trade which will give them rights and impose upon them duties of the same nature as those provided for in the Convention of June 17th, 1925, relative to the International Trade in Arms (Articles 12, 20, 21, 22, 23, 24, and paragraphs 3, 4 and 5 of Section II of Annex II), with the necessary adaptations, it being understood that this general Convention will not place the ships (even of small tonnage) of any High Contracting Parties in a position different from that of the other High Contracting Parties.

It is also understood that, before or after the coming into force of this general Convention, the High Contracting Parties are entirely free to conclude between themselves, without, however, derogating from the principles laid down in the preceding paragraph, such special agreements as, by reason of their peculiar situation, might appear to be suitable in order to bring about as soon as possible the complete disappearance of the slave trade.

### *Article 4*

The High Contracting Parties shall give to one another every assistance with the object of securing the abolition of slavery and the slave trade.

### *Article 5*

The High Contracting Parties recognise that recourse to compulsory or forced labour may have grave consequences and undertake, each in respect of the territories placed under its sovereignty, jurisdiction, protection, suzerainty or tutelage, to take all necessary measures to prevent compulsory or forced labour from developing into conditions analogous to slavery.

It is agreed that:

(1) Subject to the transitional provisions laid down in paragraph (2) below, compulsory or forced labour may only be exacted for public purposes.

(2) In territories in which compulsory or forced labour for other than public purposes still survives, the High Contracting Parties shall endeavor progressively and as soon as possible to put an end to the practice. So long as such forced or compulsory labour exists, this labour shall invariably be of an exceptional character, shall always receive adequate remuneration, and shall not involve the removal of the labourers from their usual place of residence.

(3) In all cases, the responsibility for any recourse to compulsory or forced labour shall rest with the competent central authorities of the territory concerned.

*Article 6*

Those of the High Contracting Parties whose laws do not at present make adequate provision for the punishment of infractions of laws and regulations enacted with a view to giving effect to the purposes of the present Convention undertake to adopt the necessary measures in order that severe penalties may be imposed in respect of such infractions.

*Article 7*

The High Contracting Parties undertake to communicate to each other and to the Secretary-General of the League of Nations any laws and regulations which they may enact with a view to the application of the provisions of the present Convention.

*Article 8*

The High Contracting Parties agree that disputes arising between them relating to the interpretation or application of this Convention shall, if they cannot be settled by direct negotiation, be referred for decision to the Permanent Court of International Justice. In case either or both of the States Parties to such a dispute should not be parties to the Protocol of December 16th, 1920, relating to the Permanent Court of International Justice, the dispute shall be referred, at the choice of the Parties and in accordance with the constitutional procedure of each State, either to the Permanent Court of International Justice or to a court of arbitration constituted in accordance with the Convention of October 18th, 1907, for the Pacific Settlement of International Disputes, or to some other court of arbitration.

*Article 9*

At the time of signature or of ratification or of accession, any High Contracting Party may declare that its acceptance of the present Convention does not bind some or all of the territories placed under its sovereignty, jurisdiction, protection, suzerainty or tutelage in respect of all or any provisions of the Convention; it may subsequently accede separately on behalf of any one of them or in respect of any provision to which any one of them is not a party.

*Article 10*

In the event of a High Contracting Party wishing to denounce the present Convention, the denunciation shall be notified in writing to the Secretary-General of the League of Nations, who will at once communicate a certified true copy of the notification to all the other High Contracting Parties, informing them of the date on which it was received.

The denunciation shall only have effect in regard to the notifying State, and one year after the notification has reached the Secretary-General of the League of Nations.

Denunciation may also be made separately in respect of any territory placed under its sovereignty, jurisdiction, protection, suzerainty or tutelage.

*Article 11*

The present Convention, which will bear this day's date and of which the French and English texts are both authentic, will remain open for signature by the States Members of the League of Nations until April 1st, 1927.

The Secretary-General of the League of Nations will subsequently bring the present Convention to the notice of States which have not signed it, including States which are not Members of the League of Nations, and invite them to accede thereto.

A State desiring to accede to the Convention shall notify its intention in writing to the Secretary-General of the League of Nations and transmit to him the instrument of accession, which shall be deposited in the archives of the League.

The Secretary-General shall immediately transmit to all the other High Contracting Parties a certified true copy of the notification and of the instrument of accession, informing them of the date on which he received them.

*Article 12*

The present Convention will be ratified and the instruments of ratification shall be deposited in the office of the Secretary-General of the League of Nations. The Secretary-General will inform all the High Contracting Parties of such deposit.

The Convention will come into operation for each State on the date of the deposit of its ratification or of its accession.

IN FAITH WHEREOF the Plenipotentiaries signed the present Convention.

DONE at Geneva the twenty-fifth day of September, one thousand nine hundred and twenty-six, in one copy, which will be deposited in the archives of the League of Nations. A certified copy shall be forwarded to each signatory State.

## 18. Protocol amending the Slavery Convention signed at Geneva on 25 September 1926

**Approved by General Assembly resolution 794 (VIII) of 23 October 1953**

***Entry into force*:** 7 December 1953, in accordance with article III.

*The States Parties to the present Protocol,*

*Considering* that under the Slavery Convention signed at Geneva on 25 September 1926 (hereinafter called "the Convention") the League of Nations was invested with certain duties and functions, and

*Considering* that it is expedient that these duties and functions should be continued by the United Nations,

*Have agreed* as follows:

*Article I*

The States Parties to the present Protocol undertake that as between themselves they will, in accordance with the provisions of the Protocol, attribute full legal force and effect to and duly apply the amendments to the Convention set forth in the annex to the Protocol.

*Article II*

1. The present Protocol shall be open for signature or acceptance by any of the States Parties to the Convention to which the Secretary-General has communicated for this purpose a copy of the Protocol.

2. States may become Parties to the present Protocol by:

(*a*) Signature without reservation as to acceptance;

(*b*) Signature with reservation as to acceptance, followed by acceptance;

(*c*) Acceptance.

3. Acceptance shall be effected by the deposit of a formal instrument with the Secretary-General of the United Nations.

*Article III*

1. The present Protocol shall come into force on the date on which two States shall have become Parties thereto, and shall thereafter come into force in respect of each State upon the date on which it becomes a Party to the Protocol.

2. The amendments set forth in the annex to the present Protocol shall come into force when twenty-three States shall have become Parties to the Protocol, and consequently any State becoming a Party to the Convention, after the amendments thereto have come into force, shall become a Party to the Convention as so amended.

*Article IV*

In accordance with paragraph 1 of Article 102 of the Charter of the United Nations and the regulations pursuant thereto adopted by the General Assembly, the Secretary-General of the United Nations is authorized to effect registration of the present Protocol and of the amendments made in the Convention by the Protocol on the respective dates of their entry into force and to publish the Protocol and the amended text of the Convention as soon as possible after registration.

*Article V*

The present Protocol, of which the Chinese, English, French, Russian and Spanish texts are equally authentic, shall be deposited in the archives of the United Nations Secretariat. The texts of the Convention to be amended in accordance with the annex being authentic in the English and French languages only, the English and French texts of the annex shall be equally authentic, and the Chinese, Russian and Spanish texts shall be translations. The Secretary-General shall prepare certified copies of the Protocol, including the annex, for communication to States Parties to the Convention, as well as to all other States Members of the United Nations. He shall likewise prepare for communication to States including States not Members of the United Nations, upon the entry into force of the amendments as provided in article III, certified copies of the Convention as so amended.

IN WITNESS WHEREOF the undersigned, being duly authorized thereto by their respective Governments, signed the present Protocol on the date appearing opposite their respective signatures.

DONE at the Headquarters of the United Nations, New York, this seventh day of December one thousand nine hundred and fifty-three.

**Annex to the Protocol amending the Slavery Convention signed at Geneva on 25 September 1926**

In *article 7* "the Secretary-General of the United Nations" shall be substituted for "the Secretary-General of the League of Nations".

In *article 8* "the International Court of Justice" shall be substituted for the "Permanent Court of International Justice", and "the Statute of the International Court of Justice" shall be substituted for "the Protocol of December 16th, 1920, relating to the Permanent Court of International Justice".

In the first and second paragraphs of *article 10* "the United Nations" shall be substituted for "the League of Nations".

The last three paragraphs of *article 11* shall be deleted and the following substituted:

"The present Convention shall be open to accession by all States, including States which are not Members of the United Nations, to which the Secretary-General of the United Nations shall have communicated a certified copy of the Convention.

"Accession shall be effected by the deposit of a formal instrument with the Secretary-General of the United Nations, who shall give notice thereof to all States Parties to the Convention and to all other States contemplated in the present article, informing them of the date on which each such instrument of accession was received in deposit."

In *article 12* "the United Nations" shall be substituted for "the League of Nations".

## 19. Supplementary Convention on the Abolition of Slavery, the Slave Trade, and Institutions and Practices Similar to Slavery

**Adopted by a Conference of Plenipotentiaries convened by Economic and Social Council resolution 608 (XXI) of 30 April 1956**

***Entry into force*****:** 30 April 1957, in accordance with article 13.

PREAMBLE

*The States Parties to the present Convention*,

*Considering* that freedom is the birthright of every human being,

*Mindful* that the peoples of the United Nations reaffirmed in the Charter their faith in the dignity and worth of the human person,

*Considering* that the Universal Declaration of Human Rights, proclaimed by the General Assembly of the United Nations as a common standard of achievement for all peoples and all nations, states that no one shall be held in slavery or servitude and that slavery and the slave trade shall be prohibited in all their forms,

*Recognizing* that, since the conclusion of the Slavery Convention signed at Geneva on 25 September 1926, which was designed to secure the abolition of slavery and of the slave trade, further progress has been made towards this end,

*Having regard* to the Forced Labour Convention of 1930 and to subsequent action by the International Labour Organisation in regard to forced or compulsory labour,

*Being aware*, however, that slavery, the slave trade and institutions and practices similar to slavery have not yet been eliminated in all parts of the world,

*Having decided*, therefore, that the Convention of 1926, which remains operative, should now be augmented by the conclusion of a supplementary convention designed to intensify national as well as international efforts towards the abolition of slavery, the slave trade and institutions and practices similar to slavery,

*Have agreed as follows*:

## SECTION I

## INSTITUTIONS AND PRACTICES SIMILAR TO SLAVERY

### *Article 1*

Each of the States Parties to this Convention shall take all practicable and necessary legislative and other measures to bring about progressively and as soon as possible the complete abolition or abandonment of the following institutions and practices, where they still exist and whether or not they are covered by the definition of slavery contained in article 1 of the Slavery Convention signed at Geneva on 25 September 1926:

(*a*) Debt bondage, that is to say, the status or condition arising from a pledge by a debtor of his personal services or of those of a person under his control as security for a debt, if the value of those services as reasonably assessed is not applied towards the liquidation of the debt or the length and nature of those services are not respectively limited and defined;

(*b*) Serfdom, that is to say, the condition or status of a tenant who is by law, custom or agreement bound to live and labour on land belonging to another person and to render some determinate service to such other person, whether for reward or not, and is not free to change his status;

(*c*) Any institution or practice whereby:

(i) A woman, without the right to refuse, is promised or given in marriage on payment of a consideration in money or in kind to her parents, guardian, family or any other person or group; or

(ii) The husband of a woman, his family, or his clan, has the right to transfer her to another person for value received or otherwise; or

(iii) A woman on the death of her husband is liable to be inherited by another person;

(*d*) Any institution or practice whereby a child or young person under the age of 18 years, is delivered by either or both of his natural parents or by his guardian to another person, whether for reward or not, with a view to the exploitation of the child or young person or of his labour.

### *Article 2*

With a view to bringing to an end the institutions and practices mentioned in article 1 (*c*) of this Convention, the States Parties undertake to prescribe, where appropriate, suitable minimum ages of marriage, to encourage the use of facilities whereby the consent of both parties to a marriage may be freely expressed in the presence of a competent civil or religious authority, and to encourage the registration of marriages.

## SECTION II

## THE SLAVE TRADE

### *Article 3*

1. The act of conveying or attempting to convey slaves from one country to another by whatever means of transport, or of being accessory thereto, shall be a criminal offence under the laws of the States Parties to this Convention and persons convicted thereof shall be liable to very severe penalties.

2. (*a*) The States Parties shall take all effective measures to prevent ships and aircraft authorized to fly their flags from conveying slaves and to punish persons guilty of such acts or of using national flags for that purpose.

(*b*) The States Parties shall take all effective measures to ensure that their ports, airfields and coasts are not used for the conveyance of slaves.

3. The States Parties to this Convention shall exchange information in order to ensure the practical co-ordination of the measures taken by them in combating the slave trade and shall inform each other of every case of the slave trade, and of every attempt to commit this criminal offence, which comes to their notice.

### *Article 4*

Any slave who takes refuge on board any vessel of a State Party to this Convention shall *ipso facto* be free.

## SECTION III

## SLAVERY AND INSTITUTIONS AND PRACTICES SIMILAR TO SLAVERY

### *Article 5*

In a country where the abolition or abandonment of slavery, or of the institutions or practices mentioned in article 1 of this Convention, is not yet complete, the act of mutilating, branding or otherwise marking a slave or a person of servile status in order to indicate his status, or as a punishment, or for any other reason, or of being accessory thereto, shall be a criminal offence under the laws of the States Parties to this Convention and persons convicted thereof shall be liable to punishment.

*Article 6*

1. The act of enslaving another person or of inducing another person to give himself or a person dependent upon him into slavery, or of attempting these acts, or being accessory thereto, or being a party to a conspiracy to accomplish any such acts, shall be a criminal offence under the laws of the States Parties to this Convention and persons convicted thereof shall be liable to punishment.

2. Subject to the provisions of the introductory paragraph of article 1 of this Convention, the provisions of paragraph 1 of the present article shall also apply to the act of inducing another person to place himself or a person dependent upon him into the servile status resulting from any of the institutions or practices mentioned in article 1, to any attempt to perform such acts, to bring accessory thereto, and to being a party to a conspiracy to accomplish any such acts.

## SECTION IV

### DEFINITIONS

*Article 7*

For the purposes of the present Convention:

(*a*) "Slavery" means, as defined in the Slavery Convention of 1926, the status or condition of a person over whom any or all of the powers attaching to the right of ownership are exercised, and "slave" means a person in such condition or status;

(*b*) "A person of servile status" means a person in the condition or status resulting from any of the institutions or practices mentioned in article 1 of this Convention;

(*c*) "Slave trade" means and includes all acts involved in the capture, acquisition or disposal of a person with intent to reduce him to slavery; all acts involved in the acquisition of a slave with a view to selling or exchanging him; all acts of disposal by sale or exchange of a person acquired with a view to being sold or exchanged; and, in general, every act of trade or transport in slaves by whatever means of conveyance.

## SECTION V

### CO-OPERATION BETWEEN STATES PARTIES AND COMMUNICATION OF INFORMATION

*Article 8*

1. The States Parties to this Convention undertake to co-operate with each other and with the United Nations to give effect to the foregoing provisions.

2. The Parties undertake to communicate to the Secretary-General of the United Nations copies of any laws, regulations and administrative measures enacted or put into effect to implement the provisions of this Convention.

3. The Secretary-General shall communicate the information received under paragraph 2 of this article to the other Parties and to the Economic and Social Council as part of the documentation for any discussion which the Council might undertake with a view to making further recommendations for the abolition of slavery, the slave trade or the institutions and practices which are the subject of this Convention.

## SECTION VI

### FINAL CLAUSES

*Article 9*

No reservations may be made to this Convention.

*Article 10*

Any dispute between States Parties to this Convention relating to its interpretation or application, which is not settled by negotiation, shall be referred to the International Court of Justice at the request of any one of the parties to the dispute, unless the parties concerned agree on another mode of settlement.

*Article 11*

1. This Convention shall be open until 1 July 1957 for signature by any State Member of the United Nations or of a specialized agency. It shall be subject to ratification by the signatory States, and the instruments of ratification shall be deposited with the Secretary-General of the United Nations, who shall inform each signatory and acceding State.

2. After 1 July 1957 this Convention shall be open for accession by any State Member of the United Nations or of a specialized agency, or by any other State to which an invitation to accede has been addressed by the General Assembly of the United Nations. Accession shall be effected by the deposit of a formal instrument with the Secretary-General of the United Nations, who shall inform each signatory and acceding State.

*Article 12*

1. This Convention shall apply to all non-self-governing trust, colonial and other non-metropolitan territories for the international relations of which any State Party is responsible; the Party concerned shall, subject to the provisions of paragraph 2 of this article, at the time of signature, ratification or accession declare the non-metropolitan territory or territories to which the Convention shall apply *ipso facto* as a result of such signature, ratification or accession.

2. In any case in which the previous consent of a non-metropolitan territory is required by the constitutional laws or practices of the Party or of the non-metropolitan territory, the Party concerned shall endeavour to secure the needed consent of the non-metropolitan territory within the period of twelve months from the date of signature of the Convention by the metropolitan State, and when such consent has been obtained the Party shall notify the Secretary-General.

This Convention shall apply to the territory or territories named in such notification from the date of its receipt by the Secretary-General.

3. After the expiry of the twelve-month period mentioned in the preceding paragraph, the States Parties concerned shall inform the Secretary-General of the results of the consultations with those non-metropolitan territories for whose international relations they are responsible and whose consent to the application of this Convention may have been withheld.

*Article 13*

1. This Convention shall enter into force on the date on which two States have become Parties thereto.

2. It shall thereafter enter into force with respect to each State and territory on the date of deposit of the instrument of ratification or accession of that State or notification of application to that territory.

*Article 14*

1. The application of this Convention shall be divided into successive periods of three years, of which the first shall begin on the date of entry into force of the Convention in accordance with paragraph 1 of article 13.

2. Any State Party may denounce this Convention by a notice addressed by that State to the Secretary-General not less than six months before the expiration of the current three-year period. The Secretary-General shall notify all other Parties of each such notice and the date of the receipt thereof.

3. Denunciations shall take effect at the expiration of the current three-year period.

4. In cases where, in accordance with the provisions of article 12, this Convention has become applicable to a non-metropolitan territory of a Party, that Party may at any time thereafter, with the consent of the territory concerned, give notice to the Secretary-General of the United Nations denouncing this Convention separately in respect of that territory. The denunciation shall take effect one year after the date of the receipt of such notice by the Secretary-General, who shall notify all other Parties of such notice and the date of the receipt thereof.

*Article 15*

This Convention, of which the Chinese, English, French, Russian and Spanish texts are equally authentic, shall be deposited in the archives of the United Nations Secretariat. The Secretary-General shall prepare a certified copy thereof for communication to States Parties to this Convention, as well as to all other States Members of the United Nations and of the specialized agencies.

IN WITNESS WHEREOF the undersigned, being duly authorized thereto by their respective Governments, have signed this Convention on the date appearing opposite their respective signatures.

DONE at the European Office of the United Nations at Geneva, this seventh day of September one thousand nine hundred and fifty-six.

## 20. Abolition of Forced Labour Convention*

**Convention (No. 105) concerning the Abolition of Forced Labour**

**Adopted on 25 June 1957 by the General Conference of the International Labour Organisation at its fortieth session**

***Entry into force***: 17 January 1959, in accordance with article 4.

*The General Conference of the International Labour Organisation,*

*Having been convened* at Geneva by the Governing Body of the International Labour Office, and having met in its fortieth session on 5 June 1957, and

*Having considered* the question of forced labour, which is the fourth item on the agenda of the session, and

*Having noted* the provisions of the Forced Labour Convention, 1930, and

*Having noted* that the Slavery Convention, 1926, provides that all necessary measures shall be taken to prevent compulsory or forced labour from developing into conditions analogous to slavery and that the Supplementary Convention on the Abolition of Slavery, the Slave Trade, and Institutions and Practices Similar to Slavery, 1956, provides for the complete abolition of debt bondage and serfdom, and

*Having noted* that the Protection of Wages Convention, 1949, provides that wages shall be paid regularly and prohibits methods of payment which deprive the worker of a genuine possibility of terminating his employment, and

*Having decided* upon the adoption of further proposals with regard to the abolition of certain forms of forced or compulsory labour constituting a violation of the rights of man referred to in the Charter of the United Nations and enunciated by the Universal Declaration of Human Rights, and

*Having determined* that these proposals shall take the form of an international Convention,

*adopts* this twenty-fifth day of June of the year one thousand nine hundred and fifty-seven the following Convention, which may be cited as the Abolition of Forced Labour Convention, 1957:

*Article 1*

Each Member of the International Labour Organisation which ratifies this Convention undertakes to suppress and not to make use of any form of forced or compulsory labour:

(*a*) As a means of political coercion or education or as a punishment for holding or expressing political views or views ideologically opposed to the established political, social or economic system;

(*b*) As a method of mobilising and using labour for purposes of economic development;

---

* See also Forced Labour Convention, 1930 (No. 29) which entered into force on 1 May 1932. This Convention provides for the suppression of forced or compulsory labour in all its forms within the shortest possible period subject to exceptions relating to compulsory military service, normal civil obligations, convict labour, work in emergencies and minor communal services.

(*c*) As a means of labour discipline;

(*d*) As a punishment for having participated in strikes;

(*e*) As a means of racial, social, national or religious discrimination.

*Article 2*

Each Member of the International Labour Organisation which ratifies this Convention undertakes to take effective measures to secure the immediate and complete abolition of forced or compulsory labour as specified in article 1 of this Convention.

*Article 3*

The formal ratifications of this Convention shall be communicated to the Director-General of the International Labour Office for registration.

*Article 4*

1. This Convention shall be binding only upon those Members of the International Labour Organisation whose ratifications have been registered with the Director-General.

2. It shall come into force twelve months after the date on which the ratifications of two Members have been registered with the Director-General.

3. Thereafter, this Convention shall come into force for any Member twelve months after the date on which its ratification has been registered.

*Article 5*

1. A Member which has ratified this Convention may denounce it after the expiration of ten years from the date on which the Convention first comes into force, by an act communicated to the Director-General of the International Labour Office for registration. Such denunciation shall not take effect until one year after the date on which it is registered.

2. Each Member which has ratified this Convention and which does not, within the year following the expiration of the period of ten years mentioned in the proceding paragraph, exercise the right of denunciation provided for in this article, will be bound for another period of ten years and, thereafter, may denounce this Convention at the expiration of each period of ten years under the terms provided for in this article.

*Article 6*

1. The Director-General of the International Labour Office shall notify all Members of the International Labour Organisation of the registration of all ratifications and denunciations communicated to him by the Members of the Organisation.

2. When notifying the Members of the Organisation of the registration of the second ratification communicated to him, the Director-General shall draw the attention of the Members of the Organisation to the date upon which the Convention will come into force.

*Article 7*

The Director-General of the International Labour Office shall communicate to the Secretary-General of the United Nations for registration in accordance with Article 102 of the Charter of the United Nations full particulars of all ratifications and acts of denunciation registered by him in accordance with the provisions of the preceding articles.

*Article 8*

At such times as it may consider necessary the Governing Body of the International Labour Office shall present to the General Conference a report on the working of the Convention and shall examine the desirability of placing on the agenda of the Conference the question of its revision in whole or in part.

*Article 9*

1. Should the Conference adopt a new Convention revising this Convention in whole or in part, then, unless the new Convention otherwise provides:

(*a*) The ratification by a Member of the new revising Convention shall *ipso jure* involve the immediate denunciation of this Convention, notwithstanding the provisions of article 5 above, if and when the new revising Convention shall have come into force;

(*b*) As from the date when the new revising Convention comes into force this Convention shall cease to be open to ratification by the Members.

2. This Convention shall in any case remain in force in its actual form and content for those Members which have ratified it but have not ratified the revising Convention.

*Article 10*

The English and French versions of the text of this Convention are equally authoritative.

The foregoing is the authentic text of the Convention duly adopted by the General Conference of the International Labour Organisation during its fortieth session which was held at Geneva and declared closed the twenty-seventh day of June 1957.

IN FAITH WHEREOF we have appended our signatures this fourth day of July 1957.

## 21. Convention for the Suppression of the Traffic in Persons and of the Exploitation of the Prostitution of Others

**Approved by General Assembly resolution 317 (IV) of 2 December 1949**

***Entry into force*****:** 25 July 1951, in accordance with article 24.

*Preamble*

*Whereas* prostitution and the accompanying evil of the traffic in persons for the purpose of prostitution are incompatible with the dignity and worth of the human person and endanger the welfare of the individual, the family and the community,

*Whereas,* with respect to the suppression of the traffic in women and children, the following international instruments are in force:

1. International Agreement of 18 May 1904 for the Suppression of the White Slave Traffic, as amended by the Protocol approved by the General Assembly of the United Nations on 3 December 1948,

2. International Convention of 4 May 1910 for the Suppression of the White Slave Traffic, as amended by the above-mentioned Protocol,

3. International Convention of 30 September 1921 for the Suppression of the Traffic in Women and Children, as amended by the Protocol approved by the General Assembly of the United Nations on 20 October 1947,

4. International Convention of 11 October 1933 for the Suppression of the Traffic in Women of Full Age, as amended by the aforesaid Protocol,

*Whereas* the League of Nations in 1937 prepared a draft Convention extending the scope of the above-mentioned instruments, and

*Whereas* developments since 1937 make feasible the conclusion of a convention consolidating the above-mentioned instruments and embodying the substance of the 1937 draft Convention as well as desirable alterations therein;

*Now therefore*

*The Contracting Parties*

*Hereby agree as hereinafter provided:*

*Article 1*

The Parties to the present Convention agree to punish any person who, to gratify the passions of another:

1. Procures, entices or leads away, for purposes of prostitution, another person, even with the consent of that person;

2. Exploits the prostitution of another person, even with the consent of that person.

*Article 2*

The Parties to the present Convention further agree to punish any person who:

1. Keeps or manages, or knowingly finances or takes part in the financing of a brothel;

2. Knowingly lets or rents a building or other place or any part thereof for the purpose of the prostitution of others.

*Article 3*

To the extent permitted by domestic law, attempts to commit any of the offences referred to in articles 1 and 2, and acts preparatory to the commission thereof, shall also be punished.

*Article 4*

To the extent permitted by domestic law, intentional participation in the acts referred to in articles 1 and 2 above shall also be punishable.

To the extent permitted by domestic law, acts of participation shall be treated as separate offences whenever this is necessary to prevent impunity.

*Article 5*

In cases where injured persons are entitled under domestic law to be parties to proceedings in respect of any of the offences referred to in the present Convention, aliens shall be so entitled upon the same terms as nationals.

*Article 6*

Each Party to the present Convention agrees to take all the necessary measures to repeal or abolish any existing law, regulation or administrative provision by virtue of which persons who engage in or are suspected of engaging in prostitution are subject either to special registration or to the possession of a special document or to any exceptional requirements for supervision or notification.

*Article 7*

Previous convictions pronounced in foreign States for offences referred to in the present Convention shall, to the extent permitted by domestic law, be taken into account for the purpose of:

1. Establishing recidivism;

2. Disqualifying the offender from the exercise of civil rights.

*Article 8*

The offences referred to in articles 1 and 2 of the present Convention shall be regarded as extraditable offences in any extradition treaty which has been or may hereafter be concluded between any of the Parties to this Convention.

The Parties to the present Convention which do not make extradition conditional on the existence of a treaty shall henceforward recognize the offences referred to in articles 1 and 2 of the present Convention as cases for extradition between themselves.

Extradition shall be granted in accordance with the law of the State to which the request is made.

*Article 9*

In States where the extradition of nationals is not permitted by law, nationals who have have returned to their own State after the commission abroad of any of the offences referred to in articles 1 and 2 of the present Convention shall be prosecuted in and punished by the courts of their own State.

This provision shall not apply if, in a similar case between the Parties to the present Convention, the extradition of an alien cannot be granted.

*Article 10*

The provisions of article 9 shall not apply when the person charged with the offence has been tried in a foreign State and, if convicted, has served his sentence or had it remitted or reduced in conformity with the laws of that foreign State.

*Article 11*

Nothing in the present Convention shall be interpreted as determining the attitude of a Party towards the general question of the limits of criminal jurisdiction under international law.

*Article 12*

The present Convention does not affect the principle that the offences to which it refers shall in each State be defined, prosecuted and punished in conformity with its domestic law.

*Article 13*

The Parties to the present Convention shall be bound to execute letters of request relating to offences referred to in the Convention in accordance with their domestic law and practice.

The transmission of letters of request shall be effected:

1. By direct communication between the judicial authorities; or

2. By direct communication between the Ministers of Justice of the two States, or by direct communication from another competent authority of the State making the request to the Minister of Justice of the State to which the request is made; or

3. Through the diplomatic or consular representative of the State making the request in the State to which the request is made; this representative shall send the letters of request direct to the competent judicial authority or to the authority indicated by the Government of the State to which the request is made, and shall receive direct from such authority the papers constituting the execution of the letters of request.

In cases 1 and 3 a copy of the letters of request shall always be sent to the superior authority of the State to which application is made.

Unless otherwise agreed, the letters of request shall be drawn up in the language of the authority making the request, provided always that the State to which the request is made may require a translation in its own language, certified correct by the authority making the request.

Each Party to the present Convention shall notify to each of the other Parties to the Convention the method or methods of transmission mentioned above which it will recognize for the letters of request of the latter State.

Until such notification is made by a State, its existing procedure in regard to letters of request shall remain in force.

Execution of letters of request shall not give rise to a claim for reimbursement of charges or expenses of any nature whatever other than expenses of experts.

Nothing in the present article shall be construed as an undertaking on the part of the Parties to the present Convention to adopt in criminal matters any form or methods of proof contrary to their own domestic laws.

*Article 14*

Each Party to the present Convention shall establish or maintain a service charged with the co-ordination and centralization of the results of the investigation of offences referred to in the present Convention.

Such services should compile all information calculated to facilitate the prevention and punishment of the offences referred to in the present Convention and should be in close contact with the corresponding services in other States.

*Article 15*

To the extent permitted by domestic law and to the extent to which the authorities responsible for the services referred to in article 14 may judge desirable, they shall furnish to the authorities responsible for the corresponding services in other States the following information:

1. Particulars of any offence referred to in the present Convention or any attempt to commit such offence;

2. Particulars of any search for and any prosecution, arrest, conviction, refusal of admission or expulsion of persons guilty of any of the offences referred to in the present Convention, the movements of such persons and any other useful information with regard to them.

The information so furnished shall include descriptions of the offenders, their fingerprints, photographs, methods of operation, police records and records of conviction.

*Article 16*

The Parties to the present Convention agree to take or to encourage, through their public and private educational, health, social, economic and other related services, measures for the prevention of prostitution and for the rehabilitation and social adjustment of the victims of prostitution and of the offences referred to in the present Convention.

*Article 17*

The Parties to the present Convention undertake, in connexion with immigration and emigration, to adopt or maintain such measures as are required, in terms of their obligations under the present Convention, to check the traffic in persons of either sex for the purpose of prostitution.

In particular they undertake:

1. To make such regulations as are necessary for the protection of immigrants or emigrants, and in particular, women and children, both at the place of arrival and departure and while *en route;*

2. To arrange for appropriate publicity warning the public of the dangers of the aforesaid traffic;

3. To take appropriate measures to ensure supervision of railway stations, airports, seaports and *en route,* and of other public places, in order to prevent international traffic in persons for the purpose of prostitution;

4. To take appropriate measures in order that the appropriate authorities be informed of the arrival of persons who appear, *prima facie,* to be the principals and accomplices in or victims of such traffic.

*Article 18*

The Parties to the present Convention undertake, in accordance with the conditions laid down by domestic law, to have declarations taken from aliens who are prostitutes, in order to establish their identity and civil status and to discover who has caused them to leave their State. The information obtained shall be communicated to the authorities of the State of origin of the said persons with a view to their eventual repatriation.

*Article 19*

The Parties to the present Convention undertake, in accordance with the conditions laid down by domestic law and without prejudice to prosecution or other action for violations thereunder and so far as possible:

1. Pending the completion of arrangements for the repatriation of destitute victims of international traffic in persons for the purpose of prostitution, to make suitable provisions for their temporary care and maintenance;

2. To repatriate persons referred to in article 18 who desire to be repatriated or who may be claimed by persons exercising authority over them or whose expulsion is ordered in conformity with the law. Repatriation shall take place only after agreement is reached with the State of destination as to identity and nationality as well as to the place and date of arrival at frontiers. Each Party to the present Convention shall facilitate the passage of such persons through its territory.

Where the persons referred to in the preceding paragraph cannot themselves repay the cost of repatriation and have neither spouse, relatives nor guardian to pay for them, the cost of repatriation as far as the nearest frontier or port of embarkation or airport in the direction of the State of origin shall be borne by the State where they are in residence, and the cost of the remainder of the journey shall be borne by the State of origin.

*Article 20*

The Parties to the present Convention shall, if they have not already done so, take the necessary measures for the supervision of employment agencies in order to prevent persons seeking employment, in particular women and children, from being exposed to the danger of prostitution.

*Article 21*

The Parties to the present Convention shall communicate to the Secretary-General of the United Nations such laws and regulations as have already been promulgated in their States, and thereafter annually such laws and regulations as may be promulgated, relating to the subjects of the present Convention, as well as all measures taken by them concerning the application of the Convention. The information received shall be published periodically by the Secretary-General and sent to all Members of the United Nations and to non-member States to which the present Convention is officially communicated in accordance with article 23.

*Article 22*

If any dispute shall arise between the Parties to the present Convention relating to its interpretation or application and if such dispute cannot be settled by other means, the dispute shall, at the request of any one of the Parties to the dispute, be referred to the International Court of Justice.

*Article 23*

The present Convention shall be open for signature on behalf of any Member of the United Nations and also on behalf of any other State to which an invitation has been addressed by the Economic and Social Council.

The present Convention shall be ratified and the instruments of ratification shall be deposited with the Secretary-General of the United Nations.

The States mentioned in the first paragraph which have not signed the Convention may accede to it.

Accession shall be effected by deposit of an instrument of accession with the Secretary-General of the United Nations.

For the purposes of the present Convention the word "State" shall include all the colonies and Trust Territories of a State signatory or acceding to the Convention and all territories for which such State is internationally responsible.

*Article 24*

The present Convention shall come into force on the ninetieth day following the date of deposit of the second instrument of ratification or accession.

For each State ratifying or acceding to the Convention after the deposit of the second instrument of ratification or accession, the Convention shall enter into force ninety days after the deposit by such State of its instrument of ratification or accession.

*Article 25*

After the expiration of five years from the entry into force of the present Convention, any Party to the Convention may denounce it by a written notification addressed to the Secretary-General of the United Nations.

Such denunciation shall take effect for the Party making it one year from the date upon which it is received by the Secretary-General of the United Nations.

*Article 26*

The Secretary-General of the United Nations shall inform all Members of the United Nations and non-member States referred to in article 23:

(*a*) Of signatures, ratifications and accessions received in accordance with article 23;

(*b*) Of the date on which the present Convention will come into force in accordance with article 24;

(*c*) Of denunciations received in accordance with article 25.

*Article 27*

Each Party to the present Convention undertakes to adopt, in accordance with its Constitution, the legislative or other measures necessary to ensure the application of the Convention.

*Article 28*

The provisions of the present Convention shall supersede in the relations between the Parties thereto the provisions of the international instruments referred to in sub-paragraphs 1, 2, 3 and 4 of the second paragraph of the Preamble, each of which shall be deemed to be terminated when all the Parties thereto shall have become Parties to the present Convention.

## FINAL PROTOCOL

Nothing in the present Convention shall be deemed to prejudice any legislation which ensures, for the enforcement of the provisions for securing the suppression of the traffic in persons and of the exploitation of others for purposes of prostitution, stricter conditions than those provided by the present Convention.

The provisions of articles 23 to 26 inclusive of the Convention shall apply to the present Protocol.

# G. NATIONALITY, STATELESSNESS, ASYLUM AND REFUGEES

## 22. Convention on the Nationality of Married Women

**Opened for signature and ratification by General Assembly resolution 1040 (XI) of 29 January 1957**

***Entry into force*****:** 11 August 1958, in accordance with article 6.

*The Contracting States,*

*Recognizing* that, conflicts in law in practice with reference to nationality arise as a result of provisions concerning the loss or acquisition of nationality by women as a result of marriage, of its disolution or of the change of nationality by the husband during marriage,

*Recognizing* that, in article 15 of the Universal Declaration of Human Rights, the General Assembly of the United Nations has proclaimed that "everyone has the right to a nationality" and that "no one shall be arbitrarily deprived of his nationality nor denied the right to change his nationality",

*Desiring* to co-operate with the United Nations in promoting universal respect for, and observance of, human rights and fundamental freedoms for all without distinction as to sex,

*Hereby agree* as hereinafter provided:

*Article 1*

Each Contracting State agrees that neither the celebration nor the dissolution of a marriage between one of its nationals and an alien, nor the change of nationality by the husband during marriage, shall automatically affect the nationality of the wife.

*Article 2*

Each Contracting State agrees that neither the voluntary acquisition of the nationality of another State nor the renunciation of its nationality by one of its nationals shall prevent the retention of its nationality by the wife of such national.

*Article 3*

1. Each Contracting State agrees that the alien wife of one of its nationals may, at her request, acquire the nationality of her husband through specially privileged naturalization procedures; the grant of such nationality may be subject to such limitations as may be imposed in the interests of national security or public policy.

2. Each Contracting State agrees that the present Convention shall not be construed as affecting any legislation or judicial practice by which the alien wife of one of its nationals may, at her request, acquire her her husband's nationality as a matter of right.

*Article 4*

1. The present Convention shall be open for signature and ratification on behalf of any State Member of the United Nations and also on behalf of any other State which is or hereafter becomes a member of any specialized agency of the United Nations, or which is or hereafter becomes a Party to the Statute of the International Court of Justice, or any other State to which an invitation has been addressed by the General Assembly of the United Nations.

2. The present Convention shall be ratified and the instruments of ratification shall be deposited with the Secretary-General of the United Nations.

*Article 5*

1. The present Convention shall be open for accession to all States referred to in paragraph 1 of article 4.

2. Accession shall be effected by the deposit of an instrument of accession with the Secretary-General of the United Nations.

*Article 6*

1. The present Convention shall come into force on the ninetieth day following the date of deposit of the sixth instrument of ratification or accession.

2. For each State ratifying or acceding to the Convention after the deposit of the sixth instrument of ratification or accession, the Convention shall enter into force on the ninetieth day after deposit by such State of its instrument of ratification or accession.

*Article 7*

1. The present Convention shall apply to all non-self-governing, trust, colonial and other non-metropolitan territories for the international relations of which any Contracting State is responsible; the Contracting State concerned shall, subject to the provisions of paragraph 2 of the present article, at the time of signature, ratification or accession declare the non-metropolitan territory or territories to which the Convention shall apply *ipso facto* as a result of such signature, ratification or accession.

2. In any case in which, for the purpose of nationality, a non-metropolitan territory is not treated as one with the metropolitan territory, or in any case in which the previous consent of a non-metropolitan territory is required by the constitutional laws or practices of the Contracting State or of the non-metropolitan territory for the application of the Convention to that territory, that Contracting State shall endeavour to secure the needed consent of the non-metropolitan territory within the period of twelve months from the date of signature of the Convention by that Contracting

State, and when such consent has been obtained the Contracting State shall notify the Secretary-General of the United Nations. The present Convention shall apply to the territory or territories named in such notification from the date of its receipt by the Secretary-General.

3. After the expiry of the twelve-month period mentioned in paragraph 2 of the present article, the Contracting States concerned shall inform the Secretary-General of the results of the consultations with those non-metropolitan territories for whose international relations they are responsible and whose consent to the application of the present Convention may have been withheld.

*Article 8*

1. At the time of signature, ratification or accession, any State may make reservations to any article of the present Convention other than articles 1 and 2.

2. If any State makes a reservation in accordance with paragraph 1 of the present article, the Convention, with the exception of those provisions to which the reservation relates, shall have effect as between the reserving State and the other Parties. The Secretary-General of the United Nations shall communicate the text of the reservation to all States which are or may become Parties to the Convention. Any State Party to the Convention or which thereafter becomes a Party may notify the Secretary-General that it does not agree to consider itself bound by the Convention with respect to the State making the reservation. This notification must be made, in the case of a State already a Party, within ninety days from the date of the communication by the Secretary-General; and, in the case of a State subsequently becoming a Party, within ninety days from the date when the instrument of ratification or accession is deposited. In the event that such a notification is made, the Convention shall not be deemed to be in effect as between the State making the notification and the State making the reservation.

3. Any State making a reservation in accordance with paragraph 1 of the present article may at any time withdraw the reservation, in whole or in part, after it has been accepted, by a notification to this effect addressed to the Secretary-General of the United Nations. Such notification shall take effect on the date on which it is received.

*Article 9*

1. Any Contracting State may denounce the present Convention by written notification to the Secretary-General of the United Nations. Denunciation shall take effect one year after the date of receipt of the notification by the Secretary-General.

2. The present Convention shall cease to be in force as from the date when the denunciation which reduces the number of Parties to less than six becomes effective.

*Article 10*

Any dispute which may arise between any two or more Contracting States concerning the interpretation or application of the present Convention which is not settled by negotiation, shall, at the request of any one of the Parties to the dispute, be referred to the International Court of Justice for decision, unless the Parties agree to another mode of settlement.

*Article 11*

The Secretary-General of the United Nations shall notify all States Members of the United Nations and the non-member States contemplated in paragraph 1 of article 4 of the present Convention of the following:

(*a*) Signatures and instruments of ratification received in accordance with article 4;

(*b*) Instruments of accession received in accordance with article 5;

(*c*) The date upon which the present Convention enters into force in accordance with article 6;

(*d*) Communications and notifications received in accordance with article 8;

(*e*) Notifications of denunciation received in accordance with paragraph 1 of article 9;

(*f*) Abrogation in accordance with paragraph 2 of article 9.

*Article 12*

1. The present Convention, of which the Chinese, English, French, Russian and Spanish texts shall be equally authentic, shall be deposited in the archives of the United Nations.

2. The Secretary-General of the United Nations shall transmit a certified copy of the Convention to all States Members of the United Nations and to the non-member States contemplated in paragraph 1 of article 4.

## 23. Convention on the Reduction of Statelessness

**Adopted on 30 August 1961 by a Conference of Plenipotentiaries which met in 1959 and reconvened in 1961 in pursuance of General Assembly resolution 896 (IX) of 4 December 1954**

***Entry into force*:** Not in force as of 31 December 1972 (see article 18).

*The Contracting States,*

*Acting* in pursuance of resolution 896 (IX), adopted by the General Assembly of the United Nations on 4 December 1954,

*Considering* it desirable to reduce statelessness by international agreement,

*Have agreed* as follows:

*Article 1*

1. A Contracting State shall grant its nationality to a person born in its territory who would otherwise be stateless. Such nationality shall be granted:

(*a*) At birth, by operation of law, or

(*b*) Upon an application being lodged with the appropriate authority, by or on behalf of the person concerned, in the manner prescribed by the national law. Subject to the provisions of paragraph 2 of this article, no such application may be rejected.

A contracting State which provides for the grant of its nationality in accordance with sub-paragraph (*b*) of this paragraph may also provide for the grant of its nationality by operation of law at such age and subject to such conditions as may be prescribed by the national law.

2. A Contracting State may make the grant of its nationality in accordance with sub-paragraph (*b*) of paragraph 1 of this article subject to one or more of the following conditions:

(*a*) That the application is lodged during a period, fixed by the Contracting State, beginning not later than at the age of eighteen years and ending not earlier than at the age of twenty-one years, so, however, that the person concerned shall be allowed at least one year during which he may himself make the application without having to obtain legal authorization to do so;

(*b*) That the person concerned has habitually resided in the territory of the Contracting State for such period as may be fixed by that State, not exceeding five years immediately preceding the lodging of the application nor ten years in all;

(*c*) That the person concerned has neither been convicted of an offence against national security nor has been sentenced to imprisonment for a term of five years or more on a criminal charge;

(*d*) That the person concerned has always been stateless.

3. Notwithstanding the provisions of paragraph 1 (*b*) and 2 of this article, a child born in wedlock in the territory of a Contracting State, whose mother has the nationality of that State, shall acquire at birth that nationality if it otherwise would be stateless.

4. A Contracting State shall grant its nationality to a person who would otherwise be stateless and who is unable to acquire the nationality of the Contracting State in whose territory he was born because he has passed the age for lodging his application or has not fulfilled the required residence conditions, if the nationality of one of his parents at the time of the person's birth was that of the Contracting State first above mentioned. If his parents did not possess the same nationality at the time of his birth, the question whether the nationality of the person concerned should follow that of the father or that of the mother shall be determined by the national law of such Contracting State. If application for such nationality is required, the application shall be made to the appropriate authority by or on behalf of the applicant in the manner prescribed by the national law. Subject to the provisions of paragraph 5 of this article, such application shall not be refused.

5. The Contracting State may make the grant of its nationality in accordance with the provisions of paragraph 4 of this article subject to one or more of the following conditions:

(*a*) That the application is lodged before the applicant reaches an age, being not less than twenty-three years, fixed by the Contracting State;

(*b*) That the person concerned has habitually resided in the territory of the Contracting State for such period immediately preceding the lodging of the application, not exceeding three years, as may be fixed by that State;

(*c*) That the person concerned has always been stateless.

*Article 2*

A foundling found in the territory of a Contracting State shall, in the absence of proof to the contrary, be considered to have been born within that territory of parents possessing the nationality of that State.

*Article 3*

For the purpose of determining the obligations of Contracting States under this Convention, birth on a ship or in an aircraft shall be deemed to have taken place in the territory of the State whose flag the ship flies or in the territory of the State in which the aircraft is registered, as the case may be.

*Article 4*

1. A Contracting State shall grant its nationality to a person, not born in the territory of a Contracting State, who would otherwise be stateless, if the nationality of one of his parents at the time of the person's birth was that of that State. If his parents did not possess the same nationality at the time of his birth, the question whether the nationality of the person concerned should follow that of the father or that of the mother shall be determined by the national law of such Contracting State. Nationality granted in accordance with the provisions of this paragraph shall be granted:

(*a*) At birth, by operation of law, or

(*b*) Upon an application being lodged with the appropriate authority, by or on behalf of the person concerned, in the manner prescribed by the national law. Subject to the provisions of paragraph 2 of this article, no such application may be rejected.

2. A Contracting State may make the grant of its nationality in accordance with the provisions of paragraph 1 of this article subject to one or more of the following conditions:

(*a*) That the application is lodged before the applicant reaches an age, being not less than twenty-three years, fixed by the Contracting State;

(*b*) That the person concerned has habitually resided in the territory of the Contracting State for such period immediately preceding the lodging of the application, not exceeding three years, as may be fixed by that State;

(*c*) That the person concerned has not been convicted of an offence against national security;

(*d*) That the person concerned has always been stateless.

*Article 5*

1. If the law of a Contracting State entails loss of nationality as a consequence of any change in the personal status of a person such as marriage, termination of marriage, legitimation, recognition or adoption, such loss shall be conditional upon possession or acquisition of another nationality.

2. If, under the law of a Contracting State, a child born out of wedlock loses the nationality of that State in consequence of a recognition of affiliation, he shall be given an opportunity to recover that nationality by written application to the appropriate authority, and

the conditions governing such application shall not be more rigorous than those laid down in paragraph 2 of article 1 of this Convention.

*Article 6*

If the law of a Contracting State provides for loss of its nationality by a person's spouse or children as a consequence of that person losing or being deprived of that nationality, such loss shall be conditional upon their possession or acquisition of another nationality.

*Article 7*

1. (*a*) If the law of a Contracting State entails loss of renunciation of nationality, such renunciation shall not result in loss of nationality unless the person concerned possesses or acquires another nationality.

•(*b*) The provisions of sub-paragraph (*a*) of this paragraph shall not apply where their application would be inconsistent with the principles stated in articles 13 and 14 of the Universal Declaration of Human Rights approved on 10 December 1948 by the General Assembly of the United Nations.

2. A national of a Contracting State who seeks naturalization in a foreign country shall not lose his nationality unless he acquires or has been accorded assurance of acquiring the nationality of that foreign country.

3. Subject to the provisions of paragraphs 4 and 5 of this article, a national of a Contracting State shall not lose his nationality, so as to become stateless, on the ground of departure, residence abroad, failure to register or on any similar ground.

4. A naturalized person may lose his nationality on account of residence abroad for a period, not less than seven consecutive years, specified by the law of the Contracting State concerned if he fails to declare to the appropriate authority his intention to retain his nationality.

5. In the case of a national of a Contracting State, born outside its territory, the law of that State may make the retention of its nationality after the expiry of one year from his attaining his majority conditional upon residence at that time in the territory of the State or registration with the appropriate authority.

6. Except in the circumstances mentioned in this article, a person shall not lose the nationality of a Contracting State, if such loss would render him stateless, notwithstanding that such loss is not expressly prohibited by any other provision of this Convention.

*Article 8*

1. A Contracting State shall not deprive a person of his nationality if such deprivation would render him stateless.

2. Nothwithstanding the provisions of paragraph 1 of this article, a person may be deprived of the nationality of a Contracting State:

(*a*) In the circumstances in which, under paragraphs 4 and 5 of article 7, it is permissible that a person should lose his nationality;

(*b*) Where the nationality has been obtained by misrepresentation or fraud.

3. Notwithstanding the provisions of paragraph 1 of this article, a Contracting State may retain the right to deprive a person of his nationality, if at the time of signature, ratification or accession it specifies its retention of such right on one or more of the following grounds, being grounds existing in its national law at that time:

(*a*) That, inconsistently with his duty of loyalty to the Contracting State, the person:

(i) Has, in disregard of an express prohibition by the Contracting State rendered or continued to render services to, or received or continued to receive emoluments from, another State, or

(ii) Has conducted himself in a manner seriously prejudicial to the vital interests of the State;

(*b*) That the person has taken an oath, or made a formal declaration, of allegiance to another State, or given definite evidence of his determination to repudiate his allegiance to the Contracting State.

4. A Contracting State shall not exercise a power of deprivation permitted by paragraphs 2 or 3 of this article except in accordance with law, which shall provide for the person concerned the right to a fair hearing by a court or other independent body.

*Article 9*

A Contracting State may not deprive any person or group of persons of their nationality on racial, ethnic, religious or political grounds.

*Article 10*

1. Every treaty between Contracting States providing for the transfer of territory shall include provisions designed to secure that no person shall become stateless as a result of the transfer. A Contracting State shall use its best endeavours to secure that any such treaty made by it with a State which is not a party to this Convention includes such provisions.

2. In the absence of such provisions a Contracting State to which territory is transferred or which otherwise acquires territory shall confer its nationality on such persons as would otherwise become stateless as a result of the transfer or acquisition.

*Article 11*

The Contracting States shall promote the establishment within the framework of the United Nations, as soon as may be after the deposit of the sixth instrument of ratification or accession, of a body to which a person claiming the benefit of this Convention may apply for the examination of his claim and for assistance in presenting it to the appropriate authority.

*Article 12*

1. In relation to a Contracting State which does not, in accordance with the provisions of paragraph 1 of article 1 or of article 4 of this Convention, grant its nationality at birth by operation of law, the provisions of paragraph 1 of article 1 or of article 4, as the case may be, shall apply to persons born before as well as to persons born after the entry into force of this Convention.

2. The provisions of paragraph 4 of article 1 of this Convention shall apply to persons born before as well as to persons born after its entry into force.

3. The provisions of article 2 of this Convention shall apply only to foundlings found in the territory of a Contracting State after the entry into force of the Convention for that State.

*Article 13*

This Convention shall not be construed as affecting any provisions more conducive to the reduction of statelessness which may be contained in the law of any Contracting State now or hereafter in force, or may be contained in any other convention, treaty or agreement now or hereafter in force between two or more Contracting States.

*Article 14*

Any dispute between Contracting States concerning the interpretation or application of this Convention which cannot be settled by other means shall be submitted to the International Court of Justice at the request of any one of the parties to the dispute.

*Article 15*

1. This Convention shall apply to all non-self-governing, trust, colonial and other non-metropolitan territories for the international relations of which any Contracting State is responsible; the Contracting State concerned shall, subject to the provisions of paragraph 2 of this article, at the time of signature, ratification or accession, declare the non-metropolitan territory or territories to which the Convention shall apply *ipso facto* as a result of such signature, ratification or accession.

2. In any case in which, for the purpose of nationality, a non-metropolitan territory is not treated as one with the metropolitan territory, or in any case in which the previous consent of a non-metropolitan territory is required by the constitutional laws or practices of the Contracting State or of the non metropolitan territory for the application of the Convention to that territory, that Contracting State shall endeavour to secure the needed consent of the non-metropolitan territory within the period of twelve months from the date of signature of the Convention by that Contracting State, and when such consent has been obtained the Contracting State shall notify the Secretary-General of the United Nations. This Convention shall apply to the territory or territories named in such notification from the date of its receipt by the Secretary-General.

3. After the expiry of the twelve-month period mentioned in paragraph 2 of this article, the Contracting States concerned shall inform the Secretary-General of the results of the consultations with those non-metropolitan territories for whose international relations they are responsible and whose consent to the application of this Convention may have been withheld.

*Article 16*

1. This Convention shall be open for signature at the Headquarters of the United Nations from 30 August 1961 to 31 May 1962.

2. This Convention shall be open for signature on behalf of:

(*a*) Any State Member of the United Nations;

(*b*) Any other State invited to attend the United Nations Conference on the Elimination or Reduction of Future Statelessness;

(*c*) Any State to which an invitation to sign or to accede may be addressed by the General Assembly of the United Nations.

3. This Convention shall be ratified and the instruments of ratification shall be deposited with the Secretary-General of the United Nations.

4. This Convention shall be open for accession by the States referred to in paragraph 2 of this article. Accession shall be effected by the deposit of an instrument of accession with the Secretary-General of the United Nations.

*Article 17*

1. At the time of signature, ratification or accession any State may make a reservation in respect of articles 11, 14 or 15.

2. No other reservations to this Convention shall be admissible.

*Article 18*

1. This Convention shall enter into force two years after the date of the deposit of the sixth instrument of ratification or accession.

2. For each State ratifying or acceding to this Convention after the deposit of the sixth instrument of ratification or accession, it shall enter into force on the ninetieth day after the deposit by such State of its instrument of ratification or accession or on the date on which this Convention enters into force in accordance with the provisions of paragraph 1 of this article, whichever is the later.

*Article 19*

1. Any Contracting State may denounce this Convention at any time by a written notification addressed to the Secretary-General of the United Nations. Such denunciation shall take effect for the Contracting State concerned one year after the date of its receipt by the Secretary-General.

2. In cases where, in accordance with the provisions of article 15, this Convention has become applicable to a non-metropolitan territory of a Contracting State, that State may at any time thereafter, with the consent of the territory concerned, give notice to the Secretary-General of the United Nations denouncing this Convention separately in respect to that territory. The denunciation shall take effect one year after the date of the receipt of such notice by the Secretary-General, who shall notify all other Contracting States of such notice and the date of receipt thereof.

*Article 20*

1. The Secretary-General of the United Nations shall notify all Members of the United Nations and the non-member States referred to in article 16 of the following particulars:

(*a*) Signatures, ratifications and accessions under article 16;

(*b*) Reservations under article 17;

(*c*) The date upon which this Convention enters into force in pursuance of article 18;

(*d*) Denunciations under article 19.

2. The Secretary-General of the United Nations shall, after the deposit of the sixth instrument of ratification or accession at the latest, bring to the attention of the General Assembly the question of the establishment, in accordance with article 11, of such a body as therein mentioned.

*Article 21*

This Convention shall be registered by the Secretary-General of the United Nations on the date of its entry into force.

IN WITNESS WHEREOF the undersigned Plenipotentiaries have signed this Convention

DONE at New York, this thirtieth day of August, one thousand nine hundred and sixty-one, in a single copy, of which the Chinese, English, French, Russian and Spanish texts are equally authentic and which shall be deposited in the archives of the United Nations, and certified copies of which shall be delivered by the Secretary-General of the United Nations to all Members of the United Nations and to the non-member States referred to in article 16 of this Convention.

## 24. Convention relating to the Status of Stateless Persons

**Adopted on 28 September 1954 by a Conference of Plenipotentiaries convened by Economic and Social Council resolution 526 A (XVII) of 26 April 1954**

***Entry into force*****:** 6 June 1960, in accordance with article 39.

PREAMBLE

*The High Contracting Parties*,

*Considering* that the Charter of the United Nations and the Universal Declaration of Human Rights approved on 10 December 1948 by the General Assembly of the United Nations have affirmed the principle that human beings shall enjoy fundamental rights and freedoms without discrimination,

*Considering* that the United Nations has, on various occasions, manifested its profound concern for stateless persons and endeavoured to assure stateless persons the widest possible exercise of these fundamental rights and freedoms,

*Considering* that only those stateless persons who are also refugees are covered by the Convention relating to the Status of Refugees of 28 July 1951, and that there are many stateless persons who are not covered by that Convention,

*Considering* that it is desirable to regulate and improve the status of stateless persons by an international agreement,

*Have agreed* as follows:

CHAPTER I

### GENERAL PROVISIONS

*Article 1*

DEFINITION OF THE TERM "STATELESS PERSON"

1. For the purpose of this Convention, the term "stateless person" means a person who is not considered as a national by any State under the operation of its law.

2. This Convention shall not apply:

(i) To persons who are at present receiving from organs or agencies of the United Nations other than the United Nations High Commissioner for Refugees protection or assistance so long as they are receiving such protection or assistance;

(ii) To persons who are recognized by the competent authorities of the country in which they have taken residence as having the rights and obligations which are attached to the possession of the nationality of that country;

(iii) To persons with respect to whom there are serious reasons for considering that:

(*a*) They have committed a crime against peace, a war crime, or a crime against humanity, as defined in the international instruments drawn up to make provisions in respect of such crimes;

(*b*) They have committed a serious non-political crime outside the country of their residence prior to their admission to that country;

(*c*) They have been guilty of acts contrary to the purposes and principles of the United Nations.

*Article 2*

GENERAL OBLIGATIONS

Every stateless person has duties to the country in which he finds himself, which require in particular that he conform to its laws and regulations as well as to measures taken for the maintenance of public order.

*Article 3*

NON-DISCRIMINATION

The Contracting States shall apply the provisions of this Convention to stateless persons without discrimination as to race, religion or country of origin.

*Article 4*

RELIGION

The Contracting States shall accord to stateless persons within their territories treatment at least as favourable as that accorded to their nationals with respect to freedom to practise their religion and freedom as regards the religious education of their children.

*Article 5*

RIGHTS GRANTED APART FROM THIS CONVENTION

Nothing in this Convention shall be deemed to impair any rights and benefits granted by a Contracting State to stateless persons apart from this Convention.

### *Article 6*

#### THE TERM "IN THE SAME CIRCUMSTANCES"

For the purpose of this Convention, the term "in the same circumstances" implies that any requirements (including requirements as to length and conditions of sojourn or residence) which the particular individual would have to fulfil for the enjoyment of the right in question, if he were not a stateless person, must be fulfilled by him, with the exception of requirements which by their nature a stateless person is incapable of fulfilling.

### *Article 7*

#### EXEMPTION FROM RECIPROCITY

1. Except where this Convention contains more favourable provisions, a Contracting State shall accord to stateless persons the same treatment as is accorded to aliens generally.

2. After a period of three years' residence, all stateless persons shall enjoy exemption from legislative reciprocity in the territory of the Contracting States.

3. Each Contracting State shall continue to accord to stateless persons the rights and benefits to which they were already entitled, in the absence of reciprocity, at the date of entry into force of this Convention for that State.

4. The Contracting States shall consider favourably the possibility of according to stateless persons, in the absence of reciprocity, rights and benefits beyond those to which they are entitled according to paragraphs 2 and 3, and to extending exemption from reciprocity to stateless persons who do not fulfil the conditions provided for in paragraphs 2 and 3.

5. The provisions of paragraphs 2 and 3 apply both to the rights and benefits referred to in articles 13, 18, 19, 21 and 22 of this Convention and to rights and benefits for which this Convention does not provide.

### *Article 8*

#### EXEMPTION FROM EXCEPTIONAL MEASURES

With regard to exceptional measures which may be taken against the person, property or interests of nationals or former nationals of a foreign State, the Contracting States shall not apply such measures to a stateless person solely on account of his having previously possessed the nationality of the foreign State in question. Contracting States which, under their legislation, are prevented from applying the general principle expressed in this article shall, in appropriate cases, grant exemptions in favour of such stateless persons.

### *Article 9*

#### PROVISIONAL MEASURES

Nothing in this Convention shall prevent a Contracting State, in time of war or other grave and exceptional circumstances, from taking provisionally measures which it considers to be essential to the national security in the case of a particular person, pending a determination by the Contracting State that that person is in fact a stateless person and that the continuance of such measures is necessary in his case in the interests of national security.

### *Article 10*

#### CONTINUITY OF RESIDENCE

1. Where a stateless person has been forcibly displaced during the Second World War and removed to the territory of a Contracting State, and is resident there, the period of such enforced sojourn shall be considered to have been lawful residence within that territory.

2. Where a stateless person has been forcibly displaced during the Second World War from the territory of a Contracting State and has, prior to the date of entry into force of this Convention, returned there for the purpose of taking up residence, the period of residence before and after such enforced displacement shall be regarded as one uninterrupted period for any purposes for which uninterrupted residence is required.

### *Article 11*

#### STATELESS SEAMEN

In the case of stateless persons regularly serving as crew members on board a ship flying the flag of a Contracting State, that State shall give sympathetic consideration to their establishment on its territory and the issue of travel documents to them or their temporary admission to its territory particularly with a view to facilitating their establishment in another country.

CHAPTER II

## JURIDICAL STATUS

### *Article 12*

#### PERSONAL STATUS

1. The personal status of a stateless person shall be governed by the law of the country of his domicile or, if he has no domicile, by the law of the country of his residence.

2. Rights previously acquired by a stateless person and dependent on personal status, more particularly rights attaching to marriage, shall be respected by a Contracting State, subject to compliance, if this be necessary, with the formalities required by the law of that State, provided that the right in question is one which would have been recognized by the law of that State had he not become stateless.

### *Article 13*

#### MOVABLE AND IMMOVABLE PROPERTY

The Contracting States shall accord to a stateless person treatment as favourable as possible and, in any event, not less favourable than that accorded to aliens generally in the same circumstances, as regards the acquisition of movable and immovable property and other rights pertaining thereto, and to leases and other contracts relating to movable and immovable property.

*Article 14*

ARTISTIC RIGHTS AND INDUSTRIAL PROPERTY

In respect of the protection of industrial property, such as inventions, designs or models, trade marks, trade names, and of rights in literary, artistic and scientific works, a stateless person shall be accorded in the country in which he has his habitual residence the same protection as is accorded to nationals of that country. In the territory of any other Contracting State, he shall be accorded the same protection as is accorded in that territory to nationals of the country in which he has his habitual residence.

*Article 15*

RIGHT OF ASSOCIATION

As regards non-political and non-profit-making associations and trade unions the Contracting States shall accord to stateless persons lawfully staying in their territory treatment as favourable as posible, and in any event, not less favourable than that accorded to aliens generally in the same circumstances.

*Article 16*

ACCESS TO COURTS

1. A stateless person shall have free access to the Courts of Law on the territory of all Contracting States.

2. A stateless person shall enjoy in the Contracting State in which he has his habitual residence the same treatment as a national in matters pertaining to access to the Courts, including legal assistance and exemption from *cautio judicatum solvi.*

3. A stateles person shall be accorded in the matters referred to in paragraph 2 in countries other than that in which he has his habitual residence the treatment granted to a national of the country of his habitual residence.

CHAPTER III

## GAINFUL EMPLOYMENT

*Article 17*

WAGE-EARNING EMPLOYMENT

1. The Contracting States shall accord to stateless persons lawfully staying in their territory treatment as favourable as possible and, in any event, not less favourable that that accorded to aliens generally in the same circumstances, as regards the right to engage in wage-earning employment.

2. The Contracting States shall give sympathetic consideration to assimilating the rights of all stateless persons with regard to wage-earning employment to those of nationals, and in particular of those stateless persons who have entered their territory pursuant to programmes of labour recruitment or under immigration schemes.

*Article 18*

SELF-EMPLOYMENT

The Contracting States shall accord to a stateless person lawfully in their territory treatment as favourable as possible and, in any event, not less favourable than that accorded to aliens generally in the same circumstances, as regards the right to engage on his own account in agriculture, industry, handicrafts and commerce and to establish commercial and industrial companies.

*Article 19*

LIBERAL PROFESSIONS

Each Contracting State shall accord to stateless persons lawfully staying in their territory who hold diplomas recognized by the competent authorities of that State, and who are desirous of practising a liberal profession, treatment as favourable as possible and, in any event, not less favourable than that accorded to aliens generally in the same circumstances.

CHAPTER IV

## WELFARE

*Article 20*

RATIONING

Where a rationing system exists, which applies to the population at large and regulates the general distribution of products in short supply, stateless persons shall be accorded the same treatment as nationals.

*Article 21*

HOUSING

As regards housing, the Contracting States, in so far as the matter is regulated by laws or regulations or is subject to the control of public authorities, shall accord to stateless persons lawfully staying in their territory treatment as favourable as possible and, in any event, not less favourable than that accorded to aliens generally in the same circumstances.

*Article 22*

PUBLIC EDUCATION

1. The Contracting States shall accord to stateless persons the same treatment as is accorded to nationals with respect to elementary education.

2. The Contracting States shall accord to stateless persons treatment as favourable as possible and, in any event, not less favourable than that accorded to aliens generally in the same circumstances, with respect to education other than elementary education and, in particular, as regards access to studies, the recognition of foreign school certificates, diplomas and degrees,

the remission of fees and charges and the award of scholarships.

*Article 23*

PUBLIC RELIEF

The Contracting States shall accord to stateless persons lawfully staying in their territory the same treatment with respect to public relief and assistance as is accorded to their nationals.

*Article 24*

LABOUR LEGISLATION AND SOCIAL SECURITY

1. The Contracting States shall accord to stateless persons lawfully staying in their territory the same treatment as is accorded to nationals in respect of the following matters:

(*a*) In so far as such matters are governed by laws or regulations or are subject to the control of administrative authorities: remuneration, including family allowances where these form part of remuneration, hours of work, overtime arrangements, holidays with pay, restrictions on home work, minimum age of employment, apprenticeship and training, women's work and the work of young persons, and the enjoyment of the benefits of collective bargaining;

(*b*) Social security (legal provisions in respect of employment injury, occupational diseases, maternity, sickness, disability, old age, death, unemployment, family responsibilities and any other contingency which, according to national laws or regulations, is covered by a social security scheme), subject to the following limitations:

(i) There may be appropriate arrangements for the maintenance of acquired rights and rights in course of acquisition;

(ii) National laws or regulations of the country of residence may prescribe special arrangements concerning benefits or portions of benefits which are payable wholly out of public funds, and concerning allowances paid to persons who do not fulfil the contribution conditions prescribed for the award of a normal pension.

2. The right to compensation for the death of a stateless person resulting from employment injury or from occupational disease shall not be affected by the fact that the residence of the beneficiary is outside the territory of the Contracting State.

3. The Contracting States shall exend to stateless persons the benefits of agreements concluded between them, or which may be concluded between them in the future, concerning the maintenance of acquired rights and rights in the process of acquisition in regard to social security, subject only to the conditions which apply to nationals of the States signatory to the agreements in question.

4. The Contracting States will give sympathetic consideration to extending to stateless persons so far as possible the benefits of similar agreements which may at any time be in force between such Contracting States and non-contracting States.

CHAPTER V

## ADMINISTRATIVE MEASURES

*Article 25*

ADMINISTRATIVE ASSISTANCE

1. When the exercise of a right by a stateless person would normally require the assistance of authorities of a foreign country to whom he cannot have recourse, the Contracting State in whose territory he is residing shall arrange that such assistance be afforded to him by their own authorities.

2. The authority or authorities mentioned in paragraph 1 shall deliver or cause to be delivered under their supervision to stateless persons such documents or certifications as would normally be delivered to aliens by or through their national authorities.

3. Documents or certifications so delivered shall stand in the stead of the official instruments delivered to aliens by or through their national authorities and shall be given credence in the absence of proof to the contrary.

4. Subject to such exceptional treatment as may be granted to indigent persons, fees may be charged for the services mentioned herein, but such fees shall be moderate and commensurate with those charged to nationals for similar services.

5. The provisions of this article shall be without prejudice to articles 27 and 28.

*Article 26*

FREEDOM OF MOVEMENT

Each Contracting State shall accord to stateless persons lawfully in its territory the right to choose their place of residence and to move freely within its territory, subject to any regulations applicable to aliens generally in the same circumstances.

*Article 27*

IDENTITY PAPERS

The Contracting States shall issue identity papers to any stateless person in their territory who does not possess a valid travel document.

*Article 28*

TRAVEL DOCUMENTS

The Contracting States shall issue to stateless persons lawfully staying in their territory travel documents for the purpose of travel outside their territory, unless compelling reasons of national security or public order otherwise require, and the provisions of the Schedule to this Convention shall apply with respect to such documents. The Contracting States may issue such a travel document to any other stateless person in their territory; they shall in particular give sympathetic consideration to the issue of such a travel document to stateless persons in their territory who are unable to obtain a travel document from the country of their lawful residence.

*Article 29*

FISCAL CHARGES

1. The Contracting States shall not impose upon stateless persons duties, charges or taxes, of any description whatsoever, other or higher than those which are or may be levied on their nationals in similar situations.

2. Nothing in the above paragraph shall prevent the application to stateless persons of the laws and regulations concerning charges in respect of the issue to aliens of administrative documents including identity papers.

*Article 30*

TRANSFER OF ASSETS

1. A Contracting State shall, in conformity with its laws and regulations, permit stateless persons to transfer assets which they have brought into its territory, to another country where they have been admitted for the purposes of resettlement.

2. A Contracting State shall give sympathetic consideration to the application of stateless persons for permission to transfer assets wherever they may be and which are necessary for their resettlement in another country to which they have been admitted.

*Article 31*

EXPULSION

1. The Contracting States shall not expel a stateless person lawfully in their territory save on grounds of national security or public order.

2. The expulsion of such a stateless person shall be only in pursuance of a decision reached in accordance with due process of law. Except where compelling reasons of national security otherwise require, the stateless person shall be allowed to submit evidence to clear himself, and to appeal to and be represented for the purpose before competent authority or a person or persons specially designated by the competent authority.

3. The Contracting States shall allow such a stateless person a reasonable period within which to seek legal admission into another country. The Contracting States reserve the right to apply during that period such internal measures as they may deem necessary.

*Article 32*

NATURALIZATION

The Contracting States shall as far as possible facilitate the assimilation and naturalization of stateless persons. They shall in particular make every effort to expedite naturalization proceedings and to reduce as far as possible the charges and costs of such proceedings.

CHAPTER VI

## FINAL CLAUSES

*Article 33*

INFORMATION ON NATIONAL LEGISLATION

The Contracting States shall communicate to the Secretary-General of the United Nations the laws and regulations which they may adopt to ensure the application of this Convention.

*Article 34*

SETTLEMENT OF DISPUTES

Any dispute between parties to this Convention relating to its interpretation or application, which cannot be settled by other means, shall be referred to the International Court of Justice at the request of any one of the parties to the dispute.

*Article 35*

SIGNATURE, RATIFICATION AND ACCESSION

1. This Convention shall be open for signature at the Headquarters of the United Nations until 31 December 1955.

2. It shall be open for signature on behalf of:

(*a*) Any State Member of the United Nations;

(*b*) Any other State invited to attend the United Nations Conference on the Status of Stateless Persons; and

(*c*) Any State to which an invitation to sign or to accede may be addressed by the General Assembly of the United Nations.

3. It shall be ratified and the instruments of ratification shall be deposited with the Secretary-General of the United Nations.

4. It shall be open for accession by the States referred to in paragraph 2 of this article. Accession shall be effected by the deposit of an instrument of accession with the Secretary-General of the United Nations.

*Article 36*

TERRITORIAL APPLICATION CLAUSE

1. Any State may, at the time of signature, ratification or accession, declare that this Convention shall extend to all or any of the territories for the international relations of which it is responsible. Such a declaration shall take effect when the Convention enters into force for the State concerned.

2. At any time thereafter any such extension shall be made by notification addressed to the Secretary-General of the United Nations and shall take effect as from the ninetieth day after the day of receipt by the Secretary-General of the United Nations of this notification, or as from the date of entry into force of the Convention for the State concerned, whichever is the later.

3. With respect to those territories to which this Convention is not extended at the time of signature, ratification or accession, each State concerned shall consider the possibility of taking the necessary steps in order to extend the application of this Convention to such territories, subject, where necessary for constitutional reasons, to the consent of the Governments of such territories.

*Article 37*

FEDERAL CLAUSE

In the case of a Federal or non-unitary State, the following provisions shall apply:

(*a*) With respect to those articles of this Convention that come within the legislative jurisdiction of the federal legislative authority, the obligations of the Federal Government shall to this extent be the same as those of Parties which are not Federal States;

(*b*) With respect to those articles of this Convention that come within the legislative jurisdiction of constituent States, provinces or cantons which are not, under the constitutional system of the Federation, bound to take legislative action, the Federal Goverment shall bring such articles with a favourable recommendation to the notice of the appropriate authorities of states, provinces or cantons at the earliest possible moment.

(*c*) A Federal State Party to this Convention shall, at the request of any other Contracting State transmitted through the Secretary-General of the United Nations, supply a statement of the law and practice of the Federation and its constituent units in regard to any particular provision of the Convention showing the extent to which effect has been given to that provision by legislative or other action.

*Article 38*

RESERVATIONS

1. At the time of signature, ratification or accession, any State may make reservations to articles of the Convention other than to articles 1, 3, 4, 16 (1) and 33 to 42 inclusive.

2. Any State making a reservation in accordance with paragraph 1 of this article may at any time withdraw the reservation by a communication to that effect addressed to the Secretary-General of the United Nations.

*Article 39*

ENTRY INTO FORCE

1. This Convention shall come into force on the ninetieth day following the day of deposit of the sixth instrument of ratification or accession.

2. For each State ratifying or acceding to the Convention after the deposit of the sixth instrument of ratification or accession, the Convention shall enter into force on the ninetieth day following the date of deposit by such State of its instrument of ratification or accession.

*Article 40*

DENUNCIATION

1. Any Contracting State may denounce this Convention at any time by a notification addressed to the Secretary-General of the United Nations.

2. Such denunciation shall take effect for the Contracting State concerned one year from the date upon which it is received by the Secretary-General of the United Nations.

3. Any State which has made a declaration or notification under article 36 may, at any time thereafter, by a notification to the Secretary-General of the United Nations, declare that the Convention shall cease to extend to such territory one year after the date of receipt of the notification by the Secretary-General.

*Article 41*

REVISION

1. Any Contracting State may request revision of this Convention at any time by a notification addressed to the Secretary-General of the United Nations.

2. The General Assembly of the United Nations shall recommend the steps, if any, to be taken in respect of such request.

*Article 42*

NOTIFICATIONS BY THE SECRETARY-GENERAL OF THE UNITED NATIONS

The Secretary-General of the United Nations shall inform all Members of the United Nations and non-member States referred to in article 35:

(*a*) Of signatures, ratifications and accessions in accordance with article 35;

(*b*) Of declarations and notifications in accordance with article 36;

(*c*) Of reservations and withdrawals in accordance with article 38;

(*d*) Of the date on which this Convention will come into force in accordance with article 39;

(*e*) Of denunciations and notifications in accordance with article 40;

(*f*) Of requests for revision in accordance with article 41;

IN FAITH WHEREOF the undersigned, duly authorized, have signed this Convention on behalf of their respective Governments.

DONE at New York, this twenty-eighth day of September, one thousand nine hundred and fifty-four, in a single copy, of which the English, French and Spanish texts are equally authentic and which shall remain deposited in the archives of the United Nations, and certified true copies of which shall be delivered to all Members of the United Nations and to the non-member States referred to in article 35.

## 25. Convention relating to the Status of Refugees

**Adopted on 28 July 1951 by the United Nations Conference of Plenipotentiaries on the Status of Refugees and Stateless Persons convened under General Assembly resolution 429 (V) of 14 December 1950**

***Entry into force*:** 22 April 1954, in accordance with article 43.

PREAMBLE

*The High Contracting Parties,*

*Considering* that the Charter of the United Nations and the Universal Declaration of Human Rights approved on 10 December 1948 by the General Assembly have affirmed the principle that human beings shall enjoy fundamental rights and freedoms without discrimination,

*Considering* that the United Nations has, on various occasions, manifested its profound concern for refugees and endeavoured to assure refugees the widest possible exercise of these fundamental rights and freedoms,

*Considering* that it is desirable to revise and consolidate previous international agreements relating to the status of refugees and to extend the scope of and the protection accorded by such instruments by means of a new agreement,

*Considering* that the grant of asylum may place unduly heavy burdens on certain countries, and that a satisfactory solution of a problem of which the United Nations has recognized the international scope and nature cannot therefore be achieved without international co-operation,

*Expressing* the wish that all States, recognizing the social and humanitarian nature of the problem of refugees, will do everything within their power to prevent this problem from becoming a cause of tension between States,

*Noting* that the United Nations High Commissioner for Refugees is charged with the task of supervising international conventions providing for the protection of refugees, and recognizing that the effective co-ordination of measures taken to deal with this problem will depend upon the co-operation of States with the High Commissioner,

*Have agreed as follows*:

CHAPTER I

## GENERAL PROVISIONS

### *Article 1*

DEFINITION OF THE TERM "REFUGEE"

A. For the purposes of the present Convention, the term "refugee" shall apply to any person who:

(1) Has been considered a refugee under the Arrangements of 12 May 1926 and 30 June 1928 or under the Conventions of 28 October 1933 and 10 February 1938, the Protocol of 14 September 1939 or the Constitution of the International Refugee Organization;

Decisions of non-eligibility taken by the International Refugee Organization during the period of its activities shall not prevent the status of refugee being accorded to persons who fulfil the conditions of paragraph 2 of this section;

(2) As a result of events occurring before 1 January 1951 and owing to well-founded fear of being persecuted for reasons of race, religion, nationality, membership of a particular social group or political opinion, is outside the country of his nationality and is unable, or owing to such fear, is unwilling to avail himself of the protection of that country; or who, not having a nationality and being outside the country of his former habitual residence as a result of such events, is unable or, owing to such fear, is unwilling to return to it.

In the case of a person who has more than one nationality, the term "the country of his nationality" shall mean each of the countries of which he is a national, and a person shall not be deemed to be lacking the protection of the country of his nationality if, without any valid reason based on well-founded fear, he has not availed himself of the protection of one of the countries of which he is a national.

B. (1) For the purposes of this Convention, the words "events occurring before 1 January 1951" in article 1, section A, shall be understood to mean either (*a*) "events occurring in Europe before 1 January 1951"; or (*b*) "events occurring in Europe or elsewhere before 1 January 1951"; and each Contracting State shall make a declaration at the time of signature, ratification or accession, specifying which of these meanings it applies for the purpose of its obligations under this Convention.

(2) Any Contracting State which has adopted alternative (*a*) may at any time extend its obligations by adopting alternative (*b*) by means of a notification addressed to the Secretary-General of the United Nations.

C. This Convention shall cease to apply to any person falling under the terms of section A if:

(1) He has voluntarily re-availed himself of the protection of the country of his nationality; or

(2) Having lost his nationality, he has voluntarily reacquired it; or

(3) He has acquired a new nationality, and enjoys the protection of the country of his new nationality; or

(4) He has voluntarily re-established himself in the country which he left or outside which he remained owing to fear of persecution; or

(5) He can no longer, because the circumstances in connexion with which he has been recognized as a refugee have ceased to exist, continue to refuse to avail himself of the protection of the country of his nationality;

Provided that this paragraph shall not apply to a refugee falling under section A (1) of this article who is able to invoke compelling reasons arising out of previous persecution for refusing to avail himself of the protection of the country of nationality;

(6) Being a person who has no nationality he is, because the circumstances in connexion with which he has been recognized as a refugee have ceased to exist, able to return to the country of his former habitual residence;

Provided that this paragraph shall not apply to a refugee falling under section A (1) of this article who is able to invoke compelling reasons arising out of previous persecution for refusing to return to the country of his former habitual residence.

D. This Convention shall not apply to persons who are at present receiving from organs or agencies of the United Nations other than the United Nations High Commissioner for Refugees protection or assistance.

When such protection or assistance has ceased for any reason, without the position of such persons being definitively settled in accordance with the relevant resolutions adopted by the General Assembly of the United Nations, these persons shall *ipso facto* be entitled to the benefits of this Convention.

E. This Convention shall not apply to a person who is recognized by the competent authorities of the country in which he has taken residence as having the rights and obligations which are attached to the possession of the nationality of that country.

F. The provisions of this Convention shall not apply to any person with respect to whom there are serious reasons for considering that:

(*a*) He has committed a crime against peace, a war crime, or a crime against humanity, as defined in the international instruments drawn up to make provision in respect of such crimes;

(*b*) He has committed a serious non-political crime outside the country of refuge prior to his admission to that country as a refugee;

(*c*) He has been guilty of acts contrary to the purposes and principles of the United Nations.

*Article 2*

GENERAL OBLIGATIONS

Every refugee has duties to the country in which he finds himself, which require in particular that he conform to its laws and regulations as well as to measures taken for the maintenance of public order.

*Article 3*

NON-DISCRIMINATION

The Contracting States shall apply the provisions of this Convention to refugees without discrimination as to race, religion or country of origin.

*Article 4*

RELIGION

The Contracting States shall accord to refugees within their territories treatment at least as favourable as that accorded to their nationals with respect to freedom to practice their religion and freedom as regards the religious education of their children.

*Article 5*

RIGHTS GRANTED APART FROM THIS CONVENTION

Nothing in this Convention shall be deemed to impair any rights and benefits granted by a Contracting State to refugees apart from this Convention.

*Article 6*

THE TERM "IN THE SAME CIRCUMSTANCES"

For the purpose of this Convention, the term "in the same circumstances" implies that any requirements (including requirements as to length and conditions of sojourn or residence) which the particular individual would have to fulfil for the enjoyment of the right in question, if he were not a refugee, must be fulfilled by him, with the exception of requirements which by their nature a refugee is incapable of fulfilling.

*Article 7*

EXEMPTION FROM RECIPROCITY

1. Except where this Convention contains more favourable provisions, a Contracting State shall accord to refugees the same treatment as is accorded to aliens generally.

2. After a period of three years' residence, all refugees shall enjoy exemption from legislative reciprocity in the territory of the Contracting States.

3. Each Contracting State shall continue to accord to refugees the rights and benefits to which they were already entitled, in the absence of reciprocity, at the date of entry into force of this Convention for that State.

4. The Contracting States shall consider favourably the possibility of according to refugees, in the absence of reciprocity, rights and benefits beyond those to which they are entitled according to paragraphs 2 and 3, and to extending exemption from reciprocity to refugees who do not fulfil the conditions provided for in paragraphs 2 and 3.

5. The provisions of paragraphs 2 and 3 apply both to the rights and benefits referred to in articles 13, 18, 19, 21 and 22 of this Convention and to rights and benefits for which this Convention does not provide.

*Article 8*

EXEMPTION FROM EXCEPTIONAL MEASURES

With regard to exceptional measures which may be taken against the person, property or interests of nationals of a foreign State, the Contracting States shall not apply such measures to a refugee who is formally a national of the said State solely on account of such nationality. Contracting States which, under their legislation, are prevented from applying the general principle expressed in this article, shall, in appropriate cases, grant exemptions in favour of such refugees.

*Article 9*

PROVISIONAL MEASURES

Nothing in this Convention shall prevent a Contracting State, in time of war or other grave and exceptional circumstances, from taking provisionally measures which it considers to be essential to the national security in the case of a particular person, pending a determination by the Contracting State that that person is in fact a refugee and that the continuance of such measures is necessary in his case in the interests of national security.

*Article 10*

CONTINUITY OF RESIDENCE

1. Where a refugee has been forcibly displaced during the Second World War and removed to the

territory of a Contracting State, and is resident there, the period of such enforced sojourn shall be considered to have been lawful residence within that territory.

2. Where a refugee has been forcibly displaced during the Second World War from the territory of a Contracting State and has, prior to the date of entry into force of this Convention, returned there for the purpose of taking up residence, the period of residence before and after such enforced displacement shall be regarded as one uninterrupted period for any purposes for which uninterrupted residence is required.

*Article 11*

REFUGEE SEAMEN

In the case of refugees regularly serving as crew members on board a ship flying the flag of a Contracting State, that State shall give sympathetic consideration to their establishment on its territory and the issue of travel documents to them or their temporary admission to its territory particularly with a view to facilitating their establishment in another country.

CHAPTER II

## JURIDICAL STATUS

*Article 12*

PERSONAL STATUS

1. The personal status of a refugee shall be governed by the law of the country of his domicile or, if he has no domicile, by the law of the country of his residence.

2. Rights previously acquired by a refugee and dependent on personal status, more particularly rights attaching to marriage, shall be respected by a Contracting State, subject to compliance, if this be necessary, with the formalities required by the law of that State, provided that the right in question is one which would have been recognized by the law of that State had he not become a refugee.

*Article 13*

MOVABLE AND IMMOVABLE PROPERTY

The Contracting States shall accord to a refugee treatment as favourable as possible and, in any event, not less favourable than that accorded to aliens generally in the same circumstances, as regards the acquisition of movable and immovable property and other rights pertaining thereto, and to leases and other contracts relating to movable and immovable property.

*Article 14*

ARTISTIC RIGHTS AND INDUSTRIAL PROPERTY

In respect of the protection of industrial property, such as inventions, designs or models, trade marks, trade names, and of rights literary, artistic and scientific works, a refugee shall be accorded in the country in which he has his habitual residence the same protection as is accorded to nationals of that country. In the territory of any other Contracting State, he shall be accorded the same protection as is accorded in that territory to nationals of the country in which he has his habitual residence.

*Article 15*

RIGHT OF ASSOCIATION

As regards non-political and non-profit-making associations and trade unions the Contracting States shall accord to refugees lawfully staying in their territory the most favourable treatment accorded to nationals of a foreign country, in the same circumstances.

*Article 16*

ACCESS TO COURTS

1. A refugee shall have free access to the courts of law on the territory of all Contracting States.

2. A refugee shall enjoy in the Contracting State in which he has his habitual residence the same treatment as a national in matters pertaining to access to the Courts, including legal assistance and exemption from *cautio judicatum solvi.*

3. A refugee shall be accorded in the matters referred to in paragraph 2 in countries other than that in which he has his habitual residence the treatment granted to a national of the country of his habitual residence.

CHAPTER III

## GAINFUL EMPLOYMENT

*Article 17*

WAGE-EARNING EMPLOYMENT

1. The Contracting States shall accord to refugees lawfully staying in their territory the most favourable treatment accorded to nationals of a foreign country in the same circumstances, as regards the right to engage in wage-earning employment.

2. In any case, restrictive measures imposed on aliens or the employment of aliens for the protection of the national labour market shall not be applied to a refugee who was already exempt from them at the date of entry into force of this Convention for the Contracting State concerned, or who fulfils one of the following conditions:

(*a*) He has completed three years' residence in the country;

(*b*) He has a spouse possessing the nationality of the country of residence. A refugee may not invoke the benefit of this provision if he has abandoned his spouse;

(*c*) He has one or more children possessing the nationality of the country of residence.

3. The Contracting States shall give sympathetic consideration to assimilating the rights of all refugees with regard to wage-earning employment to those of nationals, and in particular of those refugees who have entered their territory pursuant to programmes of labour recruitment or under immigration schemes.

*Article 18*

SELF-EMPLOYMENT

The Contracting States shall accord to a refugee lawfully in their territory treatment as favourable as possible and, in any event, not less favourable than that accorded to aliens generally in the same circumstances, as regards the right to engage on his own account in agriculture, industry, handicrafts and commerce and to establish commercial and industrial companies.

*Article 19*

LIBERAL PROFESSIONS

1. Each Contracting State shall accord to refugees lawfully staying in their territory who hold diplomas recognized by the competent authorities of that State, and who are desirous of practising a liberal profession, treatment as favourable as possible and, in any event, not less favourable than that accorded to aliens generally in the same circumstances.

2. The Contracting States shall use their best endeavours consistently with their laws and constitutions to secure the settlement of such refugees in the territories, other than the metropolitan territory, for whose international relations they are responsible.

CHAPTER IV

## WELFARE

*Article 20*

RATIONING

Where a rationing system exists, which applies to the population at large and regulates the general distribution of products in short supply, refugees shall be accorded the same treatment as nationals.

*Article 21*

HOUSING

As regards housing, the Contracting States, in so far as the matter is regulated by laws or regulations or is subject to the control of public authorities, shall accord to refugees lawfully staying in their territory treatment as favourable as possible and, in any event, not less favourable than that accorded to aliens generally in the same circumstances.

*Article 22*

PUBLIC EDUCATION

1. The Contracting States shall accord to refugees the same treatment as is accorded to nationals with respect to elementary education.

2. The Contracting States shall accord to refugees treatment as favourable as possible, and, in any event, not less favourable than that accorded to aliens generally in the same circumstances, with respect to education other than elementary education and, in particular, as regards access to studies, the recognition of foreign school certificates, diplomas and degrees, the remission of fees and charges and the award of scholarships.

*Article 23*

PUBLIC RELIEF

The Contracting States shall accord to refugees lawfully staying in their territory the same treatment with respect to public relief and assistance as is accorded to their nationals.

*Article 24*

LABOUR LEGISLATION AND SOCIAL SECURITY

1. The Contracting States shall accord to refugees lawfully staying in their territory the same treatment as is accorded to nationals in respect of the following matters:

(*a*) In so far as such matters are governed by laws or regulations or are subject to the control of administrative authorities: remuneration, including family allowances where these form part of remuneration, hours of work, overtime arrangements, holidays with pay, restrictions on home work, minimum age of employment, apprenticeship and training, women's work and the work of young persons, and the enjoyment of the benefits of collective bargaining;

(*b*) Social security (legal provisions in respect of employment injury, occupational diseases, maternity, sickness, disability, old age, death, unemployment, family responsibilities and any other contingency which, according to national laws or regulations, is covered by a social security scheme), subject to the following limitations:

(i) There may be appropriate arrangements for the maintenance of acquired rights and rights in course of acquisition;

(ii) National laws or regulations of the country of residence may prescribe special arrangements concerning benefits or portions of benefits which are payable wholly out of public funds, and concerning allowances paid to persons who do not fulfil the contribution conditions prescribed for the award of a normal pension.

2. The right to compensation for the death of a refugee resulting from employment injury or from occupational disease shall not be affected by the fact that the residence of the beneficiary is outside the territory of the Contracting State.

3. The Contracting States shall extend to refugees the benefits of agreements concluded between them, or which may be concluded between them in the future, concerning the maintenance of acquired rights and rights in the process of acquisition in regard to social security, subject only to the conditions which apply to nationals of the States signatory to the agreements in question.

4. The Contracting States will give sympathetic consideration to extending to refugees so far as possible the benefits of similar agreements which may at any time be in force between such Contracting States and non-contracting States.

CHAPTER V

## ADMINISTRATIVE MEASURES

### *Article 25*

#### ADMINISTRATIVE ASSISTANCE

1. When the exercise of a right by a refugee would normally require the assistance of authorities of a foreign country to whom he cannot have recourse, the Contracting States in whose territory he is residing shall arrange that such assistance be afforded to him by their own authorities or by an international authority.

2. The authority or authorities mentioned in paragraph 1 shall deliver or cause to be delivered under their supervision to refugees such documents or certifications as would normally be delivered to aliens by or through their national authorities.

3. Documents or certifications so delivered shall stand in the stead of the official instruments delivered to aliens by or through their national authorities, and shall be given credence in the absence of proof to the contrary.

4. Subject to such exceptional treatment as may be granted to indigent persons, fees may be charged for the services mentioned herein, but such fees shall be moderate and commensurate with those charged to nationals for similar services.

5. The provisions of this article shall be without prejudice to articles 27 and 28.

### *Article 26*

#### FREEDOM OF MOVEMENT

Each Contracting State shall accord to refugees lawfully in its territory the right to choose their place of residence and to move freely within its territory subject to any regulations applicable to aliens generally in the same circumstances.

### *Article 27*

#### IDENTITY PAPERS

The Contracting States shall issue identity papers to any refugee in their territory who does not possess a valid travel document.

### *Article 28*

#### TRAVEL DOCUMENTS

1. The Contracting States shall issue to refugees lawfully staying in their territory travel documents for the purpose of travel outside their territory, unless compelling reasons of national security or public order otherwise require, and the provisions of the Schedule to this Convention shall apply with respect to such documents. The Contracting States may issue such a travel document to any other refugee in their territory; they shall in particular give sympathetic consideration to the issue of such a travel document to refugees in their territory who are unable to obtain a travel document from the country of their lawful residence.

2. Travel documents issued to refugees under previous international agreements by parties thereto shall be recognized and treated by the Contracting States in the same way as if they had been issued pursuant to this article.

### *Article 29*

#### FISCAL CHARGES

1. The Contracting States shall not impose upon refugees duties, charges or taxes, of any description whatsoever, other or higher than those which are or may be levied on their nationals in similar situations.

2. Nothing in the above paragraph shall prevent the application to refugees of the laws and regulations concerning charges in respect of the issue to aliens of administrative documents including identity papers.

### *Article 30*

#### TRANSFER OF ASSETS

1. A Contracting State shall, in conformity with its laws and regulations, permit refugees to transfer assets which they have brought into its territory, to another country where they have been admitted for the purposes of resettlement.

2. A Contracting State shall give sympathetic consideration to the application of refugees for permission to transfer assets wherever they may be and which are necessary for their resettlement in another country to which they have been admitted.

### *Article 31*

#### REFUGEES UNLAWFULLY IN THE COUNTRY OF REFUGE

1. The Contracting States shall not impose penalties, on account of their illegal entry or presence, on refugees who, coming directly from a territory where their life or freedom was threatened in the sense of article 1, enter or are present in their territory without authorization, provided they present themselves without delay to the authorities and show good cause for their illegal entry or presence.

2. The Contracting States shall not apply to the movements of such refugees restrictions other than those which are necessary and such restrictions shall only be applied until their status in the country is regularized or they obtain admission into another country. The Contracting States shall allow such refugees a reasonable period and all the necessary facilities to obtain admission into another country.

### *Article 32*

#### EXPULSION

1. The Contracting States shall not expel a refugee lawfully in their territory save on grounds of national security or public order.

2. The expulsion of such a refugee shall be only in pursuance of a decision reached in accordance with due process of law. Except where compelling reasons of national security otherwise require, the refugee shall be allowed to submit evidence to clear himself, and to appeal to and be represented for the purpose before competent authority or a person or persons specially designated by the competent authority.

3. The Contracting States shall allow such a refugee a reasonable period within which to seek legal admission into another country. The Contracting States reserve the right to apply during that period such internal measures as they may deem necessary.

*Article 33*

PROHIBITION OF EXPULSION OR RETURN ("REFOULEMENT")

1. No Contracting State shall expel or return ("refouler") a refugee in any manner whatsoever to the frontiers of territories where his life or freedom would be threatened on account of his race, religion, nationality, membership of a particular social group or political opinion.

2. The benefit of the present provision may not, however, be claimed by a refugee whom there are reasonable grounds for regarding as a danger to the security of the country in which he is, or who, having been convicted by a final judgment of a particularly serious crime, constitutes a danger to the community of that country.

*Article 34*

NATURALIZATION

The Contracting States shall as far as possible facilitate the assimilation and naturalization of refugees. They shall in particular make every effort to expedite naturalization proceedings and to reduce as far as possible the charges and costs of such proceedings.

CHAPTER VI

## EXECUTORY AND TRANSITORY PROVISIONS

*Article 35*

CO-OPERATION OF THE NATIONAL AUTHORITIES WITH THE UNITED NATIONS

1. The Contracting States undertake to co-operate with the Office of the United Nations High Commissioner for Refugees, or any other agency of the United Nations which may succeed it, in the exercise of its functions, and shall in particular facilitate its duty of supervising the application of the provisions of this Convention.

2. In order to enable the Office of the High Commissioner or any other agency of the United Nations which may succeed it, to make reports to the competent organs of the United Nations, the Contracting States undertake to provide them in the appropriate form with information and statistical data requested concerning:

(*a*) The condition of refugees,

(*b*) The implementation of this Convention, and

(*c*) Laws, regulations and decrees which are, or may hereafter be, in force relating to refugees.

*Article 36*

INFORMATION ON NATIONAL LEGISLATION

The Contracting States shall communicate to the Secretary-General of the United Nations the laws and regulations which they may adopt to ensure the application of this Convention.

*Article 37*

RELATION TO PREVIOUS CONVENTIONS

Without prejudice to article 28, paragraph 2, of this Convention, this Convention replaces, as between parties to it, the Arrangements of 5 July 1922, 31 May 1924, 12 May 1926, 30 June 1928 and 30 July 1935, the Conventions of 28 October 1933 and 10 February 1938, the Protocol of 14 September 1939 and the Agreement of 15 October 1946.

CHAPTER VII

## FINAL CLAUSES

*Article 38*

SETTLEMENT OF DISPUTES

Any dispute between parties to this Convention relating to its interpretation or application, which cannot be settled by other means, shall be referred to the International Court of Justice at the request of any one of the parties to the dispute.

*Article 39*

SIGNATURE, RATIFICATION AND ACCESSION

1. This Convention shall be opened for signature at Geneva on 28 July 1951 and shall thereafter be deposited with the Secretary-General of the United Nations. It shall be open for signature at the European Office of the United Nations from 28 July to 31 August 1951 and shall be re-opened for signature at the Headquarters of the United Nations from 17 September 1951 to 31 December 1952.

2. This Convention shall be open for signature on behalf of all States Members of the United Nations, and also on behalf of any other State invited to attend the Conference of Plenipotentiaries on the Status of Refugees and Stateless Persons or to which an invitation to sign will have been addressed by the General Assembly. It shall be ratified and the instruments of ratification shall be deposited with the Secretary-General of the United Nations.

3. This Convention shall be open from 28 July 1951 for accession by the States referred to in paragraph 2 of this article. Accession shall be effected by the deposit of an instrument of accession with the Secretary-General of the United Nations.

*Article 40*

TERRITORIAL APPLICATION CLAUSE

1. Any State may, at the time of signature, ratification or accession, declare that this Convention shall extend to all or any of the territories for the international relations of which it is responsible. Such a declaration shall take effect when the Convention enters into force for the State concerned.

2. At any time thereafter any such extension shall be made by notification addressed to the Secretary-

General of the United Nations and shall take effect as from the ninetieth day after the day of receipt by the Secretary-General of the United Nations of this notification, or as from the date of entry into force of the Convention for the State concerned, whichever is the later.

3. With respect to those territories to which this Convention is not extended at the time of signature, ratification or accession, each State concerned shall consider the possibility of taking the necessary steps in order to extend the application of this Convention to such territories, subject, where necessary for constitutional reasons, to the consent of the Governments of such territories.

*Article 41*

FEDERAL CLAUSE

In the case of a Federal or non-unitary State, the following provisions shall apply:

(*a*) With respect to those articles of this Convention that come within the legislative jurisdiction of the federal legislative authority, the obligations of the Federal Government shall to this extent be the same as those of Parties which are not Federal States;

(*b*) With respect to those articles of this Convention that come within the legislative jurisdiction of constituent States, provinces or cantons which are not, under the constitutional system of the federation, bound to take legislative action, the Federal Government shall bring such articles with a favourable recommendation to the notice of the appropriate authorities of states, provinces or cantons at the earliest possible moment;

(*c*) A Federal State Party to this Convention shall, at the request of any other Contracting State transmitted through the Secretary-General of the United Nations, supply a statement of the law and practice of the Federation and its constituent units in regard to any particular provision of the Convention showing the extent to which effect has been given to that provision by legislative or other action.

*Article 42*

RESERVATIONS

1. At the time of signature, ratification or accession, any State may make reservations to articles of the Convention other than to articles 1, 3, 4, 16 (1), 33, 36-46 inclusive.

2. Any State making a reservation in accordance with paragraph 1 of this article may at any time withdraw the reservation by a communication to that effect addressed to the Secretary-General of the United Nations.

*Article 43*

ENTRY INTO FORCE

1. This Convention shall come into force on the ninetieth day following the day of deposit of the sixth instrument of ratification or accession.

2. For each State ratifying or acceding to the Convention after the deposit of the sixth instrument of ratification or accession, the Convention shall enter into force on the ninetieth day following the date of deposit by such State of its instrument of ratification or accession.

*Article 44*

DENUNCIATION

1. Any Contracting State may denounce this Convention at any time by a notification addressed to the Secretary-General of the United Nations.

2. Such denunciation shall take effect for the Contracting State concerned one year from the date upon which it is received by the Secretary-General of the United Nations.

3. Any State which has made a declaration or notification under article 40 may, at any time thereafter, by a notification to the Secretary-General of the United Nations, declare that the Convention shall cease to extend to such territory one year after the date of receipt of the notification by the Secretary-General.

*Article 45*

REVISION

1. Any Contracting State may request revision of this Convention at any time by a notification addressed to the Secretary-General of the United Nations.

2. The General Assembly of the United Nations shall recommend the steps, if any, to be taken in respect of such request.

*Article 46*

NOTIFICATIONS BY THE SECRETARY-GENERAL OF THE UNITED NATIONS

The Secretary-General of the United Nations shall inform all Members of the United Nations and non-member States referred to in article 39:

(*a*) Of declarations and notifications in accordance with section B of article 1;

(*b*) Of signatures, ratifications and accessions in accordance with article 39;

(*c*) Of declarations and notifications in accordance with article 40;

(*d*) Of reservations and withdrawals in accordance with article 42;

(*e*) Of the date on which this Convention will come into force in accordance with article 43;

(*f*) Of denunciations and notifications in accordance with article 44;

(*g*) Of requests for revision in accordance with article 45.

IN FAITH WHEREOF the undersigned, duly authorized, have signed this Convention on behalf of their respective Governments,

DONE at Geneva, this twenty-eighth day of July, one thousand nine hundred and fifty-one, in a single copy, of which the English and French texts are equally authentic and which shall remain deposited in the archives of the United Nations, and certified true copies of which shall be delivered to all Members of the United Nations and to the non-member States referred to in article 39.

## 26. Protocol relating to the Status of Refugees

**The Protocol was taken note of with approval by the Economic and Social Council in resolution 1186 (XLI) of 18 November 1966 and was taken note of by the General Assembly in resolution 2198 (XXI) of 16 December 1966. In the same resolution the General Assembly requested the Secretary-General to transmit the text of the Protocol to the States mentioned in article V thereof, with a view to enabling them to accede to the Protocol**

***Entry into force***: 4 October 1967, in accordance with article VIII.

*The States Parties* to the present Protocol,

*Considering* that the Convention relating to the Status of Refugees done at Geneva on 28 July 1951 (hereinafter referred to as the Convention) covers only those persons who have become refugees as a result of events occurring before 1 January 1951,

*Considering* that new refugee situations have arisen since the Convention was adopted and that the refugees concerned may therefore not fall within the scope of the Convention,

*Considering* that it is desirable that equal status should be enjoyed by all refugees covered by the definition in the Convention irrespective of the dateline 1 January 1951,

*Have agreed* as follows:

### *Article I*

GENERAL PROVISION

1. The States Parties to the present Protocol undertake to apply articles 2 to 34 inclusive of the Convention to refugees as hereinafter defined.

2. For the purpose of the present Protocol, the term "refugee" shall, except as regards the application of paragraph 3 of this article, mean any person within the definition of article 1 of the Convention as if the words "As a result of events occurring before 1 January 1951 and. . ." and the words ". . . as a result of such events", in article 1 A (2) were omitted.

3. The present Protocol shall be applied by the States Parties hereto without any geographic limitation, save that existing declarations made by States already Parties to the Convention in accordance with article 1 B (1) (*a*) of the Convention, shall, unless extended under article 1 B (2) thereof, apply also under the present Protocol.

### *Article II*

CO-OPERATION OF THE NATIONAL AUTHORITIES WITH THE UNITED NATIONS

1. The States Parties to the present Protocol undertake to co-operate with the Office of the United Nations High Commissioner for Refugees, or any other agency of the United Nations which may succeed it, in the exercise of its functions, and shall in particular facilitate its duty of supervising the application of the provisions of the present Protocol.

2. In order to enable the Office of the High Commissioner or any other agency of the United Nations which may succeed it, to make reports to the competent organs of the United Nations, the States Parties to the present Protocol undertake to provide them with the information and statistical data requested, in the appropriate form, concerning:

(*a*) The condition of refugees;

(*b*) The implementation of the present Protocol;

(*c*) Laws, regulations and decrees which are, or may hereafter be, in force relating to refugees.

### *Article III*

INFORMATION ON NATIONAL LEGISLATION

The States Parties to the present Protocol shall communicate to the Secretary-General of the United Nations the laws and regulations which they may adopt to ensure the application of the present Protocol.

### *Article IV*

SETTLEMENT OF DISPUTES

Any dispute between States Parties to the present Protocol which relates to its interpretation or application and which cannot be settled by other means shall be referred to the International Court of Justice at the request of any one of the parties to the dispute.

### *Article V*

ACCESSION

The present Protocol shall be open for accession on behalf of all States Parties to the Convention and of any other State Member of the United Nations or member of any of the specialized agencies or to which an invitation to accede may have been addressed by the General Assembly of the United Nations. Accession shall be effected by the deposit of an instrument of accession with the Secretary-General of the United Nations.

### *Article VI*

FEDERAL CLAUSE

In the case of a Federal or non-unitary State, the following provisions shall apply:

(*a*) With respect to those articles of the Convention to be applied in accordance with article I, paragraph 1, of the present Protocol that come within the legislative jurisdiction of the federal legislative authority, the obligations of the Federal Government shall to this extent be the same as those of States Parties which are not Federal States;

(*b*) With respect to those articles of the Convention to be applied in accordance with article I, paragraph 1, of the present Protocol that come within the legislative jurisdiction of constituent States, provinces or cantons which are not, under the constitutional system of the federation, bound to take legislative action, the Federal Government shall bring such articles with a favourable recommendation to the notice of the appropriate authorities of States, provinces or cantons at the earliest possible moment;

(*c*) A Federal State Party to the present Protocol shall, at the request of any other State Party hereto transmitted through the Secretary-General of the United

Nations, supply a statement of the law and practice of the Federation and its constituent units in regard to any particular provision of the Convention to be applied in accordance with article I, paragraph 1, of the present Protocol, showing the extent to which effect has been given to that provision by legislative or other action.

*Article VII*

RESERVATIONS AND DECLARATIONS

1. At the time of accession, any State may make reservations in respect of article IV of the present Protocol and in respect of the application in accordance with article I of the present Protocol of any provisions of the Convention other than those contained in articles 1, 3, 4, 16 (1) and 33 whereof, provided that in the case of a State Party to the Convention reservations made under this article shall not extend to refugees in respect of whom the Convention applies.

2. Reservations made by States Parties to the Convention in accordance with article 42 thereof shall, unless withdrawn, be applicable in relation to their obligations under the present Protocol.

3. Any State making a reservation in accordance with paragraph 1 of this article may at any time withdraw such reservation by a communication to that effect addressed to the Secretary-General of the United Nations.

4. Declaration made under article 40, paragraphs 1 and 2, of the Convention by a State Party thereto which accedes to the present Protocol shall be deemed to apply in respect of the present Protocol, unless upon accession a notification to the contrary is addressed by the State Party concerned to the Secretary-General of the United Nations. The provisions of article 40, paragraphs 2 and 3, and of article 44, paragraph 3, of the Convention shall be deemed to apply *mutatis mutandis* to the present Protocol.

*Article VIII*

ENTRY INTO FORCE

1. The present Protocol shall come into force on the day of deposit of the sixth instrument of accession.

2. For each State acceding to the Protocol after the deposit of the sixth instrument of accession, the Protocol shall come into force on the date of deposit by such State of its instrument of accession.

*Article IX*

DENUNCIATION

1. Any State Party hereto may denounce this Protocol at any time by a notification addressed to the Secretary-General of the United Nations.

2. Such denunciation shall take effect for the State Party concerned one year from the date on which it is received by the Secretary-General of the United Nations.

*Article X*

NOTIFICATIONS BY THE SECRETARY-GENERAL OF THE UNITED NATIONS

The Secretary-General of the United Nations shall inform the States referred to in article V above of the date of entry into force, accessions, reservations and withdrawals of reservations to and denunciations of the present Protocol, and of declarations and notifications relating hereto.

*Article XI*

DEPOSIT IN THE ARCHIVES OF THE SECRETARIAT OF THE UNITED NATIONS

A copy of the present Protocol, of which the Chinese, English, French, Russian and Spanish texts are equally authentic, signed by the President of the General Assembly and by the Secretary-General of the United Nations, shall be deposited in the archives of the Secretariat of the United Nations. The Secretary-General will transmit certified copies thereof to all States Members of the United Nations and to the other States referred to in article V above.

## 27. Statute of the Office of the United Nations High Commissioner for Refugees

**Adopted by General Assembly resolution 428 (V) of 14 December 1950**

*Chapter I*

GENERAL PROVISIONS

1. The United Nations High Commissioner for Refugees, acting under the authority of the General Assembly, shall assume the function of providing international protection, under the auspices of the United Nations, to refugees who fall within the scope of the present Statute and of seeking permanent solutions for the problem of refugees by assisting governments and, subject to the approval of the governments concerned, private organizations to facilitate the voluntary repatriation of such refugees, or their assimilation within new national communities.

In the exercise of his functions, more particularly when difficulties arise, and for instance with regard to any controversy concerning the international status of these persons, the High Commissioner shall request the opinion of an advisory committee on refugees if it is created.

2. The work of the High Commissioner shall be of an entirely non-political character; it shall be humanitarian and social and shall relate, as a rule, to groups and categories of refugees.

3. The High Commissioner shall follow policy directives given him by the General Assembly or the Economic and Social Council.

4. The Economic and Social Council may decide, after hearing the views of the High Commissioner on the subject, to establish an advisory committee on refugees, which shall consist of representatives of States Members and States non-members of the United Nations, to be selected by the Council on the basis of their demonstrated interest in and devotion to the solution of the refugee problem.

5. The General Assembly shall review, not later than at its eighth regular session, the arrangements for the Office of the High Commissioner with a view to deter-

mining whether the Office should be continued beyond 31 December 1963.

*Chapter II*

### FUNCTIONS OF THE HIGH COMMISSIONER

6. The competence of the High Commissioner shall extend to:

A. (i) Any person who has been considered a refugee under the Arrangements of 12 May 1926 and 30 June 1928 or under the Conventions of 28 October 1933 and 10 February 1938, the Protocol of 14 September 1939 or the Constitution of the International Refugee Organization;

(ii) Any person who, as a result of events occurring before 1 January 1951 and owing to well-founded fear of being persecuted for reasons of race, religion, nationality or political opinion, is outside the country of his nationality and is unable or, owing to such fear or for reasons other than personal convenience, is unwilling to avail himself of the protection of that country; or who, not having a nationality and being outside the country of his former habitual residence, is unable or, owing to such fear or for reasons other than personal convenience, is unwilling to return to it.

Decisions as to eligibility taken by the International Refugee Organizations during the period of its activities shall not prevent the status of refugee being accorded to persons who fulfil the conditions of the present paragraph;

The competence of the High Commissioner shall cease to apply to any person defined in section A above if:

(*a*) He has voluntarily re-availed himself of the protection of the country of his nationality; or

(*b*) Having lost his nationality, he has voluntarily re-acquired it; or

(*c*) He has acquired a new nationality, and enjoys the protection of the country of his new nationality; or

(*d*) He has voluntarily re-established himself in the country which he left or outside which he remained owing to fear of persecution; or

(*e*) He can no longer, because the circumstances in connexion with which he has been recognized as a refugee have ceased to exist, claim grounds other than those of personal convenience, for continuing to refuse to avail himself of the protection of the country of his nationality. Reasons of a purely economic character may not be invoked; or

(*f*) Being a person who has no nationality, he can no longer, because the circumstances in connexion with which he has been recognized as a refugee have ceased to exist and he is able to return to the country of his former habitual residence, claim grounds other than those of personal convenience for continuing to refuse to return to that country;

B. Any other person who is outside the country of his nationality or, if he has no nationality, the country of his former habitual residence, because he has or had well-founded fear of persecution by reason of his race, religion, nationality or political opinion and is unable or, because of such fear, is unwilling to avail himself of the protection of the government of the country of his nationality, or, if he has no nationality, to return to the country of his former habitual residence.

7. Provided that the competence of the High Commissioner as defined in paragraph 6 above shall not extend to a person:

(*a*) Who is a national of more than one country unless he satisfies the provisions of the preceding paragraph in relation to each of the countries of which he is a national; or

(*b*) Who is recognized by the competent authorities of the country in which he has taken residence as having the rights and obligations which are attached to the possession of the nationality of that country; or

(*c*) Who continues to receive from other organs or agencies of the United Nations protection or assistance; or

(*d*) In respect of whom there are serious reasons for considering that he has committed a crime covered by the provisions of treaties of extradition or a crime mentioned in article VI of the London Charter of the International Military Tribunal or by the provisions of article 14, paragraph 2, of the Universal Declaration of Human Rights.

8. The High Commissioner shall provide for the protection of refugees falling under the competence of his Office by:

(*a*) Promoting the conclusion and ratification of international conventions for the protection of refugees, supervising their application and proposing amendments thereto;

(*b*) Promoting through special agreements with governments the execution of any measures calculated to improve the situation of refugees and to reduce the number requiring protection;

(*c*) Assisting governmental and private efforts to promote voluntary repatriation or assimilation within new national communities;

(*d*) Promoting the admission of refugees, not excluding those in the most destitute categories, to the territories of States;

(*e*) Endeavouring to obtain permission for refugees to transfer their assets and especially those necessary for their resettlement;

(*f*) Obtaining from governments information concerning the number and conditions of refugees in their territories and the laws and regulations concerning them;

(*g*) Keeping in close touch with the governments and inter-governmental organizations concerned;

(*h*) Establishing contact in such manner as he may think best with private organizations dealing with refugee questions;

(*i*) Facilitating the co-ordination of the efforts of private organizations concerned with the welfare of refugees.

9. The High Commissioner shall engage in such additional activities, including repatriation and resettlement, as the General Assembly may determine, within the limits of the resqurces placed at his disposal.

10. The High Commissioner shall administer any funds, public or private, which he receives for assistance to refugees, and shall distribute them among the private and, as appropriate, public agencies which he deems best qualified to administer such assistance.

The High Commissioner may reject any offers which he does not consider appropriate or which cannot be utilized.

The High Commissioner shall not appeal to governments for funds or make a general appeal, without the prior approval of the General Assembly.

The High Commissioner shall include in his annual report a statement of his activities in this field.

11. The High Commissioner shall be entitled to present his views before the General Assembly, the Economic and Social Council and their subsidiary bodies.

The High Commissioner shall report annually to the General Assembly through the Economic and Social Council; his report shall be considered as a separate item on the agenda of the General Assembly.

12. The High Commissioner may invite the co-operation of the various specialized agencies.

### *Chapter III*

### ORGANIZATION AND FINANCES

13. The High Commissioner shall be elected by the General Assembly on the nomination of the Secretary-General. The terms of appointment of the High Commissioner shall be proposed by the Secretary-General and approved by the General Assembly. The High Commissioner shall be elected for a term of three years, from 1 January 1951.

14. The High Commissioner shall appoint, for the same term, a Deputy High Commissioner of a nationality other than his own.

15. (*a*) Within the limits of the budgetary appropriations provided, the staff of the Office of the High Commissioner shall be appointed by the High Commissioner and shall be responsible to him in the exercise of their functions.

(*b*) Such staff shall be chosen from persons devoted to the purposes of the Office of the High Commissioner.

(*c*) Their conditions of employment shall be those provided under the staff regulations adopted by the General Assembly and the rules promulgated thereunder by the Secretary-General.

(*d*) Provision may also be made to permit the employment of personnel without compensation.

16. The High Commissioner shall consult the governments of the countries of residence of refugees as to the need for appointing representatives therein. In any country recognizing such need, there may be appointed a representative approved by the government of that country. Subject to the foregoing, the same representative may serve in more than one country.

17. The High Commissioner and the Secretary-General shall make appropriate arrangements for liaison and consultation on matters of mutual interest.

18. The Secretary-General shall provide the High Commissioner with all necessary facilities within budgetary limitations.

19. The Office of the High Commissioner shall be located in Geneva, Switzerland.

20. The Office of the High Commissioner shall be financed under the budget of the United Nations. Unless the General Assembly subsequently decides otherwise, no expenditure, other than administrative expenditures relating to the functioning of the Office of the High Commissioner, shall be borne on the budget of the United Nations, and all other expenditures relating to the activities of the High Commissioner shall be financed by voluntary contributions.

21. The administration of the Office of the High Commissioner shall be subject to the Financial Regulations of the United Nations and to the financial rules promulgated thereunder by the Secretary-General.

22. Transactions relating to the High Commissioner's funds shall be subject to audit by the United Nations Board of Auditors, provided that the Board may accept audited accounts from the agencies to which funds have been allocated. Administrative arrangements for the custody of such funds and their allocation shall be agreed between the High Commissioner and the Secretary-General in accordance with the Financial Regulations of the United Nations and rules promulgated thereunder by the Secretary-General.

## 28. **Declaration on Territorial Asylum**

**Adopted by the General Assembly of the United Nations on 14 December 1967 (resolution 2312 (XXII))**

*The General Assembly*,

*Recalling* its resolutions 1839 (XVII) of 19 December 1962, 2100 (XX) of 20 December 1965 and 2203 (XXI) of 16 December 1966 concerning a declaration on the right of asylum,

*Considering* the work of codification to be undertaken by the International Law Commission in accordance with General Assembly resolution 1400 (XIV) of 21 November 1959,

*Adopts* the following Declaration:

### DECLARATION ON TERRITORIAL ASYLUM

*The General Assembly*,

*Noting* that the purposes proclaimed in the Charter of the United Nations are to maintain international peace and security, to develop friendly relations among all nations and to achieve international co-operation in solving international problems of an economic, social, cultural or humanitarian character and in promoting and encouraging respect for human rights and for fundamental freedoms for all without distinction as to race, sex, language or religion.

*Mindful* of the Universal Declaration of Human Rights, which declares in article 14 that:

"1. Everyone has the right to seek and to enjoy in other countries asylum from persecution.

"2. This right may not be invoked in the case of prosecutions genuinely arising from non-political crimes or from acts contrary to the purposes and principles of the United Nations",

*Recalling also* article 13, paragraph 2, of the Universal Declaration of Human Rights, which states:

"Everyone has the right to leave any country, including his own, and to return to his country",

*Recognizing* that the grant of asylum by a State to persons entitled to invoke article 14 of the Universal Declaration of Human Rights is a peaceful and humanitarian act and that, as such, it cannot be regarded as unfriendly by any other State,

*Recommends* that, without prejudice to existing instruments dealing with asylum and the status of refugees and stateless persons, States should base themselves in their practices relating to territorial asylum on the following principles:

*Article 1*

1. Asylum granted by a State, in the exercise of its sovereignty, to persons entitled to invoke article 14 of the Universal Declaration of Human Rights, including persons struggling against colonialism, shall be respected by all other States.

2. The right to seek and to enjoy asylum may not be invoked by any person with respect to whom there are serious reasons for considering that he has committed a crime against peace, a war crime or a crime against humanity, as defined in the international instruments drawn up to make provision in respect of such crimes.

3. It shall rest with the State granting asylum to evaluate the grounds for the grant of asylum.

*Article 2*

1. The situation of persons referred to in article 1, paragraph 1, is, without prejudice to the sovereignty of States and the purposes and principles of the United Nations, of concern to the international community.

2. Where a State finds difficulty in granting or continuing to grant asylum, States individually or jointly or through the United Nations shall consider, in a spirit of international solidarity, appropriate measures to lighten the burden on that State.

*Article 3*

1. No person referred to in article 1, paragraph 1, shall be subjected to measures such as rejection at the frontier or, if he has already entered the territory in which he seeks asylum, expulsion or compulsory return to any State where he may be subjected to persecution.

2. Exception may be made to the foregoing principle only for overriding reasons of national security or in order to safeguard the population, as in the case of a mass influx of persons.

3. Should a State decide in any case that exception to the principle stated in paragraph 1 of this article would be justified, it shall consider the possibility of granting to the person concerned, under such conditions as it may deem appropriate, an opportunity, whether by way of provisional asylum or otherwise, of going to another State.

*Article 4*

States granting asylum shall not permit persons who have received asylum to engage in activities contrary to the purposes and principles of the United Nations.

# H. FREEDOM OF INFORMATION

## 29. Convention on the International Right of Correction

**Opened for signature by General Assembly resolution 630 (VII) of 16 December 1952**

*Entry into force*: 24 August 1962, in accordance with article VIII.

*Preamble*

*The Contracting States,*

*Desiring* to implement the right of their peoples to be fully and reliably informed,

*Desiring* to improve understanding between their peoples through the free flow of information and opinion,

*Desiring* thereby to protect mankind from the scourge of war, to prevent the recurrence of aggression from any source, and to combat all propaganda which is either designed or likely to provoke or encourage any threat to the peace, breach of the peace, or act of aggression,

*Considering* the danger to the maintenance of friendly relations between peoples and to the preservation of peace, arising from the publication of inaccurate reports,

*Considering* that at its second regular session the General Assembly of the United Nations recommended the adoption of measures designed to combat the dissemination of false or distorted reports likely to injure friendly relations between States,

*Considering*, however, that it is not at present practicable to institute, on the international level, a procedure for verifying the accuracy of a report which might lead to the imposition of penalties for the publication of false or distorted reports,

*Considering*, moreover, that to prevent the publication of reports of this nature or to reduce their pernicious effects, it is above all necessary to promote a wide circulation of news and to heighten the sense of responsibility of those regularly engaged in the dissemination of news,

*Considering* that an effective means to these ends is to give States directly affected by a report, which they consider false or distorted and which is disseminated by an information agency, the possibility of securing commensurate publicity for their corrections,

*Considering* that the legislation of certain States does not provide for a right of correction of which foreign governments may avail themselves, and that it is therefore desirable to institute such a right on the international level, and

*Having resolved* to conclude a Convention for these purposes,

*Have agreed* as follows:

*Article I*

For the purposes of the present Convention:

1. "News dispatch" means news material transmitted in writing or by means of telecommunications, in the form customarily employed by information agencies in transmitting such news material, before publication, to newspapers, news periodicals and broadcasting organizations.

2. "Information agency" means a Press, broadcasting, film, television or facsimile organization, public or private, regularly engaged in the collection and dissemination of news material, created and organized under the laws and regulations of the Contracting State in which the central organization is domiciled and which, in each Contracting State where it operates, functions under the laws and regulations of that State.

3. "Correspondent" means a national of a Contracting State or an individual employed by an information agency of a Contracting State, who in either case is regularly engaged in the collection and the reporting of news material, and who when outside his State is identified as a correspondent by a valid passport or by a similar document internationally acceptable.

*Article II*

1. Recognizing that the professional responsibility of correspondents and information agencies requires them to report facts without discrimination and in their proper context and thereby to promote respect for human rights and fundamental freedoms, to further international understanding and co-operation and to contribute to the maintenance of international peace and security.

Considering also that, as a matter of professional ethics, all correspondents and information agencies should, in the case of news dispatches transmitted or published by them and which have been demonstrated to be false or distorted, follow the customary practice of transmitting through the same channels, or of publishing corrections of such dispatches.

The Contracting States agree that in cases where a Contracting State contends that a news dispatch capable of injuring its relations with other States or its national prestige or dignity transmitted from one country to another by correspondents or information agencies of a Contracting or non-Contracting State and published or disseminated abroad is false or distorted, it may submit its version of the facts (hereinafter called "communiqué") to the Contracting States within whose territories such dispatch has been published or disseminated. A copy of the communiqué shall be forwarded at the same time to the correspondent or information agency concerned to enable that correspondent or information agency to correct the news dispatch in question.

2. A communiqué may be issued only with respect to news dispatches and must be without comment or

expression of opinion. It should not be longer than is necessary to correct the alleged inaccuracy or distortion and must be accompanied by a verbatim text of the dispatch as published or disseminated, and by evidence that the dispatch has been transmitted from abroad by correspondent or an information agency.

*Article III*

1. With the least possible delay and in any case not later than five clear days from the date of receiving a communiqué transmitted in accordance with provisions of article II, a Contracting State, whatever be its opinion concerning the facts in question, shall:

(*a*) Release the communiqué to the correspondents and information agencies operating in its territory through the channels customarily used for the release of news concerning international affairs for publication; and

(*b*) Transmit the communiqué to the headquarters of the information agency whose correspondent was responsible for originating the dispatch in question, if such headquarters are within its territory.

2. In the event that a Contracting State does not discharge its obligation under this article, with respect to the communiqué of another Contracting State, the latter may accord, on the basis of reciprocity, similar treatment to a communiqué thereafter submitted to it by the defaulting State.

*Article IV*

1. If any of the Contracting States to which a communiqué has been transmitted in accordance with article II fails to fulfil, within the prescribed time-limit, the obligations laid down in article III, the Contracting State exercising the right of correction may submit the said communiqué, together with a verbatim text of the dispatch as published or disseminated, to the Secretary-General of the United Nations and shall at the same time notify the State complained against that it is doing so. The latter State may, within five clear days after receiving such notice, submit its comments to the Secretary-General, which shall relate only to the allegation that it has not discharged its obligations under article III.

2. The Secretary-General shall in any event, within ten clear days after receiving the communiqué, give appropriate publicity through the information channels at his disposal to the communiqué, together with the dispatch and the comments, if any, submitted to him by the State complained against.

*Article V*

Any dispute between any two or more Contracting States concerning the interpretation or application of the present Convention which is not settled by negotiations shall be referred to the International Court of Justice for decision unless the Contracting States agree to another mode of settlement.

*Article VI*

1. The present Convention shall be open for signature to all States Members of the United Nations, to every State invited to the United Nations Conference on Freedom of Information held at Geneva in 1948, and to every other State which the General Assembly may, by resolution, declare to be eligible.

2. The present Convention shall be ratified by the States signatory hereto in conformity with their respective constitutional processes. The instruments of ratification shall be deposited with the Secretary-General of the United Nations.

*Article VII*

1. The present Convention shall be open for accession to the States referred to in article VI (1).

2. Accession shall be effected by the deposit of an instrument of accession with the Secretary-General of the United Nations.

*Article VIII*

When any six of the States referred to in article VI (1) have deposited their instruments of ratification or accession, the present Convention shall come into force among them on the thirtieth day after the date of the deposit of the sixth instrument of ratification or accession. It shall come into force for each State which ratifies or accedes after that date on the thirtieth day after the deposit of its instrument of ratification or accession.

*Article IX*

The provisions of the present Convention shall extend to or be applicable equally to a contracting metropolitan State and to all territories, be they Non-Self-Governing, Trust or Colonial Territories, which are being administered or governed by such metropolitan State.

*Article X*

Any Contracting State may denounce the present Convention by notification to the Secretary-General of the United Nations. Denunciation shall take effect six months after the date of receipt of the notification by the Secretary-General.

*Article XI*

The present Convention shall cease to be in force as from the date when the denunciation which reduces the number of parties to less than six becomes effective.

*Article XII*

1. A request for the revision of the present Convention may be made at any time by any Contracting State by means of a notification to the Secretary-General of the United Nations.

2. The General Assembly shall decide upon the steps, if any, to be taken in respect of such request.

*Article XIII*

The Secretary-General of the United Nations shall notify the States referred to in article VI (1) of the following:

(*a*) Signatures, ratifications and accessions received in accordance with articles VI and VII;

(*b*) The date upon which the present Convention comes into force in accordance with article VIII;

(*c*) Denunciations received in accordance with article X;

(*d*) Abrogation in accordance with article XI;

(*e*) Notifications received in accordance with article VII.

*Article XIV*

1. The present Convention, of which the Chinese, English, French, Russian and Spanish texts shall be equally authentic, shall be deposited in the archives of the United Nations.

2. The Secretary-General of the United Nations shall transmit a certified copy to each State referred to in article VI (1).

3. The present Convention shall be registered with the Secretariat of the United Nations on the date of its coming into force.

# I. FREEDOM OF ASSOCIATION

## 30. Freedom of Association and Protection of the Right to Organise Convention

**Convention (No. 87) concerning Freedom of Association and Protection of the Right to Organise**

**Adopted on 9 July 1948 by the General Conference of the International Labour Organisation at its thirty-first session**

*Entry into force*: 4 July 1950, in accordance with article 15.

*The General Conference of the International Labour Organisation*,

*Having been convened* at San Francisco by the Governing Body of the International Labour Office, and having met in its thirty-first session on 17 June 1948,

*Having decided* to adopt, in the form of a Convention, certain proposals concerning freedom of association and protection of the right to organise which is the seventh item on the agenda of the session.

*Considering* that the Preamble to the Constitution of the International Labour Organisation declares "recognition of the principle of freedom of association" to be a means of improving conditions of labour and of establishing peace,

*Considering* that the Declaration of Philadelphia reaffirms that "freedom of expression and of association are essential to sustained progress",

*Considering* that the International Labour Conference, at its Thirtieth Session, unanimously adopted the principles which should form the basis for international regulation,

*Considering* that the General Assembly of the United Nations, at its Second Session, endorsed these principles and requested the International Labour Organisation to continue every effort in order that it may be possible to adopt one or several international Conventions,

*Adopts* this ninth day of July of the year one thousand nine hundred and forty-eight the following Convention, which may be cited as the Freedom of Association and Protection of the Right to Organise Convention, 1948:

### PART I. FREEDOM OF ASSOCIATION

*Article 1*

Each Member of the International Labour Organisation for which this Convention is in force undertakes to give effect to the following provisions.

*Article 2*

Workers and employers, without distinction whatsoever, shall have the right to establish and, subject, only to the rules of the organisation concerned, to join organisations of their own choosing without previous authorisation.

*Article 3*

1. Workers' and employers' organisations shall have the right to draw up their constitutions and rules, to elect their representatives in full freedom to organise their administration and activities and to formulate their programmes.

2. The public authorities shall refrain from any interference which would restrict this right or impede the lawful exercise thereof.

*Article 4*

Workers' and employers' organisations shall not be liable to be dissolved or suspended by administrative authority.

*Article 5*

Workers' and employers' organisations shall have the right to establish and join federations and confederations and any such organisation, federation or confederation shall have the right to affiliate with international organisations of workers and employers.

*Article 6*

The provisions of articles 2, 3 and 4 hereof apply to federations and confederations of workers' and employers' organisations.

*Article 7*

The acquisition of legal personality by workers' and employers' organisations, federations and confederations shall not be made subject to conditions of such a character as to restrict the application of the provisions of articles 2, 3 and 4 hereof.

*Article 8*

1. In exercising the rights provided for in this Convention workers and employers and their respective organisations, like other persons or organised collectivities, shall respect the law of the land.

2. The law of the land shall not be such as to impair, nor shall it be so applied as to impair, the guarantees provided for in this Convention.

*Article 9*

1. The extent to which the guarantees provided for in this Convention shall apply to the armed forces and the police shall be determined by national laws or regulations.

2. In accordance with the principle set forth in paragraph 8 of article 19 of the Constitution of the International Labour Organisation the ratification of this Convention by any Member shall not be deemed to affect any existing law, award, custom or agreement in virtue of which members of the armed forces or the police enjoy any right guaranteed by this Convention.

*Article 10*

In this Convention the term "organisation" means any organisation of workers or of employers for furthering and defending the interests of workers or of employers.

## PART II. PROTECTION OF THE RIGHT TO ORGANISE

*Article 11*

Each Member of the International Labour Organisation for which this Convention is in force undertakes to take all necessary and appropriate measures to ensure that workers and employers may exercise freely the right to organise.

## PART III. MISCELLANEOUS PROVISIONS

*Article 12*

1. In respect of the territories referred to in article 35 of the Constitution of the International Labour Organisation as amended by the Constitution of the International Labour Organisation Instrument of Amendment, 1946, other than the territories referred to in paragraphs 4 and 5 of the said article as so amended, each Member of the Organisation which ratifies this Convention shall communicate to the Director-General of the International Labour Office with or as soon as possible after its ratification a declaration stating:

(*a*) The territories in respect of which it undertakes that the provisions of the Convention shall be applied without modification;

(*b*) The territories in respect of which it undertakes that the provisions of the Convention shall be applied subject to modifications, together with details of the said modifications;

(*c*) The territories in respect of which the Convention is inapplicable and in such cases the grounds on which it is inapplicable;

(*d*) The territories in respect of which it reserves its decision.

2. The undertakings referred to in subparagraphs (*a*) and (*b*) of paragraph 1 of this article shall be deemed to be an integral part of ratification and shall have the force of ratification.

3. Any Member may at any time by a subsequent declaration cancel in whole or in part any reservations made in its original declaration in virtue of subparagraphs (*b*), (*c*) or (*d*) of paragraph 1 of this article.

4. Any Member may, at any time at which this Convention is subject to denunciation in accordance with the provisions of article 16, communicate to the Director-General a declaration modifying in any other respect the terms of any former declaration and stating the present position in respect of such territories as it may specify.

*Article 13*

1. Where the subject matter of this Convention is within the self-governing powers of any non-metropolitan territory, the Member responsible for the international relations of that territory may, in agreement with the government of the territory, communicate to the Director-General of the International Labour Office a declaration accepting on behalf of the territory the obligations of this Convention.

2. A declaration accepting the obligations of this Convention may be communicated to the Director-General of the International Labour Office:

(*a*) By two or more Members of the Organisation in respect of any territory which is under their joint authority; or

(*b*) By any international authority responsible for the administration of any territory, in virtue of the Charter of the United Nations or otherwise, in respect of any such territory.

3. Declarations communicated to the Director-General of the International Labour Office in accordance with the preceding paragraphs of this article shall indicate whether the provisions of the Convention will be applied in the territory concerned without modification or subject to modifications; when the declaration indicates that the provisions of the Convention will be applied subject to modifications it shall give details of the said modifications.

4. The Member, Members or international authority concerned may at any time by a subsequent declaration renounce in whole or in part the right to have recourse to any modification indicated in any former declaration.

5. The Member, Members or international authority concerned may, at any time at which this Convention is subject to denunciation in accordance with the provisions of article 16, communicate to the Director-General of the International Labour Office a declaration modifying in any other respect the terms of any former declaration and stating the present position in respect of the application of the Convention.

## PART IV. FINAL PROVISIONS

*Article 14*

The formal ratifications of this Convention shall be communicated to the Director-General of the International Labour Office for registration.

*Article 15*

1. This Convention shall be binding only upon those Members of the International Labour Organisation whose ratifications have been registered with the Director-General.

2. It shall come into force twelve months after the date on which the ratifications of two Members have been registered with the Director-General.

3. Thereafter, this Convention shall come into force for any Member twelve months after the date on which its ratification has been registered.

*Article 16*

1. A Member which has ratified this Convention may denounce it after the expiration of ten years from the date on which the Convention first comes into force, by an act communicated to the Director-General of the International Labour Office for registration. Such denunciation shall not take effect until one year after the date on which it is registered.

2. Each Member which has ratified this Convention and which does not, within the year following the expiration of the period of ten years mentioned in the preceding paragraph, exercise the right of denunciation provided for in this article, will be bound for another period of ten years and, thereafter, may denounce this Convention at the expiration of each period of ten years under the terms provided for in this article.

*Article 17*

1. The Director-General of the International Labour Office shall notify all Members of the International Labour Organisation of the registration of all ratifications, declarations and denunciations communicated to him by the Members of the Organisation.

2. When notifying the Members of the Organisation of the registration of the second ratification communicated to him, the Director-General shall draw the attention of the Members of the Organisation to the date upon which the Convention will come into force.

*Article 18*

The Director-General of the International Labour Office shall communicate to the Secretary-General of the United Nations for registration in accordance with Article 102 of the Charter of the United Nations full particulars of all ratifications, declarations and acts of denunciation registered by him in accordance with the provisions of the preceding articles.

*Article 19*

At the expiration of each period of ten years after the coming into force of this Convention, the Governing body of the International Labour Office shall present to the General Conference a report on the working of this Convention and shall consider the desirability of placing on the agenda of the Conference the question of its revision in whole or in part.

*Article 20*

1. Should the Conference adopt a new Convention revising this Convention in whole or in part, then, unless the new Convention otherwise provides:

(*a*) The ratification by a member of the new revising Convention shall *ipso jure* involve the immediate denunciation of this Convention, notwithstanding the provisions of article 16 above, if and when the new revising Convention shall have come into force;

(*b*) As from the date when the new revising Convention comes into force this Convention shall cease to be open to ratification by the Members.

2. This Convention shall in any case remain in force in its actual form and content for those Members which have ratified it but have not ratified the revising Convention.

*Article 21*

The English and French versions of the text of this Convention are equally authoritative.

The foregoing is the authentic text of the Convention duly adopted by the General Conference of the International Labour Organisation during its thirty-first session which was held at San Francisco and declared closed the tenth day of July 1948.

IN FAITH WHEREOF we have appended our signatures this thirty-first day of August 1948.

## 31. **Right to Organize and Collective Bargaining Convention**

**Convention (No. 98) concerning the Application of the Principles of the Right to Organise and to Bargain Collectively**

**Adopted on 1 July 1949 by the General Conference of the International Labour Organisation at its thirty-second session**

*Entry into force*: 18 July 1951, in accordance with article 8.

*The General Conference of the International Labour Organisation*,

*Having been convened* at Geneva by the Governing Body or the International Labour Office, and having met in its thirty-second session on 8 June 1949, and

*Having decided* upon the adoption of certain proposals concerning the application of the principles of the right to organise and to bargain collectively, which is the fourth item on the agenda of the session, and

*Having determined* that these proposals shall take the form of an international Convention,

*Adopts* this first day of July of the year one thousand nine hundred and forty-nine the following Convention, which may be cited as the Right to Organise and Collective Bargaining Convention 1949:

*Article 1*

1. Workers shall enjoy adequate protection against acts of anti-union discrimination in respect of their employment.

2. Such protection shall apply more particularly in respect of acts calculated to:

(*a*) Make the employment or a worker subject to the condition that he shall not join a union or shall relinquish trade union membership;

(*b*) Cause the dismissal of or otherwise prejudice a worker by reason of union membership or because of participation in union activities outside working hours or, with the consent of the employer, within working hours.

*Article 2*

1. Workers' and employers' organisations shall enjoy adequate protection against any acts of interference by

each other or each other's agents or members in their establishment, functioning or administration.

2. In particular, acts which are designed to promote the establishment of workers' organisations under the domination of employers or employers' organisations, or to support workers' organisations by financial or other means, with the object of placing such organisations under the control of employers or employers' organisations, shall be deemed to constitute acts of interference within the meaning of this article.

*Article 3*

Machinery appropriate to national conditions shall be established, where necessary, for the purpose of ensuring respect for the right to organise as defined in the preceding articles.

*Article 4*

Measures appropriate to national conditions shall be taken, where necessary, to encourage and promote the full development and utilisation of machinery for voluntary negotiation between employers or employers' organisations and workers' organisations, with a view to the regulation of terms and conditions of employment by means of collective agreements.

*Article 5*

1. The extent to which the guarantees provided for in this Convention shall apply to the armed forces and the police shall be determined by national laws or regulations.

2. In accordance with the principle set fourth in paragraph 8 of article 19 of the Constitution of the International Labour Organisation the ratification of this Convention by any Member shall not be deemed to affect any existing law, award, custom or agreement in virtue of which members of the armed forces or the police enjoy any right guaranteed by this Convention.

*Article 6*

This Convention does not deal with the position of public servants engaged in the administration of the State, nor shall it be construed as prejudicing their rights or status in any way.

*Article 7*

The formal ratifications of this Convention shall be communicated to the Director General of the International Labour Office for registration.

*Article 8*

1. This Convention shall be binding only upon those Members of the International Labour Organisation whose ratifications have been registered with the Director-General.

2. It shall come into force twelve months after the date on which the ratifications of two Members have been registered with the Director-General.

3. Thereafter, this Convention shall come into force for any Member twelve months after the date on which its ratification has been registered.

*Article 9*

1. Declarations communicated to the Director-General of the International Labour Office in accordance with paragraph 2 of article 35 of the Constitution of the International Labour Organisation shall indicate—

(*a*) The territories in respect of which the Member concerned undertakes that the provisions of the Convention shall be applied without modification;

(*b*) The territories in respect of which it undertakes that the provisions of the Convention shall be applied subject to modifications, together with details of the said modifications;

(*c*) The territories in respect of which the Convention is inapplicable and in such cases the grounds on which it is inapplicable;

(*d*) The territories in respect of which it reserves its decision pending further consideration of the position.

2. The undertakings referred to in subparagraphs (*a*) and (*b*) of paragraph 1 of this article shall be deemed to be an integral part of the ratification and shall have the force of ratification.

3. Any Member may at any time by a subsequent declaration cancel in whole or in part any reservation made in its original declaration in virtue of subparagraphs (*b*), (*c*) or (*d*) of paragraph 1 of this article.

4. Any Member may, at any time at which the Convention is subject to denunciation in accordance with the provisions of article 11, communicate to the Director-General a declaration modifying in any other respect the terms of any former declaration and stating the present position in respect of such territories as it may specify.

*Article 10*

1. Declarations communicated to the Director-General of the International Labour Office in accordance with paragraphs 4 or 5 of article 35 of the Constitution of the International Labour Organisation shall indicate whether the provisions of the Convention will be applied in the territory concerned without modification or subject to modifications; when the declaration indicates that the provisions of the Convention will be applied subject to modifications, it shall give details of the said modifications.

2. The Member, Members or international authority concerned may at any time by a subsequent declaration renounce in whole or in part the right to have recourse to any modification indicated in any former declaration.

3. The Member, Members or international authority concerned may, at any time at which this Convention is subject to denunciation in accordance with the provisions of article 11, communicate to the Director-General a declaration modifying in any other respect the terms of any former declaration and stating the present position in respect of the application of the Convention.

*Article 11*

1. A Member which has ratified this Convention may denounce it after the expiration of ten years from the date on which the Convention first comes into force, by an act communicated to the Director-General of

the International Labour Office for registration. Such denunciation shall not take effect until one year after the date on which it is registered.

2. Each Member which has ratified this Convention and which does not, within the year following the expiration of the period of ten years mentioned in the preceding paragraph, exercise the right of denunciation provided for in this article, will be bound for another period of ten years and, thereafter, may denounce this Convention at the expiration of each period of ten years under the terms provided for in this article.

*Article 12*

1. The Director-General of the International Labour Office shall notify all Members of the International Labour Organisation of the registration of all ratifications, declarations and denunciations communicated to him by the Members of the Organisation.

2. When notifying the Members of the Organisation of the registration of the second ratification communicated to him, the Director-General shall draw the attention of the Members of the Organisation to the date upon which the Convention will come into force.

*Article 13*

The Director-General of the International Labour Office shall communicate to the Secretary-General of the United Nations for registration in accordance with Article 102 of the Charter of the United Nations full particulars of all ratifications, declarations and acts of denunciation registered by him in accordance with the provisions of the preceding articles.

*Article 14*

At the expiration of each period of ten years after the coming into force of this Convention, the Governing Body of the International Labour Office shall present to the General Conference a report on the working of this Convention and shall consider the desirability of placing on the agenda of the Conference the question of its revision in whole or in part.

*Article 15*

1. Should the Conference adopt a new Convention revising this Convention in whole or in part, then, unless the new Convention otherwise provides:

(*a*) The ratification by a Member of the new revising Convention shall *ipso jure* involve the immediate denunciation of this Convention, notwithstanding the provisions of article 11 above, if and when the new revising Convention shall have come into force;

(*b*) As from the date when the new revising Convention comes into force this Convention shall cease to be open to ratification by the Members.

2. This Convention shall in any case remain in force in its actual form and content for those Members which have ratified it but have not ratified the revising Convention.

*Article 16*

The English and French versions of the text of this Convention are equally authoritative.

The foregoing is the authentic text of the Convention duly adopted by the General Conference of the International Labour Organisation during its thirty-second session which was held at Geneva and declared closed the second day of July 1949.

IN FAITH WHEREOF we have appended our signatures this eighteenth day of August 1949.

## 32. Workers' Representatives Convention

**Convention (No. 135) concerning Protection and Facilities to be Afforded to Workers' Representatives in the Undertaking**

**Adopted on 23 June 1971 by the General Conference of the International Labour Organisation at its fifty-sixth session**

***Entry into force*:** Not in force as of 31 December 1972 (see article 8).

*The General Conference of the International Labour Organisation*,

*Having been convened* at Geneva by the Governing Body of the International Labour Office, and having met in its fifty-sixth session on 2 June 1971, and

*Noting* the terms of the Right to Organise and Collective Bargaining Convention, 1949, which provides for protection of workers against acts of anti-union discrimination in respect of their employment, and

*Considering* that it is desirable to supplement these terms with respect to workers' representatives, and

*Having decided* upon the adoption of certain proposals with regard to protection and facilities afforded to workers' representatives in the undertaking, which is the fifth item on the agenda of the session, and

*Having determined* that these proposals shall take the form of an international Convention,

*Adopts* this twenty-third day of June of the year one thousand nine hundred and seventy-one the following Convention, which may be cited as the Workers' Representatives Convention, 1971:

*Article 1*

Workers' representatives in the undertaking shall enjoy effective protection against any act prejudicial to them, including dismissal, based on their status or activities as a workers' representative or on union membership or participation in union activities, in so far as they act in conformity with existing laws or collective agreements or other jointly agreed arrangements.

*Article 2*

1. Such facilities in the undertaking shall be afforded to workers' representatives as may be appropriate in order to enable them to carry out their functions promptly and efficiently.

2. In this connection account shall be taken of the characteristics of the industrial relations system of the country and the needs, size and capabilities of the undertaking concerned.

3. The granting of such facilities shall not impair the efficient operation of the undertaking concerned.

*Article 3*

For the purpose of this Convention the term "workers' representatives" means persons who are recognised as such under national law or practice, whether they are—

(*a*) trade union representatives, namely, representatives designated or elected by trade unions or by the members of such unions; or

(*b*) elected representatives, namely, representatives who are freely elected by the workers of the undertaking in accordance with provisions of national laws or regulations or of collective agreements and whose functions do not include activities which are recognised as the exclusive prerogative of trade unions in the country concerned.

*Article 4*

National laws or regulations, collective agreements, arbitration awards or court decisions may determine the type or types of workers' representatives which shall be entitled to the protection and facilities provided for in this Convention.

*Article 5*

Where there exist in the same undertaking both trade union representatives and elected representatives, appropriate measures shall be taken, wherever necessary, to ensure that the existence of elected representatives is not used to undermine the position of the trade unions concerned or their representatives and to encourage co-operation on all relevant matters between the elected representatives and the trade unions concerned and their representatives.

*Article 6*

Effect may be given to this Convention through national laws or regulations or collective agreements, or in any other manner consistent with national practice.

*Article 7*

The formal ratifications of this Convention shall be communicated to the Director-General of the International Labour Office for registration.

*Article 8*

1. This Convention shall be binding only upon those Members of the International Labour Organisation whose ratifications have been registered with the Director-General.

2. It shall come into force twelve months after the date on which the ratifications of two Members have been registered with the Director-General.

3. Thereafter, this Convention shall come into force for any Member twelve months after the date on which its ratification has been registered.

*Article 9*

1. A Member which has ratified this Convention may denounce it after the expiration of ten years from the date on which the Convention first comes into force, by an act communicated to the Director-General of the International Labour Office for registration. Such denunciation shall not take effect until one year after the date on which it is registered.

2. Each Member which has ratified this Convention and which does not, within the year following the expiration of the period of ten years mentioned in the preceding paragraph, exercise the right of denunciation provided for in this article, will be bound for another period of ten years and, thereafter, may denounce this Convention at the expiration of each period of ten years under the terms provided for in this article.

*Article 10*

1. The Director-General of the International Labour Office shall notify all Members of the International Labour Organisation of the registration of all ratifications and denunciations communicated to him by the Members of the Organisation.

2. When notifying the Members of the Organisation of the registration of the second ratification communicated to him, the Director-General shall draw the attention of the Members of the Organisation to the date upon which the Convention will come into force.

*Article 11*

The Director-General of the International Labour Office shall communicate to the Secretary-General of the United Nations for registration in accordance with Article 102 of the Charter of the United Nations full particulars of all ratifications and acts of denunciation registered by him in accordance with the provisions of the preceding articles.

*Article 12*

At such times as it may consider necessary the Governing Body of the International Labour Office shall present to the General Conference a report on the working of this Convention and shall examine the desirability of placing on the agenda of the Conference the question of its revision in whole or in part.

*Article 13*

1. Should the Conference adopt a new Convention revising this Convention in whole or in part, then, unless the new Convention otherwise provides—

(*a*) The ratification by a Member of the new revising Convention shall *ipso jure* involve the immediate denunciation of this Convention, notwithstanding the provisions of article 9 above, if and when the new revising Convention shall have come into force;

(*b*) As from the date when the new revising Convention comes into force this Convention shall cease to be open to ratification by the Members.

2. This Convention shall in any case remain in force in its actual form and content for those Members which have ratified it but have not ratified the revising Convention.

*Article 14*

The English and French versions of the text of this Convention are equally authoritative.

The foregoing is the authentic text of the Convention duly adopted by the General Conference of the International Labour Organisation during its fifty-sixth session which was held at Geneva and declared closed the twenty-third day of June 1971.

IN FAITH WHEREOF we have appended our signatures this thirtieth day of June 1971.

# J. EMPLOYMENT POLICY

## 33. Employment Policy Convention

**Convention (No. 122) concerning Employment Policy**

**Adopted on 9 July 1964 by the General Conference of the International Labour Organisation at its forty-eighth session**

***Entry into force*: 15 July 1966, in accordance with article 5.**

*The General Conference of the International Labour Organisation,*

*Having been convened* at Geneva by the Governing Body of the International Labour Office, and having met in its forty-eighth session on 17 June 1964, and

*Considering* that the Declaration of Philadelphia recognises the solemn obligation of the International Labour Organisation to further among the nations of the world programmes which will achieve full employment and the raising of standards of living, and that the Preamble to the Constitution of the International Labour Organisation provides for the prevention of unemployment and the provision of an adequate living wage, and

*Considering* further that under the terms of the Declaration of Philadelphia it is the responsibility of the International Labour Organisation to examine and consider the bearing of economic and financial policies upon employment policy in the light of the fundamental objective that "all human beings, irrespective of race, creed or sex, have the right to pursue both their material well-being and their spiritual development in conditions of freedom and dignity, of economic security and equal opportunity", and

*Considering* that the Universal Declaration of Human Rights provides that "everyone has the right to work, to free choice of employment, to just and favourable conditions of work and to protection against unemployment", and

*Noting* the terms of existing international labour Conventions and Recommendations of direct relevance to employment policy, and in particular of the Employment Service Convention and Recommendation, 1948, the Vocational Guidance Recommendation, 1949, the Vocational Training Recommendation, 1962, and the Discrimination (Employment and Occupation) Convention and Recommendation, 1958, and

*Considering* that these instruments should be placed in the wider framework of an international programme for economic expansion on the basis of full, productive and freely chosen employment, and

*Having decided* upon the adoption of certain proposals with regard to employment policy, which are included in the eighth item on the agenda of the session, and

*Having determined* that these proposals shall take the form of an international Convention,

*Adopts* this ninth day of July of the year one thousand nine hundred and sixty-four the following Convention, which may be cited as the Employment Policy Convention, 1964:

*Article 1*

1. With a view to stimulating economic growth and development, raising levels of living, meeting manpower requirements and overcoming unemployment and underemployment, each Member shall declare and pursue, as a major goal, an active policy designed to promote full, productive and freely chosen employment.

2. The said policy shall aim at ensuring that:

(*a*) There is work for all who are available for and seeking work;

(*b*) Such work is as productive as possible;

(*c*) There is freedom of choice of employment and the fullest possible opportunity for each worker to qualify for, and to use his skills and endowments in, a job for which he is well suited, irrespective of race, colour, sex, religion, political opinion, national extraction or social origin.

3. The said policy shall take due account of the stage and level of economic development and the mutual relationships between employment objectives and other economic and social objectives, and shall be pursued by methods that are appropriate to national conditions and practices.

*Article 2*

Each Member shall, by such methods and to such extent as may be appropriate under national conditions:

(*a*) Decide on and keep under review, within the framework of a co-ordinated economic and social policy, the measures to be adopted for attaining the objectives specified in article 1;

(*b*) Take such steps as may be needed, including when appropriate the establishment of programmes, for the application of these measures.

*Article 3*

In the application of this Convention, representatives of the persons affected by the measures to be taken, and in particular representatives of employers and workers, shall be consulted concerning employment policies, with a view to taking fully into account their experience and views and securing their full co-operation in formulating and enlisting support for such policies.

*Article 4*

The formal ratifications of this Convention shall be communicated to the Director-General of the International Labour Office for registration.

*Article 5*

1. This Convention shall be binding only upon those Members of the International Labour Organisation whose ratifications have been registered with the Director-General.

2. It shall come into force twelve months after the date on which the ratifications of two Members have been registered with the Director-General.

3. Thereafter, this Convention shall come into force for any Member twelve months after the date on which its ratification has been registered.

*Article 6*

1. A Member which has ratified this Convention may denounce it after the expiration of ten years from the date on which the Convention first comes into force, by an act communicated to the Director-General of the International Labour Office for registration. Such denunciation shall not take effect until one year after the date on which it is registered.

2. Each Member which has ratified this Convention and which does not, within the year following the expiration of the period of ten years mentioned in the preceding paragraph, exercise the right of denunciation provided for in this article, will be bound for another period of ten years and, thereafter, may denounce this Convention at the expiration of each period of ten years under the terms provided for in this article.

*Article 7*

1. The Director-General of the International Labour Office shall notify all Members of the International Labour Organisation of the registration of all ratifications and denunciations communicated to him by the Members of the Organisation.

2. When notifying the Members of the Organisation of the registration of the second ratification communicated to him, the Director-General shall draw the attention of the Members of the Organisation to the date upon which the Convention will come into force.

*Article 8*

The Director-General of the International Labour Office shall communicate to the Secretary-General of the United Nations for registration in accordance with Article 102 of the Charter of the United Nations full particulars of all ratifications and acts of denunciation registered by him in accordance with the provisions of the preceding articles.

*Article 9*

At such times as it may consider necessary the Governing Body of the International Labour Office shall present to the General Conference a report on the working of this Convention and shall examine the desirability of placing on the agenda of the Conference the question of its revision in whole or in part.

*Article 10*

1. Should the Conference adopt a new Convention revising this Convention in whole or in part, then, unless the new Convention otherwise provides:

(*a*) The ratification by a Member of the new revising Convention shall *ipso jure* involve the immediate denunciation of this Convention, notwithstanding the provisions of Article 6 above, if and when the new revising Convention shall have come into force;

(*b*) As from the date when the new revising Convention comes into force this Convention shall cease to be open to ratification by the Members.

2. This Convention shall in any case remain in force in its actual form and content for those Members which have ratified it but have not ratified the revising Convention.

*Article 11*

The English and French versions of the text of this Convention are equally authoritative.

# K. POLITICAL RIGHTS OF WOMEN

## 34. Convention on the Political Rights of Women

**Opened for signature and ratification by General Assembly resolution 640 (VII) of 20 December 1952**

***Entry into force***: 7 July 1954, in accordance with article VI.

*The Contracting Parties,*

*Desiring* to implement the principle of equality of rights for men and women contained in the Charter of the United Nations,

*Recognizing* that everyone has the right to take part in the government of his country directly or indirectly through freely chosen representatives, and has the right to equal access to public service in his country, and desiring to equalize the status of men and women in the enjoyment and exercise of political rights, in accordance with the provisions of the Charter of the United Nations and of the Universal Declaration of Human Rights,

*Having resolved* to conclude a Convention for this purpose,

*Hereby agree* as hereinafter provided:

*Article I*

Women shall be entitled to vote in all elections on equal terms with men, without any discrimination.

*Article II*

Women shall be eligible for election to all publicly elected bodies, established by national law, on equal terms with men, without any discrimination.

*Article III*

Women shall be entitled to hold public office and to exercise all public functions, established by national law, on equal terms with men, without any discrimination.

*Article IV*

1. This Convention shall be open for signature on behalf of any Member of the United Nations and also on behalf of any other State to which an invitation has been addressed by the General Assembly.

2. This Convention shall be ratified and the instruments of ratification shall be deposited with the Secretary-General of the United Nations.

*Article V*

1. This Convention shall be open for accession to all States referred to in paragraph 1 of article IV.

2. Accession shall be effected by the deposit of an instrument of accession with the Secretary-General of the United Nations.

*Article VI*

1. This Convention shall come into force on the ninetieth day following the date of deposit of the sixth instrument of ratification or accession.

2. For each State ratifying or acceding to the Convention after the deposit of the sixth instrument of ratification or accession the Convention shall enter into force on the ninetieth day after deposit by such State of its instrument of ratification or accession.

*Article VII*

In the event that any State submits a reservation to any of the articles of this Convention at the time of signature, ratification or accession, the Secretary-General shall communicate the text of the reservation to all States which are or may become parties to this Convention. Any State which objects to the reservation may, within a period of ninety days from the date of the said communication (or upon the date of its becoming a party to the Convention), notify the Secretary-General that it does not accept it. In such case, the Convention shall not enter into force as between such State and the State making the reservation.

*Article VIII*

1. Any State may denounce this Convention by written notification to the Secretary-General of the United Nations. Denunciation shall take effect one year after the date of receipt of the notification by the Secretary-General.

2. This Convention shall cease to be in force as from the date when the denunciation which reduces the number of parties to less than six becomes effective.

*Article IX*

Any dispute which may arise between any two or more Contracting States concerning the interpretation or application of this Convention, which is not settled by negotiation, shall at the request of any one of the parties to the dispute be referred to the International Court of Justice for decision, unless they agree to another mode of settlement.

*Article X*

The Secretary-General of the United Nations shall notify all Members of the United Nations and the non-member States contemplated in paragraph 1 of article IV of this Convention of the following:

(*a*) Signatures and instruments of ratification received in accordance with article IV;

(*b*) Instruments of accession received in accordance with article V;

(*c*) The date upon which this Convention enters into force in accordance with article VI;

(*d*) Communications and notifications received in accordance with article VII;

(*e*) Notifications of denunciation received in accordance with paragraph 1 of article VIII;

(*f*) Abrogation in accordance with paragraph 2 of article VIII.

*Article XI*

1. This Convention, of which the Chinese, English, French, Russian and Spanish texts shall be equally authentic, shall be deposited in the archives of the United Nations.

2. The Secretary-General of the United Nations shall transmit a certified copy to all Members of the United Nations and to the non-member States contemplated in paragraph 1 of article IV.

## L. MARRIAGE AND THE FAMILY, CHILDHOOD AND YOUTH

### 35. Convention on Consent to Marriage, Minimum Age for Marriage and Registration of Marriages

**Opened for signature and ratification by General Assembly resolution 1763 A (XVII) of 7 November 1962**

*Entry into force*: 9 December 1964, in accordance with article 6.

*The Contracting States,*

*Desiring*, in conformity with the Charter of the United Nations, to promote universal respect for, and observance of, human rights and fundamental freedoms for all, without distinction as to race, sex, language or religion,

*Recalling* that article 16 of the Universal Declaration of Human Rights states that:

"(1) Men and women of full age, without any limitation due to race, nationality or religion, have the right to marry and to found a family. They are entitled to equal rights as to marriage, during marriage and at its dissolution.

"(2) Marriage shall be entered into only with the free and full consent of the intending spouses.",

*Recalling further* that the General Assembly of the United Nations declared, by resolution 843 (IX) of 17 December 1954, that certain customs, ancient laws and practices relating to marriage and the family were inconsistent with the principles set forth in the Charter of the United Nations and in the Universal Declaration of Human Rights,

*Reaffirming* that all States, including those which have or assume responsibility for the administration of Non-Self-Governing and Trust Territories until their achievement of independence, should take all appropriate measures with a view to abolishing such customs, ancient laws and practices by ensuring, *inter alia*, complete freedom in the choice of a spouse, eliminating completely child marriages and the betrothal of young girls before the age of puberty, establishing appropriate penalties where necessary and establishing a civil or other register in which all marriages will be recorded,

*Hereby agree* as hereinafter provided:

*Article 1*

1. No marriage shall be legally entered into without the full and free consent of both parties, such consent to be expressed by them in person after due publicity and in the presence of the authority competent to solemnize the marriage and of witnesses, as prescribed by law.

2. Notwithstanding anything in paragraph 1 above, it shall not be necessary for one of the parties to be present when the competent authority is satisfied that the circumstances are exceptional and that the party has, before a competent authority and in such manner as may be prescribed by law, expressed and not withdrawn consent.

*Article 2*

States parties to the present Convention shall take legislative action to specify a minimum age for marriage. No marriage shall be legally entered into by any person under this age, except where a competent authority has granted a dispensation as to age, for serious reasons, in the interest of the intending spouses.

*Article 3*

All marriages shall be registered in an appropriate official register by the competent authority.

*Article 4*

1. The present Convention shall, until 31 December 1963, be open for signature on behalf of all States Members of the United Nations or members of any of the specialized agencies, and of any other State invited by the General Assembly of the United Nations to become a party to the Convention.

2. The present Convention is subject to ratification. The instruments of ratification shall be deposited with the Secretary-General of the United Nations.

*Article 5*

1. The present Convention shall be open for accession to all States referred to in article 4, paragraph 1.

2. Accession shall be effected by the deposit of an instrument of accession with the Secretary-General of the United Nations.

*Article 6*

1. The present Convention shall come into force on the ninetieth day following the date of deposit of the eighth instrument of ratification or accession.

2. For each State ratifying or acceding to the Convention after the deposit of the eighth instrument of ratification or accession, the Convention shall enter into force on the ninetieth day after deposit by such State of its instrument of ratification or accession.

*Article 7*

1. Any Contracting State may denounce the present Convention by written notification to the Secretary-General of the United Nations. Denunciation shall take effect one year after the date of receipt of the notification by the Secretary-General.

2. The present Convention shall cease to be in force as from the date when the denunciation which reduces the number of parties to less than eight becomes effective.

*Article 8*

Any dispute which may arise between any two or more Contracting States concerning the interpretation or application of the present Convention which is not settled by negotiation shall, at the request of all the parties to the dispute, be referred to the International Court of Justice for decision, unless the parties agree to another mode of settlement.

*Article 9*

The Secretary-General of the United Nations shall notify all States Members of the United Nations and the non-member States contemplated in article 4, paragraph 1, of the present Convention of the following:

(*a*) Signatures and instruments of ratification received in accordance with article 4;

(*b*) Instruments of accession received in accordance with article 5;

(*c*) The date upon which the Convention enters into force in accordance with article 6;

(*d*) Notifications of denunciation received in accordance with article 7, paragraph 1;

(*e*) Abrogation in accordance with article 7, paragraph 2.

*Article 10*

1. The present Convention, of which the Chinese, English, French, Russian and Spanish texts shall be equally authentic, shall be deposited in the archives of the United Nations.

2. The Secretary-General of the United Nations shall transmit a certified copy of the Convention to all States Members of the United Nations and to the non-member States contemplated in article 4, paragraph 1.

## 36. Recommendation on Consent to Marriage, Minimum Age for Marriage and Registration of Marriages

**(General Assembly resolution 2018 (XX) of 1 November 1965)**

*The General Assembly*,

*Recognizing* that the family group should be strengthened because it is the basic unit of every society, and that men and women of full age have the right to marry and to found a family, that they are entitled to equal rights as to marriage and that marriage shall be entered into only with the free and full consent of the intending spouses, in accordance with the provisions of article 16 of the Universal Declaration of Human Rights,

*Recalling* its resolution 843 (IX) of 17 December 1954,

*Recalling further* article 2 of the Supplementary Convention on the Abolition of Slavery, the Slave Trade, and Institutions and Practices Similar to Slavery of 1956, which makes certain provisions concerning the age of marriage, consent to marriage and registration of marriages,

*Recalling also* that Article 13, paragraph 1 b, of the Charter of the United Nations provides that the General Assembly shall make recommendations for the purpose of assisting in the realization of human rights and fundamental freedoms for all without distinction as to race, sex, language or religion,

*Recalling likewise* that, under Article 64 of the Charter, the Economic and Social Council may make arrangements with the Members of the United Nations to obtain reports on the steps taken to give effect to its own recommendations and to recommendations on matters falling within its competence made by the General Assembly,

1. *Recommends* that, where not already provided by existing legislative or other measures, each Member State should take the necessary steps, in accordance with its constitutional processes and its traditional and religious practices, to adopt such legislative or other measures as may be appropriate to give effect to the following principles:

*Principle I*

(*a*) No marriage shall be legally entered into without the full and free consent of both parties, such consent to be expressed by them in person, after due publicity and in the presence of the authority competent to solemnize the marriage and of witnesses, as prescribed by law.

(*b*) Marriage by proxy shall be permitted only when the competent authorities are satisfied that each party has, before a competent authority and in such manner as may be prescribed by law, fully and freely expressed consent before witnesses and not withdrawn such consent.

*Principle II*

Member States shall take legislative action to specify a minimum age for marriage, which in any case shall not be less than fifteen years of age; no marriage shall be legally entered into by any person under this age, except where a competent authority has granted a dispensation as to age, for serious reasons, in the interest of the intending spouses.

*Principle III*

All marriages shall be registered in an appropriate official register by the competent authority.

2. *Recommends* that each Member State should bring the Recommendation on Consent to Marriage, Minimum Age for Marriage and Registration of Marriages contained in the present resolution before the authorities competent to enact legislation or to take other action at the earliest practicable moment and, if possible, no later than eighteen months after the adoption of the Recommendation;

3. *Recommends* that Member States should inform the Secretary-General, as soon as possible after the action referred to in paragraph 2 above, of the measures taken under the present Recommendation to bring it before the competent authority or authorities, with

particulars regarding the authority or authorities considered as competent;

4. *Recommends further* that Member States should report to the Secretary-General at the end of three years, and thereafter at intervals of five years, on their law and practice with regard to the matters dealt with in the present Recommendation, showing the extent to which effect has been given or is proposed to be given to the provisions of the Recommendation and such modifications as have been found or may be found necessary in adapting or applying it;

5. *Requests* the Secretary-General to prepare for the Commission on the Status of Women a document containing the reports received from Governments concerning methods of implementing the three basic principles of the present Recommendation;

6. *Invites* the Commission on the Status of Women to examine the reports received from Member States pursuant to the present Recommendation and to report thereon to the Economic and Social Council with such recommendations as it may deem fitting.

## 37. Declaration of the Rights of the Child

**Proclaimed by the General Assembly of the United Nations on 20 November 1959 (General Assembly resolution 1386 (XIV))**

*Preamble*

*Whereas* the peoples of the United Nations have, in the Charter, reaffirmed their faith in fundamental human rights and in the dignity and worth of the human person, and have determined to promote social progress and better standards of life in larger freedom,

*Whereas* the United Nations has, in the Universal Declaration of Human Rights, proclaimed that everyone is entitled to all the rights and freedoms set forth therein, without distinction of any kind, such as race, colour, sex, language, religion, political or other opinion, national or social origin, property, birth or other status,

*Whereas* the child, by reason of his physical and mental immaturity, needs special safeguards and care, including appropriate legal protection, before as well as after birth,

*Whereas* the need for such special safeguards has been stated in the Geneva Declaration of the Rights of the Child of 1924, and recognized in the Universal Declaration of Human Rights and in the statutes of specialized agencies and international organizations concerned with the welfare of children,

*Whereas* mankind owes to the child the best it has to give,

*Now therefore,*

*The General Assembly,*

*Proclaims* this Declaration of the Rights of the Child to the end that he may have a happy childhood and enjoy for his own good and for the good of society the rights and freedoms herein set forth, and calls upon parents, upon men and women as individuals, and upon voluntary organizations, local authorities and national Governments to recognize these rights and strive for their observance by legislative and other measures progressively taken in accordance with the following principles:

*Principle 1*

The child shall enjoy all the rights set forth in this Declaration. Every child, without any exception whatsoever, shall be entitled to these rights, without distinction or discrimination on account of race, colour, sex, language, religion, political or other opinion, national or social origin, property, birth or other status, whether of himself or of his family.

*Principle 2*

The child shall enjoy special protection, and shall be given opportunities and facilities, by law and by other means, to enable him to develop physically, mentally, morally, spiritually and socially in a healthy and normal manner and in conditions of freedom and dignity. In the enactment of laws for this purpose, the best interests of the child shall be the paramount consideration.

*Principle 3*

The child shall be entitled from his birth to a name and a nationality.

*Principle 4*

The child shall enjoy the benefits of social security. He shall be entitled to grow and develop in health; to this end, special care and protection shall be provided both to him and to his mother, including adequate pre-natal and post-natal care. The child shall have the right to adequate nutrition, housing, recreation and medical services.

*Principle 5*

The child who is physically, mentally or socially handicapped shall be given the special treatment, education and care required by his particular condition.

*Principle 6*

The child, for the full and harmonious development of his personality, needs love and understanding. He shall, wherever possible, grow up in the care and under the responsibility of his parents, and, in any case, in an atmosphere of affection and of moral and material security; a child of tender years shall not, save in exceptional circumstances, be separated from his mother. Society and the public authorities shall have the duty to extend particular care to children without a family and to those without adequate means of support. Payment of State and other assistance towards the maintenance of children of large families is desirable.

*Principle 7*

The child is entitled to receive education, which shall be free and compulsory, at least in the elementary stages. He shall be given an education which will promote his general culture, and enable him, on a basis of equal opportunity, to develop his abilities, his individual judgement, and his sense of moral and social responsibility, and to become a useful member of society.

The best interests of the child shall be the guiding principle of those responsible for his education and guidance; that responsibility lies in the first place with his parents.

The child shall have full opportunity for play and recreation, which should be directed to the same purposes as education; society and the public authorities shall endeavour to promote the enjoyment of this right.

*Principle 8*

The child shall in all circumstances be among the first to receive protection and relief.

*Principle 9*

The child shall be protected against all forms of neglect, cruelty and exploitation. He shall not be the subject of traffic, in any form.

The child shall not be admitted to employment before an appropriate minimum age; he shall in no case be caused or permitted to engage in any occupation or employment which would prejudice his health or education, or interfere with his physical, mental or moral development.

*Principle 10*

The child shall be protected from practices which may foster racial, religious and any other form of discrimination. He shall be brought up in a spirit of understanding, tolerance, friendship among peoples, peace and universal brotherhood, and in full consciousness that his energy and talents should be devoted to the service of his fellow men.

## 38. Declaration on the Promotion among Youth of the Ideals of Peace, Mutual Respect and Understanding between Peoples

**Proclaimed by the General Assembly of the United Nations on 7 December 1965 (General Assembly resolution 2037 (XX))**

*The General Assembly,*

*Recalling* that under the terms of the Charter of the United Nations the peoples have declared themselves determined to save succeeding generations from the scourge of war,

*Recalling further* that in the Charter the United Nations has affirmed its faith in fundamental human rights, in the dignity of the human person and in the equal rights of men and nations,

*Reaffirming* the principles embodied in the Universal Declaration of Human Rights, the Declaration on the Granting of Independence to Colonial Countries and Peoples, the United Nations Declaration on the Elimination of All Forms of Racial Discrimination, General Assembly resolution 110 (II) of 3 November 1947 condemning all forms of propaganda designed or likely to provoke or encourage any threat to the peace, the Declaration of the Rights of the Child, and General Assembly resolution 1572 (XV) of 18 December 1960, which have a particular bearing upon the upbringing of young people in a spirit of peace, mutual respect and understanding among peoples,

*Recalling* that the purpose of the United Nations Educational, Scientific and Cultural Organization is to contribute to peace and security by promoting collaboration among nations through education, science and culture, and recognizing the role and contributions of that organization towards the education of young people in the spirit of international understanding, co-operation and peace,

*Taking into consideration* the fact that in the conflagrations which have afflicted mankind it is the young people who have had to suffer most and who have had the greatest number of victims,

*Convinced* that young people wish to have an assured future and that peace, freedom and justice are among the chief guarantees that their desire for happiness will be fulfilled,

*Bearing in mind* the important part being played by young people in every field of human endeavour and the fact that they are destined to guide the fortunes of mankind,

*Bearing in mind furthermore* that, in this age of great scientific, technological and cultural achievements, the energies, enthusiasm and creative abilities of the young should be devoted to the material and spiritual advancement of all peoples,

*Convinced* that the young should know, respect and develop the cultural heritage of their own country and that of all mankind,

*Convinced furthermore* that the education of the young and exchanges of young people and of ideas in a spirit of peace, mutual respect and understanding between peoples can help to improve international relations and to strengthen peace and security,

*Proclaims* this Declaration on the Promotion among Youth of the Ideals of Peace, Mutual Respect and Understanding between Peoples and calls upon Governments, non-governmental organizations and youth movements to recognize the principles set forth therein and to ensure their observance by means of appropriate measures:

*Principle I*

Young people shall be brought up in the spirit of peace, justice, freedom, mutual respect and understanding in order to promote equal rights for all human beings and all nations, economic and social progress, disarmament and the maintenance of international peace and security.

*Principle II*

All means of education, including as of major importance the guidance given by parents or family, instruction and information intended for the young should foster among them the ideals of peace, humanity, liberty and international solidarity and all other ideals which help to bring peoples closer together, and acquaint them with the role entrusted to the United Nations as a means of preserving and maintaining peace and promoting international understanding and co-operation.

*Principle III*

Young people shall be brought up in the knowledge of the dignity and equality of all men, without distinction as to race, colour, ethnic origins or beliefs, and in respect for fundamental human rights and for the right of peoples to self-determination.

*Principle IV*

Exchanges, travel, tourism, meetings, the study of foreign languages, the twinning of towns and universities without discrimination and similar activities should be encouraged and facilitated among young people of all countries in order to bring them together in educational, cultural and sporting activities in the spirit of this Declaration.

*Principle V*

National and international associations of young people should be encouraged to promote the purposes of the United Nations, particularly international peace and security, friendly relations among nations based on respect for the equal sovereignty of States, the final abolition of colonialism and of racial discrimination and other violations of human rights.

Youth organizations in accordance with this Declaration should take all appropriate measures within their respective fields of activity in order to make their contribution without any discrimination to the work of educating the young generation in accordance with these ideals.

Such organizations, in conformity with the principle of freedom of association, should promote the free exchange of ideas in the spirit of the principles of this Declaration and of the purposes of the United Nations set forth in the Charter.

All youth organizations should conform to the principles set forth in this Declaration.

*Principle VI*

A major aim in educating the young shall be to develop all their faculties and to train them to acquire higher moral qualities, to be deeply attached to the noble ideals of peace, liberty, the dignity and equality of all men, and imbued with respect and love for humanity and its creative achievements. To this end the family has an important role to play.

Young people must become conscious of their responsibilities in the world they will be called upon to manage and should be inspired with confidence in a future of happiness for mankind.

# M. SOCIAL WELFARE, PROGRESS AND DEVELOPMENT

## 39. Declaration on Social Progress and Development

**Proclaimed by the General Assembly of the United Nations on 11 December 1969 (resolution 2542 (XXIV))**

*The General Assembly*,

*Mindful* of the pledge of Members of the United Nations under the Charter to take joint and separate action in co-operation with the Organization to promote higher standards of living, full employment and conditions of economic and social progress and development,

*Reaffirming* faith in human rights and fundamental freedoms and in the principles of peace, of the dignity and worth of the human person, and of social justice proclaimed in the Charter,

*Recalling* the principles of the Universal Declaration of Human Rights, the International Covenants on Human Rights, the Declaration of the Rights of the Child, the Declaration on the Granting of Independence to Colonial Countries and Peoples, the International Convention on the Elimination of All Forms of Racial Discrimination, the United Nations Declaration on the Elimination of All Forms of Racial Discrimination, the Declaration on the Promotion among Youth of the Ideals of Peace, Mutual Respect and Understanding between Peoples, the Declaration on the Elimination of Discrimination against Women and of resolutions of the United Nations,

*Bearing in mind* the standards already set for social progress in the constitutions, conventions, recommendations and resolutions of the International Labour Organisation, the Food and Agriculture Organization of the United Nations, the United Nations Educational, Scientific and Cultural Organization, the World Health Organization, the United Nations Children's Fund and of other organizations concerned,

*Convinced* that man can achieve complete fulfilment of his aspirations only within a just social order and that it is consequently of cardinal importance to accelerate social and economic progress everywhere, thus contributing to international peace and solidarity,

*Convinced* that international peace and security on the one hand, and social progress and economic development on the other, are closely interdependent and influence each other,

*Persuaded* that social development can be promoted by peaceful coexistence, friendly relations and co-operation among States with different social, economic or political systems,

*Emphasizing* the interdependence of economic and social development in the wider process of growth and change, as well as the importance of a strategy of integrated development which takes full account at all stages of its social aspects,

*Regretting* the inadequate progress achieved in the world social situation despite the efforts of States and the international community,

*Recognizing* that the primary responsibility for the development of the developing countries rests on those countries themselves and acknowledging the pressing need to narrow and eventually close the gap in the standards of living between economically more advanced and developing countries and, to that end, that Member States shall have the responsibility to pursue internal and external policies designed to promote social development throughout the world, and in particular to assist developing countries to accelerate their economic growth,

*Recognizing* the urgency of devoting to works of peace and social progress resources being expended on armaments and wasted on conflict and destruction,

*Conscious* of the contribution that science and technology can render towards meeting the needs common to all humanity,

*Believing* that the primary task of all States and international organizations is to eliminate from the life of society all evils and obstacles to social progress, particularly such evils as inequality, exploitation, war, colonialism and racism,

*Desirous* of promoting the progress of all mankind towards these goals and of overcoming all obstacles to their realization,

*Solemnly proclaims* this Declaration on Social Progress and Development and calls for national and international action for its use as a common basis for social development policies:

### PART I

#### PRINCIPLES

##### *Article 1*

All peoples and all human beings, without distinction as to race, colour, sex, language, religion, nationality, ethnic origin, family or social status, or political or other conviction, shall have the right to live in dignity and freedom and to enjoy the fruits of social progress and should, on their part, contribute to it.

##### *Article 2*

Social progress and development shall be founded on respect for the dignity and value of the human person and shall ensure the promotion of human rights and social justice, which requires:

(*a*) The immediate and final elimination of all forms of inequality, exploitation of peoples and individuals, colonialism and racism, including nazism and *apartheid*, and all other policies and ideologies opposed to the purposes and principles of the United Nations;

(*b*) The recognition and effective implementation of civil and political rights as well as of economic, social and cultural rights without any discrimination.

*Article 3*

The following are considered primary conditions of social progress and development:

(*a*) National independence based on the right of peoples to self-determination;

(*b*) The principle of non-interference in the internal affairs of States;

(*c*) Respect for the sovereignty and territorial integrity of States;

(*d*) Permanent sovereignty of each nation over its natural wealth and resources;

(*e*) The right and responsibility of each State and, as far as they are concerned, each nation and people to determine freely its own objectives of social development, to set its own priorities and to decide in conformity with the principles of the Charter of the United Nations the means and methods of their achievement without any external interference;

(*f*) Peaceful coexistence, peace, friendly relations and co-operation among States irrespective of differences in their social, economic or political systems.

*Article 4*

The family as a basic unit of society and the natural environment for the growth and well-being of all its members, particularly children and youth, should be assisted and protected so that it may fully assume its responsibilities within the community. Parents have the exclusive right to determine freely and responsibly the number and spacing of their children.

*Article 5*

Social progress and development require the full utilization of human resources, including, in particular:

(*a*) The encouragement of creative initiative under conditions of enlightened public opinion;

(*b*) The dissemination of national and international information for the purpose of making individuals aware of changes occurring in society as a whole;

(*c*) The active participation of all elements of society, individually or through associations, in defining and in achieving the common goals of development with full respect for the fundamental freedoms embodied in the Universal Declaration of Human Rights;

(*d*) The assurance to disadvantaged or marginal sectors of the population of equal opportunities for social and economic advancement in order to achieve an effectively integrated society.

*Article 6*

Social development requires the assurance to everyone of the right to work and the free choice of employment.

Social progress and development require the participation of all members of society in productive and socially useful labour and the establishment, in conformity with human rights and fundamental freedoms and with the principles of justice and the social function of property, of forms of ownership of land and of the means of production which preclude any kind of exploitation of man, ensure equal rights to property for all and create conditions leading to genuine equality among people.

*Article 7*

The rapid expansion of national income and wealth and their equitable distribution among all members of society are fundamental to all social progress, and they should therefore be in the forefront of the preoccupations of every State and Government.

The improvement in the position of the developing countries in international trade resulting among other things from the achievement of favourable terms of trade and of equitable and remunerative prices at which developing countries market their products is necessary in order to make it possible to increase national income and in order to advance social development.

*Article 8*

Each Government has the primary role and ultimate responsibility of ensuring the social progress and well-being of its people, of planning social development measures as part of comprehensive development plans, of encouraging and co-ordinating or integrating all national efforts towards this end and of introducing necessary changes in the social structure. In planning social development measures, the diversity of the needs of developing and developed areas, and of urban and rural areas, within each country, shall be taken into due account.

*Article 9*

Social progress and development are the common concerns of the international community, which shall supplement, by concerted international action, national efforts to raise the living standards of peoples.

Social progress and economic growth require recognition of the common interest of all nations in the exploration, conservation, use and exploitation, exclusively for peaceful purposes and in the interests of all mankind, of those areas of the environment such as outer space and the sea-bed and ocean floor and the subsoil thereof, beyond the limits of national jurisdiction, in accordance with the purposes and principles of the Charter of the United Nations.

## PART II

### Objectives

Social progress and development shall aim at the continuous raising of the material and spiritual standards of living of all members of society, with respect for and in compliance with human rights and fundamental freedoms, through the attainment of the following main goals:

### Article 10

(*a*) The assurance at all levels of the right to work and the right of everyone to form trade unions and workers' associations and to bargain collectively; promotion of full productive employment and elimination of unemployment and under-employment; establishment of equitable and favourable conditions of work for all, including the improvement of health and safety conditions; assurance of just remuneration for labour without any discrimination as well as a sufficiently high minimum wage to ensure a decent standard of living; the protection of the consumer;

(*b*) The elimination of hunger and malnutrition and the guarantee of the right to proper nutrition;

(*c*) The elimination of poverty; the assurance of a steady improvement in levels of living and of a just and equitable distribution of income;

(*d*) The achievement of the highest standards of health and the provision of health protection for the entire population, if possible free of charge;

(*e*) The eradication of illiteracy and the assurance of the right to universal access to culture, to free compulsory education at the elementary level and to free education at all levels; the raising of the general level of life-long education;

(*f*) The provision for all, particularly persons in low-income groups and large families, of adequate housing and community services.

Social progress and development shall aim equally at the progressive attainment of the following main goals:

### Article 11

(*a*) The provision of comprehensive social security schemes and social welfare services; the establishment and improvement of social security and insurance schemes for all persons who, because of illness, disability or old age, are temporarily or permanently unable to earn a living, with a view to ensuring a proper standard of living for such persons and for their families and dependants;

(*b*) The protection of the rights of the mother and child; concern for the upbringing and health of children; the provision of measures to safeguard the health and welfare of women and particularly of working mothers during pregnancy and the infancy of their children, as well as of mothers whose earnings are the sole source of livelihood for the family; the granting to women of pregnancy and maternity leave and allowances without loss of employment or wages;

(*c*) The protection of the rights and the assuring of the weltare of children, the aged and the disabled; the provision of protection for the physically or mentally disadvantaged;

(*d*) The education of youth in, and promotion among them of, the ideals of justice and peace, mutual respect and understanding among peoples; the promotion of full participation of youth in the process of national development;

(*e*) The provision of social defence measures and the elimination of conditions leading to crime and delinquency, especially juvenile delinquency;

(*f*) The guarantee that all individuals, without discrimination of any kind, are made aware of their rights and obligations and receive the necessary aid in the exercise and safeguarding of their rights.

Social progress and development shall further aim at achieving the following main objectives:

### Article 12

(*a*) The creation of conditions for râpid and sustained social and economic development, particularly in the developing countries; change in international economic relations; new and effective methods of international cooperation in which equality of opportunity should be as much a prerogative of nations as of individuals within a nation;

(*b*) The elimination of all forms of discrimination and exploitation and all other practices and ideologies contrary to the purposes and principles of the Charter of the United Nations;

(*c*) The elimination of all forms of foreign economic exploitation, particularly that practised by international monopolies, in order to enable the people of every country to enjoy in full the benefits of their national resources.

Social progress and development shall finally aim at the attainment of the following main goals:

### Article 13

(*a*) Equitable sharing of scientific and technological advances by developed and developing countries, and a steady increase in the use of science and technology for the benefit of the social development of society;

(*b*) The establishment of a harmonious balance between scientific, technological and material progress and the intellectual, spiritual, cultural and moral advancement of humanity;

(*c*) The protection and improvement of the human environment.

## PART III

### Means and methods

On the basis of the principles set forth in this Declaration, the achievement of the objectives of social progress and development requires the mobilization of the necessary resources by national and international action, with particular attention to such means and methods as:

### Article 14

(*a*) Planning for social progress and development, as an integrated part of balanced over-all development planning;

(*b*) The establishment, where necessary, of national systems for framing and carrying out social policies and programmes, and the promotion by the countries concerned of planned regional development, taking into account differing regional conditions and needs, particularly the development of regions which are less favoured or under-developed by comparison with the rest of the country;

(*c*) The promotion of basic and applied social research, particularly comparative international research applied to the planning and execution of social development programmes.

*Article 15*

(*a*) The adoption of measures to ensure the effective participation, as appropriate, of all the elements of society in the preparation and execution of national plans and programmes of economic and social development;

(*b*) The adoption of measures for an increasing rate of popular participation in the economic, social, cultural and political life of countries through national governmental bodies, non-governmental organizations, co-operatives, rural associations, workers' and employers' organizations and women's and youth organizations, by such methods as national and regional plans for social and economic progress and community development, with a view to achieving a fully integrated national society, accelerating the process of social mobility and consolidating the democratic system;

(*c*) Mobilization of public opinion, at both national and international levels, in support of the principles and objectives of social progress and development;

(*d*) The dissemination of social information, at the national and the international level, to make people aware of changing circumstances in society as a whole, and to educate the consumer.

*Article 16*

(*a*) Maximum mobilization of all national resources and their rational and efficient utilization; promotion of increased and accelerated productive investment in social and economic fields and of employment; orientation of society towards the development process;

(*b*) Progressively increasing provision of the necessary budgetary and other resources required for financing the social aspects of development;

(*c*) Achievement of equitable distribution of national income, utilizing, *inter alia*, the fiscal system and government spending as an instrument for the equitable distribution and redistribution of income in order to promote social progress;

(*d*) The adoption of measures aimed at prevention of such an outflow of capital from developing countries as would be detrimental to their economic and social development.

*Article 17*

(*a*) The adoption of measures to accelerate the process of industrialization, especially in developing countries, with due regard for its social aspects, in the interests of the entire population; development of an adequate organizational and legal framework conducive to an uninterrupted and diversified growth of the industrial sector; measures to overcome the adverse social effects which may result from urban development and industrialization, including automation; maintenance of a proper balance between rural and urban development, and in particular, measures designed to ensure healthier living conditions, especially in large industrial centres;

(*b*) Integrated planning to meet the problems of urbanization and urban developement;

(*c*) Comprehensive rural development schemes to raise the levels of living of the rural populations and to facilitate such urban-rural relationships and population distribution as will promote balanced national development and social progress;

(*d*) Measures for appropriate supervision of the utilization of land in the interests of society.

The achievement of the objectives of social progress and development equally requires the implementation of the following means and methods:

*Article 18*

(*a*) The adoption of appropriate legislative, administrative and other measures ensuring to everyone not only political and civil rights, but also the full realization of economic, social and cultural rights without any discrimination;

(*b*) The promotion of democratically based social and institutional reforms and motivation for change basic to the elimination of all forms of discrimination and exploitation and conducive to high rates of economic and social progress, to include land reform, in which the ownership and use of land will be made to serve best the objectives of social justice and economic development;

(*c*) The adoption of measures to boost and diversify agricultural production through, *inter alia*, the implementation of democratic agrarian reforms, to ensure an adequate and well-balanced supply of food, its equitable distribution among the whole population and the improvement of nutritional standards;

(*d*) The adoption of measures to introduce, with the participation of the Government, low-cost housing programmes in both rural and urban areas;

(*e*) Development and expansion of the system of transportation and communications, particularly in developing countries.

*Article 19*

(*a*) The provision of free health services to the whole population and of adequate preventive and curative facilities and welfare medical services accessible to all;

(*b*) The enactment and establishment of legislative measures and administrative regulations with a view to the implementation of comprehensive programmes of social security schemes and social welfare services and to the improvement and co-ordination of existing services;

(*c*) The adoption of measures and the provision of social welfare services to migrant workers and their families, in conformity with the provisions of Convention No. 97 of the International Labour Organisation* and other international instruments relating to migrant workers;

(*d*) The institution of appropriate measures for the rehabilitation of mentally or physically disabled persons,

* Convention concerning Migration for Employment (Revised 1949), International Labour Office, *Convertions and Recommendations, 1919-1949* (Geneva, 1949), p. 863.

especially children and youth, so as to enable them to the fullest possible extent to be useful members of society—these measures shall include the provision of treatment and technical appliances, education, vocational and social guidance, training and selective placement, and other assistance required—and the creation of social conditions in which the handicapped are not discriminated against because of their disabilities.

*Article 20*

(*a*) The provision of full democratic freedoms to trade unions; freedom of association for all workers, including the right to bargain collectively and to strike; recognition of the right to form other organizations of working people; the provision for the growing participation of trade unions in economic and social development; effective participation of all members of trade unions in the deciding of economic and social issues which affect their interests;

(*b*) The improvement of health and safety conditions for workers, by means of appropriate technological and legislative measures and the provision of the material prerequisites for the implementation of those measures, including the limitation of working hours;

(*c*) The adoption of appropriate measures for the development of harmonious industrial relations.

*Article 21*

(*a*) The training of national personnel and cadres, including administrative, executive, professional and technical personnel needed for social development and for over-all development plans and policies;

(*b*) The adoption of measures to accelerate the extension and improvement of general, vocational and technical education and of training and retraining, which should be provided free at all levels;

(*c*) Raising the general level of education; development and expansion of national information media, and their rational and full use towards continuing education of the whole population and towards encouraging its participation in social development activities; the constructive use of leisure, particularly that of children and adolescents;

(*d*) The formulation of national and international policies and measures to avoid the "brain drain" and obviate its adverse effects.

*Article 22*

(*a*) The development and co-ordination of policies and measures designed to strengthen the essential functions of the family as a basic unit of society;

(*b*) The formulation and establishment, as needed, of programmes in the field of population, within the framework of national demographic policies and as part of the welfare medical services, including education, training of personnel and the provision to families of the knowledge and means necessary to enable them to exercise their right to determine freely and responsibly the number and spacing of their children;

(*c*) The establishment of appropriate child-care facilities in the interest of children and working parents.

**The achievements of the objectives of social progress and development finally requires the implementation of the following means and methods:**

*Article 23*

(*a*) The laying down of economic growth rate targets for the developing countries within the United Nations policy for development, high enough to lead to a substantial acceleration of their rates of growth;

(*b*) The provision of greater assistance on better terms; the implementation of the aid volume target of a minimum of 1 per cent of the gross national product at market prices of economically advanced countries; the general easing of the terms of lending to the developing countries through low interest rates on loans and long grace periods for the repayment of loans, and the assurance that the allocation of such loans will be based strictly on socio-economic criteria free of any political considerations;

(*c*) The provision of technical, financial and material assistance, both bilateral and multilateral, to the fullest possible extent and on favourable terms, and improved co-ordination of international assistance for the achievement of the social objectives of national development plans;

(*d*) The provision to the developing countries of technical, financial and material assistance and of favourable conditions to facilitate the direct exploitation of their national resources and natural wealth by those countries with a view to enabling the peoples of those countries to benefit fully from their national resources;

(*e*) The expansion of international trade based on principles of equality and non-discrimination, the rectification of the position of developing countries in international trade by equitable terms of trade, a general non-reciprocal and non-discriminatory system of preferences for the exports of developing countries to the developed countries, the establishment and implementation of general and comprehensive commodity agreements, and the financing of reasonable buffer stocks by international institutions.

*Article 24*

(*a*) Intensification of international co-operation with a view to ensuring the international exchange of information, knowledge and experience concerning social progress and development;

(*b*) The broadest possible international technical, scientific and cultural co-operation and reciprocal utilization of the experience of countries with different economic and social systems and different levels of development, on the basis of mutual advantage and strict observance of and respect for national sovereignty;

(*c*) Increased utilization of science and technology for social and economic development; arrangements for the transfer and exchange of technology, including know-how and patents, to the developing countries.

*Article 25*

(*a*) The establishment of legal and administrative measures for the protection and improvement of the human environment, at both national and international levels;

(*b*) The use and exploitation, in accordance with the appropriate international régimes, of the resources of areas of the environment such as outer space and the sea-bed and ocean floor and the subsoil thereof, beyond the limits of national jurisdiction, in order to supplement national resources available for the achievement of economic and social progress and development in every country, irrespective of its geographical location, special consideration being given to the interests and needs of the developing countries.

*Article 26*

Compensation for damages, be they social or economic in nature—including restitution and reparations—caused as a result of aggression and of illegal occupation of territory by the aggressor.

*Article 27*

(*a*) The achievement of general and complete disarmament and the channelling of the progressively released resources to be used for economic and social progress for the welfare of people everywhere and, in particular, for the benefit of developing countries;

(*b*) The adoption of measures contributing to disarmament, including, *inter alia*, the complete prohibition of tests of nuclear weapons, the prohibition of the development, production and stockpiling of chemical and bacteriological (biological) weapons and the prevention of the pollution of oceans and inland waters by nuclear wastes.

## 40. Declaration on the Rights of Mentally Retarded Persons

**Proclaimed by the General Assembly of the United Nations on 20 December 1971 (resolution 2856 (XXVI))**

*The General Assembly*,

*Mindful* of the pledge of the States Members of the United Nations under the Charter to take joint and separate action in co-operation with the Organization to promote higher standards of living, full employment and conditions of economic and social progress and development,

*Reaffirming* faith in human rights and fundamental freedoms and in the principles of peace, of the dignity and worth of the human person and of social justice proclaimed in the Charter,

*Recalling* the principles of the Universal Declaration of Human Rights, the International Covenants on Human Rights, the Declaration of the Rights of the Child and the standards already set for social progress in the constitutions, conventions, recommendations and resolutions of the International Labour Organisation, the United Nations Educational, Scientific and Cultural Organization, the World Health Organization, the United Nations Children's Fund and other organizations concerned,

*Emphasizing* that the Declaration on Social Progress and Development has proclaimed the necessity of protecting the rights and assuring the welfare and rehabilitation of the physically and mentally disadvantaged,

*Bearing in mind* the necessity of assisting mentally retarded persons to develop their abilities in various fields of activities and of promoting their integration as far as possible in normal life,

*Aware* that certain countries, at their present stage of development, can devote only limited efforts to this end,

*Proclaims* this Declaration on the Rights of Mentally Retarded Persons and calls for national and international action to ensure that it will be used as a common basis and frame of reference for the protection of these rights:

1. The mentally retarded person has, to the maximum degree of feasibility, the same rights as other human beings.

2. The mentally retarded person has a right to proper medical care and physical therapy and to such education, training, rehabilitation and guidance as will enable him to develop his ability and maximum potential.

3. The mentally retarded person has a right to economic security and to a decent standard of living. He has a right to perform productive work or to engage in any other meaningful occupation to the fullest possible extent of his capabilities.

4. Whenever possible, the mentally retarded person should live with his own family or with foster parents and participate in different forms of community life. The family with which he lives should receive assistance. If care in an institution becomes necessary, it should be provided in surroundings and other circumstances as close as possible to those of normal life.

5. The mentally retarded person has a right to a qualified guardian when this is required to protect his personal well-being and interests.

6. The mentally retarded person has a right to protection from exploitation, abuse and degrading treatment. If prosecuted for any offence, he shall have a right to due process of law with full recognition being given to his degree of mental responsibility.

7. Whenever mentally retarded persons are unable, because of the severity of their handicap, to exercise all their rights in a meaningful way or it should become necessary to restrict or deny some or all of these rights, the procedure used for that restriction or denial of rights must contain proper legal safeguards against every form of abuse. This procedure must be based on an evaluation of the social capability of the mentally retarded person by qualified experts and must be subject to periodic review and to the right of appeal to higher authorities.

# N. RIGHT TO ENJOY CULTURE; INTERNATIONAL CULTURAL DEVELOPMENT AND CO-OPERATION

## 41. Declaration of the Principles of International Cultural Co-operation

**Proclaimed by the General Conference of the United Nations Educational, Scientific and Cultural Organization at its fourteenth session, on 4 November 1966**

*The General Conference* of the United Nations Educational, Scientific and Cultural Organization, met in Paris for its fourteenth session, this fourth day of November 1966, being the twentieth anniversary of the foundation of the Organization,

*Recalling* that the Constitution of the Organization declares that "since wars begin in the minds of men, it is in the minds of men that the defences of peace must be constructed" and that the peace must be founded, if it is not to fail, upon the intellectual and moral solidarity of mankind,

*Recalling* that the Constitution also states that the wide diffusion of culture and the education of humanity for justice and liberty and peace are indispensable to the dignity of man and constitute a sacred duty which all the nations must fulfil in a spirit of mutual assistance and concern,

*Considering* that the Organization's Member States, believing in the pursuit of truth and the free exchange of ideas and knowledge, have agreed and determined to develop and to increase the means of communication between their peoples,

*Considering* that, despite the technical advances which facilitate the development and dissemination of knowledge and ideas, ignorance of the way of life and customs of peoples still presents an obstacle to friendship among the nations, to peaceful co-operation and to the progress of mankind,

*Taking account* of the Universal Declaration of Human Rights, the Declaration of the Rights of the Child, the Declaration on the Granting of Independence to Colonial Countries and Peoples, the United Nations Declaration on the Elimination of all Forms of Racial Discrimination, the Declaration on the Promotion among Youth of the Ideals of Peace, Mutual Respect and Understanding between Peoples, and the Declaration on the Inadmissibility of Intervention in the Domestic Affairs of States and the Protection of their Independence and Sovereignty, proclaimed successively by the General Assembly of the United Nations,

*Convinced* by the experience of the Organization's first twenty years that, if international cultural co-operation is to be strengthened, its principles require to be affirmed,

*Proclaims* this Declaration of the principles of international cultural co-operation, to the end that governments, authorities, organizations, associations and institutions responsible for cultural activities may constantly be guided by these principles; and for the purpose, as set out in the Constitution of the Organization, of advancing, through the educational, scientific and cultural relations of the peoples of the world, the objectives of peace and welfare that are defined in the Charter of the United Nations:

### *Article I*

1. Each culture has a dignity and value which must be respected and preserved.

2. Every people has the right and the duty to develop its culture.

3. In their rich variety and diversity, and in the reciprocal influences they exert on one another, all cultures form part of the common heritage belonging to all mankind.

### *Article II*

Nations shall endeavour to develop the various branches of culture side by side and, as far as possible, simultaneously, so as to establish a harmonious balance between technical progress and the intellectual and moral advancement of mankind.

### *Article III*

International cultural co-operation shall cover all aspects of intellectual and creative activities relating to education, science and culture.

### *Article IV*

The aims of international cultural co-operation in its various forms, bilateral or multilateral, regional or universal, shall be:

1. To spread knowledge, to stimulate talent and to enrich cultures;

2. To develop peaceful relations and friendship among the peoples and bring about a better understanding of each other's way of life;

3. To contribute to the application of the principles set out in the United Nations Declarations that are recalled in the Preamble to this Declaration;

4. To enable everyone to have access to knowledge, to enjoy the arts and literature of all peoples, to share in advances made in science in all parts of the world and in the resulting benefits, and to contribute to the enrichment of cultural life;

5. To raise the level of the spiritual and material life of man in all parts of the world.

*Article V*

Cultural co-operation is a right and a duty for all peoples and all nations, which should share with one another their knowledge and skills.

*Article VI*

International co-operation, while promoting the enrichment of all cultures through its beneficent action, shall respect the distinctive character of each.

*Article VII*

1. Broad dissemination of ideas and knowledge, based on the freest exchange and discussion, is essential to creative activity, the pursuit of truth and the development of the personality.

2. In cultural co-operation, stress shall be laid on ideas and values conducive to the creation of a climate of friendship and peace. Any mark of hostility in attitudes and in expression of opinion shall be avoided. Every effort shall be made, in presenting and disseminating information, to ensure its authenticity.

*Article VIII*

Cultural co-operation shall be carried on for the mutual benefit of all the nations practising it. Exchanges to which it gives rise shall be arranged in a spirit of broad reciprocity.

*Article IX*

Cultural co-operation shall contribute to the establishment of stable, long-term relations between peoples, which should be subjected as little as possible to the strains which may arise in international life.

*Article X*

Cultural co-operation shall be specially concerned with the moral and intellectual education of young people in a spirit of friendship, international understanding and peace and shall foster awareness among States of the need to stimulate talent and promote the training of the rising generations in the most varied sectors.

*Article XI*

1. In their cultural relations, States shall bear in mind the principles of the United Nations. In seeking to achieve international co-operation, they shall respect the sovereign equality of States and shall refrain from intervention in matters which are essentially within the domestic jurisdiction of any State.

2. The principles of this Declaration shall be applied with due regard for human rights and fundamental freedoms.

---

# LIST OF INSTRUMENTS IN CHRONOLOGICAL ORDER OF ADOPTION

| *Date of adoption* | *Instrument* |
|---|---|
| *1948* | |
| 9 July | Freedom of Association and Protection of the Right to Organise Convention |
| 9 December | Convention on the Prevention and Punishment of the Crime of Genocide |
| 10 December | Universal Declaration of Human Rights |
| *1949* | |
| 1 July | Right to Organise and Collective Bargaining Convention |
| 2 December | Convention for the Suppression of the Traffic in Persons and of the Exploitation of the Prostitution of Others |
| *1950* | |
| 14 December | Statute of the Office of the United Nations High Commissioner for Refugees |
| *1951* | |
| 29 June | Equal Remuneration Convention |
| 28 July | Convention relating to the Status of Refugees |
| *1952* | |
| 16 December | Convention on the International Right of Correction |
| 20 December | Convention on the Political Rights of Women |
| *1953* | |
| 23 October | Protocol amending the Slavery Convention signed at Geneva on 25 September 1926 |
| 23 October | Slavery Convention signed at Geneva on 25 September 1926 as amended by the Protocol of 23 October 1953 |
| *1954* | |
| 28 September | Convention relating to the Status of Stateless Persons |
| *1956* | |
| 7 September | Supplementary Convention on the Abolition of Slavery, the Slave Trade, and Institutions and Practices Similar to Slavery |
| *1957* | |
| 29 January | Convention on the Nationality of Married Women |
| 25 June | Abolition of Forced Labour Convention |
| *1958* | |
| 25 June | Discrimination (Employment and Occupation) Convention |
| *1959* | |
| 20 November | Declaration of the Rights of the Child |
| *1960* | |
| 14 December | Convention against Discrimination in Education |
| 14 December | Declaration on the Granting of Independence to Colonial Countries and Peoples |
| *1961* | |
| 30 August | Convention on the Reduction of Statelessness |
| *1962* | |
| 7 November | Convention on Consent to Marriage, Minimum Age for Marriage and Registration of Marriages |

| Date of adoption | Instrument |
|---|---|
| 1962 | |
| 10 December | Protocol Instituting a Conciliation and Good Offices Commission to be responsible for seeking a settlement of any disputes which may arise between States Parties to the Convention against Discrimination in Education |
| 14 December | General Assembly resolution 1803 (XVII) of 14 December 1962, "Permanent Sovereignty over Natural Resources" |
| *1963* | |
| 20 November | United Nations Declaration on the Elimination of All Forms of Racial Discrimination |
| *1964* | |
| 9 July | Employment Policy Convention |
| *1965* | |
| 1 November | Recommendation on Consent to Marriage, Minimum Age for Marriage and Registration of Marriages |
| 7 December | Declaration on the Promotion among Youth of the Ideals of Peace, Mutual Respect and Understanding between Peoples |
| 21 December | International Convention on the Elimination of All Forms of Racial Discrimination |
| *1966* | |
| 4 November | Declaration of the Principles of International Cultural Co-operation |
| 16 December | International Covenant on Economic, Social and Cultural Rights |
| 16 December | International Covenant on Civil and Political Rights |
| 16 December | Optional Protocol to the International Covenant on Civil and Political Rights |
| 16 December | Protocol relating to the Status of Refugees |
| *1967* | |
| 7 November | Declaration on the Elimination of Discrimination against Women |
| 14 December | Declaration on Territorial Asylum |
| *1968* | |
| 13 May | Proclamation of Teheran |
| 26 November | Convention on the Non-Applicability of Statutory Limitations to War Crimes and Crimes against Humanity |
| *1969* | |
| 11 December | Declaration on Social Progress and Development |
| *1971* | |
| 23 June | Workers' Representatives Convention |
| 20 December | Declaration on the Rights of Mentally Retarded Persons |

*CHAPTER 2*

# UNITED NATIONS COMMENTARY

Like its predecessor in Chapter 1, the document that comprises this Chapter, 'UN Action in the Field of Human Rights', published in 1974, covers a quarter of a century of experience within the United Nations family of organisations. As in the previous Chapter, the three years that have elapsed since that publication appeared are brought up to date by later documents reproduced in Chapter 3.

The Secretary General cogently states in his Preface:

> It is my hope that this new publication, indicating as it does how standards for the promotion and protection of human rights have come to be accepted by the international community over the past quarter-century, and how some of the problems of reconciling the realization of those standards with the requirements of the principle of non-intervention in matters that are essentially within the domestic jurisdiction of States have been overcome, will not only serve the academic needs but will inspire and give rise to renewed practical efforts on the part of Governments, international organizations and individuals throughout the world to ensure that human rights and fundamental freedoms are universally and effectively recognized, observed and enjoyed by everyone.

The Introduction summarises, under the main headings listed in the Contents page, the historical background of the Instruments already recorded in our Chapter 1, and analyses in detail their structure and application since the two major international Covenants were adopted in 1966. This analysis occupies most of Part I and examines every type of Instrument in terms of its legal and structural context; while Part II travels outside the Instruments themselves and goes into the methods employed by the UN and its various organs in implementing these varied tasks. This second Part is, incidentally, a gold mine for lawyers or political scientists watching the evolution, under the UN system, of the developing action by Governments and between Governments in seeking to meet their obligations under the agreements they have signed or adopted.

1948
1973

Twenty-fifth Anniversary
of the
UNIVERSAL DECLARATION
OF HUMAN RIGHTS

# UNITED NATIONS ACTION IN THE FIELD OF HUMAN RIGHTS

UNITED NATIONS
New York, 1974

## NOTE

*Human Rights: A Compilation of International Instruments of the United Nations* (United Nations publication, Sales No. E.73.XIV.2) contains the texts of conventions, declarations and certain recommendations relating to human rights adopted by the United Nations up to 31 December 1972. It also includes a number of instruments adopted by the International Labour Organisation and by the United Nations Educational, Scientific and Cultural Organization. Most of the instruments referred to in the present publication are contained in the compilation.

The publication *Multilateral Treaties in respect of which the Secretary-General Performs Depositary Functions: List of Signatures, Ratifications, Accessions, etc.* is issued annually. Information as of 31 December 1972 is contained in United Nations publication, Sales No. E.73.V.7 (ST/LEG/SER.D/6).

Symbols of United Nations documents are composed of capital letters combined with figures. Mention of such a symbol indicates a reference to a United Nations document.

ST/HR/2

UNITED NATIONS PUBLICATION

*Sales No.* E.74.XIV.2

Price: $U.S. 10.00
(or equivalent in other currencies)

## PREFACE

When the United Nations General Assembly, meeting in Paris on 10 December 1948, adopted and proclaimed the Universal Declaration of Human Rights, the world community for the first time agreed upon "a common standard of achievement for all peoples and all nations" in the field of human rights.

The Universal Declaration of Human Rights has served, since that historic occasion, as a moral imperative guiding the relationship between individuals and their Governments and as a bulwark safeguarding the human rights and fundamental freedoms and the inherent dignity of all members of the human family.

The Declaration has exercised a significant influence throughout the world and has provided a stimulant and the inspiration both within and outside the United Nations for far-reaching international action resulting in the establishment of further standards and legal obligations and for the progressive development of methods of international accountability as regards the observance of human rights.

The year 1968, the twentieth anniversary of the Universal Declaration of Human Rights, was proclaimed by the General Assembly as the International Year for Human Rights. The International Conference on Human Rights was convened that year in Teheran to provide an opportunity for States to review their legislation and practices and their international commitments against the high standards set in the Declaration.

In preparation for the Conference, two studies of a descriptive and factual nature were prepared by the Secretariat. The first (A/CONF.32/5) summarized the measures that had been taken by the United Nations in the field of human rights during the preceding twenty-year period; the second (A/CONF.32/6) set out the methods which the United Nations had employed to promote and to protect human rights and fundamental freedoms.

The studies proved invaluable, not only to participants in the Conference but also to students of the Declaration, the International Covenants on Human Rights and other international instruments relating to human rights, and to many government officials charged with responsibilities in the field. They provided a firm basis for reviewing the progress that had been made in the United Nations in the promotion and protection of human rights and for evaluating the methods and techniques employed.

The original studies covered information available up to 1 May 1967. A decision to bring those studies up to date, and to make them widely available, was taken when the General Assembly, in its resolution 2860 (XXVI) of 20 December 1971, expressed the desire to mark the twenty-fifth anniversary of the Universal Declaration of Human Rights "in a manner which would fit the occasion and serve the cause of human rights".

It is my hope that this new publication, indicating as it does how standards for the promotion and protection of human rights have come to be accepted by the international community over the past quarter-century, and how some of the problems of reconciling the realization of those standards with the requirements of the principle of non-intervention in matters that are essentially within the domestic jurisdiction of States have been overcome, will not only serve the academic needs but will inspire and give rise to renewed practical efforts on the part of Governments, international organizations and individuals throughout the world to ensure that human rights and fundamental freedoms are universally and effectively recognized, observed and enjoyed by everyone.

Kurt WALDHEIM
*Secretary-General*

## CONTENTS

CONTENTS *(continued)*

## CONTENTS *(continued)*

**CONTENTS *(continued)***

CONTENTS *(continued)*

CONTENTS *(continued)*

CONTENTS *(continued)*

CONTENTS *(continued)*

*Chapter*

CONTENTS *(continued)*

CONTENTS *(concluded)*

*Chapter*

# INTRODUCTION

The present publication reviews the activities of the United Nations in the field of human rights from the establishment of the Organization up to 31 December 1972. It is in two parts: part one deals mainly with the substantive work of the various organs concerned; part two is devoted essentially to organizational, institutional and procedural questions. These two aspects could not be separated entirely and appropriate references from one part to the other have been included so as to ensure a more useful presentation. As far as pre-1968 developments are concerned, the publication is based on two studies which were submitted by the Secretary-General to the International Conference on Human Rights, held at Teheran in 1968. Part one corresponds to the study entitled "Measures taken within the United Nations in the field of human rights" (A/CONF.32/5 and Add.1) and part two is based on "Methods used by the United Nations in the field of human rights" (A/CONF.32/6 and Add.1).

Part one consists of 12 chapters. *Chapter I* describes the origins of United Nations concern with human rights, the human rights provisions of the Charter of the United Nations and their interpretation by some of the most authoritative bodies, the contribution of the United Nations in the early years of its existence to the liquidation of certain significant problems created by the Second World War in the field of human rights and some measures taken by the United Nations before the adoption of the Universal Declaration of Human Rights on 10 December 1948, in particular in regard to United Nations Trusteeship Agreements.

*Chapter II* is devoted to an examination of the first part of the International Bill of Rights, namely the Universal Declaration of Human Rights. It deals with the origin and contents of the Universal Declaration and describes the authority and impact of that instrument. It reproduces certain general pronouncements endorsing the Universal Declaration or calling upon Governments to live up to its provisions. It analyses United Nations resolutions which invoke the Universal Declaration in support of an action on a world-wide scale for the solution of human rights problems in specific fields and in regard to concrete human rights situations in various parts of the world. It also describes the impact of the Universal Declaration on international treaties, national constitutions, municipal laws and court decisions.

*Chapter III* gives a survey of that part of the International Bill of Rights completed only on 16 December 1966, namely the International Covenant on Economic, Social and Cultural Rights, the International Covenant on Civil and Political Rights and the Optional Protocol thereto. It analyses their provisions and indicates the action taken subsequent to their adoption.

*Chapter IV* deals with action of the United Nations in regard to the right of peoples to self-determination, the recognition of self-determination as a human right, the Declaration on the Granting of Independence to Colonial Countries and Peoples of 1960 and the machinery for its implementation. The chapter describes also the application of the right to self-determination to specific territories.

*Chapter V* is devoted to United Nations action aimed at the elimination of discrimination, particularly of discrimination on grounds of race and religion, and deals in some detail with the two basic instruments so far adopted in this field by the United Nations, namely the United Nations Declaration on the Elimination of All Forms of Racial Discrimination of 1963 and the International Convention on the Elimination of All Forms of Racial Discrimination of 1965. It examines the draft Declaration on the Elimination of All Forms of Religious Intolerance and the draft Convention on the Elimination of All Forms of Religious Intolerance and Discrimination on the Ground of Religion, which are still under consideration. It also refers to certain instruments aimed at the elimination of discrimination adopted by specialized agencies.

*Chapter VI* describes United Nations measures in regard to the race problem in South Africa, the policy of *apartheid* of the Government of that country and, generally, the problem of racial discrimination in southern Africa.

*Chapter VII* deals with United Nations measures taken to bring about equality of men and women. In addition to analysing the international instruments relating to the rights of women and to describing the unified long-term United Nations programme for the advancement of women, it reviews the situation with respect to the exercise by women of their civil and political rights and of their economic, social and cultural rights.

*Chapter VIII* describes the instruments in the human rights field, other than those mentioned in chapters II, III, IV, V and VII, drawn up by or under the auspices of the United Nations since 1948. The instruments are presented in chronological order. However, where several instruments belong to a specific group, the order is governed by the first instrument belonging to that group.

*Chapter IX* deals point by point with rights proclaimed in the Universal Declaration of Human Rights for the implementation of which specific measures have been taken since 1948, without those measures necessarily resulting in the conclusion of international instruments by the United Nations.

*Chapter X* describes the action taken by the United Nations in regard to the protection of human rights in armed conflict. It deals both with the action taken by the International Conference on Human Rights, held at Teheran in 1968, and by the organs which normally act in the field of human rights and also with the action taken in the context of disarmament, limitation of armaments and weapons technology.

*Chapter XI* deals with recent United Nations concern with the question of human rights and scientific and technological developments.

*Chapter XII*, which is devoted to questions originating in events which culminated in the Second World War, deals with war crimes and crimes against humanity, the question of the non-applicability of statutory limitations to such crimes, *apartheid* as a crime against humanity, United Nations action concerning nazism and racial intolerance, and assistance to victims of persecution.

Part two is mainly devoted to organizational, institutional and procedural questions, with appropriate references, where necessary, to questions of substance dealt with essentially in part one.

*Chapter I* provides information on the United Nations organs principally or occasionally concerned with matters of human rights and on conferences convened by United Nations organs to deal with those matters.

*Chapter II* is devoted to the methods of protecting and promoting respect for human rights through the adoption of international instruments. It covers both declarations and recommendations as well as international agreements

*Chapter III* is concerned with both national and international machinery and procedures for the implementation of human rights. It describes the national measures needed to implement international agreements, declarations and recommendations.

It also describes the reporting procedures established under the provisions of the United Nations Charter, including the systems of periodic reports and reporting procedures concerning the implementation of international agreements concluded within or under the auspices of the United Nations. It analyses the procedures other than reporting procedures under these agreements. It deals with the procedure for the handling of communications concerning human rights regarding which important modifications were made in recent years. It refers to the creation of specialized agencies as a method to promote respect for certain human rights and also records recent endeavours to create regional commissions on human rights. The procedures established in the early years of the United Nations for dealing with the question of forced labour and with allegations of infringement of trade union rights are also considered. The chapter also briefly describes procedural steps taken by United Nations organs regarding specific human rights situations.

*Chapter IV* deals with the promotion of respect for human rights through the preparation of studies, the exchange of information, documentation and experience and educational and related methods. It describes the programme of advisory services in human rights, consisting of the organization of seminars, advisory services of experts and the granting of fellowships and scholarships. The public information measures, including educational activities of non-governmental organizations, are also described.

*Chapter V* deals with the methods and procedures employed by the United Nations in its struggle against racial discrimination and *apartheid*. It describes the concrete steps taken on a number of issues as well as the organs created to serve this goal.

# Part One

## MEASURES TAKEN WITHIN THE UNITED NATIONS IN THE FIELD OF HUMAN RIGHTS

# I. THE UNITED NATIONS AND HUMAN RIGHTS

## A. Origins of the United Nations concern with human rights

The United Nations interest in the promotion and encouragement of respect for human rights and fundamental freedoms corresponds to the increasing concern of the international community for the rights and aspirations for dignity of all human beings everywhere. Its roots may be traced to humanitarian traditions and the struggle for freedom and equality in all continents and, as far as more recent national developments are concerned, to the English, American, French and Russian historic pronouncements of the seventeenth, eighteenth, nineteenth and twentieth centuries. This humanitarian tradition manifested itself on the international plane in terms of positive action early in the nineteenth century when the problem of slave trade was taken up and towards the end of that century when international interest in social progress and labour legislation emerged.

The Peace Treaties by which the First World War was concluded comprised the Covenant of the League of Nations in which Members of the League accepted the obligation to endeavour to secure and maintain fair and humane conditions of labour for men, women and children. They undertook to secure the just treatment of the indigenous inhabitants of their colonies. The Peace Treaties also led to the establishment of the mandates system by which certain Powers accepted as a sacred trust of civilization responsibility for the well-being and development of the peoples which before the First World War had been under German and Turkish sovereignty. The Peace Treaties also established the International Labour Organisation in the realization that universal peace could be established only if it were based on social justice. Moreover, some of the post-1919 Peace Treaties and a number of Minorities Treaties and Declarations created a system for the protection of minorities with the League of Nations as guarantor. This system applied, however, only to a group of States in central and eastern Europe and the Middle East which had accepted obligations under these various instruments.

The specific inclusion of promotion and encouragement of respect for human rights and for fundamental freedoms for all among the purposes of the United Nations was due above all to the events which occurred during and immediately before the Second World War. The human rights provisions of the Charter reflect the reaction of the international community to the horrors of that war and of the régimes which unleashed it. The Second World War proved to many the close relationship that exists between outrageous behaviour by a Government towards its own citizens and aggression against other nations, between respect for human rights and the maintenance of peace. The experience of the war resulted in the widespread conviction that the effective international protection of human rights was a major purpose of the war, inasmuch as it is one of the essential conditions of international peace and progress. The statements to this effect made by the leaders of the victorious coalition are well known. In the Declaration of United Nations, signed on 1 January 1942 by 26 nations then at war, and subsequently adhered to by 21 other nations, the signatory Governments stated that they "subscribed to a common programme of purposes and principles embodied in the Joint Declaration of the President of the United States of America and the Prime Minister of the United Kingdom of Great Britain and Northern Ireland, dated 14 august 1941, known as the Atlantic Charter". They expressed their conviction "that complete victory over their enemies is essential to defend life, liberty, independence and religious freedom, and to preserve human rights and justice in their own lands as well as in other lands". Among the 47 signatories of this Declaration were the United States, the United Kingdom, the Union of Soviet Socialist Republics, China and France. In the "Atlantic Charter" of 14 August 1941, which was subscribed to and endorsed by the 47 nations, the President of the United States and the Prime Minister of the United Kingdom had expressed the hope "to see established a peace which will afford to all nations the means of dwelling in safety within their own boundaries, and which will afford assurance that all the men in all the lands may live out their lives in freedom from fear and want".[1]

In 1944 the Governments of the Union of Soviet Socialist Republics, the United Kingdom and the United States of America (and, subsequently, the Governments of China, the United Kingdom and the United States) met at Dumbarton Oaks and agreed upon proposals for establishing a general international organization, to be called the United Nations. The Dumbarton Oaks proposals contemplated that the United Nations should "facilitate solutions of international economic, social and other humanitarian problems and promote respect for human rights and fundamental freedoms". The proposals also contemplated that responsibility for the discharge of this function should be vested in the General Assembly and, under the authority of the General Assembly, in an Economic and Social Council, which was to be empowered to make recommendations with respect to international

---

[1] *Yearbook of the United Nations 1946-1947* (United Nations publication, Sales No. 1947.I.18), pp. 1-2.

economic, social and other humanitarian matters.[2] The Dumbarton Oaks proposals were the basis of the work of the San Francisco Conference which met in 1945 and prepared and opened for signature the Charter of the United Nations.

### B. The human rights clauses of the Charter of the United Nations

The Charter of the United Nations refers to the problem of human rights in its Preamble and in six different Articles. In the Preamble the peoples of the United Nations express their determination "to reaffirm faith in fundamental human rights, in the dignity and worth of the human person, in the equal rights of men and women and of nations large and small". The words "promoting and encouraging respect for human rights", "assisting in the realization of human rights and fundamental freedoms" appear, with certain variations, in different contexts (Article 1, paragraph 3, on purposes and principles; Article 13, subparagraph 1 (b), on the General Assembly; Article 62, paragraph 2, on the Economic and Social Council; and Article 76c on the international trusteeship system). In Article 56, read together with Article 55, "all Members pledge themselves to take joint and separate action in co-operation with the Organization for the achievement" of a number of purposes which "the United Nations shall promote", among them "universal respect for, and observance of, human rights and fundamental freedoms for all without distinction as to race, sex, language, or religion". Attention must also be drawn to the provision of Article 2, paragraph 7, which is to the effect that "nothing contained in the present Charter shall authorize the United Nations to intervene in matters which are essentially within the domestic jurisdiction of any State or shall require the Members to submit such matters to settlement under the present Charter". The Charter also provides that this principle shall not prejudice the application of enforcement measures under Chapter VII, which deals with action with respect to threats to the peace, breaches of the peace, and acts of aggression. While the Charter does not contain a precise definition or a listing of "human rights and fundamental freedoms", there is one aspect of the human rights problem which is regulated with sufficient precision in the Charter, namely, the inadmissibility of making adverse distinction based on race, sex, language or religion.

The developments which are described in the present publication find their constitutional and legal basis in some of the Charter provisions referred to in the preceding paragraph. In a recent advisory opinion the International Court of Justice interpreted the human rights clauses of the Charter and the obligations Member States had undertaken by saying—in the context of the continued presence of South Africa in Namibia — that under the Charter of the United Nations the former Mandatory (South Africa) had pledged itself to observe and respect in a territory having an international status human rights and fundamental freedoms for all without distinction as to race. The Court went on to say that "to establish instead and to enforce, distinctions, exclusions, restrictions and limitations exclusively based on grounds of race, colour, descent or national or ethnic origin which constitute a denial of fundamental human rights is a flagrant violation of the purposes and principles of the Charter.[3]

### C. Contribution of the United Nations to the liquidation of certain consequences of the Second World War

The horrors committed during the Second World War were not only instrumental in making the promotion of, and encouragement of respect for, human rights and fundamental freedoms one of the purposes of the United Nations, but they also greatly influenced some of the activities in which the United Nations has engaged, particularly in the first years of its existence. Some of these activities were devoted to the liquidation of the consequences of the events of the Second World War; they concerned the apprehension and punishment of persons guilty of war crimes and crimes against humanity, an action by which the United Nations reaffirmed the liability of such persons to punishment. This led, as will be recorded later in the present publication, to various measures in the field of the protection of human rights through resort to criminal sanctions. The General Assembly affirmed the principles of international law recognized by the Charter of the Nuremberg Tribunal (resolution 95 (I)); affirmed that genocide was a crime under international law (resolution 96 (I)); initiated studies with a view to the drafting of a convention on the crime of genocide, the formulation of the principles recognized in the Charter of the Nuremberg Tribunal and in the judgement of the Tribunal, and the drafting of a code of offences against the peace and security of mankind; and initiated studies concerning the establishment of an international criminal jurisdiction.

In 1965 United Nations organs resumed their activities in regard to war criminals and persons guilty of crimes against humanity. Action taken in this regard is described in chapter XII below.

Other activities of the Organization undertaken in the early years of its existence—and clearly connected with the liquidation of the war as well as the promotion of human rights—involved its efforts to alleviate the plight of survivors of so-called medical experiments in Nazi concentration camps and its concern with the humanitarian aspects of repatriation of prisoners of war (General Assembly resolution 427 (V)).

The organs of the United Nations showed their concern for human rights by recommending that appropriate provisions be inserted in the peace treaties which were to be concluded after the war. On the recommendation of the United Nations Nuclear Commission on Human Rights,[4]

---

[2] *Ibid.*, pp. 4-9.

[3] *Legal Consequences for States of the Continued Presence of South Africa in Namibia (South West Africa) notwithstanding Security Council Resolution 276 (1970), Advisory Opinion, I.C.J. Reports 1971*, p. 16, paras. 130 and 131.

[4] For an explanation of the status and composition of the Nuclear Commission on Human Rights, see document E/38/Rev.1 of 21 May 1946 and *Official Records of the Economic and Social Council, First Year, Second Session*, annex No. 4.

and pending the adoption of an international bill of rights, the Economic and Social Council recommended acceptance of the general principle that "international treaties embodying basic human rights, including to the fullest extent practicable treaties of peace, shall conform to the fundamental standards relative to such rights set forth in the Charter" (Economic and Social Council resolution 9 (II) of 21 June 1946). The inclusion of human rights provisions in the Peace Treaties with Bulgaria, Finland, Hungary, Italy and Romania of 10 February 1947 and the State Treaty with Austria of 15 May 1955 was the result of this recommendation of the Council. In the Preamble to the Peace Treaty with Japan (1951), Japan declared its intention to strive to realize the objectives of the Universal Declaration of Human Rights.

### D. United Nations Trusteeship Agreements and human rights

A reflection of the human rights provisions of the United Nations Charter, both before and after the adoption of the Universal Declaration, can be found in the various Trusteeship Agreements. Most of the Agreements were concluded in 1946 and 1947. Some examples are: the Trusteeship Agreements for the Territory of Togoland under British Administration (approved by the General Assembly on 13 December 1946); for the Territory of the Cameroons under British Administration (approved by the General Assembly on 13 December 1946); for the Territory of Tanganyika under British Administration (approved by the General Assembly on 13 December 1946); for the Territory of New Guinea under Australian Administration (approved by the General Assembly on 13 December 1946); for the Territory of Togoland under French Administration (approved by the General Assembly on 13 December 1946); for the Territory of the Cameroons under French Administration (approved by the General Assembly on 13 December 1946); for the Territory of Ruanda-Urundi under Belgian Administration (approved by the General Assembly on 13 December 1946); for the Territory of Western Samoa under New Zealand Administration (approved by the General Assembly on 13 December 1946); for the Territory of Nauru under the Administration of Australia, New Zealand and the United Kingdom (approved by the General Assembly on 1 November 1947); and for the former Japanese Mandated Islands under United States Administration (approved by Security Council on 2 April 1947). In the Agreements mentioned above, the Administering Authorities undertook to administer the respective territories in such a manner as to achieve the basic objectives of the International Trusteeship System laid down in Article 76 of the United Nations Charter, which are, *inter alia*, "to encourage respect for human rights and for fundamental freedoms for all without distinction as to race, sex, language or religion, and to encourage recognition of the interdependence of the peoples of the world; and ... to ensure equal treatment in social, economic and commercial matters for all Members of the United Nations and their nationals, and also equal treatment for the latter in the administration of justice...".

The Trusteeship Agreement for the Territory of Somaliland under Italian Administration (approved by the General Assembly on 2 December 1950) is of special interest for the present study because, in the Declaration of Constitutional Principles annexed to it, "the Administering Authority accepts as a standard of achievement for the Territory the Universal Declaration of Human Rights adopted by the General Assembly of the United Nations on 10 December 1948".

In its resolution 181 (II) of 29 November 1947, entitled "Future government of Palestine", the General Assembly adopted recommendations concerning the Mandated Territory of Palestine, including the Plan of Partition with Economic Union, provisions guaranteeing to all persons equal and non-discriminatory rights in civil, political, economic and religious matters and the enjoyment of human rights and fundamental freedoms were included. For the city of Jerusalem as a *corpus separatum*, comprehensive provisions purporting to guarantee freedoms of citizens, non-discrimination and equal protection of the law were also contemplated.

Another League of Nations Mandate which became a major concern of the United Nations and which has posed a serious human rights problem is the former South African Mandate for South West Africa. United Nations action on South West Africa (Namibia) is described in chapter IV, section F, below.

# II. THE INTERNATIONAL BILL OF RIGHTS: THE UNIVERSAL DECLARATION OF HUMAN RIGHTS

At the San Francisco Conference, which drafted the Charter of the United Nations, a proposal to embody an international bill of rights in the Charter itself was put forward but not proceeded with for the reason that it required more detailed consideration.[1] The idea of drafting and bringing into effect an international bill of rights was considered by many as inherent in the Charter. Even before the Charter was ratified and before it entered into force and before the United Nations as an organization was established, preliminary steps were taken towards this goal. The Preparatory Commission of the United Nations [2] and its Executive Committee,[3] meeting in the autumn of 1945, recommended that the work of the Commission on Human Rights, the establishment of which is provided for in Article 68 of the Charter, should be directed, in the first place, towards the "formulation of an international bill of rights". The General Assembly, by resolution 7 (I), adopted at the first part of its first session in 1946, concurred with that recommendation. Accordingly, when the terms of reference of the Commission on Human Rights were laid down by the Economic and Social Council in February 1956, "an international bill of rights" was the first item on its work programme.[4]

While in the beginning different views about the form the international bill of rights should take were expressed, eventually the decision emerged that the term "international bill of rights" would apply to the entirety of documents contemplated and in preparation: the Declaration, the Convention or the Covenant and the measures of implementation. This compromise solution, recommended by the Commission on Human Rights in 1947 and approved by the General Assembly in 1948 to produce the international bill of rights not by one single, comprehensive and final act, but to divide it into at least two but probably more international instruments, led to the promulgation of the Universal Declaration of Human Rights as the first of these several instruments. From 1948 to 1966 the Universal Declaration of Human Rights was the only part of the international bill of rights in existence, and it was only at the twenty-first session of the General Assembly in 1966 that the far-reaching undertaking of the international bill of rights was completed by the adoption and the opening for signature of the two Covenants and the Optional Protocol.

## A. Origin and contents of the Universal Declaration

The Universal Declaration of Human Rights was adopted in the form of a resolution of the General Assembly on 10 December 1948. Of the 58 States then Members of the United Nations 48 voted their approval, none voted against, 8 abstained and 2 were absent. One of the latter subsequently informed the Secretary-General that if its representative had not been prevented from attending the meeting, he would have voted for the Declaration.[5]

The Universal Declaration states in paragraph 1 of its preamble that recognition of the inherent dignity and of the equal and inalienable rights of all members of the human family is the foundation of freedom, justice and peace in the world. It further recalls that Member States have pledged themselves to achieve, in co-operation with the United Nations, the promotion of universal respect for and observance of human rights and fundamental freedoms. The preamble also states that a "common understanding of these rights and freedoms is of the greatest importance for the full realization of this pledge". The Declaration was proclaimed "as a common standard of achievement for all peoples and all nations, to the end that every individual and every organ of society, keeping this Declaration constantly in mind, shall strive by teaching and education to promote respect for these rights and freedoms and by progressive measures, national and international, to secure their universal and effective recognition and observance, both among the peoples of Member States themselves and among the peoples of territories under their jurisdiction".

In addition to the preamble, the Declaration consists of 30 articles. The Universal Declaration differs from the traditional catalogues of human rights which are contained in various constitutional and fundamental laws of the eighteenth and nineteenth centuries and of the beginning of the twentieth century in that it deals not only with the traditional civil and political rights but with the group of rights which have become known as economic, social and cultural rights and which have subsequently been codified in the International Covenant on Economic, Social and Cultural Rights. Article 1 of the Declaration proclaims: "All human beings are born free and equal in dignity and rights". Article 2 states that everyone is

---

[1] *Documents of the United Nations Conference on International Organization*, vol. VI, p. 705.

[2] *Report of the Preparatory Commission of the United Nations* (PC/20), chap. III, sect. 4, paras. 15-16.

[3] Executive Committee's Report on Committees and Commissions of the Economic and Social Council [PC/EX/95, sect. B, para. 21, p. 18].

[4] Economic and Social Council resolution 1/5 of 16 February 1946.

[5] Document A/1311 of 7 August 1950.

entitled to all the rights and freedoms set forth in the Declaration without distinction of any kind, such as race, colour, sex, language, religion, political or other opinion, national or social origin, property, birth or other status. In the second paragraph of article 2 the Universal Declaration provides that "no distinction shall be made on the basis of the political, jurisdictional or international status of the country or territory to which a person belongs, whether it be independent, trust, non-self-governing or under any other limitation of sovereignty". Articles 2 to 21 deal, by and large, with the traditional civil and political rights. Articles 22 to 28 of the Declaration set forth, mostly in general terms, the economic, social and cultural rights. A number of the individual provisions of the Declaration will be referred to later in this publication when the action to implement them is described.

Article 29, paragraph 1, proclaims that everyone has duties to the community in which alone the free and full development of his personality is possible. In article 29, paragraph 2, the Declaration defines the admissible limitations on the exercise of the rights and freedoms set forth in it in the following terms:

"In the exercise of his rights and freedoms, everyone shall be subject only to such limitations as are determined by law solely for the purpose of securing due recognition and respect for the rights and freedoms of others and of meeting the just requirements of morality, public order and the general welfare in a democratic society."

Article 30 of the Universal Declaration provides for an important limitation of the authority of States and of the rights of groups or persons:

"Nothing in this Declaration may be interpreted as implying for any State, group or person any right to engage in any activity or to perform any act aimed at the destruction of any of the rights and freedoms set forth herein."

The Universal Declaration of Human Rights is the result of decisions taken in 1947-1948 to produce the International Bill of Rights not by one single, comprehensive and final act, but to divide it into several instruments, of which the Universal Declaration of Human Rights was the first. The other parts of the International Bill of Rights (i.e., the two Covernants and the Optional Protocol to the International Covenant on Civil and Political Rights) were adopted by the General Assembly and opened for signature, ratification and accession on 16 December 1966, that is, 18 years after the adoption of the Universal Declaration of Human Rights. Moreover, at the time of the preparation of the present publication, the International Covenant on Economic, Social and Cultural Rights, the International Covenant on Civil and Political Rights and the Optional Protocol to the International Covenant on Civil and Political Rights are not yet in force, the required number of ratifications or accessions not having been reached yet. Because of the considerable lapse of time between the proclamation of the Universal Declaration of Human Rights and the entry into force of the other parts of the International Bill of Human Rights, the Universal Declaration has, temporarily at least. fulfilled part of the role originally contemplated for the International Bill of Rights as a whole.

The provisions of the Declaration have been used as a basis for various types of action taken by the United Nations; they have inspired a number of international conventions both within and outside the United Nations; they have exercised a significant influence on national constitutions and on municipal legislation and, in several cases, on court decisions. In some instances the text of provisions of the Declaration was actually used in international instruments or national legislation. There are also very many instances on record of the use of the Declaration as a code of conduct and as a yardstick to measure the degree of respect for and of compliance with the international standards of human rights.

In the paragraphs that follow an attempt is made to indicate some of the most significant actions of the United Nations and its organs and of individual Governments which were inspired by or based upon the Universal Declaration. By and large, one can trace three main areas in which the impact of the Universal Declaration has been felt: (*a*) decisions taken by the United Nations, its organs, the specialized agencies and other intergovernmental organizations; (*b*) international treaties and conventions; and (*c*) national constitutions, municipal legislation and court decisions.

The impact of the Universal Declaration on decisions taken by the United Nations, its organs, the specialized agencies and other intergovernmental organizations is presented under the three following headings: first, general pronouncements by United Nations organs endorsing the Universal Declaration or calling upon Governments to live up to its provisions; secondly, United Nations resolutions invoking the Universal Declaration in support of action on a world-wide scale for the solution of human rights problems in specific fields; and thirdly, United Nations resolutions invoking the Universal Declaration in regard to concrete human rights situations.

### B. General pronouncements endorsing the Universal Declaration or calling upon Governments to live up to its provisions

In its resolution 290 (IV) of 1 December 1949, entitled "Essentials of peace", the General Assembly called upon every nation: "*To promote*, in recognition of the paramount importance of preserving the dignity and worth of the human person, full freedom for the peaceful expression of political opposition, full opportunity for the exercise of religious freedom and full respect for all the other fundamental rights expressed in the Universal Declaration of Human Rights . . .".

Similarly, in resolution 377 (V) of 3 November 1950, entitled "Uniting for Peace" the General Assembly stated that a genuine and lasting peace depended upon the observance of all the Principles and Purposes of the United Nations, especially upon the respect for and observance of human rights and fundamental freedoms for all and on the establishment and maintenance of conditions of economic and social well-being in all countries. The General Assembly urged Member States "to respect fully, and to intensify joint action, in co-operation with the United Nations, to develop and stimulate universal respect for and observance of human rights and fundamental freedoms".

At its sixth session, in its resolution 540 (VI) of 4 February 1952, entitled "Observance of Human Rights" the General Assembly stated that "notwithstanding the proclamation of the Universal Declaration of Human Rights, violations of human rights have continued to occur". It emphasized that it was the responsibility of the Members of the United Nations individually and collectively to see that human rights and freedoms be enhanced throughout the world. It requested that Members intensify their efforts for the observance of human rights and freedoms in their own territories and in the Non-Self-Governing and Trust Territories. Similar statements were made by the General Assembly in 1957 (resolution 1041 (XI) of 20 February 1957) and in two resolutions (1775 (XVII) and 1776 (XVII)) adopted on 7 December 1962.

At its fifteenth session in 1960, the General Assembly adopted the Declaration on the Granting of Independence to Colonial Countries and Peoples (resolution 1514 (XV) of 14 December 1960). While the principal provisions of this Declaration are examined in another part of this publication, in the present context when recording pronouncements endorsing the Universal Declaration, reference should be made to its paragraph 7, by which the General Assembly declared: "All States shall observe faithfully and strictly the provisions of the Charter of the United Nations, the Universal Declaration of Human Rights and the present Declaration . . .".

At its eighteenth session in 1963 the General Assembly proclaimed the United Nations Declaration on the Elimination of All Forms of Racial Discrimination (resolution 1904 (XVIII) of 20 November 1963). The provisions of this instrument are examined in another part of this publication. At this stage reference should be made to article 11 of the United Nations Declaration on the Elimination of All Forms of Racial Discrimination, which is to the effect that:

> "Every State shall promote respect for and observance of human rights and fundamental freedoms in accordance with the Charter of the United Nations and shall fully and faithfully observe the provisions of the present Declaration, the Universal Declaration of Human Rights and the Declaration on the Granting of Independence to Colonial Countries and Peoples."

In 1965, the General Assembly, in resolution 2027 (XX) of 18 December 1965, entitled "Measures to accelerate the promotion of respect for human rights and fundamental freedoms", invoking the Charter, the Universal Declaration and also the Declaration on the Elimination of All Forms of Racial Discrimination and the Declaration on the Granting of Independence to Colonial Countries and Peoples, urged all Governments to make special efforts during the [first] United Nations Development Decade to promote respect for an observance of human rights and fundamental freedoms and invited them to include in their plans for economic and social development measures directed towards the achievement of further progress in the implementation of the human rights and fundamental freedoms proclaimed in the Universal Declaration of Human Rights and in subsequent declarations and instruments in the field of human rights.

At its twenty-first session, in 1966, the General Assembly, convinced that "gross violations of the rights and fundamental freedoms set forth in the Universal Declaration of Human Rights continue to occur in certain countries", called upon all States "to strengthen their efforts to promote the full observance of human rights and the right to self-determination in accordance with the Charter of the United Nations, and to attain the standards established by the Universal Declaration of Human Rights" (resolution 2144A (XXI) of 26 October 1966).

The work of the International Conference on Human Rights, held at Teheran in 1968, is described elsewhere in the present publication (chapter VIII, I). At its twenty-third session the General Assembly, in its resolution 2442 (XXIII) of 19 December 1968, expressed its conviction that the Conference had made an important constructive contribution to the cause of human rights and that its results should be translated into effective action by States, the competent organs of the United Nations and its family of organizations, and other organizations concerned. The General Assembly expressed its satisfaction with the work of the Conference, which constituted a solid foundation for further action and initiative by the United Nations and other interested international bodies, as well as by the States and national organizations concerned. The Assembly endorsed the Proclamation of Teheran[6] as an important and timely reaffirmation of the principles embodied in the Universal Declaration and in other international instruments in the field of human rights. The General Assembly also made arrangements towards the implementation of the recommendations of the Conference.

The Declaration on Social Progress and Development of 1969[7] recalled among the various United Nations pronouncements in the field of human rights, the Universal Declaration of Human Rights and called for the achievement of the common goals of development with full respect for the fundamental freedoms embodied in the Universal Declaration of Human Rights.

On 24 October 1970 the General Assembly adopted the Declaration on the Occasion of the Twenty-fifth Anniversary of the United Nations.[8] In paragraph 8 of the Declaration it is stated that the Universal Declaration of Human Rights constituted one of the landmarks in international co-operation and in the recognition and protection of the rights of every individual without any distinction and that, although some progress had been achieved, serious violations of human rights were still being committed against individuals and groups in several regions of the world. The States Members of the United Nations again pledged themselves to a continued and determined struggle against all violations of the rights

---

[6] *Final Act of the International Conference on Human Rights* (United Nations publication, Sales No. E.68.XIV.2), p. 3.

[7] Proclaimed by General Assembly resolution 2542 (XXIV) of 11 December 1969. For a summary of the provisions of the Declaration on Social Progress and Development see below, chapter VIII, section K.

[8] General Assembly resolution 2627 (XXV) of 24 October 1970.

and fundamental freedoms of human rights. The relevant provisions of the Declaration of 24 October 1970 are reproduced in chapter VIII, section L, below.

## C. United Nations resolutions invoking the Universal Declaration in support of action on a world-wide scale for the solution of human rights problems in specific fields

### 1. *General action on problems of discrimination*

Among the specific human rights problems for the solution of which the United Nations has taken action on a world-wide scale, first and foremost has been the general problem of discrimination. In its resolution 532 B (VI) of 4 February 1952, the General Assembly emphasized "that the full application and implementation of the principle of non-discrimination recommended in the United Nations Charter and the Universal Declaration of Human Rights are matters of supreme importance, and should constitute the primary objective in the work of all United Nations organs and institutions". At its fifteenth session, in its resolution 1510 (XV) of 12 December 1960, the Assembly resolutely condemned "all manifestations and practices of racial, religious and national hatred in the political, economic, social, educational and cultural spheres of the life of society as violations of the Charter of the United Nations and the Universal Declaration of Human Rights".

The Universal Declaration was, as has already been indicated, endorsed and supported in the United Nations Declaration on the Elimination of All Forms of Racial Discrimination, and also in the Declaration on the Elimination of Discrimination against Women proclaimed by the General Assembly in its resolution 2263 (XXII) of 7 November 1967.

With regard to the problem of racial prejudice and religious intolerance, the General Assembly, in its resolution 1779 (XVII) of 7 December 1962, reiterated "its condemnation of all manifestations of racial prejudice and of national and religious intolerance as violations of the Charter of the United Nations and of the Universal Declaration of Human Rights".

The Universal Declaration provided the basis of a decision of the General Assembly (resolution 315 (IV) of 17 November 1949), when it took action on the question of discrimination practised by certain States against immigrating labour: "In view of the importance of the principle of non-discrimination embodied in the Universal Declaration of Human Rights" the General Assembly decided that there should be no offensive distinctions with regard to the enjoyment of all facilities for accommodation, food, education, recreation and medical assistance against such workers and their families.

When, at its twenty-seventh session, the General Assembly decided to launch the Decade for Action to Combat Racism and Racial Discrimination, it also decided to inaugurate the activities thereof on 10 December 1973, the twenty-fifth anniversary of the Universal Declaration of Human Rights.[9]

### 2. *General action against discrimination on the grounds of sex and in matters relating to the status of women in general*

At its ninth session, the General Assembly dealt with the "status of women in private law; customs, ancient laws and practices affecting the human dignity of women" (General Assembly resolution 843 (IX) of 17 December 1954). In that resolution the Assembly recalled "the principles set forth in the United Nations Charter and in the Universal Declaration of Human Rights" and considered that in certain areas of the world women were subjected to customs, ancient laws and practices relating to marriage and the family which were inconsistent with these principles. It urged all States to take all appropriate measures with a view to abolishing such customs, ancient laws and practices. It recommended that special efforts be made to inform public opinion in all areas concerned about the Universal Declaration and existing decrees and legislation which affect the status of women.

At its twenty-second session, the General Assembly adopted resolution 2263 (XXII) whereby it proclaimed the Declaration on the Elimination of Discrimination against Women. The resolution recalled that the Universal Declaration of Human Rights asserts the principle of non-discrimination and proclaims that all human beings are born free and equal in dignity and rights and that everyone is entitled to all the rights and freedoms set forth therein without distinction of any kind, including any distinction as to sex. The resolution gave expression to the concern that, despite the Charter, the Universal Declaration, the International Covenants on Human Rights and other instruments and despite the progress made in the matter of equality of rights, there continues to exist considerable discrimination against women. The provisions of the Declaration are presented elsewhere in the present study. It concludes in its article 11 with the statement that the principle of equality of rights of men and women demands implementation in all States in accordance with the principles of the Charter and of the Universal Declaration. Governments, non-governmental organizations and individuals are urged, therefore, to do all in their power to promote the implementation of the principles contained in the Declaration on the Elimination of Discrimination against Women.

At its twenty-fifth session, the General Assembly, in its resolution 2715 (XXV) of 15 December 1970, recalled the Universal Declaration of Human Rights together with Article 101 of the Charter and the Declaration on the Elimination of Discrimination against Women in a resolution on the employment of qualified women in senior and other professional positions in the secretariats of organizations of the United Nations system.

At its twenty-seventh session, the General Assembly, in its resolution 3009 (XXVII) of 18 December 1972, again dealt with the employment of women in senior and other professional positions by the secretariats of organizations in the United Nations system. It recalled a

---

[9] General Assembly resolution 2919 (XXVII) of 15 November 1972.

number of declarations and instruments adopted by the United Nations acknowledging the equality of status of men and women, including the Charter, the Universal Declaration of Human Rights, the two Covenants and the Declaration on the Elimination of Discrimination against Women and also relevant instrument of the ILO and of UNESCO. It made arrangements for the taking of appropriate measures to ensure equal opportunities for the employment of qualified women at the senior and professional levels and in policy-making decisions.

### 3. *The right of asylum*

At the twenty-second session, by its resolution 2312 (XXII) of 14 December 1967, the General Assembly adopted the Declaration on Territorial Asylum. This Declaration invokes article 14 of the Universal Declaration of Human Rights, which provides that everyone has the right to seek and to enjoy in other countries asylum from persecution and that this right may not be invoked in the case of prosecutions generally arising from non-political crimes or from acts contrary to the purposes and principles of the United Nations. It also recalls article 13, paragraph 2, of the Universal Declaration, which states that everyone has the right to leave any country, including his own, and to return to his country. The substantive provisions of the Declaration on Territorial Asylum are summarized elsewhere in the present study.

### 4. *Administration of justice*

At its twenty-third and twenty-sixth sessions, the General Assembly dealt with a series of problems connected with the administration of justice, always invoking provisions of the Universal Declaration of Human Rights.

At its twenty-third session, the General Assembly, on the initiative of the Teheran Conference,[10] adopted a resolution on legal aid [11] in which it recalled that the Universal Declaration of Human Rights proclaims that everyone has the right to an effective remedy by the competent national tribunals for violating the fundamental rights granted him by the constitution or by law. Recalling further article 14 of the International Covenant on Civil and Political Rights, the General Assembly recommended to Member States that they should guarantee the progressive development of comprehensive systems of legal aid to those who needed it in order to protect their human rights and fundamental freedoms.

In its resolution 2393 (XXIII) of 26 November 1968, on capital punishment, the General Assembly recalled articles 3 and 5 of the Universal Declaration, providing respectively that everyone had the right to life, liberty and security of person and that no one should be subjected to torture or to cruel, inhuman or degrading treatment or punishment. In the light of these provisions of the Universal Declaration and of various studies which had been made by various United Nations organs, the General Assembly addressed recommendations to Governments and Member States concerning the legal procedures and safeguards for the accused in capital cases and concerning possible restrictions on the use of the death penalty or its total abolition.

At its twenty-sixth session, in another resolution (2857 (XXVI) of 20 December 1971), on the question of capital punishment, the General Assembly affirmed that in order fully to guarantee the right to life, provided for in article 3 of the Universal Declaration, the main objective to be pursued was the progressive restriction of the number of offences for which capital punishment might be imposed, with a view to the desirability of abolishing this punishment in all countries.

In its resolution 2858 (XXVI) of 20 December 1971, entitled "Human rights in the administration of justice", the General Assembly solemnly reaffirmed the principles concerning human rights in the administration of justice as embodied in articles 5, 10 and 11 of the Universal Declaration of Human Rights, namely those referring to the right not to be subjected to inhuman treatment or punishment; the right to a public hearing by an independent and impartial tribunal in any civil or criminal proceedings, the right, if charged with a penal offence, to be presumed innocent until proved guilty; and the right not to be subjected to retrospective criminal sanctions. In the same resolution the General Assembly invited the attention of Member States to the Standard Minimum Rules for the Treatment of Prisoners and requested action on the draft principles relating to equality in the administration of justice, which had been adopted by the Sub-Commission on Prevention of Discrimination and Protection of Minorities.

### 5. *Freedom of information*

The General Assembly has on many occasions invoked article 19 of the Declaration, which sets forth the right to freedom of opinion and expression, including the right to seek, receive and impart information and ideas through any media and regardless of frontiers.

Already at its first session in 1946, two years before the proclamation of the Universal Declaration of Human Rights, the General Assembly had stated that freedom of information was a fundamental human right and was a touchstone of all the freedoms to which the United Nations was consecrated. At the same time the General Assembly, by its resolution 59 (I) of 14 December 1946, arranged for the convocation by the Economic and Social Council of an International Conference on Freedom of Information. The results of this International Conference and the subsequent legislative action on questions of freedom of information are described later in this publication.

At its fifth session, the General Assembly adopted resolution 424 (V) of 14 December 1950 entitled "Freedom of information; interference with radio signals". In that resolution it invited the Governments of all States to refrain from interference with the reception of radio signals and at the same time invited all Governments to refrain from radio broadcasts that would mean unfair attacks or slanders against other peoples.

[10] Resolution XIX of 12 May 1968 (*Final Act of the International Conference on Human Rights*, (United Nations publication, Sales No. E.68.XIV.2), p. 15.

[11] General Assembly resolution 2449 (XXIII) of 19 December 1968.

At its seventh session the General Assembly, in its resolution 663 (VII) of 16 December 1952, dealt with the problem of information facilities in underdeveloped regions of the world. It invited the Economic and Social Council to recommend to the organizations participating in the technical assistance and other programmes providing aid or assistance at the request of Member States that they give sympathetic consideration to requests which Governments may submit with a view to improving information facilities and increasing the quantity and improving the quality of information available to the peoples of the world as one means of implementing the right of freedom of information as enunciated in article 19 of the Universal Declaration.

At its twenty-third session in a resolution (2448 (XXIII) of 19 December 1968) on freedom of information, the General Assembly again referred to article 19 of the Universal Declaration and recognized that freedom of information was indispensable to the enjoyment, promotion and protection of all the other rights and freedoms set forth in the Universal Declaration.

### 6. *Matters relating to the status of refugees*

The Statute of the Office of the United Nations High Commissioner for Refugees [12] refers to the Universal Declaration only in so far as it excludes from the competence of the High Commissioner persons who are excluded from the application of article 14 of the Universal Declaration, concerning the right to seek and to enjoy asylum.

In considering reports of the United Nations High Commissioner for Refugees, the General Assembly has, however, invoked the provisions of the Universal Declaration in a positive sense. Thus, having considered the report of the United Nations High Commissioner for Refugees submitted at the twenty-third session in 1968, the General Assembly urges States Members of the United Nations and of the specialized agencies to continue to lend their support to the High Commissioner's humanitarian task by improving the legal status of refugees residing in their territory and by treating new refugee situations in accordance with the principles and spirit of the Declaration on Territorial Asylum and the Universal Declaration of Human Rights.

### 7. *Recalling of the Universal Declaration in connexion with the rights of the child and its reaffirmation in the Declaration on the Promotion among Youth of the Ideals of Peace, Mutual Respect and Understanding between Peoples*

In the Declaration of the Rights of the Child [13] proclaimed by the General Assembly at its fourteenth session in its resolution 1386 (XIV) of 20 November 1959, the provisions of the Charter and of the Universal Declaration were invoked and it was also mentioned that the need for special safeguards for children had been recognized, *inter alia*, in the Universal Declaration.

The Declaration on the Promotion among Youth of the Ideals of Peace, Mutual Respect and Understanding between Peoples [14] was proclaimed by the General Assembly in its resolution 2037 (XX) of 7 December 1965. In the preamble, the Assembly reaffirmed the principles embodied in the Universal Declaration of Human Rights and also those of other United Nations instruments.

### 8. *The elderly and the aged*

The General Assembly was seized of the question of old age rights as early as at its third session, when it decided, by its resolution 213 (III) of 4 December 1948, to communicate the draft Declaration of Old Age Rights submitted by a Member Government to the Economic and Social Council. It was only at its twenty-sixth session that the General Assembly adopted a substantive resolution (2842 (XXVI) of 18 December 1971) on the question of the elderly and the aged. If took note with appreciation of a preliminary report of the Secretary-General (A/8364), which reviewed the major socio-economic problems of the elderly and the aged and the impact of technological and scientific advances on their well-being. It bore in mind the principles embodied in the Charter and in the Universal Declaration, with reference to respect for the dignity and worth of the human person and also recalled the Declaration on Social Progress and Development. The General Assembly also made arrangements for the continuation of the study of the changing socio-economic and cultural role and status of the aged in countries of different levels of development and requested the preparation of guidelines for national policies and international action in this field.

### 9. *Rights of mentally retarded persons*

The Declaration on the Rights of Mentally Retarded Persons, proclaimed by the General Assembly in 1971,[15] reaffirms faith in human rights and fundamental freedoms and in the principles of peace, of the dignity and worth of the human person and of social justice proclaimed in the Charter also recalled the principles of the Universal Declaration of Human Rights and other instruments of the organizations of the United Nations system.

### 10. *Outflow of trained personnel from developing to developed countries*

On 18 December 1972 at its twenty-seventh session, the General Assembly adopted resolution 3017 (XXVII) on the outflow of trained personnel from developing to developed countries. In operative paragraph 2 of this resolution, the General Assembly invited the Secretary-General, in collaboration with the organizations of the United Nations system and bearing in mind a study to be prepared under a different paragraph of the resolution, to draft, in consultation with the Member States con-

[12] Annex to General Assembly resolution 428 (V) of 14 December 1950.

[13] For a summary of the provisions of the Declaration, see below (chap. VIII, sect. F).

[14] For a summary of the provisions of the Declaration, see below (chap. VIII, sect. G).

[15] For a summary of the provisions of the Declaration, see below (chap. VIII, sect. O).

cerned, the necessary guidelines for a programme of action to be elaborated by the Committee on Science and Technology for Development, indicating viable measures that could be taken to deal with the problem and, above all, practical and effective guidance to be followed, mainly by the Governments of industrialized countries, to put an end to and to reverse that process, without prejudice to existing international agreements and in conformity with the Universal Declaration of Human Rights.

### D. United Nations resolutions invoking the Universal Declaration in regard to concrete human rights situations

As regards respect for human rights in Non-Self-Governing Territories, the General Assembly, on 12 December 1950, adopted resolution 446 (V) dealing with information on this subject, which noted the provision contained in article 2 of the Universal Declaration of Human Rights that no distinction should be made on the basis of the political, jurisdictional or international status of the country or territory to which a person belonged, whether it was independent, trust, non-self-governing or under any other limitation of sovereignty. The resolution then invited the Members responsible for the administration of Non-Self-Governing Territories to include, in the information to be transmitted to the Secretary-General under Article 73 e of the Charter, a summary of the extent to which the Universal Declaration of Human Rights was implemented in the Non-Self-Governing Territories under their administration; and requested the Special Committee dealing with this subject to include in its report to the General Assembly such recommendations as it might deem desirable relating to the application in Non-Self-Governing Territories of the principles contained in the Universal Declaration of Human Rights. In the following year, the General Assembly requested that the Administering Members describe "the manner in which human rights, in accordance with the principles set forth in the Universal Declaration of Human Rights, are protected by law, particularly in respect of *(a)* legal principles and procedures; *(b)* basic legislation and its application; *(c)* anti-discrimination legislation.[16] In 1952, the Assembly further recommended to the Members responsible for the administration of such territories "the abolition in those Territories of discriminatory laws and practices contrary to the principles of the Charter and of the Universal Declaration of Human Rights".[17]

The General Assembly, and in certain cases the Security Council, had recourse to the Declaration in various resolutions relating to the racial situation in southern Africa and in similar circumstances involving discrimination on the grounds of race and colonialism. The bulk of these instances will be recorded later in the present publication in the context of the action taken in regard to the various countries and territories concerned. In the following paragraphs only some specific decisions which occurred for the most part in the first years of the activities of the United Nations will be summarized because they are indicative of the development of the authority of the Universal Declaration of Human Rights.

Thus the Declaration was invoked in several decisions of the General Assembly concerning the treatment of people of Indian and Indo-Pakistan origin in South Africa. Repeatedly the Assembly called upon the parties to solve the dispute "in accordance with the purposes and principles of the United Nations Charter and the Universal Declaration of Human Rights".[18]

The General Assembly has had recourse to the Declaration in various decisions concerning Namibia (South West Africa). In 1957, in examining the report of the Committee on South West Africa, it noted with concern that "existing conditions in the Territory of South West Africa and the trend of the administration represent a situation contrary to the Mandates System, the Charter of the United Nations, the Universal Declaration of Human Rights, the advisory opinions of the International Court of Justice and the resolutions of the General Assembly".[19] Similar concern was expressed by the General Assembly in 1959 and 1960 when it noted that the administration of the Territory had been conducted increasingly in a manner contrary to the Mandate, the Charter of the United Nations, the Universal Declaration of Human Rights and the advisory opinions of the International Court of Justice.[20] The Assembly further, in a resolution adopted in 1960 on the same subject, considered that the *apartheid* policy applied in South West Africa was contrary to the terms of the Mandate, the provisions of the Charter of the United Nations and the Universal Declaration of Human Rights.[21] At its twenty-first session in 1966 the General Assembly, convinced that the administration of the Mandated Territory by South Africa had been conducted "in a manner contrary to the Mandate, the Charter of the United Nations and the Universal Declaration of Human Rights", decided that the Mandate was terminated and that South Africa had no other right to administer the Territory.[22]

In 1972, the Security Council was considering a situation which had arisen in Namibia in the field of labour relations. In its resolution 310 (1972),[23] it strongly condemned "the recent repressive measures against the African labourers in Namibia" and called upon the Government of South Africa "to end immediately these repressive

---

[16] See annex to General Assembly resolution 551 (VI) of 7 December 1951.

[17] General Assembly resolution 644 (VII) of 10 December 1952.

[18] General Assembly resolutions 265 (III) of 14 May 1949; 395 (V) of 2 December 1950; 511 (VI) of 12 January 1952; 615 (VII) of 5 December 1952; 719 (VIII) of 11 November 1953; 1179 (XII) of 26 November 1957; 1302 (XIII) of 10 December 1958; 1597 (XV) of 13 April 1961; 1662 (XVI) of 28 November 1961.

[19] General Assembly resolution 1142 B (XII) of 25 October 1957.

[20] General Assembly resolutions 1360 (XIV) of 17 November 1959 and 1568 (XV) of 18 December 1960.

[21] General Assembly resolution 1567 (XV) of 18 December 1960.

[22] General Assembly resolution 2145 (XXI) of 27 October 1966.

[23] Adopted by the Security Council at its 1638th meeting on 4 February 1972 at Addis Ababa by 13 votes to none, with 2 abstentions.

measures and to abolish any labour system which may be in conflict with the basic provisions of the Universal Declaration of Human Rights". In the same resolution, the Security Council further called upon all States whose nationals and corporations were operating in Namibia "to use all available means to ensure that such nationals and corporations conform, in their policies of hiring Namibian workers, to the basic provisions of the Universal Declaration of Human Rights". According to the preamble, the Council decided upon this call, being "mindful of its responsibilities to take necessary action to secure strict compliance with the obligations entered into by States Members under the relevant provisions of the Charter of the United Nations". One Government of a Member State whose nationals and companies of its nationality were operating in Namibia at the time, reported to the Secretary-General that in March 1972 it had sent, to some 40 business firms of its nationality interested in Namibian affairs, the text of Security Council resolution 310 (1972), as well as the text of the Universal Declaration of Human Rights specified in paragraph 5 of that resolution. The letter forwarding those documents stated that the Government concerned supported resolution 310 (1972) and requested the co-operation of the companies in doing everything possible to ensure that any operations in Namibia in which they had an interest were fully consonant with the Declaration. It offered its assistance in any appropriate way in dealing with that problem.[24]

At its fourth session in 1949 the General Assembly considered an item entitled "Discrimination practised by certain States against immigrating labour and in particular against labour recruited from the ranks of refugees". In view of the importance of the principle of non-discrimination embodied in the Universal Declaration of Human Rights, the General Assembly decided in its resolution 315 (IV) of 17 November 1949 to transmit the records of the discussions on the subject to the International Labour Organisation with the request that it should do all in its power to expedite the ratification and application of the relevant International Labour Convention and to promote its observance as regards the social relations of the workers and their families with the inhabitants of the region, so that no offensive distinctions might be established in regard to immigrant labourers and they might enjoy all facilities for accommodation, food, education, recreation and medical assistance, both public and private, which were provided for the community.

With regard to the problem of racial prejudice and religious intolerance, the General Assembly, in 1962, reiterated "its condemnation of all manifestations of racial prejudice and national and religious intolerance as violations of the Charter of the United Nations and of the Universal Declaration of Human Rights".

At its twenty-seventh session, the General Assembly dealt with the exploitation of labour through illicit and clandestine trafficking. In its resolution 2920 (XXVII) of 15 November 1972, the Assembly recalled the provisions of the Universal Declaration of Human Rights and of the International Convention on the Elimination of All Forms of Racial Discrimination.

The General Assembly and the Security Council have repeatedly invoked the Universal Declaration or referred to its principles in their endeavour to put an end to the policy of *apartheid* practised in South Africa. This question is dealt with in detail in another part of this publication. It may suffice here to recall Security Council resolution 182 (1963) of 4 December 1963, in which the Council urgently requested "the Government of the Republic of South Africa to cease forthwith its continued imposition of discriminatory and repressive measures, which are contrary to the principles and purposes of the charter and which are in violation of its obligations as a Member of the United Nations and of the provisions of the Universal Declaration of Human Rights". The General Assembly, in previous decisions,[25] had also considered that the racial policies practised in South Africa were "contrary to the United Nations Charter and the Universal Declaration of Human Rights". In a long series of General Assembly resolutions summarized later in this publication, the General Assembly declared that the practice of *apartheid* and similar practices constituted a crime against humanity.

In resolution 285 (III) of 25 April 1949, the Assembly recommended that one State Member withdraw the measures that prevented its nationals, wives of citizens of other nationalities, from leaving their country of origin with their husbands or in order to join them abroad. In this connexion the Assembly invoked articles 13 and 16 of the Universal Declaration, which provide that everyone has the right to leave any country, including his own, and that men and women of full age have the right to marry without any limitation due to race, nationality or religion. In opposition to this some delegations stated that the matter was exclusively within the domestic jurisdiction of the country concerned.

At its fourteenth session the General Assembly adopted a resolution in which, with reference to a specific territory, it recalled the principles regarding fundamental human rights and freedoms set forth in the Charter and in the Universal Declaration of Human Rights.[26] Delegations opposed to the resolution pointed out that it was contrary to Article 2, paragraph 7, of the Charter. At its sixteenth and twentieth sessions the General Assembly adopted resolutions on the same question in which it reaffirmed its conviction that respect for the principles of the Charter and for the Universal Declaration of Human Rights was essential for the evolution of a peaceful world order based on the rule of law.[27]

---

[24] See *Official Records of the Security Council, Twenty-seventh Year, Supplement for July, August and September 1972*, documents S/10742 and Add.1, annex.

[25] General Assembly resolutions 721 (VIII) of 8 December 1953, and 820 (IX) of 14 December 1954.

[26] General Assembly resolution 1353 (XIV) of 21 October 1959.

[27] General Assembly resolutions 1723 (XVI) of 20 December 1961, and 2079 (XX) of 18 December 1965.

### E. The influence of the Universal Declaration on international treaties

In the International Covenants which the General Assembly adopted on 16 December 1966 the provisions of the Universal Declaration of Human Rights were —with some exceptions— transformed into international conventional law. Independently from the Covenants, the drafting of which occupied the United Nations organs for many years, a considerable number of international conventions were prepared and put into effect after 1948, the purpose of which was to implement rights proclaimed in the Declaration. The text of the preambles of the Conventions often specifically refer to the Declaration or reproduce the relevant provisions thereof.

These Conventions are, in part, of a world-wide character and, in part, of territorially limited application, i.e., of a regional or bilateral character. The Conventions of world-wide application were prepared and adopted by United Nations organs, by conferences convened by the General Assembly or by the Economic and Social Council, or by specialized agencies (the International Labour Organisation and UNESCO). In chronological order these instruments are the following: the Convention relating to the Status of Refugees (1951), with a Protocol approved in 1966, the Equal Remuneration Convention (1951) (ILO), the Convention on the Political Rights of Women (1952), the Convention on the Status of Stateless Persons (1954), the Supplementary Convention on the Abolition of Slavery, the Slave Trade, and Institutions and Practices Similar to Slavery (1956), the Convention on the Nationality of Married Women (1957), the Convention on the Abolition of Forced Labour (1957) (ILO), the Discrimination (Employment and Occupation) Convention (1958) (ILO), the Convention against Discrimination in Education (1960) (UNESCO), with the Protocol of 1962; the Convention on the Reduction of Statelessness (1961), the Convention on Consent to Marriage, Minimum Age for Marriage and Registration of Marriages (1962), the Employment Policy Convention (1964) (ILO) and the International Convention on the Elimination of All Forms of Racial Discrimination (1965).

The Universal Declaration also provided the basis for action in several decisions and recommendations of the Economic and Social Council. In 1955, the Council noted article 23, paragraph 2, of the Universal Declaration of Human Rights, which, referring to all men and women workers, stated that "Everyone, without any discrimination, has the right to equal pay for equal work", and recommended that Governments give practical effect to the principle of equal pay for equal work.[28] In another resolution, the Economic and Social Council recommended to Governments that they take the necessary steps to remove legal and other obstacles impeding the access of married women to public services and functions and the exercise by them of such functions. In doing so, the Council invoked article 21 of the Universal Declaration of Human Rights, which provides that everyone has the right to take part in the government of his country and the right to equal access to public service in his country.[29] The Convention on the Non-Applicability of Statutory Limitations to War Crimes and Crimes against Humanity (1968) does not expressly refer to the Universal Declaration but more generally to the protection of human rights.

The European Convention for the Protection of Human Rights and Fundamental Freedoms, signed at Rome on 4 November 1950, states in its preamble that it was agreed to by the States Parties in order "to take the first steps for the collective enforcement of certain of the rights stated in the Universal Declaration". The Universal Declaration is listed as the first of the considerations which led the signatory Governments to conclude the Convention. As far as substance is concerned, the European Convention contains detailed provisions on most of the civil and political rights set forth in the Universal Declaration of Human Rights. Protocols to the Convention agreed to in 1952 and in 1963 give effect to a number of additional rights proclaimed in the Declaration.

The American Convention on Human Rights (Pact of San José, Costa Rica), signed at San José on 22 November 1969, states in its preamble that the American States signatory to the Convention reaffirm their intention to consolidate in the western hemisphere, within the framework of democratic institutions, a system of personal liberty and social justice based on respect for the essential rights of man. The signatory States consider that the principles to which the Convention gives effect have been set forth in the Charter of the Organization of American States and in the American Declaration of the Rights and Duties of Man and that they have been reaffirmed and refined in other international instruments, world-wide as well as regional in scope. The signatory States reiterate that in accordance with the Universal Declaration of Human Rights, the ideal of free men enjoying freedom from fear and want can be achieved only if conditions are created whereby everyone may enjoy his economic, social and cultural rights, as well as his civil and political rights.

In the Charter of the Organization of African Unity done at Addis Ababa on 25 May 1963, the Heads of African States and Governments agreed to the Charter of the Organization of African Unity, "persuaded that the Charter of the United Nations and the Universal Declaration of Human Rights, to the principles of which we reaffirm our adherence, provide a solid foundation for peaceful and positive co-operation among States". Pursuant to article II of the Charter of the Organization of African Unity, it is one of the purposes of the Organization to promote international co-operation with due regard to the Charter of the United Nations and the Universal Declaration of Human Rights.

In the Trusteeship Agreement with Italy concerning Somaliland (1950) the Administering Authority undertook to administer the Territory of Somaliland under Italian Administration in accordance with the Trusteeship Agreement, which included an annex containing a Declaration of Constitutional Principles. The annex provided that the Administering Authority should accept the

---

[28] Economic and Social Council resolution 587 (XX) of 3 August 1955.

[29] Economic and Social Council resolution 771 (XXX) of 25 July 1960.

Universal Declaration of Human Rights as standard of achievement for the Territory.

In the Peace Treaty with Japan of 1951, Japan for its part declared its intention to strive to realize the objectives of the Universal Declaration of Human Rights and the Allied Powers welcomed this intention of Japan.

In the Memorandum of Understanding between the Governments of Italy, the United Kingdom, the United States and Yugoslavia regarding the Free Territory of Trieste, initialled in London on 5 October 1954, the Italian and Yugoslav Governments agreed to enforce the Special Statute contained in the annex to the Memorandum. In the Special Statute it is provided that in the administration of their respective areas, the Italian and Yugoslav authorities shall act in accordance with the principles of the Universal Declaration of Human Rights, so that all inhabitants of the two areas of the Territory without discrimination may fully enjoy the fundamental rights and freedoms laid down in the Declaration.

### F. The influence of the Universal Declaration on national constitutions, municipal laws and court decisions

Evidence of the impact of the Universal Declaration may be found in texts of various national constitutions which were enacted after the adoption of the Universal Declaration.[30] Several of these constitutions expressly refer, either in their preambles or in their operative provisions, to the Universal Declaration. In addition, many other constitutions contain detailed provisions on a number of human rights, most of which are inspired by, or often modelled on, the text of the articles of the Declaration. Several constitutions drafted with the assistance of United Nations experts, such as those of Libya (1951) and Eritrea as an autonomous unit of Ethiopia (1952), show the marked influence of the Universal Declaration.

In the period between 1948 and 1964 the Constitutions of the following States had expressly referred to the Universal Declaration. The peoples of Algeria (1963), Burundi (1962), Cameroon (1960), Chad (1960), Democratic Republic of the Congo (1964), Republic of the Congo (1963), Dahomey (1964), Gabon (1961), Guinea (1958), Ivory Coast (1960), Madagascar (1959), Mali (1960), Mauritania (1961), Niger (1960), Senegal (1963), Sudanese Republic (later Mali) (1959), Togo (1963) and Upper Volta (1960), solemnly affirmed their devotion and adherence to the principles and ideals of the Universal Declaration. The Constitution of Somalia of 1960, in its article 7, provides that the Republic of Somalia shall comply, in so far as applicable, with the Universal Declaration of Human Rights. The Constitution of Rwanda of 1962, in its article 13, expressly provides that fundamental freedoms as set forth in the Universal Declaration of Human Rights shall be guaranteed to all citizens.

In more recent years the following developments have occurred:

[30] For the text of the human rights provisions contained in these constitutions see the volumes of the *Yearbook on Human Rights* for 1950-1969.

In the preamble to the Constitution of the Democratic Republic of the Congo, now Zaire, of 1967, the Congolese people proclaimed their adherence to the Universal Declaration of Human Rights.

The preamble to the Constitution of the Republic of Dahomey of 31 March 1968 states: "We, the People of Dahomey . . . proclaim our adherence to the principles of democracy and human rights as set out in the Declaration of the Rights of Man and of the Citizen of 1789, the Universal Declaration of 1948, and the Charter of the United Nations, and as guaranteed by this Constitution".

In 1970 a Charter of the Presidential Council of the Republic of Dahomey was proclaimed in which the political leaders of Dahomey reaffirmed Dahomey's attachment to the principles of democracy and human rights as defined in the Declaration of the Rights of Man and of the Citizen of 1789, the Universal Declaration of 1948, and the United Nations Charter.

Article 3 of the Constitution of the Republic of Equatorial Guinea of 1968 provides that the State shall recognize and guarantee the human rights and freedoms set forth in the Universal Declaration of Human Rights and shall proclaim that the freedoms of conscience and religion, association, assembly, speech, residence and domicile, and the right to property, education and decent working conditions are to be respected.

The Constitution of the Republic of Upper Volta of 1970 provides in its preamble that the People of the Upper Volta solemnly proclaim their adherence to the principles of democracy and of human rights, as set out in the Declaration of the Rights of Man and of the Citizen of 1789 and in the Universal Declaration of Human Rights.

In the years between 1949 and 1971 Constitutions of the following States were enacted which, although they do not expressly refer to the Universal Declaration, were clearly inspired by its provisions and very often reproduce its phraseology: Federal Republic of Germany (1949), Cyprus, Nigeria (1960), Sierra Leone (1961), Jamaica, Morocco, Tanganyika, Trinidad and Tobago, Uganda (1962), Dominican Republic, Yugoslavia, Zanzibar (1963), Afghanistan, Central African Republic, Haiti, Malawi, Malta, Syria (Provisional Constitution), United Arab Republic (1964), Gambia, Guatemala, Honduras, Romania, Singapore (1965), Bolivia, Brazil, Ecuador, Guyana and Nigeria (1967), Mauritius and Nauru (1968), Ghana, Kenya, Libya, provisional Constitution of Syria (1969), Fiji, the Gambia, Iraq and Madagascar (1970), Bulgaria, the Arab Republic of Egypt, Mexico (the organic law of the Territory de la Baja California Sur), Yugoslavia (amendments to various articles of the Constitution) (1971).

The impact of the Declaration in the sphere of municipal law can be found in a number of laws and decrees enacted in various countries. In 1951 Paraguay adopted an Act (No. 94) to protect scientific, literary and artistic works and to establish a public register of intellectual rights. The preamble of the Act cites article 27, paragraph 2, of the Universal Declaration which provides: "Everyone has the right to the protection of the moral and material interests resulting from any scientific, literary or artistic production of which he is the author".[31]

The Provincial Legislature of Ontario, Canada, adopted an Act to promote fair employment practices in 1951 and an Act to promote fair accommodations practices in 1954. The purpose of both was to eliminate any discrimination "because of race, creed, colour, nationality, ancestry or place of origin". The preamble of each declares that the act is "in accord with the Universal Declaration of Human Rights as proclaimed by the United Nations".[32]

The Government of Argentina issued a legislative decree (No. 1664) in 1955, which declares in its preamble that provisions purporting to deprive anyone of his nationality as a measure of political persecution are contrary to human rights as proclaimed by the General Assembly of the United Nations.[33]

The Government of Bolivia issued a legislative decree (No. 3937) in 1955 to establish a national system of education. In its preamble the decree reaffirms the principle of equality of opportunity for all Bolivians, without any discrimination, and declares that national education shall be inspired by the Universal Declaration of Human Rights.[34]

Panama enacted a law (No. 25) in 1956 to implement article 21 of its Constitution, which prohibits discrimination on account of birth, race, social origin, sex, religion or political opinion. In its preamble the law says that any discrimination on account of colour or race is "a flagrant violation" of article 21 of the National Constitution and "of the Universal Declaration of Human Rights adopted by the General Assembly of the United Nations on 10 December 1948".[35]

The Government of Costa Rica promulgated an Act (No. 2694) in 1960 prohibiting all forms of discrimination in employment. In paragraph 4 of its preamble reference is made to "the Universal Declaration of Human Rights, proclaimed by the United Nations General Assembly".[36]

In the Act of Dominican Reconciliation of 31 August 1965, the provisional Government of the Dominican Republic pledged itself to respect and to enforce respect for the human rights and public liberties set forth in the American Declaration of the Rights of Man of the Organization of American States and in the Universal Declaration of Human Rights of the United Nations.

In 1968 the Lieutenant-Governor and Legislative Assembly of the Canadian Province of Prince Edward Island enacted a Statute, which may be cited as the Human Rights code, the preamble of which contains among others the following paragraphs:

> "*Whereas* recognition of the inherent dignity and the equal and inalienable rights of all members of the human family is the foundation of freedom; justice and peace in the world and is in accord with the Universal Declaration of Human Rights as proclaimed by the United Nations; and
>
> "*Whereas* 1968 has been proclaimed by the General Assembly of the United Nations as International Year for Human Rights and it is fitting that the aforementioned principle be reaffirmed by the enactment of a measure whereby the rights of the individual may be safeguarded."

The Declaration or its individual articles have been invoked with varying effect in judicial proceedings and cited in a number of judicial decisions and opinions.

The Universal Declaration of Human Rights has been referred to by judges of the International Court of Justice, in the following instances:

In the Colombian-Peruvian asylum case, Judge Azevedo, in his dissenting opinion, invoked the Declaration in support of the right of asylum which is set forth in article 14 of the Declaration;[37]

In the Anglo-Iranian Oil Company case (jurisdiction), Judge Levi Carneiro quoted article 17 of the Universal Declaration (Right to own property);[38]

In the Nottebohm case, Mr. Guggenheim, Judge *ad hoc*, in his dissenting opinion, referred to the basic principle embodied in article 15, paragraph (1) of the Universal Declaration of Human Rights, according to which everyone has the right to a nationality;[39]

In his dissenting opinion in the South West Africa cases, Second Phase, Judge Tanaka said that the Universal Declaration of Human Rights, although not binding in itself, constituted evidence of the interpretation and application of the relevant Charter provisions.[40]

In regard to the Advisory Opinion on the Legal Consequences for States of the Continued Presence of South Africa in Namibia,[41] Vice-President Ammoun, in his separate Opinion, observed that the Advisory Opinion of the Court takes judicial notice of the Universal Declaration of Human Rights. He added that "in the case of certain of the Declaration's provisions, attracted by the conduct of South Africa it would have been an improvement to have dealt in terms with their comminatory nature, which is implied in paragraphs 130 and 131 (referred to above) of the Opinion by the references to their violation". He also said that it was not by mere chance that in article 1 of the Universal Declaration of Human Rights there stands, so worded, this primordial principle or axiom: "All human beings are born free and equal in dignity and rights" [42] Judge Ammoun's statement of the Court having taken judicial notice of the Universal

---

[31] *Yearbook on Human Rights*, 1951.
[32] *Ibid.*, 1951 and 1954.
[33] *Ibid.*, 1955.
[34] *Ibid.*, 1955.
[35] *Ibid.*, 1956.
[36] *Ibid.*, 1962.

[37] *Colombian-Peruvian asylum case, Judgement of November 20th, 1950 : I.C.J. Reports 1950*, p. 339.
[38] *Anglo-Iranian Oil Co. case (Jurisdiction), Judgement of July 22nd, 1952 : I.C.J. Reports 1952*, p. 168.
[39] *Nottebohm case (second phase), Judgement of April 6th, 1955: I.C.J. Reports 1955*, p. 63.
[40] *South West Africa (second phase), Judgement, I.C.J. Reports 1966*, pp. 288 and 293.
[41] *Legal Consequences for States of the Continued Presence of South Africa in Namibia (South West Africa) notwithstanding Security Council Resolution 276 (1970), Advisory Opinion, I.C.J. Reports, 1971*, p. 16.
[42] *Ibid.*, pp. 76-77.

Declaration is a reference to paragraph 92 on page 46 of the Advisory Opinion, in which the Court said that the terms of the preamble and operative part of General Assembly resolution 2145 (XXI), by which the South African Mandate for South West Africa was terminated, leave no doubt as to the character of the resolution. In the preamble the General Assembly had declared itself "convinced that the administration of the Mandated Territory has been conducted in a manner contrary" to the two basic international instruments directly imposing obligations upon South Africa, the Mandate and the Charter of the United Nations, as well as to the Universal Declaration of Human Rights.

At the level of national courts the Universal Declaration has been referred to in: *Fujii* v. *State of California* (California District Court of Appeals, 1950); in *Wilson* v. *Hacker* (New York Supreme Court, 1950); in *Lincoln Union* v. *Northwestern Company* and *American Federation of Labor* v. *American Sash and Door Company* (Supreme Court of the United States, 1949); in *Public Prosecutor* v. *F.A.V.A.* (Penal Chamber of the Supreme Court of the Netherlands, 1951); in *Borovski* v. *Commissioner of Immigration and Director of Prisons* and *Mejoff* v. *Director of Prisons* (Supreme Court of the Philippines, 1951); in several decisions (1951, 1952, 1954, 1956) rendered by the Civil Court of Courtrai (Belgium); in a ruling (1954) of the Court of Taranto (Italy); in *Soc. Roy Export at Charlie Chaplin* v. *Soc. Le Film Rayée Richebé* (Court of Appeal of Paris (France) (1960), in *Israel Film Studies Ltd.* v. *Films Inspection Board* (Supreme Court of Israel, 1962), *in Gold* v. *Minister of Interior* (Supreme Court of Israel, 1962), in *The Queen* v. *Liyanage* (Supreme Court of Ceylon, 1963) and in a decision (1964) handed down by the Milan (Italy) Court of Appeal (*Foro Italiano*, 1965, II, 122 pp.), and in the judgement of the Federal Constitutional Court of the Federal Republic of Germany of 15 December 1965 (Bverfge. 19, page 342, NJW 1966), which refers to the Universal Declaration of Human Rights and to the European Convention for the Protection of Human Rights and Fundamental Freedoms.

### G. Publicity for the Universal Declaration

In resolution 217 D (III), adopted on the day of adoption of the Universal Declaration itself, the General Assembly, through requests addressed to Governments of Member States, to the Secretary-General, to the specialized agencies and to non-governmental organizations, made arrangements for publicity to be given to the Declaration and for its dissemination. Similar arrangements for the publicity of important United Nations pronouncements and instruments in the human rights field were also made in regard to later documents, such as the Declaration on the Granting of Independence to Colonial Countries and Peoples (resolution 1514 (XV)), the United Nations Declaration on the Elimination of All Forms of Racial Discrimination (resolution 1904 (XVIII)), the International Convention for the Elimination of All Forms of Racial Discrimination, adopted by resolution 2106 A (XX) of 1965, and in regard to the Covenants on Human Rights.

The Secretary-General has endeavoured to have the Declaration and related documents disseminated as widely as possible. Texts of the Universal Declaration have been published and distributed in 80 languages. It has also been publicized through use of United Nations publications, posters, discussion guides, film strips, radio and television programmes, photo features, picture presentations, exhibits and numerous special events.

Each year since 1951 the United Nations and interested States and organizations have, as invited by the General Assembly in resolution 434 (V) of 4 December 1950, designated 10 December as Human Rights Day and have commemorated on that day the anniversary of the proclamation of the Universal Declaration. Special arrangements were made to commemorate the tenth, fifteenth, twentieth and twenty-fifth anniversaries in 1958, 1963, 1968 and 1973 respectively. The year 1968, the twentieth anniversary of the adoption of the Universal Declaration, was designated by resolution 1961 (XVIII) of 12 December 1963 as the International Year for Human Rights. Comprehensive arrangements to commemorate the twentieth anniversary were made, including the convening of the International Conference on Human Rights, Teheran, 1968. At the twenty-sixth session in 1971, the General Assembly expressed its desire to mark, in 1973, the twenty-fifth anniversary of the Universal Declaration in a manner which would fit the occasion and serve the cause of human rights. At its twenty-seventh session in 1972, the General Assembly reaffimed its adherence to the principles, values and ideals contained in the Universal Declaration of Human Rights and took measures for the appropriate commemoration of the twenty-fifth anniversary.

## III. THE INTERNATIONAL BILL OF RIGHTS: THE INTERNATIONAL COVENANT ON ECONOMIC, SOCIAL AND CULTURAL RIGHTS, THE INTERNATIONAL COVENANT ON CIVIL AND POLITICAL RIGHTS AND THE OPTIONAL PROTOCOL THERETO

The comprehensive undertaking started by the United Nations at the very beginning of its existence, namely, the enactment of an international bill of human rights, was completed only on 16 December 1966 when the General Assembly adopted the two Covenants and the Optional Protocol. In the present document only a few of the significant aspects of the Covenants and of the measures of implementation will be described.

### A. The substantive provisions of the two Covenants

In the International Covenant on Economic, Social and Cultural Rights each party undertakes to take steps, to the maximum of its available resources individually and through international assistance and co-operation, with a view to achieving progressively the full realization of the rights recognized in the Covenant. For this purpose it will use all appropriate means, including, particularly, legislative measures (article 2, paragraph 1, of the International Covenant on Economic, Social and Cultural Rights). In the International Covenant on Civil and Political Rights each State party undertakes to respect and to ensure to all individuals within its territory and subject to its jurisdiction the rights recognized in that Covenant (article 2, paragraph 1, of the International Covenant on Civil and Political Rights). As was stated in this respect, the obligations undertaken by the parties to the International Covenant on Civil and Political Rights are, by and large, meant to be implemented immediately upon ratification; and the rights set forth in the International Covenant on Economic, Social and Cultural Rights are to be implemented progressively.

Generally the two Covenants contain provisions on the rights set forth in the Declaration. There are, however, exceptions. Certain of the rights proclaimed in the Universal Declaration are not reflected in either of the two Covenants; on the other hand, the Covenants deal also with such rights as were not proclaimed in the Declaration.

Examples of rights set forth in the Declaration and not reflected in the Covenants are the right of everyone to own property alone as well as in association with others, and the prohibition of arbitrary deprivation of property (article 17 of the Declaration); the right of everyone to seek and to enjoy in other countries asylum from persecution (article 14 of the Declaration); and the right of everyone to a nationality and the right not to be arbitrarily deprived of one's nationality (article 15 of the Declaration). In regard to the right to a nationality, attention should be drawn, however, to article 24, paragraph 3, of the International Covenant on Civil and Political Rights, according to which every child has the right to acquire a nationality.

A right regulated in both Covenants and not contained in the Universal Declaration [1] is the right of peoples to self-determination and the related rights codified in article 1 of either Covenant, including the right of peoples freely to dispose of their natural wealth and resources. A more detailed analysis of United Nations measures in the matter of self-determination of nations and peoples will be found in chapter IV of the present publication.

While the Universal Declaration of Human Rights does not deal with the question of minorities, the General Assembly having stated in resolution 217 C (III) that it was difficult to adopt a uniform solution of the complex and delicate question which has special aspects in each State in which it arises, article 27 of the International Covenant on Civil and Political Rights provides that in those States in which ethnic, religious or linguistic minorities exist, persons belonging to such minorities shall not be denied the right, in community with the other members of their group, to enjoy their own culture, to profess and practice their own religion or to use their own language.

Owing to the fact that many of the provisions of the Covenants are more detailed than the provisions of the Declaration, the Covenants deal with aspects of matters otherwise covered by the Declaration which are not as such expressly mentioned in the Declaration. While, for example, the Declaration proclaims the right to form and to join trade unions, the regulation of the same problem in the International Covenant on Economic, Social and Cultural Rights is more detailed and specifically requires States parties to undertake to ensure the right to strike provided that it is exercised in conformity with the laws of the particular country (article 8, paragraph 1 (*d*), of the International Covenant on Economic, Social and Cultural Rights).

In the International Covenant on Economic, Social and Cultural Rights, States Parties recognize the right to work (article 6), the right to the enjoyment of just and favourable conditions of work (article 7), the right to form and to join trade unions (article 8), the right to social security including social insurance (article 9), the protection of the family, mothers, children and young persons (article 10), the right to an adequate standard

[1] See, however, *Official Records of the General Assembly, Third Session, Part I,* document A/784.

of living (article 11), the right to the enjoyment of the highest attainable standard of physical and mental health (article 12), the right of everyone to education (articles 13 and 14) and the right to take part in cultural life (article 15). Some of these rights are set forth in the covenant in considerable detail. In regard to the question of making available, e.g., compulsory primary education free of charge, States parties undertake, within two years, to work out and adopt a detailed plan of action for the progressive implementation within a reasonable number of years to be fixed in the plan of the principle of compulsory education free of charge for all (article 14).

Some of the provisions of the International Covenant on Civil and Political Rights deal with problems related to those regulated in the other Covenant. Examples are article 22 on freedom of association which also regulates the right to form and join trade unions and therefore deals with a matter also covered by article 8 of the International Covenant on Economic, Social and Cultural Rights, and articles 23 and 24 of the International Covenant on Civil and Political Rights, which deal with family, marriage and children and correspond to article 10 of the other Covenant.

The bulk of the substantive provisions of the International Covenant on Civil and Political Rights is devoted to the traditional civil and political rights as set forth in articles 3 to 13, 16 and 18 to 21 of the Universal Declaration. The International Covenant on Civil and Political Rights affords protection to the right to life (article 6), prohibits torture or cruel, inhuman or degrading treatment or punishment (article 7), prohibits slavery, the slave trade, servitude and compulsory labour (article 8), prohibits arbitrary arrest or detention (article 9); provides that all persons deprived of their liberty shall be treated with humanity (article 10); and that no one shall be imprisoned merely on the grounds of inability to fulfil a contractual obligation (article 11). The Covenant further provides for freedom of movement (article 12) and places limitations on the expulsion of aliens lawfully in the territory of a State Party (article 13). The Covenant provides in considerable detail for equality before the courts and tribunals and for guarantees in criminal and civil procedures (article 14). The Covenant prohibits retroactive criminal legislation (article 15), stipulates for the right of everyone to recognition everywhere as a person before the law (article 16) and prohibits arbitrary or unlawful interference with privacy, family, home or correspondence and unlawful attacks on honour and reputation (article 17). The Covenant states further the right to freedom of thought, conscience and religion (article 18) and to freedom of expression (article 19). It provides that propaganda for war and any advocacy of national, racial or religious hatred that constitutes incitement to discrimination, hostility or violence shall be prohibited by law (article 20). The Covenant recognizes in articles 21 and 22 the right of peaceful assembly and the right to freedom of association including the right to form and join trade unions. It stipulates that every citizen shall have the right and the opportunity to take part in the conduct of public affairs, to vote and to be elected at genuine periodic elections by universal and equal suffrage held by secret ballot and to have access on general terms of equality to public service in his country (article 25). Article 26 of the Covenant states that all persons are equal before the law and are entitled without any discrimination to equal protection of the law. The law shall also guarantee protection against discrimination.

The rights set forth in the Covenants are not absolute and are subject to limitations. The International Covenant on Civil and Political Rights, in particular, defines the admissible limitations or restrictions of the rights set forth in it. While the formulation of the limitations differs as far as details are concerned from article to article, it can be said that the Covenant, by and large, provides that the rights shall not be subject to any restrictions except those which are specified by law, are necessary to protect national security, public order *(ordre public)*, public health or morals or the rights and freedom of others (see articles 12, 14, 18, 19, 21 and 22 of the International Covenant on Civil and Political Rights). Some of the rights, however, are not subject to any specific restrictions. Examples are the right to freedom of thought, conscience and religion, as distinct from the right to manifest religion or belief, and the right to hold opinions without interference as distinct from the right to freedom of expression.

In time of public emergency which threatens the life of the nation and the existence of which is officially proclaimed the States Parties to the International Covenant on Civil and Political Rights may take measures derogating from the obligations under the Covenant to the extent strictly required by the exigencies of the situation provided that such measures are not inconsistent with the other obligations under international law and do not involve discrimination solely on the ground of race, colour, sex, language, religion or social origin. However, some of the rights are considered by the Covenant to be so essential that no derogation from them may be made even in time of public emergency. These rights are the right to life (article 6), the right not to be subjected to torture or to cruel, inhuman or degrading treatment or punishment (article 7), the prohibition of slavery and servitude (article 8, paragraphs 1 and 2), the prohibition of imprisonment merely on the ground of inability to fulfil a contractual obligation (article 11), the principle *nulla poena sine lege* (article 15), the right of everyone to recognition as a person before the law (article 16) and freedom of thought, conscience and religion (article 18).

### B. The measures of implementation of the two Covenants

The two Covenants contain measures of implementation, i.e., arrangements for the international supervision of the application of their substantive provisions. The measures of implementation of the International Covenant on Economic, Social and Cultural Rights consist in a system of reporting. States parties undertake to submit reports on the measures that they have adopted and the progress made in achieving the observance of the rights recognized in the Covenant. These reports are transmitted to the Economic and Social Council for consideration. The Council may transmit the reports to the Commission on Human Rights for study and general recommendation or, as appropriate, for information. The Covenant also provides for participation of the specialized agencies in these procedures in regard to matters falling within their respective responsibilities. States parties and the specialized agencies concerned may submit to the Council comments on any general recommendations by the Commission on Human Rights. The Economic and Social Council may submit to the General Assembly reports with recommendations of a general nature and a summary of the information it has received on the measures taken and the progress made in achieving generral observance of the rights recognized in the Covenant. In the Covenant, States parties agree that international action for the achievement of the rights recognized in it includes such methods as the conclusion of conventions, the adoption of recommendations and furnishing of technical assistance and the holding of regional meetings for the purpose of consultation and study. The International Covenant on Economic, Social and Cultural Rights also provides that nothing in it shall be interpreted as impairing the provisions of the Charter and of the constitutions of the specialized agencies, which define the respective responsibilities of the various organs of the United Nations and of the specialized agencies. It provides further that nothing in it shall be interpreted as impairing the inherent right of all peoples to enjoy and utilize fully and freely their natural wealth and resources (articles 16-25 of the International Covenant on Economic, Social and Cultural Rights). It might be added in this connexion that identical saving clauses concerning the Charter of the United Nations, the constitutions of the specialized agencies and the right of all peoples to enjoy and utilize fully and freely their natural wealth and resources are also contained in the International Covenant on Civil and Political Rights (articles 46-47).

The International Covenant on Civil and Political Rights also provides for a reporting procedure as the main method of international implementation. In this regard, the principal difference between the two Covenants is that under the International Covenant on Economic, Social and Cultural Rights the Economic and Social Council, assisted by the Commission on Human Rights and by the specialized agencies, is the instrumentality of implementation; but under the International Covenant on Civil and Political Rights the function is performed by the Human Rights Committee, an organ established by the States parties to the Covenant. The Committee consists of 18 members elected by the States parties and serving in their personal capacity. The States parties to the International Covenant on Civil and Political Rights undertake to submit reports on the measures they have adopted which give effect to the rights recognized in the Covenant and on the progress made in the enjoyment of those rights. These reports are submitted to the Human Rights Committee, the task of which is to study the reports submitted by the States parties and to transmit its reports and such general comments as it may consider appropriate to the States parties. The Committee may also transmit these comments to the Economic and Social Council, along with the copies of the reports which it has received from States parties. The States parties have the right to submit observations on any comments that may be made (articles 28, 29 and 40 of the International Covenant on Civil and Political Rights).

In addition to the reporting system, the International Covenant on Civil and Political Rights also provides for a system of inter-State proceedings in matters concerning the application of the Covenant and for the conciliation of differences arising in this regard. Under the Covenant this system is optional. It operates only if a State party declares that it recognizes the competence of the Human Rights Committee to receive and consider communications to the effect that a State party claims that another State party is not fulfilling its obligations under the Covenant. This optional system operates only on a reciprocal basis. Only a State which has made a declaration recognizing the competence of the Human Rights Committee in regard to itself is authorized to set the procedure in motion with regard to another State party which has also recognized this competence of the Committee. Moreover, the system will start operating only when ten States parties have made declarations recognizing the competence of the Committee in regard to State-to-State proceedings.

If these general conditions are complied with, a State party to the Covenant may, if it considers that another State party is not giving effect to the provisions of the Covenant, bring the matter to the attention of that State party. The receiving State shall afford the State which sent the communication an explanation or any other statement clarifying the matter. If the matter is not adjusted to the satisfaction of both States parties concerned within six months either State has the right to refer the matter to the Human Rights Committee. It is a condition for any action on the part of the Committee that all available domestic remedies have been invoked and exhausted in the matter in conformity with the generally recognized principles of international law. This is not the rule where the application of the remedies is unreasonably prolonged. The task of the Committee is to make available its good offices to the States parties concerned with a view to a friendly solution of the matter on the basis of respect for human rights and fundamental freedoms as recognized in the Covenant. The examination of State-to-State communications of the described type takes place in closed meetings of the Committee. The States concerned have the right to be represented when the matter is being considered in the Committee and to make oral and written submissions. If a solution is reached the Committee confines its report to a brief statement of the facts and of the solution reached. If a solution based on respect for human rights and fundamental freedoms as recognized in the Covenants is not reached, the Committee confines its report to a brief statement of the facts. The written submissions and the record of the oral submissions by the parties concerned are attached to the report which is communicated to the States parties (article 41).

The Covenant provides for the establishment of an additional organ: if a matter referred to the Committee is not resolved to the satisfaction of the parties concerned, the Human Rights Committee may, with the prior consent of the States parties concerned, appoint an *ad hoc* Conciliation Commission. The Commission shall consist of five persons acceptable to the States parties concerned.

if the States parties fail to reach agreement on all or part of the composition of the Commission, the Human Rights Committee is authorized to fill the vacancies on the Commission by electing the necessary number of members from among its own (the Committee's) members by secret ballot, by a two-thirds majority vote. The main task of the *ad hoc* Conciliation Commission is to make available its good offices to the States parties concerned with a view to an amicable solution on the basis of respect for the Covenant. If such a solution is not reached, the Commission's report shall embody its findings on all questions of fact as well as its views on the possibilities of an amicable solution of the matter (article 42).

The Human Rights Committee is to submit to the General Assembly through the Economic and Social Council an annual report on its activities (article 45).

## C. The Optional Protocol to the International Covenant on Civil and Political Rights

This Protocol provides, as far as the States parties to the Protocol are concerned, for a third method of implementation of the International Covenant on Civil and Political Rights, additional to the reporting procedure and the system of State-to-State communication and conciliation. A State party to the Covenant that becomes a party to the Protocol recognizes the competence of the Committee to receive and consider communications from individuals subject to its jurisdiction who claim to be victims of a violation by that State Party of any of the rights set forth in the Covenant. The right to communicate with the Committee is given to individuals claiming to be victims of a violation, irrespective of their nationality or lack of it. The right to address communications to the Committee is subject to the exhaustion by the individual concerned of all available domestic remedies. A communication which is anonymous or which the Human Rights Committee considers to be an abuse of the right of submission of such communications or to be incompatible with the provisions of the Covenant is inadmissible. The Committee is called upon to bring any communication submitted to it under the Protocol to the attention of the State party concerned. The receiving State undertakes to submit to the Committee written explanations or statenents clarifying the matter and the remedy, if any, that may have been taken by that State. The Committee considers communications received under the Protocol in the light of all written information made available to it by the individual and by the State party concerned. The Protocol provides that the Human Rights Committee shall not consider any communication unless it has ascertained that the matter is not being examined under another procedure of international investigation or settlement. The rule of exhaustion of all available domestic remedies applies under the Protocol in the same way as it applies under the Covenant. The Committee examines communications under the Protocol in closed meetings.

As a result of its consideration of communications, the Commission shall forward its views to the State party concerned and to the individual.

## D. Action subsequent to the adoption of the Covenants and the Optional Protocol

When the General Assembly adopted and opened for signature, ratification and accession the two Covenants and the Optional Protocol, it expressed the hope that the Covenants and the Optional Protocol would be signed and ratified or acceded to without delay and would come into force at an early date (resolution 2200 A (XXI) of 16 December 1966).

At its twenty-second session the General Assembly adopted a resolution (2337 (XXII) of 18 December 1967), in which, desiring to accelerate the ratification of and accession to the Covenants and the Optional Protocol and convinced that the principles and purposes of the United Nations Charter would be greatly enhanced by the coming into force of the Covenants and the Protocol, it invited States eligible to become parties to hasten their ratification of accession to these instruments.

At the twenty-sixth session, the General Assembly, desirous of making all possible efforts that might be appropriate to assist in hastening the process of ratification and, if possible in bringing into force the Covenants and the Protocol by the twenty-fifth anniversary of the proclamation of the Universal Declaration in 1973, recommended that Member States should give special attention to possibilities of accelerating as fast as possible the internal procedures that would lead to the ratification of the Covenants and of the Optional Protocol (General Assembly resolution 2788 (XXVI) of 6 December 1971). Similarly at the twenty-seventh session the General Assembly adopted unanimously a resolution (3025 (XXVII) of 18 December 1972) in which it expressed the hope that Member States would find it possible to take appropriate action with a view to accelerating the steps that would enable them to deposit their instrument of ratification or accession if possible by 10 December 1973.

# IV. UNITED NATIONS MEASURES AND PROCEDURAL ARRANGEMENTS AS REGARDS THE RIGHT TO SELF-DETERMINATION

## A. The right of peoples and nations to self-determination as a fundamental human right and measures taken by the United Nations with regard to that right

One of the purposes of the United Nations, as defined in Article 1 of the Charter, is to "develop friendly relations among nations based on respect for the principle of equal rights and self-determination of peoples". Article 55 of the Charter, which deals with international economic and social co-operation, calls for the creation of conditions of stability and well-being which are necessary for peaceful and friendly relations among nations based on the principle of equal rights and self-determination of peoples. The Universal Declaration of Human Rights does not mention self-determination specifically. The right to self-determination, however, has been recognized by the United Nations in several decisions of its organs, it has been included in the International Covenants on Human Rights and it has frequently formed the basis for action taken by the United Nations. An attempt is made in the following paragraphs to give a factual presentation of the most significant decisions taken by the United Nations in connexion with the question of self-determination, its development, its specific consideration by the *ad hoc* bodies entrusted with the problem, and in relation to the International Covenants on Human Rights.

## B. The recognition of self-determination as a human right

At its fifth session, in 1950, the General Assembly, considering certain policy questions related to the draft covenant on human rights, recognized the right of peoples and nations to self-determination as a fundamental human right. In its resolution 421 D (V) of 4 December 1950, it called upon the Economic and Social Council to request the Commission on Human Rights "to study ways and means which would ensure the right of peoples and nations to self-determination".

At its sixth session, the General Assembly, in its resolution 545 (VI) of 5 February 1952, decided to include in the International Covenants on Human Rights "an article on the right of all peoples and nations to self-determination in reaffirmation of the principle enunciated in the Charter of the United Nations". The General Assembly further decided:

> "This article shall be drafted in the following terms: 'All peoples shall have the right of self-determination', and shall stipulate that all States, including those having responsibility for the administration of Non-Self-Governing Territories, should promote the realization of that right, in conformity with the Purposes and Principles of the United Nations, and that States having responsibility for the administration of Non-Self-Governing Territories should promote the realization of that right in relation to the peoples of such Territories".[1]

At its seventh session, in 1952, the General Assembly adopted a resolution (637 (VII) of 16 December 1952), entitled "The right of Peoples and nations to self-determination". Recognizing that the right of peoples and nations to self-determination was a prerequisite to the full enjoyment of all fundamental human rights and that every Member of the United Nations should respect this right, the General Assembly adopted a series of recommendations. It recommended to all States Members of the United Nations (*a*) that they should "uphold the principle of self-determination of all peoples and nations", and (*b*) that they should "recognize and promote the realization of the right of self-determination of the peoples of Non-Self-Governing and Trust Territories which are under their administration and shall facilitate the exercise of this right by the peoples of such Territories according to the principles and spirit of the Charter of the United Nations in regard to each Territory and to the freely expressed wishes of the peoples concerned, the wishes of the people being ascertained through plebiscites or other recognized democratic means, preferably under the auspices of the United Nations". To the Member States responsible for the administration of Non-Self-Governing Territories it recommended that they should "take practical steps, pending the realization of the right of self-determination and in preparation thereof, to ensure the direct participation of the indigenous populations in the legislative and executive organs of government of those Territories, and to prepare them for complete self-government or independence". The General Assembly requested the Economic and Social Council to ask the Commission on Human Rights to continue preparing recommendations concerning international respect for the right of peoples to self-determination, and particularly recommendations relating to the steps which might be taken by the various organs of the United Nations and the specialized agencies to develop international respect for that right.

---

[1] This decision of the General Assembly was the starting point in the process of drafting what eventually became article 1 of the International Covenant on Economic, Social and Cultural Rights and of the International Covenant on Civil and Political Rights.

In 1952 and 1953, the General Assembly approved a list of factors indicative of the attainment of independence or of other systems of self-government and recommended that that list should be used by the Assembly and the Administering Members as a guide in determining whether any Non-Self-Governing Territory, due to changes in its constitutional status, was or was no longer within the scope of Chapter XI of the Charter (Declaration Regarding Non-Self-Governing Territories). The General Assembly reasserted also that in each concrete case the right of self-determination should be taken into account.[2]

### C. The Declaration on the Granting of Independence to Colonial Countries and Peoples and the machinery for its implementation

At its fifteenth session, the General Assembly adopted the Declaration on the Granting of Independence to Colonial Countries and Peoples.[3] The content of the Declaration is closely connected and interdependent with human rights, and the basic philosophy underlying the Declaration is that "the subjection to alien subjugation, domination and exploitation constitutes a denial of fundamental human rights, is contrary to the Charter of the United Nations and is an impediment to the promotion of world peace and co-operation". Using the wording of the then draft Covenants on Human Rights, the Declaration provides: "All peoples have the right to self-determination; by virtue of that right they freely determine their political status and freely pursue their economic, social and cultural development". The Declaration emphasizes: "Inadequacy of political, economic, social or educational preparedness should never serve as a pretext for delaying independence". Reference has already been made to the provision of the Declaration that states: "All States shall observe faithfully and strictly the provisions of the Charter of the United Nations, the Universal Declaration of Human Rights and the present Declaration on the basis of equality, non-interference in the internal affairs of all States, and respect for the sovereign right of all peoples and their territorial integrity".

At its sixteenth session, the General Assembly by its resolution 1654 (XVI) of 27 November 1961, established international machinery for the implementation of the Declaration of 14 December 1960 in the form of a 17-member Special Committee on the Situation with regard to the Implementation of the Declaration on the Granting of Independence to Colonial Countries and Peoples,[4] with a comprehensive system of subsidiary organs. The General Assembly requested the Special Committee to examine the application of the Declaration and make suggestions and recommendations on the progress and extent of its implementation. In the same resolution, the General Assembly reiterated and reaffirmed the objectives and principles enshrined in the Declaration and called upon States concerned to take action without further delay with a view to the faithful application and implementation of the Declaration. The General Assembly further directed the Special Committee to carry out its task by employment of all the means at its disposal for the proper discharge of its functions; authorized the Special Committee to meet elsewhere than at United Nations Headquarters whenever necessary; invited the authorities concerned to co-operate with the Committee; and requested the Trusteeship Council, the Committee on Information from Non-Self-Governing Territories and the specialized agencies concerned to assist the Special Committee.

The United Nations organs for the implementation of the Declaration on the Granting of Independence to Colonial Countries and Peoples provide machinery for the implementation of the rights set forth in article 1 of both Covenants on Human Rights. The Special Committee and its subsidiary committees have addressed themselves not only to the right of peoples to self-determination but to concrete human rights situations. In many instances, these have related to whole peoples and ethnic groups, in others to smaller groups of persons and to individuals.

In resolution 1810 (XVII), adopted on 17 December 1962, the General Assembly called upon the administering Powers concerned to cease forthwith all armed action and repressive measures directed against peoples who had not yet attained their independence, particularly, against the political activities of their rightful leaders; urged all administering Powers to take immediate steps in order that all colonial territories and peoples might accede to independence without delay in accordance with the provisions of paragraph 5 of the Declaration; and decided to enlarge the membership of the Special Committee established by resolution 1654 (XVI), by the addition of seven new members. The Special Committee was invited: *(a)* to continue to seek the most suitable ways and means for the speedy and total application of the Declaration to all Territories which have not yet attained independence; *(b)* to propose specific measures for the complete application of the Declaration; *(c)* to submit to the General Assembly a full report containing its suggestions and recommendations on all Territories which had not attained independence; and *(d)* to apprise the Security Council of any developments in those Territories which might threaten international peace and security. All Member States, especially the Administering Authorities, were requested to afford the Special Committee their fullest co-operation. The Special Committee submitted reports to the General Assembly at each of its sessions from the eighteenth to the twenty-seventh. On the basis of these reports the General Assembly adopted a number of resolutions concerning the right of nations and peoples to self-determination. Many of the resolutions relate to particular Territories and to specific tasks of the Special Committee; others are general in character. In a general resolution (1956

---

[2] General Assembly resolution 742 (VIII) of 27 November 1953. The list of factors appears in an annex to the resolution. See also General Assembly resolution 567 (VI) of 18 January 1952 and General Assembly resolution 648 (VII) of 10 December 1952.

[3] General Assembly resolution 1514 (XV) of 14 December 1960.

[4] The membership of the Special Committee was later expanded to 24 (General Assembly resolution 1810 (XVII) of 17 December 1962).

(XVIII)), adopted on 11 December 1963, the General Assembly approved the Special Committee's report, called upon the administering Powers to implement the conclusions and recommendations contained therein, and requested the Committee to continue to seek the best ways and means for the immediate and total application of the Declaration to all territories which had not attained independence. On 18 February 1965, on recommendation of the Committee, the General Assembly by its resolution 2005 (XIX) made arrangements for the supervision of elections in the Cook Islands, administered by New Zealand, by a team of observers led by a United Nations representative.[5]

The General Assembly, at its twentieth session, approved the reports of the Special Committee and again invited the administering Powers to implement its recommendations. The Committee was requested to continue to perform its task and to continue to seek the best means for the immediate and full application of resolution 1514 (XV) to all Territories which had not attained independence. Moreover, the Assembly called upon the colonial Powers to discontinue their policy of violating the right of colonial peoples through the systematic influx of foreign immigrants and the dislocation, deportation and transfer of the indigenous inhabitants; recognized the legitimacy of the struggle by the peoples under colonial rule to exercise their right to self-determination and independence; invited all States to provide material and moral assistance to the national liberation movements in colonial Territories; requested all States and international institutions, including the specialized agencies of the United Nations, to withhold assistance of any kind to the Governments of Portugal and South Africa until they renounce their policy of colonial domination and racial discrimination; and requested the colonial Powers to dismantle the military bases installed in colonial Territories and to refrain from establishing new ones.

At its twenty-first session, in 1966, the General Assembly adopted resolution 2189 (XXI) in which it deplored the negative attitude of certain colonial Powers which refused to recognize the right of colonial peoples to self-determination and independence. The Assembly further reaffirmed its recognition of the legitimacy of the struggle of the peoples under colonial rule to exercise their right to self-determination and independence. In the same resolution the Special Committee was invited to "recommend a deadline for the accession to independence of each Territory in accordance with the wishes of the people and the provisions of the Declaration". It was further invited "to pay particular attention to the small Territories and to recommend to the General Assembly the most appropriate methods and also the steps to be taken to enable the populations of those Territories to exercise fully the right to self-determination and independence". The General Assembly further requested the Special Committee "to continue to perform its tasks and to seek suitable means for the immediate and full implementation of the Declaration in all Territories which have not yet attained independence".

At its twenty-second session, in resolution 2311 (XXII) of 14 December 1967, the General Assembly recognized that the specialized agencies, the International Atomic Energy Agency and the international institutions associated with the United Nations should extend their full co-operation to the United Nations in achieving the objectives of General Assembly resolution 1514 (XV). It recommended that the specialized agencies and other international institutions concerned take urgent and effective measures to assist the peoples struggling for their liberation under colonial rule, and in particular to extend, within the scope of their respective activities, all necessary aid to the oppressed peoples of Southern Rhodesia and the Territories under Portuguese domination and to work out, in co-operation with the Organization of African Unity and through it with the national liberation movements, concrete programmes to that end. The General Assembly also recommended to the specialized agencies and international institutions not to grant any assistance to South Africa and Portugal until they renounced their policy of racial discrimination and colonial domination.

At the same session, in resolution 2326 (XXII), the General Assembly reaffirmed its recognition of the legitimacy of the struggle of the colonial peoples to exercise their right to self-determination and independence. It requested the United Nations High Commissioner for Refugees, the specialized agencies concerned and other international relief organizations to increase their economic, social and humanitarian assistance to the refugees from Territories under colonial domination. It requested the colonial Powers to dismantle their bases and installations in colonial Territories, and condemned once again the policies, pursued by certain administering Powers in the Territories under their domination, of imposing non-representative régimes and constitutions, strengthening the position of foreign economic and other interests. The General Assembly in resolution 2326 (XXII) further requested the Special Committee to make concrete suggestions with a view to assisting the Security Council in considering appropriate measures under the United Nations Charter with regard to developments in colonial Territories which were likely to threaten international peace and security, and it recommended that the Security Council take such suggestions fully into consideration. The General Assembly further invited the Special Committee to pay particular attention to the small Territories and to recommend to the General Assembly the most appropriate methods and also the steps to be taken to enable the populations of those Territories to exercise fully their right to self-determination and independence. It also requested the Special Committee to submit recommendations regarding the holding of a special conference of representatives of colonial peoples for the purpose of considering the most effective means by which the international community could intensify its assistance to them in their efforts to achieve self-determination.

At the twenty-third session in 1968, the General Assembly in resolution 2465 (XXIII) reviewed the implementation of the Declaration on the Granting of In-

---

[5] It may be noted that plebiscites under United Nations supervision were held in several Trust Territories on the eve of their independence.

dependence to Colonial Countries and Peoples and recalled and reaffirmed earlier resolutions adopted on the matter. It stated that the continuation of colonialism and its manifestations, including racism and *apartheid* and the attempts of some colonial Powers to suppress national liberation movements by repressive activities against colonial peoples were incompatible with the Charter, the Universal Declaration of Human Rights and the Declaration on the Granting of Independence to Colonial Countries and Peoples. It declared that the practice of using mercenaries against movements for national liberation and independence was punishable as a criminal act and that the mercenaries themselves were outlaws, and called upon the Governments of all countries to enact legislation declaring the recruitment, financing and training of mercenaries in their territory to be a punishable offence and prohibiting their nationals from serving as mercenaries. In the same resolution 2465 (XXIII) the General Assembly also initiated preparations for the commemoration of the tenth anniversary of the Declaration on the Granting of Independence to Colonial Countries and Peoples.

In its resolution 2426 (XXIII) of 1968, the General Assembly addressed itself again to the specialized agencies and appealed in particular to the International Bank for Reconstruction and Development and the International Monetary Fund to take all necessary steps to withhold from the Governments of Portugal and South Africa financial, economic, technical and other assistance until they renounce their policies of racial discrimination and colonial domination. It recommended that the Bank should withdraw the loans and credits it had granted to the Governments of Portugal and South Africa which were being used by those Governments to suppress the national liberation movement in the Portuguese colonies and in Namibia, and against the African population of South Africa.

In resolution 2548 (XXIV), adopted at the twenty-fourth session in 1969, the General Assembly reaffirmed its previous resolutions, particularly those provisions thereof which related to the continuation of colonial rule as a threat to international peace and security and to the dismantling of military bases established by colonial Powers in colonial Territories. In resolution 2555 (XXIV), the General Assembly reiterated its appeals to the specialized agencies in the matter of implementing resolution 1514 (XV) and called again for concrete programmes for assisting the oppressed peoples of Southern Rhodesia, Namibia and the Territories under Portuguese administration. It requested the Economic and Social Council to continue to consider, in consultation with the Special Committee, appropriate measures for the co-ordination of the policies and activities of the specialized agencies in implementing the relevant General Assembly resolutions. Its recommendations were addressed particularly to the International Civil Aviation Organization, The International Telecommunication Union, the Universal Postal Union and the Inter-Governmental Maritime Consultative Organization.

In resolution 2621 (XXV) the General Assembly adopted a programme of action to assist in the full implementation of the Declaration on the Granting of Independence to Colonial Countries and Peoples. Among the items of the programme of action thus adopted was the drawing of the attention of the Security Council to the need to continue to give special attention to the problems of southern Africa and in particular to widen the scope of the sanctions against the illegal régime of Southern Rhodesia by declaring mandatory all the measures laid down in Article 41 of the Charter; the General Assembly also requested the Security Council to give careful consideration to the question of imposing sanctions upon South Africa and Portugal, and to give urgent consideration to the question of imposing fully and unconditionally an embargo on arms of all kinds to the Government of South Africa and the illegal régime of Southern Rhodesia. The programme of action further called for according to all freedom fighters under detention the treatment laid down in the Geneva Convention relative to the Treatment of Prisoners of War, of 12 August 1949.[6] Representatives of liberation movements should be invited, whenever necessary, by the United Nations and other international organizations within the United Nations system to participate in an appropriate capacity in the proceedings of those organs relating to their countries. The Special Committee was directed to assist the General Assembly in making arrangements, in co-operation with the administering Powers, for securing a United Nations presence in the colonial Territories. Where resolution 1514 (XV) had not been fully implemented with regard to a given Territory, the General Assembly would continue to bear responsibility for that Territory until such time as the people concerned had had an opportunity to exercise freely its right to self-determination and independence. In resolution 2704 (XXV), the General Assembly reiterated its urgent appeal to the specialized agencies and the other organizations within the United Nations system to render all possible moral and material assistance to the peoples struggling for their liberation. It recommended increased assistance to refugees from colonial Territories in particular by the United Nations Development Programme and the International Bank for Reconstruction and Development.

The various condemnations, requests and recommendations contained in earlier resolutions were reaffirmed in resolutions 2878 (XXVI) and 2874 (XXVI) adopted at the twenty-sixth session in 1971.

The determinations, condemnations, requests and recommendations of earlier sessions were reiterated with increased emphasis in 1972 in resolutions 2908 (XXVII) and 2980 (XXVII).

In accordance with the General Assembly's request to the Special Committee to apprise the Security Council of any developments in any Territory it examined which might threaten international peace and security, the Special Committee in 1963 drew the Council's attention to the situation existing in Southern Rhodesia, Aden, South West Africa and the Territories under Portuguese administration. In 1965 it drew the Council's attention to the "grave situation prevailing" in both Southern

---

[6] United Nations, *Treaty Series*, vol. 75 (1950), No. 972.

Rhodesia and Aden, to the "continued deterioration of the situation in the Territories under Portuguese domination", to the "serious situation prevailing in South West Africa", and to "the threat to territorial integrity" of what then were Basutoland, Bechuanaland and Swaziland.

### D. The development of the status of the Trust Territories

As of the end of 1947, the following Territories had been placed under the trusteeship system of the United Nations: the Cameroons under French administration; the Cameroons under British administration; Togoland under French administration; Togoland under British administration; Ruanda-Urundi under Belgian administration; Tanganyika under British administration; Western Samoa under New Zealand administration; New Guinea under Australian administration; Nauru under the joint administration of Australia, New Zealand and the United Kingdom; The Pacific Islands Trust Territory (Marshalls, Marianas and Carolines) under United States administration. The former Italian colony of Somalia was placed under Trusteeship in 1950, with Italy as the Administering Authority (General Assembly resolution 442 (V) of 2 December 1950).

Togoland under British administration joined the Gold Coast when the latter became the independent sovereign nation of Ghana on 6 March 1957.[7] Ghana was admitted to membership in the United Nations on 8 March 1957 (General Assembly resolution 1118 (XI)).

In March 1959, the General Assembly voted to end the Trusteeship Agreement for the Cameroons under French administration. On 20 September 1960 the Republic of Cameroon was admitted to United Nations membership (General Assembly resolution 1476 (XV)).

On 14 November 1958, in its resolution 1253 (XIII) the General Assembly resolved that the Trusteeship Agreement for Togoland under French administration would be terminated on 27 April 1960. Togo was admitted to the United Nations on 20 September 1960 (General Assembly resolution 1477 (XV)).

The Trusteeship of Somaliland was ended on 1 July 1960 when Italian-administered Somaliland joined British Somaliland, which had acceded to independence a few days before. The Republic of Somalia was admitted to membership in the United Nations on 20 September 1960 (General Assembly resolution 1479 (XV) of 20 September 1960).

As far as the Cameroons under British administration was concerned the Teusteeship in regard to its northern part (Northern Cameroons) came to an end on 1 June 1961 when Northern Cameroons became a part of Nigeria as a separate province of the northern region of Nigeria. As far as the Southern Cameroons under British administration was concerned the Trusteeship came to an end on 1 October 1961 when Southern Cameroons, formerly under British administration, became part of the Federal Republic of Cameroon. (General Assembly resolution 1608 (XV) of 21 April 1961.)

The Trusteeship Agreement for Tanganyika was terminated when it attained independence on 9 December 1961.

On 1 July 1962 Ruanda-Urundi achieved independence as Rwanda and Burundi.[8] The Republic of Rwanda and the Kingdom of Burundi were admitted to membership in the United Nations on 18 September 1962 (General Assembly resolutions 1748 (XVII) and 1749 (XVII)).

In its resolution 2347 (XXII) of 19 December 1967, the General Assembly resolved that the Trusteeship Agreement for Nauru should cease to be in force upon the accession to independence by Nauru on 31 January 1968. Nauru did not apply for membership in the United Nations.

By December 1972 only two of the original 11 Territories under Trusteeship had not yet reached the Charter's goal: New Guinea and the Pacific Islands Trust Territories. With regard to New Guinea, the General Assembly by its resolution 2865 (XXVI) of 20 December 1971 decided that the name to be applied for United Nations purposes to the Non-Self-Governing Territory of Papua and the Trust Territory of New Guinea would henceforth be "Papua New Guinea". In its resolution 2977 (XXVII) of 14 December 1972, the General Assembly welcomed the establishment of a time-table for the attainment of full self-government by Papua New Guinea and called upon the administering Power to prepare, in consultation with the Government of Papua New Guinea, a further time-table for independence.

### E. Non-Self-Governing Territories

In 1946, eight member States (Australia, Belgium, Denmark, France, the Netherlands, New Zealand, the United Kingdom and the United States) undertook to transmit information on the following Territories under their administration:

*Australia:* Papua

*Belgium:* Belgian Congo

*Denmark:* Greenland

*France:* French West Africa, French Equatorial Africa, French Somaliland, Madagascar and dependencies, French Establishments in Oceania, Indo-China, French Establishments in India, New Caledonia and dependencies, St. Pierre and Miquelon, Morocco, Tunisia, the New Hebrides under Anglo-French Condominium, Martinique, Guadeloupe, and dependencies, French Guiana and Réunion

*Netherlands:* Netherlands Indies, Surinam and Curaçao

*New Zealand:* Cook Islands and the Tokelau Islands

*United Kingdom:* Aden (Colony and Protectorate), Bahamas, Basutoland, Bechuanaland Protectorate, British Somaliland Protectorate, Brunei, Cyprus, Dominica, Falkland Islands, Gold Coast (Colony and Protectorate), Grenada, Hong Kong, Jamaica, Kenya (Colony and Protectorate), Malayan Union, Malta, Nigeria,

---

[7] General Assembly resolution 1044 (XI) of 13 December 1956, on the result of the plebiscite held in Togoland under British administration.

[8] General Assembly resolution 1746 (XVI) of 27 June 1962 on the future of Ruanda-Urundi.

North Borneo, Northern Rhodesia, Nyasaland, St. Helena and dependencies, St. Vincent, Sarawak, Seychelles, Sierra Leone, Singapore, Swaziland, Trinidad and Tobago, Uganda Protectorate, the High Commission Territories of the Western Pacific (Gilbert and Ellice Islands Colony, British Solomon Islands Protectorate, Pitcairn Island), Barbados, Bermuda, British Guiana, British Honduras, Fiji, Gambia, Gibraltar, Leeward Islands, Mauritius, St. Lucia, and Zanzibar Protectorate.

*United States:* Alaska, American Samoa, Guam, Hawaii, Panama Canal Zone, Puerto Rico and the Virgin Islands.

By the end of 1954, France ceased submitting information on the following Territories on the ground that they enjoyed self-government either as overseas departments or under analogous arrangements within the French Republic: French Establishments in Oceania, New Caledonia, French Guiana, Guadeloupe and Martinique, Réunion and St. Pierre and Miquelon.

It also ceased submitting information on the French Establishments in India which became part of India. At the same time other Non-Self-Governing Territories achieved self-government: Indonesia and the States of Indochina, which won their Independence; Puerto Rico, now a Commonwealth associated with the United States; Greenland, which joined the Kingdom of Denmark on an equal basis with other parts of the realm; the Netherlands Antilles and Surinam, now partners in the Kingdom of the Netherlands.

Since 1955 there has been an increasingly rapid advance of the peoples of both Trust and Non-Self-Governing Territories towards self-government and independence. In 1956, Morocco and Tunisia became independent. In the same year, the French Government informed the Secretary-General of the United Nations that beginning with the year 1957, by reason of constitutional and political changes, France had decided to stop transmitting information under Article 73 *e* for French West Africa, French Equatorial Africa, Madagascar, the Comoro Archipelago and French Somaliland. In 1957, the Gold Coast became the independent State of Ghana and in 1958 the former French Guinea became independent as the Republic of Guinea. The Federation of Malaya achieved independence in 1957 and in 1959 Alaska and Hawaii attained statehood as states of the United States of America.

During 1960, the newly independent nations that emerged from independent status (including, as already noted, three Trust Territories) [9] were: Malagasy Republic, Republic of the Congo (Leopoldville), Republic of Dahomey, Republic of the Niger, Republic of the Upper Volta, Republic of the Ivory Coast, Republic of Chad, Republic of the Congo (Brazzaville), Gabon Republic, Central African Republic, Republic of Cyprus, Federation of Nigeria, Senegal, Mali, and the Islamic Republic of Mauritania. British Somaliland joined with the Trust Territory of Somaliland under Italian Trusteeship as the Republic of Somalia.

[9] Republic of Cameroon, Republic of Togo, Somalia.

In 1960, the General Assembly [10] declared the following Territories to be Non-Self-Governing Territories: the Cape Verde Archipelago, Portuguese Guinea, São Tomé and Príncipe, São João Batista da Ajudá, Angola, Mozambique, Goa,[11] Macau and Timor. In the same resolution the General Assembly noted that the Government of Spain agreed to transmit information on the following Territories: Fernando Poo, Ifni, Rio Muni and Spanish Sahara.

Among the dependent Territories that became independent between 1961 and 1972 were the following: Bahrain, Barbados, Bhutan, Botswana, Burundi, Equatorial Guinea, Fiji, Gambia, Guyana, Jamaica, Kenya, Kuwait, Lesotho, Malawi, Maldives, Malta, Mauritius, Oman, People's Republic of Southern Yemen, Qatar, Rwanda, Sierra Leone, Singapore, Swaziland, Trinidad and Tobago, Uganda, United Arab Emirates, Zambia and Zanzibar, which later formed, with Tanganyika, the United Republic of Tanzania.

### F. The question of South West Africa (Namibia) in particular

In 1946, when the question of implementing the provisions of Chapter IX (Non-Self-Governing Territories) and XII (Trusteeship) of the Charter was being discussed, South Africa proposed to the first session of the General Assembly the incorporation of the Territory into the Union of South Africa

The Assembly in resolution 65 (I) of 14 December 1946, declared that it was unable to accede to the incorporation of South West Africa into the Union of South Africa and recommended instead that the Territory be placed under the Trusteeship System and invited the Union Government to propose a Trusteeship Agreement for the Territory. Claiming that it was under no obligation to place its Mandate for South West Africa under the United Nations Trusteeship System, South Africa as the only former Mandatory Power refused to do so. The United Nations has been concerned with the question of this former Mandated Territory since 1946.

In 1947, and again in 1948, the General Assembly reaffirmed its recommendation that South West Africa be placed under the Trusteeship System.[12] It also recommended that the Union continue reporting annually on its administration of South West Africa until it had reached agreement with the United Nations on the future status of the Territory. In 1949, the Union Government, objecting to the method of dealing with the one report submitted, notified the United Nations that it had decided not to forward any further reports on its administration of South West Africa.

The General Assembly at its fourth session in 1949, asked the International Court of Justice for an opinion on the legal aspects of the question, inquiring whether:

[10] General Assembly resolution 1542 (XV) of 15 December 1960.

[11] Goa became a part of India in 1961.

[12] General Assembly resolution 141 (II) of 1 November 1947 and General Assembly resolution 227 (III) of 26 November 1948.

(*a*) The Union of South Africa continued to have international obligations under the Mandate for South West Africa;

(*b*) The provisions of Chapter XII of the Charter were applicable to the Territory;

(*c*) The Union of South Africa had competence to modify the international status of the Territory or, in the event of a negative reply, where such competence would rest.[13]

The International Court of Justice, in rendering its opinion,[14] stated that:

(*a*) South Africa continued to have the international obligations laid down in the Mandate for South West Africa;

(*b*) The United Nations should exercise supervisory functions over the administration of the Territory;

(*c*) South Africa continued to have the obligation to promote the material and moral well-being and social progress of the inhabitants of the Territory;

(*d*) Although the Charter did not impose on South Africa the legal obligation to place South West Africa under the International Trusteeship System, Chapter XII of the Charter applied to the Territory in the sense that it provided a means by which the Territory might be brought under the Trusteeship System;

(*e*) South Africa, acting alone, was not competent to modify the international status of the Terrritory.

The advisory opinion of the International Court of Justice was accepted by the General Assembly at its fifth session.[15] The Assembly also established a five-member *Ad Hoc* Committee (Denmark, Syria, Thailand, the United States and Uruguay) to confer with the Union Government concerning the procedural measures for implementing the Court's opinion and to examine reports and petitions concerning South West Africa.

The *Ad Hoc* Committee met with representatives of the Union Government from 1951 to 1953. The Union Government did not accept the opinion of the International Court of Justice and was unwilling to accept any form of United Nations supervision over the Territory's administration, contending that such supervision would automatically impose upon it greater obligations than it had assumed under the League of Nations Mandate. It was, however, prepared to reassume some of its international obligations under the League Mandate by negotiating a new agreement with France, the United Kingdom and the United States. Such an agreement would be subject to the approval of the United Nations, but South Africa would be directly responsible to the three Powers and not to the United Nations.

This proposal was found unacceptable by the *Ad Hoc* Committee and was rejected in 1953 by the General Assembly.[16]

In 1953 and in subequent years additional subsidiary bodies were established, such as a seven-member Committee by General Assembly resolution 749 (VIII) of 1953 and a Good Offices Committee by General Assembly resolution 1143 (XII) of 1958. In 1960 the Committee on South West Africa was invited by General Assembly resolution 1568 (XV) to go to South West Africa immediately and to investigate the situation there and to make proposals on steps which would enable the Territory's indigenous inhabitants to achieve a wide measure of internal self-government designed to lead them to complete independence. Another special committee for South West Africa was established in 1961 by General Assembly resolution 1702 (XVI).

On 4 November 1960, Ethiopia and Liberia filed concurrent applications in the International Court of Justice instituting contentious proceedings against the Union of South Africa under the Mandate for South West Africa. The two States were seeking a judgement of the International Court of Justice requiring the Union Government to carry out its obligations under the League of Nations Mandate. The Union of South Africa raised objections to the jurisdiction of the International Court of Justice to hear the dispute brought by Ethiopia and Liberia. In its judgement[17] on the preliminary objections, delivered on 21 December 1962, the Court decided, by 8 votes to 7, that it had jurisdiction to adjudicate upon the merits of the dispute brought before it by Ethiopia and Liberia.

On 18 July 1966 the International Court of Justice delivered its judgement (second phase)[18] on the action instituted in 1960 by Ethiopia and Liberia against South Africa. The Court found that Ethiopia and Liberia could not be considered as having established any legal rights or interest appertaining to them in the subject matter considered. By the President's casting vote—the votes being equally divided—the Court decided to reject the claim of both applicants.

At its twenty-first session in 1966 the General Assembly adopted resolution 2145 (XXI) of 27 October 1966, in which it expressed its conviction that the administration of the Mandated Territory by South Africa had been conducted in a manner contrary to the Mandate, the Charter of the United Nations and the Universal Declaration of Human Rights. The General Assembly reaffirmed: "that the provisions of General Assembly resolution 1514 (XV) are fully applicable to the people of the Mandated Territory of South West Africa and that, therefore, the people of South West Africa have the inalienable right to self-determination, freedom, and independence in accordance with the Charter of the United Nations". The General Assembly decided that South Africa had failed to fulfil its obligations with respect to the administration of the Territory, that the Mandate was therefore terminated, that South Africa "has no

---

[13] General Assembly resolution 338 (IV) of 6 December 1949.

[14] *International status of South West Africa, Advisory Opinion: I.C.J. Reports 1950*, p. 128.

[15] General Assembly resolution 449 (V) of 13 December 1950.

[16] General Assembly resolution 749 (VIII) of 28 November 1953.

[17] *South West Africa Cases (Ethiopia* v. *South Africa; Liberia* v. *South Africa), Preliminary Objections, Judgment of 21 December 1962: I.C.J. Reports 1962*, p. 319.

[18] *South West Africa, Second Phase, Judgment, I.C.J. Reports 1966*, p. 6.

other right to administer the Territory and that henceforth South West Africa comes under the direct responsibility of the United Nations". The General Assembly further resolved that the United Nations must discharge its responsibility with respect to this Territory and for this purpose established an *Ad Hoc* Committee for South West Africa to recommend practical means by which South West Africa should be administered, to enable the people of the Territory to exercise the right of self-determination and to achieve independence.[19]

At its fifth special session the General Assembly in its resolution 2248 (S-V) of 19 May 1967, reaffirmed the territorial integrity of South West Africa and the inalienable right of its people to freedom and independence. It decided to establish the United Nations Council for South West Africa and entrusted to it the following powers and functions to be discharged in the Territory: (*a*) to administer South West Africa until independence, with the maximum possible participation of the people of the Territory; (*b*) to promulgate such laws, decrees and administrative regulations as are necessary for the administration of the Territory until a legislative assembly is established following elections conducted on the basis of universal adult suffrage; (*c*) to take as an immediate task all the necessary measures, in consultation with the people of the Territory, for the establishment of a constituent assembly to draw up a constitution on the basis of which elections will be held for the establishment of a legislative assembly and a responsible government; (*d*) to take all the necessary measures for the maintainance of law and order in the Territory; and (*e*) to transfer all powers to the people of the Territory upon the declaration of independence. The General Assembly also provided that the Council should entrust such executive and administrative tasks as it deemed necessary to a United Nations Commissioner for South West Africa, who should be responsible to the Council. The General Assembly further decided that the Council should be based in South Africa and should proceed to South West Africa with a view, *inter alia*, to taking over the administration of the Territory.

In November 1967 the United Nations Council for South West Africa submitted its first report to the General Assembly.[20] In this report, the Council stated, *inter alia*, that the Foreign Minister of the Republic of South Africa had informed the Secretary-General that his Government was unwilling to comply with the terms of resolution 2145 (XXI) of the General Assembly and would continue to administer South West Africa notwithstanding that resolution, which it considered to be "illegal". The Council concluded that the refusal of the Government of South Africa to co-operate in the implementation of General Assembly resolutions 2145 (XXI) and 2248 (S-V) made it impossible for the Council to discharge effectively all of the functions and responsibilities entrusted to it by the Assembly.

At its twenty-second session, the General Assembly adopted resolution 2325 (XXII) of 16 December 1967, in which it noted with appreciation the report of the United Nations Council for South West Africa and requested the Council to fulfil by every available means the mandate entrusted to it by the General Assembly. The General Assembly also condemned the refusal of the Government of South Africa to comply with General Assembly resolutions 2145 (XXI) and 2248 (S-V). The General Assembly also requested the Security Council to take effective steps to enable the United Nations to fulfil the responsibilities it had assumed with respect to South West Africa and also to take all appropriate measures to enable the United Nations Council for South West Africa to discharge fully its functions and responsibilities.

The General Assembly also dealt with the question of Namibia (South West Africa) in resolutions 2372 (XXII) of 12 June 1968, 2403 (XXIII) of 16 December 1968, 2498 (XXIV) of 31 October 1969, 2678 (XXV) of 9 December 1970 and 2871 (XXVI) of 20 December 1971.

The Security Council in its resolution 245 (1968) of 25 January 1968 took note of General Assembly resolution 2145 (XXI) by which the Assembly had terminated South Africa's mandate over South West Africa and had decided that South Africa had no other right to administer the Territory and that henceforth South West Africa would came under the direct responsibility of the United Nations. In its resolution 246 (1968) of 14 March 1968 which, like the previous resolution 245 (1968) was adopted unanimously, the Security Council took into account General Assembly resolution 2145 (XXI) terminating the mandate. In its resolution 264 (1969) the Security Council recognized that the General Assembly had terminated the mandate of South Africa over Namibia. It declared the continued presence of South Africa in Namibia illegal and called upon the Government of South Africa to withdraw immediately its administration from the Territory.

By its resolution 269 (1969), the Security Council reaffirmed its resolution 264 (1969), condemned the Government of South Africa for its refusal to comply with that resolution and called upon the Government of South Africa to withdraw its administration from the Territory immediately and in any case before 4 October 1969. The resolution reminded South Africa of its obligations under Article 25 of the Charter and characterized the continued occupation of Namibia by South Africa as constituting an aggressive encroachment on the authority of the United Nations. The Security Council also recognized the legitimacy of the struggle of the people of Namibia against the South African authorities in the Territory.

In its resolution 276 (1970), the Security Council repeated that the continued presence of South African authorities in Namibia was illegal and took additional decisions with a view to the effective implementation of its relevant resolutions.

In its resolution 283 (1970), the Security Council requested States to refrain from any relations with South Africa that implied recognition of the authority of the South African Government over Namibia and called

[19] For the work of the *Ad Hoc* Committee see its report (*Official Records of the General Assembly, Fifth Special Session, Annexes*, agenda item 7, document A/6640).

[20] *Official Records of the General Assembly, Twenty-second Session, Annexes*, agenda item 64, document A/6897.

upon all States to take appropriate measures in regard to diplomatic and consular relations and commercial and industrial enterprises and concessions.

By its resolution 284 (1970), the Security Council submitted the following question to the International Court of Justice with the request for an advisory opinion:

"What are the legal consequences for States of the continued presence of South Africa in Namibia, notwithstanding Security Council resolution 276 (1970) ?"

On 21 June 1971 the International Court of Justice gave the following reply to this question:[21]

"(1) That the continued presence of South Africa in Namibia being illegal, South Africa is under the obligation to withdraw its administration from Namibia immediately and thus put an end to its occupation of the Territory;

"(2) That States Members of the United Nations are under obligation to recognize the illegality of South Africa's presence in Namibia and the invalidity of its acts on behalf of and concerning Namibia, and to refrain from any acts and in particular any dealings with the Government of South Africa implying recognition of the legality of, or lending support or assistance to, such presence and administration;

"(3) That it is incumbent upon States which are not Members of the United Nations to give assistance, within the scope of sub-paragraph (2) above, in the action which has been taken by the United Nations with regard to Namibia".

In its resolution 301 (1971) the Security Council took note with appreciation of this advisory opinion and endorsed the Court's opinion expressed in paragraph 133 of the advisory opinion. The General Assembly in its resolution 2871 (XXVI) noted the advisory opinion with satisfaction.

In its resolution 309 (1972) of 4 February 1972, the Security Council invited the Secretary-General, in consultation and close co-operation with a group of the Security Council, to initiate as soon as possible contacts with all parties concerned, with a view to establishing the necessary conditions to enable the people of Namibia, freely and with strict regard to the principles of human equality, to exercise their right to self-determination and independence. It called on the Government of South Africa to co-operate fully with the Secretary-General in the implementation of the resolution and requested the Secretary-General to report not later than 31 July 1972. In another resolution adopted on 4 February 1972 (resolution 310 (1972)) the Security Council reaffirmed that the continued occupation of Namibia by the South African authorities was illegal, reaffirmed earlier strong condemnations of action taken by the South African authorities and decided that in the event of failure on the part of the Government of South Africa to comply with the resolution, the Security Council would meet immediately to decide upon effective steps or measures, in accordance with the relevant Chapters of the Charter, to secure the full and speedy implementation of that resolution.

In its resolution 319 (1972) adopted on 1 August 1972, the Security Council considered the report submitted by the Secretary-General,[22] in accordance with resolution 309 (1972) referred to above. It invited the Secretary-General to continue his contacts with all parties concerned and to proceed, after necessary consultations, with the appointment of a representative to assist him in the discharge of his mandate. It requested the Secretary-General to report by 15 November 1972.

### G. The question of Southern Rhodesia in particular

Since 1962 the question of Southern Rhodesia has been repeatedly examined by both the General Assembly and the Security Council. In its resolution 2138 (XXI) of 22 October 1966 concerning the question of Southern Rhodesia, the General Assembly condemned any arrangement reached between the administering Power and the illegal racist minority régime that would not recognize the inalienable rights of the people of Zimbabwe to self-determination and independence. In its resolution 2151 (XXI) of 17 November 1966, the General Assembly recalled a series of its own resolutions and also resolution 217 (1965) of 20 November 1965 in which the Security Council had declared that the racist minority régime in Southern Rhodesia was illegal. Subsequently, the General Assembly adopted on the question of Southern Rhodesia, *inter alia*, resolutions 2262 (XXII), 2383 (XXIII), 2508 (XXIV), 2652 (XXV), 2769 (XXVI), 2945 (XXVII) and 2946 (XXVII). At its twenty-seventh session the General Assembly, in consultation with the Organization of African Unity, invited representatives of the national liberation movements of Zimbabwe to participate in an observer capacity in its consideration of the situation in the Territory. Having heard those representatives, the Assembly reaffirmed the principle that there should be no independence before majority rule in Zimbabwe and affirmed that any settlement relating to the future of the Territory must be worked out with the full participation of the genuine political leaders representing the majority of the people of Zimbabwe and must be endorsed fully and freely by the people (General Assembly resolution 2945 (XXVII)). The General Assembly also noted with satisfaction the rejection by the African population of Zimbabwe of the "proposals for a settlement" agreed upon between the Government of the United Kingdom and the illegal régime. It called upon the Government of the United Kingdom under no circumstances to transfer or accord to the illegal régime any of the powers or attributes of sovereignty and requested that Government to ensure the country's attainment of independence by a democratic system of Government. It urged the United Kingdom to convene as soon as possible a national constitutional conference where the genuine political representatives of the people of Zimbabwe would be able to work out a settlement relating to the future of the territory for

[21] *Legal Consequences for States of the Continued Presence of South Africa in Namibia (South West Africa) notwithstanding Security Council resolution 276 (1970), Advisory Opinion, I.C.J. Reports 1971*, para. 133.

[22] *Official Records of the Security Council, Twenty-seventh Year, Supplement for July, August and September 1972*, document S/10738.

subsequent endorsement by the people through free and democratic processes. In another resolution also adopted at the twenty-seventh session (2946 (XXVII) of 7 December 1972), the General Assembly strongly condemned the policies of the Governments—particularly those of South Africa and Portugal—which, in violation of the relevant resolutions of the United Nations and contrary to their specific obligations under Article 25 of the Charter, continued to collaborate with the illegal racist minority régime in its racialist and repressive domination of the people of Zimbabwe, and called upon those Governments to cease forthwith all such collaboration. It condemned all violations of, as well as the failure of certain States to enforce strictly, the mandatory sanctions imposed by the Security Council, as being contrary to the obligations assumed by them under article 25 of the Charter. It condemned the continued importation by the Government of a Member State of chrome and nickel from Zimbabwe in open contravention of the provisions of Security Council resolutions 253 (1968), 277 (1970), 288 (1970), and 314 (1972) and contrary to the specific obligations assumed by that Government under Article 25 of the Charter. The General Assembly called upon the Government concerned to desist forthwith from further violations of the sanctions and to observe faithfully and without exception the provisions of the above-mentioned resolutions.

The action taken by the Security Council on Southern Rhodesia in and after 1965 can be summarized as follows: in its resolution 202 (1965) of 6 May 1965 the Security Council requested the United Kingdom Government and all States Members of the United Nations not to accept a unilateral declaration of independence for Southern Rhodesia by the minority Government. It requested the United Kingdom also to take all necessary action to prevent a unilateral declaration of independence and not to transfer under any circumstances to its colony of Southern Rhodesia, as at present governed, any of the powers or attributes of sovereignty, but to promote the country's attainment of independence by the democratic system of government in accordance with the aspirations of the majority of the population. When the unilateral declaration of independence had been made, the Security Council by resolution 216 (1965) of 12 November 1965 decided to condemn it and to call upon all States not to recognize the illegal racist minority régime and to refrain from rendering any assistance to it.

In resolution 217 (1965) of 20 November 1965 the Security Council determined that the situation resulting from the Proclamation of Independence by the illegal authorities in Southern Rhodesia was extremely grave, that the Government of the United Kingdom should put an end to it and that its continuance in time constituted a threat to international peace and security. The Security Council reaffirmed the provisions of its resolution 216 (1965) and of General Assembly resolution 1514 (XV); called upon the Government of the United Kingdom to quell the rebellion of the racist minority and called upon all States not to recognize that illegal authority and not to entertain any diplomatic or other relations with it. The Security Council also called upon the Organization of African Unity to do all in its power to assist in the implementation of resolution 217 (1965), in conformity with Chapter VIII of the Charter.

In its resolution 221 (1966) of 9 April 1966, the Security Council expressed its grave concern that substantial supplies of oil might reach Southern Rhodesia. Determined that the resulting situation constituted a threat to the peace, it called upon the Government of the United Kingdom to prevent, by the use of force if necessary, the arrival at Beira of vessels reasonably believed to be carrying oil destined for Southern Rhodesia. In its resolution 232 (1966) of 16 December 1966, the Security Council, acting in accordance with Articles 39 and 41 of the Charter, determined that the situation in Southern Rhodesia constituted a threat to international peace and security, decided upon a series of measures to be taken by States to prevent the import of certain products originating in Southern Rhodesia into their respective countries and decided on additional measures to be taken to contribute to the effectiveness of the sanctions.

In resolution 253 (1968) of 29 May 1968, the Security Council determined in considerable detail the measures to be taken by States Members of the United Nations in applying the sanctions against Southern Rhodesia. In adopting this resolution as well as resolution 277 (1970) of 18 March 1970, the Security Council expressly stated that it was acting under Chapter VII of the Charter. In the latter resolution the Security Council decided *inter alia* in accordance with Article 41 of the Charter and in furthering the objectives of ending the rebellion that Member States should immediately sever all diplomatic, consular, trade, military and other relations that they might have with the illegal régime in Southern Rhodesia, should terminate any representation that they may maintain in the Territory and should immediately interrupt any existing means of transportation to and from Southern Rhodesia. In resolution 288 (1970) of 17 November 1970 the Security Council, again acting under the previous decisions taken under Chapter VII of the Charter, decided that the sanctions against Southern Rhodesia should remain in force.

In resolutions 314 (1972) of 28 February 1972 and 318 (1972) of 28 July 1972 the Security Council again called upon States to refrain from taking any measures that would in any way permit or facilitate the importation from Southern Rhodesia of commodities falling within the scope of the obligations imposed by resolution 253 (1968) and drew the attention of all States to the need for increasing vigilance in implementing its provisions. It demanded that all Member States should scrupulously carry out their obligations to implement fully the Council resolutions of 1968, 1970 and 1972 and condemned all acts violating their provisions.

### H. The question of the people of Palestine

The right to self-determination of the people of Palestine has been emphasized by the General Assembly in several resolutions.

In resolution 2535 B (XXIV) the General Assembly, on 10 December 1969, had recognized that the problem of the Palestine Arab refugees had arisen from the denial of their inalienable rights under the Charter of the United Nations and the Universal Declaration of Human Rights. In resolution 2628 (XXV) of 4 November 1970 on the situation in the Middle East, the General Assembly had recognized that respect for the rights of the Palestinians was an indispensable element in the establishment of a just and lasting peace in the Middle East.

In resolution 2649 (XXV) of 30 November 1970, the General Assembly recognized the right of peoples under colonial and alien domination in the legitimate exercise of their right to self-determination to seek and receive all kinds of moral and material assistance, in accordance with the resolutions of the United Nations and the spirit of the Charter of the United Nations; called upon all Governments that denied the right to self-determination to observe that right in accordance with the relevant international instruments and the principles and spirit of the Charter; condemned those Governments that denied the right to self-determination of peoples recognized as being entitled to it, especially the peoples of southern Africa and Palestine.

In resolution 2672 C (XXV) of 8 December 1970, on the subject of Palestine refugees, the General Assembly, bearing in mind the principle of equal rights and self-determination of peoples, recognized that the people of Palestine were entitled to "equal rights and self-determination" in accordance with the Charter and declared that full respect for those rights was an indispensable element in the establishment of a just and lasting peace in the Middle East.

On 6 December 1971, the General Assembly adopted resolution 2787 (XXVI) which confirmed the legality of, among others, the Palestinian people's struggle for self-determination and liberation from foreign domination and alien subjugation by all available means consistent with the Charter.

In resolution 2792 D (XXVI) of 6 December 1971, the General Assembly recognized that the people of Palestine were entitled to equal rights and self-determination and expressed its grave concern that they had not been permitted to enjoy their inalienable rights and to exercise their right to self-determination.

By its resolution 2963 E (XXVII) of 13 December 1972, the General Assembly affirmed that the people of Palestine were entitled to equal rights and self-determination, in accordance with the Charter of the United Nations, and it expressed once more its grave concern that the people of Palestine had not been permitted to exercise their right to self-determination.

## I. The right of self-determination in the International Covenants on Human Rights

The right to self-determination is recognized in article 1 [23] of the International Covenant on Economic, Social and Cultural Rights and in article 1 of the International Covenant on Civil and Political Rights, both of which provide that all peoples have the right of self-determination and that by virtue of that right they freely determine their political status and freely pursue their economic, social and cultural development. This language as already indicated in section C above, had also been incorporated in the Declaration on the Granting of Independence to Colonial Countries and Peoples of 1960. Article 1 of each Covenant further provides that all peoples may, for their own ends, freely dispose of their natural wealth and resources without prejudice to any obligations arising out of international economic co-operation based upon the principle of mutual benefit, and international law and that in no case may a people be deprived of its own means of subsistence. Article 25 of the International Covenant on Economic, Social and Cultural Rights and article 47 of the International Covenant on Civil and Political Rights provide that nothing in the Covenants shall be interpreted as impairing the inherent right of all peoples to enjoy and utilize fully and freely their natural wealth and resources. The natural wealth and resources aspect of the right to self-determination has been elaborated in the Declaration on Permanent Sovereignty over Natural Resources dealt with in section I below.

Article 1, paragraph 3, of each Covenant further provides that the States Parties, including those having responsibility for the administration of Non-Self-Governing and Trust Territories, shall promote the realization of the right of self-determination and shall respect that right, in conformity with the provisions of the Charter of the United Nations.

## J. Permanent sovereignty over natural resources

In connexion with the question of permanent sovereignty of peoples and nations over their natural wealth and resources, the General Assembly decided, by resolution 1314 (XIII) of 12 December 1958, to establish a commission to conduct a full survey of the status of this basic constituent of the right of self-determination. At its seventeenth session in 1962, it adopted the Declaration on Permanent Sovereignty over Natural Resources.[24] In this Declaration the General Assembly stated that it was desirable to promote international co-operation for the economic development of developing countries and stated that economic and financial agreements between the developed and the developing countries must be based on the principles of equality and of the right of peoples and nations to self-determination. The Assembly declared that the right of peoples and nations to permanent sovereignty over their natural wealth and resources must be exercised in the interest of their national development and of the well-being of the people of the State concerned; that the exploration, development and disposition of such resources, as well as the imported capital, should be in conformity with rules and conditions which the

[23] Article 1 of both Covenants was considered and adopted by the Third Committee at the tenth session of the General Assembly in 1955. For the proceedings on this matter and the issues discussed see *Official Records of the General Assembly, Tenth Session, Annexes*, agenda item 28, part I, document A/3077, in particular, paras. 17-77 thereof. The Covenants were adopted and opened for signature, ratification and accession by General Assembly resolution 2200 (XXI) of 16 December 1966 and are annexed thereto.

[24] General Assembly resolution 1803 (XVII) of 14 December 1962.

peoples or nations freely consider to be necessary or desirable; that nationalization, expropriation or requisitioning should be based on grounds of public utility, security or national interest; and that international co-operation for the economic development of developing countries should be such as to further their independent national development and should be based upon respect for their sovereignty over their natural wealth and resources.

At its twenty-first session, the General Assembly reaffirmed by resolution 2158 (XXI) of 25 November 1966, the inalienable right of all countries to exercise permanent sovereignty over their natural resources in the interest of their national development, in conformity with the spirit and principles of the Charter of the United Nations and as recognized in General Assembly resolution 1803 (XVII); and declared "that the United Nations should undertake a maximum concerted effort to channel its activities so as to enable all countries to exercise that right fully".

At its twenty-third session, the General Assembly, in its resolution 2386 (XXIII) of 19 November 1968, reaffirmed the principles and recommendations contained in its resolution adopted at the twenty-first session and expressed the view that the full exercise of permanent sovereignty over natural resources would play an important role in the achievement of the goals of the Second United Nations Development Decade. At its twenty-fifth session, after having taken note of a further report of the Secretary-General (A/8058) on the subject of permanent sovereignty over natural resources, the General Assembly, in its resolution 2692 (XXV) of 11 December 1970, recognized that the exercise of permanent sovereignty over their natural resources by developing countries was indispensable in order that they might, *inter alia*, accelerate their industrial development, and in that connexion stressed the important role of the appropriate organizations of the United Nations system in the promotion of specific industrial projects dealing with the natural resources of developing countries. It made arrangements through the Economic and Social Council and the latter's Committee on Natural Resources for the preparation of periodic reports on the advantages derived from the exercise by developing countries of permanent sovereignty over natural resources. In those reports particular reference should be made to the impact of such exercise on the increased mobilization of resources, especially of domestic resources, for the economic and social development, on the out-flow of capital therefrom as well as on the transfer of technology. It arranged for continued studies and reports by the Secretary-General.

The United Nations Conference on the Human Environment adopted at Stockholm on 16 June 1972 a Declaration setting forth a series of principles, several of which endorse the principle of national sovereignty over the natural resources of States. Thus, under principle 21, States have, in accordance with the Charter of the United Nations and the principles of international law, the sovereign right to exploit their own resources pursuant to their own environmental policies, and the responsibility to ensure that activities within their jurisdiction or control do not cause damage to the environment of other States. At its twenty-seventh session, the General Assembly, in resolution 2994 (XXVII) of 15 December 1972, took note with satisfaction of the report of the United Nations Conference on the Human Environment containing the Declaration adopted by the Conference and drew the attention of Governments to that Declaration.

The United Nations Conference on Trade and Development adopted at its third session in 1972 principles relevant to the subject here under consideration. The Conference also adopted a resolution providing for the preparation of a "Charter of Economic Rights and Duties of States" which would set forth, among other rights, the right of nations to permanent sovereignty over natural resources.[25]

In its resolution 3016 (XXVII) of 18 December 1972 on permanent sovereignty over natural resources of developing countries, adopted at the twenty-seventh session, the General Assembly took into account the relevant principles adopted both by the United Nations Conference on Trade and Development at its third session and by the Conference on the Human Environment and reaffirmed the right of States to permanent sovereignty over all their natural resources, on land within their international boundaries, as well as those found in the sea-bed and the sub-soil thereof within their national jurisdiction and in the superjacent waters. The General Asembly declared that actions, measures or legislative regulations of States aimed at coercing, directly or indirectly other States engaged in the change of their structure or in the exercise of their sovereign rights over their natural resources, both on land and in their coastal waters, were in violation of the Charter and of the Declaration on Principles of International Law concerning Friendly Relations and Co-operation among States (General Assembly resolution 2625 (XXV)) and contradicted the targets, objectives and policy measures of the International Strategy for Development for the Second United Nations Development Decade (General Assembly resolution 2626 (XXV)).

---

[25] *Proceedings of the United Nations Conference on Trade and Development, Third Session*, vol. I, *Report and Annexes* (TD/180).

# V. UNITED NATIONS ACTION AIMED AT THE ELIMINATION OF DISCRIMINATION ON GROUNDS OF RACE AND RELIGION

At its first session the General Assembly adopted resolution 103 (I) of 19 November 1946, entitled "Persecution and discrimination", reading as follows:

"*The General Assembly declares* that it is in the higher interests of humanity to put an immediate end to religious and so-called racial persecution and discrimination, and calls on the Governments and responsible authorities to conform both to the letter and to the spirit of the Charter of the United Nations, and to take the most prompt and energetic steps to that end."

## A. United Nations Declaration on the Elimination of All Forms of Racial Discrimination

A comprehensive solemn statement on the United Nations philosophy and policy in regard to discrimination on the grounds of race, colour or ethnic origin is contained in the United Nations Declaration on the Elimination of All Forms of Racial Discrimination (General Assembly resolution 1904 (XVIII)) proclaimed on 20 November 1963. In this Declaration the General Assembly affirmed that discrimination between human beings on the grounds of race, colour or ethnic origin was an offence to human dignity, a denial of the principles of the Charter, a violation of the rights proclaimed in the Universal Declaration, an obstacle to friendly and peaceful relations among nations capable of disturbing peace and security among peoples. The Declaration addresses itself to States as well as to institutions, groups or individuals. The Declaration of 1963 elaborates upon the provisions of the Universal Declaration of Human Rights and covers in several respects situations which are not dealt with in that Declaration. Thus, the Declaration of 1963 provides that particular efforts shall be made to prevent discrimination based on race, colour or ethnic origin, especially in the fields of civil rights, access to citizenship, education, religion, employment, occupation and housing. Everyone shall have equal access to any place or facility intended for use by the general public. All States shall take effective measures to revise governmental and other public policies and to rescind offending laws and regulations. They should also pass legislation prohibiting discrimination by private persons and groups. All propaganda and organizations based on ideas or theories of the superiority of one race or group of persons of one colour or ethnic origin, with a view to justifying or promoting racial discrimination, shall be severely condemned. All incitement to or acts of violence against any race or group of persons shall be punishable under law. All States shall take immediate and positive measures to prosecute and/or outlaw organizations which promote or incite to racial discrimination or incite to or use violence for purposes of discrimination based on race, colour and ethnic origin.

## B. International Convention on the Elimination of All Forms of Racial Discrimination

The International Convention on the Elimination of All Forms of Racial Discrimination was adopted by the General Assembly by resolution 2106 A (XX) on 21 December 1965. It was opened for signature on 7 March 1966. Together with the Discrimination (Employment and Occupation) Convention adopted by the International Labour Conference in 1958, the Convention against Discrimination in Education adopted by the General Conference of UNESCO in 1960 and the articles prohibiting discrimination of the two International Covenants on Human Rights, this Convention constitutes the expression of the international conventional law on the subject. Its most important features are described below.

In the Convention (article 2), States parties condemn racial discrimination and undertake to pursue by all appropriate means and without delay a policy of eliminating it in all its forms. Each State party undertakes to amend, rescind or nullify any laws and regulations which have the effect of creating or perpetuating racial discrimination wherever it exists. States parties undertake not only not to engage in any act or practice of racial discrimination themselves, but also to prohibit and bring to an end by all appropriate means, including legislation, as required by circumstances, racial discrimination by any persons, group or organization. The Convention provides that when the circumstances so warrant States parties shall take specific and concrete measures to ensure the adequate development and protection of certain racial groups or individuals belonging to them for the purpose of guaranteeing them the full and equal enjoyment of human rights and fundamental freedoms.

States parties also undertake (article 4) to adopt immediate and positive measures designed to eradicate all incitement to or acts of racial discrimination. To this end the States parties undertake to declare an offence punishable by law all dissemination of ideas based on racial superiority or hatred, incitement to racial discrimination, as well as all acts of violence or incitement to such acts. They further undertake to declare illegal and prohibit organizations and propaganda activities which promote and incite racial discrimination, and to recognize participation in such organizations or activities as an offence punishable by law.

Article 5 of the Convention contains a long list of rights and freedoms in the enjoyment of which racial discrimination shall be prohibited and eliminated. The list contains, in addition to the rights set forth in the Universal Declaration of Human Rights, also some rights on which the Universal Declaration does not contain any express provisions, such as the right to inherit and the right of access to any place or service intended for use by the general public such as transport, hotels, restaurants, cafés, theatres and parks. Article 5 lists specifically, among the rights in regard to which discrimination is prohibited, the right to work, the right to join trade unions and the right to housing.

The Convention provides for comprehensive measures of implementation (articles 8 to 16). It provides for the establishment of a Committee on the Elimination of Racial Discrimination and of an *ad hoc* Conciliation Commission. The Committee's tasks are to consider reports on the legislative, judicial, administrative or other measures States parties have adopted and that give effect to the provisions of the Convention; to make suggestions and general recommendations based on the examination of the reports and information received from the States parties; to perform functions with a view to settling disputes among States parties concerning the application of the Convention; to receive and consider communications from individuals or groups of individuals within the jurisdiction of States parties which have recognized the competence of the Committee to this effect, and to forward suggestions and recommendations in regard to such communications. The Committee is also to co-operate with various United Nations bodies in regard to petitions from the inhabitants of non-independent territories.

The functions of the *ad hoc* Conciliation Commission are to make available its good offices to States parties in disputes concerning the application of the Convention with a view to an amicable solution on the basis of respect for the Convention. The *ad hoc* Conciliation Commission is called upon to present a report embodying its findings on all questions of fact relevant to the issue between the parties and containing such recommendations as it may think proper for the amicable solution of the dispute.

The reports of the *ad hoc* Conciliation Commission are to be communicated to the States parties to the dispute and, eventually, to the other parties to the Convention. The Committee on the Elimination of Racial Discrimination reports annually to the General Assembly.

A more detailed description of the measures of implementation of the Convention on the Elimination of All Forms of Racial Discrimination are described in part two of the present publication.

The General Assembly repeatedly urged States to become parties to the Convention. Thus at its twenty-second session, in resolution 2332 (XXII) the General Assembly urged all eligible Governments to sign, ratify and implement this as well as other conventions directed against discrimination in employment, occupation and education. In its resolution 2647 (XXV) the General Assembly invited countries which were not yet parties to the Convention to take any steps necessary to ratify it or accede to it, if possible in 1971, on the occasion of the International Year for Action to Combat Racism and Racial Discrimination. In resolution 2648 (XXV) the General Assembly, having received the first report of the Committee on the Elimination of Racial Discrimination covering the first year of its activities, stressed the significance, for the fulfilment of the objectives of the United Nations in the field of human rights, of the fact that the Convention had come into force and that the Committee on the Elimination of Racial Discrimination had been brought into being. In resolution 2783 (XXVI) the General Assembly urged all States not yet parties to the Convention to ratify or accede to it as soon as possible. At its twenty-seventh session again the General Assembly in resolution 2921 (XXVII) urgently requested all States not yet parties to the Convention to ratify or accede to it, if possible by 10 December 1973, the twenty-fifth anniversary of the adoption of the Universal Declaration of Human Rights.

### C. Draft Declaration and draft Convention on the Elimination of All Forms of Religious Intolerance

At the seventeenth session of the General Assembly in 1962 it was decided that in addition to a Declaration and Convention on the Elimination of All Forms of Racial Discrimination, a draft Declaration and a draft Convention on the Elimination of All Forms of Religious Intolerance should be prepared.[1] While the United Nations Declaration on the Elimination of All Forms of Racial Discrimination was proclaimed on 20 November 1963[2] and the International Convention on the Elimination of All Forms of Racial Discrimination was adopted and opened for signature and ratification or accession on 21 December 1965,[3] the instruments relating to the elimination of all forms of religious intolerance are still in the process of being prepared.

At its twentieth session in 1964 the Commission on Human Rights began work on the draft Declaration on the Elimination of All Forms of Religious Intolerance on the basis of a preliminary draft submitted to it by the Sub-Commission on Prevention of Discrimination and Protection of Minorities.[4] In its resolution 1015 C (XXXVII) of 30 July 1964 the Economic and Social Council noted the report of a working party set up by the Commission on Human Rights for the purpose of preparing the draft Declaration. The Council decided to refer to the General Assembly the relevant documents of the Commission on Human Rights and of the Council itself and suggested to the General Assembly that it take a decision on the further course to be followed on the matter of the draft Declaration on the Elimination of All Forms of Religious Intolerance. Further developments on the draft Declaration are summarized below.

As far as the draft Convention on the Elimination of All Forms of Religious Intolerance is concerned, a preli-

---

[1] General Assembly resolutions 1780 (XVII) and 1781 (XVII).

[2] General Assembly resolution 1904 (XVIII) of 20 November 1963; see sect. A above.

[3] General Assembly resolution 2106 (XX).

[4] E/CN.4/873, para. 142, resolution 3 (XVI), annex. For the printed text, see *Official Records of the Economic and Social Council, Thirty-seventh Session, Supplement No. 8*, para. 294.

minary draft was submitted to the Commission by the Sub-Commission on Prevention of Discrimination and Protection of Minorities in the report of its seventeenth session.[5] The Sub-Commission also submitted a preliminary draft as an expression of the general views of the Sub-Commission on additional measures of implementation. The Sub-Commission's draft was examined and revised at the twenty-first, twenty-second and twenty-third sessions of the Commission on Human Rights in 1965, 1966 and 1967, respectively.[6]

In its resolution 3 (XXIII) the Commission on Human Rights transmitted to the Economic and Social Council a preamble and 12 articles of the draft International Convention on the Elimination of All Forms of Religious Intolerance, additional draft articles proposed by one delegation and by the Sub-Commission on Prevention of Discrimination and Protection of Minorities, and the preliminary draft of additional measures of implementation submitted by the Sub-Commission. The Commission on Human Rights recommended to the Economic and Social Council that it transmit these documents to the General Assembly.

In the substantive articles of the draft Convention prepared by the Commission on Human Rights it is provided, *inter alia*, that the expression "religion or belief" shall include theistic, non-theistic and atheistic beliefs. Neither the establishment nor the recognition of a religion or belief by a State nor the separation of Church from State, shall by itself be considered religious intolerance or discrimination on the ground of religion or belief. The States parties to the draft Convention will undertake to ensure to everyone within their jurisdiction the right to freedom of thought, conscience, religion or belief. They will also undertake to respect the right of parents to bring up their children in the religion or belief of their choice. The exercise of this right carries with it the duty of parents to inculcate in their children tolerance for the religion of others. States parties will undertake the obligation to ensure to everyone freedom to enjoy and to exercise political, civic, economic, social and cultural rights without discrimination on the ground of religion or belief. The States parties shall take effective measures to prevent and eliminate discrimination on the ground of religion or belief, including the enactment or abrogation of laws or regulations where necessary to prohibit such discrimination by any person, group or organization. States parties will undertake to ensure to everyone within their jurisdiction effective protection and remedies against any acts which violate his human rights contrary to the Convention, as well as the right to seek just and adequate reparation or satisfaction for any damage suffered as a result of such acts.

The draft Convention also provides that nothing in it shall be interpreted as giving to any person, group, organization or institution the right to engage in activities aimed at prejudicing national security, friendly relations between nations or the purposes and principles of the United Nations. Nor shall the Convention be construed to preclude a State party from prescribing by law such limitations as are necessary to protect public safety, order, health or morals or the individual rights and freedoms of others or the general welfare in a democratic society.

At its twenty-second session in 1967, the General Assembly (Third Committee) was unable to complete the consideration of the draft Convention owing to its heavy agenda and for lack of time. The Third Committee decided to change the title of the draft Convention to "International Convention on the Elimination of All Forms of Intolerance and of Discrimination based on Religion or Belief". The Committee also revised the preamble and article I of the draft Convention as prepared by the Commission on Human Rights and furthermore decided not to mention in the draft Convention any specific examples of religious intolerance. The General Assembly in resolution 2295 (XXII) of 11 December 1967 bore in mind these decisions of the Third Committee.[7]

In the preamble, as revised by the Third Committee, the States parties to the Convention would give expression to the consideration that the disregard and infringement of human rights and fundamental freedoms, and in particular of the right to freedom of thought, conscience, religion or belief had brought, directly or indirectly, wars and great suffering to mankind, especially when manifestations of religion or belief had served and were still serving as a means or as an instrument of foreign interference in the internal affairs of other States and peoples. The States parties would also proclaim that religion or belief, for anyone who professed either, was one of the fundamental elements in his conception of life, and that freedom of religion or belief should be fully respected and guaranteed. Governments, organizations and private persons should strive to combat any exploitation or abuse of religion or belief for political or other ends. The States parties would express their conviction that the right to freedom of religion or belief should not be abused so as to impede any measures aimed at the elimination of colonialism and racialism.

In the revised draft article I, as amended by the Third Committee, it is stated that neither the establishment of a religion nor the recognition of a religion or belief by a State nor the separation of Church from State "shall" by itself be considered religious intolerance or discrimination on the ground of religion or belief.

The General Assembly, by its resolution 2295 (XXII), decided to accord priority, during the twenty-third session in 1968, to the item relating to elimination of all forms of religious intolerance which would include both the draft Declaration on the Elimination of All Forms of Religious Intolerance and the draft International Convention on the Elimination of All Forms of Intolerance and of Discrimination Based on Religion or Belief.

However, at the twenty-third session, as well as the three succeeding ones, the General Assembly always post-

---

[5] E/CN.4/882 and Corr.1, para. 321, resolution I (XVII), annex.

[6] *Official Records of the Economic and Social Council, Thirty-ninth Session, Supplement No. 8*, (E/4024); *ibid., Forty-first Session, Supplement No. 8*, (E/4184); *ibid., Forty-second Session, Supplement No. 6*, (E/4322).

[7] See *Official Records of the General Assembly, Twenty-second Session, Annexes*, agenda item 54, document A/6934.

poned the consideration of the item relating to religious intolerance to its next session. At the twenty-seventh session the General Assembly adopted resolution 3027 (XXVII), in which it affirmed the equal importance of both a Declaration and an International Convention on the Elimination of All Forms of Racial Intolerance. Convinced of the need to give new momentum to this work by initially concentrating on the completion of one of these instruments and noting that the consideration of the item had been deferred at each session of the General Assembly without proper discussion since the twenty-second session, the Assembly decided to accord priority to the completion of the Declaration on the Elimination of All Forms of Religious Intolerance before resuming consideration of the draft International Convention on the subject. It further decided to give priority at its twenty-eighth session to the elaboration of the Declaration with a view to the adoption, it possible, of such a Declaration as part of the observance of the twenty-fifth anniversary of the Universal Declaration of Human Rights.

### D. Instruments for the elimination of descrimination adopted by the specialized agencies

Arising out of discussions initiated within United Nations organs, various aspects of discrimination falling within the competence of specialized agencies, were referred to the agencies for consideration. As a result, important instruments aimed at the elimination of discrimination have been adopted by several specialized agencies. These include the ILO Convention and Recommendation on discrimination in respect of employment and occupation, adopted in 1958, and the UNESCO Convention and Recommendation against Discrimination in Education, adopted in 1960. The provisions of these instruments are briefly indicated below.

States parties to the ILO Discrimination (Employment and Occupation) Convention undertake to declare and pursue a national policy designed to promote, by methods appropriate to national conditions and practice, equality of opportunity and treatment in respect of employment and occupation with a view to eliminating any discrimination in respect thereof. Among the concretely defined obligations undertaken by States parties is the obligation to seek the co-operation of employers' and workers' organizations in promoting the acceptance and observance of this policy. States parties undertake to enact such legislation and to promote such educational programmes as may be calculated to secure the acceptance and observance of the policy. They are obliged to repeal any statutory provisions and to modify any administrative instructions or practices which are inconsistent with the policy of the promotion of equality of opportunity. In respect of employment under the direct control of a national authority, States parties undertake not merely to seek the co-operation of workers' and employers' organizations in promoting the acceptance and observance of the policy, but to pursue it. The policy shall also be observed in the activities of vocational guidance, vocational training and placement services under the direction of a national authority. Those States parties to the Convention of 1958 which also are or intend to become parties to the International Convention on the Elimination of All Forms of Racial Discrimination undertake to prohibit and bring to an end racial discrimination by any persons, group or organization and thereby to prohibit such discrimination in employment not under the direct control of a national authority. The definition of discrimination in the Convention of 1958 comprises any distinction, exclusion or preference made on the basis of race, colour, sex, religion, political opinion, national extraction or social origin, which has the effect of nullifying or impairing equality of opportunity or treatment in employment or occupation. The terms "employment" and "occupation" include access to vocational training, access to employment and to particular occupations and terms and conditions of employment. Any distinction, exclusion or preference in respect of a particular job based on the inherent requirements thereof shall not be deemed to be discrimination. The Convention also provides that any measures affecting an individual who is justifiably suspected of or engaged in activities prejudicial to the security of the State shall not be deemed to be discrimination, provided that the individual concerned shall have the right to appeal to a competent body. The Discrimination (Employment and Occupation) Recommendation elaborates in greater detail the action to be taken to implement the national non-discrimination policy laid down in the Convention.

States parties to the UNESCO Convention against Discrimination in Education undertake among other things to abrogate any statutory provisions and any administrative instructions and to discontinue any administrative practices which involve discrimination in education. They commit themselves to ensure, by legislation where necessary, that there is no discrimination in the admission of pupils to educational institutions and not to allow any differences of treatment by the public authorities between nationals, except on the basis of merit or need, in the matter of school fees and the granting of scholarships or other forms of assistance. They undertake to give foreign nationals resident within their territory the same access to education as that given to their own nationals. The States parties undertake to develop and to apply a national policy which will tend to promote equality of opportunity and of treatment in the matter of education. Among the aspects of this policy which the Convention stresses is the policy to make primary education free and compulsory; to make secondary education generally available and accessible to all; to make higher education equally accessible to all on the basis of individual capacity. States are to ensure that their standards of education are equivalent in all public educational institutions of the same level. These and related provisions of the Convention are now paralleled by the provisions of articles 13 and 14 of the International Covenant on Economic, Social and Cultural Rights. Both the Convention of 1960 and the Covenant also implement the provision of article 26, paragraph 2, of the Universal Declaration of Human Rights that education shall be directed to the full development of the human personality and to the strengthening of respect for human rights and fundamental freedoms. The definition of "discrimination" in the Convention of 1960 includes any distinction, exclusion, limitation or preference which being based on race, colour, sex, language, religion, political or other opinion, national or social origin, economic condition or birth, has the purpose or effect of nullifying or impairing equality of treatment in education. However, the establishment or maintenance of separate educational systems or institutions for pupils of the two sexes shall not be deemed to constitute discrimination if they offer equivalent access to education, provide a teaching staff with qualifications of the same standards as well as school premises and equipment of the same quality and afford the opportunity to take the same or equivalent courses of study. Similarly, the establishment or maintenance, for religious or linguistic reasons, of separate educational systems or institutions is permitted if participation in such system or attendance at such institutions is optional and if the education provided conforms to standards laid down by the competent authorities. Subject to certain conditions, the establishment or maintenance of private educational institutions is also deemed not to be discrimination within the meaning of the Convention. Under a Protocol which the General Conference of UNESCO adopted in 1962, a Conciliation and Good Offices Commission was instituted. It is responsible for seeking the settlement of any dispute which may arise between States parties to the Convention of 1960. Its procedure may be set into motion by a State party to the Protocol which considers that another State party is not giving effect to a provision of the Convention of 1960. The measures of implementation provided for in the Protocol of 1962 are by and large similar to those which the Commission on Human Rights had proposed for the implementation of the International Covenant on Civil and Political Rights. There are, however, considerable differences between the Protocol of 1962 and the measures of implementation of the International Covenant on Civil and Political Rights as approved by the General Assembly in 1966.

## VI. MEASURES AS REGARDS *APARTHEID* AND RACIAL DISCRIMINATION

### A. Action by the General Assembly

Since the beginning of its activities the United Nations has been concerned with the racial policies of the Government of South Africa. The matter was raised at the first session of the General Assembly in 1946 by the Government of India in the form of a complaint relating to the treatment of people of Indian origin in the Union of South Africa. This question was further considered by the General Assembly as a separate agenda item until 1962. The contention that the General Assembly was not competent to deal with it was mentioned by some delegations and continued to be raised during several of the following sessions. At its first session the General Assembly adopted resolution 44 (I), by which it stated that owing to the treatment of people of Indian origin in the Union, "friendly relations between the two Member States have been impaired and might be further impaired in the future" and therefore requested the two Governments to report at its following session what action they had taken to deal with the situation.

During the third session, the First Committee of the General Assembly rejected a draft resolution presented by South Africa recommending that the General Assembly should decide that the question came essentially within the domestic jurisdiction of the Union and was not within the competence of the General Assembly. Instead the General Assembly, by its resolution 265 (III), invited the Governments of India, Pakistan and South Africa to enter into discussion at a round-table conference, taking into consideration the purposes and principles of the Charter of the United Nations and the Universal Declaration of Human Rights. At the fifth session of the General Assembly, the *Ad Hoc* Political Committee, to which the examination of the matter had been referred, decided that it was competent to deal with the matter and recommended certain specific proposals for adoption by the General Assembly. At the same session the General Assembly adopted resolution 395 (V) of 2 December 1950, in which it expressed the opinion that "a policy of 'racial segregation' *(apartheid)* is necessarily based on doctrines of racial discrimination". It recommended once again a round-table discussion and stated that if the Governments concerned should fail to hold a round-table conference within a reasonable time, a commission of three members should be established to assist the parties. The General Assembly also called upon the Governments concerned to "refrain from taking any steps which would prejudice the success of their negotiations, in particular, the implementation or enforcement of the provisions of the 'Group Areas Act', pending the conclusion of such negotiations". In its resolution 511 (VI) of 12 January 1952, the General Assembly, noting that the promulgation, on 30 March 1951, of five proclamations under the Group Areas Act rendered operative thereby the provisions of that Act in direct contravention of paragraph 3 of resolution 395 (V), called upon the Government of the Union of South Africa to suspend the implementation of the Group Areas Act.

In resolution 615 (VII) adopted at its seventh session on 5 December 1952 the General Assembly emphasized the consideration and recommendations contained in its previous resolutions on the subject and established a Good Office Commission to facilitate the negotiations between the Governments concerned.

At the sixth session the General Assembly also had considered the question of the racial situation in South Africa not limited to the treatment of persons of Indian and Pakistani origin under an agenda item entitled "The question of race conflict in South Africa resulting from the policies of *apartheid* of the Government of the Union of South Africa". The representative of the Union of South Africa protested against the inclusion of the item in the agenda. He introduced a motion that, having regard to the provision of Article 2, paragraph 7, of the Charter, the Assembly should declare itself incompetent to consider the item. The motion was rejected, and when repeated on various later occasions, it was consistently rejected. On 5 December 1952 the General Assembly adopted two resolutions on this problem. In one of them (resolution 616 A (VII)) the General Assembly, referring to its previous resolutions to the effect that a policy of racial segregation *(apartheid)* was necessarily based on doctrines of racial discrimination, established a commission of three members to study the racial situation in the Union of South Africa. It also stipulated that the study was to be carried out in the light of the purposes and principles of the Charter, with due regard to the provisions of several Articles of the Charter specifically mentioned, and the resolutions of the United Nations on racial persecution and discrimination. In resolution 616 B (VII) the General Assembly solemnly called upon all Member States to bring their policies into conformity with their obligations under the Charter to promote the observance of human rights and fundamental freedoms.

Following the adoption of the resolution the representative of the Union of South Africa declared that he had been instructed to state that his Government would continue to claim the protection inscribed in Article 2, paragraph 7, of the Charter and that it must therefore regard any resolution emanating from a discussion on or the consideration of the item as *ultra vires*, and therefore as null and void.

In resolution 616 A (VII) the General Assembly invited the Government of the Union of South Africa to extend its full co-operation to the United Nations Commission on the Racial Situation in the Union of South Africa. In a communication to the Secretary-General and to the Commission, the Government of South Africa pointed out that since it had consistently regarded the question of the Union's racial policy as a domestic matter it regarded resolution 616 A (VII) as unconstitutional and could not therefore recognize the Commission established thereunder.[1] Under these circumstances the Commission decided to try to make up for the lack of direct contact with South African realities on the spot by examining the declarations of Union politicians, by studying thoroughly the principal legislative texts governing the life of individuals and groups in South Africa and, lastly, by studying whatever memoranda were submitted to it and by hearing witnesses in a position to inform it on the problems under study.

The Commission submitted three reports, which were dealt with in General Assembly resolutions 721 (VIII), 820 (IX) and 917 (X). The General Assembly took note of the conclusions of the Commission that the continuance of the policies of *apartheid* would make peaceful solution increasingly difficult and endanger friendly relations among States (resolution 721 (VIII) of 8 December 1953). It also shared the profound conviction of the Commission that these policies constituted a grave threat to the peaceful relations between ethnic groups in the world (resolution 820 (IX) of 14 December 1954).

In resolutions adopted at later sessions the General Assembly expressed its concern over the fact that the Government of South Africa was continuing to give effect to the policies of *apartheid*. It deplored the attitude of that Government which had not observed its obligations under the Charter and had pressed forward with discriminatory measures. By its resolution 1663 (XVI) of 28 November 1961, the General Assembly recommended that all States take separate and collective action, in conformity with the United Nations Charter, to bring about the abandonment by the South African Government of the policies of racial discrimination.

During the seventeenth session of the General Assembly in 1962, the consideration of *apartheid* by the United Nations entered a new phase. At this session the General Assembly considered the wider question of the "policies of *apartheid* of the Government of the Republic of South Africa", which was to cover both the discrimination practised against the population of Indian and Pakistani origin and the race conflict involving the African population. Recalling its previous resolutions regarding the racial situation in that country, the General Assembly in its resolution 1761 (XVII) of 6 November 1962, strongly deprecated the continued and total disregard of the Government of South Africa of its obligations under the Charter of the United Nations and its determined aggravation of racial issues by enforcing measures of increasing ruthlessness. The General Assembly requested the Security Council to take appropriate measures, including sanctions, to secure South Africa's compliance with the resolutions of the General Assembly and of the Security Council on this subject and, if necessary, to consider action under Article 6 of the Charter, which deals with expulsion of Members from the United Nations. By the same resolution (1761 (XVII)) Member States were requested to take the following diplomatic and economic measures to bring about the abandonment of those policies:

"(*a*) Breaking off diplomatic relations with the Government of the Republic of South Africa or refraining from establishing such relations;

"(*b*) Closing their ports to all vessels flying the South African flag;

"(*c*) Enacting legislation prohibiting their ships from entering South African ports;

"(*d*) Boycotting all South African goods and refraining from exporting goods, including all arms and ammunition, to South Africa;

"(*e*) Refusing landing and passage facilities to all aircraft belonging to the Government of South Africa and companies registered under the laws of South Africa."

In the same resolution the General Assembly decided to establish a Special Committee on the Policies of *Apartheid* of the Government of the Republic of South Africa, which was later renamed the Special Committee on *Apartheid*.

On 11 October 1963 the General Assembly "considering reports to the effect that the Government of South Africa was arranging the trial of a large number of political prisoners under arbitrary laws prescribing the death sentence", adopted resolution 1881 (XVIII), in which it condemned the South African Government for its failure to comply with repeated resolutions of the United Nations calling for an end to the repression of persons opposing *apartheid*. The General Assembly requested the Government of South Africa to abandon the arbitrary trial and "forthwith to grant unconditional release to all political prisoners and to all persons imprisoned, interned or subject to other restrictions for having opposed the policy of *apartheid*".

By resolution 1978 A (XVIII) of 16 December 1963 the General Assembly strengthened the mandate of the Special Committee by requesting it "to continue to follow constantly the various aspects of this question and to submit reports to the General Assembly and the Security Council whenever necessary". This resolution further requested the Secretary-General to furnish the Special Committee with all the necessary means for the effective accomplishment of its task and invited the specialized agencies and all Member States to give it their assistance and co-operation in the fulfilment of its mandate. The General Assembly in the same resolution also appealed to all States to take appropriate measures and intensify their efforts with a view to dissuading the South African Government from pursuing its policies of *apartheid* and requested them in particular to implement fully the Security Council resolution of 4 December 1963. In resolution 1978 B (XVIII) the General Assembly requested the Secretary-General to seek ways and means of providing relief and assistance, through the appropriate inter-

[1] See *Official Records of the General Assembly, Eighth Session, Supplement No. 16*, documents A/2505 and Add.1.

national agencies, to the families of all persons persecuted by the Government of the Republic of South Africa for their opposition to the policies of *apartheid* and invited Member States and organizations to contribute to such relief and assistance.

Subsequently, at its twentieth session in 1965, the General Assembly, in resolution 2054 A (XX), drew the attention of the Security Council to the fact that the situation in South Africa constituted a threat to international peace and security, that action under Chapter VII of the Charter was essential in order to solve the problem of *apartheid*, and that universally applied economic sanctions were the only means of achieving a peaceful solution. In the same resolution the General Assembly deplored the actions of certain States which, through political, economic and military collaboration with South Africa, were encouraging it to persist in its racial policies and urgently appealed to such States to cease their increasing relations with the Government of South Africa. The Assembly invited the specialized agencies to deny technical and economic assistance to the Government of South Africa, without, however, interfering with humanitarian assistance to the victims of the policies of *apartheid*. In response to the request of the United Nations Special Committee on the Policies of *Apartheid* of the Government of the Republic of South Africa, made in accordance with General Assembly resolution 1978 A (XVIII), the Executive Board of UNESCO, at its seventieth session in May 1965, authorized the Director-General to prepare a report on the effects of the policy of *apartheid* in the fields of education, culture, science and the dissemination of information in the Republic of South Africa. The report was submitted to the Special Committee in December 1966.[2] At its fourteenth session, the General Conference of UNESCO defined anew the tasks of UNESCO in the light of the United Nations General Assembly resolutions relating to the elimination of colonialism, racialism and racial discrimination. After declaring its conviction that the practice of *apartheid* and all other forms of racial discrimination constituted a threat to international peace and security and were a crime against humanity, the General Conference, in its resolution No. 11, decided: (1) to continue, within the framework of UNESCO's programme, to organize meetings and research projects on the harmful effects of colonialism, neo-colonialism and racialism on the social and economic life of countries and on the development of their education, science and culture, with a view to assisting in the application of practical measures to eradicate such after-effects; (2) to make more active use of the Organization's information and publications programme and other forms of activity in order to unmask and to help eradicate, with all possible speed, colonialism, neo-colonialism, the policy and practice of *apartheid* and racial discrimination, and also to give wide publicity to the relevant resolutions of the United Nations General Assembly and the UNESCO General Conference.

[2] The report was subsequently published as *Apartheid: Its Effects on Education, Science, Culture and Information* (UNESCO, Paris, 1967).

At its twenty-first session the General Assembly, in its resolution 2202 A (XXI) of 16 December 1966, declared that action under Chapter VII of the Charter of the United Nations was essential in order to solve the problem of *apartheid* and that universally applied mandatory economic sanctions were the only means of achieving a peaceful solution. At the same session, the General Assembly in resolution 2144 A (XXI) requested that the Secretary-General establish within the Secretariat of the United Nations a unit to deal exclusively with the policies of *apartheid*, in order that maximum publicity might be given to the evils of those policies.

At the twenty-first and following sessions the General Assembly repeatedly and with ever increasing emphasis expressed its condemnation and abhorrence of the policy of *apartheid*. Elsewhere in this publication, reference is made to the General Assembly resolutions which condemn the policies of *apartheid* as constituting a crime against humanity (General Assembly resolutions 2074 (XX), 2202 A (XXI), 2184 (XXI), 2189 (XXI), 2307 (XXI), 2506 B (XXIV), 2671 F (XXV) and 2775 F (XXVI)).

At the twenty-sixth and twenty-seventh sessions the General Assembly (resolutions 2786 (XXVI) and 2922 (XXVII)) considered a draft Convention on the Suppression and Punishment of the Crime of *Apartheid*. At the time of the preparation of the present publication, the Assembly has not yet taken final action on a draft international instrument devoted to *apartheid*.

Of the many resolutions on the policies of *apartheid* of the Government of South Africa which the General Assembly adopted at its twenty-third to twenty-seventh sessions, the following might be especially mentioned (some of them have already been listed above in relation to the condemnation of *apartheid* as a crime against humanity). In resolution 2396 (XXIII) the General Assembly drew the attention of the Security Council to the grave situation in South Africa and in southern Africa as a whole, with special reference to Chapter VII of the Charter. It condemned the actions of those States, particularly the main trading partners of South Africa, and the activities of foreign, financial and other interests, all of which were encouraging the South African Government which persisted in its racial policies. The General Assembly reaffirmed its recognition of the legitimacy of the struggle of the people of South Africa for all human rights, and in particular political rights and fundamental freedoms for all people of South Africa irrespective of race, colour or creed. In resolution 2506 A (XXIV) the General Assembly condemned the Government of South Africa for its repressive acts against the political movement of the oppressed people of South Africa and, in particular, for its enactment of the Terrorism Act, 1967. In resolution 2506 B (XXIV) the General Assembly invited all States, in recognition of their obligations under the Charter and in support of the legitimate struggle of the oppressed people of South Africa, to desist from collaborating with the Government of South Africa, by taking steps to prohibit financial and economic interests under their national jurisdiction from co-operating with the South African Government and companies registered in South Africa. States were also invited to prohibit airlines and shipping lines from providing services to and from South Africa and to refrain from extending loans, investments and technical assistance to South Africa and to companies registered there. The General Assembly invited all States and organizations to observe with appropriate ceremonies the International Day for the Elimination of Racial Discrimination of 21 March 1970.

At its twenty-fifth session the General Assembly adopted seven resolutions dealing with the policies of *apartheid* of the Government of South Africa (2624 (XXV) and 2671 A-F (XXV)). In these resolutions, the General Assembly called upon all States to take immediate steps to implement fully the provisions of Security Council resolution 282 (1970), which will be dealt with below in section B of this chapter, gave detailed instructions to the Special Committee on *Apartheid,* arranged for co-operation with the Organization of African Unity, invited the co-operation of the trade unions of the world, dealt with the United Nations Trust Fund for South Africa and urged all States to terminate diplomatic consular and other official relations with the Government of South Africa, to terminate all military, economic, technical and other co-operation with South Africa and reiterated and re-emphasized the various measures of an economic character and the arms embargo which has been recommended in earlier resolutions.

At the twenty-sixth session the General Assembly adopted a series of nine resolutions (2764 (XXVI) and 2775 A-H (XXVI)). Appealing to all States to exert their influence to secure the repeal of all legislation to give effect to the oppressive policies of *apartheid* and the liberation of all persons imprisoned or detained for opposition to *apartheid,* the General Assembly addressed itself with the same aim in view to national and international associations of jurists and to all religious organizations. It elaborated on earlier provisions concerning the arms embargo, dealt with *apartheid* in sports, the establishment of Bantustans and appealed to all national and international trade union organizations to intensify their action against *apartheid.* Action on similar lines was also taken at the twenty-seventh session of the General Assembly in 1972 (resolutions 2923 A-F (XXVII)). These resolutions dealt with the maltreatment and torture in South Africa of prisoners and detainees, with the United Nations Trust Fund for South Africa, with instructions to the Special Committee on *Apartheid,* with the dissemination of information on *apartheid.* The General Assembly reaffirmed its conviction that economic and other sanctions under Chapter VII of the Charter, universally applied, constituted one of the essential means of achieving a peaceful solution of the grave situation in South Africa. It repeated its request to the specialized agencies and other organizations within the United Nations system to discontinue all collaboration with the Government of South Africa until it renounced its policies of *apartheid.* It appealed to States members of international agencies and organizations, particularly the members of the European Economic Community, the General Agreement on Tariffs and Trade and the International Monetary Fund, to take the necessary steps to deny all assistance and other facilities to the Government of South Africa so long as it continued to defy the resolutions of the General Assembly and of the Security Council. The General Assembly welcomed the decision taken by the Workers' Group at the International Labour Conference to convene at Geneva in 1973, an international conference of trade unions to work out a common programme of action against *apartheid.*

### B. Action by the Security Council

The question of *apartheid* came before the Security Council for the first time in 1960. After having considered the complaint of 29 Member States concerning "the situation arising out of large-scale killings of unarmed and peaceful demonstrators against racial discrimination and segregation in the Union of South Africa", the Security Council, in its resolution 134 (1960) of 7 April 1960, recognized that the situation in that country was one that had led to international friction and, if continued, might endanger international peace and security. It called upon the Government of the Union of South Africa to abandon its policies of *apartheid* and racial discrimination and requested the Secretary-General, in consultation with that Government, to make adequate arrangements to uphold the purposes and principles of the Charter. In January 1961 the Secretary-General visited South Africa at the invitation of the Government. However, no mutually acceptable arrangement was found in the discussions of the Secretary-General with the Prime Minister of South Africa.

In its resolution 181 (1963) of 7 August 1963 the Security Council strongly deprecated the policies of South Africa in its perpetuation of racial discrimination and called upon the South African Government to liberate all persons imprisoned, interned or subject to other restrictions for having opposed the policy of *apartheid.* The Council also solemnly called upon all States to cease forthwith the sale and shipment of arms, ammunition of all types and military vehicles to South Africa.

On 4 December 1963, in resolution 182 (1963), the Security Council unanimously reaffirmed resolution 181 (1963) and decided on the establishment, by the Secretary-General, of a group of recognized experts "to examine methods of resolving the present situation in South Africa through full, peaceful and orderly application of human rights and fundamental freedoms to all inhabitants of the territory as a whole, regardless of race, colour or creed, and to consider what part the United Nations might play in the achievement of that end". The Group of Experts established by the Secretary-General suggested in its report [3] that the Security Council should invite the South African Government to take part in discussions under the auspices of the United Nations on the formation of a National Convention fully representative of all people of South Africa. The Group of Experts expressed the view that if no satisfactory reply was given by the South African Government, the Security Council would be left with no peaceful means for assisting to resolve the situation, except to apply economic sanctions.

---

[3] *Official Records of the Security Council, Nineteenth Year, Supplement for April, May and June 1949,* document S/5658, annex.

In 1964 the Security Council adopted two resolutions (190 (1964) of 9 June 1964 and 191 (1964) of 18 June 1964) on the question. Noting with grave concern that the verdict to be delivered in the Rivonia trial instituted against the leaders of the anti-*apartheid* movement under arbitrary laws might have serious consequences, the Council urged the South African Government to renounce the execution of persons sentenced to death, to end forthwith the trial in progress and to grant amnesty to all persons subject to penal measures for having opposed the policy of *apartheid.* Further, in its resolution 190 (1964) the Council condemned the *apartheid* policies of the South African Government and the legislation supporting these policies, such as the General Law Amendment Act and, in particular, the 90-day detention clause. In resolution 191 (1964) the Security Council endorsed the main conclusions of the Group of Experts established by resolution 182 (1963), that "all people of South Africa should be brought into consultation to decide the future of their country at the national level". It appealed to the Government of South Africa to accept this conclusion and to co-operate with the Secretary-General and to submit its views to him. The South African Government, however, refused to respond to the above invitation and claimed that the resolution represented intervention in matters falling within its domestic jurisdiction. Following a recommendation in the report of the Group of Experts the Security Council, in operative paragraph 8 of resolution 191 (1964), decided to establish an Expert Committee, composed of representatives of each current member of the Security Council, to undertake a technical and practical study and report to the Council as to the feasibility, effectiveness, and implications of measures which could, as appropriate, be taken by the Security Council under the United Nations Charter.

The Expert Committee sought to obtain the views of Member States on issues relating to the subject of its deliberations. To this end it also circulated a questionnaire,[4] to which 34 replies were received. The report [5] of the Expert Committee contained conclusions approved by majority vote and also a dissenting vote submitted by two members of the Committee.

In its resolution 282 (1970) of 23 July 1970, the Security Council stated that it was convinced of the need to strengthen the arms embargo called for in its earlier resolutions and that the situation in South Africa constituted a potential threat to international peace and security. It reaffirmed its earlier resolutions, condemned the violations of the arms embargo called for in them and called for additional measures in the economic and military fields to be taken by States.

In resolution 311 (1972) of 4 February 1972 the Security Council deplored again the persistent refusal of the Government of South Africa to implement the resolutions adopted by the Security Council to promote a peaceful solution in accordance with the Charter and expressed its grave concern that the situation in South Africa seriously disturbed international peace and security in southern Africa. It decided, as a matter of urgency, to examine methods of resolving the present situation arising out of the policies of *apartheid* of the Government of South Africa.

### C. Action by other United Nations organs

The action taken by organs other than the General Assembly and the Security Council, in particular that of the Economic and Social Council, of the Commission on Human Rights and organs established by it, the Sub-Commission on Prevention of Discrimination and Protection of Minorities, and the Special Committee on *Apartheid* is reflected in the resolutions of the General Assembly, which are summarized in a different context, because the General Assembly resolutions are mostly based on the recommendations of these organs.

Many of the decisions and other activities referred to have not been restricted to South Africa but have in addition applied either to other countries and territories in southern Africa or to events involving racial discrimination and segregation "wherever they may occur". Most of the decisions of the Economic and Social Council and its subsidiary organs and of the Committee on *Apartheid* have a bearing mostly on the establishment of machinery and procedures created to combat *apartheid* and are therefore treated in part two of the present publication.

In the present context it has to be pointed out however that the approach of the Commission on Human Rights and its superior bodies to questions of gross violations of human rights and particularly the question of *apartheid* took a turn towards intensified activities in 1967, when the Commission established an *Ad Hoc* Working Group of Experts to investigate the charges of torture and illtreatment of prisoners, detainees or persons in police custody in South Africa and to recommend action to be taken in concrete cases.[6] The Economic and Social Council in its resolution 1236 (XLII) of 1967 welcomed that decision. In the following year the Commission on Human Rights enlarged the mandate of the *Ad Hoc* Working Group to cover, in addition to South Africa, also Namibia (South West Africa), Southern Rhodesia and the Portuguese Territories in Africa.[7] On the basis of reports submitted by the *Ad Hoc* Working Group and on the recommendation of the Commission on Human Rights and of the Economic and Social Council, the General Assembly adopted at successive sessions comprehensive resolutions calling upon South Africa and the authorities of the other Territories in the south of Africa to change their legislation, to release prisoners, to punish persons guilty of the ill-treatment of prisoners, to pay compensation, etc. (General Assembly resolution 2240 (XXIII) of 1968; 2547

---

[4] For the text of the questionnaire and the replies thereto, see *Official Records of the Security Council, Twentieth Year, Special Supplement No. 2.*

[5] *Ibid.*

[6] Resolution 2 (XXIII) of the Commission on Human Rights, *Official Records of the Economic and Social Council, Forty-second Session, Supplement No. 6* (E/4322), para. 268.

[7] Resolution 2 (XXIV) of the Commission on Human Rights, 1968. *Official Records of the Economic and Social Council, Forty-fourth Session, Supplement No. 4* (E/4475), chapter XVIII.

(XXIV) of 1969; 2714 (XXV) of 1970). By way of example, reference is made to resolution 2714 (XXV), in which the General Assembly, acting on recommendations originally made by the *Ad Hoc* Working Group of Experts on the treatment of political prisoners in South Africa, established by resolution 2 (XXIII) of the Commission on Human Rights, condemned any and every practice of torture and ill-treatment of prisoners, detainees and captured freedom fighters in Namibia and the other Territories, as well as of persons in police custody in those Territories, again condemned the practice of torture and ill-treatment of prisoners in South Africa and addressed a series of very concrete recommendations to the Government of South Africa, based on recommendations contained in reports of the *Ad Hoc* Working Group of Experts and calling for, *inter alia*, the following: the immediate disbanding of the Bureau of State Security of South Africa; the discontinuance of the practice by which political detainees were compelled to testify against their former colleagues; the immediate and unconditional release of certain Africans who had been re-arrested under the Terrorism Act; the granting of full access at all trials of political opponents of the régime to independent outside observers; a full and impartial investigation into the deaths of political prisoners and detainees in its gaols as well as the full indemnification of the families of the deceased.

The Economic and Social Council and the Governing Body of the International Labour Office agreed in 1949 on arrangements for the protection of trade union rights (freedom of association) according to which the International Labour Organisation established, on behalf of the United Nations as well as on its own behalf, a Fact Finding and Conciliation Commission on Freedom of Association to which allegations regarding infringements of trade union rights against States members of the International Labour Organisation are to be referred. When South Africa ceased to be a member of that specialized agency, a difficulty arose to which the International Labour Office drew the attention of the Economic and Social Council, when it transmitted to it a complaint of the infringement of trade union rights in South Africa, submitted to the International Labour Office by an international trade union organization. The Economic and Social Council decided in resolution 1216 (XLII) of 1 June 1967 to transmit the communication to the *Ad Hoc* Working Group established by resolution 2 (XXIII) of the Commission on Human Rights. By this and by the later resolution 1302 (XLIV) of 28 May 1968, the Economic and Social Council extended the terms of reference of the *Ad Hoc* Working Group to examine further the question of infringements of trade union rights in South Africa and to include in its examination the infringements of trade union rights in South West Africa (Namibia).

# VII. MEASURES TAKEN BY THE UNITED NATIONS FOR THE PROMOTION OF EQUALITY OF MEN AND WOMEN

## A. Introduction

The provisions of the Charter cited in chapter I, section B, above laid the foundation for measures which have been taken by the United Nations in regard to the status of women. While all the provisions cited in chapter I are relevant, particular mention may be made in the present chapter of the Preamble to the Charter, which sets forth the principle of "the dignity and worth of the human person" and of "equal rights of men and women"; of Article 1, paragraph 3, which lists among the purposes and principles of the United Nations the promotion of universal respect for and observance of human rights and fundamental freedoms without distinction as to sex; and of Articles 55 and 56, under which all Member States of the United Nations pledge themselves to take joint and separate action in co-operation with the United Nations to promote universal respect for and observance of human rights and fundamental freedoms for all without distinction as to sex. Article 8 may also be noted, which provides: "The United Nations shall place no restrictions on the eligibility of men and women to participate in any capacity and under conditions of equality in its principal and subsidiary organs".

The measures taken in regard to the status of women have also been inspired by the Universal Declaration of Human Rights, especially articles 2, 7, 15, 16, 17, 21, 22, 23, 25 and 26. The International Covenants and the implementation procedures they provide will also be of considerable significance for the work of the United Nations in the field of the status of women.

Most of the measures designed to raise the status of women have emanated from the Commission on the Status of Women, a functional commission of the Economic and Social Council. The Commission was given a specific mandate to prepare recommendations and reports to the Council "on promoting women's rights in political, economic, civil, social and educational fields" and to make recommendations to the Council" on urgent problems requiring immediate attention in the field of women's rights, with the object of implementing the principle that men and women shall have equal rights, and to develop proposals to give effect to such recommendations".

Important initiatives for the adoption of measures to promote the status of women have also been taken by the General Assembly itself. Examples are: (*a*) the initiation of a study of the establishment of a unified long-term United Nations programme for the advancement of women, which was proposed in General Assembly resolution 1777 (XVII) of 7 December 1962; and (*b*) the elaboration of the Declaration on the Elimination of Discrimination against Women, which was requested by the General Assembly in resolution 1921 (XVIII) of 5 December 1963 and eventually proclaimed in 1967 (General Assembly resolution 2263 (XXII)). On both of these matters the preparatory work was undertaken by the Commission on the Status of Women.

In recent years the Social Development Commission has also taken certain initiatives, especially within the context of the development and utilization of human resources. These have included the organization of an expert group meeting to discuss the integration of women in development. This meeting, held in June 1972, was a joint project of the Social Development Commission and the Commission on the Status of Women (see section P below) and it brought together for the first time experts on questions of development and experts on questions of women's rights.

The Commission on the Status of Women is concerned not only with women's rights as such, and their universal recognition and acceptance, which was the principal focus of its work in the early years, but also with the opportunities available to women to exercise these rights once they have been written into law. In other words, the Commission seeks to promote the equal rights of men and women *de jure* and *de facto*, and much of its present work is directed towards the elimination of the wide discrepancies existing between the legal status of women and the role they play in practice. These concerns have led the Commission, in the last decade or so, into a number of new fields of enquiry, including particularly the study of women's role in, and the contribution they make or should be making to, the development of their countries. The expansion in the work programme dates back to the study of the establishment and implementation of a unified long-term United Nations programme for the advancement of women, initiated by the General Assembly in 1962. These developments in the work of the Commission on the Status of Women have paralleled developments in other United Nations bodies stressing the importance of balanced social and economic development for all countries.

In general terms, the measures taken by the United Nations aimed at improving the status of women to date have included the elaboration of international conventions, a formal recommendation and a declaration, and the establishment of procedures for the implementation of such instruments; the adoption of resolutions addressing recommendations for action to Governments, and also, in some instances, to specialized agencies and to non-governmental organizations in consultative status;

the preparation of studies and reports on a variety of questions relating to all the fields of concern to the Commission on the Status of Women; the development of operational programmes especially through the use of technical assistance and advisory services programmes to promote the advancement of women; and the dissemination of information concerning the work of the United Nations and other educational measures in this field. Details of the various measures adopted are given under appropriate substantive headings below.

### B. A unified long-term United Nations programme for the advancement of women

#### 1. *Origin and scope of the programme*

The General Assembly, in resolution 1777 (XVII) of 7 December 1962, requested the Secretary-General "to study in co-operation with Member States, the specialized agencies, the United Nations Children's Fund and appropriate non-governmental organizations, the possibility of providing and developing new resources aimed especially at the initiation and implementation of a unified long-term United Nations programme for the advancement of women"; and "within the scope of the programme of advisory services in the field of human rights and the advisory social services welfare programme to study especially the possiblity of expanding the assistance that can be rendered through seminars, fellowships and the services of experts for the advancement of women in developing countries". The Commission on the Status of Women was invited to co-operate with the Secretary-General to these ends.

In a report which the Secretary-General presented to the Commission on the Status of Women at its nineteenth session (February/March 1966) and which the Commission approved, it was suggested that the basic objectives of a unified, long-term United Nations programme for the advancement of women should be: [1]

(*a*) To promote the universal recognition of the dignity and worth of the human person and of the equal rights of men and women in accordance with the Charter of the United Nations and the Universal Declaration of Human Rights;

(*b*) To enable women to participate fully in the development of society in order that society may benefit from the contribution of all its members;

(*c*) To stimulate an awareness among both men and women of women's full potential and of the importance of their contribution to the development of society

It was also suggested that the programme be developed in stages and that during the initial stage particular emphasis be placed on: [2]

(*a*) The establishment of specific goals to be achieved;

(*b*) The determination of the special needs and problems of women in relation to these goals and in relation to economic and social development;

(*c*) The intensification of action to meet these needs and overcome these problems in order to achieve the goals established.

During the initial phase of the long-term programme for the advancement of women the proclamation by the General Assembly of the Declaration on the Elimination of Discrimination against Women—which eventually took place at the twenty-second session of the General Assembly, by resolution 2263 (XXII) of 7 November 1967—was considered an important objective so that the Declaration, along with the conventions and other instruments relating to the status of women, adopted under the auspices of the United Nations and of the specialized agencies, may provide guidelines for action by Governments and other bodies concerned with the advancement of women. (The relevant conventions and other instruments are dealt with in section C below.)

At the time of the adoption of General Assembly resolution 1777 (XVII) of 1962 the basic aim of its sponsors was to expand technical assistance activities that would help women, especially those in the developing countries, and to co-ordinate the efforts of the various organs and agencies within the United Nations system in this respect. This has remained an important objective of the unified long-term programme for the advancement of women and a number of recommendations have subsequently been addressed to Governments with this end in view. As the discussions have evolved however the unified long-term programme has come to mean an international programme in which all interested organs and agencies would be encouraged to participate, and in which all the various methods and techniques available, including technical assistance, would be used to equip women and to encourage their active participation in all aspects of national and international life.

#### 2. *Recommendations of the International Conference on Human Rights*

The general objective above is apparent in the guidelines for the long-term programme adopted by the International Conference on Human Rights at Teheran in 1968 (resolution IX, entitled "Measures to promote women's rights in the modern world including a unified long-term United Nations programme for the advancement of women").[3]

The Conference invited Governments to draw up long-term programmes for the advancement of women within the context of national development plans where they existed, and it requested the United Nations bodies and the specialized agencies to contribute, through appropriate technical assistance, to such programmes, and to establish or review their budgetary priorities with a view to meeting the requirements of the programmes.

The Teheran Conference specifically recommended that the Commission on the Status of Women should: (*a*) give priority to the examination of problems concerning the education of women and their contribution to develop-

[1] *United Nations Assistance for the Advancement of Women* (United Nations publication, Sales No. 67.IV.2), chap. IV.

[2] *Ibid.*

[3] *Final Act of the International Conference on Human Rights* (United Nations publication, Sales No. E.68.XIV.2), p. 10.

ment; (*b*) consider drafting conventions relating to the status of women in any fields where they are lacking; and (*c*) reconsider and adapt its programme and methods of work to meet the needs of women in the contemporary world.

### 3. *A programme of concerted international action for the advancement of women*

It was in 1966 at its nineteenth session, after concluding the report of the Secretary-General referred to in section B 2 above, that the Commission on the Status of Women first turned its attention actively to the question of women's role in national development. It called for the preparation of a questionnaire seeking the views of Governments and non-governmental organizations "on the role women can play in the economic and social development of their countries, the degree of priority which should be given to the contribution of women to the various areas of national, economic and social development, the problems encountered, possible ways of surmounting those problems and the kind of assistance that might be required". This request was endorsed by the Economic and Social Council in its resolution 1133 (XLI) of 26 July 1966.

Common observations made by most of the countries replying to the relevant questions were, *inter alia*:[4] (*a*) that the participation of women was increasing considerably in many areas and that their access to higher posts was improving, although their level of responsibility was generally low; (*b*) that the number of married women entering the labour market was increasing; (*c*) that in many countries there was a growing demand among married women for part-time work; (*d*) that there was a need for women and men to adapt themselves to the characteristics of modern society, for example, to the changing role of the home as a consumer rather than a producer of goods; (*e*) that there was a growing realization that the upbringing of children should be a joint responsibility of both parents; (*f*) that traditional attitudes hampered women from fully utilizing their talents and skills; (*g*) that much progress had been made in legislation according men and women equal rights in the political, social and economic fields; (*h*) that the advancement of the position of women must be viewed in terms of the rapid economic and social progress that could be achieved if greater equality between the sexes existed; (*i*) that greater economic progress and efficiency could be achieved if the scale of evaluation used in the labour market, based on physical characteristics of sex, were abandoned; (*j*) that the unified long-term programme for women and United Nations assistance in that field must be integrated within the context of the development of each individual country, and that the role of women should be aimed at benefiting all members of society.

Several Governments had indicated that they considered measures to increase women's contribution to the economic and social development of their countries as part of the goals of national plans for development. The Commission's attention was also drawn to the different measures which Member States had undertaken with a view to advancing the position of women in their countries, particularly the establishment of bodies to study the problems of women.

At the twenty-third session of the Commission on the Status of Women in 1970[5] it was stated that General Assembly resolution 1777 (XVII), which had initiated all the activities concerning the unified long-term programme, had resulted in the extension in the scope of work of the Commission, especially in the social field. At that session the Commission prepared a comprehensive draft resolution for consideration by the Economic and Social Council and the General Assembly entitled: Programme of concerted international action for the advancement of women. The Commission recommended in particular that certain general objectives and minimum targets should be achieved by the end of the Second United Nations Development Decade. These recommendations were the basis for resolution 2716 (XXV), unanimously adopted by the General Assembly on 15 December 1970.

In the annex to the resolution the General Assembly set forth, as recommended by the Commission on the Status of Women and by the Economic and Social Council, both the general objectives and the minimum targets to be achieved in this field during the Second United Nations Development Decade.

Among the general objectives recommended by the General Assembly is the ratification of, or accession to, the relevant international conventions relating to the status of women and the enactment of legislation to bring national laws into conformity with international instruments relating to the status of women, including in particular the Declaration on the Elimination of Discrimination against Women. The General Assembly further lists among the general objectives the taking of effective legal and other measures to ensure the full implementation of these instruments and the development of effective large-scale educational and informational programmes to make all sectors of the population fully aware of the norms which were established. Among the general objectives is further the assessment and evaluation of the contribution of women to the various economic and social sectors in relation to the country's over-all development plans and programmes with view to establishing specific objectives and minimum targets that might realistically be achieved by 1980. The General Assembly further enjoins the study of the positive and negative effects of scientific and technological change on the status of women and also the establishment of machinery and procedures to make possible the continuous review and evaluation of women's integration into all sectors of economic and social life and their contribution to development.

---

[4] See the report of the Commission on the Status of Women on the twenty-second session (*Official Records of the Economic and Social Council, Forty-sixth Session*, E/4619), paras. 79 *et seq.*

[5] Report of the Commission on the Status of Women on the twenty-third session (*Official Records of the Economic and Social Council, Forty-eighth Session, Supplement No. 6*), para. 32 *et seq.* and draft resolution II.

Among the minimum targets to be achieved during the Second United Nations Development Decade in the field of education, the General Assembly calls for the progressive elimination of illiteracy, ensuring equality in literacy between the sexes; equal access of boys and girls to education; decisive progress in achieving free and compulsory education at the primary level and in achieving free education at all levels; the establishment of educational policies that take account of employment needs and opportunities and of scientific and technological change.

In the matter of training and employment, the General Assembly calls for the provision of the same vocational advice and guidance to members of both sexes; equal access of girls and women to vocational training; universal acceptance of the principle of equal pay for equal work; full acceptance of the policy of non-discrimination in relation to the employment and treatment of women; a substantial increase in the numbers of qualified women in skilled and technical work, and at all higher levels of economic life and in posts of responsibility.

Under the heading "Health and maternity protection" the General Assembly calls for ensuring paid maternity leave; the development and extension of adequate child care facilities; and the development of a wide network of special medical establishments for the protection of the health of the mother and child. Among the minimum targets there is also the making available to all persons who so desire the necessary information and advice to enable them to decide freely and responsibly on the number and spacing of their children, including information on the ways in which women can benefit from family planning.

As far as administration and public life are concerned the annex calls for a substantial increase in the number of women participating in public and government life at the local, national and international levels. Special attention might be paid to training women for such participation, expecially in middle-level and higher posts. The number of qualified women holding responsible posts at the executive and policy-making levels, including those related to over-all development planning should also be substantially increased.

## C. International instruments relating to the rights of women and the implementation of such instruments

In addition to the Charter, the Universal Declaration of Human Rights and the International Covenants on Human Rights, the following international instruments are specifically devoted to matters concerning the status of women:

Declaration on the Elimination of Discrimination against Women, 1967;

Convention on the Political Rights of Women, 1952;

Convention on the Nationality of Married Women, 1957;

Convention on Consent to Marriage, Minimum Age for Marriage and Registration of Marriages, 1962, and the Recommendation on the same subject, 1965.

The following instruments are also of particular importance as regards the status of women:

Equal Remuneration Convention, 1951, of the ILO;

Discrimination (Employment and Occupation) Convention, 1958, of the ILO;

Convention against Discrimination in Education and Recommendation on the same subject, 1960, of UNESCO;

Recommendation concerning the Employment of Women with Family Responsibilities, 1965, of the ILO;

Recommendation concerning the Status of Teachers, 1966, of UNESCO;

Proclamation of Teheran, 1968;

Declaration on Social Progress and Development, 1969.

### 1. *Declaration on the Elimination of Discrimination against Women, 1967*

The Declaration on the Elimination of Discrimination against Women was adopted unanimously by the General Assembly in resolution 2263 (XXII) on 9 November 1967. It was adopted after four years of debate and detailed drafting work in the Commission on the Status of Women and in the Assembly itself. The need for this Declaration is stated in the preamble, which expresses concern that despite the Charter, the Universal Declaration of Human Rights, the International Covenants on Human Rights and other instruments and despite progress made in the equality of rights "there continues to exist considerable discrimination against women".

The Declaration of 1967 represents an up-to-date general pronouncement of United Nations policy in regard to equality of men and women and the elimination of discrimination based on sex. In the paragraphs that follow it will be shown that the Declaration restates and consolidates a series of principles, many of which were embodied in earlier international instruments emanating from the United Nations and the specialized agencies. However, before proceeding to recall the earlier instruments reflected in the provisions of the Declaration, it is necessary to emphasize that in this case at least the whole is more than the sum of its parts. It must be added, moreover, that the Declaration of 1967 also sets forth a series of important principles not, or not concretely and in detail, contained in the earlier treaties and recommendations.

The declaration contains eleven articles, seven of them dealing with substantive rights of women. These are concerned with: political rights (article 4); right to a nationality (article 5); rights under civil law (article 6); discriminatory provisions under penal law (article 7); traffic in women (article 8); educational rights (article 9); and economic rights (article 10).

By providing that all appropriate measures shall be taken to ensure to women, on equal terms with men and without any discrimination, the right to vote in all elections and the right to hold public office and to exercise all public functions, the Declaration restates the provisions of the Convention on Political Rights of Women adopted in 1952, but includes specific reference to participation in referenda, which is not mentioned in the Convention. In proclaiming the principle that women shall have the same rights as men to acquire, change or retain their nationality, and in providing that marriage to an alien shall not automatically affect the nationality of the wife, the Declaration restates the provisions of the Convention on the Nationality of Married Women, 1957, although in the latter provisions the Declaration is less far-reaching than the Convention.

In providing that all appropriate measures, particularly legislative measures, shall be taken to ensure to women, married or unmarried, equal rights with men in the field of civil law, the Declaration lists the fields in which this equality shall particularly apply. It consolidates a series of solemn statements by the General Assembly and the Economic and Social Council, adopted over the years on the initiative of the Commission on the status of Women. Article 6 also restates provisions of earlier instruments such as the Convention on Consent to Marriage, Minimum Age for Marriage and Registration of Marriages of 1962 and the Recommendation on these subjects of 1965.

The Declaration provides that all appropriate measures shall be taken to ensure to girls and women equal rights with men in education at all levels. Thereby the Declaration incorporates principles on which the Convention against Discrimination in education was based, which was adopted by the General Conference of UNESCO in 1960.

In proclaiming that all appropriate measures shall be taken to ensure to women equal rights with men in the field of economic and social life, the Declaration incorporates, among other principles, also those to which various International Labour Conventions have given expression, in particular the Equal Remuneration Convention of 1951 and the Discrimination (Employment and Occupation) Convention of 1958.

The Declaration adds the categorical injunction that all appropriate measures shall be taken to combat all forms of traffic in women and exploitation or prostitution of women. In this regard the Declaration reaffirms provisions of earlier instruments, including the Convention on the Suppression of Traffic in Persons and the Exploitation of the Prostitution of Others of 1949, referred to below in chapter VIII B. The Declaration also calls for the abolition of all provisions in penal law that are discriminatory against women.

In its more general provisions the Declaration states that discrimination against women, denying or limiting as it does their equality of rights with men, is fundamentally unjust and constitutes an offence against human dignity. The Declaration calls for the abolition of existing laws, customs, regulations and practices which are discriminatory against women. The principle of equality of rights, it proclaims, shall be embodied in the constitution or otherwise guaranteed by law. The Declaration also calls for the ratification or accession to, or full implementation as soon as practicable, of the international instruments of the United Nations and specialized agencies relating to the elimination of discrimination against women.

One year after the adoption of the Declaration, the Economic and Social Council, in resolution 1325 (XLIV) of 31 May 1968, adopted on the recommendation of the Commission on the Status of Women, outlined certain measures for its implementation. These included the initiation of a reporting system. Governments, interested specialized agencies and non-governmental organizations were invited to report on measures taken to give publicity to the Declaration and to comply with its provisions.

At its twenty-fourth session (1972), the Commission recommended that the reporting system applicable to the Declaration be expanded and consolidated to include information on the implementation of other United Nations conventions dealing with women's rights, and that these reports be submitted in accordance with a four-year cycle. In future the Commission on the Status of Women will consider at alternate sessions information relating to civil and political rights, and information relating to economic, social and cultural rights. Detailed guidelines have been prepared to assist Governments in submitting the information requested.

### 2. *Convention on the Political Rights of Women, 1952*

The Convention on the Political Rights of Women was adopted by the General Assembly in its resolution 640 (VII) of 20 December 1952 and entered into force on 7 July 1954. It is the first world-wide international treaty in which States parties have undertaken a legal obligation concerning the exercise of political rights by their citizens and in which the Charter principle of equal rights of men and women has been applied to a concrete problem. The preamble to the Convention expresses the desire of the States parties to implement the principle of equality of rights for men and women and recognizes, in paraphrasing article 21 of the Universal Declaration of Human Rights, that everyone has the right to take part in the government of his country directly or through freely chosen representatives, and has right to equal access to public service in his country. It is the stated intention of the Contracting Parties to equalize the status of men and women in the enjoyment and exercise of political rights, in accordance with the provisions of the Charter and of the Universal Declaration of Human Rights.

The substantive provisions of the Convention on the Political Rights of Women are to the effect that women shall be entitled to vote in all elections on equal terms with men, without any discrimination; that women shall be eligible for election to all publicly elected positions, established by national law on equal terms with men without any discrimination; and that women shall be entitled to hold public office and to exercise all public functions established by national law on equal terms with men without any discrimination. A voluntary reporting procedure concerning the implementation of the Convention on the Political Rights of Women has been in operation since 1953, when the Economic and Social Council, in its resolution 504 E (XVI) of 23 July 1953, requested that States parties to the Convention report every two years to the Economic and Social Council on the measures taken by them to implement the provisions of the Convention.

At its thirty-sixth session the Economic and Social Council, in its resolution 961 B (XXXVI) of 12 July 1963, noting that while States parties to the Convention on the Political Rights of Women had been requested by Council resolution 504 E (XVI) to submit reports on measures taken by them to implement its provisions, no similar information was at that time requested from States Members of the United Nations not parties to the Convention, addressed a request for reports to those States not parties to the Convention. It invited the Government of each State Member of the United Nations to supply the Secretary-General every two years with information it considered appropriate with regard to implementation of the principles stated in the Convention, including particularly whether any women have been elected to the national parliament and have been appointed to high governmental, judicial or diplomatic posts, such as minister or head of department, ambassador or member of delegation to sessions of the United Nations General Assembly or of corresponding organs of the specialized agencies. The Council reiterated this invitation at its thirty-ninth session in its resolution 1068 B (XXXIX) of 16 July 1965.

Fourteen years after the adoption and opening for signature of the Convention on the Political Rights of Women the General Assembly, by adopting and opening for signature and ratification the International Covenant on Civil and Political Rights, extended the prohibition to discrimination in regard to political rights on the ground of sex, which is set forth in the 1952 Convention, by providing in article 25 of the Covenant, that every citizen should have the rights and the opportunity without distinction of any kind, such as race, colour, sex, language, religion, political or other opinion, national or social origin, property, birth or other status, and without unreasonable restrictions, to take part in the conduct of public affairs directly or through freely chosen representatives; to vote and to be elected at genuine periodic elections, which should be by universal and equal suffrage and should be held by secret ballot, guaranteeing the free expression of the electors; and to have access, on general terms of equality, in public service to his country.

### 3. *Convention on the Nationality of Married Women, 1957*

The Convention on the Nationality of Married Women was adopted by the General Assembly in its resolution 1040 (XI) of 29 January 1957 and entered into force on 11 August 1958. This Convention is a further step in a development which had been foreshadowed in The Hague Convention on Certain Questions Relating to the Conflict of Nationality Laws of 1930 [6] and which tends to replace the traditional principle of the unity of the family with the principle of the independence of the nationality of the wife from that of the husband. Under the Convention of 1957 each Contracting State agrees that neither the celebration nor the dissolution of marriage between one of its nationals and an alien, nor the change of nationality by the husband during marriage, shall automatically affect the nationality of the wife. Each Contracting State, however, agrees that the alien wife of one of its nationals may, at her request, acquire the nationality of her husband through specially privileged naturalization procedures. The Convention shall not be construed as affecting any legislation or judicial practice by which the alien wife of one of its nationals may, at her request, acquire her husband's nationality as a matter of right.

### 4. *Convention on Consent to Marriage, Minimum Age for Marriage and Registration of Marriages, 1962*

This Convention, which the General Assembly adopted in its resolution 1763 A (XVII) of 7 November 1962, entered into force on 9 December 1964. It is the result of the initiative taken by the Commission on the Status of Women and the Economic and Social Council, on the one hand, and the 1956 Diplomatic Conference, which prepared and adopted the Supplementary Convention on the Abolition of Slavery, the Slave Trade, and Institutions and Practices Similar to Slavery, on the other. The Convention, the purpose of which is to guarantee that no marriage shall be legally entered into without the full and free consent of both parties, provides for three measures intended to achieve this aim. The consent must be expressed by the two intending spouses in person after due publicity and in the presence of the authority competent to solemnize the marriage and of witnesses as prescribed by law. The second measure provided for in the Convention is that States parties shall take legislative action to specify a minimum age for marriage. Thirdly, all marriages shall be registered in an appropriate official register by the competent authority.

The Convention provides for a limited exception from the rule requiring the presence of both parties at the solemnization of the marriage. It is not necessary for one of the parties to be present when the competent authority is satisfied that the circumstances are exceptional and that the party has, before a competent authority and in such manner as may be prescribed by law, expressed and not withdrawn consent.

The Convention also permits an exception from the rule that no marriage shall be legally entered into by a person under the specified age. This exception applies where a competent authority has, in the interest of the intending spouses and for serious reasons, granted a dispensation as to age.

### 5. *Recommendation on Consent to Marriage, Minimum Age for Marriage and Registration of Marriages, 1965*

This Recommendation, which the General Assembly adopted on 1 November 1965 (resolution 2018 (XX)), deals with the same problems as the Convention adopted three years earlier and is intended to be taken into consideration by such States as may not be in a position to become parties to the Convention of 1962. The requirements for permitting a marriage by proxy are not as stringent in the Recommendation as they are in the Convention. On the other hand, while the Convention does not itself specify a minimum age for marriage and imposes upon States parties only the obligation to take legislative action to this effect, the Recommendation expressly provides that the minimum age for marriage to be specified by Member States shall not be less than 15 years of age.

---

[6] League of Nations, *Treaty Series*, vol. CLXXIX, p. 89.

While the Convention of 1962 does not provide for any international machinery of implementation (except a settlement of disputes clause which requires the request of all parties to the dispute for its referral to the International Court of Justice) the Recommendation is more specific in this regard. The General Assembly recommended that each Member State should bring the Recommendation before the authorities competent to enact legislation or to take other action at the earliest practicable moment and should inform the Secretary-General as soon as possible after this action of the measures taken to bring the question before the competent authority or authorities, with particulars regarding the authority or authorities considered as competent. The Recommendation further provides for a reporting procedure. States Members were expected to report to the Secretary-General at the end of three years and thereafter at intervals of five years on the law and practice with regard to the matter dealt with in the Recommendation, showing the extent to which effect had been given or was proposed to be given to the provisions of the Recommendation and such modifications as had been found or might be found necessary in adapting or applying it. The reports received from Governments were to be presented to the Commission on the Status of Women, which was expected to examine them and to report to the Economic and Social Council with such recommendation as it might deem fitting. As of the beginning of 1973 only one series of such reports has been submitted to the Commission on the Status of Women. The second series will be submitted within the framework of the reporting system on the implementation of the Declaration on the Elimination of Discrimination against Women (see above, section 1).

### 6. *The elaboration of a new instrument or instruments*

At its recent sessions the Commission on the Status of Women has considered the question whether a new instrument or instruments in the field of the status of women should be elaborated. At its twenty-third session in March-April 1970 the Commission, in resolution 4 (XXIII), requested the Secretary-General to undertake a study showing to what extent existing international conventions already contained provisions relating to rights covered by the Declaration on the Elimination of Discrimination against Women, the measures of implementation provided under such conventions, and the status of ratifications and accessions to them.

At its twenty-fourth session (February-March 1972) the report prepared by the Secretary-General pursuant to that resolution of the Commission (E/CN.6/552) was before the Commission. At that session a proposal was made by one delegation providing that the Commission on the Status of Women should begin the preparation of a draft convention for the elimination of discrimination against women at its next (twenty-fifth) session in 1974. After an extensive debate in which also opposing view points were expressed, the Commission in its resolution 5 (XXIV) invited the Secretary-General to call upon the States Members of the United Nations to transmit their views or proposals concerning the nature and content of a new instrument or instruments of international law to eliminate discrimination against women. The Commission also resolved to place an item entitled "Consideration of proposals concerning a new instrument or instruments of international law to eliminate discrimination against women" on the agenda of its twenty-fifth (1974) session and in order to facilitate this work decided to establish a working group to meet before the beginning of the twenty-fifth session and begin work on the preparation of a new draft instrument or instruments of international law. It also requested the Secretary-General, the ILO and UNESCO to assist the working group and the Commission in their work.

## D. Political rights of women [7]

### 1. *The right to vote and to hold public office*

In 1948 the Economic and Social Council (resolution 120 A(VI) of 3 March 1948) requested the Secretary-General to being up to date annually information on the political rights of women and their eligibility for public office. Since that time the Secretary-General has prepared and circulated, each year, reports on progress achieved in the field of political rights of women, including the available provisions taken from constitutions, electoral laws and other legal instruments which granted, restricted or denied women the right to vote and to be elected to public office on equal terms with men. [8]

In 1966, pursuant to Economic and Social Council resolution 1132 (XLI) of 26 July 1966, the Secretary-General consolidated into a single report all the information available on the political rights of women, including the information received from Governments on the implementation of the Convention on Political Rights of Women.

At its resumed forty-eighth session, the Economic and Social Council, on the recommendation of the Commission on the Status of Women, adopted resolution 1510 (XLVIII) of 28 May 1970, which contained a draft resolution for adoption by the General Assembly on the employment of qualifed women in senior and other professional positions by the secretariats of organizations in the United Nations system. The General Assembly adopted the resolution recommended to it by the Economic and Social Council as resolution 2715 (XXV) of 15 December 1970. In that resolution the General Assembly recalled Article 101 of the United Nations Charter, the Universal Declaration of Human Rights and the Declaration on the Elimination of Discrimination against Women. The Assembly expressed the hope that the United Nations, including its special bodies and all intergovernmental agencies in the United Nations system of organizations, would set an example with regard to opportunities for the employment of women at senior and other profes-

---

[7] See also section C 2 above with regard to the Convention on the Political Rights of Women of 1952.

[8] See documents A/619 and Add.1 and 2 and Corr.1; A/1163; A/1342 and Corr.1; A/1911; A/2154 and Add.1 and 2; A/2462; A/2692 and Corr.1; A/2952 and Add.1; A/3145 and Add.1; A/3627 and Corr.1; A/3889; A/4159; A/4407; A/4824 and Corr.1; A/5153; A/5456 and Add.1; A/5735; A/6036.

sional levels. It urged the United Nations and the other bodies concerned to take or continue to take appropriate measures to ensure equal opportunities for the employment of qualified women in senior and other professional positions. It requested the Secretary-General to include in his report on the composition of the Secretariat data relevant to this question.

When, on the proposal of the Commission on the Status of Women, the question of employment of women in senior and other professional positions by the secretariats of organizations in the United Nations system was again taken up by the Economic and Social Council at its fifty-second session, the Council again recommended to the General Assembly the adoption of a resolution on the problem. On the basis of the draft resolution submitted to it by the Council in its resolution 1676 (LII), the General Assembly adopted at its twenty-seventh session resolution 3009 (XXVII) of 18 December 1972, which differs somewhat from the text submitted by the Council. Most, but not all, of the changes were due to the necessity to take into account, particularly in the statistical statements of the preamble, developments that had occurred between the session of the Council in June 1972 and the adoption of the General Assembly resolution in December 1972. In resolution 3009 (XXVII) the General Assembly noted with satisfaction the appointment by the Secretary-General of a woman to the rank of Assistant Secretary-General and expressed the hope that more women would be appointed to positions at high levels of the United Nations Secretariat. Once again it urged the organizations in the United Nations system to take or continue to take appropriate measures, including more extensive publicizing of the right of individuals personally to apply for vacant positions, in order to ensure equal opportunities for the employment of qualified women at the senior and professional levels and in policy-making positions. The General Assembly called upon Member States, when proposing nationals for appointment to the senior and professional positions in the secretariats, to give full consideration to submitting the candidatures of qualified women for all positions, particularly at the policy-making level.

### 2. *Civic and political education*

In 1948, the Economic and Social Council, acting on recommendations of the Commission, drew attention, in resolution 154 A (VII) to the fact that opportunities for the exercise of political rights and a greater measure of activity by women voters in making use of their right to take part in elections, as well as the introduction of a more general system of electing women to key posts in national, public, municipal and other institutions, would serve as an effective method of stimulating the interest of women voters, would increase their interest in social and political work, and would ensure a fuller use by women voters of their right to take part in elections. The Council also requested the Secretary-General to continue, for the benefit of women who have recently acquired the vote, the collection of information about effective programmes of political education; to give favourable consideration to measures for technical advice to such countries; and to prepare for general use a popular pamphlet showing the extent to which women have been accorded equal political rights.

## E. Nationality of married women

The problem of the nationality of married women has been the concern of the United Nations since the Commission on the Status of Women decided to study this question in 1948. On the recommendation of the Commission, the Economic and Social Council decided in 1949 that a convention on the nationality of married women, which would assure women equality with men in the exercise of rights set out in article 15 of the Universal Declaration of Human Rights, and especially prevent a woman from becoming stateless or otherwise suffering hardships arising out of these conflicts in law, should be prepared as soon as possible.[9]

In 1955 the Commission on the Status of Women completed its preparation of a draft convention on the nationality of married women and forwarded the draft to the Economic and Social Council, which in turn forwarded it to the General Assembly for final approval. The Convention on the Nationality of Married Women was adopted by the General Assembly in its resolution 1040 (XI) of 29 January 1957 and was opened for signature, ratification and accession by States on 20 February of that year (see above, section C 3).

Under a resolution which the Economic and Social Council adopted in 1954 (resolution 547 D (XVIII)) the Secretary-General has continued the collection of information on recent changes in national legislation affecting the nationality of married women. Reports on this question are currently presented to the Commission on the Status of Women every four years under the reporting system established by the Commission at its twenty-fourth session (1972) in connexion with the implementation of the Declaration on the Elimination of Discrimination against Women (see section C, above).

## F. Status of women in private law and related questions concerning the rights and dignity of women

The legal status of married women has been the concern of the Commission on the Status of Women since the beginning of its work in 1946. In June of that year the Economic and Social Council, in its resolution 11 (II), requested the Secretary-General "to make arrangements for a complete and detailed study of the legislation concerning the status of women and the practical application of such legislation". Subsequently, the Secretary-General prepared a questionnaire on the legal status and treatment of women covering, among other fields, nationality, family law and property rights. The questionnaire was circulated to Governments, and a series of reports based on the replies received, was prepared and submitted to the Commission from 1946 to 1965.

Reports on selected subjects in the field of private law have also been requested by the Commission and prepared

[9] Economic and Social Council resolution 242 (IX) of 1 Augus 1949.

by the Secretariat on the basis of special questionnaires addressed to Governments or on the basis of information available to the Secretariat, including documentation prepared by participants attending seminars organized under the human rights advisory services programme.

In examining these various reports the Commission on the Status of Women, over a period of years, has made a series of recommendations addressed to Governments through the Economic and Social Council. It has been inspired in much of its work in this field by the terms of article 16 of the Universal Declaration of Human Rights, and more recently by article 6 of the Declaration on the Elimination of Discrimination against Women. At its twenty-first session, the Commission on the Status of Women initiated a long-term programme of further studies in the field of family law, based on article 6 of the above Declaration and focusing especially on the changes which have occurred in the intervening years. The first of those studies will deal with the legal capacity and property rights of women. Details of the resolutions adopted to date by the Council on the recommendation of the Commission on the Status of Women are given below.

### 1. *Rights and duties of men and women during marriage and at its dissolution*

In resolution 504 D (XVI) of 23 July 1953, adopted on the recommendation of the Commission on the Status of Women, the Economic and Social Council expressed the belief that the sharing by the spouses of the authority, prerogatives and responsibilities involved in marriage were not only of benefit to the status of women but to the family as an institution. With this in view the Council recommended that Governments take all possible measures to ensure equality of rights and duties of husband and wife in family matters and to ensure to the wife full legal capacity, the right to engage in work outside the home and the right on equal terms with her husband to acquire, administer, enjoy and dispose of property.

*Matrimonial régimes.* The following year the Council, upon recommendation of the Commission on the Status of Women, in resolution 547 I (XVIII) drew attention to the desirability of a statutory régime which would take account of the rights of the wife over community and separate property during marriage and at its dissolution. It recommended that discriminatory provisions affecting the property rights of the wife should be removed from national legislation and that the property belonging to the spouses at the time of marriage should remain separate, any property acquired during a marriage being held separately or in common with joint management. In case of dissolution of marriage, property acquired during the marriage should be divided equally.

*Right of married women to engage in independent work.* In resolution 547 J (XVIII) of the same year the Council noted that under some legal systems the husband has the power to prevent his wife from engaging in independent work, and in some systems he has control over her earnings. It recommended that Governments take all the necessary measures to ensure the rights of a married woman to undertake independent work and to administer and dispose of her earnings without the necessity of securing her husband's authorization.

*Domicile of married women.* In resolution 587 D III (XX), the Council, accepting the proposals of the Commission relating to the domicile of married women, noted that in the legal systems of many countries the domicile of the wife follows that of her husband; that in these countries the wife upon marriage loses her original domicile and acquires the domicile of her husband, which she retains until the dissolution of the marriage even if residing separately. The Council expressed the belief that such legal systems were incompatible with the principle of equality of spouses during the marriage, proclaimed in the Universal Declaration of Human Rights, and noted that their application resulted in particular hardships for married women in countries where domicile determined the jurisdiction of courts in matrimonial matters and where the law in the place of domicile governs a person's status. The Council recommended that Governments take all necessary measures to ensure the right of a married woman to an independent domicile.

*Parental rights and duties.* In 1955 in resolution 587 D II (XX) the Council, endorsing proposals of the Commission on the Status of Women, noted that in some legal systems parental authority belongs exclusively or primarily to the father; that in some countries in the event of loss of such authority it does not automatically pass to the mother; and in some instances on dissolution of marriage the custody of the children is awarded to the father, regardless of the merits of the case. The Council was of the opinion that these limitations were incompatible with the principle of equality of the spouses during marriage and at its dissolution and accordingly recommended that States Members of the United Nations take steps to ensure equality between parents in the exercise of rights and duties with respect to their children. At its fifteenth session (1961), the Commission on the Status of Women decided to study this question further. It asked the Secretary-General to prepare a preliminary report on parental rights and duties, including guardianship, based on information available to him, including the documentation of the seminars on the status of women in family law. When considering the preliminary report at its nineteenth session (1966), the Commission decided to forward it to Governments, together with an explanatory note, and to invite them to provide supplementary information on the basis of which the report would be revised. The revised report was presented to the Commission at its twentieth session in 1967. After considering this report the Commission recommended—and the Economic and Social Council eventually adopted—a resolution, "Parental rights and duties, including guardianship" (resolution 1207 (XLII) of 29 May 1967), in which it welcomed the generally discernible trend in many legal systems towards a sharing on a basis of equality of the parental authority. The Council recommended that Governments of Member States take all possible measures to ensure equality between men and women in the exercise of parental rights and duties. It further recommended the following principles for ensuring such equality, taking account of the special characteristics of legislation in different countries and bearing in mind that in all cases the interest of the children should be paramount:

"(*a*) Women shall have equal rights and duties with men in respect to guardianship of their minor children and the exercise of parental authority over them, including care, custody, education and maintenance;

"(*b*) Both spouses shall have equal rights and duties with regard to the administration of the property of their minor children, with the legal limitations necessary to ensure as far as possible that it is administered in the interest of the children;

"(*c*) The interest of the children shall be the paramount consideration in proceedings regarding custody of children in the event of divorce, annulment of marriage or judicial separation;

"(*d*) No discrimination shall be made between men and women with regard to decisions regarding custody of children and guardianship or other parental rights in the event of divorce, annulment of marriage or judicial separation."

*Inheritance laws as they affect the status of women.* In 1962 at its sixteenth session, the Commission on the Status of Women had before it a report of the Secretary-General on inheritance laws as they affect the status of women which had been prepared at the request of the Commission in 1961 on the basis of a special questionnaire addressed to Governments. It was noted in this report that in some systems the inheritance rights of women are not equal to those of men. For example, in some a male heir is preferred to the female in the order of succession; and in others women receive a fraction of the share of the male in the same degree of relationship. In resolution 884 D I (XXXIV) adopted on the recommendation of the Commission on the Status of Women in 1962, the Economic and Social Council recommended that Governments take measures to ensure equality of inheritance rights of men and women by providing that men and women in the same degree of relationship to the deceased should be entitled to equal shares in the estate and should have equal rank in the order of succession. Furthermore, it recommended that Governments provide that the inheritance rights and the capacity of women to make a will, to accept or refuse an inheritance and to be administrators or executors of estates should not be affected by marriage and that the interest of the widow in the estate should be equal to that of the widower.

*Dissolution of marriage, annulment and judicial separation.* In 1965, the Commission on the Status of Women considered a report prepared by the Secretary-General at its request on the dissolution of marriage, annulment of marriage and judicial separation. This report was based on a special questionnaire submitted to Governments. After considering this report, the Commission recommended in a draft resolution, which was subsequently endorsed by the Economic and Social Council as resolution 1068 F (XXXIX), that Governments of Member States take all possible measures to ensure equality of rights between men and women in the event of dissolution of marriage, annulment of marriage or judicial separation. The following principles were recommended for ensuring such equality, taking account of the special characteristics of legislation in differing countries:

"(*a*) Facilities for reconciliation should be made available;

"(*b*) A divorce or judicial separation shall be granted only by a competent judicial authority and shall be legally recorded;

"(*c*) Both spouses shall have the same rights and shall have available the same legal grounds and legal defences in proceedings for divorce, annulment of marriage and judicial separation;

"(*d*) The right of either spouse to give or withhold full and free consent should be ensured by law in the event of divorce on the ground of mutual consent in countries where mutual consent is a ground for divorce;

"(*e*) In proceedings regarding custody of children, the interest of the children shall be the paramount consideration;

"(*f*) Divorce, annulment of marriage, judicial separation or dissolution of marriage by death shall not have as a consequence an inequality in legal status and capacity of men and women."

### 2. *Consent to marriage, minimum age for marriage and registration of marriages*

The Conference of Plenipotentiaries, convened in 1956 to prepare the Supplementary Convention on the Abolition of Slavery, the Slave Trade, and Institutions and Practices Similar to Slavery, in addition to adopting such a Convention, recommended that the Economic and Social Council consider "the appropriateness of initiating a study of the question of marriage, with the object of drawing attention to the desirability of free consent of both parties to a marriage and of the establishment of a minimum age for marriage, preferably of not less than fourteen years". In 1957, the Economic and Social Council decided to entrust the study of this question to the Commission on the Status of Women.

There was considerable discussion in both the Commission and the Council as to whether an international instrument prescribing standards in these fields should take the form of a recommendation or of a convention. It was decided to prepare both a convention and a recommendation. At its sessions in 1960 and in 1961, the Commission prepared a preliminary draft convention and draft recommendation on these subjects.

In 1962, the General Assembly adopted and opened for signature the Convention on Consent to Marriage, Minimum Age for Marriage and Registration of Marriages,[10] and in 1965 the General Assembly adopted a Recommendation [11] on the same subject. The substantive provisions of both these instruments are analysed in section C 4 and 5 above.

---

[10] General Assembly resolution 1763 A (XVII) of 7 November 1962.

[11] General Assembly resolution 2018 (XX) of 1 November 1965.

### 3. *Customs, ancient laws and practices affecting the human dignity of women*

Since 1946, the Commission has regularly received and continues to receive reports on the status of women in Trust and in Non-Self-Governing Territories. These reports, which are based on information annually transmitted to the United Nations by the Administering Authorities in answer to questionnaires, deal with the legal, social, economic and educational status of women in these Territories.

In 1954, after considering such reports, the Commission through the Economic and Social Council, made certain recommendations to the General Assembly and to the Trusteeship Council on "customs, ancient laws and practices affecting the human dignity of women". The Commission felt that, in certain areas of the world, including Trust and Non-Self-Governing Territories, women are subject to customs, laws and practices regarding marriage and the family, which are inconsistent with the principles set forth in the Charter of the United Nations and the Universal Declaration of Human Rights. The Trusteeship Council (at its fifteenth session in 1955) decided to take note of the Commission's resolution. The General Assembly adopted a resolution (resolution 843 (IX) of 17 December 1954) based on the Commission's recommendations, the operative paragraphs of which read as follows:

"*The General Assembly,*

"...

"1. *Urges* all States, including States which have or assume responsibility for the administration of Non-Self-Governing and Trust Territories, to take all appropriate measures in the countries and Territories under their jurisdiction with a view to abolishing such customs, ancient laws and practices by ensuring complete freedom in the choice of a spouse; abolishing the practice of the bride-price; guaranteeing the right of widows to the custody of their children and their freedom as to remarriage; eliminating completely child marriages and the betrothal of young girls before the age of puberty and establishing appropriate penalties where necessary; establishing a civil or other register in which all marriages and divorces will be recorded; ensuring that all cases involving personal rights be tried before a competent judicial body; ensuring also that family allowances, where these are provided, be administered in such a way as to benefit directly the mother and child;

"2. *Recommends* that special efforts be made through fundamental education, in both private and public schools, and through various media of communication, to inform public opinion in all areas mentioned in the second paragraph of the preamble above concerning the Universal Declaration of Human Rights and existing decrees and legislation which affect the status of women."

### 4. *Operations based on customs*

The question of operations based on customs was first discussed by the Commission in 1952 in connexion with the status of women in Trust and Non-Self-Governing Territories. On this occasion, the Commission requested the Trusteeship Council to revise its questionnaire to the Administering Authorities, in order to obtain from them pertinent information on the existence of such customs, and to invite the Member States concerned to take immediate action with a view to abolishing them. During the twelfth session of the Trusteeship Council, in 1953, a resolution was adopted noting the inclusion in the questionnaire of questions regarding the violation of the physical integrity of women as suggested by the Commission on the Status of Women.

The Commission has often expressed the view that operations based on customs performed on girls and young women, as carried out in certain parts of the world, are not only dangerous to health but seriously impair the human dignity of women. It has been noted that individual Governments concerned are working towards the elimination of these practices, and the hope has been expressed that they would continue to accelerate these efforts, with a view to complete abolition of those practices. In this connexion, the Economic and Social Council in 1960 in resolution 771 D (XXX) expressed the hope that Governments would take advantage of available services of the United Nations and of the specialized agencies which they considered appropriate for this purpose.

In 1958, on the initiative of the Commission, the Economic and Social Council (resolution 680 B II (XXVI)) invited the World Health Organization to undertake a study "of the persistence of customs which subject girls to ritual operations" and of the measures adopted or planned to put an end to these practices.

The question of these operations was discussed at the United Nations seminar on the participation of women in public life which was held in 1960 in Addis Ababa for African participants. The summary of the debate on this subject is contained in paragraphs 60, 61 and 62 of the report of the seminar (ST/TAO/HR/9). Subsequently, the Economic and Social Council drew the attention of the World Health Organization to this report and asked the agency whether it would undertake a study of the medical aspects of operations based on customs to which many women were still being subjected (resolution 821 II (XXXII) of 19 July 1961).

The World Health Organization took the position that the operations in question were based on "social and cultural backgrounds" and therefore were outside its competence. It stated that it would supply medical information as part of any wider socio-economic study undertaken (E/3592). To date no such study has been made, nor has any further action been taken.

## G. Tax legislation

Tax legislation as it affects women, especially married women who work, was discussed at several sessions of the Commission on the Status of Women. Two reports, in particular, formed the basis of the Commission's consideration of this question. The first was a preliminary study by the Secretary-General containing relevant information from Governments and non-governmental organizations based on the questionnaire on the legal status and treatment of women (E/CN.6/297). This report was submitted to the Commission at its eleventh session (1957). The second report dealing with tax legislation applicable to women, submitted to the Commission at its thirteenth session (1959), was prepared by consultants.

After considering these reports the Commission on the Status of Women recommended a draft resolution for adoption by the Economic and Social Council, which was endorsed by the Council and became resolution 821 (IV) C (XXXII) of 19 July 1961. In that resolution, the Council called the attention of Member States to the need in tax legislation to provide for equal treatment for men and women in respect to taxation of earned income and invited them to consider the desirability of giving effect to this principle by ensuring that married persons do not pay tax on earned income at a higher rate than single persons.

### H. Status of the unmarried mother

At its twentieth session in 1967, the Commission on the Status of Women considered the study of discrimination against persons born out of wedlock prepared by a Special Rapporteur of the Sub-Commission on Prevention of Discrimination and Protection of Minorities, and the draft general principles on equality and non-discrimination in respect of persons born out of wedlock and draft principles relating to the study, which had been adopted by the Sub-Commission at its nineteenth session, January 1967.[12] The Commission on the Status of Women expressed its general support for the principles on equality and non-discrimination in respect of persons born out of wedlock adopted by the Sub-Commission and requested the Secretary-General to prepare a report concerning law and practice with respect to unmarried mothers.

The requested study (E/CN.6/540) was presented to the Commission on the Status of Women at its twenty-third session in 1970. At that session and at the twenty-fourth session in 1972 the Commission prepared two draft resolutions, which were eventually adopted by the Economic and Social Council. In one of them, which was adopted by the Economic and Social Council at its forty-eighth session in 1970 (resolution 1514 (XLVIII)), the Council expressed the consideration that as a human being the unmarried mother was entitled to respect for her dignity and for her well-being and that of her child and that the integration of the unmarried mother and her child was a complex problem which called for thorough study. The Council urged States Members or members of the specialized agencies that had not yet done so to take adequate measures of social assistance in favour of the unmarried mother and the child born out of wedlock.

In resolution 1679 (LII) of 2 June 1972, the Council recommended to Governments of States Members of the United Nations a set of general principles for securing the unmarried mother and her child acceptance on an equal footing with other members of society. Among the principles thus adopted and recommended by the Council were the following: maternal filiation shall be recognized in law in all cases, automatically as a consequence of the fact of birth. If maternal filiation alone is established, the nationality and surname of the mother shall be transmitted to her child, if possible in such a manner as not to reveal the fact of birth out of wedlock. If both maternal and paternal filiation is established, the nationality of the child shall be governed by the same rules as those which apply in the case of birth in wedlock. The unmarried mother shall be vested in law with full parental authority over her child. When both paternal and maternal filiation is established, the maintenance obligations of the parents to the child shall be the same as if the child were born in wedlock. There shall be no discrimination against the offspring of unmarried mothers in any matters of inheritance, employment, education or training, or in access to child-care facilities.

### I. Discrimination against women in penal law

At its third session in 1949, the Commission on the Status of Women resolved to include among the questions to be examined by it the application to women of penal law, police statutes and prison administration. Subsequently, at its eleventh session in 1950, the Economic and Social Council, acting on recommendations of the Commission on the Status of Women, invited the Social Commission to bear in mind, in its study of the prevention of crime and the treatment of offenders, the concern for women, so that there should be no discrimination against women in penal law and its application and that there should be provision for the particular needs of women in all parole, probation, welfare, vocational training and rehabilitation services. The Council further invited the Social Commission to refer to the Commission on the Status of Women, for its consideration and comment, any question arising in the special field referred to above.

Except for the provisions contained in article 7 of the Declaration on the Elimination of Discrimination against Women, the question of discrimination against women in penal law has not been subsequently discussed by any organ of the United Nations, including the Commission on the Status of Women.

### J. Access of women to education, science and culture

#### 1. *Access of women to education*

In the early years, the Commission on the Status of Women adopted a number of general resolutions relating to the access of girls and women to education, basing its considerations on information furnished by the Secretariat of the United Nations, as well as on reports prepared by UNESCO. More recently a pattern has evolved whereby UNESCO submits a report to the Commission on the Status of Women at each session on some aspect of the access of girls and women to education (literacy, out-of-school education, education in rural areas, co-education, primary, secondary, technical and vocational, higher education, teaching profession). In

[12] Report of the Sub-Commission on the work of its nineteenth session, (E/CN.4/930); *Study of discrimination against persons born out of wedlock* (United Nations publication, Sales No. E.68.XIV.3).

addition to reports on such special topics, UNESCO submits reports on its activities of special interest to women.

Consideration of all these reports by the Commission on the Status of Women has resulted in the adoption of a large number of resolutions, many of them addressing recommendations to Governments, and, in some instances, to non-governmental organizations. Examples are cited below.

In 1948, the Economic and Social Council, on the recommendation of the Commission on the Status of Women, adopted resolution 154 F (VII) requesting Members of the United Nations "to grant women equal educational rights with men and to ensure that they are offered genuine educational opportunities, irrespective of nationality, race or religion". The Council also suggested that UNESCO include in its reports, information on progress achieved and plans for improving educational opportunities for women. The Council further suggested that UNESCO, upon request, be ready to make suggestion for programmes for the education of adults, where such programmes would help to solve the problem of illiteracy, and for other educational programmes.

In 1953, in resolution 504 H (XVI), adopted on the recommendation of the Commission on the Status of Women, the Economic and Social Council drew the attention of Governments and of the specialized agencies to the need for ensuring that pupils of both sexes have the same opportunity to take basic school curricula, including curriculum choices. In a second resolution of the same date (resolution 504 I (XVI)), the Council recommended to Member States that laws and regulations regarding the distribution of scholarships provide equal opportunities for girls and women and that such scholarships be made available to them in education in any field and in preparation for all careers. The Council also expressed the hope that in countries where native and official languages exist, attention would be given in programmes of education to the importance of providing equal opportunities for women to acquire the language in addition to their own, which would permit them access to the resources and knowledge in the general culture of the country.

In the following year, the Economic and Social Council in resolution 547 K (XVIII), recommended that States, both Members and non-members of the United Nations, should:

"(*a*) Take the necessary steps to ensure that women have equal access with men to all types of education without any of the distinctions mentioned in article 2 of the Universal Declaration on Human Rights;

"(*b*) Enact the necessary laws and regulations to eliminate all forms of discrimination against women in education and to ensure access for women to all types of education, including vocational and technical education, and equal opportunities to obtain state scholarships for education in any field in preparation for all careers;

"(*c*) Take the necessary measures to institute free, compulsory, primary education and take full advantage of the facilities and resources of UNESCO in developing additional educational opportunities for girls and women as needed."

In 1957, the Economic and Social Council, in resolution 652 C (XXIV) recommended that States Members of the United Nations or members of the specialized agencies should, in their programmes of educational advancement:

"(*a*) Make provisions for equal participation in fundamental educational programmes by all who have not received primary education and for an intensified campaign against illiteracy among the female population of areas where the general development of education is not advanced;

"(*b*) Make the necessary provision for increased attendance by girls at primary schools by instituting or extending universal, free and compulsory primary education for all, and by providing a sufficient number of schools, teachers and general education facilities."

As already indicated, progressive elimination of illiteracy, ensuring equality in literacy between the sexes and equal access of boys and girls to education is also set forth authoritatively in the annex of General Assembly resolution 2716 (XXV) already referred to above and in the resolutions of the Commission on the Status of Women and of the Economic and Social Council which were the bases of the General Assembly's resolution on programme of concerted international action for the advancement of women.

*Out-of-school and adult education*

A series of reports by UNESCO on the access of girls and women to education at different levels was presented to the Commission in 1960. The first one dealt with the access of women to out-of-school education (E/CN.6/361). The Commission adopted at its fourteenth session recommendations addressed to Governments, subsequently endorsed by the Council in resolution 771 G (XXX).

In resolution 821 V B (XXXII) of 19 July 1961, the Economic and Social Council, after inviting Governments of Member States to apply the provisions of the UNESCO Convention and Recommendation against Discrimination in Education as fully as possible and to provide full opportunities for young persons of both sexes to take the same or equivalent courses of study, recommended that such Governments and the competent education authorities give special attention to problems of illiteracy among women by adopting the necessary measures to increase, so far as may be necessary for this purpose, their budgetary appropriations for education, and to introduce, wherever it does not exist, the principle of free and compulsory primary education and to take appropriate steps to build schools as necessary. The Council also invited UNESCO to pursue steadily and to develop its plans for assistance in the fight against illiteracy; to assist all initiatives or actions by States aimed at increasing the opportunities for women to obtain education and all necessary educational material.

In 1965, the Council, in resolution 1068 H (XXXIX), which was also adopted on the recommendation of the Commission on the Status of Women, recommended that Member States should give a permanent place to programmes for women in planning their national literacy programmes and should take account of the special problems affecting women in rural areas. The Council invited UNESCO to devote particular attention to problems relating to the literacy education and continuing education of women and to encourage the inclusion, in the experimental programme to be launched in various countries, of projects relating particularly to the literacy education of women and directed towards the civic, social and economic education of women.

*Access of women to the teaching profession.* In 1961, the Commission on the Status of Women, after considering a report by UNESCO on the access of women to the teaching profession (E/CN.6/375), made certain recommendations later endorsed by the Council in resolution 821 A V (XXXII). The Council called upon the educational authorities in States Members of the United Nations and members of the specialized agencies to ensure, in law and in fact, equal pay and equal in-service training and promotional opportunities for women teachers, equal access to posts of responsiblity and authority, abolishing obstacles to the employment or re-employment of women in the teaching profession, crèches etc. The Council invited UNESCO and the other specialized agencies concerned to lend their assistance to Member States to this end.

*Primary education.* In 1962, the report dealing with the access of girls to primary education (E/CN.6/396 and Corr.1 and 2) was presented to the Commission at its sixteenth session.

In resolution 884 C (XXXIV) of 16 July 1962, adopted on the Commission's initiative, the Council recommended that States Members, of the United Nations and of the specialized agencies expand, where necessary, universal, compulsory and free elementary education for children of both sexes, to increase the attendance in elementary schools, especially by girls, to develop adult education, especially for women, to implement fully the Convention and Recommendation against Discrimination in Education especially for women, to implement fully the Convention and Recommendation against Discrimination in Education, adopted by the General Conference of UNESCO.

*Education in rural areas.* In 1963, the Commission on the Status of Women at its seventeenth session considered a report by UNESCO on the education of women in rural areas (E/CN.6/408) and a report by the ILO on the employment and conditions of work of women in agriculture (E/CN.6/422), on which it based recommendations subsequently approved by the Economic and Social Council in resolution 961 D (XXXVI). In that resolution the Council recommended that Governments of Member States give due priority to programmes of activities directed towards the development of education and vocational training of all types and at all levels for girls and women of rural areas, and that they include proper provisions to that end in their national development plans.

*Secondary education.* A report by UNESCO on the access of girls and women to secondary education (E/CN.6/433) was before the Commission on the Status of Women at its eighteenth session (1965). In resolution 1068 I (XXXIX), the Council endorsed proposals of the Commission based on that report and recommended that Member States:

"(*a*) Make provision, in planning their education systems, for all such measures—including schools, boarding schools and scholarships—as will assure girls, on a footing of complete equality with boys, access to secondary education, whether ordinary, teacher-training, vocational or technical;

"(*b*) Adopt the necessary measures to ensure that pupils of all secondary establishments, boys and girls, can obtain guidance to enable them to proceed to the type of secondary education, whether ordinary, teacher-training, vocational or technical, best suited to their aptitudes;

"(*c*) Ensure that girls who have completed their secondary studies have equal opportunities with boys of access to jobs and occupation for which these studies fit them, and that those qualified for higher education have equal opportunities with boys of access to it;

"(*d*) Take advantage, in developing the educational institutions required for increasing the number of women teachers in secondary education, of all the possiblities offered by technical assistance."

*Higher education*

At its twentieth session (1967), the Commission on the Status of Women considered a report by UNESCO on the access of girls and women to higher education (E/CN.6/451 and Add.1 and 2).

Acting on a recommendation submitted by the Commission on the Status of Women, the Economic and Social Council adopted resolution 1327 (XLIV) of 31 May 1968 on access of women to education. In that resolution the Economic and Social Council recalled the principles set out in the preamble and articles 9 and 10 of the Declaration on the Elimination of Discrimination against Women and the principles contained in the Convention against Discrimination in Education. The Council also recalled the suggestions and conclusions of the seminar on civic and political education of women held at Helsinki, Finland in 1967. It took into account the general trend of the UNESCO programme and pilot projects for encouraging girls and women to take up scientific and technical studies. It noted with satisfaction that an increasing number of girls and women were attending institutions for technical and vocational education.

*Technical and vocational education*

In 1952, the Economic and Social Council, acting on recommendations of the Commission on the Status of Women, recommended in resolution 445 D (XIV) that Governments take all possible measures to ensure provision of adequate facilities and opportunities for vocational training and guidance for all workers without regard to sex, and to give girls and women access to all forms of training and apprenticeship; and that they bear in mind the needs of women in making requests for technical assistance to the United Nations and the specialized agencies to develop vocational guidance and vocational and technical education. In 1960, a similar recommendation was made by the Council in resolution 771 E (XXX).

In 1962, the Commission itself, in resolution 6 (XVI),[13] expressed the hope that the competent authorities would:

"(*a*) Consider how to improve effectively the vocational guidance and counselling, as well as the vocational and technical training of women and girls, and achieve free educational facilities in that field;

"(*b*) Ensure to men and women equal access to existing vocational and professional schools and other facilities;

"(*c*) Establish new centres, where necessary, for equal vocational guidance and counselling, as well as vocational and professional training of men and women;

"(*d*) Encourage on-the-job vocational training of women in industrial and other establishments.

The Commission also expressed the hope that non-governmental organizations in consultative status would develop facilities for assisting, as appropriate, the vocational guidance, as well as the vocational and technical training, of women and girls.

In 1965, the Council, on the recommendation of the Commission on the Status of Women, in resolution 1068 G (XXXIX) recommended that Member States take all possible steps to promote the access of women to education at all levels and to vocational and technical training; it urged them to promote by all possible means a full and active role for women in economic and social fields. The Council also invited Member States which had not already done so to ratify the Discrimination (Employment and Occupation) Convention of 1958 and the Convention against Discrimination in Education of 1960 and to accept the principles laid down in the Vocational Training Recommendation adopted by the International Labour Conference in 1962, and the Recommendation concerning Technical and Vocational Education adopted by the General Conference of UNESCO in 1962.

The report of UNESCO on the access of women to technical and vocational education (E/CN.6/498) was submitted to the Commission at its twenty-first session (1968). In resolution 1327 ((XLIV) the Council endorsed proposals of the Commission and noted:

"The insufficient number of technical institutions admitting female students, the unsuitability of school curricula, in both the developed and developing countries and in both rural and urban areas, for providing training in a wide range of occupations relevant to employment possiblities, the inadequacy or lack of information given to families regarding the types of training available, and inadequate orientation adapted to the potentialities of girls, the persistent orientation of courses towards so-called feminine occupations for which there is a limited demand, and the lack of a clear distinction between training for an occupation and training for family responsiblities."

The Council also noted "that in some parts of the world illiteracy and wastage among girls and women" still constituted "major obstacles to their access to technical and vocational education".

*Co-education.* At its twenty-third session (1970) the Commission considered a report by UNESCO on co-education (E/CN.6/537 and Add.1). In resolution 6 (XXIII), the Commission recommended "that scholarships, loans and adequate facilities be provided to ensure the enrolment of girls and women in co-educational establishments and that a public education campaign in favour of equal access to education and vocational training be undertaken".

*Literacy.* At its twenty-third session, the Commission also considered a report by UNESCO on equal access of women to literacy (E/CN.6/538). On the recommendation of the Commission, the Economic and Social Council adopted resolution 1512 (XLVIII) of 28 May 1970 in which it requested UNESCO "to assign an important place in its functional literacy programmes to women who are still illiterate and to give assistance to all governmental and non-governmental literacy undertakings, *inter alia*, by acquainting them with modern techniques and methods for overcoming illiteracy".

### 2. *Long-term UNESCO programme for the advancement of women through access to education, science and culture*

A development of considerable importance in UNESCO's activities in the field of access of girls and women to education is the elaboration by the organization of a long-term programme for the advancement of women through access to education, science and culture. The programme was approved by the General Conference of UNESCO at its fourteenth session in 1966.

The Director-General of UNESCO was authorized by the General Conference, in co-operation with the United Nations and the appropriate specialized agencies, to intensify long-term action to achieve full equality for women and, consequently, to hasten the advancement of women and their full participation in the economic and social development of their countries through access to education, science and culture, and to assist member States at their request in their efforts to elaborate and apply a general policy directed to this end, in particular:

"(*a*) To implement a study, research and training programme, carried out in co-operation with member States in the field of education, the social and natural sciences and communication;

"(*b*) To aid government projects within UNESCO's sphere of activity which are designed to meet the need for the advancement of women and girls in various regions both rural and urban and to participate, in co-operation with a member State, in the implementation of an experimental project, and to this end to participate in the activities, of member States;

"(*c*) To give technical and financial support to activities planned and carried out by international non-governmental organizations working within the field of UNESCO's activities to facilitate the full participation of women and girls in the economic and social development of their countries."[14]

---

[13] *Official Records of the Economic and Social Council, Thirty-fourth Session, Supplement No. 7* (E/3606/Rev.1), para. 71.

[14] *Records of the General Conference, Fourteenth Session, Resolutions* (Paris, UNESCO, 1966), resolution 1.1322.

United Nations organs welcomed the initiative taken by UNESCO and expressed their support for the programme. For example, the Economic and Social Council in resolution 1134 (XLI) of 26 July 1966, noted with appreciation UNESCO's work on a long-term programme for the advancement of women.

At its twenty-second session in 1969, the Commission on the Status of Women considered a UNESCO report on its activities of particular interest to women (E/CN.6/520) according to the basic subjects of the long-term programme referred to in the preceding paragraph during the first two years of the implementation of the programme. The report showed that the number of women students receiving technical vocational education and scientific education was still very small in spite of the various UNESCO activities to encourage access of women to these fields. The report also indicated that regarding literacy work the Organization applied the principle of functional literacy. Another aim of the programme was to ensure that women took part in the preparation and implementation of educational development plans, and that more women attended teacher training institutions established or assisted by UNESCO. On the recommendation of the Commission on the Status of Women, the Economic and Social Council in resolution 1396 (XLVI) of 5 June 1969 invited Member States to apply to the United Nations Development Programme for technical assistance to develop opportunities for girls and women, particularly in the fields of literacy, of technical and vocational education and scientific studies, of teacher-training and of educational planning and administration. The Council invited UNESCO to seek means of further developing its programme for equal access of girls and women to education, science and culture, in co-operation with the other agencies concerned in the United Nations family and in co-ordination with the United Nations long-term programme for the advancement of women.

In the report (E/CN.6/557) on its activities covering the period 1970-1971, which the Commission on the Status of Women considered at its twenty-fourth session in 1972, UNESCO gave an account of various experimental projects for equal access of girls and women to education undertaken by the Organization. It stressed that the priority areas were literacy, technical and vocational education and education in the contact of rural development, that three regional conferences had been held during the period under review and that 20 States members of UNESCO had selected equal access of girls and women to education as one of the priority topics for the International Education Year. In resolution 1686 (LII) of 2 June 1972, adopted on the recommendation of the Commission on the Status of Women, the Economic and Social Council recommended that UNESCO should continue its studies on questions of priority interest to the younger generation, in the belief that the development of a sense of civic responsibility among girls is of primary importance in order to accelerate their full integration into all spheres of society. The Secretary-General and the Director-General of UNESCO were requested to give particular attention to measures for the advancement of education programmes for boys and girls, as a means of ensuring the fulfilment of the human personality and the effective and practical enjoyment of the rights belonging to every human being.

### K. Economic rights of women

The Commission on the Status of Women has also been very active in the field of economic rights and opportunities for women in which it has been greatly assisted by the work of the International Labour Organisation. As in the case of the access of girls and women to education, the Commission studies at each session some aspect, or aspects, of economic rights and opportunities for women on the basis of reports which are furnished in this case primarily by the ILO. Reports on ILO activities of special interest from the standpoint of women's employment are also submitted to the Commission at each session. The question of equal pay for equal work has been of particular concern to the Commission on the Status of Women since 1948, and developments on the application of this principle are considered every four years on the basis of ILO reports.

In its work to promote equal rights for men and women in the economic field, the Commission on the Status of Women has been influenced by the provisions of article 23 of the Universal Declaration of Human Rights. As indicated above, two ILO Conventions are of particular importance for the status of women and may be noted here. They are the Equal Remuneration Convention, 1951 (See section 2 below) and the Discrimination (Employment and Occupation) Convention, 1958 (see chapter V B above). Both the Economic and Social Council and the Commission on the Status of Women have expressed their support for these conventions in resolutions dealing with economic rights and opportunities of women. Another ILO instrument of particular importance for women is the Recommendation on Employment (Women with Family Responsibilities), adopted by the International Labour Conference in 1965 (see section 4 below).

The Economic and Social Council, in resolution 587 F III (XX) of 3 August 1955, adopted on the initiative of the Commission on the Status of Women, recommended that all States Members and non-members of the United Nations should adopt legislative and other measures to provide women with suitable economic opportunities by granting them equal rights with men to employment, pay, education, rest and material security in case of old age, illness or loss of capacity to work; and encourage such action as will secure for women, in the economic field, equal rights with men in all countries, including the Trust and Non-Self-Governing Territories. In another part of the same resolution the Council also urged non-governmental organizations to work for the eradication of all possible obstacles in the way of economic emancipation of women.

In 1961, the Council in resolution 821 IV A (XXXII) also adopted on the recommendation of the Commission on the Status of Women, recommended that Governments of States Members of the United Nations and of the specialized agencies, take the necessary measures to eliminate restrictions on the right of women, including married women and women contracting marriage, to work in conformity with the principles laid down in the ILO Convention concerning Discrimination in Respect of Employment and Occupation.

In 1966, the Commission called for a study by the ILO of the repercussions of scientific and technical progress on the position of women in the matter of labour and employment. The Commission felt that the constant increase in the prominence and importance of science and technology in the life of society made such a study of particular importance at the present time. The Economic and Social Council endorsed the Commission's request in resolution 1136 (XLI).

Examples of action taken on specific questions in the field of economic rights and opportunities are given below.

### 1. *Access of women to training and employment in the principal professional fields*

Specific studies on the access of women to employment and occupation in certain fields have been prepared for the Commission on the Status of Women in accordance with resolution 652 E (XXIV) of the Economic and Social Council, adopted in 1957 on the Commission's recommendation. The Council decided to undertake a global study of the access of women to training and employment in the principal professional and technical fields. Subsequently, a series of reports was submitted by the United Nations Secretariat, dealing with the access of women to training and employment in the fields of architecture, engineering, law (E/CN.6/343 and Add.1-5), draughtsmanship, science and engineering, accountancy and statistics (E/CN.6/347 and Add.1 and 2).

In 1961 and the following years, the Commission on the Status of Women and the Economic and Social Council re-examined their approach to the study of this question on the basis of reports submitted by the Secretariat (E/CN.6/411) and by the ILO (E/CN.6/412) and on the recommendations of the Commission, the Economic and Social Council suggested that Governments, non-governmental organizations and industrial concerns, when determining their requirements in regard to specialists of differing degrees of scale and preparing plans for training them, take into account the need to give women a place on an equal footing with men (Council resolution 961 E II (XXXVI) of 12 July 1963).

The general objectives and minimum targets set forth in the annex to General Assembly resolution 2715 (XXV) in the field of training and employment have already been referred to above.

### 2. *Equal pay for work of equal value*

The question of equal pay for equal work for men and women workers as indicated above in the beginning of this section has been a concern of the Commission of the Commission on the Status of Women, the Economic and Social Council and the International Labour Organisation for many years.

In 1948, in resolution 121 (VI) adopted on the Commission's recommendation, the Economic and Social Council reaffirmed the principle of equal rights of men and women laid down in the Preamble of the United Nations Charter, approved the principle of equal remuneration for work of equal value for men and women workers, and called upon Member States to implement that principle in every way, irrespective of nationality, race, language and religion.

The Council at the same time transmitted a memorandum of the World Federation of Trade Unions on the subject to the International Labour Organisation —inviting the latter to proceed as rapidly as possible with the further consideration of the subject—and to the Commission on the Status of Women for its consideration and any suggestions it might wish to make to the Council.

In 1949, the Commission on the Status of Women recommended that the following principles be included in the International Labour Organisation discussions of equal pay for equal work:

"(*a*) Adoption of the principle of rate-for-the-job rather than rate-based-on-sex;

"(*b*) Granting to women the same technical training and guidance, access to jobs, and promotion procedures as to men;

"(*c*) Abolition of the legal or customary restrictions on the pay of women workers;

"(*d*) Provision of measures to lighten the tasks that arise from women's home responsiblities, as well as the tasks relating to maternity."

The Economic and Social Council, in resolution 242 D (IX) of the same year decided to transmit the above recommendations and other relevant documentation to the ILO for its information and consideration in connexion with the action it had already initiated on the question of equal pay for equal work.

The International Labour Conference, as a result of its consideration of the matter, adopted the Equal Remuneration Convention and Recommendation in 1951. By that Convention, States parties have undertaken, by means appropriate to the methods in operation for determining rates of remuneration, to promote and, in so far as is consistent with such methods, to ensure the application to all workers of the principle of equal remuneration for men and women workers for work of equal value. This principle may be applied by means of national laws or regulations, legally established or recognized machinery for wage determination, collective agreements between employers and workers or a combination of these various measures. Different rates between workers which correspond, without regard to sex, to differences, as determined by objective appraisal, in the work to be performed shall not be considered as being contrary to this principle. The Equal Remuneration Recommendation lays down more detailed rules concerning the measures and methods for implementing the equal remuneration principle, and also calls for action to facilitate the application of this principle through measures in regard to vocational guidance and training, vocational placement, the provision of social welfare services to meet the needs of women workers, particularly those with family responsibilities, and promotion of equality as regards access to employment and posts.

In 1952, the Economic and Social Council (resolution 445 E (XIV)) commended the action taken by the International Labour Conference at its thirty-fourth Conference in June 1951, in the adoption of a Convention, supplemented by a Recommendation, on Equal Remuneration for Men and Women Workers for Work of Equal Value, and recommended that States members of the ILO introduce as soon as possible, by means of proper legislation or other measures, equal remuneration for equal work for men and women workers, in accordance with the ILO Convention and Recommendation. At the same time, the Council urged the adoption and implementation, in all countries not members of the ILO, of the principle of equal pay for equal work without discrimination on the basis of sex.

In 1953, acting on recommendations of the Commission on the Status of Women, the Council (in resolution 504 G (XVI)), noting that some progress had been achieved, urged increased efforts towards widespread implementation of the principle of equal remuneration in all countries, whether or not members of the ILO, by means appropriate to their systems of wage-fixing. In 1954, the Council (resolution 547 E (XVIII)) recommended that all States, both Members and non-members of the United Nations, which had not yet done so, take legislative and other action, in accordance with their respective constitutional procedures, to establish and carry into effect the principle of equal pay for equal work for all classes of men and women wage-earners.

In 1955, the Council (resolution 587 C (XX)) again urged the Governments of all States, whether or not they were Members of the United Nations, to take legislative and other measures for the application of the principle of equal pay for equal work for men and women. At that time the Council recommended that Governments, in making plans for technical assistance, include in such plans projects for utilization of technical advisory services designed to develop appropriate methods where such methods did not exist, for giving practical effect to the principle of equal pay, and that high priority be given to such projects.

Two years later, in 1957, the Council (resolution 652 D (XXIV)) urged all Member States of the United Nations to expedite the ratification of the Equal Remuneration Convention or otherwise to carry out their responsibilities with respect to the Convention; and recommended that the Governments of Member States implement the principle of equal pay for men and women for equal work, by legislation, by collective bargaining or by other measures. At that time the Council invited the International Labour Office to continue to provide current information to the Commission on the Status of Women on the results of the efforts undertaken by Member States to eliminate wage discrimination and to ensure the practical application of the principle of equal pay for equal work.

In 1962, the Council called upon the Governments of Member States which had not ratified or otherwise implemented the principles of the Equal Remuneration Convention to do so, as appropriate under the Constitution of the International Labour Organisation, and also to implement the provisions of the Equal Remuneration Recommendation, and, by the adoption of the relevant legislative and practical measures in all economic fields, to apply and promote consistently the principle of equal pay for equal work in accordance with the said convention. At the same time the Council called upon the ILO to continue to follow the introduction of the principle of equal pay for equal work on a world scale and to bear this principle in mind in considering working and social questions on an international level.

In the International Covenant on Economic, Social and Cultural Rights, the States Parties recognize the right of everyone to the enjoyment of just and favourable conditions of work which ensure, among other things, fair wages and equal remuneration for work of equal value without distinction of any kind; in particular, women being guaranteed conditions of work not inferior to those enjoyed by men, with equal pay for equal work.

The right to equal remuneration with men and to equality of treatment in respect of work of equal value is to be ensured to women, married or unmarried, under article 10 of the Declaration on the Elimination of Discrimination against Women.

More recently at its twenty-fourth session in February-March 1972 the Commission on the Status of Women adopted a resolution on equal pay for work of equal value [15] in which it expressed its conviction that the implementation of the Equal Remuneration Convention constituted a major step in advancing the state of women workers, noted that while progress had been made in that regard, much remained to be done and expressed its awareness of the difficulties of implementing the Equal Remuneration Convention without objective job-analysis and job-evaluation. The Commission conveyed its appreciation to the International Labour Office for its progress report on equal pay for work of equal value (E/CN.6/550), prepared for the consideration of the Commission, and expressed the hope that States Members of the United Nations who had not yet ratified the Convention would do so without further delay. The Commission on the Status of Women requested the International Labour Office to continue to study measures to promote objective appraisal of jobs on the basis of the work to be performed with a view to developing objective analysis, evaluation and classification criteria. It further requested the International Labour Office to analyse the concept of pay and the factors determining its level and structure (including deferred pay) with a view to the effective application of the principle of equal remuneration of men and women. The Commission asked the International Labour Office further to include in its periodic reports to the Commission information relating to the progress of its research on the subject.

### 3. *Age of retirement and pension rights*

Two subjects studied by the Commission on the Status of Women at several sessions between the years 1958-1963

---

[15] Report of the Commission on the Status of Women on the twenty-fourth session, February/March 1972, *Official Records of the Economic and Social Council, Fifty-second Session, Supplement No. 6* (E/5109), resolution 4 (XXIV).

were the age of retirement and pension rights, which in many countries are not the same for men and women workers. After preliminary consideration of the question on the basis of information furnished by the United Nations Secretariat and by the ILO, the Commission recognized that the question was one of some complexity on which differences of opinion existed; and it decided in 1960 to recommend that the Economic and Social Council invite the ILO to make a complete study of the subject. The Council endorsed this recommendation in resolution 771 F (XXX). The ILO submitted a comprehensive report to the Commission, which was first discussed in 1963 (E/CN.6/394 and Corr.1; E/CN.6/410). The Commission noted that although there was a trend towards equal provisions in retirement for men and women, a divergence of views existed among Governments and women's organizations in various countries about the pensionable ages for men and women. It recommended that the provisions on age of retirement and right to a pension "should be sufficiently flexible to meet a variety of changing circumstances, individual preferences as regard effective retirement, bearing in mind the encouraging trend towards equal economic conditions for the work of men and women, including equal provisions in the matter of age of retirement and the right to pension".[16]

### 4. *Working women with family responsibilities*

A significant development in this field was the unanimous adoption by the International Labour Conference in 1965 of the Recommendation on Employment (Women with Family Responsibilities). The Commission on the Status of Women expressed its great interest in this Recommendation at all stages of its preparation. The objectives of the Recommendation are defined in section I, which provides that the competent authorities should, in co-operation with the public and private organizations concerned, in particular employers' and workers' organizations, and in accordance with national and local needs and possibilities, (*a*) pursue an appropriate policy with a view to enabling women with family responsibilities who work outside their home to exercise their right to do so without being subject to discrimination and in accordance with the principles laid down in the Discrimination (Employment and Occupation) Convention, 1958, as well as in other standards adopted by the International Labour Conference relating to women; and (*b*) encourage, facilitate or themselves undertake the development of services to enable women to fulfil their various responsiblities at home and at work harmoniously.

Under section II the competent authorities, in co-operation with the public and private organizations concerned, are requested to take appropriate steps, with a view towards (*a*) encouraging the consideration of the problems of women workers with family responsibilities to help them to become effectively integrated in the labour force on the basis of equal rights; (*b*) researching into the various aspects of the employment of women workers with family responsiblities in order to present objective information on which sound policies may be based; and (*c*) engendering broader public understanding of the problems of these workers, so that a climate of opinion will develop conducive to helping them meet their family and employment responsibilities.

Section III of the Recommendation deals with child-care services and facilities and recommends that the competent authorities, in co-operation with public and private organizations concerned, and within the scope of their resources for collecting information, (*a*) collect and publish adequate statistics on the number of mothers engaged in or seeking employment and on the age of their children; (*b*) ascertain through surveys the needs and preference for child-care arrangements organized outside the family; (*c*) take appropriate steps to ensure that child-care services and facilities meet the needs and preferences so revealed; (*d*) establish adequate standards for child-care services, with supervision by the competent authorities, to ensure safeguarding the health and welfare of the child; and (*e*) ensure public understanding and support for efforts made to meet the special needs of working parents in respect of child-care services and facilities.

The provisions under section IV are intended to facilitate women's entry into employment, or re-entry after a comparatively long absence, so that they may enjoy equality of opportunity and training to enable them to become integrated into the labour force on a footing of equality. It is recommended that the competent authorities take all measures necessary to ensure general education for girls and vocational guidance and training without discrimination on grounds of sex, to encourage girls to obtain a sound vocational preparation as a basis for their future work lives and to convince parents and educators of the need to give girls a sound vocational preparation. Also included in this section are proposals for the provision of services that may be necessary to facilitate the entry or re-entry into employment of women who have been out of the labour force because of family responsibilities. It is proposed that these services include adequate counselling, information and placement. The section also provides that in the case of women who, on account of their family responsibilities arising out of maternity, do not find themselves in a position to return to their employment immediately following exhaustion of the normal period of maternity leave established by law or practice, appropriate measures should be taken to the extent possible to allow them a reasonable further period of leave of absence without relinquishing their employment.

Section V of the Recommendation urges attention to matters of particular relevance for women workers with family responsibilities, such as the organization of public transport, dovetailing of school and child-care hours and work hours, facilities to simplify household tasks and home aid services.

The International Labour Conference at its fifty-seventh session in 1972 adopted a resolution concerning women workers inviting the Governing Body of the International Labour Office to request the Director-General to work

[16] *Official Records of the Economic and Social Council, Thirty-sixth Session, Supplement No. 7* (E/3749), resolution 9 (XVII), para. 118.

out a programme of activities designed to promote equality of treatment and opportunity for women workers, to bring up to date the report on women workers in the changing world prepared for the forty-eighth session of the International Labour Conference in 1964 and to consider placing the question of equality of treatment of women workers on the agenda of the session of the International Labour Conference to be held in 1975, International Women's Year.

At its nineteenth session in 1966, the Commission on the Status of Women expressed the belief that the adoption of the Recommendation was "of fundamental importance to the work of international organizations engaged in combating and eliminating discrimination against women".[17]

The Declaration on the Elimination of Discrimination against Women provides in article 10, paragraph 2, that in order to prevent discrimination against women on account of marriage or maternity and to ensure the effective right to work, measures shall be taken to prevent their dismissal in the event of marriage or maternity and to provide paid maternity leave, with the guarantee of returning to former employment, and to provide the necessary social services, including child-care facilities. The minimum targets to be achieved during the Second United Nations Development Decade set forth in the annex to General Assembly resolution 2716 (XXV) also provide for the progressive extension of measures to ensure maternity protection, with a view to ensuring paid maternity leave with the guarantee of returning to former or equivalent employment and for the development and extension of adequate child-care and other facilities to assist parents with family responsibilities.

#### 5. *Questions of special employment opportunities for women (part-time work, handicrafts, cottage industries, employment of older women workers)*

At its twentieth session in 1955, the Economic and Social Council adopted, on the recommendation of the Commission on the Status of Women and on the basis of a report prepared by the ILO, resolution 587 F (XX), recommending that Member States make intensive use of the ILO experience when plans for the development of handicraft and cottage industries were contemplated. In its resolution 625 B (I) (XXII) of 1956, also adopted on the recommendation of the Commission, the Economic and Social Council invited the ILO to give special attention to methods found useful for the avoidance of the abuse of industrial home work.

Partly as a result of interest expressed by the Commission on the Status of Women, the ILO prepared a comprehensive international survey on part-time employment in 1963 and submitted the report (E/CN.6/428) to the Commission in 1965.

The survey pointed out that while part-time employment is by no means limited to women, in most countries the great majority of the part-time labour force are women and that nearly everywhere a considerable proportion of women part-time workers are married. The survey referred to some of the special problems part-time work presents for workers and employers concerned and noted that the ILO proposed to continue to study the question. A further study is now in progress, on the basis of replies to a questionnaire to Governments and the analytical report will be made available by the ILO to the Commission.

In considering the question of older women workers, the Commission on the Status of Women called for a series of reports by the ILO in 1955, 1956 and 1957, and it observed from the information furnished to it that special difficulties are often encountered by older women in obtaining or sometimes in retaining employment. The Commission has expressed its belief that older women workers and women in part-time employment should be accorded conditions of work, including social security benefits, as favourable as those enjoyed by other workers, taking account of their respective situation.[18]

At its twenty-third session in 1970 the Commission on the Status of Women requested the Secretary-General to suggest to Governments that they organize, in collaboration with the specialized agencies concerned and non-governmental organizations interested in the problem, surveys in their respective countries with a view to obtaining direct information and opinions from working women themselves concerning their family responsibilities, particularly on (*a*) their actual position with respect to the sharing of household duties; (*b*) the obstacles, if any, preventing them from duly carrying out both activities; (*c*) their views on the problem itself, when it exists; and (*d*) their suggestions concerning practical measures to deal with obstacles to the smooth running of the home. The Commission decided that once the results of these surveys were obtained, it would carry out, in the light thereof, the relevant studies and consider the need for an educational campaign on the subject which could provide guidance on the sharing of responsibilities within the family, bearing in nind the rapid changes that are taking place in the structure of labour in human society owing to the growth of women's participation in paid work.

### L. The condition of women in special situations

#### 1. *Status of women in Trust and Non-Self-Governing Territories*

The Commission on the Status of Women has always been interested in the status of women in all areas of the world, including Trust and Non-Self-Governing Territories. Since its third session in 1949, it has reviewed at each session reports relating to the status of women in these territories on the basis of relevant information contained in the annual reports made by the Administering Authorities under the procedure established pursuant to Articles 73 (e) and 88 of the Charter. An example of action taken is General Assembly resolution 731 (VIII),

---

[17] *Official Records of the Economic and Social Council, Forty-first Session, Supplement No. 7* (E/4175), resolution 14 (XIX), para. 337.

[18] *Official Records of the Economic and Social Council, Twenty-fourth Session, Supplement No. 3* (E/2968), resolution 6 (XI), para. 147.

adopted in 1953 on the recommendation of the Commission on the Status of Women through the Economic and Social Council. In this resolution the General Assembly urged States to take all necessary measures, particularly educational and legislative measures, leading to the development of political rights of women in all territories in which women do not enjoy full political rights including Trust and Non-Self-Governing Territories. Following the request made by the Commission on the Status of Women at its third session in 1949, reports were submitted annually to the Commission from 1950 to 1968. These consisted primarily of excerpts from the reports of the Governments concerned and were, consequently, restricted to those Territories for which Governments did furnish reports. At its twenty-first session in 1968 (resolution 1 (XXI)) the Commission asked that reports be submitted to it at every other session based on information from Governments and also on any relevant reports and records of the Trusteeship Council and of the Special Committee on the Situation with regard to the Implementation of the Declaration on the Granting of Independence to Colonial Countries and Peoples. This request had the effect of extending the scope of the information considered, both as regards the Territories covered and the documentation consulted. More recently, reports on the status of women in Trust and Non-Self-Governing Territories were submitted to the Commission at its twenty-second session in 1969 (E/CN.6/509) and at the twenty-fourth session in 1972 (E/CN.6/560). In resolution 2 (XXII) the Commission, *inter alia*, expressed special concern for the status of women and children in the Territories and requested the Secretary-General to draw the attention of the Administering Authorities to the importance of seminars on civic and political education of women.

### 2. *Protection of women and children in emergency and armed conflict*

At its twenty-second session in January-February 1969, the Commission on the Status of Women considered the protection of women and children in emergency or war time, fighting for peace, national liberation and independence. The Commission adopted resolution 4 (XXII), in which it took note of resolutions I and XXIII adopted by the International Conference on Human Rights,[19] Teheran, 1968, and General Assembly resolutions 2443 (XXIII) and 2444 (XXIV) of 19 December 1968 concerning respect for and implementation of human rights in occupied territories, and human rights in armed conflicts. It expressed the hope that women in increasing numbers would be consulted or sent on missions by the International Committee of the Red Cross in occupied territories and territories ravaged by war or struck by natural disasters. The Commission solemnly appealed to all women throughout the world to make every effort to contribute, in their families and in their communities, to the establishment of peace and justice and towards finding a just solution to armed conflicts. The Commission recommended that the protection of women and children against inhuman practices in time of armed conflict or occupation should more than ever receive the attention of the United Nations, the International Committee of the Red Cross and the United Nations Children's Fund.

At its twenty-third session, in March-April, 1970, the Commission on the Status of Women continued its consideration of the problem. On a recommendation by the Commission, the Economic and Social Council adopted resolution 1515 (XLVIII) of 28 May 1970 in which it called upon States to abide fully by their obligations under the Geneva Convention relative to the Protection of Civilian Persons in Time of War, of 1949[20] and other rules of international law concerning respect for human rights in armed conflicts.

The initiative taken in the matter by the Commission on the Status of Women was of course parallel to, and integrated with, the comprehensive activities that the United Nations had undertaken on the problem of the protection of human rights in armed conflicts since 1968, which is described in detail in chapter X below. The Commission on the Status of Women and, on its recommendation, the Economic and Social Council, stressed mainly that aspect of the over-all problem which affects women in particular. Thus in resolution 1515 (XLVIII) of 1970, the Economic and Social Council requested the Secretary-General to give particular attention, in pursuing his study on respect for human rights in armed conflicts, to the question of protection of women and children in emergency or wartime. The Council also requested the General Assembly to consider the possibility of drafting a declaration on the protection of women and children in emergency or wartime.

The Commission on the Status of Women continued its examination and study of the problem of the protection of women and children in emergency and armed conflict at its twenty-fourth session in February-March 1972 and on its recommendation the Economic and Social Council adopted resolution 1687 (LII) of 2 June 1972. In that resolution the Council expressed appreciation to the Secretary-General for giving special consideration, in his reports to the General Assembly on respect for human rights in armed conflicts, to the suggestion made by the Commission on the Status of Women at its twenty-second session regarding the necessity of taking specific measures for the protection of women and children in periods of armed conflict and in occupied territories. The Council welcomed the fact that the Conference of Government Experts, convened by the International Committee of the Red Cross, which at the time of the adoption of the Council resolution was in session, was giving consideration to the problem of special measures for the protection of women and children in periods of armed conflict and occupation. The Council also decided to include this question on the programme of work of the Commission on the Status of Women.

[19] *Final Act of the International Conference on Human Rights* (United Nations publication, Sales No. E.68.XIV.2), pp. 5 and 18.

[20] United Nations, *Treaty Series*, vol. 75, p. 287.

### M. The interrelationship of the status of women and family planning

The question of family planning was first discussed in the Commission on the Status of Women in connexion with the United Nations assistance for the advancement of women and the establishment of a unified long-term programme. In two resolutions, adopted at its eighteenth session in 1965 and at its nineteenth session in 1966, the Commission stressed the importance of making information on family planning available to married couples. It suggested that non-governmental organizations in consultative status, each in accord with its own programmes, objectives and policies, study the possibility of making available the increasing fund of knowledge in the field of family planning as a source of assistance to married couples in fulfilling their parental responsiblities (resolution 7 (XVIII)). The Commission also requested the Secretary-General to prepare a report on the relationship between family planning and the advancement of women. Subsequently, it asked that a brief summary of pertinent research and resources available through the United Nations should be included in this report, with special emphasis on material that might be used in conferences of non-governmental as well as official bodies (resolution 4 (XIX)).

The study initiated at the sessions referred to in the preceding paragraph was one of the most significant and one of the most difficult on which the United Nations has embarked in recent years in the status of women field. Other United Nations organs concerned with the population question have expressed interest in the Commission's initiative, and have made certain preliminary studies of the status of women as one factor, among others, that has been found to affect fertility.

Since this study was initiated there has been increasing emphasis in various United Nations bodies on the human rights aspects of population questions. In its resolution on population growth and economic development (resolution 2211 (XXI) of 17 December 1966) for example, the General Assembly recognized the sovereignty of nations in formulating and promoting their own population policies, with due regard to the principle that the size of the family should be the free choice of each individual family. In his address [21] delivered at the opening of the International Conference on Human Rights in Teheran, the Secretary-General, U Thant, stated that on Human Rights Day 1967, Heads of State or Prime Ministers of 30 countries had transmitted to him a "Declaration on Population". These world leaders had stated their belief that a great majority of parents desired to have the knowledge and means to plan their families and that the opportunity to decide the number and spacing of children was a fundamental human right. The Teheran Conference itself, in its resolution XVIII of 12 May 1968,[22] noted the Declaration on Population of 10 December 1966, and expressed the belief that it was timely to draw attention to the connexion between population growth and human rights. The Conference observed that the present rate of population growth in some areas of the world hampered the struggle against hunger and poverty and in particular reduced the possibilities of rapidly achieving adequate standards of living, thereby impairing the full realization of human rights. The Conference recognized that moderation of the present rate of population growth in such areas would enhance the conditions for offering greater opportunities for the enjoyment of human rights and the improvement of living conditions for each person. The Conference considered that couples had a basic human right to decide freely and responsibly on the number and spacing of their children and a right to adequate education and information in this respect.

The Declaration on Social Progress and Development proclaimed by General Assembly resolution 2542 (XXIV) of 11 December 1969 provides in its article 4 that parents have the exclusive right to determine freely and responsibly the number and spacing of their children. In article 22 (*b*) the Declaration further calls for programmes which include the provision to families of the knowledge and means necessary to enable them to exercise that right. Article 9 (*e*) of the Declaration on the Elimination of Discrimination against Women calls for the right of girls and women to have access to eductional information to help in ensuring the health and well-being of families. Similarly the minimum targets to be achieved during the Second United Nations Development Decade set forth in the annex to General Assembly resolution 2715 (XXV) include the making available to all persons who so desire the necessary information and advice to enable them to decide freely and responsibly on the number and spacing of their children.

At its forty-fourth session in May 1968, the Economic and Social Council approved the decision taken by the Commission on the Status of Women at its twenty-first session in January-February 1968 to appoint a Special Rapporteur to continue the study of the status of women and family planning.[23]

At its twenty-third session in March/April 1970 the Commission on the Status of Women received a progress report by its Special Rapporteur (E/CN.6/542). It requested the Special Rapporteur to prepare guidelines to assist Governments in undertaking national surveys and to aid United Nations bodies and non-governmental organizations in further work on this subject.

At its twenty-fourth session in February-March 1972 the Commission on the Status of Women considered a second progress report by the Special Rapporteur (E/CN.6/564). The detailed guidelines prepared by the Special Rapporteur in co-operation with the Secretary-General focused attention on three interrelated factors: (*a*) the influence of family planning on the status of women, which is interpreted to mean the extent to which family planning has helped or hindered, or may be expected to help or hinder, women as individuals in the exercise of

[21] See *Final Act of the International Conference on Human Rights* (United Nations publication, Sales No. E.68.XIV.2), annex II.B.

[22] *Ibid.*, p. 14.

[23] *Offiicial Records of the Economic and Social Council, Forty-fourth session, Supplement No. 1*, resolution 1326 (XLIV).

their rights, irrespective of the population factor in the country concerned; (*b*) the status of women as a factor influencing fertility which will take into account the extent to which the exercise by women of their various rights has been found to influence, or may be expected to influence, fertility; and (*c*) the implications for the status of women of current trends in population growth, under which would be examined the effects of the population factor—whether over-population or under-population—on the exercise by women of their various rights, and its implications for national development.[24]

Replies on the basis of these guidelines have been received from over 50 Governments. In addition, the Special Rapporteur undertook consultations with a number of Governments in Asia, Africa and Latin America. Four in-depth studies were initiated with private organizations in India, Indonesia, Egypt and Nigeria. Others are expected to follow in Latin America. An international seminar, organized within the framework of the human rights advisory services programme, was held at Istanbul, Turkey in July 1972. Regional seminars in the western hemisphere, Asia and Africa are also contemplated as part of the study to be submitted to the Commission in 1974.

### N. Effect of the recommendations of the Commission on the Status of Women on national legislation

In the years between 1962 and 1967 the Commission on the Status of Women requested and received from the Secretary-General reports (E/CN.6/437 and Add.1) on the effect of resolutions and recommendations of the Commission on national legislation.

At its twenty-fourth session in 1972 the Commission decided that, in future, such reports should form part of the documentation relating to the implementation of the Declaration on the Elimination of Discrimination against Women and related instruments, to enable the Commission to consider information furnished by Governments, specialized agencies and non-governmental organizations, and information available to the Secretary-General from other sources.

### O. The participation of women in community development

In 1965 the Commission on the Status of Women called for a study on "the participation of women in community development and the possiblity of increasing the scope and content of their contribution", noting at the same time "the great importance of community development in stimulating the advancement of women".

Community development has been defined as: "the processes by which the efforts of the people themselves are united with those of governmental authorities to improve the economic, social and cultural conditions of communities, to integrate these communities into the life of the nation, and to enable them to contribute fully to national progress. This complex of processes is then made up of two essential elements: the participation by the people themselves in efforts to improve their level of living with as much reliance as possible on their own initiative; and the provision of technical and other services in ways which encourage the initiative, self-help and mutual help, and make these more effective. It is expressed in programmes designed to achieve a wide variety of specific improvements".[25]

The goals of community development may be said, therefore, to be twofold: (*a*) the comprehensive improvement of conditions in communities; and (*b*) the integration of the development of communities with national development. The methods used emphasize: (*a*) the initiative and voluntary efforts of local people to raise their own levels of living; and (*b*) the provision, mainly by the Government, of the measures, services and facilities needed for local programmes and projects. Community development then is essentially a partnership between the local people and the Government.

The interest of the Commission on the Status of Women in community development is focused on three main points: (*a*) the examination of the extent to which women are participating at the present time in community development programmes, especially in rural areas; (*b*) the consideration of ways in which existing programmes have helped to advance the status of women; and (*c*) the making of recommendations that would both improve the status of women and benefit the programmes themselves.

The studies made for the Commission on the Status of Women on this subject have been based primarily on information furnished by Governments. It is apparent from the information received that women participate with enthusiasm and interest in community development programmes in many countries, and that their contribution is considered highly valuable. The community development programmes include activities connected with education and training, especially literacy and adult education, vocational training and civic and political education; activities in the economic and social fields aimed at raising levels of living, such as health, nutrition, social welfare, housing and home management, family planning, agriculture, small-scale industry and handicrafts and co-operatives; and activities which provide training for community development work.

These various questions are still under study by the Commission on the Status of Women and by the Secretariat.

### P. The integration of women in the total development effort

The International Development Strategy for the Second United Nations Development Decade (General Assembly resolution 2626 (XXV) of 24 October 1970) includes among its goals and objectives the encouragement of the full integration of women in the total development

[24] Report on the twenty-fourth session of the Commission on the Status of Women, February/March 1972; *Official Records of the Economic and Social Council, Fifty-second Session, Supplement No. 6* (E/5109), resolution 6 (XXIV).

[25] *Official Records of the Economic and Social Council, Twenty-fourth Session, Annexes,* agenda item 4, document E/2931, annex III, paras. 1-2.

effort. It is one of the three objectives of International Women's Year, 1975, which was proclaimed by the General Assembly resolution 3010 (XXVII) of 18 December 1972, to intensify action to "ensure the full integration of women in the total development effort, especially by emphasizing women's responsibility and important role in economic, social and cultural development at the national, regional and international levels, particularly during the Second United Nations Development Decade".

In compliance with General Assembly resolutions 2626 (XXV) on the International Development Strategy mentioned above and 2716 (XXV) on the Programme of Concerted International Action for the Advancement of Women, an interregional meeting of experts on the integration of women in development was held in June 1972 at United Nations Headquarters.[26] It was part of the work programme of the Commission for Social Development as well as that of the Commission on the Status of Women.

UNICEF, UNDP, the Economic Commission for Africa, the Office for Technical Co-operation and the Centre for Development Planning, Projections and Policies, as well as FAO, WHO and UNESCO, were represented at the meeting. The participants were experts from different regions of the world, representing the fields of social and economic planning, industry, employment, agriculture, law and social welfare.

Several recommendations relating to national strategies and international action for the integration of women in development were made, and the necessity of national policy taking into account the economic and social structure and the national stage of development—rather than seeking to apply a uniform world strategy—was emphasized. The participants recommended:

(*a*) Concerning rural areas, training and modernization should be combined with land reform and give to women an opportunity to increase their productivity as well as their earnings. This might stop the rural migration and reduce urban unemployment.

(*b*) Integrated programmes for women in small-scale business should include literacy as well as management co-operatives. Measures should be also taken to ensure women mobility and allow them to acquire business acumen.

(*c*) Simultaneously with the creation of co-ordinated programmes of training and vocational guidance, job opportunities for women should be created to utilize their acquired knowledge.

(*d*) Statistical studies should be made on women's employment in all fields at the national level; manpower studies should include all activities of women.

(*e*) At the national level, existing recommendations of the Commission on the status of women in private law, and particularly family law, as well as the provisions of article 6 of the Declaration on the Elimination of Discrimination against Women, should be implemented as an essential part of the integration of women in development.

[26] For the report of the meeting, see United Nations publication, Sales No. E.73.IV.12.

(*f*) Exchange of knowledge and experience at regional and international levels should be pursued. In this regard, the role of the specialized agencies within the United Nations system was pointed out, as well as the key role of the UNDP resident representatives, in collaboration with United Nations organs, in advising Governments on the integration of women in national development, especially in such areas as agricultural development, regional development, industrialization and urbanization.

(*g*) Supplementary efforts should be made in order to recruit more women, including those who would serve at the policy-making level, in the United Nations system, to focus attention on the need for projects to integrate women in national development. The group also recommended an exchange of information on development problems at both national and international levels in order to facilitate more effective co-ordination.

In recent years, the Commission on the Status of Women has also shown great concern for the advancement of women in rural areas, to whom previously insufficient attention had been given. On the recommendation of the Commission on the Status of Women, the Economic and Social Council adopted resolution 1678 (LII) of 2 June 1972 on participation of women in rural development programmes, in which it urged Governments in their planning for development and effective utilization of human resources, to make possible the effective participation of national women's organizations and other non-governmental organizations that had programmes for the advancement of women, particularly in the rural areas. It also requested the United Nations Development Programme and all other appropriate organizations of the United Nations system, and the regional organizations, to consider allocating more of their technical assistance funds for the purpose of more effective planning and implementation of rural development programmes for women.

On the recommendation of the Commission, the Economic and Social Council adopted at its fifty-second session in 1972 resolution 1684 (LII) on the integration of women at all levels of development. In that resolution the Economic and Social Council noted that, because of differing cultural traditions and of stages of socio-economic progress of countries all the world over and also within each of those countries, women were found at several levels of development. The Council considered that there might be a tendency, in the implementation of the programme of concerted international action for the advancement of women, to concentrate solely on the most elementary stages of development of women, which might lead to neglect of the needs and requirements of women at the middle and higher levels of development. The Council recommended that the objectives and targets set forth in the annex to General Assembly resolution 2716 (XXV) should be realized in such a way as to benefit women at all levels of development.

The Council adopted, also on the recommendation of the Commission on the Status of Women, resolution 1682 (LII) of 2 June 1972 on increased activities relating to the status of women at the regional level. In that resolution the Council invited intergovernmental organizations outside the United Nations system to consider the establishment of regional commissions on the status of women in order to make more effective the resolutions and measures adopted in favour of women and to promote the wider integration of women in all sectors of development and progress of their countries. The Council also invited the United Nations regional economic commissions to take action to incorporate in their regional activities programmes designed to increase the participation of women.

### Q. The use of technical co-operation for the advancement of women, including the human rights advisory services programme

The Commission on the Status of Women has for many years held the view that technical co-operation programmes within the United Nations system might be used to greater advantage to benefit the advancement of women, and it has adopted several resolutions inviting Governments to make fuller use of the services available under these programmes. Prior to the establishment of the advisory services programme in the field of human rights by the General Assembly in 1956 (resolution 926 (X)), a resolution emanating from the Commission on the Status of Women in 1953 had authorized the Secretary-General to render at the request of Member States certain services that did not fall within the scope of existing technical assistance programmes, to assist States in promoting and safeguarding the rights of women (General Assembly resolution 729 (VIII)).

Since the establishment of the advisory services programme in 1956, the Commission on the Status of Women has always been extremely interested in the seminars organized under that programme and in the award of fellowships.[27] It has also felt that greater use might be made of the services of experts in the field of the status of women.

In resolution 2716 (XXV) on the programme of concerted international action for the advancement of women, which has been repeatedly referred to above, the General Assembly recommended that conferences, seminars and similar meetings at the regional and international levels should be organized with the participation, wherever possible, of ministers, high government officials and specialists concerned with problems of development, and of representatives of non-governmental organizations concerned with this problem, to consider ways and means of promoting the status of women within the framework of over-all development. On the recommendation of the Commission on the Status of Women made at its twenty-fourth session, the Economic and Social Council in resolution 1683 (LII) of 2 June 1972 welcomed the organization of an interregional meeting of experts on the role of women in development as a joint project of the Commission for Social Development and the Commission on the Status of Women.

[27] For a list of seminars organized under the advisory services programme, see annex below.

### R. Dissemination of information concerning the work of the United Nations in regard to the status of women and other educational measures to promote equality of men and women

The need to influence public opinion throughout the world in favour of the principle of equality of status between men and women has been emphasized on many occasions by the Commission on the Status of Women since its establishment in 1946. At its second session in 1948, for example, the Commission recommended through the Economic and Social Council that the Secretary-General call upon the press, radio, film and other information agencies to help in removing prejudices against the principle of equality between men and women, that he assist, in accordance with his means and possiblity, all such information agencies in those efforts to the fullest possible extent, and that he prepare suitable information material of all kinds for that purpose. Over the years many pamphlets and other publications have been issued by the United Nations.[28]

At its fourth and fifth sessions in 1950 and 1951, the Commission on the Status of Women requested the Secretary-General to prepare and circulate to members of the Commission and other interested individuals and organizations a newsletter containing information on activities undertaken by the other United Nations organs of interest to the status of women and containing information on recent developments on the advancement of the status of women throughout the world. The newsletter is issued twice a year and receives very wide circulation at the present time.

Throughout the years non-governmental organizations in consultative status have also undertaken many activities to inform the public of the work of the United Nations in regard to the status of women, and the Commission has always greatly welcomed the assistance it has received in its work from such organizations. In a decision relating to the establishment of a long-term programme for the advancement of women, the Economic and Social Council, in resolution 1334 (XLI), adopted on 26 July 1966 on the recommendation of the Commission on the Status of Women, asked the Secretary-General to study the possibilities of joint consultations, exchanges of information and collaboration between the Commission on the Status of Women and the international non-governmental organizations in consultative status which are interested in the long-term programme for the advancement of women.

The Declaration on the Elimination of Discrimination against Women of 1967, while in itself an important and central part of the work of the United Nations in regard to the status of women, is also a means for drawing international attention to that work. It urges Governments, non-governmental organizations and individuals to do all in their power to promote the implementation of the principles contained in the Declaration.

[28] For a list of United Nations publications relating to the status of women, see annex below.

General Assembly resolution 2716 (XXV) calls for the development of effective large-scale educational and informational programmes using all mass media and other available means to make all sectors of the population in rural as well as urban areas fully aware of the norms established by the United Nations and the specialized agencies in the conventions, recommendations, declarations and resolutions adopted under their auspices, and to educate public opinion and enlist its support for all measures aimed at achieving the realization of the standards set forth.

A consistent effort has been made since the proclamation of the Declaration on the Elimination of Discrimination against Women, to have its text distributed in as many languages and as widely as possible. Thus on the recommendation of the Commission on the Status of Women, the Economic and Social Council in resolution 1325 (XLIV) requested the Secretary-General and the specialized agencies to take steps to ensure the immediate circulation of the text of the Declaration through their respective services; it invited Member States, competent national organizations and non-governmental organizations to take all measures for the recognition, in law and in fact, of the principles contained in the Declaration and, to this end: (*a*) to publicize the text of the Declaration in their national languages as widely as possible, to issue pamphlets, articles and commentaries on the Declaration and to use all other appropriate media of communication; (*b*) to undertake studies on the rapid evolution in the traditional roles of men and women with regard to their participation in the life of the family and of society as a whole; (*c*) to encourage within the entire country, programmes designed to give effect to the provisions of the Declaration. The Council invited the full participation of international non-governmental organizations in the activities for publicizing the Declaration and in the implementation of the principles contained therein.

At its twenty-fourth session the Commission on the Status of Women in resolution 1 (XXIV) [29] referred to the great influence of mass communication media in the determination of cultural patterns that affected the full development of women and noted that all the Commission's efforts to promote the advancement of women encountered a serious obstacle in the deep-rooted attitudes in men and women which tend to perpetuate the *status quo*. The Commission observed that these attitudes were due to cultural patterns, which to a certain extent determined the way of thinking and feeling and which were disseminated on a vast scale today as a result of the technical advances in mass communication media. The Commission therefore resolved to include in the agenda of its twenty-fifth session in 1974 an item entitled "Influence of mass communication media on the formation of a new attitude towards the role of women in present-day society". The Commission also invited UNESCO to consider the possibility of carrying out inter-disciplinary studies on the subject.

[29] *Official Records of the Economic and Social Council, Fifty-second Session, Supplement No. 6*, chap. VIII.

## S. International Women's Year

At its twenty-seventh session, by resolution 3010 (XXVII) of 18 December 1972, the General Assembly proclaimed the year 1975 International Women's Year and decided to devote this year to intensified action to promote equality between men and women, to ensure the full integration of women in the total development effort, especially by emphasizing women's responsibility and important role in economic, social and cultural development at the national, regional and international levels, particularly during the Second United Nations Development Decade, and to recognize the importance of women's increasing contribution to the development of friendly relations and co-operation among States and to the strengthening of world peace.

It invited all Member States and all interested organizations to take steps to ensure the full realization of the rights of women and their advancement on the basis of the Declaration on the Elimination of Discrimination against Women, and requested the Secretary-General to prepare, in consultation with Member States, specialized agencies and interested non-governmental organizations, within the limits of existing resources, a draft programme for the International Women's Year.

In making these decisions the General Assembly was bearing in mind the aims and principles of the Declaration on the Elimination of Discrimination against Women (adopted by the General Assembly in resolution 2269 (XXII) of 7 November 1967) and recognized the effectiveness of the work done by the Commission on the Status of Women in the 25 years since its establishment, and the important contribution which women have made to the social, political, economic and cultural life of their countries.

The General Assembly also considered that it was necessary to strengthen universal recognition of the principle of the equality of men and women, *de jure* and *de facto*, and that both legal and social measures have to be taken by Member States which have not yet done so to ensure the implementation of women's rights.

The Assembly recalled that resolution 2626 (XXV) of 24 October 1970, containing the International Development Strategy for the Second United Nations Development Decade, includes among the goals and objectives of the Decade the encouragement of the full integration of women in the total development effort, and drew attention to the general objectives and minimum targets to be attained in the course of the Second United Nations Development Decade, as defined by the Commission on the Status of Women and adopted by the General Assembly in its resolution 2716 (XXV) of 15 December 1970.

The General Assembly considered that, with those ends in view, the proclamation of an international women's year would serve to intensify the action required to advance the status of women.

## ANNEX

### United Nations publications relating to the status of women

#### A. *Miscellaneous publications*

*Legal Status of Married Women;* Sales No. 1957.IV.8 (revised)

*Nationality of Married Women;* Sales No. 64.IV.1

*Equal Pay for Equal Work;* Sales No. 60.IV.4

*Convention on the political rights of women, History and commentary;* Sales No. 55.IV.17

*Convention on the Nationality of Married Women: Historical background and commentary;* Sales No. 62.IV.3

*Civic and Political Education of Women;* Sales No. 64.IV.7

*Resources available to Member States for the Advancement of Women;* Sales No. 66.IV.6

*United Nations Assistance for the Advancement of Women;* Sales No. 67.IV.2

*Constitutions, electoral laws and other legal instruments relating to political rights of women;* Sales No. 69.IV.2

*Declaration on the Elimination of Discrimination against Women;* OPI-297

*Participation of women in the economic and social development of their countries;* Sales No. 70.IV.4

*The Status of the Unmarried Mother: Law and Practice;* Sales No. E.71.IV.4

*Participation of women in community development;* Sales No. 72.IV.8

*The United Nations and the Status of Women;* Sales No. 64.I.10

*Parental Rights and Duties, including Guardianship;* Sales No. E.68.IV.3

*Equal Rights for Women: a call for Action;* OPI/494

#### B. *Reports of seminars on the status of women*

*1957 Seminar on the Civic Responsibilities and Increased Participation of Asian Women in Public Life* (organized by the United Nations in co-operation with the Government of Thailand). United Nations reference: ST/TAO/HR/1.

*1959 Seminar on the Participation of Women in Public Life* (organized by the United Nations in co-operation with the Government of Colombia). United Nations reference: ST/TAO/HR/5

*1960 Seminar on the Participation of Women in Public Life* (organized by the United Nations in co-operation with the Government of Ethiopia). United Nations reference: ST/TAO/HR/9

*1965 Seminar on the Participation of Women in Public Life* (organized by the United Nations in co-operation with the Government of Mongolia). United Nations reference: ST/TAO/HR/24

*1961 Seminar on the Status of Women in Family Law* (organized by the United Nations in co-operation with the Government of Romania). United Nations reference: ST/TAO/HR/11

*1962 Seminar on the Status of Women in Family Law* (organized by the United Nations in co-operation with the Government of Japan). United Nations reference: ST/TAO/HR/14

*1963 Seminar on the Status of Women in Family Law* (organized by the United Nations in co-operation with the Government of Colombia). United Nations reference: ST/TAO/HR/18

*1964 Seminar on the Status of Women in Family Law* (organized by the United Nations in co-operation with the Government of Togo). United Nations reference: ST/TAO/HR/22

*1966 Seminar on United Nations Assistance for the Advancement of Women: Measures Required for the Advancement of Women with Special Reference to the Establishment of a Long-Term Programme* (organized by the United Nations in co-operation with the Government of the Philippines). United Nations reference: ST/TAO/HR/28

*Civic and Political Education of Women;* Sales No. 64.IV.7

*1967 Seminar on the Civic and Political Education of Women* (organized by the United Nations in co-operation with the Government of Finland). United Nations reference: ST/TAO/HR/3

*1968 Seminar on the Civic and Political Education of Women* (organized by the United Nations in co-operation with the Government of Ghana), United Nations reference: ST/TAO/HR/35

*1969 Seminar on the effects of scientific and technological developments on the status of women* (organized by the United Nations in co-operation with the Government of Romania). United Nations reference: ST/TAO/HR/37

*1970 Seminar on the Participation of Women in the Economic Life of Their Countries* (organized by the United Nations in co-operation with the Government of the Union of Soviet Socialist Republics). United Nations reference: ST/TAO/HR/41

*1971 Seminar on the Participation of Women in Economic Life* (organized by the United Nations in co-operation with the Government of Gabon), United Nations reference: ST/TAO/HR/43

*1972 Seminar on the Status of Women and Family Planning* (organized by the United Nations in co-operation with the Government of Turkey), United Nations reference: ST/TAO/HR/46

*1973 Seminar on the Status of Women and Family Planning* (organized by the United Nations in co-operation with the Government of the Dominican Republic). United Nations reference: (not yet available).

*1973 Seminar on the Status of Women and Family Planning* for Countries within the Economic Commission for Asia and the Far East Region (organized by the United Nations in co-operation with the Government of Indonesia). United Nations reference: (not yet available).

*1973 Seminar on the Family in a changing society: Problems and responsibilities of its members* on a world-wide basis (organized by the United Nations in co-operation with the Government of the United Kingdom of Great Britain and Northern Ireland.) United Nations reference: (not yet available).

# VIII. OTHER UNITED NATIONS HUMAN RIGHTS INSTRUMENTS

A number of United Nations instruments in the field of human rights have been dealt with in earlier chapters of this publication. These are: the International Bill of Rights consisting of the Universal Declaration of Human Rights of 1948, the International Covenant on Economic, Social and Cultural Rights, the International Covenant on Civil and Political Rights, and the Optional Protocol to the latter of 1966, the United Nations Declaration on the Elimination of All Forms of Racial Discrimination (1963), the International Convention on the Elimination of All Forms of Racial Discrimination (1965), the Discrimination (Employment and Occupation) Convention (1958), the Convention against Discrimination in Education (1960), the Protocol to the latter instituting a Conciliation and Good Offices Commission (1962), the Equal Remuneration Convention (1951), the Convention on the Political Rights of Women (1952), the Convention on the Nationality of Married Women (1957), the Convention on Consent to Marriage, Minimum Age for Marriage and Registration of Marriages (1962) and Recommendation on the same subjects (1965) and the Declaration on the Elimination of Discrimination against Women (1967).

In addition to those mentioned above, a number of other instruments have been drawn up since 1948 by, or under the auspices of, the United Nations, which are dealt with in this chapter.

## A. Convention on the Prevention and Punishment of the Crime of Genocide

The concern of the United Nations with the problem of "genocide" stems from its dealing with certain consequences of the Second World War. As stated in chapter I, section C above, and in chapter XII, section A below, the General Assembly, at its first session, at the same time that it decided to affirm the principles of international law recognized by the Charter of the Nuremberg Tribunal and the Judgement of the Tribunal (resolution 95 (I) of 11 December 1946), also affirmed that genocide was a crime under international law which the civilized world condemned and for the commission of which principals and accomplices—whether private individuals, public officials or statesmen and whether the crime is committed on religious, racial, political or any other grounds—were punishable (resolution 96 (I) of 11 December 1946). In that resolution the General Assembly stated that genocide was the denial of the right of existence of entire human groups, a denial which shocked the conscience of mankind, resulted in great losses to humanity and was contrary to moral law and to the spirit and aims of the United Nations. At the same time the General Assembly initiated studies with a view to drawing up a draft Convention on the crime of genocide.

The Economic and Social Council arranged for a draft Convention on the crime of genocide to be prepared by the Secretariat and revised by a committee of the Council. The draft was submitted to the General Assembly at its third session, revised at the General Assembly level and approved and proposed for signature and ratification or accession by resolution 260 (III) of 9 December 1948. It entered into force on 12 January 1951.

In the Genocide Convention the Contracting Parties confirm that genocide is a crime under international law which they undertake to prevent and to punish. Genocide is defined as meaning "any of the following acts committed with intent to destroy, in whole or in part, a national, ethnical, racial or religious group, as such:

"(*a*) Killing members of the group;

"(*b*) Causing serious bodily or mental harm to members of the group;

"(*c*) Deliberately inflicting on the group conditions of life calculated to bring about its physical destruction in whole or in part;

"(*d*) Imposing measures intended to prevent births within the group;

"(*e*) Forcibly transferring children of the group to another group."

In the Convention, States parties place it beyond doubt that genocide (and conspiracy, incitement and attempts to commit it and complicity in it), even if perpetrated by a Government in its own territory against its own citizens, is not a matter essentially within the domestic jurisdiction of States but a matter of international concern. Any Contracting Party can call upon United Nations organs to intervene. Genocide is a crime whether it is committed in time of peace or in time of war. Persons committing genocide or conspiracy, incitement and attempts to commit it and complicity in it shall be punished, whether they are constitutionally responsible rulers, public officials or private individuals. Persons charged with genocide shall be tried by a competent tribunal of the State in the territory in which the act was committed or by such international penal tribunal as may have jurisdiction with respect to those Contracting Parties which will have accepted its jurisdiction. The attempts to establish an international criminal court are described in chapter X below.

The Convention specifies that genocide (and conspiracy, incitement and attempts to commit it and complicity in it) shall not be considered as political crimes for the purpose of extradition. The Contracting Parties pledge themselves in such cases to grant extradition in accordance with their laws and treaties in force. The Convention further provides that any Contracting Party may call upon the competent organs of the United Nations to take such action under the Charter as they consider appropriate for the prevention and suppression of acts of genocide and related acts defined in the Convention.

In 1953, the General Assembly in its resolution 795 (VIII), reiterated its appeal to States to accelerate their ratifications of, or accessions to, the Convention, and requested the Secretary-General to continue to take all necessary measures designed to ensure the widest possible diffusion of the nature, contents and purposes of the Convention. In 1965, the Economic and Social Council (resolution 1074 D (XXXIX) invited eligible States which had not done so to accede as soon as possible to the Convention.

The Sub-Commission on Prevention of Discrimination and Protection of Minorities expressed the belief in 1965 (in resolution 8 (XVII) that there might exist a need for further measures to prevent and punish the crime of genocide, and it requested the Commission on Human Rights to give consideration to such further measures. In 1967, at its twentieth session the Sub-Commission decided to include in its future work, and to undertake as soon as possible, a study of the question of the prevention and punishment of the crime of genocide. On the recommendation of the Commission on Human Rights, the Economic and Social Council, by resolution 1420 (XLVI) of 6 June 1969, approved the Sub-Commission's decision to undertake the study and authorized the Sub-Commission to designate a Special Rapporteur to carry it out. In 1971, at its twenty-fourth session, the Sub-Commission appointed Mr. Nicodème Ruhashyankiko as Special Rapporteur. In 1972, at its twenty-fifth session, the Sub-Commission examined the preliminary report submitted by the Special Rapporteur (E/CN.4/Sub.2/L. 565) and requested him to continue his study.

The work undertaken by the United Nations to draft a Convention on the Suppression and Punishment of the Crime of *Apartheid* is described below.

## B. Convention for the Suppression of the Traffic in Persons and of the Exploitation of the Prostitution of others

The Convention for the Suppression of the Traffic in Persons and of the Exploitation of the Prostitution of Others was approved by the General Assembly in its resolution 317 (IV) of 2 December 1949 and entered into force on 25 July 1951. This Convention, while not part of the human rights programme of the United Nations in a narrower sense, was adopted by the General Assembly with a view to the suppression of institutions and practices which, in the words of the preamble, "are incompatible with the dignity and worth of the human person and endanger the welfare of the individual, the family and the community".

The purpose of the Convention has been to consolidate a series of older international instruments relating to white slave traffic, traffic in women and children and traffic in women of full age and to extend the scope of these instruments (listed in the preamble to the Convention) partly on the basis of a League of Nations draft of 1937.

The States parties to the Convention agree, in particular, to punish any person who, to gratify the passions of another, procures, entices or leads away, for purposes of prostitution, another person or exploits the prostitution of another person, even with the consent of the persons concerned. Parties further agree to make the management of financing of a brothel or the renting of a building or parts thereof for the prostitution of others a criminal offence. Attempts of, and participation in, these acts shall also be punishable. The protection of the law shall be afforded to aliens upon the same terms as to nationals.

Laws, regulations or administrative provisions by which persons engaged in prostitution are subject to special registration or to the possession of special documents or to exceptional requirements for supervision or notification shall be abolished. The main offences stipulated for in the Convention shall be regarded as extraditable offences.

The Convention does not affect the principle that the offences to which it refers shall in each State be defined, prosecuted and punished in conformity with its domestic law.

## C. Conventions relating to refugees, statelessness and nationality

Under the auspices of the United Nations five international instruments have been adopted with respect to the question of nationality, statelessness and of refugees. Three of them, the Conventions relating to the Status of Refugees, the Status of Stateless Persons and the Reduction of Statelessness, were adopted by conferences convened by the General Assembly and the Economic and Social Council, respectively; the Convention on the Nationality of Married Women was adopted by the General Assembly. The Protocol relating to the Status of Refugees, on the recommendation of the Executive Committee of the Programme of the United Nations High Commissioner for Refugees was noted with approval by the Economic and Social Council in its resolution 1186 (XLI) of 18 November 1966. In resolution 2198 (XXI) of 16 December 1966 the General Assembly took note of the Protocol relating to the Status of Refugees, which entered into force on 4 October 1967.

The preambles to the Convention relating to the Status of Refugees of 1951 and that relating to the Status of Stateless Persons of 1954 invoke the Charter and the Universal Declaration of Human Rights, which "have affirmed the principle that human beings shall enjoy fundamental rights and freedoms without discrimination". They recall that the United Nations has endeavoured to assure for refugees and for stateless persons the widest possible exercise of these fundamental rights and freedoms. Two principles form the basis of both Conventions: first, that there should be as little discrimination as possible between nationals, on the one hand, and refugees or stateless persons on the other; secondly, that there should be no discrimination based on race, religion or country of origin at all among refugees and among stateless persons.

In the Convention relating to the Status of Refugees of 1951, which entered into force on 22 April 1954, States parties have undertaken to apply to refugees, as defined in the instrument, "national treatment", i.e., treatment at least as favourable as that accorded to their own nationals with regard to certain rights, such as freedom of religion, access to courts, elementary education and public relief. With regard to other rights (wage-earning, employment and the right of association), refugees are entitled to most-favoured-nation treatment, i.e., the most favourable treatment accorded to nationals of a foreign country. In other respects (e.g., self-employment, education other than elementary education) they receive treatment as favourable as possible and, in any event, not less favourable than that accorded to aliens generally. The Convention applies only to persons who have become refugees as a result of events occurring before 1 January 1951. By the Protocol relating to the Status of Refugees, the dateline requirement was omitted and the States parties to the Protocol undertook to apply it without any geographic limitation.

The Convention relating to the Status of Stateless Persons of 1954, which entered into force on 6 June 1960, applies to "a person who is not considered as a national by any State under the operation of its law". With regard to most matters, the treatment accorded to stateless persons is the same as that accorded to refugees under the Convention relating to the Status of Refugees. As regards certain rights, however, the Stateless Persons Convention places stateless persons in a position less favourable than that provided for refugees; e.g., with regard to wage-earning employment and the right of association, they enjoy treatment not less favourable than that accorded to aliens generally and are not entitled to most-favoured-nation treatment.

The Convention on the Nationality of Married Women, adopted by the General Assembly on 29 January 1957 (resolution 1040 (XI)), is summarized in chapter VII above. It entered into force on 11 August 1958.

With regard to the Convention on the Reduction of Statelessness of 1961,[1] in 1953 and 1954 the International Law Commission prepared a draft Convention on the Elimination of Future Statelessness, the purpose of which was to solve the problem of statelessness and to eliminate statelessness as regards States Parties. Some members of the International Law Commission took the view that a less ambitious instrument constituted a more practicable solution of the problem and the Commission therefore prepared, as an alternative, a draft Convention on the Reduction of Future Statelessness.[2] In 1954 the General Assembly decided by resolution 896 (IX) upon the convening of an international conference of plenipotentiaries to conclude a Convention on the subject. This Conference convened in 1959 and again in 1961. On 30 August 1961 the Conference adopted the Convention on the Reduction of Statelessness (1961).

[1] Not in force as of 31 December 1972.

[2] See reports of the International Law Commission on the work of its fifth and sixth sessions *(Official Records of the General Assembly, Eighth Session, Supplement No. 9; ibid., Ninth Session, Supplement No. 9)*.

The essential provisions of the Convention can be summarized as follows: a contracting State shall grant its nationality to a person born in its territory who would otherwise be stateless. It may, however, make the granting of this nationality subject to certain conditions. A child born in wedlock in a territory of a contracting State whose mother has been a national of that State shall acquire at birth that nationality if it otherwise would be stateless. A foundling found in the territory of a contracting State shall, in the absence of proof to the contrary, be considered to have been born within that territory of parents possessing the nationality of that State. Subject to certain conditions a contracting State shall grant its nationality to a person born in the territory of a contracting State who would otherwise be stateless if the nationality of one of the parents at the time of the person's birth was that of that State. If the law of a contracting State entails loss of nationality as a consequence of any change in the personal status of a person, such as marriage, termination of marriage, legitimation, recognition or adoption, such loss shall be conditional upon possession or acquisition of another nationality. A contracting State shall not deprive a person of his nationality if such deprivation would render him stateless. The Convention, however, recognizes certain exceptions to this rule. A contracting State may not deprive any person or group of persons of their nationality on racial, ethnic, religious or political grounds.

### D. Convention on the International Right of Correction

The idea underlying the Convention on the International Right of Correction, which entered into force on 24 August 1962, is an attempt to transfer to the international level an institution which has been part of the national law of some countries. Its basic idea is that embodied in the maximum *audiatur et altera pars*, i.e., that the person referred to in a printed report shall have the right to convey to the readers his side of the question. In the Convention of 1952 the Contracting States agree that in cases where a Contracting State contends that a news dispatch capable of injuring its relations with other States or its national prestige or dignity transmitted from one country to another by correspondents or information agencies and published or disseminated abroad is false or distorted, it may submit its version of the facts (called "communiqué") to the contracting States within whose territories such dispatch has been published or disseminated. The receiving State has the obligation to release the communiqué to the correspondents and the information agencies operating in its territory through the channels customarily used for the release of news concerning international affairs for publication. The Convention does not impose a legal obligation on the Press or other media of information to publish the communiqué. The obligation of the receiving State to release the communiqué arises, however, whatever may be its opinion of the facts dealt with in the news dispatch or in the communiqué which purports to correct it. In the event that the receiving State does not discharge its obligation with respect to a communiqué of another State, the latter may accord, on the basis of reciprocity, similar treatment to a communiqué submitted to it by the defaulting State. The complaining State further has the right to seek relief through the Secretary-General of the United Nations, who shall give appropriate publicity, through the information channels at his disposal, to the communiqué, together with the original dispatch and the comments, if any, submitted to him by the State complained against. The Convention also contains a compromise clause referring disputes to the International Court of Justice.

### E. Supplementary Convention on the Abolition of Slavery, the Slave Trade, and Institutions and Practices Similar to Slavery

As one of the results of the intensive preoccupation of the United Nations with the question of slavery (see chapter IX, section E), the Supplementary Convention on the Abolition of Slavery, the Slave Trade, and Institutions and Practices Similar to Slavery was adopted in 1956 by a United Nations Conference of Plenipotentiaries convened by the Economic and Social Council and entered into force on 30 April 1957. The preamble makes it clear that the Convention is an instrument of international legislation for the purpose of implementing the Charter and giving effect to the Universal Declaration of Human Rights, both of which it invokes. The Convention outlaws certain institutions and practices similar to slavery, such as debt bondage, serfdom, purchase of brides and exploitation of child labour; it encourages the prescription of suitable minimum of marriage; it emphasizes the criminality of the slave trade and provides for penal sanctions for other practices, such as mutilating, branding or otherwise marking a slave, or a person of servile status. The Convention also provides for the co-operation between States parties directed to giving effect to its provisions. The Parties also undertake to communicate to the Secretary-General copies of any laws, regulations and administrative measures enacted or put into effect to implement the provisions of the Convention. This information is submitted, in addition to the States parties, also to the Economic and Social Council as part of the documentation for any discussion which the Council might undertake with a view to making further recommendations for the abolition of the objectionable institutions with which the Convention deals.

### F. Declaration of the Rights of the Child

The Declaration of the Rights of the Child, proclaimed in 1959 by the General Assembly in its resolution 1386 (XIV), recalls the Geneva Declaration of the Rights of the Child of 1924. As far as the work of the United Nations is concerned, it goes back to the initiative of the Social Commission (now the Commission for Social Development) of the Economic and Social Council, which prepared a draft in 1950. In 1956 the Commission on Human Rights, basing itself on the draft of the Social Commission, started working on the Declaration and prepared at its fifteenth session in 1959 a draft on the basis of which the General Assembly completed the preparation of the Declaration and adopted it. The Declaration of the Rights of the Child elaborates upon the human rights provisions of the Charter and of those of the Universal Declaration of Human Rights, particularly article 25 of the latter, according to which motherhood and childhood are entitled to special care and assistance and all children, whether born in or out of wedlock, shall enjoy the same social protection.

The Declaration of the Rights of the Child sets forth in the form of ten principles a code for the well-being of every child without any exception whatsoever. Every child shall be entitled to the rights set forth in the Declaration without distinction or discrimination on account of race, colour, sex, language, religion, political or other opinion, national or social origin, property, birth or other status, whether of himself or of his family. The Declaration provides that the child shall be given opportunities and facilities by law and by other means to enable him to develop physically, mentally, morally, spiritually and socially in a healthy and normal manner and in conditions of freedom and dignity. The Declaration emphasizes that in the enactment of laws for this purpose the best interests of the child shall be the paramount consideration. The child shall be entitled from his birth to a name and a nationality. The latter principle and that providing for measures of protection of the child without any discrimination have subsequently been incorporated in article 24 of the International Covenant on Civil and Political Rights.

The Declaration of the Rights of the Child also deals with the enjoyment by the child of the benefits of social security and the right to adequate nutrition, housing, recreation and medical services. A special provision deals with physically, mentally or socially handicapped children. The Declaration proclaims that the child is entitled to receive education which will be free and compulsory, at least in the elementary stages, and which will promote his general culture and enable him to develop his abilities, his sense of moral and social responsibility and to become a useful member of society. The child shall be protected against all forms of neglect, cruelty and exploitation and shall not be the subject of traffic in any form. The Declaration provides that a child in no case shall be caused or permitted to engage in any occupation or employment which would prejudice his health or education or interfere with his physical, mental or moral development. The child shall be protected from practices which foster racial, religious or any other form of discrimination and shall be brought up in a spirit of understanding, toleration, friendship among peoples, peace and universal brotherhood. This aspect of the care for children and young persons has been further elaborated in the Declaration on the Promotion Among Youth of the Ideals of Peace, Mutual Respect and Understanding between Peoples of 1965, which is dealt with in section G, below.

### G. Declaration on the Promotion Among Youth of the Ideals of Peace, Mutual Respect and Understanding between Peoples

The Declaration, which was adopted by resolution 2037 (XX) on 7 December 1965, is the reaffirmation of, and elaboration upon, principles which are embodied in the Universal Declaration of Human Rights of 1948, the

Declaration of the Rights of the Child of 1959, the Declaration on the Granting of Independence to Colonial Countries and Peoples of 1960, the United Nations Declaration on the Elimination of All Forms of Racial Discrimination of 1963 and other pronouncements of the United Nations condemning propaganda designed or likely to provoke or encourage any threat to the peace and having bearing upon the upbringing of young persons in a spirit of peace, mutual respect and understanding among peoples. In the Declaration the General Assembly calls upon Governments, non-governmental organizations and youth movements to ensure the observance of its principles by appropriate measures. The purpose of the Declaration is to promote equal rights for all human beings and all nations, economic and social progress, disarmament and the maintenance of international peace and security. Education should acquaint young peoples with the role entrusted to the United Nations as a means of preserving and maintaining peace and promoting international understanding and co-operation. The Declaration encourages exchanges, travel, tourism, meetings, the study of foreign languages and the twinning of towns and universities without discrinination. It appeals particularly to youth organizations to make their contribution to the work of educating the young generation in accordance with the ideals set forth in the Declaration. It stresses that the family has an important role to play in implementing its aims.

### H. Declaration on Territorial Asylum

The question of the right of asylum and related problems occupied the United Nations during the very first years of its activities in connexion with refugees and persons displaced as a consequence of the events of the Second World War. These aspects of the question are treated elsewhere in this publication among the questions connected with the liquidation of certain problems created by the Second World War. However, the United Nations also dealt with the question of the right of asylum on a general plane, as is illustrated by article 14 of the Universal Declaration of Human Rights, according to which everyone has the right to seek and to enjoy in other countries asylum from persecution, a right which may not be invoked in the case of prosecution arising genuinely from non-political crimes or from acts contrary to the purposes and principles of the United Nations.

Early in the proceedings of the Commission on Human Rights the question was also raised of the possibility of inserting an article on this right either in one of the draft International Covenants on Human Rights or in a special convention. At its second session in 1947 the Commission on Human Rights decided to examine at an early opportunity the question of the inclusion of the right of asylum of refugees from persecution in the international bill of human rights or in a special convention for the purpose. In its resolution 421 B (V) of 4 December 1950 the General Assembly called upon the Commission on Human Rights, through the Economic and Social Council, to consider the inclusion in the draft Covenant then before the General Assembly of "other rights", including the right of asylum, the insertion of which had been proposed by one Government. At the eighth session of the Commission on Human Rights in 1952 various proposals concerning the right of asylum were made, but none of them was accepted.[3]

As no article on the right of asylum had been included in the draft International Covenants on Human Rights, one Member Government submitted to the Commission, at its thirteenth session in 1957, a draft Declaration on the Right of Asylum. After Member Governments and the United Nations High Commissioner for Refugees had been consulted, the Commission on Human Rights, at its fifteenth session in 1959, decided to undertake the drafting of such a declaration. At its sixteenth session in 1960 the Commission on Human Rights had before it the comments of Governments, of the United Nations High Commissioner for Refugees and of non-governmental organizations on the draft Declaration on the Right of Asylum. The Commission on Human Rights was also notified that the General Assembly, at its fourteenth session in 1959, had adopted resolution 1400 (XIV) regarding the codification of the principles and rules of international law relating to the right of asylum. The Commission on Human Rights adopted the draft Declaration on the Right of Asylum at its sixteenth session. The draft was transmitted to the General Assembly by resolution 772 E (XXX) of the Economic and Social Council.

At the fifteenth, sixteenth and seventeenth sessions of the General Assembly the draft Declaration was referred to the Third Committee, which, at the seventeenth session in 1962, approved texts for the preamble and article 1 of the draft Declaration. No work was done on the draft Declaration at the eighteenth and nineteenth sessions of the General Assembly in 1963 and 1964-1965 respectively.

At the twentieth session of the General Assembly the question was referred to the Sixth Committee, which dealt with the problem at the twentieth and twenty-first sessions of the General Assembly. At the twenty-first session a working group of the Sixth Committee prepared a draft Declaration on Territorial Asylum on the basis of the work done previously by the Third Committee and the Commission on Human Rights, respectively. By resolution 2203 (XXI) of 16 December 1966 the General Assembly arranged for the transmission of the draft to Member States for their further consideration and decided to place an item relating to it on the provisional agenda of the twenty-second session (1967) with a view to the final adoption of a declaration on this subject.

The Declaration on Territorial Asylum was adopted by the General Assembly on 14 December 1967 (resolution 2312 (XXII)). The Declaration provides that asylum granted by a State in the exercise of its sovereignty to persons entitled to invoke article 14 of the Universal Declaration of Human Rights, including persons struggling against colonialism, shall be respected by all other States. The Declaration goes on to state that the right to seek and enjoy asylum may not be invoked by any

[3] See E/CN.4/SR.316-318.

person with respect to whom there are serious reasons for considering that he has committed a crime against peace, a war crime or a crime against humanity as defined in the international instruments drawn up to make provision in respect of such crimes. It rests with the State granting asylum to evaluate the grounds for the granting of asylum.

The Declaration also provides that the situation of persons entitled to invoke article 14 of the Universal Declaration of Human Rights, including persons struggling against colonialism, is of concern to the international community. This is without prejudice to the sovereignty of States and the purposes and principles of the United Nations. Where a State finds difficulty in granting or continuing to grant asylum, States individually or jointly or through the United Nations shall consider, in a spirit of international solidarity, appropriate measures to lighten the burden on that State.

The instrument further states that no person who is entitled to invoke article 14 of the Universal Declaration of Human Rights shall be subjected to measures such as rejection at the frontier or, if he has already entered the territory in which he seeks asylum, expulsion or compulsory return to any State where he may be subjected to persecution. The Declaration provides for exceptions to be made to this principle. These are permissible only for overriding reasons of national security or in order to safeguard the population, as in the case of a mass influx of persons. In such cases the State shall consider the possibility of granting to the person concerned, under such conditions as it may deem appropriate, an opportunity, whether by way of provisional asylum or otherwise, of going to another State. States granting asylum shall not permit persons who have received asylum to engage in activities contrary to the purposes and principles of the United Nations.

## I. Proclamation of Teheran

The International Conference on Human Rights, convened by the General Assembly as part of the commemoration of the twentieth anniversary of the proclamation of the Universal Declaration of Human Rights, was held at Teheran from 22 April to 13 May 1968. The composition and activities of the Conference are described in part two, chapter I C below. The Conference solemnly proclaimed that it was imperative that the members of the international community fulfil their solemn obligations to promote and encourage respect for human rights and fundamental freedoms for all. The Proclamation said that the Universal Declaration of Human Rights stated a common understanding of the peoples of the world concerning the inalienable and inviolate rights of all members of the human family and constituted an obligation for the members of the international community. The Proclamation of Teheran emphasized that the International Covenants on Human Rights, the Declaration on the Granting of Independence to Colonial Countries and Peoples, the International Convention on the Elimination of All Forms of Racial Discrimination, as well as other conventions and declarations in the field of human rights, had created new standards and obligations to which States should conform. It added that much remained to be done in regard to the implementation of human rights and fundamental freedoms. The Declaration expressed the gravest concern of the international community in regard to the repugnant policy of *apartheid* and called for the use of every possible means to eradicate this evil. It recorded that problems of colonialism still preoccupied the international community and that massive and gross denials of human rights had tragic consequences and endangered the foundations of freedom, justice, and peace in the world. The Declaration referred to the failure of the (first) Development Decade to reach its modest objectives. It stressed the necessity of effective national and international policies of economic and social development. It stated that international action aimed at eradicating illiteracy from the face of the earth and promoting education at all levels required urgent attention. It stated that the full implementation of the Declaration on the Elimination of Discrimination against Women was a necessity for the progress of mankind. The Proclamation emphasized that the protection of the family and of the child remained the concern of the international community and repeated that parents had a basic human right to determine freely and responsibly the number and the spacing of their children. It also expressed concern in regard to the aspirations of the younger generation aud the endangering by recent scientific discoveries and technological advances of the rights and freedoms of individuals, and called for disarmament, which would release immense human and material resources.

## J. Convention on the Non-Applicability of Statutory Limitations to War Crimes and Crimes against Humanity

The Convention on the Non-Applicability of Statutory Limitations to War Crimes and Crimes against Humanity was adopted and opened for signature, ratification and accession by General Assembly resolution 2391 (XXIII) of 26 November 1968. The Convention entered into force on 11 November 1970.

Article I of the Convention provides that no statutory limitation shall apply to war crimes and crimes against humanity. War crimes within the meaning of the Convention are war crimes as they are defined in the Charter of the International Military Tribunal of 8 August 1945 and confirmed by resolutions 3 (I) and 95 (I) of 1946 of the General Assembly, particularly the "grave breaches" enumerated in the Geneva Conventions of 1949 for the protection of war victims. The Convention applies further to crimes against humanity, whether committed in time of war or in time of peace, as they are defined in the Charter of the International Military Tribunal and in the General Assembly resolutions of 1946 just referred to, the eviction by armed attack or occupation and inhuman acts resulting from the policy of *apartheid*, and the crime of genocide as defined in the Convention of 1948, even if such acts do not constitute a violation of the domestic law of the country in which they were committed.

Pursuant to article II, the provisions of the Convention apply to representatives of State authority and private individuals, who participate in or who directly incite others to the commission of any of those crimes, or who conspire to commit them, irrespective of the degree of completion, and to representatives of the State authority who tolerate their commission.

Under article III the States parties to the Convention undertake to adopt all necessary domestic measures, legislative or otherwise, with a view to making possible the extradition, in accordance with international law, of the persons referred to in article II.

By virtue of article IV the States parties undertake to adopt, in accordance with their respective constitutional processes, any legislative or other measures necessary to ensure that statutory or other limitations shall not apply to the prosecution and punishment of the crimes referred to in articles I and II of the Convention and that, where they exist, such limitations shall be abolished.

### K. Declaration on Social Progress and Development

At its twenty-fourth session, the General Assembly, in its resolution 2542 (XXIV) of 11 December 1969, adopted and solemnly proclaimed the Declaration on Social Progress and Development and called for national and international action for its use as a common basis for social development policies.

The Declaration on Social Progress and Development reaffirms faith in human rights and fundamental freedoms and in the principles of peace, of the dignity and worth of the human person, and of social justice proclaimed in the Charter. It recalls the principles of the earlier international instruments in the human rights field and states in its article 1:

> "All peoples and all human beings, without distinction as to race, colour, sex, language, religion, nationality, ethnic origin, family or social status, or political or other conviction, shall have the right to live in dignity and freedom and to enjoy the fruits of social progress and should, on their part, contribute to it".

The Declaration further states that:

> "Social progress and development shall be founded on respect for the dignity and value of the human person and shall ensure the promotion of human rights and social justice, which requires:
>
> "(*a*) The immediate and final elimination of all forms of inequality, exploitation of peoples and individuals, colonialism and racism, including nazism and *apartheid*, and all other policies and ideologies opposed to the purposes and principles of the United Nations;
>
> "(*b*) The recognition and effective implementation of civil and political rights as well as of economic, social and cultural rights without any discrimination."

The following are considered primary conditions of social progress and development:

> "(*a*) National independence based on the rights of peoples to self-determination;
>
> "(*b*) The principle of non-interference in the internal affairs of States;
>
> "(*c*) Respect for the sovereignty and territorial integrity of States;
>
> "(*d*) Permanent sovereignty of each nation over its natural wealth and resources;
>
> "(*e*) The rights and responsiblity of each State and, as far as they are concerned, each nation and people to determine freely its own objectives of social development, to set its own priorities and to decide in conformity with the principles of the Charter of the United Nations the means and methods of their achievement without any external interference;
>
> "(*f*) Peaceful coexistence, peace, friendly relations and co-operation among States irrespective of differences in their social, economic or political systems."

The Declaration further provides:

> "The family as a basic unit of society and the natural environment for the growth and well-being of all its members, particularly children and youth, should be assisted and protected so that it may fully assume its responsiblities within the community. Parents have the exclusive right to determine freely and responsibly the number and spacing of their children."

The Declaration stresses that social progress and development require the full utilization of human resources with full respect for the fundamental freedoms embodied in the Universal Declaration of Human Rights. It stresses that social development requires assurance to everyone of the right to work and the free choice of employment. Social progress and development require the participation of all members of society in productive and socially useful labour and the establishment in conformity with human rights and fundamental freedoms and with the principles of justice and the social function of property, of forms of ownership of land and of the means of production which preclude any kind of exploitation of man, ensure equal rights to property for all and create conditions leading to genuine equality among people.

The Declaration on Social Progress and Development aims at the continuous raising of the material and spiritual standards of living of all members of society, with respect for and in compliance with human rights and fundamental freedoms, and proceeds to set forth the main goals as well as the means and methods for the achievement of the objectives of social progress and development.

Among many other goals the Declaration calls for the establishment of legal and administrative measures for the protection and improvement of the human environment. The Declaration also calls for the achievement of general and complete disarmament and the channelling of the progressively released resources to be used for economic and social progress for the welfare of people everywhere and, in particular, for the benefit of developing countries. It also calls for adoption of measures contributing to disarmament, including among others, the complete prohibition of nuclear weapons, the prohibition of the development, production and stockpiling of (biological) weapons and the prevention of the pollution of oceans and inland waters by nuclear wastes.

### L. Declaration on the Occasion of the Twenty-fifth Anniversary of the United Nations

On 24 October 1970, the General Assembly (resolution 2627 (XXV)) adopted the Declaration on the Occasion of the Twenty-fifth Anniversary of the United Nations, in which the representatives of the States Members of the United Nations, assembled at United Nations Headquarters on 24 October 1970 on the occasion of the twenty-fifth anniversary of the coming into force of the Charter, made a series of solemn declarations.

The Declaration acclaims the role of the United Nations in the process of the liberation of peoples of colonial, Trust and other Non-Self-Governing Territories. It states that despite these achievements, many Territories and peoples continue to be denied their right to self-determination and independence. In recognizing the legitimacy of the struggle of colonial peoples for their freedom by all appropriate means at their disposal, the Declaration of 24 October 1970 calls upon all Governments to comply in this respect with the provisions of the Charter, taking into account the Declaration on the Granting of Independence to Colonial Countries and Peoples adopted in 1960. The Declaration strongly condemns the evil policy of *apartheid*, which is a crime against the conscience and dignity of mankind and, like nazism, is contrary to the principles of the Charter.

The Declaration contains the following general statement on human rights and fundamental freedoms:

"The United Nations has endeavoured in its first twenty-five years to further the Charter objectives of promoting respect for, and observance of, human rights and fundamental freedoms for all. The international conventions and declarations concluded under its auspices give expression to the moral conscience of mankind and represent humanitarian standards for all members of the international community. The Universal Declaration of Human Rights, the International Covenants on Human Rights, the International Convention on the Elimination of All Forms of Racial Discrimination and the Convention on the Prevention and Punishment of the Crime of Genocide constitute a landmark in international co-operation and in the recognition and protection of the rights of every individual without any distinction. Although some progress has been achieved, serious violations of human rights are still being committed against individuals and groups in several regions of the world. We pledge ourselves to a continued and determined struggle against all violations of the rights and fundamental freedoms of human beings, by eliminating the basic causes of such violations, by promoting universal respect for the dignity of all people without regard to race, colour, sex, language or religion, and in particular, through greater use of the facilities provided by the United Nations in accordance with the Charter."

### M. Declaration on Principles of International Law concerning Friendly Relations and Co-operation among States in accordance with the Charter of the United Nations

Also on 24 October 1970, the General Assembly (in resolution 2625 (XXV)) adopted the Declaration on Principles of International Law concerning Friendly Relations and Co-operation among States in accordance with the Charter of the United Nations. In this Declaration the General Assembly solemnly proclaimed a series of principles, among them the duty of States to co-operate with one another in accordance with the Charter.

In this context the General Assembly declared that the States had the duty to co-operate with one another irrespective of the differences in their political, economic and social systems in the various fields of international relations, in order to maintain international peace and security and to promote international economic stability and progress, the general welfare of nations and international co-operation free from discrimination based on such differences. The General Assembly proclaimed that, to this end, States should co-operate in various fields, including co-operation in the promotion of universal respect for and observance of human rights and fundamental freedoms for all, and in the elimination of all forms of racial discrimination and all forms of religious intolerance.

The General Assembly also stated that:

"By virtue of the principle of equal rights and self-determination of peoples enshrined in the Charter of the United Nations, all peoples have the right freely to determine, without external interference, their political status and to pursue their economic, social and cultural development, and every State has the duty to respect this right in accordance with the provisions of the Charter.

"Every State has the duty to promote, through joint and separate action, realization of the principle of equal rights and self-determination of peoples, in accordance with the provisions of the Charter, and to render assistance to the United Nations in carrying out the responsibilities entrusted to it by the Charter regarding the implementation of the principle, in order:

"(*a*) To promote friendly relations and co-operation among States; and

"(*b*) To bring a speedy end to colonialism, having due regard to the freely expressed will of the peoples concerned;

and bearing in mind that subjection of peoples to alien subjugation, domination and exploitation constitutes a violation of the principles, as well as a denial of fundamental human rights, and is contrary to the Charter.

"Every State has the duty to promote through joint and separate action universal respect for and observance of human rights and fundamental freedoms in accordance with the Charter.

"The establishment of a sovereign and independent State, the free association or integration with an independent State or the emergence into any other political status freely determined by a people constitute modes of implementing the right of self-determination by that people.

"Every State has the duty to refrain from any forcible action which deprives peoples referred to above in the elaboration of the present principle of their right to self-determination and freedom and independence. In their actions against, and resistance to, such forcible action in pursuit of the exercise of their right to self-determination, such peoples are entitled to seek and to receive support in accordance with the purposes and principles of the Charter.

"The territory of a colony or other Non-Self-Governing Territory has, under the Charter, a status separate and distinct from the territory of the State administering it; and such separate and distinct status under the Charter shall exist until the people of the colony or Non-Self-Governing Territory have exercised their right of self-determination in accordance with the Charter, and particularly its purposes and principles.

"Nothing in the foregoing paragraphs shall be construed as authorizing or encouraging any action which would dismember or impair, totally or in part, the territorial integrity or political unity of sovereign and independent States conducting themselves in compliance with the principles of equal rights and self-determination of peoples as described above and thus possessed of a government representing the whole people belonging to the territory without distinction as to race, creed or colour."

### N. Declaration on the Strengthening of International Security

In the Declaration on the Strengthening of International Security, the General Assembly (in resolution 2734 (XXV) of 16 December 1970) solemnly reaffirmed that universal respect for and full exercise of human rights and fundamental freedoms and the elimination of the violation of those rights were urgent and essential to the strengthening of international security, and hence resolutely condemned all forms of oppression, tyranny and discrimination, particularly racism and racial discrimination, wherever they occurred.

The General Assembly further condemned the criminal policy of *apartheid* of the Government of South Africa and reaffirmed the legitimacy of the struggle of the oppressed peoples to attain their human rights and fundamental freedoms and self-determination.

### O. Declaration on the Rights of Mentally Retarded Persons

At its twenty-sixth session the General Assembly (in resolution 2856 (XXVI) of 20 December 1971), mindful of the pledge of Member States under the Charter which is expressed in Article 56 and reaffirming faith in human rights and fundamental freedoms and in the dignity and worth of the human person and of social justice, adopted the Declaration on the Rights of Mentally Retarded Persons. The General Assembly recalled the principles of the Universal Declaration of Human Rights, of the two Covenants, and of the Declaration of the Rights of the Child. It recalled the constititions, conventions, recommendations and resolutions of various specialized agencies and other organs and organizations. It also invoked the Declaration on Social Progress and Development. It proclaimed the Declaration on the Rights of Mentally Retarded Persons and called for national and international action to ensure that it would be used as a common basis and frame of reference for the protection of the rights set forth in it. The Declaration provides, *inter alia*, that the mentally retarded person has, to the maximum degree of feasibility, the same rights as other human beings, a right to proper medical care and physical therapy and to such education, training, rehabilitation and guidance as will enable him to develop his ability and maximum potential. The mentally retarded person has a right to economic security and to a decent standard of living and a right to protection from exploitation, abuse and degrading treatment.

### P. Declaration of the United Nations Conference on the Human Environment

The United Nations Conference on the Human Environment, convened by the General Assembly in its resolution 2398 (XXIII) of 3 December 1968 and supplemented by later General Assembly resolutions, met at Stockholm from 5 to 16 June 1972 and, having considered the need for a common outlook and for common principles to inspire and guide the peoples of the world in the preservation and enhancement of the human environment, adopted the Declaration of the United Nations Conference on the Human Environment.[4] In that Declaration the Conference proclaimed:

"Man is both creature and moulder of his environment, which gives him physical sustenance and affords him the opportunity for intellectual, moral, social and spiritual growth. In the long and tortuous evolution of the human race on this planet a stage has been reached when, through the rapid acceleration of science and technology, man has acquired the power to transform his environment in countless ways and on an unprecedented scale. Both aspects of man's environment, the natural and the man-made, are essential to his well-being and to the enjoyment of basic human rights—even the right to life itself."

The Conference also adopted a series of Principles, in which it stated the common conviction that:

"Man has the fundamental right to freedom, equality and adequate conditions of life, in an environment of a quality that permits a life of dignity and well-being, and he bears a solemn responsibility to protect and improve the environment for present and future generations. In this respect, policies promoting or perpetuating *apartheid*, racial segregation, discrimination, colonial and other forms of oppression and foreign domination stand condemned and must be eliminated."

Among the Principles stated by the Conference were also the following:

"Economic and social development is essential for ensuring a favourable living and working environment for man and for creating conditions on earth that are necessary for the improvement of the quality of life."

---

[4] A/CONF.48/14 and Corr.1, chap. I.

"...

"Man and his environment must be spared the effects of nuclear weapons and all other means of mass destruction. States must strive to reach prompt agreement, in the relevant international organs, on the elimination and complete destruction of such weapons."

In resolution 2994 (XXVII) of 15 December 1972, the General Assembly took note with satisfaction of the report of the United Nations Conference on the Human Environment [5] and drew the attention of Governments and the Governing Council of the United Nations Environment Programme to the Declaration of the Conference.

## Q. Principal instruments in the human rights field adopted by the specialized agencies

It may be appropriate to recall that certain instruments have been adopted by the specialized agencies on questions closely related to instruments and other measures in the human rights field adopted by the United Nations, frequently as a result of initiatives originally taken in United Nations organs. Reference has already been made in chapter V to the Conventions and Recommendations adopted by the ILO and UNESCO regarding discrimination in employment and occupation and in education. The ILO Convention and Recommendation on equal remuneration have been considered in chapter VII. Other major instruments which may be briefly mentioned here are those concerned with the abolition of forced labour and with freedom of association.

The International Labour Conference, which had already in 1930 adopted a Forced Labour Convention providing for the progressive abolition of forced labour [6] —adopted the Abolition of Forced Labour Convention in 1957. Each member of the International Labour Organisation which ratifies this Convention undertakes to suppress and not to make use of any form of forced or compulsory labour for the following purposes: (*a*) as a means of political coercion or education or as a punishment for holding or expressing political views or views ideologically opposed to the established political, social or economic system; (*b*) as a method of mobilizing and using labour for purposes of economic development; (*c*) as a means of labour discipline; (*d*) as a punishment for having participated in strikes and (*e*) as a means of racial, social, national or religious discrimination. It must take effective measures to secure the immediate and complete abolition of forced or compulsory labour for any such purposes. Article 8 of the International Covenant on Civil and Political Rights also contains an absolute prohibition of forced or compulsory labour. At its fifty-fourth session in 1970 the International Labour Conference adopted the Special Youth Schemes Recommendation, 1970 (No. 136) which deals, amongst other things, with the compatibility of such schemes with the provisions of the two ILO forced labour Conventions. The Recommendation provides that participation in special youth employment and training schemes should be voluntary, but that exceptions to this rule may be permitted where there is full compliance with the terms of existing international labour Conventions on forced labour and employment policy, and, *inter alia*, in respect of (*a*) schemes of education and training involving obligatory enrolment of unemployed young people within a definite period after the age limit of regular school attendance; and (*b*) schemes for young people who have previously accepted an obligation to serve for a definite period as a condition of being enabled to acquire education or technical qualifications of special value to the community for development.

The principal ILO instruments in the fields of freedom of association and protection of the right to organize are the Freedom of Association and Protection of the Right to Organize Convention, 1948, the Right to Organise and Collective Bargaining Convention, 1949 and the Workers' Representatives Convention, 1971. The guarantees to which the first of these Conventions requires States parties to give effect include the following: workers and employers, without distinction whatsoever, shall have the right to establish and, subject only to the rules of the organization concerned, to join organizations of their own choosing without previous authorization for furthering and defending their interests. Organizations of workers or of employers shall have the right to draw up their constitutions and rules, to elect their representatives in full freedom, to organize their administration and activities and to formulate their programmes. The public authorities shall refrain from any interference which would restrict this right or impede the lawful exercise thereof. Workers' and employers' organizations shall not be liable to be dissolved or suspended by administrative authority. They shall have the right to establish and join federations and confederations which shall have the right to affiliate with international organizations of workers and employers. In exercising the rights provided for in the Convention, workers and employers and their respective organizations, like other persons or organized collectivities, shall respect the law of the land. The law of the land shall not be such as to impair, nor shall it be so applied as to impair, the guarantees provided for in the Convention.

The Right to Organise and Collective Bargaining Convention requires States parties to provide protection for workers against acts of anti-union discrimination and for workers' and employers' organizations against mutual acts of interference in their establishment, functioning and administration. States parties must establish appropriate machinery to ensure respect for these rights, and take measures to encourage and promote voluntary collective negotiation between employers or employers' organizations and workers' organizations.

---

[5] A/CONF.48/14 and Corr.1.

[6] The Forced Labour Convention, 1930 (No. 29) — which was adopted primarily in the light of practices then current in colonial territories — provides for the suppression of forced or compulsory labour in all its forms within the shortest possible period and lays down specific conditions and guarantees subject to which, in the transitional period pending total abolition, forced or compulsory labour might be used as an exceptional measure for public purposes only.

The Workers' Representatives Convention, 1971, supplements the terms of the Right to Organise and Collective Bargaining Convention, 1949, which provides for protection of workers against anti-union discrimination in respect of their employment. Under the new Convention, workers' representatives in the undertaking will enjoy effective protection against any act prejudicial to them, including dismissal, based on their status or activities as a workers' representative or on union membership or participation in union activities, in so far as they act in conformity with existing laws or collective agreements or other jointly agreed arrangements. Workers' representatives will be afforded such facilities in the undertaking as may be appropriate in order to enable them to carry out their functions promptly and efficiently. The granting of such facilities shall not impair the efficient operation of the undertaking concerned. For the purpose of the Convention the term "workers' representatives" means persons recognized as such under national law or practice, whether they be trade union representatives —namely representatives designated or elected by trade unions or by members of such unions—or elected representatives, namely representatives freely elected by the workers of the undertaking whose functions do not include activities recognized as the exclusive prerogative of trade unions in the country concerned. Where there exist in the same undertaking both trade union representatives and elected representatives, appropriate measures shall be taken, wherever necessary, to ensure that the existence of elected representatives is not used to undermine the position of the trade unions concerned or of their representatives.

In 1964 the General Conference of the International Labour Organisation adopted the Employment Policy Convention, 1964, which entered into force on 15 July 1966. In the preamble the Convention states: that "the Declaration of Philadelphia recognises the solemn obligation of the International Labour Organisation to further, among the nations of the world, programmes which will achieve full employment and the raising of standards of living. . .". It refers further to the fact that:

> "under the terms of the Declaration of Philadelphia it is the responsiblity of the International Labour Organisation to examine and consider the bearing of economic and financial policies upon employment policy in the light of the fundamental objective that 'all human beings, irrespective of race, creed or sex, have the right to pursue both their material well-being and their spiritual development in conditions of freedom and dignity, of economic security and equal opportunity'".

The Convention quotes article 23 from the Universal Declaration of Human Rights, which provides that "everyone has the right to work, to free choice of employment, to just and favourable conditions of work and to protection against unemployment". The Employment Policy Convention provides that:

> "with a view to stimulating economic growth and development, raising levels of living, meeting manpower requirements and overcoming unemployment and underemployment, each Member shall declare and pursue, as a major goal, an active policy designed to promote full, productive and freely chosen employment".

The policy shall aim at ensuring that:

> "(*a*) there is work for all who are available for and seeking work; (*b*) such work is as productive as possible; (*c*) there is freedom of choice of employment and the fullest possible opportunity for each worker to qualify for, and to use his skills and endowments in, a job for which he is well suited, irrespective of race, colour, sex, religion, political opinion, national extraction or social origin."

Article 3 of the Convention states that:

> "In the application of this Convention, representatives of the persons affected by the measures to be taken, and in particular representatives of employers and workers, shall be consulted concerning employment policies, with a view to taking fully into account their experience and views and securing their full co-operation in formulating and enlisting support for such policies."

In 1970 the International Labour Conference revised the Holidays with Pay Convention, 1936 and the Holidays with Pay (Agriculture) Convention, 1952 and adopted the Holidays with Pay Convention (Revised), 1970. It applies to all employed persons, with the exception of seafarers, and provides that they shall be entitled to an annual paid holiday of a length to be specified by each State party. The holiday shall be no less than three working weeks for one year of service. A minimum period of service not exceeding six months may be required for entitlement. This Convention regulates in detail the exercise of a right which is also set forth in general human rights instruments, particularly in article 24 of the Universal Declaration of Human Rights and in article 7 (*d*) of the International Covenant on Economic, Social and Cultural Rights.

# IX. IMPLEMENTATION OF RIGHTS PROCLAIMED IN THE UNIVERSAL DECLARATION OF HUMAN RIGHTS

## A. General action concerning the promotion of respect for human rights

Throughout their existence the organs of the United Nations have repeatedly expressed their concern about the State of respect for human rights in the world and formulated recommendations to States. These acts of the United Nations organs were either recommendations favouring positive action or statements critical of the general situation or of specific situations. Recommendations of this type were cited in chapter II above and include among others the resolutions, "Essentials of peace", "Uniting for peace", "Observance of human rights" and "Measures to accelerate the promotion of respect for human rights and fundamental freedoms". The International Conference on Human Rights of 1968 and the solemn declarations adopted by the General Assembly on 24 October 1970 were additional major events in this field.

### 1. *The International Conference on Human Rights, 1968*

The convening of the International Conference on Human Rights, at Teheran in 1968, must also be mentioned as a major event in the course of United Nations action for the promotion of respect for human rights. The Conference was decided upon by General Assembly resolutions 2081 (XX) of 1965, 2217 C (XXI) of 1966 and 2339 (XXII) of 1967 and was held at Teheran, Iran, from 22 April to 13 May 1968.[1]

*The scope and work of the Conference*

The Conference adopted a series of resolutions which dealt with respect for and implementation of human rights in occupied territories; measures to be taken against nazism and racial intolerance; measures to achieve rapid and total elimination of all forms of racial discrimination in general and the policy of *apartheid* in particular; the treatment of persons who oppose racist régimes; observance of the principle of non-discrimination in employment; measures to eliminate all forms and manifestations of racial discrimination; establishment of a new, additional United Nations programme on racial discrimination; the importance of the universal realization of the right of peoples to self-determination and of the speedy granting of independence to colonial countries and peoples for the effective guarantee and observance of human rights. The Conference further urged that measures be taken to promote women's rights in the modern world and endorsed the drawing up and execution of a unified long-term United Nations programme for the advancement of women. It initiated action for the preparation of model rules of procedure for bodies dealing with violations of human rights. It urged the undertaking of thorough and continuous interdisciplinary studies of the problems of human rights and scientific and technological developments. It invited Governments to take action to combat illiteracy. It considered that all Governments should concern themselves with the situation of refugees in the world and called for co-operation with the United Nations High Commissioner for Refugees. It initiated action on the rights of detained persons. It appealed for greater support to international activities in the interest of the child and expressed its appreciation of the efforts of the United Nations Children's Fund. The Conference, recognizing the world-wide economic and social consequences which a general and complete disarmament could have in the implementation of human rights and fundamental freedoms, appealed to all States to co-operate actively with the competent organs of the United Nations towards an immediate conclusion of an agreement on general and complete disarmament. In a resolution on economic development and human rights, the Conference addressed recommendations to the economically developed countries and called urgently for the preparation of a global strategy.

In a resolution on human rights aspects of family planning, the Conference drew attention to the fact that the present rapid rate of population growth in some areas hampered the struggle against hunger and poverty and considered that couples had a basic human right to decide freely and responsibly on the number and spacing of their children and a right to adequate education and information in that respect. The Conference made recommendations in the matter of legal aid. It made a strong plea for the education of youth in respect for human rights and fundamental freedoms. It went on record in favour of intensified action for the realization of economic, social and cultural rights. It called for universal accession by States to international instruments relating to human rights. It initiated the subsequent comprehensive studies and action by the United Nations organs on the question of human rights in armed conflicts. It urged that an International Year for Action to Combat Racism and Racial Discrimination be declared and suggested additional publicity for the Universal Declaration of Human Rights. It also endorsed a certain decision taken in the field of sports as a measure to achieve the elimination of racial discrimination.

[1] *Final Act of the International Conference on Human Rights* (United Nations publication, Sales No. E.68.XIV.2).

2. *Solemn declarations adopted by the General Assembly on 24 October 1970*

The solemn declaration adopted by the General Assembly at its twenty-fifth session, i.e. the Declaration on the Occasion of the Twenty-fifth Anniversary of the United Nations and the Declaration on Principles of International Law concerning Friendly Relations and Co-operation among States in accordance with the Charter of the United Nations, were intended to serve among other purposes that of promoting and encouraging human rights and fundamental freedoms.

The General Assembly resolutely condemned the criminal policy of *apartheid* of the Government of South Africa and reaffirmed the legitimacy of the struggle of the oppressed peoples to attain their human rights and fundamental freedoms and self-determination.

On 24 October 1970 the General Assembly further proclaimed the Second United Nations Development Decade, starting from 1 January 1971, and adopted the International Development Strategy for that Decade (resolution 2626 (XXV)).

In the preamble to the International Development Strategy for the Decade, the Governments dedicated themselves anew to the fundamental objectives enshrined in the Charter 25 years earlier to create conditions of stability and well-being and to ensure a minimum standard of living consistent with human dignity through economic and social progress and development. The General Assembly declared that the success of the international development activities would depend in large measure on improvement in the general international situation, particularly the elimination of colonialism, racial discrimination, *apartheid* and occupation of territories of any State, and the promotion of equal political, economic, social and cultural rights for all members of society.

In its section entitled "Human development" the International Development Strategy states that those developing countries which consider that their rate of population growth hampers their development will adopt measures which they deem necessary in accordance with their concept of development. Developed countries, consistent with their national policies, will upon request provide support through the supply of means for family planning and further research.

Developing countries will formulate and implement educational programmes taking into account their developing needs.

Developing countries will establish at least a minimum programme of health facilities comprising an infrastructure of institutions, including those for medical training and research to bring basic medical services withih the reach of a specified proportion of their population by the end of the Decade.

Developing countries will take steps to provide improved housing and related community facilities in both urban and rural areas, especially for low-income groups.

3. *Increased United Nations activities against violations of human rights*

On the initiative of the Special Committee on the Situation with regard to the Implementation of the Declaration on the Granting of Independence to Colonial Countries and Peoples, the Economic and Social Council in its resolution 1104 (XL) invited the Commission on Human Rights in 1966 to consider as a matter of importance and urgency the question of the violation of human rights and fundamental freedoms, including policies of racial discrimination and segregation and of *apartheid* in all countries with particular reference to colonial and other dependent countries and territories. On 26 October 1966, the General Assembly (in its resolution 2144 (XXI)) reaffirmed its strong condemnation of the violations of human rights and fundamental freedoms wherever they occurred, especially in all colonial and dependent territories, including the policies of *apartheid* in South Africa, South West Africa and racial discrimination in various colonies listed by name in the Assembly resolution. The General Assembly called upon all States to strengthen their efforts to promote the full observance of human rights and the right to self-determination and to take effective measures for the suppression of the policies of *apartheid* and segregation and for the elimination of racial discrimination wherever it might occur, especially in colonial and other dependent countries and territories. It invited States to become parties to all Conventions which aim at protecting human rights and fundamental freedoms, including, in particular, the International Convention on the Elimination of All Forms of Racial Discrimination.

The General Assembly also invited the Economic and Social Council and the Commission on Human Rights to give urgent consideration to ways and means of improving the capacity of the United Nations to put a stop to violations of human rights wherever they may occur.

Further developments in this field, in particular the adoption by the Economic and Social Council of resolution 1503 (XLVIII) in 1970 and the procedure relating to communications in the human rights field, based on that resolution, are described in part two of this publication.

4. *Respect for human rights during the vicissitudes of war*

In resolution 237 (1967), adopted on 14 June 1967 in connexion with the conflict in the Middle East, the Security Council emphasized that the essential and inalienable human rights should be respected even during the vicissitudes of war. The Security Council considered that all the obligations of the Geneva Convention relative to the Treatment of Prisoners of War of 12 August 1949 [2] should be complied with by the parties involved in the conflict. It called upon the Government concerned to ensure the safety, welfare and security of the inhabitants of the areas where military operations had taken place and to facilitate the return of those inhabitants who had fled the areas since the outbreak of hostilities. The Security Council further recommended to the Governments concerned the scrupulous respect of the humanitarian principles

---

[2] United Nations, *Treaty Series*, vol. 75 (1950), No. 972.

governing the treatment of prisoners of war and the protection of civilian persons in time of war, contained in the Geneva Conventions of 12 August 1949.[3] This resolution of the Security Council was welcomed with great satisfaction by the General Assembly in its resolution 2252 (ES-V) adopted on 4 July 1967, during the fifth emergency special session of the General Assembly. The General Assembly reaffirmed its resolution of 4 July 1967 at its twenty-second session (resolution 2341 B (XXII) of 19 December 1967.) The contents of these resolutions of the Security Council and of the General Assembly have been repeatedly recalled and reaffirmed; the delay in their implementation has been deplored.[4]

### B. Advisory services in the field of human rights

In 1955 the General Assembly decided to consolidate earlier programmes of technical advice in the field of women's rights (General Assembly resolution 729 (VIII) of 23 October 1953); the eradication of discrimination (General Assembly resolution 730 (VIII) of 23 October 1953); and freedom of information (General Assembly resolution 839 (IX) of 17 December 1954) with a broader programme to be known as "advisory services in the field of human rights", established by resolution 926 (X) of 14 December 1955. In this resolution the General Assembly authorized the Secretary-General, subject to the directions of the Economic and Social Council, to make provision at the request of Governments for the following forms of assistance with respect to the field of human rights: *(a)* advisory services of experts; *(b)* fellowships and scholarships; *(c)* seminars. The programme is designed to give Governments an opportunity to share their experiences and exchange knowledge on the promotion of human rights.

A more detailed description of the programme and of its operation will be found in part two of this publication. There will also be found a description of the arrangements made by United Nations organs concerning the handling of communications related to human rights, communications related to the status of women and similar subjects.

### C. The work of the United Nations against discrimination (articles 2 and 7 of the Universal Declaration)

A large part of the preceding chapters is devoted to the fight of the United Nations against discrimination. Chapter V above is exclusively devoted to describing United Nations actions aimed at the elimination of discrimination and chapter VI describes in considerable detail the measures taken as regards *apartheid* and racial discrimination in South Africa. Therefore in the present chapter, which is devoted to the implementation of specific rights proclaimed in the Universal Declaration, it remains to deal with arrangements for acting against discrimination in two specific fields, i.e., employment and occupation, and education.

[3] United Nations, *Treaty Series*, vol. 75 (1950), Nos. 970-973.

[4] Security Council resolutions 248 (1968) and 259 (1968); General Assembly resolutions 2443 (XXIII), 1968; 2452 B (XXIII) 1968; 2535 B (XXIV), 1969; 2546 (XXIV), 1969; 2727 (XXV), 1970; 2851 (XXVI), 1971; 3005 (XXVII), 1972.

#### 1. *Discrimination in employment and occupation*

On the initiative of the Sub-Commission on Prevention of Discrimination and Protection of Minorities and with the authorization of the Commission on Human Rights and the Economic and Social Council, preliminary studies of the question of discrimination in employment and occupation were undertaken between 1952 and 1954. At its 1954 session the Sub-Commission noted that the International Labour Organisation was willing to undertake the study of discrimination in that field. On the recommendation of the Commission on Human Rights, the Economic and Social Council at its eighteenth session in 1954 requested the ILO to undertake the study.

In November 1955 the Governing Body of the ILO decided to place the question of discrimination in the field of employment and occupation on the agenda of the fortieth session of the International Labour Conference to be held in 1957, with a view to the adoption of an international instrument on the subject.

In 1958 the Sub-Commission on Prevention of Discrimination and Protection of Minorities considered the provisional texts of two instruments prepared by the ILO and formulated its observations.

In the same year the International Labour Conference adopted the Convention and the Recommendation concerning discrimination in the field of employment and occupation. The provisions of these instruments are summarized in chapter V.

The International Labour Conference at its fifty-sixth session in 1971 considered a general survey prepared by the ILO Committee of Experts on the Application of Conventions and Recommendations concerning the Discrimination (Employment and Occupation) Convention and Recommendation, 1958. The survey, based on reports supplied by Governments under articles 19 and 22 of the ILO Constitution concerned the position of law and practice in regard to matters dealt with in the Convention and Recommendation both in non-ratifying and ratifying countries as well as with difficulties preventing or delaying ratification of the Convention.

In 1972 the Governing Body of the International Labour Office approved proposals concerning the preparation of special surveys on national situations within the framework of the ILO's special programme of action for the elimination of discrimination in employment and occupation. Such surveys would be undertaken at the request of a Government or of a workers' or employers' organization on the understanding that the decision to undertake such a survey and the arrangements for carrying it out would be made in agreement with the Government concerned.

#### 2. *Discrimination in education*

The Sub-Commission on Prevention of Discrimination and Protection of Minorities at its fifth session decided to initiate a study of discrimination in the field of education and appointed a Special Rapporteur for that purpose. The action was approved by the Commission on Human Rights and by the Economic and Social Council and in due course a copy of the Special Rapporteur's draft study was, at the request of the Sub-Commission, sent to the Director-General of UNESCO, inviting that specialized agency to comment on the draft report and to lend such assistance to the work of the Sub-Commission and its Special Rapporteur as might be considered appropriate.

Following the consideration of a revised report, the Sub-Commission recommended that UNESCO should be asked to consider the possibility of drafting and adopting an appropriate international instrument or instruments for the prevention of discrimination in education, taking into account the fundamental principles set forth by the Sub-Commission. The study and the proposals made by the Sub-Commission were, at the request of the Commission on Human Rights (thirteenth session), transmitted to Governments for comments and suggestions.

In resolution 2 (XIV), adopted at its fourteenth session, the Commission on Human Rights noted the decision of the Executive Board of UNESCO to consider, at its fiftieth session (April 1958), the question of the possible inclusion in the agenda of the tenth session of the UNESCO General Conference (November 1958) of an item relating to the advisability of preparing one or more international instruments designed to eliminate or prevent discrimination in the field of education. The General Conference of UNESCO, at its tenth session (November 1958), decided to take responsibility for drafting recommendations to Member States and an international convention on the various aspects of discrimination in education. The General Conference requested the Director-General:

(*a*) To prepare a preliminary report, draft recommendations and a draft convention to be circulated to Member States for comments;

(*b*) To convene in 1960 a committee of technical and legal experts appointed by Member States, with a view to submitting revised drafts of such recommendations and of a convention, to the eleventh session of the General Conference.

In resolution 9 (XVI) of 16 March 1960 the Commission on Human Rights noted with appreciation the efforts made by UNESCO to establish international instruments on discrimination in education and requested UNESCO to submit to the Commission, at its seventh session, the Convention and Recommendation which the General Conference was expected to adopt at its eleventh session, and to keep it regularly informed of any subsequent developments on this subject.

At its seventeenth session, the Commission on Human Rights, in resolution 4 (XVII), noted with satisfaction that the General Conference of UNESCO had adopted (on 14 December 1960) a Convention and a Recommendation against Discrimination in Education, which marked a very important step towards the eradication of discrimination in this field. The provisions of the Convention are summarized in chapter V.

Article 7 of the Convention and an equivalent clause in the Recommendation require States to submit to the General Conference, in a manner to be determined by it, periodic reports giving information on the legislative and administrative provisions which they have adopted and other action which they have taken for the application of the instruments. In 1965, the Executive Board, which the General Conference had requested to give effect to the requirements of article 7, considered that Governments should present reports at regular intervals in a standardized form on the basis of specific questionnaires. As from 1966 a Special Committee established by the Executive Board examined the reports sent by Governments.

At its fifteenth session (1968), the General Conference considered that the presentation of such periodic reports by member States and their examination by the Organization constituted a particularly important task which should be continued and carried out regularly, but that it might prove necessary, in the light of the experience gained, to introduce certain changes into the procedure and methods to be followed. Accordingly, in subsequent years, the questionnaires were revised with a view to eliciting more detailed and meaningful information from Governments.

### D. Seminars relating to discrimination and protection of minorities

Under the programme of advisory services in human rights the United Nations, in co-operation with the host Governments concerned, organized the following seminars:

Seminar on the multilateral society, Ljubljana, Yugoslavia, 8-21 June 1965 (ST/TAO/HR/23);

Seminar on the subject of *apartheid*, Brasilia, Brazil, 23 August-4 September 1966 (ST/TAO/HR/27);

Seminar on the question of the elimination of all forms of racial discrimination, New Delhi, India, 27 August-9 September 1968 (ST/TAO/HR/34);

Seminar on measures to be taken on the national level for the implementation of United Nations instruments aimed at combating and eliminating racial discrination and for the promotion of harmonious race relations, Yaoundé, Cameroon, 16-29 June 1971 (ST/TAO/HR/42);

Seminar on the dangers of a recrudescence of intolerance in all its forms and the search for means of preventing and combating it, Nice, France, 24 August-6 September 1971 (ST/TAO/HR/44).

Pursuant to General Assembly resolution 2202 A (XXI) of 16 December 1966 an international seminar on *apartheid*, racial discrimination and colonialism in southern Africa was held at Kitwe, Zambia, from 25 July to 4 August 1967.[5]

### E. Measures relating to the eradication of slavery and the slave trade (article 4 of the Universal Declaration)

In its resolution 228 (III) of 13 May 1949, the General Assembly requested the Economic and Social Council to study the problem of slavery. Since that time a number

[5] The report of the seminar is to be found in document A/6818.

of comprehensive surveys have been prepared and studied by the Council.

The first survey was prepared by the *Ad Hoc* Committee on Slavery appointed by the Secretary-General in accordance with the Economic and Social Council resolution 238 (IX).[6] The survey was based upon replies to a questionnaire on slavery from Governments and information collected from other sources. The Committee's main proposals were that a protocol should be prepared whereby the United Nations would assume the functions and powers formerly exercised by the League of Nations under the International Slavery Convention of 1926; that a supplementary convention should be prepared which would cover forms of servitude other than slavery; and that a standing body of experts should be established to study and report on further measures required to eradicate slavery. As will be seen below, these proposals, with the exception of the last, were eventually approved and acted upon.

In its resolution 388 (XIII) of 10 September 1951 the Council, to which the report of the *Ad Hoc* Committee was submitted, noted that the material was not in such a form as to allow the Council to act upon it at its thirteenth session and requested the Secretary-General to obtain further information and to report to the Council indicating what action the United Nations and specialized agencies could most appropriately take in order to achieve the elimination of slavery, the slave trade and forms of servitude resembling slavery in their effects.

Pursuant to this resolution the Secretary-General prepared and submitted to the Council, at its fifteenth session in 1953, the Second survey (E/2357), completing the one prepared by the *Ad Hoc* Committee. The Council at that session (in its resolution 475 (XV)) requested the Secretary-General to urge those Governments which had failed to supply information or had supplied incomplete information to reply accurately and fully to the questionnaire already transmitted to them.

The same year the General Assembly (in resolution 794 (VIII) of 23 October 1953), acting upon the recommendation of the *Ad Hoc* Committee which had been transmitted to it by the Economic and Social Council, approved a Protocol amending the Slavery Convention signed at Geneva on 25 September 1926, urged all States parties to the Slavery Convention to sign or accept the Protocol, and recommended to all other States to accede at their earliest opportunity to the Slavery Convention as amended by the Protocol.[7] The third survey of the problem of slavery, prepared by Mr. Hans Engen (Norway), the Special Rapporteur appointed by decision of the Council in resolution 525 (XVII) of 24 April 1964, was submitted to the Council at its nineteenth session in 1955. At that session the Council, by resolution 564 (XIX), appointed a Committee consisting of the representatives of 10 Governments to prepare a text of a draft supplementary convention on slavery. In 1956 the Council, in resolution 608 (XXI), decided that a conference of plenipotentiaries should be convened to complete the drafting of the supplementary convention and to open it for signature.

The Conference of Plenipotentiaries was held at Geneva from 13 August to 4 September 1956 and used as the basis of its discussions the draft supplementary convention on the abolition of slavery, the slave trade, and institutions and practices similar to slavery, which had been prepared by the *Ad Hoc* Committee. On 4 September 1956 the Conference adopted the Supplementary Convention on the Abolition of Slavery, the Slave Trade, and Institutions and Practices Similar to Slavery by 40 votes in favour, none against, with 3 abstentions, and opened it for signature.[8]

In 1960, 1961 and 1962 the Council urged those Governments of States Members of the United Nations and members of the specialized agencies which had not already done so to adhere to the Conventions. The General Assembly (in its resolution 1941 (XVII) of 19 December 1962) made a similar appeal and, at the same time, urged all States parties to the Conventions on Slavery to co-operate fully in carrying out their terms, in particular, by furnishing the Secretary-General, if they had not already done so, the information called for under article 8 of the Supplementary Convention on Abolition of Slavery.

In 1963, the Council, feeling a need for accurate, comprehensive and up-to-date information on the extent to which slavery, the slave trade, and institutions and practices similar to slavery persisted, requested (in its resolution 960 (XXXVI) of 12 July 1963) the Secretary-General to appoint a Special Rapporteur on slavery to bring the Engen report up to date. The Secretary-General accordingly appointed Mr. Mohammed Awad (United Arab Republic) as Special Rapporteur.

After considering and noting the Special Rapporteur's report (E/4168 and Add.1-5) which was based on replies received to a questionnaire formulated by the Secretary-General in consultation with the Special Rapporteur, the Council (in resolution 1126 (XLI) of 26 July 1966) referred the question of slavery and the slave trade in all their practices and manifestations, including the slavery-like practices of *apartheid* and colonialism, to the Commission on Human Rights and requested the Commission to submit to it a report containing specific proposals for effective and immediate measures which the United Nations could adopt to put an end to slavery in all its practices and manifestations. At the same time the Council called again upon all Member States which were not parties to become parties as soon as possible to the International Slavery Convention of 1926 and to the Supplementary Convention of 1956. The Council also invited UNESCO to continue its programme of education designed to correct a social outlook that tolerated the existence of slavery or forms of servitude similar to slavery.

Pursuant to Economic and Social Council resolution 1126 (XLI) the Commission on Human Rights (in the report on its twenty-third session[9] (1967)) recommended

[6] *Official Records of the Economic and Social Council, Thirteenth Session, Annexes*, agenda item 21, document E/1988.

[7] For the text of the Slavery Convention of 1926 and the Protocol amending it, see *Human Rights: A Compilation of International Instruments of the United Nations* (United Nations publication, Sales No. E.73.XIV.2).

[8] For the contents of this Convention, see chapter VIII.

[9] *Official Records of the Economic and Social Council, Forty-second Session, Supplement No. 6.*

to the Economic and Social Council a series of measures for combating slavery. On the recommendation of the Commission, the Economic and Social Council adopted a resolution (1232 (XLII) of 6 June 1967) on the subject at its forty-second session in which it expressed the view that both the International Slavery Convention of 1926 and the Supplementary Convention of 1956 on the Abolition of Slavery, the Slave Trade, and Institutions and Practices Similar to Slavery should be reconsidered in order to embrace the contemporary manifestations of slavery exemplified by *apartheid* and colonialism.

The Council also requested the Commission on the Status of Women, the Commission on Social Development, the ILO, UNESCO and WHO to give attention to the problem of slavery and the slave trade in their work. It also called upon the Republic of South Africa to put an end to the practice of *apartheid* in South Africa and in the Territory of South West Africa under the direct responsibility of the United Nations.

At its twenty-third session the Commission on Human Rights (in resolution 13 (XXIII)) also requested the Sub-Commission on Prevention of Discrimination and Protection of Minorities to undertake regular consideration of the question of slavery in all its forms, including the slavery-like practices of *apartheid* and colonialism, taking into account the study and recommendations prepared by the Council's Special Rapporteur and such other material as it believed pertinent, and to consider information submitted by the States parties to the Supplementary Convention of 1956 in accordance with article 8 of that Convention.

At its twentieth session in September-October 1967, the Sub-Commission on Prevention of Discrimination and Protection of Minorities adopted two resolutions (E/CN.4/947, para. 111) on the problem, one relating to further study of the question of slavery and the other relating to technical assistance and other resources that might be used in eliminating slavery. In the first of these resolutions (4 A (XX)) the Sub-Commission, *inter alia*, requested the Commission to recommend to the Economic and Social Council:

(*a*) That the Sub-Commission be authorized to undertake a study of the measures which might be taken in the case of States failing to carry out their obligations under the Conventions of 1926 and 1956;

(*b*) That a study of the proposals of international police action to interrupt and punish the transportation of persons in danger of being enslaved be initiated;

(*c*) That a list of experts in economic, sociological, legal and other relevant disciplines, "whose advice shall be available to States concerned" with the liquidation of slavery and the slave trade in all their practices and manifestations, be established.

It also requested the Secretary-General to take a series of steps with a view to obtaining information, particularly that called for under the Supplementary Convention of 1956, and to assign one or more officers in the Division of Human Rights to the exclusive study of slavery and the slave trade including the slavery-like practices of *apartheid* and colonialism. In resolution 4 B (XX) the Sub-Commission requested the Secretary-General to undertake the promotion and co-ordination of measures to be taken by the specialized agencies and other competent United Nations bodies to eliminate slavery, the slave trade and similar institutions and practices.

At its forty-fourth session, the Economic and Social Council, on the recommendation of the Commission on Human Rights, adopted resolution 1330 (XLIV) of 31 May 1968, by which it authorized the Sub-Commission to undertake a study of the measures that might be taken to implement the Slavery Convention of 1926 and the Supplementary Convention of 1956 and the various recommendations included in the resolutions of the General Assembly, the Economic and Social Council and the Commission on Human Rights relating to the slavery-like practices of *apartheid* and colonialism. The Council further authorized the Sub-Commission to initiate a study of the possibilities of international police co-operation to interrupt and punish the transportation of persons in danger of being enslaved. The Council requested the Secretary-General to establish a list of experts in economic, sociological, legal and other relevant disciplines, whose advice would be available to States concerned with the liquidation of slavery and the slave-trade in all their practices and manifestations, including the slavery-like practices of *apartheid* and colonialism. It also reminded Governments of the facilities available under the technical assistance programmes for assisting Governments in eliminating slavery and slavery-like practices and in helping them to solve resulting economic and social problems. The Council requested all Governments to exert their full influence and resources to assist in the total eradication of *apartheid* and colonialism. The Council affirmed that the master-and-servant laws currently enforced in Southern Rhodesia, South West Africa and South Africa constituted clear manifestations of slavery and the slave-trade. In another resolution (1331 (XLIV)), which had been recommended to the Council by the Commission on the Status of Women, the Council expressed its concern that the *Report on Slavery* prepared by the Special Rapporteur [10] indicated that slavery and the slave-trade and similar institutions and practices still existed in many parts of the world and that women especially were among the victims of such institutions and practices. The Council condemned slavery, *apartheid*, colonialism, the slave-trade and similar institutions and practices such as marriages without consent, traffic in persons for purposes of prostitution, transference and inheritance of women and other similar degrading practices. The Council noted with satisfaction the recommendations of the Sub-Commission (E/CN.4/947, para. 111) and addressed a number of appeals to Governments concerning their becoming parties to the relevant international instruments and requested the assistance of the specialized agencies in solving the problem.

At its forty-sixth session the Economic and Social Council (in resolution 1419 (XLVI) of 6 June 1969), on the recommendation of the Commission on Human Rights, confirmed the designation by the Sub-Commission of the Special Rapporteur to carry out a study within the terms of Council resolution 1330 (XLIV).

---

[10] United Nations publication, Sales No. 67.XIV.2.

### F. Measures relating to forced labour (article 4 of the Universal Declaration)

At its sixth session, in 1948, the Economic and Social Council included in its agenda, at the request of the American Federation of Labor formulated in a letter dated 24 November 1947 (E/596), an item entitled: "Survey of forced labour and measures for its abolition". The American Federation of Labor suggested, in its letter, that the Council should ask the ILO to undertake a comprehensive survey on the extent of forced labour in all Member States of the United Nations and to suggest positive measures, including a revised convention and measures for its implementation for eliminating forced labour.

At its eighth session the Council adopted resolution 195 (VIII) of 7 March 1949, in which it requested the Secretary-General to co-operate closely with the International Labour Organisation in its work on forced labour questions, to approach all Governments and to inquire in what manner and to what extent they would be prepared to co-operate in an impartial investigation into the extent of forced labour in their countries, including the reasons for which persons were made to perform forced labour and the treatment accorded to them. The Secretary-General was also requested to inform and consult the ILO regarding the progress being made on this question.

At its ninth session, in 1949, the Council adopted resolution 237 (IX) in which it took note of the communication of the ILO on the conclusions arrived at by the Governing Body of the International Labour Office at its 109th session. The Governing Body, in a resolution adopted at that session, recommended that close contact should be established with the Secretary-General with a view to the setting up of an impartial commission of inquiry. The Council considered that the replies received from Governments up to its ninth session did not provide the conditions under which a commission of inquiry could operate effectively. It requested the Secretary-General to ask Governments which had not as yet replied, whether they would be prepared to co-operate in an inquiry.

In resolution 350 (XII), adopted on 19 March 1951, the Economic and Social Council, considering the replies furnished by Member States in accordance with resolutions 195 (VIII) and 237 (IX), and taking note of the communications from the International Labour Organisation which set forth the discussions on the question of forced labour at the 111th and 113th sessions of the Governing Body, decided to establish, in co-operation with the ILO, the *Ad Hoc* Committee on Forced Labour, composed of independent persons qualified by their competence and impartiality The resolution required the *Ad Hoc* Committee to make a survey and a study of systems of forced labour.

In its report (E/2431) the *Ad Hoc* Committee stated that its inquiry had revealed the existence of facts relating to systems of forced labour of so grave a nature that they seriously threatened fundamental human rights and jeopardized the freedom and status of workers in contravention of the obligations and provisions of the Charter of the United Nations. The Committee felt, therefore, that those systems of forced labour, in any of their forms' should be abolished. It suggested that, wherever necessary, international action should be taken, either by framing more conventions or by amending existing conventions.

In December 1953 the General Assembly adopted resolution 740 (VIII) in which it affirmed the importance it attached to the abolition of all systems of forced or "corrective" labour and invited the Economic and Social Council and the International Labour Organisation, as a matter of urgency, to give early consideration to the report of the *Ad Hoc* Committee on Forced Labour. At its seventeenth session the Economic and Social Council examined the report of the *Ad Hoc* Committee and, in resolution 524 (XVII) of 27 April 1954, condemned systems of forced labour which were employed as a means of political coercion or punishment for holding or expressing political views and which were on such a scale as to constitute an important element in the economy of a given country. The Council, in the same resolution, appealed to all Governments to re-examine their laws and administrative practices in the matter. The General Assembly (in its resolution 842 (IX) of 17 December 1954) endorsed the Council's condemnation and supported its appeals to Governments.

In November 1954 the Governing Body of the ILO decided unanimously to place the question of forced labour on the agenda of the thirty-ninth session of the International Labour Conference (Geneva, June 1956), for double discussion, with a view to the adoption, in 1957, of a new international instrument on forced labour, Furthermore, in June 1955, at its 129th session, the Governing Body of the ILO decided to set up an independent *Ad Hoc* Committee on Forced Labour.

In 1956 the Economic and Social Council considered a second report (E/2815 and Add.1-5 and Add.4/Corr.1) on forced labour, prepared jointly by the Secretary-General of the United Nations and the Director-General of the ILO, pursuant to resolution 524 (XVII) of the Council. On this occasion, the Council (in its resolution 607 (XXI) of 1 May 1956) again condemned all forms of forced labour contrary to the principles of the United Nations Charter and the Universal Declaration of Human Rights, and urged that action be taken towards the elimination of forced labour wherever it might exist. The Council, in the same resolution, commended the ILO for the action it had taken and expressed its interest in further action to be taken by the ILO. Recognizing that the ILO had special responsibilities in this field and giving particular attention to measures designed to assist in the elimination of forced labour, the Council requested the Secretary-General to transmit to the Director-General of the International Labour Office any information which might be received concerning forced labour. The ILO was, at the same time, invited to include in its annual report to the Council an account of the action taken in this field.

At its fortieth session the International Labour Conference adopted unanimously a new convention (the Abolition of Forced Labour Convention, 1957) which outlawed the use of any form of forced or compulsory labour for five specified purposes. The provisions of the

Convention are summarized in chapter VIII. Later the same year the Governing Body of the ILO, at its 137th session, decided to establish a new independent committee on forced labour with a view to continuing the fact-finding activities of the previous *Ad Hoc* Committee. The new Committee met in March 1959, and its report was noted by the Governing Body of the ILO at its 142nd session.

The Abolition of Forced Labour Convention, 1957, is one of a series of instruments emanating from the League of Nations, the United Nations and the International Labour Organisation which give expression to the determination of these organizations and their membership to combat slavery and forced labour.

While in some of the earlier instruments in this field States parties had undertaken to bring about the abolition or abandonment of the objectionable institutions and practices "progressively and as soon as possible", the parties to the Convention of 1957 undertook to take effective measures to secure "the immediate and complete" abolition of forced or compulsory labour.

Article 8 of the International Covenant on Civil and Political Rights contains the prohibition of forced or compulsory labour. The provision of the Covenant that no one shall be required to perform forced or compulsory labour shall not be held to preclude, in countries where imprisonment with hard labour may be imposed as a punishment for a crime, the performance of hard labour in pursuance of a sentence to such punishment by a competent court. The Covenant also lists certain types of work which shall not be included within the term of forced or compulsory labour for the purposes of the provision such as work or service normally required of a person who is under detention, any service of a military character and any national service required by law of conscientious objectors; any service exacted in cases of emergency or calamity; and any work or service which forms part of normal civil obligations (article 8, para. 3 of the International Covenant on Civil and Political Rights).

### G. Measures relating to torture or to cruel, inhuman or degrading treatment or punishment (article 5 of the Universal Declaration)

The United Nations position on this question is formulated in the provisions of article 5 of the Universal Declaration of Human Rights and articles 7 and 10 of the International Covenant on Civil and Political Rights. Article 7 of the Covenent provides that no one shall be subjected to torture or to cruel, inhuman or degrading treatment or punishment. Article 10 provides that all persons deprived of their liberty shall be treated with humanity and with respect for the inherent dignity of the human person. Article 10 also provides that the penitentiary system shall comprise treatment of prisoners the essential aim of which shall be their reformation and social rehabilitation.

In 1949 the Trusteeship Council recommended that corporal punishment should be abolished immediately in the Cameroons and Togoland under British administration and that corporal punishment should be formally abolished in New Guinea.[11] The General Assembly gave its full support to this recommendation and itself recommended the adoption of strong and effective measures to abolish immediately the corporal punishment of whipping in Ruanda-Urundi.[12]

In the following year the General Assembly recommended that measures be taken immediately to bring about the complete abolition of corporal punishment in all Trust Territories where it still existed [13] and requested the Administering Authorities to report on the matter.

Two years later the Assembly reviewed the reports which it had received. It noted that measures had been taken to reduce the number of offences in respect of which corporal punishment was applied, noted the arguments presented by the Administering Authorities concerned to explain why that penalty had not yet completely disappeared, and expressed the opinion that the considerations presented should not prevent the complete abolition of corporal punishment in the Trust Territories where it still existed. The Assembly repeated its previous recommendations and urged the Administering Authorities concerned to apply them without delay.[14]

In 1955 the First United Nations Congress on the Prevention of Crime and the Treatment of Offenders [15] adopted the Standard Minimum Rules for the Treatment of Prisoners [16] worked out by an Advisory Committee of Experts established in accordance with the plan prepared by the Secretary-General and approved by General Assembly resolution 415 (V). In resolution 663 C I (XXIV) of 31 July 1957 the Economic and Social Council approved those Rules and recommended them to States Members.

The purpose of the Standard Minimum Rules for the Treatment of Prisoners is not to describe in detail a model system of penal institutions but, on the basis of the general consensus of contemporary thought and the essential elements of the most adequate systems of today, to set out what is generally accepted as being good principle and practice in the treatment of prisoners and management of institutions. One of the Standard Minimum Rules (Rule 31) is to the effect that corporal punishment, punishment by placing in a dark cell, and all cruel, inhuman or degrading punishment shall be completely prohibited as punishments for disciplinary offences.

The draft Principles on Freedom from Arbitrary Arrest prepared by a committee established by the Commission on Human Rights pursuant to resolution 2 (XVII) of

---

[11] See *Official Records of the General Assembly, Fourth Session, Supplement No. 4.*

[12] General Assembly resolution 323 (IV) of 15 November 1949.

[13] General Assembly resolution 440 (V) of 2 December 1950.

[14] General Assembly resolution 562 (VI) of 18 January 1952.

[15] General Assembly resolution 415 (V) of 1 December 1950 and annex on the transfer to the United Nations of the functions of the International Penal and Penitentiary Commission.

[16] See A/CONF/6/1, annex I A (United Nations publication, Sales No. 1956.IV.4).

that Commission (1962)[17] contain the provision that no arrested or detained person shall be subjected to physical or mental compulsion, torture, violence, threats or inducement of any kind . . . administration of drugs or any other means which tend to impair or to weaken his freedom of action or decision, his memory or his judgement. Article 10 and article 26 of the draft Principles, by limiting the time for which the arrested person can be kept in police custody, aim at minimizing the risk that he might be subjected to improper treatment or pressures by the police. To safeguard, among other things, against improper methods of interrogation, article 22, paragraph 2, requires that counsel must be present at any examination of the arrested or detained person. In more general terms, article 27 also provides that the treatment accorded to the arrested or detained person, whether in police custody or in prison custody, must not be less favourable than that stipulated by the Standard Mininum Rules for the Treatment of Prisoners.

The question of capital punishment is dealt with under section H below in connexion with the protection of human rights in criminal law.

### H. Protection of human rights in criminal law and in criminal, civil and administrative procedure (articles 7, 8, 9, 10 and 11 of the Universal Declaration)

The principles proclaimed in articles 7, 8, 9, 10 and 11 of the Declaration have been set forth in one form or another in the International Covenant on Civil and Political Rights (see articles 9, 14 and 15 of the Covenant). The measures taken within the United Nations to promote respect for and observance of these rights and freedoms have included several studies and a series of seminars.

At its twelfth session, in 1956, the Commission on Human Rights, recognizing that studies of specific rights or groups of rights were necessary for the purpose of ascertaining the existing conditions, the results obtained and the difficulties encountered in the work of States Members for the wider observance of, and respect for, human rights and fundamental freedoms, decided to undertake such studies "to stress in these studies general developments, progress achieved and measures taken to safeguard human liberty, with such recommendations of an objective and general character as may be necessary".

As its first subject for study the Commission decided to select the right of everyone to be free from arbitrary arrest, detention and exile. In resolution 624 B (II) (XXII) of 1 August 1956 the Economic and Social Council approved the subject for special study as selected by the Commission.

For the purpose of the study the Commission appointed a committee of four representatives of States members of the Commission. The Committee decided to prescribe the rules and practices under different legal systems in respect of the subject of the study to the end that nations may share experiences and may work individually or jointly toward the achievement of the common standards set forth in the Universal Declaration of Human Rights. The Committee also agreed to be particularly interested in such rules and practices as contribute significantly to the protection and enhancement of the dignity, liberty and security of the human person.[18]

The Committee consulted the *travaux preparatoires* of the Universal Declaration of Human Rights and the then draft International Covenants on Human Rights; reports of the seminars held under the Advisory Services Programme in Human Rights on the protection of human rights in criminal laws or procedure; the work of the social defence programme of the Social Commission and the Standard Minimum Rules for the Treatment of Prisoners adopted in 1955.

The *Study of the Right of Everyone to be Free from Arbitrary Arrest, Detention and Exile* was originally submitted to the Commission in 1961. In 1962 the Committee revised the study and prepared, in accordance with the Commission's request (in resolution 2 (XVII)), draft principles on freedom from arbitrary arrest.[19]

The study and the draft principles on freedom from arbitrary arrest and detention have been on the agenda of several sessions of the Commission on Human Rights, including the twenty-third session 1967, the twenty-fourth session in 1968, and the twenty-fifth session in 1969. At the latter session the Commission on Human Rights (resolution 23 (XXV)),[20] considering that the study as prepared by the four-member Committee had been submitted to the Commission in 1962 and that by resolution 2 (XVIII) the Commission had transmitted the draft principles adopted by the Committee to States Members of the United Nations and members of the specialized agencies for their comments, noted that 47 Governments had submitted their comments on the draft Principles. At its seventeenth session in 1961 (in resolution 2 (XVII)) the Commission on Human Rights had also requested the four-member Committee to undertake a separate study on the right of arrested persons to communicate with those necessary for them to consult in order to ensure their defense or to protect their essential interests. At its twenty-fifth session in 1969 the Commission on Human Rights received the report of the Committee on the further study (E/CN.4/996). Noting that the separate new study suggests modifications/revisions of some of the draft principles contained in the study on the Right of Everyone to be Free from Arbitrary Arrest, Detention and Exile, and desiring to obtain the views of as many Governments as possible on both studies and also on the suggested modifications of the draft principles, it arranged for a further consultation of States Members of the United Nations and the specialized agencies.

---

[17] The draft principles were elaborated as the outcome of the *Study of the Right of Everyone to be Free from Arbitrary Arrest, Detention and Exile* (United Nations publication, Sales No. 65.XIV.2). For this study in general and the action taken on it, see section H below.

[18] Preliminary report of the Committee, E/CN.4/739.

[19] See United Nations publication, Sales No. 65.XIV.2, part VI.

[20] *Official Records of the Economic and Social Council, Forty-sixth Session*, document E/4621.

The consideration of the question was again postponed at the twenty-seventh session in 1971 and at the twenty-eighth session in 1972.[21]

The International Covenant on Civil and Political Rights contains a series of provisions which embody principles that have also been the basis for the work of the Committee on Arbitrary Arrest, Detention and Exile. It provides that everyone has the right to liberty and security of person, that no one shall be subjected to arbitrary arrest or detention and that no one shall be deprived of his liberty except on such grounds and in accordance with such procedures as are established by law (article 9, paragraph 1). Article 14, paragraph 2, of the Covenant provides that everyone charged with a criminal offence shall have the right to be presumed innocent until proved guilty according to law.

The International Covenant on Civil and Political Rights provides (article 14, paragraph 3) that, in the determination of any criminal charge against him, everyone shall be entitled, as a minimum guarantee, to have adequate time and facilities for the preparation of his defence and to communicate with counsel of his own choosing.

Article 14 of the International Covenant on Civil and Political Rights contains provisions relating to equality in the administration of justice. It states, *inter alia*, that in the determination of any criminal charge against him, or of his rights and obligations in a suit at law, everyone shall be entitled to a fair and public hearing by a competent, independent and impartial tribunal established by law and that everyone convicted of a crime shall have the right to his conviction and sentence being reviewed by a higher tribunal according to law.

At its fifteenth session in 1963 the Sub-Commission on Prevention of Discrimination and Protection of Minorities decided (in resolution 1 (XV)) to undertake a study of equality in the administration of justice, in accordance with article 10 of the Universal Declaration, and it appointed a Special Rapporteur to carry out the study. On the recommendation of the Commission on Human Rights, the Economic and Social Council, in resolution 958 (XXXVI) of 12 July 1963 approved the Sub-Commission's decisions. The Rapporteur submitted to the Sub-Commission a series of progress reports and a draft report. The Rapporteur's final report (E/CN.4/Sub.2/296) was examined by the Sub-Commission at its twenty-second session in 1969. At that session, in its resolution 3 (XXII), the Sub-Commission transmitted the final report to the Commission on Human Rights for its earliest practicable consideration and at its twenty-third session in 1970, by resolution 3 (XXIII), the Sub-Commission considered, revised and adopted the draft principles on equality in the administration of justice which were contained in paragraph 596 of the report by the Special Rapporteur.[22]

The reports of the twenty-second and twenty-third sessions of the Sub-Commission were before the Commission on Human Rights at its twenty-seventh and twenty-eighth sessions in 1971 and 1972 respectively. At its twenty-seventh session the Commission on Human Rights recommended that the Economic and Social Council request the Secretary-General to print the Special Rapporteur's study together with the General Principles adopted by the Sub-Commission. The Economic and Social Council accepted this recommendation and in its resolution 1594 (L) of 21 May 1971 recommended that the Commission on Human Rights should at its twenty-eighth session examine the draft Principles relating to equality in the administration of justice and take a decision on further action. At its twenty-eighth session in 1972 the Commission on Human Rights noted with regret that owing to lack of time it had been unable to examine the draft Principles in detail. Emphasizing the importance and urgency of consideration in depth of those Principles, with a view to considering the elaboration of an international instrument on the subject, the Commission requested Member States to communicate their comments and views concerning the draft Principles and the form of the instrument on those Principles. The Government comments so far received have been reproduced in document E/CN.4/1112 and addenda.

### 1. *The question of capital punishment*

At its fourteenth session in 1959 and at its eighteenth session in 1963, the General Assembly addressed itself to both the human rights and social aspects of the question of capital punishment.[23] Accordingly, studies of the problem of capital punishment were undertaken, covering developments from 1956 to 1960, and a second study covering developments from 1961 to 1965.[24] However, the workload at its twenty-second session did not permit the General Assembly to consider the substance of the item on capital punishment. The Assembly (in resolution 2334 (XXII) of 18 December 1967) therefore decided to consider the question of capital punishment at its twenty-third session in 1968, and invited the Secretary-General to provide it with pertinent information and requested the Economic and Social Council to instruct the Commission to seek the views of the Consultative Group on the Prevention of Crime and the Treatment of Offenders concerning certain proposals submitted by delegations at the forty-second session of the Economic and Social Council.

At the twenty-third session the General Assembly (resolution 2393 (XXIII) of 26 November 1968) considered part I of the report, *Capital Punishment*, in the light of the Comments thereon of the *Ad Hoc* Advisory Committee of Experts on the Prevention of Crime and the Treatment of Offenders, and part II of the report covering developments from 1961 to 1965. Taking note of the conclusion

[21] Decisions taken at the 1136th meeting of 25 March 1971 and at the 1182nd meeting of 6 April 1972.

[22] For the revised text see *Study of Equality in the Administration of Justice* (United Nations publication, Sales No. E.71.XIV.3).

[23] See General Assembly resolutions 1396 (XIV) of 20 November 1959 and 1918 (XVIII) of 10 December 1963.

[24] *Capital Punishment* (United Nations publication, Sales No. E.67.IV.15).

drawn by the Advisory Committee from part I of the report, namely that, if one looked at the whole problem of capital punishment in historical perspective, it became clear that there was a world-wide tendency towards a considerable reduction in the number and categories of offences for which capital punishment might be imposed and taking note of the view expressed in part II of that report, that there was an over-all tendency in the world towards fewer executions, taking note also of the report of the meeting of the Consultative Group on the Prevention of Crime and the Treatment of Offenders held in 1968, in so far as it related to the question of capital punishment,[25] the General Assembly invited Governments of Member States:

"(*a*) To ensure the most careful legal procedures and the greatest possible safeguards for the accused in capital cases in countries where the death penalty obtains, *inter alia*, by providing that:

(i) A person condemned to death shall not be deprived of the right to appeal to a higher judicial authority or, as the case may be, to petition for pardon or reprieve;

(ii) A death sentence shall not be carried out until the procedures of appeal or, as the case may be, of petition for pardon or reprieve have been terminated;

(iii) Special attention be given in the case of indigent persons by the provision of adequate legal assistance at all stages of the proceedings;

"(*b*) To consider whether the careful legal procedures and safeguards referred to in sub-paragraph (*a*) above may not be further strengthened by the fixing of a time-limit or time-limits before the expiry of which no death sentence shall be carried out, as has already been recognized in certain international conventions dealing with specific situations;"

The General Assembly further, in its resolution 2393 (XXIII), asked Governments for information on their present attitude to possible further restriction of the use of the death penalty or to its total abolition. At the same time the General Assembly adopted a separate resolution (2394 (XXIII) of 26 November 1968) on capital punishment in southern Africa. In that resolution the General Assembly condemned the illegal régime in Southern Rhodesia, the equally illegal South African régime in Namibia and the racist Government in South Africa for resorting to the application of the death penalty and the threat or use of capital punishment in their attempts to suppress the natural aspirations of the peoples of southern Africa to social and economic justice, civil rights and political freedom.

At its fiftieth session the Economic and Social Council examined the report submitted by the Secretary-General in accordance with General Assembly resolution 2393 (XXIII). The Council in its resolution 1574 (L) of 20 May 1971, took note with satisfaction of the measures already taken by a number of States to ensure the most careful legal procedures and the greatest possible safeguards for the accused in capital cases in countries where the death penalty still obtained. The Council considered that further efforts should be made by Member States to ensure the full and strict observance anywhere of the principles contained in articles 5, 10 and 11 of the Universal Declaration of Human Rights, reaffirmed by articles 7, 14 and 15 of the International Covenant on Civil and Political Rights. The Council affirmed that the main objective to be pursued was that of progressively restricting the number of offences for which capital punishment might be imposed with a view to the desirability of abolishing that punishment in all countries so that the right to life might be fully guaranteed.

The General Assembly, in its resolution 2857 (XXVI) of 20 December 1971, took note of the Council's resolution and expressed the desirability of continuing and extending the consideration of the question of capital punishment by the United Nations. The General Assembly adopted recommendations based on those of the Council resolution and requested the Secretary-General, on the basis of material furnished by Governments of Member States where capital punishment still existed, to prepare a separate report regarding practices and statutory rules which might govern the right of a person sentenced to capital punishment to petition for pardon, commutation or reprieve, and to submit that report to the General Assembly.

At its fifty-second session the Economic and Social Council considered additional information provided by some Member States on the legal procedures and safeguards applied in capital cases and on their attitude to possible further restriction of the use of the death penalty or its total abolition. In its resolution 1656 (LII) of 1 June 1972, the Council invited those Member States which had not yet provided the requested information to do so as soon as possible so that the Secretary-General could submit to the Council at its fifty-fourth session in 1973 the available information on the subject. The General Assembly, in its resolution 3011 (XXVII) of 18 December 1972 requested the Secretary-General to inform the Council of the progress made in collecting the relevant information and invited it to consider at its fifty-fourth session the present situation and trends with regard to capital punishment.

## 2. *Seminars*

Ten regional seminars, organized under the programme of advisory services in the field of human rights, have considered matters relating to the protection of human rights in criminal law and criminal procedure and protection against the illegal exercise or the abuse of administrative authority, including the role of the police in the protection of human rights:

Seminar on the protection of human rights in criminal law and procedure, Baguio City, Philippines, 17-28 February 1958 (ST/TAO/HR/2);

Seminar on the protection of human rights in criminal law and procedure, Santiago, Chile, 19-30 May 1958 (ST/TAO/HR/3);

[25] *Official Records of the General Assembly, Twenty-third Session, Annexes*, agenda item 59, document A/7243, annex.

Seminar on judicial and other remedies against the illegal exercise or abuse of administrative authority, Peradeniya (Kandy), Ceylon, 4-15 May 1959 (ST/TAO/HR/4);

Seminar on judicial and other remedies against the illegal exercise or abuse of administrative authority, Buenos Aires, Argentina, 31 August-11 September 1959 (ST/TAO/HR/6);

Seminar on the role of substantive criminal law in the protection of human rights, and the purposes and legitimate limits of penal sanctions, Tokyo, Japan, 10-24 May 1960 (ST/TAO/HR/7);

Seminar on the protection of human rights in criminal procedure, Vienna, Austria, 20 June-4 July 1960 (ST/TAO/HR/8);

Seminar on the protection of human rights in the administration of criminal justice, Wellington, New Zealand, 6-20 February 1961 (ST/TAO/HR/10);

Seminar on *amparo, habeas corpus* and other similar remedies, Mexico City, Mexico, 15-28 August 1961 (ST/TAO/HR/12);

Seminar on judicial and other remedies against the abuse of administrative authority, with special emphasis on the role of parliamentary institutions, Stockholm, Sweden, 12-25 June 1962 (ST/TAO/HR/15).

Seminar on the role of the police in the protection of human rights, Canberra, Australia, 30 April-14 May 1963 (ST/TAO/HR/16);

## I. The preparation of additional international instruments for the protection of human rights by applying criminal penalties

### 1. *Study of the question of* apartheid *from the point of view of international penal law*

At its twenty-eighth session in 1972, the Commission on Human Rights examined the study of its *Ad Hoc* Working Group concerning the question of *apartheid* from the point of view of international penal law (E/CN.4/1075 and Corr.1), submitted in accordance with Commission resolution 8 (XXVI). The study dealt with the relevant doctrine, with international instruments relating to international penal law and with practices and manifestations of *apartheid* which could be considered as crimes under international law. On the recommendation of the Commission, the Economic and Social Council, at its fifty-second session, decided on 2 June 1972 to transmit to Member States, the Special Committee on *Apartheid* and the International Law Commission the report of the *Ad Hoc* Working Group of Experts for their comments.

### 2. *Draft Convention on the Suppression and Punishment of the Crime of* Apartheid

At the twenty-sixth session of the General Assembly in 1971 two delegations submitted to the Third Committee a draft Convention on the Suppression and Punishment of the Crime of *Apartheid*.[26] By its resolution 2786 (XXVII) of 6 December 1971, the Assembly transmitted to the Commission on Human Rights the draft Convention, together with the relevant records of the discussion. The Commission on Human Rights considered the question at its twenty-eighth session in 1972 when it had before it in addition to a draft Convention, also a draft Protocol (E/CN.4/L.1189) which was intended to be annexed to the International Convention on the Elimination of All Forms of Racial Discrimination. Pursuant to a General Assembly directive, the Commission on Human Rights also decided that the pertinent documents should be sent to the Special Committee on *Apartheid* so that it could examine them and prepare comments.[27]

At the twenty-seventh session of the General Assembly a revised version of the draft Convention was submitted to the Third Committee. Under this draft the States parties to the Convention would declare that inhuman acts resulting from the policies and practices of *apartheid* and similar racial segregation were crimes violating the principles of international law, and in particular the purposes and principles of the Charter constituting a serious threat to international peace and security. The States parties to the Convention would declare criminal those organizations, institutions and individuals which pursued a policy of *apartheid.* The Convention would contain a detailed definition of the acts which came under the term, when committed for the purpose of establishing and maintaining domination by one racial group of persons over any other racial group of persons and of systematically suppressing them. International criminal responsiblity would apply to individuals, members of organizations and institutions, and representatives of the State whenever they participated in, directly inspired or conspired in the commission of the acts defined in the Convention or when they abetted or encouraged such participation, inspiration or conspiracy. States parties would undertake to co-operate on the international level in combating the crime of *apartheid* and also to send reports to the Commission on Human Rights on various relevant events. Disputes between States parties arising out of the interpretation, application or implementation of the Convention which had not been settled by negotiation, would, at the request of (all) the States parties to the dispute be brought before the International Court of Justice save where the parties to the dispute had agreed to some other form of settlement.

In the course of the proceedings of the Third Committee an amendment was moved to the revised draft resolution under which a Committee consisting of experts would be elected by States parties. That Committee would have functions comparable to those of the Committee on the Elimination of Racial Discrimination established under the International Convention on the Elimination of Racial Discrimination.

---

[26] *Official Records of the General Assembly, Twenty-sixth Session, Annexes*, agenda item 54, document A/8542, para. 32.

[27] See *Official Records of the Economic and Social Council, Fifty-second Session, Supplement No. 7* (E/5113), paras. 37-48 and chap. XIII, resolution 4 (XXVIII).

The General Assembly (in its resolution 2922 (XXVII) of 15 November 1972) reaffirmed its firm conviction that *apartheid* constituted a total negation of the purposes and principles of the Charter and was a crime against humanity, and also that the conclusion of an international convention on the subiect would be an important contribution to the struggle against *apartheid*, racism, economic exploitation, colonial domination and foreign occupation. The Assembly decided to transmit to the Special Committee on *Apartheid* and to States the revised draft Convention [28] and the amendments thereto [29] for their comments and views, and invited the Commission on Human Rights, through the Economic and Social Council, to consider as a priority item the revised draft Convention and the amendments thereto, and to submit the results of its consideration to the General Assembly at its twenty-eighth session.

## J. Measures relating to the right of everyone to leave any country, including his own, and to return to his country (article 13 (2) of the Universal Declaration)

In 1964 the United Nations published the *Study of Discrimination in Respect of the Right of Everyone to Leave Any Country, Including His Own, and to Return to His Country*, prepared by Mr. José D. Ingles (Philippines), Special Rapporteur of the Sub-Commission on Prevention of Discrimination and Protection of Minorities.[30] The study includes a summary of trends with respect to recognition and observance of these rights, a series of conclusions and proposals drawn up by the Special Rapporteur (chapters V and VI). After examining the proposals submitted by the Special Rapporteur (contained in chapter VI of the *Study*) the Sub-Commission on Prevention of Discrimination and Protection of Minorities formulated, at its fifteenth session (1963), draft principles on the subject and transmitted these general principles to the Commission on Human Rights for further consideration.

The draft [31] submitted by the Sub-Commission provides that every national of a country is entitled, without discrimination of any kind to leave his country temporarily or permanently; that no one shall be forced to renounce his nationality as a condition for the exercise of the right to leave his country; that no one shall be arbitrarily deprived of the right to enter his own country and that no one shall be denied the right to return to his own country on the ground that he has no passport or other travel document.

The study and the draft principles have been on the agenda of the twenty-third, twenty-fourth, twenty-fifth, twenty-seventh and twenty-eighth sessions of the Commission on Human Rights. The Commission has so far taken no action on them.

It might be mentioned in conclusion that the right set forth in article 13 (2) of the Universal Declaration is also contained in the International Covenant on Civil and Political Rights, article 12 of which provides in paragraph 2 that "everyone shall be free to leave any country, including his own" and in paragraph 4 that "no one shall be arbitrarily deprived of the right to enter his own country". Article 5 of the International Convention on the Elimination of All Forms of Racial Discrimination guarantees the right of everyone, without distinction as to race, colour, or national or ethnic origin, to equality before the law, notably in the enjoyment of the right, among others, to leave any country, including one's own, and to return to one's country.

### 1. *Migration*

Within the United Nations, the Economic and Social Council has allocated responsibilities in the field of migration between the Population and the Social Commissions, but has recalled that "all the other functional commissions of the Council may have to deal with aspects of migration which fall within their respective assignments".[32] The over-all co-ordination of responsibilities in the field of migration is achieved through a technical Working Group on Migration established under the auspices of the Administrative Committee on Co-ordination, now convened by the International Labour Organisation, which assumes, under the Administrative Committee on Co-ordination, the responsiblity at the international level for promoting co-operation and co-ordination in this field. Non-governmental organizations have also contributed to the study of migration, particularly by their participation in sessions of the Conference of Non-Governmental Organizations Interested in Migration, convened jointly by the United Nations and the ILO. Standards adopted by the ILO for the protection of migrant workers are laid down in the Migration for Employment Convention (Revised) and Recommendation (Revised), 1949, and the Protection of Migrant Workers (Underdeveloped Countries) Recommendation, 1955.

## K. The United Nations High Commissioner for Refugees

Among the measures which the United Nations took to alleviate the plight of refugees, in addition to initiating the establishment of the International Refugee Organization as a specialized agency of the United Nations, and in addition to the preparation and the putting into effect of the Convention relating to the Status of Refugees of 1951 and the Convention relating to the Status of Stateless Persons of 1954, was the establishment in 1949 of the Office of the United Nations High Commissioner for Refugees by resolution 319 (IV) of 3 December 1949. The Statute of the Office of the United Nations High Commissioner for Refugees is contained in the annex to General Assembly resolution 428 (V) of 14 December 1950.

[28] *Official Records of the General Assembly, Twenty-seventh session, Annexes*, agenda item 50, document A/8880, para. 42.

[29] *Ibid.*, para. 43.

[30] United Nations publication, Sales No. 64.XIV.2.

[31] See *Study*, annex VI.

[32] Economic and Social Council resolution 156 (VII) of 10 August 1948.

The function of the High Commissioner is to provide international protection, under the auspices of the United Nations, to refugees who fall within the scope of the Statute and to seek a permanent solution for the problem of refugees by assisting Governments and, under certain conditions, private organizations in the voluntary repatriation of such refugees or their assimilation within new national communities. A description of the organization and activities of the Office of the United Nations High Commissioner for Refugees is contained in part two of this publication.

## L. Measures relating to the right to a nationality (article 15 of the Universal Declaration)

### 1. *Nationality and statelessness*

In its resolution 116 D (VI) of 1 March 1948, the Economic and Social Council stated that the problem of stateless persons demanded action "to ensure that everyone shall have an effective right to a nationality". The following year, by its resolution 242 C (IX) of 1 August 1949, the Council decided that a convention on the nationality of married women, which would assure women equality with men in the exercise of the rights set out in article 15 of the Universal Declaration of Human Rights, and especially prevent a woman from becoming stateless or otherwise suffering hardships arising out of these conflicts in law, should be prepared as soon as possible.

In 1949 the United Nations published the *Study of Statelessness*,[33] prepared by the Secretary-General at the request of the Economic and Social Council (resolution 116 D (VI). The study included information and recommendations relating to the improvement of the status of stateless persons and the elimination of statelessness. The recommendations called for the universal recognition of the two following principles as a means of eliminating the sources of statelessness: (*a*) every child must receive a nationality at birth; (*b*) no person throughout his life should lose his nationality until he has acquired a new one.[34] Concerning the reduction of the number of existing losses of statelessness the recommendations set forth principles and invited all Governments of States Members to bring their legislation into conformity with these principles.

At its ninth session, in resolution 248 B (IX) of 8 August 1949, the Economic and Social Council, having considered the study prepared by the Secretary-General and the resolution on nationality of married women [35] adopted by the Council at the same session and taking note of the recommendations contained therein, decided to appoint an *ad hoc* committee consisting of representatives of 13 Governments with special competence in this field in order to: (*a*) consider the desirability of preparing a revised and consolidated convention relating to the international status of refugees and stateless persons; and, if they considered such a course desirable, draft the text of such a convention; (*b*) consider means of eliminating the problem of statelessness, including the desirability of requesting the International Law Commission to prepare a study and make recommendations on that subject; and (*c*) make any other suggestions they deemed suitable for the solution of the problems, taking into account recommendations of the Secretary-General to submit the report of the Committee to Governments for comments and, subsequently, to submit both report and comments to the Council.

### 2. *The elimination and reduction of future statelessness*

At its fifth and sixth sessions in 1953 and 1954 the International Law Commission prepared a draft Convention on the Elimination of Future Statelessness and a draft Convention on the Reduction of Future Statelessness.[36]

In 1954 the General Assembly decided to convene an International Conference of Plenipotentiaries to consider the two draft Conventions.[37] The Conference met in 1959 and again in 1961, when it prepared and opened for signature and ratification the Convention on the Reduction of Statelessness, the provisions of which are analysed in chapter VIII.

### 3. *The nationality of married women*

The efforts of the United Nations concerning the nationality of married women and the Convention on the subject, adopted in 1957, are dealt with in chapter VII.

### 4. *The status of stateless persons*

In connexion with the work of the United Nations relating to the status of refugees and stateless persons a Conference of Plenipotentiaries which met in 1951 adopted the Convention relating to the Status of Refugees. Another conference, which convened in 1954, adopted the Convention relating to the Status of Stateless Persons.[38]

## M. Measures relating to freedom of thought, conscience and religion (article 18 of the Universal Declaration)

In the Charter of the United Nations, Members have pledged themselves to promote universal respect for and

[33] United Nations publication, Sales No. 1949.XIV.2.

[34] It will be noted that the first of these two principles suggested in the Secretary-General's study of 1949 has been incorporated in article 24, paragraph 3, of the International Covenant on Civil and Political Rights, which provides that every child has the right to acquire a nationality.

[35] Economic and Social Council resolution 242 C (IX); see also chap. VII above, relating to the status of women.

[36] For the report of the International Law Commission covering the work of its fifth session, see *Official Records of the General Assembly, Eighth Session, Supplement No. 9* (A/2456) and for the report of the International Law Commission covering the work of its sixth session, see *Official Records of the General Assembly, Ninth Session, Supplement No. 9* (A/2693).

[37] General Assembly resolution 896 (IX) of 4 December 1954.

[38] For the provisions of these two Conventions, see A/CONF.2/108 (United Nations publication, Sales No. 1951.IV.4) and E/CONF.17/5/Rev.1 (United Nations publication, Sales No. 1956.XIV.1).

observance of human rights and fundamental freedoms for all without discrimination as to, *inter alia*, religion. Article 18 of the Universal Declaration of Human Rights proclaims the right of everyone to freedom of thought, conscience and religion. The United Nations has taken a series of measures with regard to this fundamental freedom.

In 1953 the Sub-Commission on Prevention of Discrimination and Protection of Minorities included in its list of projects, later approved by the Commission on Human Rights and the Economic and Social Council, a study of discrimination in the matter of religious rights and practices. The Sub-Commission, in 1955, examined a preliminary report on this topic prepared by Mr. Halpern, and in 1956 it appointed as Special Rapporteur, Mr. Arcot Krishnaswami, who, in 1959, completed the *Study of Discrimination in the Matter of Religious Rights and Practices.*[39] The study traces the development of the concept of the right to freedom of thought, conscience and religion to the tenets of tolerance inherent in almost all religious disciplines of the world; it devotes attention to the gradual evolution of this concept in various national laws that led to its eventual international recognition. It defines the nature of the right (chapter I); explains its essential elements, such as freedom to maintain or to change religion (chapter II) and as freedom to manifest religion or belief (chapter III). It discusses the status of religions in relation to the State (chapter IV) and gives a summary of trends observed and conclusions submitted by the Special Rapporteur (chapter V). The study further elaborates a programme for action that relates a series of basic rules and suggests guidelines on freedom and non-discrimination in the matter of religious rights and practices (chapter VI).

On the basis of proposals submitted by the Special Rapporteur, the Sub-Commission drew up a series of draft principles on freedom and non-discrimination in this matter. The Commission on Human Rights noted the draft principles in its resolution 4 (XVI)[40] and requested the Secretary-General to transmit these to the Governments of States Members of the United Nations and of the specialized agencies for their comments. On the recommendation of the Commission on Human Rights at its sixteenth session, the Economic and Social Council, in resolution 772 C (XXX), drew the attention of the General Assembly, in connexion with the consideration by the Assembly of article 18 of the draft Covenant on Civil and Poiltical Rights, to the study prepared by the Special Rapporteur and to the fact that the principles drawn up by the Sub-Commission had been submitted to Governments for their observations.

The draft principles prepared by the Sub-Commission state that everyone shall be free to adhere or not to adhere to a religion or belief in accordance with the dictates of his conscience; that parents shall have the prior right to decide the religion or belief in which their child should be brought up; that no one shall be subjected to material or moral coercion likely to impair his religious or non-religious belief, shall be free from any discrimination on account of his religion or belief; that no one shall be compelled to take an oath contrary to his convictions and that a priest who receives information in confidence in the performance of his duties shall not be compelled to divulge it.

The draft principles contain a number of other provisions, including provisions relating to freedom to travel for religious purposes, to observe dietary practices; freedom from any adverse distinctions based on religion in obtaining dissolution of marriage; freedom from compulsory religious or atheistic instruction contrary to one's belief.

The draft Declaration and draft Convention on the Elimination of All Forms of Religious Intolerance are dealt with above in chapter V. In the preparation of these two drafts due account was taken of the draft Principles prepared by the Sub-Commission and discussed in the Commission.

### N. Right of property (article 17 of the Universal Declaration)

In the course of the consideration by the Commission on Human Rights of the draft Covenants on Human Rights, the question of including an article on the right of property in the draft Covenants was the subject of considerable discussion, particularly at the seventh, eighth and tenth sessions of the Commission. No agreement was reached on a text or on whether the right should be included in the International Covenant on Civil and Political Rights or in the International Covenant on Economic, Social and Cultural Rights or in both.[41] After attempts had been made to come to an agreement through the appointment of a sub-committee of the Commission on Human Rights and the text proposed by the sub-committee had been rejected, the Commission, at its tenth session, decided to adjourn indefinitely consideration of the question of the inclusion of an article on the right of property in the draft Covenant on Economic, Social and Cultural Rights.

During the consideration of the draft Covenants by the General Assembly, suggestions for the inclusion of an article on the right of property in one or the other of the two Covenants were made, but none was pressed to the vote. As a consequence, the Covenants, as adopted on 16 December 1966, do not contain a provision concerning this right.

In article 5 of the International Convention on the Elimination of All Forms of Racial Discrimination, States parties undertake to guarantee the right of everyone

[39] United Nations publication, Sales No. 60.XIV.2.

[40] *Official Records of the Economic and Social Council, Thirtieth Session, Supplement No. 8* (E/3335), p. 20.

[41] For a summary of the proceedings relating to the inclusion of an article on the right to own property in either Covenant, see Annotations on the text of the draft International Covenants on Human Rights, *Official Records of the General Assembly, Tenth Session, Annexes*, agenda item 28, part II, chap. VIII, paras. 195-212, and Report of the Tenth Session of the Commission on Human Rights, *Official Records of the Economic and Social Council, Eighteenth Session, Supplement No. 7* (E/2573), paras. 40-71.

without distinction as to race, colour, or national or ethnic origin, to equality before the law in the enjoyment of a number of rights including "the right to own property alone as well as in association with others" and "the right to inherit".

The Declaration on the Elimination of Discrimination against Women of 1967 provides that all appropriate measures shall be taken to ensure to women, married or unmarried, equal rights with men in the field of civil law, and in particular, the right to acquire, administer, enjoy, dispose of and inherit property, including property acquired during marriage.

Aspects of the right to property have repeatedly been considered and dealt with by the General Assembly and the Economic and Social Council in connexion with the problem of land reform.[42] To the extent that it deals with nationalization, expropriation and requisitioning the Declaration on Permanent Sovereignty over Natural Resources of 1962 [43] deals with aspects of the right of property against the background of the right of peoples and nations to permanent sovereignty over their natural wealth and resources.

### O. Measures relating to freedom of opinion and expression (article 19 of the Universal Declaration)

At its first session in 1946 the General Assembly stated that freedom of information was a fundamental human right and the touchstone of all the freedoms to which the United Nations was consecrated. At the same time the General Assembly requested the Economic and Social Council to undertake the convocation of an International Conference on Freedom of Information (General Assembly resolution 59 (I) of 14 December 1946). Accordingly, the Economic and Social Council, by resolution 74 (V) of 15 August 1947, convened the United Nations Conference on Freedom of Information, which met in Geneva in March-April 1948. The Conference prepared three draft Conventions—on the Gathering and International Transmission of News, the Institution of an International Right of Correction, and Freedom of Information, respectively—as well as draft articles for inclusion in the Universal Declaration of Human Rights and a great number of resolutions. The Final Act of the Conference [44] was referred to the Economic and Social Council, which in turn referred it to the General Assembly for action. The General Assembly adopted at its third session the draft Convention on the International Transmission of News and the Right of Correction, which consisted of an amalgamation of the provisions of the draft Conventions on the Gathering and International Transmission of News and on the Institution of an International Right of Correction which had been prepared by the Conference of 1948. The General Assembly, however, decided that the Convention it had approved should not be open for signature until the General Assembly had taken definite action on the draft Convention on Freedom of Information (General Assembly resolution 277 A and C (III) of 13 May 1949).

At its seventh session in 1952 the General Assembly decided to open the substantive provisions of the Convention that it had approved in 1949 which dealt with the international right of correction as a separate international instrument. Consequently, it adopted and opened for signature the Convention on the International Right of Correction (General Assembly resolution 630 (VII) of 16 December 1952). This Convention has been in force since 24 August 1962.

The "definite action" on the draft Convention on Freedom of Information which the General Assembly contemplated in its resolution 277 A (III) of 1949 has not yet been taken by the General Assembly. However, a Committee established by the General Assembly in resolution 426 (V) of 14 December 1950 prepared a new version of the draft Convention (A/AC.42/7 and Corr.1, annex). On the basis of the work done by that Committee, the Third Committee of the General Assembly, at the fourteenth, fifteenth and sixteenth sessions of the General Assembly in 1959, 1960 and 1961, approved the preamble and four operative paragraphs of the draft Convention on Freedom of Information.[45]

By article 1 of the draft Convention on Freedom of Information as approved by the Third Committee each contracting State undertakes to respect and protect the right of every person to have at his disposal diverse sources of information. Each contracting State shall secure to its own nationals and to such of the nationals of every other Contracting State as are lawfully within its territory freedom to gather, receive and impart without governmental interference, save as provided in article 2, and regardless of frontiers, information and opinions orally, in writing or in print, in the form of art or by duly licensed visual or auditory devices. The draft Convention prohibits discrimination in regard to this right on political grounds or on the basis of race, sex, language or religion.

Article 2 of the draft Convention as approved by the Third Committee provides that the exercise of the freedoms referred to in article 1 (summarized in the preceding paragraph) carries with it duties and responsibilities. These freedoms may, however, be subject only to such necessary restrictions as are clearly defined by law and applied in accordance with the law in respect of national security and public order *(ordre public)*; systematic dissemination of false reports harmful to friendly relations among nations and of expressions inciting to war or national, racial or religious hatred; attacks on founders of religion; incitement to violence and crime, public health or morals; the rights, honour or reputation of others and the fair administration of justice. These res-

[42] See, e.g., General Assembly resolutions 1426 (XIV) of 5 December 1959 and 1828 (XVII) of 18 December 1962, and Economic and Social Council resolution 887 (XXXIV) of 24 July 1962.

[43] General Assembly resolution 1803 (XVII) of 14 December 1962.

[44] United Nations publication, Sales No. 48.XIV.2.

[45] See *Official Records of the General Assembly, Fourteenth Session, Third Committee, Annexes,* agenda item 35, document A/4341; *ibid., Fifteenth Session, Annexes,* agenda item 35, document A/4636; *ibid., Sixteenth Session, Annexes,* agenda item 36, document A/5041.

trictions shall not be deemed to justify the imposition by any State of prior censorship on news, comments and political opinions and may not be used as grounds for restricting the right to criticize the Government.

Article 3 of the draft Convention is a saving clause for rights and freedoms to which the Convention refers which may be guaranteed under the laws of any contracting State or any Conventions to which it is a party. In article 4 the contracting States recognize that the right of reply is a corollary of freedom of information and may establish appropriate means for safeguarding that right.

At the sessions of the General Assembly held between 1962 and 1972, the General Assembly was unable to consider the draft Convention on Freedom of Information and the draft Declaration on the same subject and always decided to postpone the consideration to the next session.[46]

At its twenty-seventh session, the General Assembly considered a special aspect of the over-all problem of freedom of information in connexion with a proposal for the preparation of an international convention on the principles governing the use by States of artificial earth satellites for direct television broadcasting. In resolution 2916 (XXVII) of 9 November 1972, the General Assembly reaffirmed the common interest of all mankind in furthering the peaceful exploration and use of outer space for the benefit of all States and for the development of friendly relations and mutual understanding, and bore in mind that direct television broadcasting should help to draw the peoples of the world closer together, to widen the exchange of information and cultural values and to enhance the educational level of people in various countries. The General Assembly considered at the same time that direct television broadcasting by means of satellites should take place under conditions in which that new form of space technology would serve only the lofty goals of peace and friendship among peoples. The General Assembly referred to the need to prevent the conversion of direct television broadcasting into a source of international conflict and of aggravation of the relations among States, and to protect the sovereignty of States from any external interference. It noted the draft Convention on the subject submitted to the General Assembly by a Member State [47] and stated its belief that the activity of States in this field must be based on the principles of mutual respect for sovereignty, non-interference in domestic affairs, equality, co-operation and mutual benefit. The General Assembly stated at the same time that the introduction of direct television broadcasting by means of satellites could raise significant problems connected with the need to ensure the free flow of communications on a basis of strict respect for the sovereign rights of States. It resolved that it was necessary to elaborate principles governing the use by States of artificial earth satellites for direct television broadcasting with a view to concluding an international agreement or agreements. The General Assembly requested the Committee on the Peaceful Uses of Outer Space to undertake the elaboration of such principles as soon as possible.

In a second resolution (2917) (XXVII)) the General Assembly noted that the work done on the draft Convention on Freedom of Information and deliberations thereon in the General Assembly might be useful in the discussion and elaboration of international instruments or United Nations arrangements relative to direct television broadcasts.

In 1954, the General Assembly took action with regard to an instrument in the field of information which had been adopted under the auspices of the League of Nations, namely the International Convention concerning the Use of Broadcasting in the Cause of Peace, Geneva, 1936.[48] A study on the 1936 Convention had been prepared by the Secretary-General for use by the Sub-Commission on Freedom of Information and of the Press in 1950 (E/CN.4/Sub.1/104). In resolution 841 (IX) of 17 December 1954, the General Assembly requested States parties to the Convention of 1936 to state whether they wished to transfer to the United Nations the functions which were performed under the terms of the 1936 Convention by the League of Nations. The General Assembly requested the Secretary-General to prepare for this purpose a draft Protocol and to include in it new articles which would provide that each Party should refrain from radio broadcasts that would mean unfair attacks or slanders against other people anywhere and also that each Party should not interfere with the reception within its territory of foreign radio broadcasts. An appropriate draft Protocol was prepared by the Secretary-General and circulated to the States parties to the Convention of 1936. Final action has not yet been taken on the draft; however, in resolution 1903 (XVIII) of 18 November 1963 on participation in general multilateral treaties concluded under the auspices of the League of Nations, the General Assembly requested the Secretary-General to invite each State which was a Member of the United Nations or of a specialized agency or a Party to the Statute of the International Court of Justice or had been designated for this purpose by the General Assembly and which otherwise was not eligible to become a Party to the League of Nations treaty concerned, to accede thereto. In the annex to resolution 2021 (XX) of 5 November 1965 on general multilateral treaties concluded under the auspices of the League of Nations, the General Assembly listed the International Convention concerning the Use of Broadcasting in the Cause of Peace, 1936, among those which might be of interest for accession by additional States.

The Economic and Social Council also prepared at its twenty-seventh and twenty-eighth sessions in 1959-1960 a draft Declaration on Freedom of Information and transmitted it to the General Assembly for its consideration (Economic and Social Council resolutions 720

[46] General Assembly resolution 1840 (XVII); decision of the 1279th plenary meeting at the eighteenth session; General Assembly resolutions 2061 (XX), 2216 (XXI), 2336 (XXII), 2448 (XXIII), 2596 (XXIV), 2722 (XXV), 2844 (XXVI) and decision adopted at the 2114th plenary meeting at the twenty-seventh session. On the origin of the draft Declaration on Freedom of Information, see below.

[47] See *Official Records of the General Assembly, Twenty-seventh Session, Annexes*, agenda items 28, 29 and 37, document A/8771.

[48] League of Nations, *Treaty Series*, vol. CLXXXVI, p. 301.

(XXVII), 732 (XVIII) and 756 (XXIX)). The General Assembly has not yet taken action on the draft Declaration prepared by the Council.[49]

The provisions of the International Covenant on Civil and Political Rights relating to freedom of opinion, freedom of expression and freedom to seek, receive and impart information are contained in its article 19. Article 20 of the Covenant deals with the prohibition of propaganda for war and of advocacy of national, racial or religious hatred. The International Convention on the Elimination of All Forms of Racial Discrimination prohibits in article 5 expressly racial discrimination in regard to the right to freedom of opinion and expression.

In 1948 the United Nations Conference on Freedom of Information recommended that the question of drawing up an international code of ethics be referred to the Sub-Commission on Freedom of Information and of the Press. In 1952 the Sub-Commission transmitted to the Economic and Social Council the text of the draft International Code of Ethics (ST/SOA/12). The Council and the General Assembly adopted a number of resolutions concerning this draft. At its ninth session, in resolution 838 (IX) of 17 December 1954, the General Assembly, noting the Secretary-General's report [50] on the question of organizing an international professional conference to prepare the final text of the Code, decided, at that time, to take no further action in regard to the organization of such a conference and requested the Secretary-General to transmit the text of the draft International Code to enterprises and associations for their information and for such action as they might deem proper.

Apart from drafting the various international instruments referred to in the preceding paragraphs the various United Nations organs also took certain concrete measures to contribute to the promotion of respect for freedom of expression and information by recommending to Governments that they refrain from radio broadcasts containing unfair attacks or slanders against other peoples and by inviting all Member States to give every possible facility so that their peoples may know objectively the activities of the United Nations in promoting peace. The General Assembly and the Economic and Social Council advised against the interference with the reception of radio signals originating beyond their territories. The General Assembly recommended to all Member States that when they were compelled to declare a state of emergency, measures to limit freedom of information and of the Press should be taken only in the most exceptional circumstances and then only to the extent strictly required by the situation. (General Assembly resolutions 424 (V) and 425 (V) of 14 December 1950). The Economic and Social Council also made recommendations to Governments to do all within their power to safeguard the right of correspondents freely and faithfully to gather and transmit news (Economic and Social Council resolution 387 B (XIII) of 1 September 1951). The General Assembly recommended that Governments should open their countries to greater freedom of communication by facilitating access to United Nations information programmes, supporting activities of United Nations information centres and facilitating the free flow of accurate information through all media (General Assembly resolution 1313 B (XIII) of 12 December 1958).

### 1. *Development of information media in developing countries*

The development of information media in developing countries is an aspect of freedom of information which, with the special co-operation of UNESCO, the United Nations has considered in some detail.

At its thirteenth session, in 1957, the Commission on Human Rights had before it a note (E/CN.4/732) submitted by the Secretary-General outlining the activities of the United Nations and the specialized agencies in the field of freedom of information and surveying the results and progress achieved in that field. At the same session the Commission adopted resolution 9 (XIII) in which it decided to appoint a five-member committee for the purpose of reviewing the work of the United Nations and the specialized agencies and reporting to the Commission on Human Rights what action should be taken to develop information media, to improve their utilization and to promote the widest possible implementation of the recommendations and decisions made in the various organs of the United Nations, including those relating to developing countries and territories.

In 1957 the Economic and Social Council considered a study (E/2947 and Add.1) on this question made by the Secretary-General in consultation with UNESCO pursuant to Economic and Social Council resolution 574 D (XIX) of 25 May 1955. In that resolution the Council requested the Secretary-General, in consultation with UNESCO, to prepare an analysis of the information and recommendations received from Governments and, on the basis of this analysis, to present elements necessary for the formulation by the Council of a programme of concrete action. In resolution 643 (XXIII) of 27 April 1957 the Council having considered the above-mentioned study in media of information in developing countries, reaffirmed its resolution 574 D (XIX) and invited the Secretary-General to complete the study in co-operation with specialized agencies as appropriate. In resolution 1189 B (XII) of 11 December 1957 the General Assembly recommended that special consideration should be given to the problem of developing media of information in developing countries.

In resolution 1313 A (XIII) of 12 December 1958, the General Assembly requested the Economic and Social Council to formulate a programme of concrete action and measures on the international plane which could be undertaken for the development of information enterprises in developing countries. At its twenty-seventh session the Council, in resolution 718 (XXVII) of 24 April 1959, requested UNESCO to undertake a survey designed to provide the elements for the programme of concrete action desired by the Assembly. The reports of the survey, carried out by UNESCO in a series of

[49] In regard to the postponement of action on the draft Declaration see footnote 46 above.

[50] *Official Records of the General Assembly, Ninth Session,* documents A/2691 and Add.1 and 2.

regional meetings in Asia, Africa and Latin America, held in co-operation with the respective United Nations regional economic commissions were transmitted to the Assembly by the Council by its resolution 888 E (XXXIV) of 24 April 1962.

In resolution 1778 (XVII) of 7 December 1962, the Assembly invited the Governments concerned to include adequate provision in their economic plans for the development of national information media and recommended that the Governments of the more developed countries should co-operate with less developed countries with a view to meeting the urgent needs of the latter in connexion with programmes for the development of independent and national information media, with due regard for the culture of each country. The Technical Assistance Board, the Special Fund, the specialized agencies concerned, the regional economic commissions and other public and private agencies and institutions were invited to assist, as appropriate, the less developed countries in developing and strengthening their national information media.

UNESCO was requested by the Assembly to continue to further the programme for the development of information media, including the application of new techniques of communication for achievement of rapid progress in education; to keep up to date, as far as possible, its survey on this subject; and to report, as appropriate, to the Commission on Human Rights and to the Economic and Social Council.

At its forty-third session, the Economic and Social Council dealt again with the problems of the development of information media (resolution 1278 (XLIII) of 4 August 1967). It noted that there had been significant advances in the techniques of communication that would warrant a further report of UNESCO on the application of these techniques for the advancement of rapid progress in education and for the economic and social development generally. The Council noted with satisfaction that UNESCO had intensified its activities in this field and in particular had recently initiated long-term programmes in space communication and book development.

The Council therefore invited UNESCO in consultation with the Member States, the United Nations, the specialized agencies concerned and the competent professional organizations, to prepare the further report indicated in General Assembly resolution 1778 (XVII) on the application of new techniques of communication for the achievement of rapid progress in education, notably in the field of book development and, within its competence, in the field of space communication.

### 2. *Reports on freedom of information*

The first report on freedom of information [51] was presented in 1953 by Mr. Salvador P. Lopez (Philippines), Rapporteur appointed by the Economic and Social Council in its resolution 442 C (XIV) of 13 June 1952. The second, entitled "Report on developments in the field of freedom of information",[52] was prepared by Dr. Hilding Eek (Sweden), a consultant appointed by the Secretary-General. Pursuant to a decision taken by the Economic and Social Council in 1959 (resolution 718 (XXVII), section II), the Secretary-General prepared and submitted to the Commission on Human Rights a series of annual reports on developments affecting freedom of information.[53] The series of reports was discontinued, however, in 1965. Reports on freedom of information were to be submitted, under the system of periodic reports on human rights, every three years, the first such reports to cover the period ending 30 June 1967. However, by resolution 1596 (L) the Economic and Social Council decided on 21 May 1971 that, with effect from the date of that resolution, Member States shall be asked to submit periodic reports once every two years in a continuing cycle: the first, on civil and political rights to be submitted in 1972; the second, on economic, social and cultural rights, in 1974; the third, on freedom of information, in 1976.

### 3. *Seminars*

Two regional seminars, organized under the programme of advisory services in the field of human rights, have considered matters relating to freedom of information: the seminar on freedom of information, New Delhi, India, 20 February-4 March 1962 (ST/TAO/HR/13) and the seminar on freedom of information, Rome, Italy, 7-20 April 1964 (ST/TAO/HR/20).

## P. Measures relating to freedom of association (article 20 of the Universal Declaration)

At its fourth session, in 1947, the Economic and Social Council, having taken note of the item regarding trade union rights placed on its agenda at the request of the World Federation of Trade Unions and the memoranda (A/374) submitted by the World Federation of Trade Unions and the Amercian Federation of Labor, resolved to transmit these documents to the ILO for consideration and report to the Economic and Social Council. The Council further resolved (resolution 52 (IV) of 24 March 1947) to transmit the documents to the Commission on Human Rights, in order that it might consider those aspects of the subject which might appropriately form part of the bill or Declaration of Human Rights.

In pursuance of the Council's request made at its fourth session, the ILO transmitted to the Council a report entitled "Decisions Concerning Freedom of Association Adopted Unanimously by the Thirtieth Session of the International Labour Conference in July 1947" (A/374/Add.1). The Economic and Social Council in resolution 84 (V), adopted at its fifth session, decided to transmit this report to the General Assembly, to recognize the principles proclaimed by the International Labour Conference and to request the ILO to continue its efforts

[51] *Official Records of the Economic and Social Council, Sixteenth Session, Supplement No. 12.*

[52] *Ibid., Thirty-first Session, Annexes*, agenda item 10 (part II), document E/4443.

[53] See E/CN.4/822 and Add.1-3; E/CN.4/838 and Add.1-3; E/CN.4/862 and Add.1 and 2.

in order that one or several international conventions might be adopted. The General Assembly, at its second session, in resolution 128 (II) of 17 November 1947, approved Economic and Social Council resolutions 52 (IV) and 84 (V) and endorsed the principles proclaimed by the ILO. The General Assembly also decided to transmit the report of the ILO to the Commission on Human Rights with the same objects as those stated in Economic and Social Council resolution 52 (IV).

At its thirty-first session, held in San Francisco in June-July 1948, the International Labour Conference had before it a report on freedom of association based on the replies of the Governments to a questionnaire submitted to them by the International Labour Office.[54] The conclusions of that report contained, as a basis for discussion by the Conference, a draft of a proposed convention concerning freedom of association and protection of the right to organize. The Conference adopted the Convention in the course of its thirty-first session, in July 1948. In resolution 279 (III) of 13 May 1949 the General Assembly expressed the earnest hope that Governments would take prompt action for the early ratification of that Convention. At its thirty-second session in 1949, the International Labour Conference adopted a further Convention concerning the application of the principles of the right to organize and to bargain collectively. At its fifty-sixth session in 1971, the International Labour Conference adopted a Convention concerning the protection and facilities to be afforded to workers' representatives in the undertaking. The provisions of these three Conventions are summarized in chapter VIII.

The provisions to which each member of the International Labour Organisation, for which the Convention on Freedom of Association and Protection of the Right to Organize of 1948 is in force, undertakes to give effect include the following: Workers and employers, without distinction whatsoever, shall have the right to establish and, subject only to the rules of the organization concerned, to join organizations of their own choosing without previous authorization. Organizations of workers or of employers for furthering and defending the interests of workers or of employers shall have the right to draw up their constitutions and rules, to elect their representatives in full freedom, to organize their administration and activities and to formulate their programmes. The public authorities shall refrain from any interference which would restrict this right or impede the lawful exercise thereof. Workers' and employers' organizations shall not be liable to be dissolved or suspended by administrative authority. They shall have the right to establish and join federations and confererations which shall have the right to affiliate with international organizations of workers and employers. In exercising the rights provided for in the Convention, workers and employers and their respective organizations, like other persons or organized collectivities, shall respect the law of the land. The law of the land shall not be such as to impair, nor shall it be so applied as to impair, the guarantees provided for in the Convention.

In 1949 the Economic and Social Council (resolution 239 (IX) of 2 August 1949), after examining a report by the Secretary-General on his consultations with the Director-General of the International Labour Office with regard to the question of enforcement of trade union rights (freedom of association) (E/1405 and E/1405/Corr.2) requested the International Labour Organisation to proceed, on behalf of the United Nations, in accordance with its relationship agreement, as well as on its own behalf, with the establishment of a Fact-Finding and Conciliation Commission on Freedom of Association. The Council in its resolution 277 (X) of 17 February 1950 decided to accept on behalf of the United Nations the services of the ILO and the Fact-Finding and Conciliation Commission which it had established and to forward to the Governing Body of the International Labour Office, for its consideration as to referral to the Commission, all allegations regarding infringements of trade union rights received from Governments or trade unions or employers' organizations against member States of the International Labour Organisation. In 1951, the Governing Body of the International Labour Office decided to establish a Governing Body Committee on Freedom of Association for the preliminary examination of such allegations and to consider the appropriateness of referral of particular cases to the Fact-Finding and Conciliation Commission.

In 1970 and 1971 the ILO Governing Body Committee on Freedom of Association had under consideration a complaint alleging infringements of trade union rights in a member State of the ILO. Before the substance of the complaint had been examined by the Committee the country concerned withdrew from the ILO while remaining a Member of the United Nations. The Committee then recommended to the ILO Governing Body that, in conformity with the procedure for the examination of complaints of infringement of freedom of association instituted in 1950, the allegations of the complainants be forwarded for examination to the Economic and Social Council to decide, with the consent of the Government concerned, whether to refer the case to the ILO Fact-Finding and Conciliation Commission on Freedom of Association. The Government having replied that it had no objection to the submission of the matter to the Commission, the Economic and Social Council decided in June 1972 to refer the case to the Commission.

Since its establishment in 1951, the ILO Governing Body Committee on Freedom of Association has considered many hundreds of allegations of the infringement of trade union rights. In a few cases the complaint was referred on the recommendation of the Committee on Freedom of Association to the Fact-Finding and Conciliation Commission.

The Council, in its resolution 474 (XV) of 9 April 1953, requested the Secretary-General to forward to the Governing Body of the ILO all such allegations received in the future. This procedure applies only in regard to allegations of the infringement of trade union rights directed against members of the International Labour Organisation.

---

[54] ILO, thirty-first session, San Francisco, 1948, report VII ("Freedom of Association and Protection of the Right to Organize") (Geneva, 1948).

The question of what action to take in regard to allegations of the infringement of trade union rights in States not members of the International Labour Organisation became of great practical importance when South Africa ceased to be a member of that specialized agency. The solution adopted by the Economic and Social Council by its resolutions 1216 (XLII) of 1967 and 1302 (XLIV) of 1968 was that it extended the terms of reference of the *ad hoc* Working Group of Experts on the Treatment of Political Prisoners in South Africa, which had been established by the Commission on Human Rights in 1967 by resolution 2 (XXIII), to deal also with allegations of the infringement of trade union rights in South Africa and in South West Africa (Namibia).

## Q. Measures relating to the right to take part in government (article 21 of the Universal Declaration)

### 1. *Studies*

In 1963 the United Nations published the *Study of Discrimination in the Matter of Political Rights*,[55] prepared by Mr. Hernán Santa Cruz (Chile), Special Rapporteur of the Sub-Commission on Prevention of Discrimination and Protection of Minorities. The study includes a summary of trends and conclusions drawn up by the Special Rapporteur (chapter VI) and a series of draft principles on freedom and non-discrimination in the matter of political rights. At its fourteenth session, in 1962, the Sub-Commission, after examining the draft principles submitted by the Special Rapporteur, formulated general principles on freedom and non-discrimination in the matter of political rights [56] and transmitted them to the Commission on Human Rights for further consideration.

The general principles proclaimed by the Sub-Commission to ensure recognition of the right of everyone to take part in the government of his country and other related political rights, and to prevent discrimination in the enjoyment of these rights, state that all people have the right to self-determination; that every national of a country is entitled within that country to full and equal political rights without distinction of any kind, such as race, colour, sex, language, religion, political or other opinion, national or social origin, property, birth or other status; that freedom of opinion and expression and freedom of peaceful assembly and association are essential to the enjoyment of political rights; and that these freedoms, and access to the facilities and means for their exercise, shall be ensured to all persons at all times. Other principles relate to the universality of suffrage, the equality of suffrage, the secrecy of vote, the periodicity of elections, the genuine character of elections and other public consultations, and the access to elective and non-elective public office.

The *Study of discrimination in the matter of political rights* and the draft principles have been on the agenda of several sessions of the Commission on Human Rights, including the twenty-eighth session in 1972; the Commission on Human Rights has not yet taken action on them.

In 1971 the United Nations published, in connexion with the observance in 1971 of the International Year for Action to Combat Racism and Racial Discrimination, the *Special Study on Racial Discrimination in the Political, Economic, Social and Cultural Spheres*,[57] also prepared by Mr. Hernán Santa Cruz as Special Rapporteur of the Sub-Commission. This second study also deals, as its title indicates, with racial discrimination in the political sphere. As the Special Rapporteur states in paragraph 1079 of this Study, general principles relating to the elimination of all forms of racial discrimination are set out clearly in the United Nations Declaration on the Elimination of All Forms of Racial Discrimination, while practical measures to implement those principles are contained in the provisions of the International Convention on that subject.

### 2. *The right to take part in government in United Nations instruments*

Article 25 of the International Covenant on Civil and Political Rights contains the following provisions:

"Every citizen shall have the right and the opportunity, without any of the distinctions mentioned in article 2 and without unreasonable restrictions:

"(*a*) To take part in the conduct of public affairs, directly or through freely chosen representatives;

"(*b*) To vote and to be elected at genuine periodic elections which shall be by universal and equal suffrage and shall be held by secret ballot, guaranteeing the free expression of the will of the electors;

"(*c*) To have access, on general terms of equality, to public service in his country."

The United Nations Declaration on the Elimination of All Forms of Racial Discrimination of 1963 provides in its article 6 that:

"No discrimination by reason of race, colour or ethnic origin shall be admitted in the enjoyment by any person of political and citizenship rights in his country, in particular the right to participate in elections through universal and equal suffrage and to take part in the government. Everyone has the right of equal access to public service in his country."

By article 5 of the International Convention on the Elimination of All Forms of Racial Discrimination, States parties undertake to guarantee the right of everyone, without distinction as to race, colour or national or ethnic origin, to equality before the law in the enjoyment of a series of rights including:

"Political rights, in particular the rights to participate in elections—to vote and to stand for election—on the basis of universal and equal suffrage, to take part in the Government as well as in the conduct of public affairs at any level and to have equal access to public service."

---

[55] United Nations publication, Sales No. 63.XIV.2.

[56] United Nations publication, Sales No. 63.XIV.2, annex I.

[57] United Nations publication, Sales No. E.71.XIV.2.

### 3. *Political rights of women*

In 1946, before the adoption of the Universal Declaration of Human Rights, the General Assembly (resolution 56 (I) of 11 December 1946) recommended "that all Member States, which have not already done so, adopt measures necessary to fulfil the purposes and aims of the Charter . . . by granting to women the same political rights as to men". The interest of the United Nations in extending political rights to women has continued since that time.

In 1948, the Economic and Social Council (resolution 154 A (VII) of 20 August 1948) requested the Member States in which women had not yet been given the same political rights as men to grant such rights to women in all spheres of economic, national, cultural, social and political life; it drew attention to the fact that opportunities for the exercise of these rights and a greater measure of activity by women voters in making use of their right to take part in elections, as well as the introduction of a more general system of electing women to key posts in national, public, municipal and other institutions, would serve as an effective method of stimulating the interest of women voters, would increase their interest in social and political work, and would ensure a fuller use by women voters of their right to take part in elections.

At the same time the Council (resolution 154 B (VII) of 20 August 1948) recommended that Member States (*a*) grant women, whether married or unmarried, access on equal terms with men to posts in the public service at all levels, including diplomatic, consular, legal and judicial office, and to all liberal and other professions; and (*b*) consider women equally with men when appointing their delegations to organs and agencies of the United Nations and to international bodies and conferences.

The Commission on the Status of Women requested the Secretary-General, in 1950, "to prepare for submission to this Commission a draft convention on the granting to women of equal political rights with men". [58] The Commission considered the Secretary-General's draft in 1951 and presented its own draft to the Economic and Social Council in August of that year. By its resolution 445 B (XIV) of 26 May 1952, the Council forwarded that draft to the General Assembly in 1952.

On 20 December 1952 the General Assembly by its resolution 640 (VII) adopted the Convention on the Political Rights of Women and opened it for signature and ratification at the end of its session. The contents of the Convention are described in chapter VII above.

In its resolution 731 (VIII) of 23 October 1953 the General Assembly urged States "to take all necessary measures, particularly educational and legislative measures, leading to the development of the political rights of women in all Territories in which women do not enjoy full political rights, including Trust and Non-Self-Governing Territories".

[58] *Official Records of the Economic and Social Council, Eleventh Session, Supplement No. 6*, para. 25.

In 1955 the United Nations published a booklet, entitled *The Convention on the Political Rights of Women: History and Commentary.*[59] The publication traces the history and background of the Convention and contains a commentary on its provisions.

### 4. *Seminars*

Eight regional seminars, organized under the programme of advisory services in the field of human rights, have considered matters relating to the right to take part in government:

- Seminar on the civic responsibilities and increased participation of Asian women in public life, Bangkok, Thailand, 5-16 August 1957 (ST/TAO/HR/1)
- Seminar on participation of women in public life, Bogotá, Colombia, 18-29 May 1959 (ST/TAO/HR/5)
- Seminar on the participation of women in public life, Addis Ababa, Ethiopia, 12-23 September 1960 (ST/TAO/HR/9)
- Seminar on the participation of women in public life, Ulan Bator, Mongolia, 3-17 August 1965 (ST/TAO/HR/24)
- Seminar on participation in local administration as a means of promoting human rights, Budapest, Hungary, 14-27 June 1966 (ST/TAO/HR/26)
- Seminar on the effective realization of civil and political rights at the national level, Kingston, Jamaica, 25 April - 8 May 1967 (ST/TAO/HR/28)
- Seminar on the civic and political education of women, Helsinki, Finland, 1-14 August 1967 (ST/TAO/HR/30)
- Seminar on the civic and political education of women, Accra, Ghana, 19 November - 2 December 1968 (ST/TAO/HR/35)

### 5. *Reports on the political rights of women*

A survey of reports on the political rights of women will be found in chapter VII above.

## R. Measures relating to the right to education (article 26 of the Universal Declaration)

### 1. *Eradication of illiteracy*

Both the General Assembly and the Economic and Social Council, in a number of resolutions,[60] have recommended the establishment of free and compulsory education and the raising of such education to the level enjoyed by the peoples of the advanced countries. In 1961 the Assembly, feeling that even greater efforts were called for with a view to eradicating mass illiteracy throughout the world as speedily as possible, invited the United Nations Educational, Scientific and Cultural Organiz-

[59] United Nations publication, Sales No. 1955.IV.17.

[60] General Assembly resolutions 330 (IV) of 2 December 1949, 743 (VIII) of 27 November 1953, 1049 (XI) of 20 February 1957 and 1463 (XIV) of 12 December 1962; and Economic and Social Council resolutions 652 C (XXIV) of 24 July 1957 and 821 V B (XXXII) of 19 July 1961.

ation (*a*) to make a general review of the question of the eradication of mass illiteracy throughout the world, with the object of working out concrete and effective measures at the international and national levels, for such education; and (*b*) to present to the General Assembly a survey of the position in the world with regard to the extention of universal literacy, together with recommendations on measures which might be taken within the framework of the United Nations for co-operation in the eradication of illiteracy. At the same time the Assembly called for the extension of effective assistance for the eradication of illiteracy and the promotion of education of all kinds to the developing countries, both bilaterally and within the framework of the United Nations and its specialized agencies, and expressed the hope that the Governments of those countries would assign, in their programmes of social development, prime importance to the problem of eradicating illiteracy.[61]

Subsequently, the General Assembly and the Economic and Social Council, on the one hand, and the UNESCO, on the other, developed a very intensive activity and started the World Campaign for Universal Literacy. The regional economic commissions of the Economic and Social Council have also been active. In its resolutions 1937 (XVIII) of 11 December 1963 and 2043 (XX) of 8 December 1965 the General Assembly commended the far-flung activities in the campaign and addressed appropriate recommendations to Member States and to UNESCO. In resolution 2192 (XXI) of 15 December 1966 the General Assembly, in the name of human solidarity, invited Member States, international organizations, non-governmental organizations, foundations, institutions and private enterprises to provide continuing and effective financial material and technical support for the World Campaign for Universal Literacy.

By its resolution 2263 (XXII) of 7 November 1967, the General Assembly approved the Declaration on the Elimination of Discrimination against Women that stipulates that, among other rights, women shall have equal opportunities for access to programmes of continuing education, including adult literacy programmes. The Declaration on Social Progress and Development, proclaimed by the General Assembly in its resolution 2542 (XXIV) of 11 December 1969, includes the eradication of illiteracy as one of the goals to be attained in the raising of the material and spiritual standards of living of all members of society.

### 2. *Action against discrimination in education*

In 1957 the United Nations published the *Study of Discrimination in Education*,[62] prepared by the late Mr. Charles D. Ammoun (Lebanon), Special Rapporteur of the Sub-Commission on Prevention of Discrimination and Protection of Minorities. The history of this study and the description of the subsequent action taken by the United Nations organs which was to lead to the adoption, in 1960, by the General Conference of UNESCO of a Convention and a Recommendation against discrimination in education, are given above in section D of this chapter.

### 3. *The role of youth in promoting universal respect for human rights and other purposes of the United Nations*

Article 66 of the Universal Declaration of Human Rights provides that education shall be directed to the full development of the human personality and to the strengthening of respect for human rights and fundamental freedoms. It shall promote understanding, tolerance and friendship among all nations, racial or religious groups, and shall further the activities of the United Nations for the maintenance of peace. Guided by, *inter alia*, this provision of the Declaration the General Assembly has in recent years paid considerable attention to the role of youth in promoting the purposes of the Charter and the objectives of peace, international security and co-operation among nations, social and economic progress and, in particular, universal respect for human rights. Reference has already been made to the Declaration on the Promotion among Youth of the Ideals of Peace, Mutual Respect and Understanding between Peoples adopted by General Assembly resolution 2037 (XX), on 7 December 1965 (see chapter VIII, section G, above).

Acting upon resolution XX on education of youth in the respect for human rights and fundamental freedoms, adopted on 12 May 1968 by the International Conference on Human Rights,[63] the General Assembly resumed the consideration of the question of the role of youth in promoting respect for human rights at its twenty-third session in 1968 and on later occasions. At its twenty-third session it adopted resolution 2447 (XXIII) of 19 December 1968 in which it endorsed the appeal made by the International Conference on Human Rights to States to ensure that all means of education should be employed so that youth might grow up and develop in a spirit of respect for human dignity and equal rights of man without discrimination as to race, colour, language, sex or faith. The General Assembly endorsed the recommendations made by the Conference to States, international organizations and youth organizations. It requested the Economic and Social Council to invite the Commission on Human Rights in co-operation with UNESCO to study the question of the education of youth all over the world with a view to the development of its personality and the strengthening of its respect for the rights of man and fundamental freedoms.

Implementing the request addressed to it by the General Assembly, the Commission on Human Rights took up the question at its twenty-fifth session in 1969 and subsequently considered it at its twenty-sixth (1970) and twenty-seventh (1971) sessions. In resolution 11 (XXVII) the Commission addressed a number of recommendations to Governments, initiated a study on the question of conscientious objection to military service and requested UNESCO to undertake activities aimed at facilitating

[61] General Assembly resolutions 1677 (XVI) and 1710 (XVI) of 18 and 19 December 1961, respectively.

[62] United Nations publication, Sales No. 57.XIV.3.

[63] *Final Act of the International Conference on Human Rights* (United Nations publication, Sales No. E.68.XIV.2), p. 15.

the teaching of human rights in universities and to consider the possible development of an independent scientific discipline of human rights.

In 1969 the General Assembly again dealt with the question, endorsed recommendations of the Economic and Social Council and addressed a series of recommendations to Governments on the subject of youth, its education in the respect for human rights and fundamental freedoms, its problems and needs and its participation in national development (General Assembly resolution 2497 (XXIV)). At the twenty-fifth session in 1970, the General Assembly again adopted a comprehensive resolution on the subject (resolution 2633 (XXV)) and it did so again at the twenty-sixth session in 1971 by adopting resolution 2770 (XXVI).

Within the programme of advisory services in the field of human rights a seminar on the role of youth in the promotion and protection of human rights was held at Belgrade from 2 to 12 June 1970 (ST/TAO/HR/39). The Commission on Human Rights in 1971, in resolution 11 A (XXVII), expressed the hope that further seminars on the same subject would be organized, if possible in all regions of the world, and invited the Secretary-General to explore, through such seminars and other techniques available, ways and means by which youth might be encouraged to participate constructively and to assist in the effective implementation of United Nations principles concerning human rights at the national and international level.

At its twenty-seventh session in 1972 the General Assembly adopted a resolution on channels of communication with youth and international youth organizations (resolution 3022 (XXVII)). In that resolution it, *inter alia*, considered that the United Nations University would serve as one of the important channels of communication with youth and would provide a free forum for the teaching, and for the discussion among young people, of subjects relating to international law, human dignity and human rights, and also to the role of youth in promoting economic and social progress, world peace, understanding and co-operation among peoples. The project of the United Nations University is discussed in section 5 below.

### 4. *International Education Year*

By resolution 2306 (XXII) of 13 December 1967, the General Assembly decided to observe an International Education Year and provisionally designated the year 1970 for that purpose. The Economic and Social Council, in its resolution 1355 (XLV) of 2 August 1968, invited all United Nations agencies, bodies and organs to participate in the preparation of programmes of concerted action in close co-operation with UNESCO. On 19 November 1968 the General Conference of UNESCO adopted a resolution on International Education Year stating that UNESCO would assume primary responsibility for the preparation and execution of an international concerted programme in that field.

At its twenty-third session in resolution 2412 (XXIII), the General Assembly decided to designate 1970 as International Education Year, endorsed the programme of action for the International Education Year set out in resolution 4.2.2. adopted by the General Conference of UNESCO [64] and recommended that States take stock of the situation with respect to education and training in their countries and plan and initiate or stimulate action and studies linked to the objectives and themes of the International Education Year in the context of their preparation for the Second United Nations Development Decade. The implementation of the idea was pursued by the Economic and Social Council and the Secretary-General, in co-operation with UNESCO, submitted a report (E/4707 and Corr.1 and 2 and Add.1 and 2) on the project. In resolution 1436 (XLVII) of 13 July 1969, the Economic and Social Council requested UNESCO and the organizations of the United Nations system concerned to intensify their co-ordinated effort to pursue the objectives of the International Education Year, within the context of the over-all strategy for development during the Second United Nations Development Decade by further specifying concrete means to realize those objectives. The Council considered that International Education Year was above all an occasion for reflection and action by Member States with a view to improving and expanding their educational systems. It recommended to Governments appropriate action.

The General Assembly, at its twenty-fourth session by resolution 2572 (XXIV) of 13 December 1969, took note of the Secretary-General's report and endorsed Economic and Social Council resolution 1436 (XLVII).

In the International Development Strategy for the Second United Nations Development Decade adopted by General Assembly resolution 2626 (XXV) of 24 October 1970 it is proclaimed in paragraph (67) that developing countries will formulate and implement educational programmes taking into account their development needs. Particular emphasis will be placed on teacher-training programmes and on the development of curriculum materials to be used by teachers. Increasing use will be made of modern equipment, mass media and new teaching methods to improve the efficiency of education. Necessary facilities will be provided for improving the literacy and technical competence of groups that are already productively engaged as well as for adult education.

### 5. *Establishment of the United Nations University*

The idea of a United Nations University was brought before the General Assembly for the first time in the Introduction to the Annual Report of the Secretary-General on the Work of the Organization 1968/1969 and was subsequently repeatedly discussed by the General Assembly and by the Economic and Social Council.[65]

After the question had been thoroughly studied also by the United Nations Educational, Scientific and Cultural

---

[64] Resolution 4.2.2 adopted by the Executive Board of UNESCO at its 82nd Session, April/May 1969.

[65] See *Official Records of the General Assembly, Twenty-fourth Session, Supplement No. 1A*, paras. 196-197; General Assembly resolutions 2573 (XXIV), 1969; 2691 (XXV), 1970; 2822 (XXVI), 1971; Economic and Social Council resolution 1731 (LIII), 1972.

Organization, by the United Nations Institute for Training and Research and by a Panel of Experts on the Establishment of an International University, the General Assembly adopted at its twenty-seventh session, on the recommendation of the Economic and Social Council, resolution 2951 (XXVII), by which it decided to establish an international university under the auspices of the United Nations to be known as the United Nations University.

The General Assembly also decided that the United Nations University should be guided by a series of objectives and principles among which are the following: the concept of the University should be that of a system of academic institutions and not of an intergovernmental organization; binding guarantees, under law, of academic freedom and autonomy should be written into the charter of the University; the structure of the University should consist of a programming and co-ordinating central organ and a decentralized system of affiliated institutions, devoted to action-oriented research into the pressing global problems of human survival, development and welfare; the research programmes of the institutions of the University should include, among other matters, coexistence between peoples of differing cultures, tongues and social systems, peaceful relations between States and the maintenance of peace and security, human rights, economic and social change and development, the environment and the proper use of resources, basic scientific research and the application of the results of science and technology in the interests of development.

The General Assembly requested the Secretary-General, in close co-operation with the Director-General of UNESCO, to establish a Founding Committee of the United Nations University to define further the objectives and principles of the University and to draft its charter. The Secretary-General was also requested to commence efforts for raising the necessary funds in order to permit the launching of the University at the earliest possible date. He was also requested to submit to the General Assembly at its twenty-eighth session in 1973, through the Economic and Social Council, the draft charter of the University as well as a report on the implementation of resolution 2951 (XXVII).

# X. PROTECTION OF HUMAN RIGHTS IN ARMED CONFLICTS

The protection of human rights in armed conflicts has been one of the preoccupations of the United Nations and of its various organs in recent years. The present chapter, devoted to these activities, is divided into two sections: section A describes the activities that originated in organs whose main concern is action in the realization of human rights and fundamental freedoms for all; section B deals with efforts made in the matter of humanizing the conduct of armed conflicts in connexion with the handling of political and international security matters, including the regulation and restriction of armaments.

## A. The question of human rights in armed conflicts as dealt with by the organs active in the field of human rights and fundamental freedoms for all

### 1. *The work of the International Conference on Human Rights, 1968*

The fact that the prevention and removal of threats to the peace and the suppression of acts of aggression is the principal responsibility of the United Nations explains the reluctance shown during the first years of the existence of the Organization to deal with questions which presupposed the persistence of war and occurrence of hostilities. The Security Council and the General Assembly, in the exercise of their powers and responsibilities under the Charter, and various subsidiary organs have, of course, repeatedly concerned themselves with concrete questions involving human rights in armed conflicts. However, the initiative for acting on humanizing the effect of armed conflicts from the standpoint of the United Nations human rights programme was taken only at the International Conference on Human Rights, held at Teheran in April/May 1968.

The International Conference on Human Rights in its resolution XXIII,[1] observed that armed conflicts continued to plague humanity; considered that the widespread violence and brutality of the times, including massacres, summary executions, tortures, inhuman treatment of prisoners, killing of civilians in armed conflicts and the use of chemical and biological means of warfare—including napalm bombing—eroded human rights and engendered counter-brutality; expressed the conviction that even during periods of armed conflict, humanitarian principles must prevail; and decided to recommend certain types of action.

The Conference noted that the provisions of the Hague Conventions of 1899 and 1907 were intended to be only a first step in the provision of a code prohibiting or limiting the use of certain methods of warfare and that they were adopted at a time when the present means and methods of warfare did not exist.

It pointed out that the Geneva Protocol of 1925, prohibiting the use of "asphyxiating, poisonous or other gases and of all analogous liquids, materials and devices", had not been universally accepted or applied and might need a revision in the light of modern development. It also expressed the opinion that the Geneva Conventions of 1949 were not sufficiently broad in scope to cover all armed conflicts.

The Conference noted that States parties to the Geneva Conventions of 1949 sometimes failed to appreciate their responsibilities to take steps to ensure respect of these humanitarian rules in all circumstances by other States, even if they were not themselves directly involved in an armed conflict.

The Conference also noted that minority racist or colonial régimes which refused to comply with the decisions of the United Nations and the principles of the Universal Declaration of Human Rights, frequently resorted to executions and inhuman treatment of those who struggled against such régimes. The Conference considered that such persons should be protected against inhuman or brutal treatment and also that such persons, if detained, should be treated as prisoners of war or political prisoners under international law.

The Conference therefore requested the General Assembly to invite the Secretary-General to study:

"(*a*) Steps which could be taken to ensure the better application of existing humanitarian international conventions and rules in all armed conflicts;

"(*b*) The need for additional humanitarian international conventions or for possible revision of existing conventions to ensure the better protection of civilians, prisoners and combatants in all armed conflicts and the prohibition and limitation of the use of certain methods and means of warfare."

The Conference expressed itself in favour of consultation with the International Committee of the Red Cross. It requested that the attention of all States members of the United Nations system be drawn to the existing rules of international law on the subject and that States be urged, pending the adoption of new rules of international law relating to armed conflicts, to ensure the protection of the inhabitants and belligerents in all armed conflicts.

[1] *Final Act of the International Conference on Human Rights* (United Nations publication, Sales No. E.68.XIV.2), p. 18.

The Conference called on all States which had not yet done so to become parties to the Hague Conventions of 1899 and 1907, the Geneva Protocol of 1925 and the Geneva Conventions of 1949.

### 2. *Action by the General Assembly at its twenty-third session in 1968*

At its twenty-third session the General Assembly, in its resolution 2444 (XXIII) of 19 December 1948, took note of resolution XXIII adopted by the International Conference on Human Rights. The General Assembly affirmed that the provisions of that resolution needed to be implemented effectively as soon as possible. In its resolution 2444 (XXIII) the General Assembly affirmed a resolution adopted at the International Conference of the Red Cross, held at Vienna in 1965, which laid down a series of principles for observance by all governmental and other authorities for action in armed conflicts.

The General Assembly affirmed the following principles:

"(*a*) That the rights of the parties to a conflict to adopt means of injuring the enemy is not unlimited;

"(*b*) That it is prohibited to launch attacks against the civilian populations as such;

"(*c*) That distinction must be made at all times between persons taking part in the hostilities and members of the civilian population to the effect that the latter be spared as much as possible."

The General Assembly invited the Secretary-General, in consultation with the International Committee of the Red Cross and other appropriate international organizations, to study steps which could be taken to secure the better application of existing humanitarian international conventions and rules in all armed conflicts, and the need for additional humanitarian international conventions or for other appropriate legal instruments to ensure the better protection of civilians, prisoners and combatants in all armed conflicts and the prohibition and limitation of the use of certain methods and means of warfare.

### 3. *First report by the Secretary-General and action taken by the General Assembly at its twenty-fourth session in 1969*

At its twenty-fourth session in 1969 the General Assembly had before it the first report of the Secretary-General (A/7720) on respect for human rights in armed conflicts, which it had requested in its resolution 2444 (XXIII) of 1968. The Secretary-General's report presented to the General Assembly an historical survey of international instruments of a humanitarian character relating to armed conflicts, beginning with the Geneva Convention of 1864, the Declaration of St. Petersburg of 1868 and many other instruments including the Hague Conventions of 1899 and 1907 already referred to, the International Convention for the Amelioration of the Condition of the Wounded and Sick in Armies in the Field of 1906, the Geneva Protocol of 1925, the 1929 Conventions on the Wounded and Sick and on Prisoners of War, the Geneva Conventions of 1949 and the Hague Convention for the Protection of Cultural Property in the Event of Armed Conflict of 1954.

The study also referred to more recent instruments in the field of armament limitations such as the Treaty Banning Nuclear Weapon Tests in the Atmosphere, in Outer Space and Under Water of 1963, the Treaty on Principles Governing the Activities of States in the Exploration and Use of Outer Space of 1967 and the Treaty on the Non-proliferation of Nuclear Weapons of 1968.

The Secretary-General's study also examined the relations between the Geneva Conventions of 1949 and the United Nations human rights instruments, and raised the question of the humanitarian law applicable in conflicts not of an international character.

The Secretary-General's study further dealt with steps to secure respect of humanitarian principles in all armed conflicts through the better application and reaffirmation of existing conventions and the adoption of additional legal instruments, with the question of penal sanctions for violations of humanitarian rules and with other measures.

The principal aspects considered from that point of view were the protection of civilians including the planning and co-ordination of relevant action, the protection of prisoners, guerrilla warfare, internal armed conflicts, the protection of combatants and the prohibition and limitation of the use of certain methods and means of warfare. The study also examined problems of international assistance in, and supervision of, the application of humanitarian measures.

In its resolution 2597 (XXIV) of 16 December 1969, the General Assembly noted the Secretary-General's report with appreciation and noted also relevant resolutions concerning human rights in armed conflicts adopted at the twenty-first International Conference of the Red Cross. It requested the Secretary-General to continue the study, giving special attention to the need for protection of the rights of civilians and combatants in conflicts arising from the struggles of peoples under colonial and foreign rule for liberation and self-determination, and to the better application of existing humanitarian international conventions and rules to such conflicts. The Secretary-General was again requested to consult and co-operate closely with the International Committee for the Red Cross. In its resolution 2597 (XXIV), the General Assembly also decided to transmit the report of the Secretary-General to the Commission on Human Rights and to the Economic and Social Council.

Pursuant to the decision taken by the Commission on Human Rights [2] at its twenty-sixth session and approved by the Economic and Social Council at its resumed forty-eighth session in 1970, the observations of the members of the Commission and of the Social Committee on the report of the Secretary-General (A/7720) were transmitted to the General Assembly.

---

[2] *Official Records of the Economic and Social Council, Forty-eighth Session, Supplement No. 5* (E/4816), chap. XXIII.

4. *Second report by the Secretary-General and action taken by the General Assembly at its twenty-fifth session in 1970*

In 1970 the Secretary-General, pursuant to the request addressed to him in General Assembly resolution 2957 (XXIV), submitted to the Assembly at its twenty-fifth session a second report on respect for human rights in armed conflicts (A/8053). This report addressed itself to the subjects which had been in the forefront of the discussions of the General Assembly, the Economic and Social Council and the Commission on Human Rights.

It examined the protection of human rights in armed conflicts which derived from the international instruments on human rights adopted under the auspices of the United Nations. The report pointed out that there were instances in which the protection ensured by the human rights instruments of the United Nations was more far-reaching than that derived from the Geneva Conventions and other humanitarian instruments. It emphasized, in particular, that the International Covenant on Civil and Political Rights contained provisions from which derogation was not permitted. These were intended to apply at all times and everywhere, in time of peace as well as in time of war and to the full range of conceivable conflicts, irrespective of whether or not they were of an international character. The Covenant and other human rights instruments of the United Nations applied to all individuals subject to qualifications less restrictive than those provided for under some of the Geneva Conventions of 1949. Also as to substance, in many respects the protection to be derived from the Covenant was wider and more extensive.

The above-mentioned general statements of the report were elaborated in greater detail in annex I, entitled "General norms concerning respect for human rights in their applicability to armed conflicts".

The Secretary-General's second report dealt in considerable detail with the protection of civilians, with the protection of combatants in international armed conflicts. with the protection of prisoners, with the prohibition and limitation of certain methods and means of warfare and with non-international armed conflicts and guerrilla warfare.

Special emphasis was placed in a separate chapter on the protection of civilians and combatants in conflicts arising from the struggles of peoples under colonial and foreign rule for liberation and self-determination. The report considered the international supervision of the application of humanitarian laws. It also emphasized the necessity of publicity, dissemination and teaching.

The Secretary-General's second report contained a large number of observations, suggestions and recommendations on the whole field of the protection of human rights in armed conflict. both *de lege lata* and *de lege ferenda.* These included considerations relating to the establishment of civilian sanctuaries concerning the prohibition of the use of certain weapons such as chemical and bacteriological weapons, suggestions for the possible extension of the scope of article 3 of the Geneva Conventions of 1949 containing rules applicable in conflicts not of an international character, observations on the persons to be protected in internal conflicts and in situations concerning guerrilla warfare, on conditions for privileged belligerency and the applicability of Geneva Convention 4 (on civilian persons) to freedom fighters.

At its twenty-fifth session, the General Assembly considered extensively the question of human rights in armed conflicts and on 9 December 1970 adopted five resolutions relating to it.

In its resolution 2673 (XXV) the General Assembly initiated work on a draft international agreement ensuring the protection of journalists engaged in dangerous missions. The action taken pursuant to this resolution will be described in greater detail below.

In its resolution 2674 (XXV) the General Assembly solemnly reaffirmed the necessity to avert the unleashing of agressive wars and armed conflicts and condemned the actions of countries which, in flagrant violation of the Charter, continue to conduct aggressive wars and defy the generally accepted principles of the Geneva Protocol of 1925 and the Geneva Conventions of 1949. It considered that States violating these instruments should be condemned and held responsible to the world community. The resolution also affirmed that the participants in resistance movements and freedom fighters should be treated in case of their arrest as prisoners of war. It also strongly condemned bombardements of civilian populations and the use of chemical and bacteriological weapons.

In its resolution 2675 (XXV), the General Assembly affirmed the following basic principles for the protection of civilian populations in armed conflicts:

"1. Fundamental human rights, as accepted in international law and laid down in international instruments, continue to apply fully in situations of armed conflict.

"2. In the conduct of military operations during armed conflicts, a distinction must be made at all times between persons actively taking part in the hostilities and civilian populations.

"3. In the conduct of military operations, every effort should be made to spare civilian populations from the ravages of war, and all necessary precautions should be taken to avoid injury, loss or damage to civilian populations.

"4. Civilian populations as such should not be the object of military operations.

"5. Dwellings and other installations that are used only by civilian populations should not be the object of military operations.

"6. Places or areas designated for the sole protection of civilians, such as hospital zones or similar refuges, should not be the object of military operations.

"7. Civilian populations, or individual members thereof, should not be the object of reprisals, forcible transfers or other assaults on their integrity.

"8. The provision of international relief to civilian populations is in conformity with the humanitarian principles of the Charter of the United Nations, the Universal Declaration of Human Rights and other international instruments in the field of human rights. The Declaration of Principles for International Humanitarian Relief to the Civilian Population in

Disaster Situations, as laid down in resolution XXVI adopted by the twenty-first International Conference of the Red Cross, shall apply in situations of armed conflict, and all parties to a conflict should make every effort to facilitate this application."

In its resolution 2676 (XXV) the General Assembly addressed itself in particular to the treatment of prisoners of war. The General Assembly noted a relevant resolution adopted by the twenty-first International Conference of the Red Cross held at Istanbul in 1969. Considering that the direct repatriation of seriously wounded and seriously sick prisoners of war and the repatriation or internment in a neutral country of prisoners of war who have undergone a long period of captivity constituted important aspects of human rights as advanced and preserved under the Geneva Conventions of 1949 and the Charter of the United Nations, the General Assembly called upon all parties to any armed conflict to comply with the terms and provisions of the Geneva Convention relative to the Treatment of Prisoners of War, of 12 August 1949, in order to ensure the humane treatment of all persons entitled to the protection of the Convention and, *inter alia*, to permit regular inspection, in accordance with the Convention, of all places of detention of prisoners of war by a protecting Power or humanitarian organization such as the International Committee of the Red Cross. It endorsed the continuing efforts of the International Committee of the Red Cross to secure the effective application of the Geneva Convention of 1949, urged compliance with article 109 of the Geneva Convention of 1949, which requires the repatriation of seriously wounded and seriously sick prisoners of war and which provides for agreements with a view to the direct repatriation or internment in a neutral country of able-bodied prisoners of war who have undergone a long period of captivity, and urged that combatants in all armed conflicts not covered by article 4 of the Geneva Convention of 1949 be accorded the same humane treatment defined by the principles of international law applied to prisoners of war.

In its resolution 2677 (XXV), the General Assembly laid down a programme for further work in this field. In particular it welcomed the decision of the International Committee of the Red Cross to convene in 1971 a conference on the reaffirmation and development of international humanitarian law applicable to armed conflicts, to be attended by government experts. The General Assembly expressed the view that one or more plenipotentiary diplomatic conferences might be convened in order to adopt international legal instruments for the reaffirmation and development of humanitarian law applicable to armed conflicts. It emphasized the importance of continued close co-operation between the United Nations and the International Committee of the Red Cross

Pursuant to General Assembly resolution 2673 (XXV) the Commission on Human Rights considered at its twenty-seventh session in 1971 the question of a draft international agreement ensuring the protection of journalists engaged in dangerous missions.[3]

[3] See *Official Records of the Economic and Social Council, Fiftieth Session, Supplement No. 4* (E/4949), chap. IX and chap. XIX, resolution 15 (XXVII).

5. *Third report of the Secretary-General and action taken by the General Assembly at its twenty-sixth session in 1971*

The third report of the Secretary-General (A/8370 and Add.1) on respect for human rights in armed conflicts, submitted to the General Assembly at its twenty-sixth session, was mainly devoted to reporting on the work of the Conference of Government Experts on the Reaffirmation and Development of International Humanitarian Law Applicable in Armed Conflicts which had been held at Geneva in May and June 1971.

The Secretary-General's report also contained the text of the two draft protocols adopted by the Conference of Government Experts: the draft Protocol on the Protection of the Wounded and Sick, additional to the Geneva Convention relative to the Protection of Civilian Persons in Time of War of 12 August 1949; and the draft Protocol on the Protection of the Wounded and Sick, additional to article 3 of the four Geneva Conventions of 1949, relative to armed conflicts not international in character.

At its twenty-sixth session in 1971 the General Assembly again adopted a number of resolutions on respect for human rights in armed conflicts. Resolution 2854 (XXVI) of 20 December 1971 dealt with the protection of journalists engaged in dangerous missions in areas of armed conflict (see section 7 below).

In resolution 2852 (XXVI) of 20 December 1971 the General Assembly expressed its determination to continue its efforts to achieve better application of existing rules relating to armed conflicts as well as the reaffirmation and development of these rules. The General Assembly invited the International Committee of the Red Cross to continue the work that was begun with the assistance of government experts in 1971, and taking into account all relevant United Nations resolutions on human rights in armed conflicts to devote special attention to:

"(*a*) The need to ensure better application of existing rules relating to armed conflicts, particularly the Hague Conventions of 1899 and 1907, the Geneva Protocol of 1925 and the Geneva Conventions of 1949, including the need for strengthening the system of protecting Powers contained in such instruments;

"(*b*) The need for a reaffirmation and development of relevant rules, as well as other measures to improve the protection of the civilian population during armed conflicts, including legal restraints and restrictions on certain methods of warfare and weapons that have proved particularly perilous to civilians, and also arrangements for humanitarian relief;

"(*c*) The need to evolve norms designed to increase the protection of persons struggling against colonial and alien domination, foreign occupation and racist régimes;

"(*d*) The need for development of the rules concerning the status, protection and humane treatment of combatants in international and non-international armed conflicts and the question of guerrilla warfare;

"(*e*) The need for additional rules regarding the protection of the wounded and the sick".

The General Assembly also requested the Secretary-General to prepare as soon as possible a report on napalm and other incendiary weapons.

Addressing itself to the work of the 1971 Conference of Government Experts, the General Assembly in resolution 2853 (XXVI) of 29 December 1971, welcomed the progress made as regards:

"(*a*) Protection of the wounded and the sick;

"(*b*) Protection of victims of non-international armed conflicts;

"(*c*) Rules applicable in guerrilla warfare;

"(*d*) Protection of civilian population against dangers of hostilities;

"(*e*) Strengthening of the guarantees afforded by international humanitarian law for non-military civil defence organizations;

"(*f*) Rules relative to the behaviour of combatants;

"(*g*) Measures intended to reinforce the implementation, in armed conflicts, of existing international humanitarian law;"

The General Assembly also expressed in resolution 2853 (XXVI) the hope that the second session of the Conference of Government Experts on the Reaffirmation and Development of International Humanitarian Law applicable in Armed Conflicts would make recommendations for the further development of international humanitarian law in that field, including, as appropriate, draft protocols to the Geneva Conventions of 1949, for subsequent consideration at one or more plenipotentiary diplomatic conferences. It also called upon States parties to the existing international instruments to review, as a matter of priority, any reservations they might have made to those instruments.

### 6. *Developments in 1972*

In September 1972 the Secretary-General provided the General Assembly with a survey (A/8781 and Corr.1) of the results of the second (1972) session of the Conference of Government Experts and of some other relevant developments. The second session of the Conference of Experts was held at Geneva in May-June 1972. The Secretary-General's report contained an analysis of the comprehensive proceedings of the Conference and the text of a draft Additional Protocol to the four Geneva Conventions of 1949, part II (Wounded, sick and shipwrecked persons) which had been submitted by Commission I of the Conference to the plenary session of the Conference.

In the course of the debates of the Conference, many government experts made reference to the first two reports of the Secretary-General on respect for human rights in armed conflicts (A/7720 and A/8052), and several experts expressed support for various observations and suggestions contained in those reports. The Director of the Division of Human Rights, representing the Secretary-General, elaborated on a number of those suggestions. He said, in particular, that in the work required to adapt the basic rules of international humanitarian law to current conditions in armed conflicts, full account should be taken of the Universal Declaration of Human Rights and other international instruments adopted by the United Nations, general rules relating to human rights which, in accordance with their provisions, were applicable in time of war as in time of peace. With regard to the strengthening of the procedures of the implementation and supervision of international humanitarian law, the representative of the Secretary-General emphasized that it was important to make the system of protecting Powers effective as far as possible, particularly by preparing in peace-time for its smooth operation. In reply to some observations made during the debate, the representative of the Secretary-General pointed out that the proposed protocols being considered by the Conference would not limit the possibilities for action of United Nations organs under the Charter, which, by its very terms, must prevail over any other international agreement.

In addition to the Secretary-General's report, the General Assembly took cognizance of the report prepared by the International Committee of the Red Cross on the work of the Conference of Government Experts.

In its resolution 3032 (XXVII) of 18 December 1972, the General Assembly expressed appreciation to the International Committee of the Red Cross for its dedicated efforts to promote the reaffirmation and development of international humanitarian law applicable in armed conflicts and welcomed the progress achieved at the second session of the Conference of Government Experts.

The General Assembly noted with concern, nevertheless, that agreement had not emerged among government experts on drafts concerning a number of fundamental issues, such as:

"(*a*) Methods to ensure a better application of existing rules relating to armed conflicts;

"(*b*) Definitions of military objectives and protected objects, in order to counter the tendency in armed conflicts to regard ever growing categories of objects as permissible targets for attack;

"(*c*) Definitions of protected persons and combatants, responsive to the need for improved protection of civilians and of combatants in modern armed conflicts;

"(*d*) The question of guerrilla warfare;

"(*e*) Prohibition of use of weapons and methods of warfare which indiscriminately affect civilians and combatants;

"(*f*) Prohibition or restriction of the use of specific weapons which are deemed to cause unnecessary suffering;

"(*g*) Rules facilitating humanitarian relief in armed conflicts;

"(*h*) Definition of those armed conflicts of a non-international character which should be subject to rules additional to those contained in the Geneva Conventions of 1949."

The General Assembly considered that substantial progress on fundamental issues such as those enumerated above was indispensable if the efforts to supplement international humanitarian law by new rules were to become significant for the alleviation of the suffering brought by modern armed conflicts.

It welcomed the readiness of the Swiss Federal Council, as communicated to the Secretary-General, to convoke a diplomatic conference on the reaffirmation and development of international humanitarian law applicable in armed conflicts.

It expressed the belief that the further preparations for that conference as well as its organization must be such that substantial progress be achieved on fundamental issues which were as yet unresolved.

The General Assembly urged all Governments and invited the International Committee of the Red Cross to continue to seek through consultations to achieve a rapprochement in the positions of Governments to ensure that the diplomatic conference envisaged would adopt rules which would mark substantial progress on fundamental legal issues connected with modern armed conflicts and which would contribute significantly to the alleviation of the suffering brought about by such conflicts. The Assembly decided to include in the provisional agenda of its twenty-eighth session the item entitled "Human rights in armed conflicts: respect for human rights in armed conflicts".

### 7. *The question of the protection of journalists engaged in dangerous missions in areas of armed conflict*

As already indicated, the initiative to provide for the protection of journalists engaged in dangerous missions was taken by the General Assembly at its twenty-fifth session, when in resolution 2673 (XXV) it stated that it was essential for the United Nations to obtain complete information concerning armed conflicts and that journalists, whatever their nationality, had an important role to play in that regard. The General Assembly noted with regret that journalists engaged in missions in areas where an armed conflict was taking place sometimes suffered as a result of their professional duty. The General Assembly listed the provisions of the Geneva Conventions of 1949, in the protection of which journalists partake, but added that these provisions did not cover some categories of journalists engaged in dangerous missions and did not correspond to their present needs. Convinced of the need for an additional humanitarian international instrument to ensure the better protection of journalists engaged in dangerous missions, the General Assembly in resolution 2673 (XXV) invited the Economic and Social Council to request the Commission on Human Rights to consider the possiblity of preparing a draft international agreement on the question which would provide, *inter alia*, for the creation of a universally recognized and guaranteed identification document.

The Commission on Human Rights accordingly considered this question at its twenty-seventh session in 1971 when it had before it a preliminary draft international convention on the protection of journalists engaged in dangerous missions presented by one delegation (E/CN.4/L.1149) and a revised text thereof co-sponsored by six delegations (E/CN.4/L.1149/Rev.1).

In its resolution 15 (XXVII) [4] the Commission recommended that the Economic and Social Council consider the transmission of the preliminary draft convention to the General Assembly, to States members of the Organizations of the United Nations system and—through the International Committee of the Red Cross—to the parties of the Geneva Conventions of 1949 as well as to the Intergovernmental Conference of Experts of the International Committee of the Red Cross.

The Secretary-General was requested to establish a group of experts to consider the appropriate composition for an international professional committee for the protection of journalists engaged in dangerous missions and to consider the conditions, procedure and criteria for the issue and withdrawal of the safe-conduct card.

The Working Group of Experts established under Commission resolution 15 (XXVIII) met in September 1971 and submitted in its report (A/8438) a number of conclusions and recommendations concerning the contemplated International Professional Committee for the protection of journalists engaged in dangerous missions and the issuance, withdrawal and recognition of the contemplated safe-conduct card and also a draft Protocol relating to the composition and functions of the International Professional Committee.

At its fiftieth session the Economic and Social Council (resolution 1597 (L) of 21 May 1971) transmitted to the General Assembly the preliminary draft convention on the protection of journalists and the pertinent documentation.

At its twenty-sixth session the General Assembly dealt with the protection of journalists engaged in dangerous missions in its resolution 2854 (XXVI) of 20 December 1971. It expressed the belief that it was necessary to adopt a convention providing for the protection of journalists engaged in dangerous missions in areas of armed conflict and invited the Commission on Human Rights, through the Economic and Social Council, to consider as a matter of priority the preliminary draft convention, taking also into consideration the draft convention submitted by one Government, the working paper submitted by another, the observations of Governments, and subsequent documents including the draft protocol prepared by the Working Group. It arranged also for the submission of the text to the Conference of Government Experts at its second session, convened in 1972 by the International Committee of the Red Cross.

The Commission on Human Rights at its twenty-eighth session in March/April 1972 approved as a basis for further work the draft articles of an international convention on the protection of journalists engaged in dangerous professional missions in areas of armed conflict.[5] It also decided to transmit the draft articles to the second session of the Conference of Government Experts convened by the International Committee of the Red Cross in order that they might be brought to the notice

[4] *Official Records of the Economic and Social Council, Fiftieth Session, Supplement No. 4* (E/4949), chap. XIX.

[5] *Ibid., Fifty-second session, Supplement No. 7* (E/5113), chap. XIII, resolution 6 (XXVIII), annex.

of the Conference for its observations. On the recommendation of the Commission, the Economic and Social Council, by resolution 1690 (LII), transmitted to the General Assembly the draft articles and relevant other documentation.

The draft convention annexed to resolution 6 (XXVIII) of the Commission on Human Rights provides, *inter alia*, that the States parties to it and, as far as possible, all the States parties to the conflict in the territories of a State party, having identified a journalist as one who holds a card certifying his status, shall do all that is necessary to protect him from the danger of death or injury or from any other danger inherent in the conflict; inform him to the extent compatible with military requirements of the areas and circumstances in which he may be exposed to danger; recognize, in case of internment, that the relevant regulations for the treatment of internees set forth in the Fourth Geneva Convention of 1949 shall apply; ensure that if a journalist who holds a card is killed or injured, falls seriously ill, is reported missing, or is arrested or imprisoned, the information concerning him will be communicated forthwith to his next of kin or to the State party that issued the card or be made public. The application of the Convention shall have no legal effect under international law on the situation of the Parties to a conflict; nor shall it affect the sovereignty of States in so far as concerns national laws with respect to the crossing of frontiers or the movement or residence of aliens.

At its twenty-seventh session in 1972, the General Assembly (Third Committee) conducted a thorough and extensive examination of the draft Convention before it. Many amendments were proposed and after an informal working group had studied the various texts with a view to reconciling the differences, a number of delegations submitted a new text of the revised draft articles (A/C.3/L.1963/Rev.1) to which additional amendments were also proposed. Eventually, on the recommendation of the Third Committee, the General Assembly, at its 2117th plenary meeting on 12 December 1972, decided to include the item "Human rights in armed conflicts: protection of journalists engaged in dangerous missions in areas of armed conflict" in the provisional agenda of its twenty-eighth session and to consider it as a matter of high priority.[6]

### B. The question of human rights in the light of instruments dealing with disarmament, limitation of armaments and problems of weapons technology

In section A above, information was given on measures initiated by those organs of the United Nations whose main responsibility is United Nations action in the field of human rights. Measures intended to protect human rights in armed conflicts have also been achieved in the context of the work of the political organs of the United Nations. Some of the important measures in this category will be described ih the paragraphs that follow.

#### 1. *Declaration on the Prohibition of the Use of Nuclear and Thermo-nuclear Weapons of 1961*

At its sixteenth session in 1961 the General Assembly adopted by a majority vote the Declaration on the Prohibition of the Use of Nuclear and Thermo-nuclear Weapons (resolution 1653 (XVI) of 24 November 1961). In that document the General Assembly declared:

"(*a*) The use of nuclear and thermo-nuclear weapons is contrary to the spirit, letter and aims of the United Nations and, as such, a direct violation of the Charter of the United Nations;

"(*b*) The use of nuclear and thermo-nuclear weapons would exceed even the scope of war and cause indiscriminate suffering and destruction to mankind and civilization and, as such, is contrary to the rules of international law and to the laws of humanity;

"(*c*) The use of nuclear and thermo-nuclear weapons is a war directed not against an enemy or enemies alone but also against mankind in general, since the peoples of the world not involved in such a war will be subjected to all the evils generated by the use of such weapons;

"(*d*) Any State using nuclear and thermo-nuclear weapons is to be considered as violating the Charter of the United Nations, as acting contrary to the laws of humanity and as committing a crime against mankind and civilization."

#### 2. *Treaty Banning Nuclear Weapon Tests in the Atmosphere, in Outer Space and Under Water of 1963*

In 1963 the Treaty Banning Nuclear Weapon Tests in the Atmosphere, in Outer Space and Under Water was signed. It entered into force on 10 October 1963. This Treaty was not concluded under direct United Nations auspices. It was noted with approval by the General Assembly in resolution 1910 (XVIII).

In the preamble to the Treaty the parties state that they seek to achieve the discontinuance of all test explosions of nuclear weapons for all time, are determined to continue negotiations to that end, and desire to put an end to the contamination of man's environment by radioactive substances. In the Treaty itself, each of the parties undertakes to prohibit, to prevent and not to carry out any nuclear weapon test explosion or any other nuclear explosion at any place under its jurisdiction or control in the atmosphere, in outer space or under water.

#### 3. *Treaty on Principles Governing the Activities of States in the Exploration and Use of Outer Space, including the Moon and Other Celestial Bodies of 1967*

By resolution 2222 (XXI) of 19 December 1966, the General Assembly commended the Treaty on Principles Governing the Activities of States in the Exploration and Use of Outer Space, including the Moon and Other Celestial Bodies. In that Treaty the States Parties undertake not to place in orbit around the earth any objects carrying nuclear weapons or any other kinds of weapons of mass destruction, not to install such weapons on celestial bodies, or station weapons in outer space in any other manner. The moon and other celestial bodies are to be used exclusively for peaceful purposes.

---

[6] Report of the Secretary-General on human rights in armed conflicts, protection of journalists engaged in dangerous missions in areas of armed conflict (A/8777 and Add.1 and 2).

### 4. *Treaty on the Non-Proliferation of Nuclear Weapons of 1968*

By resolution 2373 (XXII) of 12 June 1968 the General Assembly commended the Treaty on the Non-Proliferation of Nuclear Weapons. By that Treaty each nuclear-weapon State party undertakes not to transfer to any recipient whatsoever nuclear weapons or other nuclear explosive devices or control over such weapons or explosive devices, directly or indirectly; and in no way to assist, encourage or induce any non-nuclear-weapon State to manufacture or otherwise acquire nuclear weapons or other nuclear explosive devices.

### 5. *Treaty on the Prohibition of the Emplacement of Nuclear Weapons and Other Weapons of Mass Destruction on the Sea-Bed and the Ocean Floor and in the Subsoil Thereof*

The Treaty on the Prohibition of the Emplacement of Nuclear Weapons and Other Weapons of Mass Destruction on the Sea-Bed and the Ocean Floor and in the Subsoil Thereof was commended by the General Assembly in resolution 2660 (XXV) of 7 December 1970, and opened for signature on 11 February 1971. Parties to the Treaty are bound not to emplant or emplace nuclear weapons or other weapons of mass destruction—or facilities designed for launching or testing of such weapons—on the sea-bed and the ocean floor and in the subsoil thereof beyond the outer limit of the sea-bed zone.

The prohibitions do not apply either to the coastal State or to the sea-bed beneath its territorial waters.

### 6. *Chemical and bacteriological weapons*

Over many years repeatedly the General Assembly has dealt with the question of chemical and bacteriological (biological) weapons and has strongly recommended the accession of States not yet parties to it to the Protocol for the Prohibition of the Use in War of Asphyxiating, Poisonous or Other Gases, and of Bacteriological Methods of Warfare, signed at Geneva on 17 June 1925.[7]

At the request of the General Assembly the Secretary-General engaged in studies concerning chemical and bacteriological (biological) weapons and the effects or their possible use, the most comprehensive and recent one being the Secretary-General's report submitted in 1969.[8]

It was only at the twenty-sixth session of the General Assembly in 1971 that the Assembly was in a position to consider and to commend, by its resolution 2826 (XXVI) of 16 December 1971, the Convention on the Prohibition of the Development, Production and Stockpiling of Bacteriological (Biological) and Toxin Weapons and on Their Destruction.

By this Convention each State Party

"Undertakes never in any circumstances to develop, produce, stockpile or otherwise acquire or retain:

"(1) Microbial or other biological agents, or toxins whatever their origin or method of production, of types and in quantities that have no justification for prophylatic, protective or other peaceful purposes;

"(2) Weapons, equipment or means of delivery designed to use such agents or toxins for hostile purposes or in armed conflict."

Each State party further

"undertakes to destroy, or to divert to peaceful purposes, as soon as possible but not later than nine months after the entry into force of the Convention, all agents, toxins, weapons, equipment and means of delivery specified in article I of the Convention, which are in its possession or under its jurisdiction or control. In implementing the provisions of this article all necessary safety precautions shall be observed to protect populations and the environment."

#### *Report on napalm and other incendiary weapons*

In his report (A/8052) to the General Assembly at the twenty-fifth session, referred to above, the Secretary-General recalled that in its resolution XXIII the International Conference on Human Rights had referred to the question of napalm bombing and had added that the question would call for study. The idea of undertaking and pursuing a study of the legality or otherwise of napalm bombing had received the support of a number of experts consulted by the Secretary-General and of those of the International Committee of the Red Cross. The Secretary-General's report added that if the General Assembly accepted the merit of such a study, it might consider requesting the Secretary-General to prepare, with the assistance of qualified consultant experts, a report on napalm weapons and the effects of their possible use (A/8052, para. 126). In its resolution 2852 (XXVI) of 20 December 1971 the General Assembly, on the report of the Third Committee, requested the Secretary-General, in line with paragraph 126 of his report, to prepare as soon as possible a report on napalm and other incendiary weapons and all aspects of their possible use.

The Secretary-General's report entitled *Napalm and Other Incendiary Weapons and All Aspects of their Possible Use*[9] was submitted to the General Assembly at its twenty-seventh session. The report concluded that the massive spread of fire through incendiary weapons was largely indiscriminate in its effects on military and civilian targets and that a number of injuries, whether directly from the action of incendiary or as a result of fires initiated by them, were intensely painful and required exceptional resources for their medical treatment far beyond the reach of most countries (paras. 186-187 of the report, A/8803/Rev.1). The General Assembly deplored the use of napalm and other incendiary weapons in all armed conflicts and commended the report to the attention of all Governments and peoples.

---

[7] League of Nations, *Treaty Series*, vol. XCIV, 1929, No. 2138.

[8] United Nations publication, Sales No. E.69.I.24.

[9] United Nations publication, Sales No. E.73.I.3.

## XI. HUMAN RIGHTS AND SCIENTIFIC AND TECHNOLOGICAL DEVELOPMENTS

Paragraph 18 of the Proclamation of Teheran,[1] adopted by the International Conference on Human Rights, Teheran, on 13 May 1968, reads:

> "While recent scientific discoveries and technological advances have opened vast prospects for economic, social and cultural progress, such developments may nevertheless endanger the rights and freedoms of individuals and will require continuing attention."

The Conference dealt with the question of human rights and scientific and technological developments at greater length in its resolution XI.[2]

On the basis of this conference resolution, the General Assembly adopted resolution 2450 (XXIII) of 19 December 1968, paragraph 1 of which invited the Secretary-General to undertake, with the assistance, among others, of the Advisory Committee on the Application of Science and Technology to Development and in co-operation with the executive heads of competent specialized agencies, a study of the problems in connexion with human rights arising from developments in science and technology, in particular from the following standpoints: (*a*) respect for the privacy of individuals and the integrity and sovereignty of nations in the light of advances in recording and other techniques; (*b*) protection of the human personality and its physical and intellectual integrity, in the light of advances in biology, medicine and biochemistry; (*c*) uses of electronics which might affect the rights of the person and the limits which should be placed on such uses in a democratic society; and (*d*) more generally, the balance which should be established between scientific and technological progress and the intellectual, spiritual, cultural and moral advancement of humanity.

At the same time the General Assembly requested the Secretary-General to prepare, on a preliminary basis, a report comprising a summary account of studies already made or in progress on the aforementioned subjects, emanating in particular from governmental and intergovernmental sources, the specialized agencies and the competent non-governmental organizations, and a draft programme of work which might be undertaken in fields in which subsequent surveys would be necessary for the attainment of the objectives of the present resolution 2450 (XXIII).

At its twenty-sixth session in 1970, the Commission on Human Rights received the preliminary report (E/CN.4/1028 and Add.1-4) requested by the General Assembly. At that session, however, it did not have the time necessary to study the substantial documentation compiled and examined in that report (Commission on Human Rights resolution 14 (XXVI)). The Commission proceeded to a thorough examination of the whole problem at its twenty-seventh session in 1971, when in its resolution 10 (XXVII) it laid down further details concerning the scope of the study to be undertaken. These are set forth below.

It may be noted that existing international instruments of the United Nations deal with two aspects connected with the problem of human rights in scientific and technological developments.

Article 12 of the Universal Declaration of Human Rights provides that no one shall be subjected to arbitrary interference with his privacy, family, home or correspondence. It also provides that everyone has the right to the protection of the law against such interference. Similarly, article 17 of the International Covenant on Civil and Political Rights is to the effect that no one shall be subjected to arbitrary or unlawful interference with his privacy, family, home or correspondence. Under article 17 of the Covenant everyone has the right to the protection of the law against such interference or attacks.

Article 7 of the International Covenant on Civil and Political Rights, which prohibits torture and cruel, inhuman or degrading treatment or punishment, deals in this context with medical or scientific experimentation in the following words: "In particular, no one shall be subjected without his free consent to medical or scientific experimentation."

In its resolution 10 (XXVII) of 1971, referred to above, the Commission on Human Rights recognized the need during the Second United Nations Development Decade to concentrate its attention on the most important and basic problems of protecting human rights and fundamental freedoms in the context of scientific and technological progress, and in particular on: (*a*) protection of human rights in the economic, social and cultural fields in accordance with the structure and resources of States and the scientific and technological level they have reached, as well as protection of the right to work in conditions of the automation and mechanization of production; (*b*) the use of scientific and technological developments to foster respect for human rights and the legitimate interests of other peoples and respect for generally recognized moral standards and standards of international law; and (*c*) prevention of the use of scientific and technological achievements to restrict fundamental democratic rights and freedoms. The Commission requested the Secretary-General to continue his study of the consequences, for the observance of human rights, of current developments in science and technology, taking into account also

[1] *Final Act of the International Conference on Human Rights* (United Nations publication, Sales No. E.68.XIV.2), p. 3.

[2] *Ibid.*, p. 12.

the possibility of using them to improve living conditions and the enjoyment of economic, social and cultural rights. The Commission further requested the Secretary-General, bearing in mind the information received from Governments and in the light of the discussions at the twenty-seventh session of the Commission, to supplement his studies, so as to present a balanced picture of all basic problems arising in connexion with the exercise of human rights and fundamental freedoms in conditions of scientific and technological progress, and to submit to the Commission one or more reports, in fields where sufficient documentation and studies were available, which could be used as a basis for exploring the possibility of preparing international instruments designed to strengthen the protection of the human rights proclaimed in the Universal Declaration of Human Rights.

The first report of the Secretary-General on the impact of recent scientific and technological developments on economic, social and cultural rights is contained in document E/CN.4/1084. It deals with the right to food and the right to clothing as aspects of the rights to an adequate standard of living laid down by article 25 of the Universal Declaration of Human Rights. In connexion with each of the two rights, the report describes existing international standards, the favourable impact of recent scientific and technological developments and the problems created thereby, and legislation and other standards and guidelines.

Besides the relevant documentation submitted at its twenty-eighth session (E/CN.4/1083 and Add.1 and 2 and E/CN.4/1084), the Commission on Human Rights is to have before it at its twenty-ninth session in 1973 a preliminary report by the Secretary-General on the impact on recent scientific and technological developments on certain further economic, social and cultural rights, namely the rights to work, to just and favourable conditions of work, to favourable remuneration, to equal pay for equal work, to form and join trade unions, and to housing (E/CN.4/1115).

In regard to the impact of scientific and technological developments on civil and political rights the Commission on Human Rights, at its twenty-ninth session in 1973, is to have before it the report of the Secretary-General under paragraph 1 (*a*) of Assembly resolution 2450 (XXIII) dealing with respect for the privacy of individuals and the integrity and sovereignty of nations in the light of advances in recording and other techniques (E/CN.4/1116).

In 1972 the Secretary-General organized, in co-operation with the Government of Austria under the programme of advisory services in the field of human rights, a seminar on human rights and scientific and technological developments, which was held at Vienna from 19 June to 1 July 1972. The participants in the seminar conducted a thorough investigation of the impact of recent scientific and technological developments on certain specific human rights; on national measures and policies to protect and promote human rights in the light of recent scientific and technological developments and to ensure the utilization of scientific discoveries and their technological applications in the interest of society as a whole; on the impact of recent scientific and technological developments on peoples and nations, with particular attention to the developing countries; and on international programmes and action, including technical co-operation, to ensure the use of scientific and technological development to promote human rights with due respect to the legitimate interests of other nations and peoples. The seminar did not however adopt recommendations on the subjects with which it had dealt.[3] Earlier, the Secretary-General had organized, in co-operation with the Government of Romania, a seminar on the effects of scientific and technological developments on the status of women, which was held in Iasi, Romania, from 5 to 18 August 1969. That seminar agreed on a number of conclusions and suggestions emanating from its debates.[4]

When the General Assembly, at its twenty-seventh session in 1972, considered the question of human rights and scientific and technological developments, the significance of the question relating to it and their complex nature was generally stressed. The importance of the studies undertaken by the Secretary-General was underlined and it was said that science and technology were part of the intellectual heritage of all mankind and they were not to be monopolized by any country, any group of countries or any group within a country. They should serve mankind as a whole. In one of two resolutions it adopted on the question (3026 A (XXVII)), the General Assembly expressed the view that mankind had reached the point where the acceleration of scientific and technological progress might, depending on its use, either be conducive to the enhancement and dissemination of the artistic and cultural values constituting part of the heritage of mankind, or add to the risk of debasing them. It invited Governments to make provision as far as possible, in their national development plans and programmes, for the preservation and development of cultural values. In a second resolution (3026 B (XXVII)), the General Assembly recognized that the scope of the problem, consisting of the establishment of a balance between scientific and technological progress and the intellectual, spiritual, cultural and moral advancement of humanity, was of such a comprehensive nature as to cover every aspect of the question of human rights and scientific and technological development. It requested the Secretary-General to accelerate and complete preparation of relevant reports on the subject, paying more attention to the programmes of an equitable and just distribution of incomes, the protection of the right to work and to health, the preparation and retraining of personnel, the raising of standards of living and the educational and cultural level of people in the light of scientific and technological development. The General Assembly also requested the Commission on Human Rights to proceed with and accelerate its work with a view, in particular, to examining the possibility of preparing draft instruments designed to strengthen respect for human rights proclaimed in the Universal Declaration of Human Rights in the light of developments of science and technology.

---

[3] See Report of the seminar on human rights and scientific and technological developments (ST/TAO/HR/45).

[4] See Report of the seminar on the effects of scientific and technological developments on the status of women (ST/TAO/HR/37).

# XII. QUESTIONS ORIGINATING IN EVENTS WHICH CULMINATED IN THE SECOND WORLD WAR

## A. War crimes and crimes against humanity

As part of the liquidation of the consequences of the Second World War various United Nations organs were compelled to engage in activities dealing with the problem of persons suspected of having committed war crimes or crimes against humanity. This preoccupation led the United Nations to promote the progressive development and codification of the law relating to these subjects.

One of the results of these efforts was the preparation and opening for signature, ratification or accession of the Convention on the Prevention and Punishment of the Crime of Genocide (1948). For details of the Convention, see chapter VIII above.

At the request of the General Assembly the International Law Commission proceeded to formulate the Nuremberg Principles, i.e., the principles which had been applied by the International Military Tribunal in the trial of the major German war criminals. Among the principles thus formulated there is the statement that any person who commits an act which constitutes a crime under international law is responsible therefor and liable to punishment. The fact that internal law does not impose a penalty for an act which constitutes a crime under international law does not relieve the person who committed the act from responsibility under international law. Nor does the fact that a person who committed an act which constitutes a crime under international law acted as Head of State or responsible Government official relieve him from such responsibility. The fact that a person acted pursuant to order of his Government or of a superior does not relieve him from responsibility under international law, provided a moral choice was in fact possible to him. Any person charged with a crime under international law has the right to a fair trial on the facts and law. The Nuremberg Principles—as did the Charter of the International Military Tribunal and Judgment of the Tribunal—deal with three types of international crimes, namely, crimes against peace, war crimes and crimes against humanity. War crimes are violations of the laws or customs of war which include, but are not limited to, murder, ill-treatment or deportation to slave labour or for any other purpose of civilian population of or in occupied territory, murder or ill-treatment of prisoners of war, of persons on the seas, killing of hostages, plunder of public or private property, wanton destruction of cities, towns, or villages, or devastation not justified by military necessity. Crimes against humanity are murder, extermination, enslavement, deportation and other inhuman acts done against any civilian population, or persecutions on political, racial or religious grounds, when such acts are done or such persecutions are carried on in execution of or in connexion with any crime against peace or any war crime.[1]

The International Law Commission, at the request of the General Assembly, also prepared at its third session in 1951 the draft Code of Offences against the Peace and Security of Mankind. The draft Code defines the offences against the peace and security of mankind and states that they are crimes under international law for which the responsible individuals shall be punishable. The draft Code embodies provisions which are based on both the Genocide Convention and the Nuremberg Principles but is not limited to them. It also contains a detailed definition of the term "act of aggression" and lists a series of activities which come within this definition, such as the employment of armed force for any purpose other than national or collective self-defence or in pursuance of a decision or recommendation of a competent organ of the United Nations. A threat to resort to an act of aggression, the preparation by the authorities of a State for the employment of armed force against another State, the incursion into the territory of a State from the territory of another State by armed bands, the undertaking or encouragement by the authorities of a State of activities calculated to foment civil strife in another State or the toleration of organized activities to this effect are all proscribed as offences against the peace and security of mankind The Code of Offences also lists the undertaking or encouragement or toleration of terrorist activities in another State, acts violating treaty obligations designed to ensure international peace and security and acts resulting in the annexation contrary to international law of territory belonging to another State or of territory under an international régime.[2]

At the request of the General Assembly the International Law Commission also dealt with the question of international criminal jurisdiction and decided by majority that it would be desirable to establish an international judicial organ for the trial of persons charged with genocide or other crimes under which jurisdiction would be conferred upon that organ by international convention. By majority decision the Commission also decided that the establishment of such an international judicial organ would be possible.[3]

---

[1] *Official Records of the General Assembly, Fifth Session, Supplement No. 12,* document A/1316.

[2] *Ibid., Sixth Session, Supplement No. 9,* document A/1858.

[3] *Ibid., Fifth Session, Supplement No. 12,* document A/1360.

Thereupon, two Committees on International Criminal Jurisdiction, which were appointed by the General Assembly and met in 1951 and 1953, respectively, prepared the draft of a statute of an International Criminal Court.[4] By resolutions 1186 and 1187 (XII) of 11 December 1957 the General Assembly decided to defer consideration of the question of an international criminal jurisdiction until such time as it would take up again the question of defining aggression and the question of a draft Code of Offences against the Peace and Security of Mankind. Although a Committee on the question of defining aggression has met on several occasions, the General Assembly has not yet taken up again the question of defining aggression and the question of the draft Code of Offences, with the consequence that it has not yet taken any decision on the draft Statute of an International Criminal Court.

United Nations organs resumed action in regard to war criminals and persons guilty of crimes against humanity in 1965 when the Commission on Human Rights requested the Secretary-General to undertake a study of the problems raised in international law by war crimes and crimes against humanity, and, by priority, a study of legal procedures to ensure that no period of limitation shall apply to such crimes.[5] In regard to the terms "war crimes" and "crimes against humanity" reference is made to the formulation by the International Law Commission of the Nuremberg Principles, which are based on the Charter of the International Military Tribunal of 1945[6] and the Judgment of the Tribunal. The Economic and Social Council, at its thirty-ninth session in 1965, *inter alia*, urged all States to continue their efforts to ensure that the criminals responsible for war crimes and crimes against humanity are traced, apprehended and equitably punished by the competent courts (resolution 1074 D (XXXIX)).

The Study requested by the Commission was presented to it at its twenty-second session in 1966 (E/CN.4/906). At the recommendation of the Commission, the Economic and Social Council, at its forty-first session in 1966,[7] took a series of decisions on the problem. Among them was the decision to urge all States to take any measures necessary to prevent the application of statutory limitation to war crimes and crimes against humanity. The Council also invited the Commission on Human Rights to prepare, as a matter of priority, a draft convention to the effect that no statutory limitation should apply to war crimes and crimes against humanity irrespective of the date of their commission. It requested the Secretary-General to prepare a preliminary draft for such a convention (resolution 1158 (XLI) of 5 August 1966).

### B. The question of the non-applicability of statutory limitations to war crimes and crimes against humanity

On the basis of the Secretary-General's draft Convention submitted to the Commission on Human Rights in document E/CN.4/928 of 25 January 1967, what was eventually to become the Convention on the Non-Applicability of Statutory Limitations to War Crimes and Crimes against Humanity was worked out by the Commission on Human Rights, the Economic and Social Council and the General Assembly. At the twenty-second session the Third Committee and the General Assembly were, owing to lack of time, unable to complete the consideration and adoption of the Convention in 1967. At the twenty-second session, the General Assembly adopted however resolution 2338 (XXII) in which it recommended that pending the adoption of a Convention by the General Assembly no legislative or other action be taken which might be prejudicial to the aims and purposes of a Convention on the subject. The Convention was adopted and opened for signature, ratification and accession in the following year (1968) by General Assembly resolution 2391 (XXIII) of 26 November 1968. The Convention on the Non-Applicability of Statutory Limitations to War Crimes and Crimes against Humanity is summarized in chapter VIII, section J above.

### C. *Apartheid* as a crime against humanity

The law relating to internationally criminal behaviour elaborated at the end of the Second World War and in the first years of existence of the United Nations has recently been invoked also in regard to contemporary activities which the General Assembly has declared to be criminal under the earlier principles.

In its resolution on the question of Southern Rhodesia (2022 (XX) of 5 November 1965), the General Assembly condemned the policies of racial discrimination and segregation practised in Southern Rhodesia and stated that they constituted a crime against humanity. It made a similar finding in resolution 2074 (XX) of 17 December 1965 on the question of South West Africa by condemning the policies of *apartheid* and racial discrimination practised by the Government of South Africa in South West Africa as constituting a crime against humanity.

In resolution 2202 A (XXI) of 16 December 1966 on the policies of *apartheid* of the Government of the Republic of South Africa, the General Assembly condemned the policies of *apartheid* practised by the Government of South Africa as a crime against humanity. At the same session, in resolution 2184 (XXI) of 12 Decem-

---

[4] *Ibid., Seventh Session, Supplement No. 11*, A/2136; and *ibid., Ninth Session, Supplement No. 12* (A/2645).

[5] *Official Records of the Economic and Social Council, Thirty-ninth Session, Supplement No. 8*, E/4024, resolution 3 (XXI).

[6] Article 6 of the Charter of the International Military Tribunal of 1945 reads, in part :

"(*b*) *War crimes :* namely, violations of the laws or customs of war. Such violations shall include, but not be limited to, murder, ill-treatment or deportation to slave labour or for any other purpose of civilian population of or in occupied territory, murder or ill-treatment of prisoners of war or persons on the seas, killing of hostages, plunder of public or private property, wanton destruction of cities, towns or villages, or devastation not justified by military necessity;

"(*c*) *Crimes against humanity :* namely, murder, extermination, enslavement, deportation, and any other inhumane acts committed against any civilian population, before or during the war, or persecutions on political, racial or religious grounds in execution of or in connexion with any crime within the jurisdiction of the Tribunal, whether or not in violation of the domestic law of the country where perpetrated."

[7] *Official Records of the Economic and Social Council, Forty-first Session, Supplement No. 8* (E/4184), resolution 3 (XXII).

ber 1966 on the question of territories under Portuguese administration, the General Assembly condemned as a crime against humanity the policy of the Government of Portugal, which violated the economic and political rights of indigenous population by the settlement of foreign immigrants in the territories under Portuguese administration and by the exporting of African workers to South Africa. In its resolution 2189 (XXI) of 13 December 1966 the General Assembly declared that the practice of *apartheid*, as also all forms of racial discrimination, constituted a crime against humanity.

In resolution 2307 (XXII) on the policies of *apartheid* of the Government of the Republic of South Africa, the General Assembly reiterated its condemnation of the policies of *apartheid* as a crime against humanity and in resolution 2396 (XXIII) of 2 December 1968 it repeated the condemnation as stated in resolution 2307 (XXII). At the same twenty-third session, the General Assembly adopted the Convention on the Non-Applicability of Statutory Limitations to War Crimes and Crimes against Humanity, in article I (*b*) of which inhuman acts resulting from the policies of *apartheid* are listed as crimes against humanity.

At its twenty-fourth and twenty-fifth sessions, the General Assembly again adopted resolutions characterizing the policy of *apartheid* as a crime against humanity. At the twenty-fourth session, the General Assembly did this by adopting resolution 2506 B (XXIV) on the policies of *apartheid* of the Government of South Africa, in which it reaffirmed its resolution 2396 (XXIII) and its other resolutions on the question of *apartheid.* In resolution 2671 F (XXV) of 8 December 1970, the General Assembly declared that the policies of *apartheid* of the Government of South Africa were a negation of the Charter of the United Nations and constituted a crime against humanity. Resolution 2671 (XXV) was reaffirmed by resolution 2775 F (XXVI) of 29 November 1971. In the Declaration on the Occasion of the Twenty-fifth Anniversary of the United Nations, adopted by General Assembly resolution 2627 (XXV), the representatives of the States Members of the United Nations declared (in paragraph 7), that they strongly condemned "the evil policy of *apartheid* which is a crime against the conscience and dignity of mankind".

### D. Recent action concerning the punishment of war crimes and crimes against humanity, both of the period of the Second World War and that of contemporary events

In its resolution 2583 (XXIV) of 13 December 1969 on the "question of the punishment of war criminals and of persons who have committed crimes against humanity", the General Assembly recalled its resolutions 3 (I) of 13 February 1946 and 170 (II) of 31 October 1947 on the extradition and punishment of war criminals, and also declarations on the subject made by the Allied Powers during the Second World War on 13 January 1942 and 30 October 1943. The General Assembly expressed its conviction that the thorough investigation of war crimes and crimes against humanity and the detection, arrest, extradition and punishment of persons responsible for war crimes and crimes against humanity, constituted an important element in the prevention of such crimes, the protection of human rights and fundamental freedoms, the encouragement of confidence, the furtherance of co-operation among peoples and the promotion of international peace and security. The General Assembly called upon all the States concerned to take the necessary measures for the thorough investigation of war crimes and crimes against humanity and for the detection, arrest, extradition and punishment of all war criminals and persons guilty of crimes against humanity who had not yet been brought to trial or punished.

The General Assembly took the matter up again at the twenty-fifth session when, in resolution 2712 (XXV), it drew attention to the fact that many war criminals and persons who had committed crimes against humanity were continuing to take refuge in the territories of certain States and were enjoying protection. It condemned "the war crimes and crimes against humanity at present being committed as a result of aggressive wars and the policies of racism, *apartheid* and colonialism" and called upon the States concerned to bring to trial persons guilty of such crimes. It also called upon all the States concerned to intensify their co-operation in the collection and exchange of information which would contribute to the detection, arrest, extradition, trial and punishment of persons guilty of such crimes. It also requested the Secretary-General to continue to study the question of the punishment of war crimes and crimes against humanity as well as the criteria for determining compensation to the victims of such crimes. The Secretary-General submitted his study on these subjects in document A/8345 of 28 September 1971.

In its resolution 2840 (XXVI) of 18 December 1971 the General Assembly again recalled its resolutions 3 (I) of 1946 and 170 (II) of 1947 on the extradition and punishment of war criminals. It also requested the Commission on Human Rights to consider the principles of international co-operation in the detection, arrest, extradition and punishment of persons guilty of war crimes and crimes against humanity. The question was examined by the Commission on Human Rights at its twenty-eighth session (March/April 1972) and by the Economic and Social Council at its fifty-second session.[8]

When the General Assembly (Third Committee) at the twenty-seventh session considered the question of "Principles of international co-operation in the detection, arrest, extradition and punishment of persons guilty of war crimes and crimes against humanity", a draft resolution containing draft principles was submitted to the Third Committee by three delegations (A/C.3/L. 1975). The General Assembly adopted resolution 3020 (XXVII) of 18 December 1972, by which it decided to transmit these draft principles for further elaboration to the Commission on Human Rights and requested the Commission to prepare and to submit to the General Assembly at its twenty-eighth session in 1973 a set of

[8] See *Official Records of the Economic and Social Council, Fifty-second Session, Supplement No. 7,* and Economic and Social Council resolution 1691 (XLII) of 2 June 1972, and General Assembly resolutions 2712 (XXV) of 1970, 2840 (XXVI) of 1971 and 3020 (XXVII) of 1972.

draft principles. The General Assembly decided to include the item relating to these principles in the provisional agenda of the twenty-eighth session.

### E. United Nations action concerning nazism and racial intolerance

As far as the substance is concerned the action taken by the United Nations concerning nazism and racial intolerance is related to the action which has been taken on *apartheid* and other forms of racial discrimination.

At its twenty-second session, the General Assembly adopted resolution 2331 (XXII) of 18 December 1967, entitled "Measures to be taken against nazism and racial intolerance". In that resolution, the General Assembly resolutely condemned any ideology, including nazism, based on racial intolerance and terror as a gross violation of human rights and fundamental freedoms and of the purposes and principles of the Charter of the United Nations and called upon all States to take immediate and effective measures against any such manifestations. The resolution also confirmed that nazism was incompatible with the objectives of the Charter, the Universal Declaration of Human Rights, the Convention on the Prevention and Punishment of the Crime of Genocide, the United Nations Declaration on the Elimination of All Forms of Racial Discrimination, the International Convention on the Elimination of All Forms of Racial Discrimination and other international instruments.

Guided by the provisions of General Assembly resolution 2331 (XXII), noting the concern that had been expressed at recent activities of groups and organizations propagating nazism and other ideologies based on racial intolerance and terror, which had been decisively condemned by the United Nations, the Commission on Human Rights in its resolution 15 (XXIV) of 1968 noted resolution 1 (XX), adopted in 1967 by the Sub-Commission on Prevention of Discrimination and Protection of Minorities (Special study of racial discrimination in the political, economic, social and cultural spheres), in which the Sub-Commission had invited the Special Rapporteur to give due consideration in his report to the problem of measures which should be taken to halt Nazi activities wherever they occurred. The Commission on Human Rights once again resolutely condemned all ideologies, including nazism and *apartheid*, which were based on racial intolerance and terror, as a gross violation of human rights and fundamental freedoms, of the principles and purposes of the United Nations Charter and as a serious threat to world peace and the security of peoples. It addressed a request to the Sub-Commission to submit recommendations for measures which could be taken on the problem. The Commission on Human Rights, through the Economic and Social Council, recommended to the General Assembly the adoption of a resolution on the question, which is summarized below.[9] In the meantime the International Conference on Human Rights held at Teheran, April/May 1968 had, on its part, adopted a resolution [10] in which it expressed its profound alarm at the recent renewal of activities by groups and organizations engaged in propaganda for nazism and other similar ideologies based on terrorism and racial intolerance. The Conference stressed that nazism and similar ideologies were incompatible with the Charter, the Universal Declaration of Human Rights, the Genocide Convention, the Declaration and International Convention on the Elimination of All Forms of Racial Discrimination and other international instruments. Considering that that ideology and that practice had in the past led to barbarous acts outraging the conscience of mankind and recalling that the Universal Declaration on Human Rights and the two Covenants stipulated that nothing in those instruments might be interpreted as implying for any State, group or person any right to engage in any activity or to perform any act, such as racist or Nazi practices, aimed at the destruction of any of the rights set forth therein, the Conference strongly condemned nazism, neo-nazism, racism and similar ideologies and practices as a blatant violation of the basic human rights and freedoms. The Conference urged all States, with due regard to the principles contained in the Universal Declaration, to declare illegal and to prohibit Nazi and racist organizations and groups, any organized or other activity based on Nazi ideology and any similar ideology based on terrorism and racial intolerance, and to declare participation in such organizations and activities to be a criminal act punishable by law.

Acting on the recommendation of the Commission on Human Rights, the Economic and Social Council and the Teheran Conference, the General Assembly adopted at its twenty-third session the resolution already referred to on measures to be taken against nazism and racial intolerance (resolution 2438 (XXIII) of 19 December 1968). In that resolution the General Assembly accepted the recommendations of both the Commission on Human Rights and the Council, on the one side, and of the Conference on the other, and called upon all States and peoples, as well as national and international organizations, to strive for the eradication as soon as possible and once and for all of racism, nazism and similar ideologies and practices including *apartheid.*

At its twenty-fifth session in 1969, the Commission on Human Rights had again before it the question of measures to be taken against nazism and racial intolerance, In its resolution 10 (XXV) it requested the Sub-Commission to deal, in the study which it was carrying out, with the danger of revival of that ideology. It again submitted, through the Economic and Social Council, a draft resolution to the General Assembly which, after endorsement by the Economic and Social Council, became General Assembly resolution 2545 (XXIV). The General Assembly urgently called upon those States concerned which had not yet done so, to take immediate and effective measures, with due regard to the principles contained in the Universal Declaration, for the complete prohibition of the Nazi and racist organizations and

---

[9] General Assembly resolution 2438 (XXIII) of 19 December 1968; see also resolution of the Economic and Social Council 1335 (XLIV) of 31 May 1968.

[10] *Final Act of the International Conference on Human Rights* (United Nations publication, Sales No. E.68.XIV.2), p. 5.

groups and for their prosecution in the courts. The General Assembly also called upon all States and national and international organizations to set aside a day, to be observed each year on an appropriate day in memory of the victims of the struggle against nazism and similar ideologies.[11]

At its twenty-sixth session in 1970 the Commission on Human Rights had before it a report on the question prepared by the Secretary-General (A/7683) which it studied with satisfaction. It requested the Sub-Commission to continue its study, placing special emphasis on measures to be taken to detect and effectively to prevent contemporary activities that might be inspired by nazism and any other totalitarian ideology based on incitement to hatred and racial intolerance. In resolution 2713 (XXV) the General Assembly urged the States concerned to implement without delay the earlier resolutions of the General Assembly on the question and in particular to take legislative and other effective measures with a view to the speedy and final eradication of nazism, including its contemporary forms, of racism and similar ideologies. It called upon States during 1971, the International Year for Action to Combat Racism and Racial Discrimination, to take effective measures to combat contemporary manifestations of nazism and other forms of racial intolerance.

At its twenty-seventh session in February/March 1971, the Commission on Human Rights had before it, among other documents, the report of the Sub-Commission on its twenty-third session (E/CN.4/1040) which, in chapter VIII, contained a draft resolution submitted by the Sub-Commission on the danger of a revival of nazism and racial intolerance. The Commission on Human Rights adopted draft resolution IV, for adoption by the Economic and Social Council and the General Assembly.[12] It also recommended to the Economic and Social Council that it invite the General Assembly to resume, as soon as possible, its study of the question of international criminal jurisdiction and the question of the draft code of offences against the peace and security of mankind with a view to the preparation of effective measures to eliminate any possibility of revival of nazism. No action was taken on this particular recommendation by either the Economic and Social Council or the General Assembly.

The General Assembly adopted, however, a comprehensive resolution on the danger of a revival of nazism and racial intolerance (resolution 2839 (XXVI) of 18 December 1971. In it the General Assembly recognized that there still existed in the world convinced adherents of nazism and racial intolerance whose activities, if they were not opposed in sufficient time, could bring about a resurgence of those ideologies. The General Assembly considered that contemporary manifestations of resurgent nazism, like the earlier ones, combined racial prejudice and discrimination with terrorism, and that in some cases racism had been raised to the level of State policy, as in the case of South Africa. The General Assembly further expressed its conviction that the best bulwark against nazism and racial discrimination was the establishment and maintenance of democratic institutions, that the existence of genuine political, social and economic democracy was an effective vaccine and an equally effective antidote against the formation or development of nazi movements and that a political system based on freedom and effective participation by the people in the conduct of public affairs, and under which economic and social conditions were such as to ensure a decent standard of living for the population, made it impossible for fascism, nazism or other ideologies based on terror to succeed. The General Assembly invited all States Members of the United Nations or members of specialized agencies to review their legislation with a view to determining whether, in the light of their circumstances, further legal measures were required. The General Assembly also recommended to those States which were unable, for serious constitutional or other reasons, to implement immediately and fully the provisions of the United Nations Declaration and of the International Convention on the Elimination of All Forms of Racial Discrimination, which condemned and outlawed all propaganda and all organizations based on ideas or theories of the superiority of one race or group of persons of one colour or ethnic origin, to take certain defined measures. Those measures should provide that:

"(*a*) Such organizations should not be allowed to receive financial subsidies from organs of the State, private companies or individuals;

"(*b*) Such organizations should not be allowed the use of public premises in which to establish their headquarters or conduct meetings of their members, the use of streets and squares in populated areas for holding demonstrations, or the use of public information media for disseminating propaganda;

"(*c*) Such organizations should not be allowed to form militarized detachments on any pretext, and offenders should be subject to prosecution in the courts;

"(*d*) Persons employed by the State, particularly in the armed forces, should not be permitted to belong to such organizations."

The General Assembly stated that all those measures should be taken only in so far as they were compatible with the principles of the Universal Declaration. The General Assembly also requested the specialized agencies, regional intergovernmental organizations and Governments to assist in the fight against the resurgence of nazism and of similar ideologies.

### F. Assistance to victims of persecution

#### 1. *Plight of survivors of concentration camps*

At its eleventh session, the Economic and Social Council, in its resolution 305 (XI) of 14 July 1950, took note of the report of the fourth session of the Commission on the Status of Women[13] referring to the tragic fate

[11] Resolution of the Economic and Social Council 1417 (XLVI) of 6 June 1969 and General Assembly resolution 2545 (XXIV) of 11 December 1969.

[12] See *Official Records of the Economic and Social Council, Fiftieth Session, Supplement No. 4*, chap. XX.

[13] *Official Records of the Economic and Social Council, Eleventh Session, Supplement No. 16* (E/1712).

of survivors of concentration camps who, under the Nazi régime, had been the victims of so-called scientific experiments and requested the Secretary-General to consider as soon as possible, with the competent authorities and institutions, means for alleviating the plight of such victims. After considering a preliminary report by the Secretary-General, the Council, in resolution 353 (XII) adopted in March 1951, appealed to the competent German authorities to consider making the fullest possible reparations for the injuries suffered, under the Nazi régime, by persons subjected to so-called scientific experiments in concentration camps; invited the International Refugee Organization and the World Health Organization to assist in dealing with the problem; and requested the Secretary-General to study the possiblity of securing such voluntary support and contributions as might appear necessary to supplement the reparations proposed, if they proved inadequate.

In a letter dated 30 July 1951, the Government of the Federal Republic of Germany stated that it was prepared, in special cases of need, to afford practical assistance to such surviving victims of experiments on human beings then living abroad and persecuted on grounds of race, religion, opinions or political convictions as were ineligible for reparation under the compensation laws in force in the *Länder* of the Federal Republic; either because they lacked residential qualifications or because the time-limit for submission of applications had expired. That Government also stated that victims of experiments who were ineligible for reparation on other grounds would not be denied assistance if their health had been permanently impaired through gross disregard of human rights, and that it was prepared, on humanitarian grounds, to provide assistance in all cases where such assistance was required and appeared justified.

The Council in its resolution 386 (XIII) of 15 September 1951 welcomed the decision taken by the Government of the Federal Republic of Germany in assuming responsibility for this problem and appealed to that Government to render on the most generous scale possible the assistance which it had undertaken. At the Council's request, the Secretary-General has since made available to the Government of the Federal Republic of Germany the information that had been collected concerning the number and nature of the various cases, and he has kept that Government supplied with new information as it has been received. The Government has further been informed of the view of the Council expressed in resolution 386 (XIII) that the investigation and certification of individual claims is a matter of primary responsibility for that Government.

### 2. *Financial assistance to refugees persecuted by reason of their nationality*

On October 1960 an Agreement was concluded between the United Nations High Commissioner for Refugees and the German Federal Government in favour of refugees who had been persecuted under the Nazi régime by reason of their nationality, in disregard of human rights. The Office of the High Commissioner for Refugees established a secretariat of the United Nations High Commissioner for Refugees Indemnification Fund to decide on the applications. It also established a consultative committee on which welfare agencies and the refugees themselves are represented and advise the High Commissioner in matters connected with the fund. On 21 December 1966 the High Commissioner for Refugees announced that a formal agreement had been concluded with the Federal Republic of Germany for the creation of a new fund for those refugees persecuted by Nazi Germany for reason of nationality but who were excluded under the terms of the fund established in 1960 (under the 1960 fund, which was disbursed to 12,000 national refugees in 35 countries, applicants had to be refugees on October 1953 in order to qualify). The new fund is entrusted to benefit refugees persecuted by reason of their nationality, who either acquired a new nationality prior to that date or became refugees after that date.

### 3. *Assistance to victims of racial discrimination in southern Africa*

The comprehensive activities of the United Nations family of organizations to render financial and other assistance to victims of racial discrimination in southern Africa are described in part one, chapter VI, above and in part two, chapter V below.

# Part Two

# METHODS USED BY THE UNITED NATIONS IN THE FIELD OF HUMAN RIGHTS

# I. INSTITUTIONAL AND ORGANIZATIONAL ARRANGEMENTS

The provisions of the Charter of the United Nations relating to human rights are summarized in part one, chapter I, section B of the present publication. Under Article 60 of the Charter, responsiblity for the discharge of the functions of the Organization, a concept which under the Charter includes co-operation in promoting respect for the observance of human rights in the field of international economic and social co-operation, is vested in the General Assembly and, under the authority of the General Assembly, in the Economic and Social Council which, for this purpose, has the powers set forth in Chapter X of the Charter, entitled "The Economic and Social Council".

Under Article 60 of the Charter "Responsiblity for the discharge of the functions of the Organization set forth in this Chapter shall be vested in the General Assembly and, under the authority of the General Assembly, in the Economic and Social Council, which shall have for this purpose the powers set forth in Chapter X".

The General Assembly and the Economic and Social Council are listed in Article 7 of the Charter among "the principal organs of the United Nations". Under Article 7, paragraph 2, such subsidiary organs as may be found necessary may be established in accordance with the Charter. Under Article 22 the General Assembly may establish such subsidiary organs as it deems necessary for the performance of its functions.

Under Article 68 of the Charter "the Economic and Social Council shall set up commissions in economic and social fields and for the promotion of human rights, and such other commissions as may be required for the performance of its functions".

This chapter will first provide data on each of the organs of the United Nations established under the Charter to deal specifically with matters of protection of human rights and will then refer to some of the other organs of the United Nations which occasionally consider such matters in relation to other functions which are entrusted to them under the United Nations Charter.

## A. United Nations organs principally concerned with matters of human rights

### 1. *The General Assembly*

In addition to the Charter provisions mentioned above, it may be recalled that under Article 10 of the Charter the General Assembly may discuss and make recommendations on "any questions or any matters within the scope of the present Charter or relating to the powers and functions of any organs provided for in the present Charter".

It is one of the functions of the General Assembly to "initiate studies and make recommendations" for the purpose of

"promoting international co-operation in the economic, social, cultural, educational, and health fields, and assisting in the realization of human rights and fundamental freedoms for all without distinction as to race, sex, language, or religion" (Article 13.1 b).

Under Article 15, the General Assembly receives and considers reports from the other organs of the Organization, some of which are in various ways concerned with human rights.

*Composition and functioning*

The General Assembly consists of all the Members of the United Nations (Article 9 of the Charter). Each Member of the Assembly has one vote (Article 18). Decisions of the General Assembly on important questions are taken by a majority of two thirds of the Members present and voting, and decisions on other questions are taken by a simple majority. Article 18 enumerates several specific questions to which the two-thirds rule applies, including such questions as the election of the non-permanent members of the Security Council, the election of the members of the Economic and Social Council, the election of members of the Trusteeship Council and the operation of the international Trusteeship System. Decisions on the determination of additional categories of questions to be decided by a two-thirds majority are made by a majority of the Members present and voting.

Questions concerning human rights as such are not listed among the categories of questions the decisions on which require a two-thirds majority for adoption under paragraph 2 of article 18.[1] The record of voting at past sessions of the Assembly indicates that, without the question of the "importance" of the item and of the majority required being raised, a two-thirds majority was

[1] When the draft Convention on the Political Rights of Women was considered by the General Assembly at its 409th plenary meeting on 20 December 1952, one delegation, pointing out that the draft prepared by the Third Committee contained a colonial application clause, claimed that a two-thirds majority on that clause was "absolutely necessary". The President ruled that the draft convention and the draft resolution attached to it constituted a question of importance and required a two-thirds majority. Eventually, the draft colonial application clause received a simple, but not a two-thirds, majority and was therefore not adopted. The draft convention as a whole was adopted, having obtained the required two-thirds majority. (See General Assembly (VII), Plenary, 409th meeting, pp. 439 and 440). In another case, the Assembly, at its 401st meeting on 5 December 1952, assented to a

*(Continued on next page)*

actually obtained and in most cases considerably exceeded. A number of important decisions were in fact reached without dissenting votes. The International Covenant on Economic, Social and Cultural Rights was adopted by 105 votes to none; the International Covenant on Civil and Political Rights was adopted by 106 votes to none (A/PV.1496).

Pursuant to Article 20 of the Charter, the General Assembly shall meet in regular annual sessions and in such special sessions as occasion may require. The regular annual session commences on the third Tuesday in September (rule 1 of the rules of procedure of the General Assembly).[2]

The General Assembly adopts its own rules of procedure (Article 21 of the Charter). At each session it elects its President and 17 Vice-Presidents who hold office until the close of the session at which they are elected (Article 21 of the Charter and rule 31 of the rules of procedure of the General Assembly).

The provisional agenda of the General Assembly, which is submitted to the Assembly for approval as soon as possible after the opening of the session, includes, in accordance with rule 13 of the rules of procedure:

"(*a*) The report of the Secretary-General on the work of the Organization;

"(*b*) Reports from the Security Council, the Economic and Social Council, the Trusteeship Council, the International Court of Justice, the subsidiary organs of the General Assembly, specialized agencies (where such reports are called for under agreements entered upon);

"(*c*) All items the inclusion of which has been ordered by the General Assembly at a previous session;

"(*d*) All items proposed by other principal organs of the United Nations;

"(*e*) All items proposed by any Member of the United Nations;

"(*f*) All items pertaining to the budget for the next financial year and the report on the accounts for the last financial year;

"(*g*) All items which the Secretary-General deems it necessary to put before the General Assembly; and

"(*h*) All items proposed under Article 35, paragraph 2, of the Charter by States not members of the United Nations".

In addition, provision is made for any Member or principal organ of the United Nations or the Secretary-General to request the inclusion of supplementary items in the agenda (Rule 14); and for additional items to be placed on the agenda of the session if the General Assembly so decides by a majority of the Members present and voting (Rule 15).

Many human rights items on the agenda of the General Assembly originated in sections of the report of the Economic and Social Council or in decisions of the General Assembly at earlier sessions to take up particular matters relating to human rights. Special items relating to human rights have also been proposed for inclusion in the agenda of the General Assembly by the Economic and Social Council, the Trusteeship Council, by a Member State or by the Secretary-General.

*Methods of dealing with matters of human rights*

Most items relating to human rights are referred to the Social, Humanitarian and Cultural or Third Committee of the General Assembly. Items referred to other Main Committees may however, also relate to questions of protection of human rights and fundamental freedoms such as certain items of an essentially political character which are referred either to the First or to the Special Political Committees [3] of the General Assembly (some of them are considered by the General Assembly in plenary meetings) [4] or items of an essentially economic

*(Foot-note 1 continued)*

statement of the President that the question of the race conflict in South Africa resulting from the policies of *apartheid* of the Union of South Africa was an important one. (See General Assembly, Plenary, 401st meeting, pp. 333 and 334.) The question whether the problems of colonialism and racial discrimination are "important questions" within the meaning of Article 18, paragraph 2, of the Charter has remained controversial.

[2] The rules of procedure of the General Assembly, embodying amendments and additions adopted by the General Assembly up to 31 December 1971, are contained in document A/520/Rev.11 (United Nations publication, Sales No. E.72.I.13). After 1 January 1972, at the twenty-seventh session of the General Assembly, one rule (rule 160), dealing with the composition of the Committee on Contributions, was amended (General Assembly resolution 2913 (XXVII) of 9 November 1972).

[3] Examples of items which have a bearing on human rights and were considered by the Political and Security Committee (First Committee) are the various actions which the General Assembly took on questions of the development, production and stockpiling of bacteriological (biological) and toxin weapons and the question of chemical weapons and the question of the suspension of nuclear and thermo-nuclear tests. An example of an item relating to human rights considered by the *Ad hoc* Political Committee as it was then known (fifth session, 1950) was the item entitled "Observance in Bulgaria, Hungary and Romania of human rights and fundamental freedoms". For many years the question of the policies of *apartheid* of the Government of South Africa has been referred to the Special Political Committee. The Special Political Committee has regularly dealt with the reports of the Special Committee to investigate Israeli Practices Affecting the Human Rights of the Population of the Occupied Territories.

[4] The following are examples of items relating to human rights which have been considered by the General Assembly without reference to a Main Committee, i.e., which have been dealt with by the General Assembly in plenary:

At the fourteenth, sixteenth and twentieth sessions, the General Assembly adopted without reference to a Main Committee resolutions on the question of human rights within the territory of a Member State (resolutions 1353 (XIV), 1723 (XVI) and 2079 (XX));

At its eighteenth session, the General Assembly considered directly in plenary the item "The violation of human rights in South Vietnam";

The problem of the human environment, which has an important bearing on human rights, was originally (at the twenty-third session) considered by the General Assembly in plenary;

The Declaration on the Occasion of the Twenty-fifth Anniversary of the United Nations, which contains important pronouncements on human rights, was considered by the General Assembly directly in plenary without reference to a Main Committee;

*(Continued on next page)*

character which are referred to the Economic and Financial or Second Committee.[5] Items on the agenda of the General Assembly relating to Non-Self-Governing or Trust Territories are usually referred to the Fourth Committee of the General Assembly, which is called the Trusteeship Committee (including Non-Self-Governing Territories). The Administrative and Budgetary or Fifth Committee deals with the financial aspects and budgetary provisions concerning the United Nations relating to human rights items. Some items relating to human rights have been dealt with by the Legal or Sixth Committee.[6] The above-mentioned Committees, being Main Committees of the General Assembly, consist, like the Assembly itself, of all States Members of the United Nations. In the early years of the Organization a few items were considered by the Joint First and Third Committee,[7] the Joint Second and Third Committee, the Joint First and Sixth Committee [8] etc., but this practice has not been followed in recent years.

The reports of the Main Committees, which generally contain the text of all proposals and amendments introduced in the Committee, the results of votes on such proposals and amendments and in the case of some Committees a brief summary of issues discussed as well as draft recommendations for consideration and approval by the Assembly, are considered by the Assembly in plenary meetings. The Assembly adopts after considering them, the draft resolutions proposed by the Main Committee concerned. Occasionally, a draft resolution proposed by the Committee may be rejected, amended, or another one may be substituted for it.

*Terminology and addressees of decisions*

In acting on matters of human rights, the General Assembly has followed a varied pattern in its use of terminology. While the word "recommends" has been used in a number of resolutions, several other wordings have been employed, among them: "urges", "requests", "invites", "once again invites", "asks", "affirms", "is of the opinion", "decides", "resolves therefore", "endorses", "recognizes", "endeavours", "approves", "refers", "calls upon", "solemnly calls upon", "supports", "appeals", "deplores", "condemns", "resolutely condemns", "expresses regret and concern", "notes", "notes with appreciation", "notes with regret", "declares", "declares again", "expresses the earnest hope", "expresses its satisfaction".

Most recommendations of the General Assembly relating to human rights have been addressed to States, Governments, the Security Council, the Economic and Social Council and its commissions, the Trusteeship Council, the Secretary-General and the specialized agencies in respect of matters within the jurisdiction of these organs. Recommendations have also been addressed to subsidiary bodies of the General Assembly and, in a few cases, to non-governmental organizations and voluntary agencies and individuals.

*Subsidiary bodies*

The General Assembly has, on various occasions, established subsidiary organs of a temporary or an *ad hoc* character, as well as special committees, to assist it in the performance of its functions with respect to human rights. Examples of such bodies are the Committee established [9] to prepare a draft Convention on Freedom of Information, the *ad hoc* Commission on Prisoners of War,[10] the United Nations Commission on the Racial Situation in the Union of South Africa,[11] the United Nations Good Offices Commission established [12] in connexion with the question of the treatment of people of Indian origin in the Union of South Africa and the Special Committee on the Policies of *Apartheid* of the Government of the Republic of South Africa.[13] The latter Committee was later (8 December 1970, 1921st meeting) renamed "Special Committee on *Apartheid*".

The General Assembly's Special Committee on the Situation with regard to the Implementation of the Decla-

---

*(Foot-note 4 continued)*

At its twenty-seventh session, the General Assembly dealt, without reference to a Main Committee, with the question of an international conference of experts for the support of victims of colonialism and *apartheid* and with the question of a Week of Solidarity with the Colonial Peoples of Southern Africa and Guinea (Bissau) and Cape Verde Fighting for Freedom, Independence, and Equal Rights (General Assembly resolutions 2910 and 2911 (XXVII)).

5 An example indicative of the fact that there are no hard and fast rules on the allocation of items to various committees is the item concerning permanent sovereignty over natural resources, which originated in the Commission on Human Rights and in the Third Committee; in recent years the question has consistently been referred to the Second Committee. The questions of the International Education Year and of the International University (United Nations University) were also referred to the Second Committee. It was the Second Committee to which the report of the United Nations Conference on the Human Environment was referred and which recommended the action taken by the Assembly on the recommendations of the Conference.

6 The item "Draft Declaration on the Right of Asylum" was referred at the twentieth and twenty-first sessions of the General Assembly to the Sixth Committee. Previously it had been referred to and considered by the Third Committee. The Declaration on Territorial Asylum was adopted at the twenty-second session after the final text had been established by a joint drafting committee of the Third and Sixth Committees. The question of respect for human rights in armed conflicts was, at the twenty-third to twenty-sixth sessions of the General Assembly, referred to the Third Committee. At the twenty-seventh session, the General Assembly decided to allocate part of the item to the Third Committee, another part to the Sixth Committee, while other aspects were dealt with by the First Committee.

7 e.g., the item concerning the "Draft Declaration on Fundamental Human Rights and Freedoms" was considered by the Joint First and Third Committee at the second part of the first session of the General Assembly.

8 e.g., the item concerning the "Treatment of Indians in the Union of South Africa" was referred to the Joint First and Sixth Committee by the General Assembly at the second part of the first session.

9 General Assembly resolution 426 (V).

10 Established by the Secretary-General in accordance with the request and the directives of the General Assembly contained in its resolution 427 (V).

11 General Assembly resolution 616 (VII).

12 General Assembly resolution 615 (VII).

13 General Assembly resolution 1761 (XVII).

ration on the Granting of Independence to Colonial Countries and Peoples is discussed later in the present publication.

### 2. *The Economic and Social Council*

*Composition and membership*

The Economic and Social Council is, in accordance with Article 7 of the Charter, a principal organ of the United Nations. The Council originally was composed of 18 Members of the United Nations, elected by secret ballot by the General Assembly in accordance with articles 146 and 147 of its rules of procedure for a term of office of three years, and eligible for immediate re-election. By an amendment to Article 61 of the Charter, adopted by the General Assembly on 17 December 1963 (General Assembly resolution 1991 B (XVIII)), which came into force on 31 August 1965, the membership of the Council was increased from 18 to 27. The Assembly decided that, without prejudice to the distribution of Council seats that was in effect at the time of the adoption of the aforementioned resolution, the 9 additional members should be elected according to the following pattern: 7 from African and Asian States; 1 from Latin American States; and 1 from Western European and other States. The members of the Council are therefore at present elected according to the following pattern: 12 from African and Asian States; 3 from Eastern European States; 5 from Latin American States; and 7 from Western European and other States.

By resolution 2847 (XXVI) of 20 December 1971, the General Assembly decided to amend once more Article 61 of the Charter to the effect that the membership of the Economic and Social Council was to be increased from 27 to 54. Under Article 108 of the Charter, amendments have to be ratified in accordance with their respective constitutional processes by two thirds of the Members of the United Nations, including all the permanent members of the Security Council. As of 31 December 1972, 46 Members, including one permanent member of the Security Council, had ratified the amendment to Article 61 adopted in 1971. In resolution 2847 (XXVI) the General Assembly further decided that the members of the Economic and Social Council should be elected according to the following pattern: 14 members from African States; 11 members from Asian States; 10 members from Latin American States; 13 members from Western European and other States; and 6 members from socialist States of Eastern Europe. The General Assembly welcomed the decision of the Economic and Social Council, pending the receipt of the necessary ratifications to permit the enlargement of the Council's membership, to enlarge its sessional committees to 54 members and invited the Council to elect the 27 additional members as soon as possible. The Economic and Social Council elected the additional 27 members at the organizational meetings of its fifty-second session in January 1972 and since then the sessional committees, i.e. the Economic Committee, the Social Committee and the Co-ordination Committee, have consisted of 54 members.[14]

*Function and methods of work*

As already indicated, the Economic and Social Council is directed by the Charter to set up commissions for the promotion of human rights. Under Article 64 of the Charter, the Council may make arrangements with the Members of the United Nations and with the specialized agencies to obtain reports on the steps taken to give effect to its own recommendations and to recommendations on matters falling within its competence made by the General Assembly. The Council may communicate its observations on these reports to the General Assembly. In accordance with Article 66, the Council may, with the approval of the General Assembly, perform services at the request of Members of the United Nations and at the request of the specialized agencies and is also to perform such functions as may be assigned to it by the General Assembly.

In a number of its resolutions, the Council has sought to define its role and methods of work. An example is resolution 1156 (XLI) of 5 August 1966 in which the Council expressed the view that it has an important role to play in: *(a)* Acting as governing body for the United Nations work programme in the economic, social and human rights fields; *(b)* Ensuring the co-ordination of the activities of the United Nations system of organizations in these same fields; and *(c)* Providing a forum for the discussion of issues of international economic and social policy, and formulating recommendations for the United Nations system of organizations. In recent years the Council has devoted considerable efforts to the improvement of the organization of its work. The recommendation to the General Assembly to adopt the 1971 amendment to Article 61 of the Charter was one of the results of those efforts (Council resolution 1621 (LI) of 30 July 1971). In its resolution 1623 (LI) of 30 July 1971, the Council decided that in its review of the over-all economic and social situation it should formulate new policy recommendations to meet the challenges of development.

In addition to the above there are other Charter provisions concerning the Council and procedures based on these provisions which are relevant to the Council's work in the field of human rights.

*Co-ordination with specialized agencies*

Under Article 57 of the Charter, the various specialized agencies, established by intergovernmental agreement and having wide international responsiblities, as defined in their basic instrument, in economic, social, cultural, educational, health and related fields, are to be brought into relationship with the United Nations in accordance with the provisions of Article 63.

Under Article 63 paragraph 1, of the Charter, the Economic and Social Council enters into agreements with the specialized agencies bringing the latter into a relation-

[14] By resolution 1193 (XLI) of 27 December 1966, the Council had decided that each sessional committee would have as its Chairman one of the three Vice-Presidents of the Council.

ship with the United Nations. These agreements are subject to the approval of the General Assembly. The agreements concluded by the United Nations with the specialized agencies contain general provisions on: reciprocal representation at meetings of organs; proposal of agenda items; action to be taken by the specialized agencies as regards recommendations of the General Assembly and of the Economic and Social Council; exchange of information and documentation; assistance to the Security Council and the Trusteeship Council; co-operation with regard to implementation of Chapter XI of the Charter relating to Non-Self-Governing Territories; relations with the International Court of Justice; headquarters and regional offices; personal arrangements; statistical services; interagency agreements; liaison etc.[15]

The Economic and Social Council is authorized, by Article 63, paragraph 2, of the Charter, to co-ordinate the activities of the specialized agencies through consultation with and recommendations to such agencies and through recommendations to the General Assembly and to the Members of the United Nations. In accordance with Article 64, paragraph 1, the Council receives regularly reports from the specialized agencies on their activities.

Arrangements have been made, in accordance with Article 70 of the Charter, for representatives of the specialized agencies to participate, without vote, in the deliberations of the Council and its commissions and for the United Nations representatives to participate in the deliberations of the specialized agencies. Under the rules of procedure of the Council, specialized agencies thus participating may submit proposals regarding items of concern to them, which may be put to the vote upon the request of any member of the Council or of the committee concerned (rule 78 (2)).

Specialized agencies have the right to propose items for inclusion in the Council's provisional agenda (rule 10 (1.g.)).

When proposals are made in the Council for new activities to be undertaken by the United Nations relating to matters which are of direct concern to specialized agencies, the Secretary-General is to enter into consultation with the agencies concerned and to report to the Council on the means of achieving co-ordinated use of the respective agencies.

*The Administrative Committee on Co-ordination*

A standing Administrative Committee on Co-ordination, consisting of the Secretary-General of the United Nations and the directors general of the specialized agencies, was established "for the purpose of taking all appropriate steps, under the leadership of the Secretary-General, to ensure the fullest and most effective implementation of the agreements entered into between the United Nations and the specialized agencies".[16]

*Co-operation with the Security Council*

Under Article 65 of the Charter, the Economic and Social Council may furnish information to the Security Council and is to assist that Council upon its request.

*Co-operation with the Trusteeship Council*

Article 91 of the Charter provides that the Trusteeship Council shall, when appropriate, avail itself of the assistance of the Economic and Social Council and of the specialized agencies in regard to matters with which they are respectively concerned.

The Trusteeship Council may propose items for inclusion in the Economic and Social Council's provisional agenda (rule 10 (1.*d*.)) of the Economic and Social Council's rules of procedure. The President of the Trusteeship Council or his representative may participate, without the right to vote, in the deliberations on matters of particular concern to that Council, including questions it proposed for inclusion in the Economic and Social Council's agenda (rule 77).

The Council and the International Court of Justice. Under Article 96 of the Charter, the General Assembly, by resolution 89 (I) of 11 December 1946, has authorized the Council to request of the International Court of Justice advisory opinions on legal questions arising within the scope of its activities. The Council so far has not availed itself of this possibility.

*Consultation with non-governmental organizations*

Article 71 of the Charter provides that the Economic and Social Council may make "arrangements for consultation with non-governmental organizations which are concerned with matters within its competence". Such arrangements may be made "with international organizations and, where appropriate, national organizations after consultation with the Member of the United Nations concerned". The basic arrangements for consultation with non-governmental organizations were originally laid down in Council resolution 288 (X) of 27 February 1950. The arrangements made in 1950 were superseded by the arrangements for consultation with non-governmental organizations set forth in Council resolutions 1296 (XLIV) of 23 May 1968. Some of the provisions of resolution 1296 (XLIV) are summarized below.

The arrangements made by resolution 1296 (XLIV) contain the principles to be applied in the establishment of consultative relations. Among those principles are the following:

"1. The organization shall be concerned with matters falling within the competence of the Economic and Social Council with respect to international economic, social, cultural, educational, health, scientific, technological and related matters and to questions of human rights.

[15] The agreements with the ILO and UNESCO which are the two specialized agencies mostly concerned with specific questions of human rights may be found on pages 1-10 and 21-31, respectively, of *Agreements between the United Nations and the Specialized Agencies and the International Atomic Energy Agency* (United Nations publication, Sales No. 61.X.1.). The same volume contains the agreements with FAO, WHO, ITU and other specialized agencies.

[16] Economic and Social Council resolution 13 (III) of 21 September 1946. See also *Official Records of the Economic and Social Council, Thirty-ninth Session, Annexes,* agenda item 5, document E/4040, chap. IV.

"2. The aims and purposes of the organization shall be in conformity with the spirit, purposes and principles of the Charter of the United Nations.

"3. The organization shall undertake to support the work of the United Nations and to promote knowledge of its principles and activities, in accordance with its own aims and purposes and the nature and scope of its competence and activities.

"4. The organization shall be of representative character and of recognized international standing; it shall represent a substantial proportion, and express the views of major sections, of the population or of the organized persons within the particular field of its competence, covering, where possible, a substantial number of countries in different regions of the world. Where there exist a number of organizations with similar objectives, interests and basic views in a given field, they shall, for the purposes of consultation with the Council, form a joint committee or other body authorized to carry on such consultation for the group as a whole. It is understood that when a minority opinion develops on a particular point within such a committee, it shall be presented along with the opinion of the majority.

"...

"7. Subject to paragraph 9 below, the organization shall be international in its structure, with members who exercise voting rights in relation to the policies or action of the international organization. Any international organization which is not established by intergovernmental agreement shall be considered as a non-governmental organization for the purpose of these arrangements, including organizations which accept members designated by governmental authorities, provided that such membership does not interfere with the free expression of views of the organization.

"8. The basic resources of the international organization shall be derived in the main part from contributions of the national affiliates or other components or from individual members. Where voluntary contributions have been received, their amounts and donors shall be faithfully revealed to the Council Committee on Non-Governmental Organizations. Where, however, the above criterion is not fulfilled and an organization is financed from other sources, it must explain to the satisfaction of the Committee its reasons for not meeting the requirements laid down in this paragraph. Any financial contribution or other support, direct or indirect, from a Government to the international organization shall be openly declared to the Committee through the Secretary-General and fully recorded in the financial and other records of the organization and shall be devoted to purposes in accordance with the aims of the United Nations.

"...

"11. In considering the establishment of consultative relations with a non-governmental organization, the Council will take into account whether the field of activity of the organization is wholly or mainly within the field of a specialized agency, and whether or not it could be admitted when it has, or may have, a consultative arrangement with a specialized agency."

In establishing consultative relations with organizations the Council made the following distinctions:

"(*a*) Organizations which are concerned with most of the activities of the Council and can demonstrate to the satisfaction of the Council that they have marked and sustained contributions to make to the achievement of the objectives of the United Nations in the fields set out in paragraph 1 above, and are closely involved with the economic and social life of the peoples of the areas they represent and whose membership, which should be considerable, is broadly representative of major segments of population in a large number of countries (to be known as organizations in general consultative status, category I);

"(*b*) Organizations which have a special competence in, and are concerned specifically with, only a few of the fields of activity covered by the Council, and which are known internationally within the fields for which they have or seek consultative status (to be known as organizations in special consultative status, category II)."

Organizations accorded consultative status in category II because of their interest in the field of human rights should have a general international concern with this matter, not restricted to the interest of a particular group of persons, a single nationality or the situation in a single State or restricted group of States. Special consideration shall be given to the applications of organizations in this field whose aims place stress on combating colonialism, *apartheid*, racial intolerance and other gross violations of human rights and fundamental freedoms.

Other organizations which do not have general or special consultative status but which the Council, or the Secretary-General of the United Nations, in consultation with the Council or its Committee on Non-Governmental Organizations, considers can make occasional and useful contributions to the work of the Council or its subsidiary bodies or other United Nations bodies within their competence shall be included in a list (to be known as the Roster). This list may also include organizations in consultative status or similar relationship with a specialized agency or a United Nations body. These organizations shall be available for consultation at the request of the Council or its subsidiary bodies.

Decisions on the establishment of consultative relationships with non-governmental organizations and the listing of organizations on the Roster are taken by the Economic and Social Council upon recommendation of the Council Committee on Non-Governmental Organizations. Organizations in categories I and II may designate authorized representatives to sit as observers at public meetings of the Council and of subsidiary bodies. Those on the Roster may have representatives present at such meetings dealing with matters within their field of competence.

Organizations in category I may propose to the Council Committee on Non-Governmental Organizations that the Committee request the Secretary-General to place items of special interest to the organizations on the provisional agenda of the Council.

Organizations in categories I and II may submit written statements of specified maximum length on subjects in which these organizations have a special competence. The Secretary-General, in consultation with the President of the Council, or the Council or its Committee on Non-Governmental Organizations, may invite organizations on the Roster to submit written statements.

On the recommendation of the Council Committee on Non-Governmental Organizations, organizations in category I may be heard by the Council or by its sessional committees. In special circumstances an organization in category II may also be heard. Whenever the Council discusses the substance of an item presented by a non-governmental organization in category I, such an organization is entitled to present orally to the Council or to a sessional committee of the Council, as appropriate, an introductory statement of an expository nature.

Similar rules apply to consultation with commissions of the Council or other subsidiary organs of the Council. Subject to certain conditions, organizations in category I may propose items for the provisional agenda of commissions. The arrangements for consultation between *ad hoc* committees of the Council authorized to meet between sessions of the Council and organizations in categories I and II and on the Roster follow those approved for commissions of the Council unless the Council or the Committee decides otherwise.

Paragraphs 43 to 46 of resolution 1296 (XLIV) provide for consultation between the organizations in question and the Secretariat as follows:

"43. The Secretariat should be so organized as to enable it to carry out the duties assigned to it concerning the consultative arrangements as set forth in the present resolution.

"44. All organizations in consultative relationship shall be able to consult with officers of the appropriate sections of the Secretariat on matters in which there is a mutual interest or a mutual concern. Such consultation shall be upon the request of the non-governmental organization or upon the request of the Secretary-General of the United Nations.

"45. The Secretary-General may request organizations in categories I and II and those on the Roster to carry out specific studies or prepare specific papers, subject to the relevant financial regulations.

"46. The Secretary-General shall be authorized, within the means at his disposal, to offer to non-governmental organizations in consultative relationship facilities which include:

"(*a*) Prompt and efficient distribution of such documents of the Council and its subsidiary bodies as shall in the judgement of the Secretary-General be appropriate;

"(*b*) Access to the press documentation services provided by the United Nations;

"(*c*) Arrangements of informal discussions on matters of special interest to groups or organizations;

"(*d*) Use of the libraries of the United Nations;

"(*e*) Provision of accommodation for conferences or smaller meetings of consultative organizations on the work of the Economic and Social Council;

"(*f*) Appropriate seating arrangements and facilities for obtaining documents during public meetings of the General Assembly dealing with matters in the economic and social fields."

The Council may invite non-governmental organizations in categories I and II and on the Roster to take part in conferences called by the Council under Article 62 (4) of the Charter. The organizations shall undertake the same responsiblities as at sessions of the Council itself, unless the Council decides otherwise.

By resolution 1392 (XLVI) of 3 June 1969 the Economic and Social Council made amendments in its rules of procedure consequential to the new arrangements which it had made by resolution 1296 (XLIV).

*Organizational and procedural arrangements of the Economic and Social Council.*

Under Article 72 (1) of the Charter the Council adopts its own rules of procedure.[17]

Under rule 1 of the rules of procedure of the Council the Economic and Social Council shall normally hold two regular sessions a year. Pursuant to rule 4, special sessions may be held by decision of the Council or at the request of a majority of the Members of the Council, the General Assembly, the Security Council and, subject to certain conditions, also at the request of the Trusteeship Council.

The Secretary-General draws up and submits to the Council at each regular session the provisional agenda for the following regular session. The provisional agenda includes all items proposed by: (*a*) the Council; (*b*) the General Assembly; (*c*) the Security Council; (*d*) the Trusteeship Council; (*e*) a Member of the United Nations; (*f*) the Secretary-General; (*g*) a specialized agency.

Some agenda items are considered by the Council directly in plenary meeting; others are allocated to the committees of the Council. However it may refer items without preliminary debate in the Council to certain organs or bodies, including one or more of its commissions or to specialized agencies for examination and report at a subsequent session of the Council.

Each member of the Council is represented by an accredited representative, who may be accompanied by such alternate representatives and advisers as may be required. By resolution 412 B (XIII), the Council invited to its sessions as observers international regional organizations accorded similar privileges by the General Assembly.[18] These organizations are: the Organization of American States, the League of Arab States, and the

[17] Council resolution 217 (VIII) of 18 March 1949, as repeatedly amended. For the most recent edition, which does not contain the amendments referred to above, adopted at the forty-sixth session (resolution 1392 (XLVI)), see United Nations publication, Sales No. 67.I.32.

[18] See also General Assembly resolutions 253 (III), 477 (V) and 2011 (XX).

Organization of African Unity. On the question of the representation of the Council of Europe, see below.

Each member of the Economic and Social Council has one vote. Decisions of the Council are made by a majority of the members present and voting.

In accordance with the provisions of the Charter the Secretary-General acts in that capacity in all meetings of the Council and of its committees. He designates the officers concerned of the Secretariat to act as his representatives.

The Secretary-General is responsible for keeping the members of the Council informed of any question which may be brought before it for consideration. He is also responsible for providing services in connexion with the Council's meetings, including submission of appropriate documentation, interpretation, translation, the keeping of records etc.

The Secretary-General, or his representative, may make oral as well as written statements to the Council, its committees or subsidiary bodies concerning any question under consideration.

*Consideration by the Council of questions of human rights*

*The Social Committee*

Human rights items are normally referred for consideration to the Council's Social Committee. At its seventh session, however, because of its heavy agenda, the Council established a Sessional Human Rights Committee. The reports of the Social Committee, which include draft resolutions, are submitted to the Council in plenary meetings, where draft resolutions are presented for final approval.

*Ad hoc committees, working groups and rapporteurs*

In connexion with its consideration of questions of human rights, the Council has, from time to time, set up *ad hoc* committees of governmental representatives (whether or not these Governments were represented on the Council), of experts, or of representatives of members appointed in their individual capacity, which were directed to report at a subsequent session on matters defined in the resolution establishing them. For example, by resolution 564 (XIX), the Council set up the *ad hoc* committee composed of representatives of States Members of the United Nations, which was charged with the preparation of the text of a draft supplementary convention on slavery. By resolution 350 (XII), the Council set up the *Ad Hoc* Committee on Forced Labour,[19] which was composed of members appointed in their individual capacity.

The Council has also been assisted upon occasion by rapporteurs appointed in their individual capacity. Examples are the Rapporteur on Freedom of Information elected by the Council at its 660th meeting on 25 July 1952 and the Special Rapporteur on Slavery appointed by the Secretary-General under Council resolution 960 (XXVI) of 12 July 1963.

[19] This Committee was a joint organ of the United Nations and the ILO.

*Recommendations of the Council*

Recommendations of the Economic and Social Council under Article 62 of the Charter (see above) were made by the Council or as a result of referrals by the General Assembly, by subsidiary bodies of the Council, by the Secretary-General, by specialized agencies or by international conferences convened by the United Nations. Recommendations have also been made on the basis of such matters as have come before the Council pursuant to its own decision, some of which have contained requests for certain tasks to be performed by other bodies. The Council has made many recommendations on the basis of numerous draft recommendations submitted to it by its functional commissions, and on the basis of studies and reports submitted to it.

These recommendations have been addressed to, among others, States (States Members of the United Nations, States Members and non-Members of the United Nations, States Members of the United Nations and of the specialized agencies and States parties to the Statute of the International Court of Justice, groups of States or individual States, various State authorities); Governments; the General Assembly; the Trusteeship Council; the specialized agencies in general; specific specialized agencies; the IAEA; and non-governmental bodies. Some recommendations have been addressed in more general terms, such as the one contained in resolution 607 (XXI), which called for the elimination of forced labour "wherever it exists".

The subjects of the resolutions of the Council have varied widely. They have included: respect for human rights in general; violations of human rights; racial discrimination, including *apartheid*; the punishment of war criminals; freedom of information, freedom of association (trade-union rights), the status of women, refugees and stateless persons, slavery and servitude, forced labour, prevention of discrimination, protection of minorities, conventions in the field of human rights, the celebration of certain anniversaries of the Universal Declaration of Human Rights, the teaching of the principles of the Declaration, the submission of reports on human rights, advisory services in the field of human rights, discrimination in respect of employment and occupation, the problem of indigenous populations, the danger of a revival of nazism and racial intolerance, employment of women in senior and other professional positions by the secretariats of the United Nations system, protection of journalists engaged in dangerous missions, and the exploitation of labour through illicit and clandestine trafficking.

In its resolutions, the Council has not only used the word "recommends" but also such expressions as "calls upon", "suggests", "proposes", "expresses the hope", "invites", "requests", "urges", "urges strongly", "appeals to", "views with extreme concern", "condemns", etc.

The Council submits an annual report to the General Assembly. One part or several parts of this report deal with the Council's consideration or an action on questions of human rights.

### 3. *The functional commissions of the Economic and Social Council*

#### (a) *The Commission on Human Rights*

*Establishment*

Article 68 of the United Nations Charter provides that "The Economic and Social Council shall set up commissions in economic and social fields and for the promotion of human rights, and such other commissions as may be required for the performance of its functions". The Charter does not contain provisions concerning the composition or specifying the functions of the Commission on Human Rights.

The Commission on Human Rights, a subsidiary organ of the Economic and Social Council, is one of six functional commissions set up by the Council in 1946. It was established, by Council resolution 5 (I) of 16 February 1946, to render the required advice and assistance enabling the Council to discharge the responsibility assigned to it by the Charter of promoting universal respect for, and observance of, human rights and fundamental freedoms for all without distinction as to race, sex, language or religion.

*Functions and competence*

The terms of reference of the Commission, approved by the Council in resolution 5 (I) of 16 February 1946, as amended by Council resolution 9 (II) of 21 June 1946, are as follows:

"The work of the Commission shall be directed towards submitting proposals, recommendations and reports to the Council regarding:

"(*a*) An international bill of rights;

"(*b*) International declarations or conventions on civil liberties, the status of women, freedom of information and similar matters;

"(*c*) The protection of minorities;

"(*d*) The prevention of discrimination on grounds of race, sex, language or religion;

"(*e*) Any other matter concerning human rights not covered by items (*a*), (*b*), (*c*) and (*d*).

"The Commission shall make studies and recommendations and provide information and other services at the request of the Economic and Social Council.

"The Commission may propose to the Council any changes in its terms of reference.

"The Commission may make recommendations to the Council concerning any sub-commission which it considers should be established."

Under paragraph 3 of resolution 9 (II) of the Economic and Social Council, the Commission is authorized "to call in *ad hoc* working groups of non-governmental experts in specialized fields or individual experts, without further reference to the Council, but with the approval of the President [of the Economic and Social Council] and the Secretary-General".

The Commission made use of this authorization for the first time at its twenty-third session in 1967 when, by resolution 2 (XXIII) it established an *Ad Hoc* Working Group of Experts composed of eminent jurists and prison officials to investigate the charges of torture and ill-treatment of prisoners, detainees or persons in police custody in South Africa. The terms of reference of this *Ad Hoc* Working Group were later extended by decisions of the Commission and of the Economic and Social Council to cover also other territories in the south of Africa and to deal also with the question of violation of trade union rights. At its twenty-fifth session in 1969 the Commission decided to establish a special Working Group of Experts with the mandate to investigate allegations concerning Israel's violations of the Geneva Convention relative to the Protection of Civilian Persons in Time of War of 1949, in the Middle East.

The terms of reference of the Commission on Human Rights as laid down in 1946 were widened by Council resolutions 1235 (XLII) of 1967 and 1503 (XLVIII) of 1970, dealing with gross violations of human rights and communications relating to them. These recent arrangements are described below.

The Commission executes the directives of its parent organ, the Economic and Social Council and of the General Assembly. It also submits proposals and recommendations to the Council. The Commission's interaction with other United Nations organs or bodies which are not subordinate to the Commission is usually channelled through the Council.[20]

---

[20] There have been instances of the General Assembly addressing the Commission on Human Rights directly. The following are some examples : By resolution 545 (VI) in 1952, the General Assembly decided to include in the international covenant or covenants on human rights an article on the self-determination of peoples. It specified some of the terms of the article, and requested the Commission on Human Rights to submit to the General Assembly at its seventh session recommendations "concerning international respect for the self-determination of peoples". At its ninth session, the General Assembly by resolution 837 (IX), made a direct request to the Commission on Human Rights to complete its recommendations concerning international respect for the right of peoples and nations concerning self-determination. The General Assembly in this decision did not address itself to the Economic and Social Council except for a request to transmit the recommendations of the Commission on Human Rights to the General Assembly. By resolution 1041 (XI), the General Assembly decided to transmit directly to the Commission on Human Rights the official records and other documents relating to its discussion of interim measures to be taken with respect to the violation of human rights. In response to the above request, the Commission reported to the General Assembly through the Economic and Social Council. By resolution 2673 (XXV) the General Assembly invited the Commission to consider the question of the protection of journalists engaged in dangerous missions in areas of armed conflict as a matter of priority at its next (twenty-seventh) session. By resolution 2840 (XXVI) the General Assembly requested the Commission on Human Rights to consider the principles of international co-operation in the detection, arrest, extradition and punishment of persons guilty of war crimes and crimes against humanity and to submit a report on this question to the General Assembly. The General Assembly in its resolution 2854 (XXVI) requested the Commission on Human Rights to transmit its report on its twenty-eighth session to the Conference of Government Experts on the Reaffirmation and Development of International Humanitarian Law Applicable in Armed Conflicts. In resolution 2920 (XXVII) the General Assembly recommended that the Commission on Human Rights should consider the question of the exploitation of labour through illicit and clandestine trafficking as a matter of priority.

*Composition and membership*

Initially, the Commission consisted of a nucleus of nine members appointed by the Council in their individual capacity. The Commission thus constituted was asked to make recommendations on the definitive composition of the Commission to the Council at its second session.

Resolutions 9 (II) and 12 (II) of 21 June 1946, adopted by the Economic and Social Council after consideration of the report of the nuclear Commission on Human Rights, provide, *inter alia*, for the Commission to consist of one representative from each of 18 Member States of the United Nations selected by the Council. Members of the Commission are elected by secret ballot. The resolutions further provide that, with a view to securing a balanced representation in the various fields covered by the Commission, the Secretary-General shall consult with the Governments of the States selected to serve on the Commission before the representatives are finally nominated by these Governments and confirmed by the Economic and Social Council.

The membership of the Commission on Human Rights remained at 18 until 1961. Since then it has been enlarged twice, as follows: in its resolution 845 (XXXII) of 3 August 1961, the Economic and Social Council, noting that there had been a considerable increase in the membership of the United Nations since the establishment of the functional commissions of the Council, and believing in the importance of ensuring an equitable geographical distribution in the membership of the functional commissions, decided, *inter alia*, to increase the membership of the Commission on Human Rights from 18 to 21 members to be elected by the Council from among the Members of the United Nations. In its resolution 1147 (XLI) of 4 August 1966, the Economic and Social Council, noting that since its thirty-second session there had been a further increase in the membership of the United Nations, and taking into consideration the deep interest of many States Members of the United Nations in participating in, and contributing to, the work of the subsidiary bodies of experts, decided *inter alia*, to enlarge, with effect from 1 January 1967, the Commission on Human Rights from 21 to 32 members, those members to be elected on the basis of an equitable geographical distribution according to the following pattern:

(*a*) Eight members from African States;

(*b*) Six members from Asian States;

(*c*) Six members from Latin American States;

(*d*) Eight members from Western European and other States;

(*e*) Four members from socialist States of Eastern Europe.

The term of office of the members of the Commission on Human Rights is three years. A staggered arrangement of terms of service, arrived at by drawing lots for the initial periods following the establishment of the Commission and each one of its two enlargements, makes it possible for one third of the members to be elected every year, thus ensuring a certain continuity of membership. Moreover, retiring members of the Commission are eligible for immediate re-election. In the event that a member of the Commission is unable to serve for the full three-year term, the vacancy thus arising is filled by the Member Government after consultation with the Secretary-General and subject to confirmation by the Economic and Social Council.

*Procedural and operational arrangements*

The frequency of the sessions of the Commission on Human Rights is regulated by the Economic and Social Council. In resolution 1156 (XLI), the Council decided that the Commission should continue to meet annually as in the past. In its resolution 1165 (XLI), the Council, sharing the belief of the Commission on Human Rights that more than a four-week session each year would be needed to enable it to cope with its heavy agenda, decided to authorize the Commission to have a longer session, but one not exceeding six weeks, beginning in 1967. The Commission on Human Rights is subject to the provision of resolution 1156 (XLI) whereby the Council may decide to convene a special session of a Commission between its regular sessions, if the need arises.[21] The Commission normally meets at the Headquarters of the United Nations in New York or at the European Office of the Organization in Geneva.

The Commission operates under the rules of procedure of the functional commissions of the Economic and Social Council. These rules of procedure were initially adopted by the Economic and Social Council in its resolution 100 (V) of 1947 and revised by the Council in resolution 289 (X) of 1950. Subsequently a great number of amendments were adopted.[22]

In accordance with Council resolution 48 A (IV), the Commission on Human Rights invites the Commission on the Status of Women to send a representative to participate in its deliberations when items relating to discrimination based on sex are to be discussed. Such representatives usually make statements to the Commission on matters of interest to them and they may also reply to questions relating to such matters.

Each representative of a State member of the Commission may be accompanied by advisers and may be replaced during the session by an alternate designated by his Government. Alternates are designated by Governments in consultation with the Secretary-General.

In addition, the sessions of the Commission may be attended by the following:

(*a*) Representatives of any Members of the United Nations which are not represented on the Commission who are invited by the Commission to participate in its deliberations;

(*b*) Representatives of any Members of the United Nations which are not represented on the Commission who are designated by their Governments to sit as observers;

(*c*) Representatives of the specialized agencies;

---

[21] A special session of the Commission was held in 1949 in pursuance of Council resolution 197 (VIII) to elect new members of the Sub-Commission on Freedom of Information and of the press. Administratively, this meeting has been treated as the fourth session of the Commission (see E/1315).

[22] For text as of 31 December 1972, see United Nations publication, Sales No. E.70.I.90.

(*d*) Representatives of the Office of the United Nations High Commissioner for Refugees;

(*e*) Representatives of non-governmental organizations in consultative status with the Economic and Social Council in Category A or B or on the Register.

In resolution 1159 (XLI) of 5 August 1966, the Economic and Social Council invited the Secretary-General to make arrangements for the presence of observers as appropriate from the Council of Europe, the Inter-American Commission on Human Rights, the Organization of African Unity and the League of Arab States, and from other regional inter-governmental bodies particularly concerned for human rights at sessions of the Commission on Human Rights and of the Sub-Commission on Prevention of Discrimination and Protection of Minorities, and to arrange for the exchange of information between the Commission and these bodies on matters relating to human rights.

The Secretary-General or his representative acts in that capacity at all meetings of the Commission and of its committees. The Secretary-General is normally represented by the Director of the Division of Human Rights.

The Secretary-General or his representative may make oral as well as written statements to the Commission or its subsidiary bodies concerning any question under consideration.

The meetings of the Commission are public unless the Commission decides otherwise. Meetings held to consider communications concerning human rights under resolution 728 F (XXVIII) are private.

Economic and Social Council resolution 1503 (XLVIII) of 1970 established a new procedure for handling communications which appear to reveal a consistent pattern of gross and reliably attested violations of human rights and fundamental freedoms within the terms of reference of the Sub-Commission on Prevention of Discrimination and Protection of Minorities. The procedure of the Commission on Human Rights and its subsidiary organs under this Council resolution shall remain confidential until such time as the Commission may decide to make recommendations to the Economic and Social Council.

Summary records of the public meetings of the Commission are prepared and distributed by the Secretariat. The records of private meetings of the Commission are to be made available to the Members of the United Nations upon decision of the Commission and may be made public at such time and under such conditions as the Commission may decide.[23]

The provisional agenda for each session of the Commission, drawn up by the Secretary-General in consultation with the Commission Chairman whenever possible, may include items proposed by:

(1) The Commission at a previous session;

(2) The General Assembly, the Economic and Social Council, the Security Council or the Trusteeship Council;

(3) Members of the United Nations, the specialized agencies, and the International Atomic Energy Agency, provided such items are submitted with basic documents in sufficient time to reach the Secretary-General not less than forty-nine days before the first meeting of each session. Any such item submitted to the Secretary-General for inclusion in the provisional agenda less than forty-nine days before the date of the first meeting of the session shall also be accompanied by a statement of urgency and of the reasons which precluded its submission within the period of time specified;

(4) A sub-commission of the Commission;

(5) The Chairman or the Secretary-General; and

(6) Non-governmental organizations in consultative status in Category I, subject to the provisions of rule 7.[24]

Each year, at the commencement of its first meeting, the Commission elects a Chairman and one or more Vice-Chairmen, and other officers, from among its members.

All decisions of the Commission are made by a majority of the members present and voting.

Whenever the Commission recommends action by the Council, it is expected, under its rules of procedure, to frame, so far as practicable, its recommendation as a draft resolution of the Council.

*The Commission's report*

The Commission on Human Rights reports to the Economic and Social Council on the work of each session of the Commission. The report of the Commission is divided into several chapters. In accordance with the pattern which has so far prevailed, the first chapter usually deals with the organization of the session. Subsequent chapters deal separately with each of the agenda items considered by the Commission. These chapters contain a summary of the debate and the proposals in connexion with each topic and a record of any decision or action taken thereon by the Commission. One chapter is devoted to the adoption of the Commission's report and another contains the text of the draft resolutions recommended by the Commission for action by the Economic and Social Council.

---

[23] At various sessions the Commission has decided to make public the records of the private meetings devoted to consideration of the item relating to communications. For example, see report of the fifteenth session of the Commission (*Official Records of the Economic and Social Council, Twenty-eighth Session, Supplement No. 8*, para. 247).

[24] Rule 7 of the rules of procedure of the functional commissions of the Economic and Social Council reads as follows : "Non-governmental organizations in Category I may propose items for the provisional agenda of commissions subject to the following conditions :

(*a*) An organization which intends to propose such an item shall inform the Secretary-General at least sixty-three days before the commencement of the session, and before formally proposing an item shall give due consideration to any comments the Secretariat may make;

(*b*) The proposal shall be formally submitted with the relevant basic documentation not less than forty-nine days before the commencement of the session. The item shall be included in the agenda of the Commission if it is adopted by a two-thirds majority of those present and voting."

*Decisions and action taken by the Commission*

In the course of each session, the Commission deals with several categories of items: some of them are questions referred to the Commission by the General Assembly directly (on rare occasions, see foot-note 35 *supra*.) or through the Economic and Social Council, or by the Council itself. Others pertain to the work of the Commission's subordinate bodies and the consideration of their reports. Still others consist in the consideration, alone or in conjunction with a broader examination of an item, of reports of the Secretary-General submitted to the Commission. Yet another category covers the various aspects of the conduct of the Commission's business. The Commission adopts its own resolutions and also recommends draft resolutions for adoption by the Economic and Social Council. Those to whom parts of the Commission's own resolutions have been addressed directly include States Members of the United Nations or their Governments, the Secretary-General, specialized agencies, and non-governmental organizations with competence in the field of human rights.

The terminology used in the resolutions and texts reflecting the Commission's action and decisions has varied, depending on the nature of the question or item or aspects thereof acted upon; or on the terms of the Commission's mandate to deal with the question; or on whether the Commission addressed its decision to a higher or a subordinate body; or on a combination of the preceding factors. For example: The Commission on Human Rights adopted, at its twenty-second session, resolution 2 (XXII) on the question of the "violation of human rights and fundamental freedoms, including policies of racial discrimination and segregation and of *apartheid* in all countries, with particular reference to colonial and other dependent countries and territories". In this resolution the Commission, bearing in mind its special responsibilities for the promotion of human rights and fundamental freedoms everywhere, considering that the Economic and Social Council, in its resolution 1102 (XL) asked that the Commission should consider as a matter of importance and urgency the question and submit to the Council at its forty-first session its recommendation on measures to halt those violations, *inter alia*, condemned violations of human rights and fundamental freedoms whenever they occur; requested the Economic and Social Council to recommend to the General Assembly certain measures aiming at halting violations; instructed the Sub-Commission on Prevention of Discrimination and Protection of Minorities to examine all relevant United Nations materials and to submit to the Commission at its twenty-third session such recommendations or comments as it considers appropriate; requested the Economic and Social Council to transmit the resolution of the Commission to the Special Committee on the Implementation of the Declaration on the Granting of Independence to Colonial Countries and Peoples; informed the Council that, in order completely to deal with the question of violation of human rights and fundamental freedoms in all countries, it will be necessary for the Commission to consider fully the means by which it may be more fully informed of violations of human rights with a view to devising recommendations for measures to halt them; and decided to consider at its twenty-third session the question of the Commission's tasks and functions and its role in relation to violation of human rights in all countries.

In its resolution 3 (XXVI) section B of 1970, the Commission on Human Rights declared that the policy of *apartheid* was the most reprehensible manifestation of racial discrimination and urged all Governments to proclaim and reaffirm their abhorrence and condemnation of *apartheid* and racial discrimination in southern Africa, in particular. In resolution 9 (XXVII) relating to the question of the violation of human rights in the territories occupied as a result of hostilities in the Middle East, the Commission condemned the continued violation of human rights in the occupied territories and specifically listed the policies and practices which it was condemning. In resolution 2 (XXVIII) of 1972, the Commission on Human Rights stated that it was determined to bring about the complete elimination of racial discrimination in all its forms and manifestations and that it was disturbed at the situation in southern Africa and elsewhere in which racial discrimination continued and was in many cases intensified.

In respect of the reports on the sessions of its subordinate bodies, the Commission usually takes note of them as a whole and acts as it deems appropriate on any parts thereof.

*Subsidiary bodies*

The functional commissions of the Economic and Social Council may establish subsidiary bodies of their own to examine certain questions falling within their general province and competence. These subsidiary bodies may be of two kinds: permanent sub-commissions to deal with a whole category of questions (for the establishment of which the authorization of the Council is needed) and *ad hoc* or special committees to deal with a particular question [25]—for example, to draw up a draft convention. The existence of such a committee may cease as soon as it has carried out its terms of reference.

The Commission on Human Rights set up two sub-commissions of the first of the types mentioned above: a Sub-Commission on Freedom of Information and of the Press (which was discontinued in 1952), and a Sub-Commission on the Prevention of Discrimination and Protection of Minorities.

The Committee on Periodic Reports is one of the bodies of the second type which the Commission on Human Rights set up during the period 1964-1966. It is dealt with separately below.

Earlier, at its twelfth session, the Commission on Human Rights had established a committee [26] composed of four of its members, it being agreed that they would

[25] An example is the Working Group established by Commission resolution 4 (XXII) to study all relevant questions concerning the proposal to create the institution of a United Nations High Commissioner for Human Rights and to report to the Commission at its twenty-third session.

[26] See *Official Records of the Economic and Social Council, Twenty-second Session, Supplement No. 3*, para. 49; also Economic and Social Council resolution 624 B (XXII).

be serving as representatives of States and not as individuals, to prepare a *Study of the Right of Everyone to be Free from Arbitrary Arrest, Detention and Exile*.[27] At its seventeenth session, the Commission requested the Committee to prepare a study on the right of arrested persons to communicate with those whom it is necessary for them to consult in order to ensure their defence or to protect their essential interests.

### (i) *The Sub-Commission on Prevention of Discrimination and Protection of Minorities*

*Establishment*

By resolution 9 (II) of the Economic and Social Council, the Commission on Human Rights was authorized to establish sub-commissions on the protection of minorities and on the prevention of discrimination. The Council issued certain directives concerning the functions of the two sub-commissions whose establishment it authorized, but left the final decision on this matter to the Commission on Human Rights.

The Commission, at its first session held from 27 January to 10 February 1947, decided to establish one Sub-Commission on Prevention of Discrimination and Protection of Minorities instead of creating separate sub-commissions, as empowered to do by the Council.

*Functions and competence*

The Sub-Commission's initial terms of reference were clarified and extended in scope at the fifth session of the Commission on Human Rights in 1949. They are as follows: [28]

"(*a*) To undertake studies, particularly in the light of the Universal Declaration of Human Rights, and to make recommendations to the Commission on Human Rights concerning the prevention of discrimination of any kind relating to human rights and fundamental freedoms and the protection of racial, national, religious and linguistic minorities; and

"(*b*) To perform any other functions which may be entrusted to it by the Economic and Social Council or the Commission on Human Rights."

By resolution 1235 (XLII) on the "Question of the violation of human rights and fundamental freedoms, including policies of racial discrimination and segregation and of *apartheid*, in all countries, with particular reference to colonial and other dependent countries and territories" the Economic and Social Council welcomed the decision of the Commission on Human Rights to give annual consideration to the item relating to violation of human rights and concurred with the request for assistance in this regard addressed to the Sub-Commission on Prevention of Discrimination and Protection of Minorities. It authorized the Commission on Human Rights and the Sub-Commission to examine information relevant to gross violations of human rights and fundamental freedoms contained in the communications listed by the Secretary-General pursuant to Economic and Social Council resolution 728 F (XXVIII) of 1959. In resolution 1503 (XLVIII) of 1970 the Economic and Social Council authorized the Sub-Commission on Prevention of Discrimination and Protection of Minorities to appoint a working group to meet once a year in private meetings to consider all communications including replies of Governments thereon with a view to bringing to the attention of the Sub-Commission those communications together with the replies of Governments, if any, which appeared to reveal a consistent pattern of gross and reliably attested violations of human rights and fundamental freedoms within the terms of reference of the Sub-Commission. The Council also decided that the Sub-Commission should devise appropriate procedures for dealing with the question of admissibility of communications received by the Secretary-General under Council resolution 728 F (XXVIII) and in accordánce with Council resolution 1235 (XLII). It requested the Sub-Commission to consider the communications brought before it in accordance with the decision of a majority of the members of the working group and any replies of Governments relating thereto and other relevant information with a view to determining whether to refer to the Commission on Human Rights particular situations which appeared to reveal a consistent pattern of gross and reliably attested violations of human rights requiring consideration by the Commission.

The Sub-Commission on Prevention of Discrimination and Protection of Minorities gave effect to the request addressed to it by the Economic and Social Council by adopting resolution 1 (XXIV) of 14 August 1971 containing provisional procedures for dealing with the question of admissibility of communications.

*Composition and membership*

The Sub-Commission is composed of persons selected by the Commission on Human Rights to serve normally for three years [29] in their capacity as individuals and not as representatives of States. The selection is made in consultation with the Secretary-General and is subject to the consent of the Governments of the States of which the persons are nationals. Not more than one person may be selected from any single country.

Originally the Sub-Commission had 12 members. Following the increase in the membership of the United Nations, the Sub-Commission was subsequently enlarged. By Commission resolution 11 (XV) and Council resolution 728 E (XXVIII), it was increased to 14 in 1959; by Commission resolution 4 (XXI) and Council resolution 1074 G (XXXIX), it was raised in 1965 to 18, "in order to ensure adequate representation to different regions, legal systems and cultures"; and by Commission resolution 9 (XXIV) and Council resolution 1334 (XLIV) it was increased as from 1969 to 26.

---

[27] The study was submitted to the Commission together with draft principles on freedom from arbitrary arrest and detention. See United Nations publication, Sales No. 65.XIV.2.

[28] *Official Records of the Economic and Social Council, Ninth Session, Supplement No. 10*, para. 13.

[29] *Official Records of the Economic and Social Council, Fourth Session, Supplement No. 3*, chap. IV, and *ibid., Ninth Session, Supplement No. 10*, para. 13.

By resolution 1334 (XLIV) of 31 May 1968 the Council further decided that the 26 members of the Sub-Commission shall be elected from nominations of experts made by States Members of the United Nations on the following basis:

From the Afro-Asian group of States, 12 members;
From Western European and other States, 6 members;
From Latin American States, 5 members;
From Eastern European States, 3 members.

In resolution 502 A (XVI) of 3 August 1953, the Economic and Social Council decided that the Sub-Commission should meet at least once a year for three weeks. Since that time the Sub-Commission has held annual sessions.[30]

*Procedural and operational arrangements*

The proceedings of the Sub-Commission are governed by the rules of procedure of the functional commissions of the Economic and Social Council in so far as these rules are applicable. (Rule 71 of the rules of procedure of the functional commissions.)

Under rule 68, the Sub-Commission elects its own officers "unless otherwise directed" by the Commission on Human Rights. In practice, the Sub-Commission has always elected its Chairman, one or more (at recent sessions three) Vice-Chairmen and a Rapporteur.

A member of the Sub-Commission who is unable to attend the whole or part of a session may, with the consent of his Government and in consultation with the Secretary-General, designate an alternate who then has the same status as a member of the Sub-Commission. This provision was resorted to on a number of occasions.

In accordance with Council resolution 48 (IV), the Sub-Commission invites the Commission on the Status of Women to send a representative to participate in its deliberations when items relating to discrimination based on sex are to be discussed.

In addition, the meetings of the Sub-Commission are attended by the following: Observers designated by Governments of Member States; representatives of specialized agencies; and representatives of interested non-governmental organizations in consultative status with the Economic and Social Council. Following the adoption of Economic and Social Council resolution 1159 (XLI) of 5 August 1966, the session of the Sub-Commission may also be attended by observers as appropriate from the Council of Europe, the Inter-American Commission on Human Rights, the Organization of African Unity and the League of Arab States, and from other regional intergovernmental bodies particularly concerned with human rights, in accordance with the operative paragraph of the said resolution.

The Secretary-General is represented at the meetings of the Sub-Commission by the Director or the Deputy Director of the Division of Human Rights.

*Studies by special rapporteurs*

In connexion with the various studies which it has undertaken under its terms of reference and the authorization of the Council, the Sub-Commission has made frequent use of the method of appointing special rapporteurs from among its own members, who have submitted for consideration by the Sub-Commission reports on such questions as discrimination in education; discrimination in the matter of religious rights and practices; discrimination in the matter of political rights; discrimination in respect of the right of everyone to leave any country, including his own, and to return to his country; discrimination against persons born out of wedlock; equality in the administration of justice; and racial discrimination in the political, economic, social and cultural spheres.[31]

The standard directives relating to the preparation of such studies were set out in Sub-Commission resolution B of 15 January 1954[32] as amended by Commission resolution III adopted at the tenth session of the Commission on Human Rights.[33] As decided therein, the "study" or the "report" (the two terms seem to be used interchangeably) should be carried out in three stages:

I. Collection, analysis and verification of material;
II. Production of a report;
III. Recommendations for action.

The three stages are detailed by the resolution:

"I

"*Collection, analysis and verification of material*

"The main sources of material will be the following:

"(*a*) Governments; (*b*) the Secretary-General; (*c*) specialized agencies; (*d*) non-governmental organizations; (*e*) writings of recognized scholars and scientists, though the collection of material should not be limited to these sources.

[30] In 1950 the Economic and Social Council, by resolution 414 (XIII), decided to discontinue the Sub-Commission after a final session in October 1951, until 31 December 1954, its work to be taken over by the Council, the Commission on Human Rights, the Secretary-General and *ad hoc* bodies as appropriate. The General Assembly, at its sixth session, adopted resolution 532 B (VI), in which, "considering that the prevention of discrimination and protection of minorities are two of the most important branches of the positive work undertaken by the United Nations", it invited the Council (*a*) to authorize the Sub-Commission on Prevention of Discrimination and Protection of Minorities "to continue its work so that it may fulfil its mission, and especially to convene a session in 1952", and "(*b*) to take any practical steps that may be necessary for the continuance, within the framework of the United Nations, of the work on prevention of discrimination and protection of minorities". Accordingly a fifth session of the Sub-Commission was held in 1952. In 1953 the Council decided that the Sub-Commission should meet once a year, and it has done so ever since.

[31] The *Study of Discrimination in Education*, first of the series, was published in 1957 (Sales No. 57.XIV.3); the *Study of Discrimination in the Matter of Religious Rights and Practices*, the second, was published in 1960 (Sales No. 60.XIV.2); the *Study of Discrimination in the Matter of Political Rights*, the third, was published in 1963 (Sales No. 63.XIV.2); the *Study of Discrimination in Respect of the Right of Everyone to Leave any Country, Including His Own, and to Return to His Country*, the fourth, was published in 1964 (Sales No. 64.XIV.2); the *Study of Discrimination Against Persons Born out of Wedlock*, the fifth, was published in 1968 (Sales No. 68.XIV.3) and the *Study of Equality in the Administration of Justice*, the sixth, was published in 1972 (Sales No. E.71. XIV.3).

[32] See E/CN.4/703, para. 97.

[33] *Official Records of the Economic and Social Council, Eighteenth Session, Supplement No. 7*, para. 418.

"Summaries of material dealing with each country will be prepared and forwarded to the Governments concerned for comment and supplementary data.

"II

"Production of a report

"(*a*) *Nature of the report*

"(i) It should be undertaken on a global basis and with respect to all the grounds of discrimination condemned by the Universal Declaration of Human Rights, but special attention should be given to instances of discrimination that are typical of general tendencies and instances where discrimination has been successfully overcome.

"(ii) The report should be factual and objective and should deal with the *de facto* as well as the *de jure* situation regarding discrimination in . . .

"(iii) The report should point out the general trend and development of legislation and practices with regard to discrimination stating whether their tendency is toward an appreciable elimination or reduction of discrimination, whether they are static, or whether they are retrogressive.

"(iv) The report should also point out the factors which in each instance have led to the discriminatory practices, pointing out those which are economic, social, political, or historic in character and those resulting from a policy evidently intended to originate, maintain or aggravate such practices.

"(v) The report should be drawn up not only to serve as a basis for the Sub-Commission's recommendations, but also with a view to educating world opinion.

"(vi) In drawing up the report full advantage should be taken of the conclusions already reached with respect to discrimination by other bodies of the United Nations or by the specialized agencies.

"(*b*) *Method of production*

"(i) A special rapporteur shall draw up a draft report along the lines laid down in paragraph (a), bearing in mind the observations made in the debates by members of the Sub-Commission. . . . The rapporteur shall proceed with expedition with a view to submitting the report at [a session of the Sub-Commission].

"Should he fail to complete his work for that date, he shall submit a progress report in which he shall give an account of the material assembled and of the methods adopted or which he intends to adopt in carrying out his work.

"(ii) In addition to the material and information which he is able to collect and which he shall embody in his report in the form of an analysis, the special rapporteur shall include such conclusions and proposals as he may judge proper to enable the Sub-Commission to make recommendations for action to the Commission on Human Rights.

"III

"*Recommendations for action*

"These shall be made following the consideration of the report by the Sub-Commission."

At its twelfth session in 1956, the Commission on Human Rights decided "that materials and studies in the field of discrimination should relate to States Members of the United Nations and of the specialized agencies, and that such recommendations as may be made should be of an objective and general character, in accordance with the Charter of the United Nations".[34]

Studies carried out by a special rapporteur appointed by the Sub-Commission may provide the basis for the preparation of draft instruments or the formulation of principles on the problem under consideration. Thus, the first study, on discrimination in education, provided the basis for the preparation of the UNESCO Convention on this subject. The second, on discrimination in religious rights and practices, has been used in the drafting of the declaration and convention against all forms of religious intolerance, which are still under consideration by United Nations organs. The formulation of the "General Principles on Equality and Non-Discrimination in Respect of Persons Born out of Wedlock" adopted by the Sub-Commission at its nineteenth session was based on the study on the same subject conducted by a special rapporteur appointed by the Sub-Commission.[35]

*Decisions and action by the Sub-Commission*

On some questions, including those which relate to the various facets of the conduct of its work and the discharge of its functions, the Sub-Commission adopts its own resolutions. On others, it formulates draft resolutions and requests their adoption by the Commission on Human Rights. As to the terminology employed, resolutions of the Sub-Commission have contained, by way of illustration, requests addressed to various parties (e.g., the Commission on Human Rights, the specialized agencies, the Secretary-General, the special rapporteurs appointed by the Sub-Commission); expressions of gratitude or appreciation to various parties or of hope or gratification in connexion with certain developments; condemnation of certain practices; and decisions to initiate certain studies or to consider certain questions.

The Sub-Commission has in some cases prepared, at the request of higher organs, drafts of instruments in the field of human rights.

(ii) *The* ad hoc *committee on periodic reports of the Commission on Human Rights*

To assist the Commission on Human Rights in considering the periodic reports by States submitted under Economic and Social Council resolution 624 B (XXII)

[34] *Official Records of the Economic and Social Council, Twenty-second Session, Supplement No. 3*, resolution IX.

[35] On the subject of studies prepared by the Sub-Commission, see also the section of this publication dealing with studies in the field of human rights in general.

of 1956 and under later resolutions which amended and supplemented it, various *ad hoc* committees were established. The activities under the system of periodic reports on human rights are described in chapter III below. In the present context it is only appropriate to state that the Commission on Human Rights had originally, in 1956, proposed a system of annual reports on human rights (Commission resolution 1 (XII) of 1956). Under the system as established by the Economic and Social Council, reports were to be submitted every three years (Economic and Social Council resolution 624 B (XII) of 1956). By its resolution 1596 (L) of 1971 the Economic and Social Council changed the cycle for periodic reports previously in force by asking States to submit periodic reports once every two years in a continuing cycle, the first on civil and political rights, the second on economic, social and cultural rights and the third on freedom of information.

(iii) *The* ad hoc *committee envisaged under Council resolution 1503 (XLVIII)*

Council resolution 1503 (XLVIII) of 27 May 1970, which establishes a new procedure for certain communications relating to violations of human rights and fundamental freedoms, requests the Commission on Human Rights after it has examined any situation referred to it by the Sub-Commission to determine whether it may be a subject of an investigation by an *ad hoc* committee to be appointed by the Commission, which shall be undertaken only with the express consent of the State concerned and shall be conducted in constant co-operation with that State and under conditions determined by agreement with it. The composition of the Committee shall be determined by the Commission, the members of the Committee shall be independent persons whose competence and impartiality is beyond question. Their appointment shall be subject to the consent of the Government concerned.

(b) *The Commission on the Status of Women*

*Establishment*

The Economic and Social Council, at its first session in 1946, established a nuclear Sub-Commission on the Status of Women as a sub-commission of the nuclear Commission on Human Rights. This Sub-Commission was instructed to submit proposals to the Council through the Commission on Human Rights regarding, *inter alia*, its terms of reference and the scope of its future work.

The Council, having considered at its second session the reports of the nuclear Commission on Human Rights and of the nuclear Sub-Commission on the Status of Women, decided, by resolution 11 (II) of 21 June 1946, to confer upon the latter the status of a full Commission to be known as the Commission on the Status of Women.

*Functions and competence*

The functions of the Commission were initially set out in resolution 11 (II) of the Economic and Social Council. They were subsequently defined, in Council resolution 48 (IV) of 29 March 1947, as follows:

"The functions of the Commission shall be to prepare recommendations and reports to the Economic and Social Council on promoting women's rights in political, economic, civil, social and educational fields. The Commission shall also make recommendations to the Council on urgent problems requiring immediate attention in the field of women's rights with the object of implementing the principle that men and women shall have equal rights, and to develop proposals to give effect to such recommendations."

*Composition and membership*

The Commission is composed of representatives of States Members of the United Nations elected by the Council. The States elected to serve on the Commission nominate, after consultation with the Secretary-General, their representatives, and these nominations are confirmed by the Economic and Social Council. The members of the Commission are normally elected for three years and are eligible for re-election.

The membership of the Commission was originally set at 15 but was expanded in 1951 to 18 members, and then to 21 in 1961. By Council resolution 1147 (XLI) of 4 August 1966, the membership of the Commission was further increased, with effect from 1 January 1967, from 21 to 32 members, those members to be elected on the basis of an equitable geographical distribution according to the same pattern as established for the Commission on Human Rights.

*Procedural and operational arrangements*

By resolution 1156 (XLI) of 5 August 1966, the Council decided that the Commission should continue to meet annually. According to this decision, the Commission on the Status of Women held its twentieth, twenty-first, twenty-second and twenty-third sessions in 1967, 1968, 1969 and 1970, respectively. However, at its forty-seventh session in 1969, the Economic and Social Council decided that, starting in 1971, the Commission should meet biennially (1637th meeting of the Council, 8 August 1969). According to that decision the Commission held its twenty-fourth session in 1972 and will hold its twenty-fifth session in 1974. The sessions of the Commission are usually of three weeks' duration. The place of meeting has normally been the Headquarters of the United Nations in New York or the United Nations Office at Geneva. The Commission however has occasionally been invited by a Member State to hold a session in its territory.[36] Thus, the third session of the Commission in 1949 was held in Beirut, at the invitation of the Government of Lebanon; the fourteenth session in 1960 in Buenos Aires, at the invitation of the Government of Argentina and the eighteenth in 1965 in Teheran, at the invitation of the Government of Iran.

[36] It will be recalled in this connexion that the General Assembly adopted resolution 1202 (XII) of 13 December 1957, entitled "Pattern of Conferences", operative para. 2 (*e*) of which reads as follows: "Meetings may be held away from the established headquarters of any body in other cases where a Government issuing an invitation for a meeting to be held within its territory has agreed to defray, after consultations with the Secretary-General as to their nature and possible extent, the additional costs involved."

The Commission operates under the rules of procedure of the functional commissions of the Economic and Social Council.

Sessions of the Commission on the Status of Women may be attended by observers designated by Member States of the United Nations which are not members of the Commission, but which have a particular interest in its work. At the Commission's twenty-fourth session, a State member of several specialized agencies, not a Member of the United Nations, was represented by an observer.

Specialized agencies have also the right to be represented at sessions of the Commission. Representatives of the ILO and UNESCO have played an active part in the Commission's deliberations with respect to items of concern to them. The Commission has frequently requested the assistance of these agencies in preparing documentation relating to items within their competence. Each agency also submits regularly to the Commission a report on its activities concerning women.

The Council at its forty-first session, in its resolution 1134 (XLI) of 26 July 1966, entitled "Co-operation in the unified long-term United Nations programme for the advancement of women", invited two specialized agencies (the Food and Agriculture Organization of the United Nations and the World Health Organization) and the United Nations Children's Fund to submit to the Commission reports on those of their activities which were of particular interest for the advancement of women.

In accordance with resolution 48 (IV) of the Economic and Social Council, observers from inter-governmental organizations in the field of women's rights may attend sessions of the Commission in an advisory and informative capacity and arrangements can be made for the exchange of information between the Commission and such regional inter-governmental organizations on subjects relating to the status of women. The Inter-American Commission of Women has been represented at the Commission since the above Council resolution was adopted in 1947; the Inter-American Commission submits a report on its activities to the Commission every year.

Observers from international non-governmental organizations which enjoy consultative status with the Economic and Social Council also attend regularly sessions of the Commission. At the invitation of the Chairman, they make oral statements on items being discussed by the Commission. In accordance with resolution 1296 (XLIV) of the Economic and Social Council, non-governmental organizations with consultative status are entitled to circulate statements pertinent to the Commission's deliberations.

At the commencement of the first meeting of each session the Commission elects a Chairman and one or more Vice-Chairmen and a Rapporteur. Since its twenty-first session in 1968 the Commission has always elected three Vice-Chairmen.

At the end of each session, the Commission adopts, for submission to the Council, a report summarizing its debates, decisions and recommendations. This is presented in the same form as the report of the Commission on Human Rights.

*Decisions of the Commission*

The Commission on the Status of Women which utilizes similar methods of work as the Commission on Human Rights deals with several categories of items, including items referred to it by the General Assembly (through the Economic and Social Council), or by the Council itself. It has also been the practice of the Commission on the Status of Women to deal, at each session, with aspects of political rights of women, of the status of women in private law, of the access of girls and women to education and of economic rights and opportunities for women. It normally bases its consideration of these items on reports furnished by the Secretary-General or by the appropriate specialized agency (i.e., the ILO and UNESCO).

In addition to preparing conventions, declarations, and recommendations, and considering the implementation of such instruments, primarily through reporting systems, the Commission adopts a variety of resolutions, many containing recommendations for action by Governments, specialized agencies and non-governmental organizations.

As in the case of the Commission on Human Rights, the Commission on the Status of Women adopts its own resolutions and recommends draft resolutions for adoption by the Economic and Social Council. The Commission's own internal resolutions have been addressed: to the Secretary-General; to the Commission on Human Rights in certain circumstances (for example, recommendations concerning periodic reports on human rights); to the Economic and Social Council; to States Members of the United Nations and of the specialized agencies in certain special circumstances, usually in connexion with requests for information;[37] to specialized agencies (the ILO and UNESCO) in certain circumstances, especially in connexion with reports which are submitted on a continuing basis; and to non-governmental organizations.

Resolutions recommended by the Commission for adoption by the Economic and Social Council and internal resolutions adopted by the Commission at recent sessions related, among other subjects, to periodic reports on human rights, the status of women and family planning, parental rights and duties, the status of the unmarried mother, the implementation of the Declaration on the Elimination of Discrimination against Women, protection of women and children in emergency and armed conflict, employment of women in senior and other professional positions by the secretariats of the organizations in the United Nations system, the status of women agricultural workers, employment of women with family responsibilities and the employment of domestic workers.

### 4. *The Secretariat*

Under the Charter, the Secretariat is a principal organ of the United Nations, comprising the Secretary-General,

[37] The Commission has adopted many resolutions containing recommendations to Governments to take certain action. These have always been addressed to Governments through the Economic and Social Council.

who is the chief administrative officer of the Organization, and a staff appointed by him under regulations established by the General Assembly (Articles 97-101). The Secretary-General and the staff may not seek or receive instructions from any Government or from any other authority external to the Organization, and each Member of the United Nations has undertaken in the Charter to respect the exclusively international character of the Secretary-General and the staff and not to seek to influence them in the discharge of their responsibilities (Article 101).

Under Article 98 of the Charter the Secretary-General acts in that capacity in all meetings of the General Assembly, of the Security Council, of the Economic and Social Council, and of the Trusteeship Council. He performs such other functions as are entrusted to him by these organs. He makes an annual report to the General Assembly on the work of the Organization. The report reviews developments during the period covered in the various fields of activities. It contains in part three (Economic, social and humanitarian activities) a section on human rights questions. In addition to the Report of the Secretary-General on the work of the Organization proper, the Secretary-General regularly also publishes an introduction to the report in which he comments on various questions and issues which in his opinion are of special concern to the Organization.

The Report of the Secretary-General on the work of the organization for the period 16 June 1971 to 15 June 1972 appeared as document A/8701.[38] The introduction to the report of the Secretary-General, dated August 1972, appeared as document A/8701/Add.1.[39]

Under Article 99 of the Charter, the Secretary-General may bring to the attention of the Security Council any matter which in his opinion may threaten the maintenance of international peace and security.

*Division of Human Rights*

One of the divisions of the Secretariat is the Division of Human Rights. In the early years of the United Nations it was part of the Department of Social Affairs and later of the Department of Economic and Social Affairs. With effect as from April 1958, responsibility for the functions and staff of the Division of Human Rights was transferred from the Under-Secretary for Economic and Social Affairs to the Under-Secretary in Charge of Special Political Affairs. Since that time the Division of Human Rights has reported to the Chef de Cabinet, Under-Secretaries-General for Special Political Affairs and, since 1 May 1972, to the Under-Secretary-General for Political and General Assembly Affairs.

The Division of Human Rights is headed by a Director. These is also a Deputy Director. The Division is divided into sections and units which are headed by a Principal Officer or by senior officers as Chiefs of Sections and Chiefs of Units, respectively.

[38] *Official Records of the General Assembly, Twenty-seventh Session, Supplement No. 1.*

[39] *Ibid., Supplement No. 1A.*

*Other departments of the Secretariat which deal with matters relating to human rights*

The Centre for Social Development and Humanitarian Affairs was recently established within the Department of Economic and Social Affairs. Among its functions are those previously entrusted to the Section on the Status of Women of the Division of Human Rights, for which now the Promotion of Equality of Men and Women Branch of the Centre, headed by a Deputy Director, is responsible.

Various other units of the Secretariat may, of course, have to be concerned with matters relating to human rights in connexion with their activities. The Office of Legal Affairs is responsible, *inter alia*, for advising the Secretariat and other organs of the United Nations on legal questions, and has dealt with human rights matters referred by the General Assembly to its Sixth Committee, such as the Convention on the Prevention and Punishment of the Crime of Genocide and the Declaration on the Right of Asylum. The Department of Political and Security Council Affairs has been concerned with matters relating to human rights which have been considered by the Security Council or subsidiary bodies of the Security Council and the General Assembly, the First and the Special Political Committees of the General Assembly, and with some items of a mainly political character which have been directly considered by the plenary meetings of the General Assembly. The Department of Trusteeship and Information from Non-Self-Governing Territories has dealt with matters relating to human rights which have arisen in the Trusteeship Council, the Fourth Committee of the General Assembly and the Special Committee on the Situation with regard to the Implementation of the Declaration on the Granting of Independence to Colonial Countries and Peoples. The Non-Governmental Organizations Section of the Department of Economic and Social Affairs is responsible for the arrangements for consultation with non-governmental organizations established by the Economic and Social Council; reviews and processes applications from non-governmental organizations for consultative status; and arranges briefing of non-governmental organizations and attendance at conferences of non-governmental organizations in a liaison capacity with the United Nations. The Office of Public Information prepares and disseminates materials of various kinds to acquaint the public with the work and the activities of the United Nations in the field of human rights.

### 5. *The Office of the United Nations High Commissioner for Refugees*

Among the measures which the United Nations has taken to alleviate the plight of refugees after the International Refugee Organization, a specialized agency of the United Nations, terminated its activities in 1952, were the preparation and adoption of the Convention relating to the Status of Refugees which came into effect on 22 April 1954, the Protocol relating to the Status of Refugees which came into effect on 4 October 1967 and the Convention relating to the Status of Stateless Persons of 1954 which came into force on 6 June 1960, and the establishment as of 1 January 1951 of the Office of the United Nations High Commissioner for Refugees (UNHCR) by General Assembly resolution 319 (IV) of 3 December 1949.[40]

The functions of the High Commissioner are to provide, under the auspices of the United Nations, international protection to refugees who fall within the scope of the Statute, and to seek permanent solutions for the problem of refugees by assisting Governments and, under certain conditions, private organizations to facilitate the voluntary repatriation of refugees or their assimilation within new national communities. Under the Statute, those within the High Commissioner's competence are not only persons who have become refugees as a result of events occurring before 1 January 1951 but also persons who have become refugees as a result of events occurring after that date.

Since the date of the Statute the General Assembly has adopted various resolutions relating to the functions and competence of the High Commissioner's Office, and in certain cases the General Assembly has called upon the High Commissioner to assist specific groups of refugees not covered by the strict terms of the Statute. Thus in resolution 1388 (XIV) of 20 November 1959, the General Assembly authorized the High Commissioner in respect of refugees who did not come within the competence of the United Nations to use his good offices in the transmission of contributions designed to provide assistance to these refugees.

At its twenty-seventh session the General Assembly on 12 December 1972 adopted resolution 2958 (XXVII) on assistance to Sudanese refugees returning from abroad. In that resolution the General Assembly noted with appreciation the efforts of the Government of the Sudan to achieve a peaceful and lasting settlement in the southern part of the country and commended the United Nations High Commissioner for Refugees for the efficient manner in which he had been co-ordinating the relief, resettlement and rehabilitation operations in southern Sudan.

The competence of the Office of the High Commissioner extends to persons covered by the Convention relating to the Status of Refugees, adopted on 28 July 1951 by a Conference of Plenipotentiaries convened under General Assembly resolution 429 (V) of 1950. The Convention of 1951 applies only to persons who have become refugees as a result of events occurring before 1 January 1951. With the passage of time and the emergence of new refugee situations the need was increasingly felt to broaden the scope of the Convention *ratione personae*. As a result a Protocol relating to the Status of Refugees was prepared and submitted to the United Nations General Assembly in 1966. The General Assembly took note of the Protocol in resolution 2198 (XXI) of 16 December 1966 and requested the Secretary-General to submit the text thereof to States to enable them to accede. The Protocol entered into force on 4 October 1967 upon the deposit of the sixth instrument of accession.

As mentioned above, in accordance with the Statute of his Office the High Commissioner is called upon to provide international protection for refugees falling within his competence. An important aspect of this activity specifically mentioned in the Statute is promoting the conclusion and ratification of international conventions for the protection of refugees. The principal international instrument of this type is the Convention relating to the Status of Refugees of 28 July 1951 which defines the basic rights of refugees and lays down the minimum standards for their treatment in their countries of asylum as regards a variety of matters affecting their day-to-day existence. The provision of international protection by the United Nations High Commissioner for Refugees by promoting the adoption of such international instruments, and constant efforts to ensure that refugees are treated in accordance with the minimum standards which they incorporate is an example of practical action in the field of human rights.

In resolution 1167 (XII) of 26 November 1957 the General Assembly, having considered the problem of the Chinese refugees in Hong Kong, recognized that the problem was such as to be of concern to the international community and authorized the High Commissioner to use his good offices to encourage arrangements for contributions with a view to alleviating the distress of these refugees. In resolution 1784 (XVII) of 7 December 1962 the General Assembly recalled resolution 1167 (XII) and requested the High Commissioner to continue to use his good offices, in agreement with the Governments of the countries concerned, to provide assistance to the Chinese refugees in Hong Kong.

In resolution 1286 (XIII) of 5 December 1958 the General Assembly noted the action taken in 1958 by the High Commissioner on behalf of refugees from Algeria in Tunisia and considered that a similar problem existed in Morocco. It recommended therefore that the High Commissioner continue his action on behalf of the refugees in Tunisia on a substantial scale and that he undertake similar action in Morocco. In resolutions 1389 (XIV) of 20 November 1959, 1500 (XV) of 5 December 1960 and 1672 (XVI) of 18 December 1961 the General Assembly repeated its recommendation that the High Commissioner should continue his efforts on behalf of these refugees pending their return home.

At its twenty-sixth session the General Assembly on 6 December 1971 adopted resolution 2790 (XXVI) on United Nations assistance to East Pakistan refugees through the United Nations focal point and United Nations humanitarian assistance to East Pakistan. In that resolution the General Assembly noted the report of the United Nations High Commissioner for Refugees on his activities as the focal point in co-ordinating international relief assistance for refugees from East Pakistan in India. It endorsed the designation by the Secretary-General of the United Nations High Commissioner for Refugees to be the focal point for the co-ordination of assistance to East Pakistan refugees in India, from and through the United Nations system. It requested the Secretary-General and the High Commissioner to continue their efforts and to ensure that international assis-

[40] The Statute of the Office forms an annex to General Assembly resolution 428 (v) of 14 December 1950.

tance be used to the maximum advantage to relieve the suffering of the refugees in India and of the people of East Pakistan.

In the above-mentioned resolution 429 (V) of 14 December 1950 the General Assembly called upon Governments to co-operate with the United Nations High Commissioner for Refugees. This request has on several occasions been repeated by the General Assembly, e.g., in its resolution 2956 A (XXVII) of 12 December 1972, when it urged Governments to continue to lend their support to the High Commissioner's humanitarian action by:

(*a*) Facilitating his efforts in the field of international protection;

(*b*) Co-operating in the promotion of permanent solutions to refugee problems;

(*c*) Providing the necessary means to attain the financial targets established with the approval of the Executive Committee.

Finally, in the above-mentioned resolution 2956 A (XXVII) of 12 December 1972, the General Assembly (*a*) noted with appreciation the manner in which the High Commissioner had, at the request of the Secretary-General and in accordance with the relevant resolutions of the Economic and Social Council and the General Assembly, co-ordinated, or participated in, essential humanitarian actions undertaken by the organizations in the United Nations system and (*b*) requested the High Commissioner to continue to participate, at the invitation of the Secretary-General, in those humanitarian endeavours of the United Nations for which his Office had particular expertise and experience.

### 6. *The Special Committee on the Situation with regard to the Implementation of the Declaration on the Granting of Independence to Colonial Countries and Peoples*

*Establishment and composition*

The General Assembly, at its fifteenth session, by resolution 1514 (XV) of 14 December 1960, adopted the Declaration on the Granting of Independence to Colonial Countries and Peoples.

At its sixteenth session [41] the General Assembly established a Special Committee of 17 members (later extended to 24 members) with the task "to examine the application of the Declaration and to make suggestions and recommendations on the progress and extent of the implementation of the Declaration".

The General Assembly directed the Special Committee to carry out its tasks by all means at its disposal within the framework of the procedures and modalities to be adopted for the proper discharge of its functions. In resolutions adopted at subsequent sessions of the General Assembly, the Special Committee was invited to continue to seek the most suitable ways and means for the speedy [42] (in later resolutions the word "speedy" was changed to "immediate") [43] and total application of the Declaration to all territories which had not yet attained independence.

In resolution 1810 (XVII), and in a subsequent resolution [44] the General Assembly requested the Special Committee to apprise the Security Council of developments in any territory examined by it which might threaten international peace and security and to make suggestions which might assist the Council in considering appropriate measures under the Charter of the United Nations.

By resolutions adopted at its seventeenth and eighteenth sessions the General Assembly entrusted to the Special Committee a series of functions which up to that time had been performed by other subsidiary bodies concerned with dependent Territories.[45] The Committees whose functions were taken over by the Special Committee, namely, the Special Committee for South West Africa, the Special Committee on Territories under Portuguese Administration and the Committee on Information from Non-Self-Governing Territories, were dissolved by the General Assembly at those sessions.

*Place of meetings*

By paragraph 6 of its resolution 1654 (XVI), the General Assembly authorized the Special Committee to meet elsewhere than the United Nations Headquarters, whenever and wherever such meetings might be required for the effective discharge of its functions, in consultation with the appropriate authorities. In pursuance of this provision the Committee has repeatedly availed itself of invitations from Member States and has often held meetings away from United Nations Headquarters.

*Collection of information by the Special Committee*

At its eighth meeting on 5 March 1962, the Special Committee agreed to a statement of its Chairman summing up the main points which would form the basis of its work.[46] In that work programme it was contemplated that information relevant to the task of the Committee should be collected and necessary documentation prepared by the Secretariat. In order to assist in the submission of information by the Administering Authorities, it was agreed that the Special Committee should instruct a Sub-Committee to draw up a questionnaire to be addressed to those authorities. As a consequence, the

---

[41] General Assembly resolution 1654 (XVI) of 27 November 1961; the membership of the Committee was extended to 24 by General Assembly resolution 1810 (XVII) of 17 December 1962.

[42] See paragraph 8 (a) of resolution 1810 (XVII) of 17 December 1962.

[43] See paragraph 4 of General Assembly resolution 1956 (XVIII) of 11 December 1963; paragraph 6 of General Assembly resolution 2105 (XX) of 20 December 1965; paragraph 17 of General Assembly resolution 2189 (XXI) of 13 December 1966.

[44] See paragraph 13 of General Assembly resolution 2105 (XX).

[45] General Assembly resolutions 1805 (XVII) of 14 December 1962; 1806 (XVII) of 14 December 1962 and 1970 (XVIII) of 16 December 1963.

[46] For explanations and reservations relating to the Chairman's summary, see the Report of the Committee, (*Official Records of the General Assembly, Seventeenth Session, Annexes*, agenda item 25, addendum, document A/5238, paras. 16-111).

Special Committee, on the recommendation of a five-member sub-committee, approved a questionnaire.[47] The following parts of the questionnaire are of particular interest for the present study:

Section IV of the questionnaire relates to suffrage and asks the Administering Authority to state whether and to what extent suffrage exists in the Territory concerned, and to explain its statutory and other bases.

Section VIII of the questionnaire reads as follows:

"*Human rights and fundamental freedoms*

" (*a*) Describe the statutory and constitutional safeguards, if any, in regard to the observance of human rights and fundamental freedoms. Describe the restraints, if any, on the exercise of any of these rights (furnish relevant texts or extracts);

" (*b*) Describe the rights of the indigenous inhabitants to establish political parties and the actual existence of political parties, freedom of expression, freedom of assembly and freedom of the press, etc.;

" (*c*) Describe the rights of the workers to form and join trade unions and to otherwise protect their interests;

" (*d*) Describe the situation with regard to effectively guaranteed security of person and of the community with reference to the foregoing rights and freedoms. What are the restraints, if any, on civil liberties, in particular, the right to form political parties and trade unions and to hold public meetings, etc. (give relevant texts and extracts of statutes and regulations)."

*Written petitions and hearing of petitioners*

The programme of work as summarized by the Chairman on 5 March 1962[48] provided that the Special Committee might hear petitioners and receive written petitions as additional and supplementary means of acquiring information on the Territories concerned. It was understood that petitioners would be heard at the discretion of the Committee and not as a matter of course and that the Committee would have the discretion to screen petitions. Accordingly, in March 1962 a seven-member Sub-Committee on Petitions was established. Without prejudice to the right of the Committee to decide otherwise for exceptional reasons in any particular case, the Special Committee agreed on its policy in regard to petitions procedure by providing that all petitions should be examined in the first instance by the Sub-Committee on Petitions. The final authority to take decisions would rest with the Special Committee. Copies of all petitions for oral hearings should be circulated not only to the members of the Sub-Committee but to all members of the Special Committee. In regard to other petitions, the Sub-Committee on Petitions should make suitable recommendations to the Committee for adoption.[49]

[47] For the text of the questionnaire, see A/AC.109/6.

[48] See foot-note 46, above.

[49] For certain observations by members of the Special Committee on these arrangements, see *Official Records of the General Assembly, Seventeenth Session, Annexes*, agenda item 25, addendum, document A/5238, paras. 16-111.

The Sub-Committee on Petitions decides which communications it receives shall be circulated as petitions.

*Visiting missions*

One of the means of assisting in the operation of the Special Committee has been the sending out of visiting groups to various Territories. In considering that method the Committee recognized the limitations inherent in that procedure and the need for securing the co-operation of the administering Powers concerned. As this method developed, the Special Committee sent visiting missions to a number of Territories. When, in a specific case, the administering Power did not admit the visiting mission, the visiting group visited neighbouring countries. In other cases the visiting mission was admitted to the Territories concerned.[50]

*Co-operation between the Special Committee and the Commission on Human Rights*

In a resolution adopted on 18 June 1965 the Special Committee drew the attention of the Commission on Human Rights to the evidence submitted by petitioners concerning violations of human rights committed in various Territories and expressed its profound shock at the violations of human rights committed in order to stifle legitimate aspirations of the African population to self-determination and independence. This initiative of the Special Committee led to action by the Economic and Social Council, the Commission on Human Rights, the Sub-Commission on Prevention of Discrimination and Protection of Minorities and the General Assembly.[51]

The relevant action of the Commission on Human Rights included the adoption at its twenty-third session under the item concerning violations of human rights and fundamental freedoms of five resolutions[52] one of which recommended that the Economic and Social Council should confirm the inclusion in the terms of reference of the Commission of "the power to recommend and adopt general and specific measures to deal with violations of human rights".[53] This action by the Special Committee on the Situation with regard to the Implementation of the Declaration on the Granting of Independence to Colonial Countries and Peoples led eventually to the elaboration of the new procedure for dealing with communications concerning human rights, particularly by resolution 1503 (XLVIII) of the Economic and

[50] The General Assembly approved the programme of sending visiting groups to various Territories and requested the administering Powers to admit them and to extend to them full co-operation and assistance (General Assembly resolutions 2069 (XX) of 16 December 1965 and 2105 (XX) of 20 December 1965).

[51] Resolutions of the Economic and Social Council 1102 (XL) of 4 March 1966 and 1164 (XLI) of 5 August 1966; resolution of the General Assembly 2144 A (XXI) of 26 October 1966, para. 12, and resolutions of the Commission on Human Rights 2 (XXII); resolution 5 (XIX) of 1967 of the Sub-Commission (502nd meeting); and paras. 103-104 of this study.

[52] See report of the Commission on Human Rights on its twenty-third session, *Official Records of the Economic and Social Council, Forty-second Session, Supplement No. 6*, chap. V, paras. 271-404.

[53] Commission on Human Rights resolution 9 (XXIII) of 16 March 1967.

Social Council, which development has been described in section D above.

*Relationships of the Special Committee with other principal and subsidiary organs of the United Nations and with the specialized agencies*

In resolution 1654 (XVI) the General Assembly requested the Trusteeship Council, and also the Committee on Information from Non-Self-Governing Territories (the functions of which were subsequently taken over by the Special Committee) and the specialized agencies concerned, to assist the Special Committee in its work within their respective fields.

Following upon the directive it received from the General Assembly in resolution 1956 (XVIII) to apprise the Security Council of any developments in any Territories examined by it which may threaten international peace and security, the Committee has repeatedly reported to the Security Council on relevant developments.

The Special Committee has submitted to the General Assembly each year comprehensive reports on its activities. These reports were regularly considered and acted upon in part by the General Assembly in plenary without reference to one of the Main Committees, while the chapters of the Special Committee's reports relating to specific territories were regularly referred to for consideration and report to the Fourth Committee of the General Assembly.

To give some examples, in resolution 2189 (XXI) of 13 December 1966 the General Assembly noted with satisfaction the work accomplished by the Special Committee, expressed its appreciation to that Committee for its efforts to secure the implementation of the Declaration, approved the report of the Special Committee for the past year and also the programme envisaged for the coming year. Similar resolutions were adopted at the twenty-second session in 1967 when by resolution 2326 (XXII) the General Assembly also urged the Administering Powers to give effect to the recommendations contained in the Special Committee's report; at the twenty-third session by resolution 2465 (XXIII) of 20 December 1968, when it also requested the Special Committee to make concrete suggestions which could assist the Security Council in considering appropriate measures under the Charter with regard to developments in colonial territories likely to threaten international peace and security, and recommended that the Security Council take such suggestions fully into consideration; at the twenty-fourth session when in resolution 2548 (XXIV) of 11 December 1969 it also urged the specialized agencies and international institutions associated with the United Nations, including the various programmes in the United Nations system, to give effect to the recommendations contained in the report of the Special Committee. In that resolution the General Assembly requested the Special Committee to continue to examine the compliance of Member States with the Declaration and with other relevant resolutions on the question of decolonization, particularly those relating to the Territories under Portuguese domination, Southern Rhodesia and Namibia. It also invited the Special Committee to continue to pay particular attention to the small Territories and to recommend to the General Assembly the most appropriate methods and also the steps to be taken to enable the population of those Territories to exercise fully their right to self-determination and independence. Another resolution which has to be mentioned in this context is resolution 2708 (XXV) of 14 December 1970, in which the General Assembly, in addition to expressing satisfaction and approval in regard to the work of the Special Committee, requested the Special Committee to make concrete suggestions which could assist the Security Council in considering appropriate measures under the Charter. The General Assembly called upon the administering Powers to co-operate fully with the Special Committee by permitting the access of visiting groups to the colonial Territories in order to secure first-hand information concerning the Territories and to ascertain the wishes and aspirations of the inhabitants.

In resolution 2908 (XXVII) of 2 November 1972, the General Assembly, in addition to expressing satisfaction with the work of the Special Committee and approving its report, called upon the administering Powers to co-operate with the Special Committee in the discharge of its mandate and, in particular, to participate in the work of the Committee relating to the Territories under their administration. At its resumed fifty-first session, the Economic and Social Council by resolution 1651 (LI) of 29 October 1971 had instructed its Committee on Non-Governmental Organizations to study how non-governmental organizations in consultative status with the Council assisted in the achievement of the objectives of the Declaration and other relevant resolutions of the General Assembly. In resolution 2908 (XXVII) the General Assembly requested the Special Committee to continue to enlist the support of national and international organizations having a special interest in the field of decolonialization, in the achievement of the objectives of the Declaration and in the implementation of the relevant resolutions of the United Nations, and in particular to assist the Economic and Social Council in the study envisaged in Council resolution 1651 (LI).

In resolution 2311 (XXII) of 14 December 1967 the General Assembly recognized that the specialized agencies, the International Atomic Energy Agency and the international institutions associated with the United Nations should extend their full co-operation to the United Nations in achieving the objectives of General Assembly resolution 1514 (XV). In resolution 2426 (XXIII) of 18 December 1968, the General Assembly noted with regret that some of these organizations, in particular the International Bank for Reconstruction and Development and the International Monetary Fund, had not so far implemented General Assembly resolution 2311 (XXII) and it appealed again to all the specialized agencies and international institutions, in particular the Bank and the Fund, to take the necessary steps to withhold from the Governments concerned financial, economic, technical and other assistance until they renounced their policies of racial discrimination and colonial domination. These appeals were repeated in resolution 2555 (XXIV) of 12 December 1969, 2704 (XXV) of 14 December 1970, 2874 (XXVI) of 20 December 1971 and in resolution 2980 (XXVII) of 4 December 1972. In resolution 2704

(XXV), the General Assembly noted that while several of the specialized agencies had rendered considerable assistance to refugees from the colonial territories of Africa, they perhaps had not extended their full co-operation with the United Nations.

## B. Other organs which have dealt with matters of human rights

### 1. *The Security Council*

*Functions and powers*

The Security Council is the principal organ of the United Nations on which the Charter confers primary responsibility for the maintenance of international peace and security. In the discharge of this responsibility, the Security Council is empowered by the Charter to take appropriate measures, including action aiming at pacific settlement of disputes and preventive and enforcement action. Allegations of violations or denial of human rights and fundamental freedoms have repeatedly given rise to situations of which the Security Council has become seized.

In discharging its duties the Security Council is required to act in accordance with the purposes and principles of the United Nations Charter (Article 24, paragraph 2), which include the purpose mentioned in Article 1, paragraph 3: "To achieve international co-operation in . . . promoting and encouraging respect for human rights and for fundamental freedoms for all without distinction as to race, sex, language, or religion".

The Security Council may investigate any dispute, or any situation which might give rise to a dispute, in order to determine whether the continuance of the dispute or situation is likely to endanger the maintenance of international peace and security (Article 34). Any Member of the United Nations may bring any such dispute or situation to the attention of the Security Council or the General Assembly. Also a State not a Member of the United Nations may bring to the attention of the Security Council or of the General Assembly any dispute to which it is a party if it accepts in advance, for the purposes of the dispute, the obligation of pacific settlement provided in the Charter.

The General Assembly may discuss any such dispute or situation. The Assembly, however, may make no recommendation with regard to a dispute or situation in respect of which the Security Council is exercising the functions assigned to it in the Charter, unless the Security Council so requests (Articles 35, paragraph 1; 11, paragraph 2; 12, paragraph 1).

The General Assembly may call the attention of the Security Council to situations which are likely to endanger international peace and security (Article 11, paragraph 3). The Secretary-General may also bring to the attention of the Security Council any matter which in his opinion may threaten the maintenance of international peace and security (Article 99).

All functions of the United Nations relating to strategic areas in Trust Territories, including the approval of the terms of Trusteeship Agreements and of their alteration or amendment, are exercised by the Security Council. The Security Council avails itself of the assistance of the Trusteeship Council to perform those functions of the United Nations under the Trusteeship System relating to political, economic, social and educational matters in the strategic areas.

*Composition*

The Security Council is composed of 15 members. By Article 23 of the Charter, as amended, China, France, the USSR, the United Kingdom and the United States of America are permanent members of the Council, and the General Assembly elects 10 other Members of the United Nations as non-permanent members of the Council [54] to serve for two years. Each member of the Council has one representative.

*Operational and procedural arrangements*

Decisions of the Security Council on procedural matters are made by an affirmative vote of nine members. Decisions on all other matters are made by an affirmative vote of nine members including the concurring votes of the permanent members; [55] provided that a party to a dispute shall abstain from voting in decisions with respect to the pacific settlement of such a dispute. It is established that the voluntary abstention of a permanent member of the Security Council does not amount to a negative vote of that member.

*Security Council action in the field of human rights*

Among the problems of which the Security Council has been seized and which contain important human rights elements, the *apartheid* policies of the Government of South Africa, the situation in the Territories under Portuguese administration, the situation in Southern Rhodesia, the situation in the Territories occupied in the course of the 1967 Middle East conflict and the question of Namibia (South West Africa) must be mentioned.

As examples of pronouncements by the Security Council on issues of human rights the following may be cited.

In 1960 the Security Council considered the complaint of 29 Member States [56] concerning "the situation arising out of the large-scale killings of unarmed and peaceful demonstrators against racial discrimination and segregation in the Union of South Africa" and recognized that the situation had been brought about by "the racial policies of the Government of the Union of South Africa and the continued disregard by that Government of the

---

[54] In connexion with the election of the non-permanent members of the Security Council, the Charter stipulates that due regard should be specially paid, in the first instance to the contribution of Members of the United Nations to the maintenance of international peace and security and to the other purposes of the Organization, and also to equitable geographical distribution. This latter criterion is applied by electing members in accordance with the following pattern : (*a*) five from African and Asian States; (*b*) one from East European States; (*c*) two from Latin American States; (*d*) two from West European and other States.

[55] In accordance with Security Council practice, the abstention from voting of one or more permanent members does not prevent the adoption of a decision which has received the required majority.

[56] *Official Records of the Security Council, Fifteenth Year, Supplement for January, February and March 1960*, documents S/4279 and Add.1.

resolutions of the General Assembly calling upon it to revise its policies and bring them into conformity with its obligations and responsibilities under the Charter of the United Nations". The Security Council recognized that the situation in South Africa had "led to international friction and if continued might endanger international peace and security". It deplored "that the recent disturbances in the Union of South Africa should have led to the loss of life of so many Africans" and deplored also "the policies and actions of the Government of the Union of South Africa which have given rise to the present situation". The Security Council called upon the Government of South Africa "to initiate measures aimed at bringing about racial harmony based on equality in order to ensure that the present situation does not continue or recur, and to abandon its policies of *apartheid* and racial discrimination".

In its resolution 181 (1963) the Security Council expressed its conviction that the situation in South Africa was seriously disturbing international peace and security. It strongly deprecated the policies of South Africa in its perpetuation of racial discrimination as being inconsistent with the principles contained in the Charter and contrary to South Africa's obligations as a Member of the United Nations. The Security Council called upon the Government of South Africa to abandon the policies of *apartheid* and discrimination and to liberate all persons imprisoned, interned or subjected to other restrictions for having opposed the policy of *apartheid*.

In resolution 182 (1963) of 4 December 1963, the Security Council, "recognizing the need to eliminate discrimination in regard to basic human rights and fundamental freedoms for all individuals within the territory of the Republic of South Africa without distinction as to race, sex, language or religion", and "expressing the firm conviction that policies of *apartheid* and racial discrimination as practised by the Government of the Republic of South Africa are abhorrent to the conscience of mankind. . .", urgently requested "the Government of the Republic of South Africa to cease forthwith its continued imposition of discrimination and repressive measures which are contrary to the principles and purposes of the Charter and which are in violation of its obligations as a Member of the United Nations and of the provisions of the Universal Declaration of Human Rights".

In resolution 190 (1964) of 9 June 1964 the Security Council noted with grave concern that an arbitrary trial instituted against the leaders of the anti-*apartheid* movement had been resumed and urged the Government of South Africa to end forthwith the trial in progress, to renounce the execution of persons sentenced to death for acts resulting from the opposition to the policy of *apartheid* and to grant an amnesty to all persons already imprisoned, interned or subjected to other restrictions for having opposed the policy of *apartheid*. In its resolution 191 (1964) of 18 June 1964 the Security Council repeated its previous declarations that the policies of *apartheid* were contrary to the principles and purposes of the Charter of the United Nations, inconsistent with the provisions of the Universal Declaration of Human Rights as well as with South Africa's obligations under the Charter. It repeated its earlier urgent appeals to renounce the executions, to grant immediate amnesty and to abolish the practice of imprisonment without charges. The Council endorsed and subscribed in particular to the main conclusion of the group of experts which it had appointed earlier, namely that all the people of South Africa should be brought into consultation and should thus be enabled to decide the future of their country at the national level.

By resolution 282 (1970) the Security Council reiterated its condemnation of the evil and abhorrent policies of *apartheid* and recognized the legitimacy of the struggle of the oppressed people of South Africa in pursuance of their human and political rights as set forth in the Charter and the Universal Declaration of Human Rights. It expressed its conviction that the situation resulting from the continued application of the policies of *apartheid* and the constant build-up of the South Africa military and police forces constituted a potential threat to international peace and security.

In resolution 311 (1972) the Security Council noted with grave concern the aggravation of the situation in South Africa resulting from the continued intensification and expansion of the policies of *apartheid*. The Security Council heard statements of individuals invited to address the Council on the question. It expressed its grave concern that the situation in South Africa seriously disturbed international peace and security in southern Africa, repeated its condemnation of the Government of South Africa for continuing its policies of *apartheid* in violation of its obligations under the Charter and reiterated its total opposition to the policies of *apartheid* of the Government of South Africa.

In resolution 163 (1961) of 9 June 1961 the Security Council recalled General Assembly resolution 1542 (XV) by which Angola, among others, had been declared a Non-Self-Governing Territory within the meaning of Chapter XI of the Charter and it invoked the Declaration on the Granting of Independence to Colonial Countries and Peoples (General Assembly resolution 1514 (XV) of 14 December 1960). The Security Council in particular invoked that part of resolution 1514 (XV) by which the General Assembly had declared without dissent that the subjection of peoples to alien subjugation, domination and exploitation constituted a denial of fundamental human rights, was contrary to the Charter and an impediment to world peace and co-operation. The Security Council quoted further the General Assembly's call for immediate steps to be taken to transfer all powers to the peoples of those Territories (covered by resolution 1514 (XV)) without any conditions or reservations in accordance with their freely expressed wills and desires, without any distinction as to race, creed or colour, in order to enable them to enjoy complete independence and freedom. The Security Council called upon the Portuguese authorities to desist forthwith from repressive measures in Angola. By resolution 180 (1963) on the situation in the Territories under Portuguese administration, the Security Council affirmed that the policy of Portugal in claiming the Territories under its administration as "overseas Territories" and as integral parts of metropolitan Portugal was contrary to the principles of the Charter. It deprecated the repeated violations by the Portuguese Government of the principles of the Charter and called for the promulgation of an unconditional political amnesty and the establishment of conditions that would allow the free functioning of political parties. In resolution 218 (1965) the Security Council reaffirmed its earlier statements and demands to Portugal in regard to the Territories under Portuguese administration. In resolution 312 (1972) of 4 February 1972 the Security Council again expressed the grave concern that the Government of Portugal was continuing its measures of repression and its military operations against the African peoples of Angola, Mozambique and Guinea (Bissau). It recognized the legitimacy of the struggle of the liberation movements in those three Territories and reaffirmed the inalienable right of the peoples of those Territories to self-determination and independence. It called upon Portugal to promulgate an unconditional political amnesty and the restoration of democratic political rights and to transfer power to political institutions freely elected and representative of the peoples. In resolution 322 (1972) of 22 November 1972 the Security Council again examined the situation in Angola, Guinea (Bissau) and Mozambique and also in Cape Verde and again called upon the Government of Portugal to cease forthwith all acts of repression against the peoples of those Territories.

The Security Council repeatedly acted on the question of Southern Rhodesia. Detailed references have been made in part one of this publication to the various resolutions the Security Council adopted on the problem of Southern Rhodesia. These were: resolutions 202 (1965), 216 (1965), 217 (1965), 221 (1966), 232 (1966), 253 (1968), 277 (1970), 288 (1970), 314 (1972), and 318 (1972). All these resolutions have been summarized in part one of the present publication.

In resolution 237 (1967) adopted on 15 June 1967 in connexion with the conflict in the Middle East, the Security Council proclaimed the necessity of respect for essential and inalienable human rights even during the vicissitudes of war. It also called for the scrupulous respect for the humanitarian principles embodied in the Geneva Conventions of 1949 governing the treatment of prisoners of war and the protection of civilian persons in time of war.

In resolution 258 (1968) the Security Council recalled its resolution 237 (1967), deplored the delay in its implementation and requested the Secretary-General to report thereon. In resolution 271 (1969) the Security Council called upon Israel scrupulously to observe the provisions of the Geneva Conventions and international law governing military occupation.

Three of the principal organs of the United Nations have acted on the question of Namibia (South West Africa), namely the General Assembly, the Security Council and the International Court of Justice. The action by all three organs is summarized in chapter IV, section F of part one of this publication. The Security Council became involved in the problem in 1968 when in resolutions 245 (1968) and 246 (1968) it took note of and took into account the termination of the South African mandate over South West Africa by General Assembly resolution 2145 (XXI) of 1966. By resolutions 264 (1969), 269 (1969) and 276 (1970) the Security Council recognized the termination of the mandate, declared the continued presence of South Africa in Namibia to be illegal and called upon the Government of South Africa to withdraw immediately its administration from the Territory. By resolution 284 (1970) the Security Council asked the International Court of Justice for an advisory opinion on the legal consequences for States of the continued presence of South Africa in Namibia. The Court's reply is reproduced in part one, chapter IV, section F, of the present publication. In its resolution 301 (1971) the Security Council endorsed the Court's opinion. By resolution 309 (1972) of 4 February 1972 the Security Council invited the Secretary-General to initiate contacts with all parties concerned. After having received the Secretary-General's report, the Security Council invited the Secretary-General by resolution 319 (1972) to continue his contacts. After having received and considered a further report by the Secretary-General, the Security Council, by resolution 323 (1972) of 6 December 1972, invited the Secretary-General to continue his efforts and requested him to report no later than 30 April 1973.

### 2. *The Trusteeship Council*

The Trusteeship Council is a principal organ of the United Nations, set up to assist the General Assembly, under whose authority it operates, in carrying out its functions relating to the International Trusteeship System provided for in Chapter XII of the United Nations charter. One of "the basic objectives of the trusteeship system" is "to encourage respect for human rights and for fundamental freedoms for all without distinction as to race, sex, language or religion". The work of the Trusteeship Council, therefore, involves important aspects and issues of human rights.

The composition, functions and powers of the Trusteeship Council are laid down in Chapter XIII of the Charter.

*Composition*

Under the terms of Article 86, paragraph 1, of the Charter, the Trusteeship Council consists of three categories of Members of the United Nations: 1. Those Members administering Trust Territories; 2. Such of those Members mentioned by name in Article 23, i.e. the permanent members of the Security Council, as are not administering Trust Territories; 3. Members elected for three-year terms by the General Assembly, in sufficient numbers to "ensure that the total number of members of the Trusteeship Council is equally divided between those Members of the United Nations which administer Trust Territories and those which do not".

By January 1973, only two of the original Territories under trusteeship had not yet reached the Charter's goal, namely New Guinea under Australian administration and the Trust Territories of the Pacific Islands under United States administration. As a consequence it has not been possible to retain the composition of the Trusteeship Council as laid down in Article 86 of the Charter or to ensure that the total number of members of the Council is equally divided between those Members of the United

Nations which administer Trust Territories and those which do not. At the beginning of 1973 the Trusteeship Council consisted of the five permanent members of the Security Council and of Australia.

It may therefore at present be sufficient to recall that the functions of the Trusteeship Council are laid down in Articles 87 and 88 of the Charter and that under Article 83 of the Charter all functions of the United Nations relating to strategic areas are to be exercised by the Security Council. One of the remaining two Trust Territories, the Trust Territory of the Pacific Islands, has been designated as a strategic area. In accordance with the relevant Charter provisions and resolutions of the Security and Trusteeship Councils, the Trusteeship Council has, with regard to the Trust Territory of the Pacific Islands, carried out and continued to carry out on behalf of the Security Council the functions of the United Nations under the International Trusteeship System that apply to strategic areas.

*Procedural and operational arrangements*

In accordance with Article 89 of the Charter, each member of the Trusteeship Council has one vote, and the decisions of the Trusteeship Council are made by a majority of the members present and voting.

The Council's rules of procedure and its decisions have elaborated certain of its functions and processes which have been of relevance to human rights and fundamental freedoms in Trust Territories. Among these have been the consideration of annual reports of Administering Authorities, the despatch of visiting missions and the supervision of plebiscites and elections. The co-operation of the Trusteeship Council with the Economic and Social Council was also regulated.

*Report of the Trusteeship Council*

The Trusteeship Council presents to the General Assembly an annual general report on its activities and on the discharge of its responsibilities under the International Trusteeship System. The report includes a review of the conditions in each Trust Territory. The Council also reports to the Security Council on conditions in the Trust Territory designated as a strategic area.

Since the entry into force of the International Convention on the Elimination of Racial Discrimination, the question of the co-operation between the Committee on the Elimination of Racial Discrimination established under that Convention and the Trusteeship Council and other United Nations bodies dealing with petitions and receiving reports from Trust and Non-Self-Governing Territories has been initiated pursuant to article 15 of the Convention. The Trusteeship Council and the Special Committee on the Situation with regard to the Implementation of the Declaration on the Granting of Independence to Colonial Countries and Peoples have, on the request of the Committee and following a recommendation of the General Assembly (resolution 2784 (XXVI) of 1971), agreed to participate in this work.

### 3. *The International Court of Justice*

Under Article 92 of the United Nations Charter, the International Court of Justice is the principal judicial organ of the United Nations. The Court functions in accordance with the Statute of the International Court of Justice, which forms an integral part of the Charter of the United Nations.

Under Article 93 of the Charter, all Members of the United Nations are *ipso facto* parties to the Statute of the International Court of Justice. A State which is not a Member of the United Nations may become a party to the Statute of the International Court of Justice on conditions determined in each case by the General Assembly upon the recommendation of the Security Council. At present there are three States parties to the Statute of the International Court of Justice which are not Members of the United Nations.

Under Article 94 of the Charter, each Member of the United Nations undertakes to comply with the decision of the International Court of Justice in any case to which it is a party.

Article 95 of the Charter reads as follows: "Nothing in the present Charter shall prevent Members of the United Nations from entrusting the solution of their differences to other tribunals by virtue of agreements already in existence or which may be concluded in the future."

Under Article 95 of the Charter, the General Assembly or the Security Council may request the International Court of Justice to give an advisory opinion on any legal question. Other organs of the United Nations and specialized agencies, which may at any time be so authorized by the General Assembly, may also request advisory opinions of the Court on legal questions arising within the scope of their activities. The General Assembly has requested and obtained from the Court several advisory opinions; the Security Council requested and obtained one advisory opinion. Acting under Article 96, the General Assembly has authorized, by resolution 89 (I) of 11 December 1946, the Economic and Social Council to request advisory opinions of the International Court of Justice on legal questions arising within the scope of the activities of the Council. By agreements concluded with the United Nations and approved by the General Assembly, each of the specialized agencies with the exception of the Universal Postal Union has been authorized to request advisory opinions of the International Court of Justice on Legal questions arising within the scope of its competence or activities other than questions concerning mutual relationships of the specialized agency concerned and the United Nations or other specialized agencies. The International Atomic Energy Agency has also been so authorized. So far, only UNESCO has made such a request.

*Composition of the Court and election of members*

The Court is composed of a body of independent judges, elected regardless of their nationality from among persons of high moral character, who possess the qualifications required in their respective countries for appointment to the highest judicial offices or are jurisconsults of recognized competence in international law (Article 2 of the Statute).

The Court consist of 15 members, no two of whom may be nationals of the same State (Article 2.1.).

Article 4 (1) of the Statute states that the members of the Court are to be elected by the General Assembly and by the Security Council in accordance with a procedure detailed in paragraphs 2 and 3 of Article 4 and also in Articles 5-7 of the Statute. Article 4 (3) of the Statute of the Court provides that the conditions under which a State which is a party to the Statute but not a Member of the United Nations may participate in electing the members of the Court are, in the absence of a special agreement, to be laid down by the General Assembly upon the recommendation of the Security Council.

The members of the Court are elected for nine years and may be re-elected (Article 13). The terms of the members are so distributed as to make possible the renewal of one third of the membership every three years.

*Functioning*

The Court elects its President and Vice-President for three years. They may be re-elected. The Court appoints its Registrar and may provide for the appointment of such officers as may be necessary (Article 21).

The Court has its seat at The Hague. The Court, however, is not prevented from sitting and exercising its functions elsewhere whenever the Court considers it desirable (Article 22).

A quorum of nine judges suffices to constitute the Court (Article 25.3.).

The Court may from time to time form one or more chambers, composed of three or more judges as the Court may determine, for dealing with particular categories of cases (Article 26.1), and a judgement given by any such chamber is to be considered as rendered by the Court (Article 27).

The Court frames rules for carrying out its functions. In particular, it lays down rules of procedure (Article 30.1.).

*Competence*

Only States may be parties in cases before the Court. The Court is open to the States parties to its Statute. The conditions under which the Court is to be open to other States are, subject to the special provisions contained in treaties in force, to be laid down by the Security Council, but in no case shall such conditions place the parties in a position of inequality before the Court (Article 35, paragraphs 1 and 2).

Whenever a treaty or convention in force provides for reference of a matter to a tribunal to have been instituted by the League of Nations, or to the Permanent Court of International Justice, the matter is, as between the parties to the Statute, to be referred to the International Court of Justice (Article 37).

In accordance with Article 36 of the Statute of the Court, the jurisdiction of the Court comprises all cases which the parties refer to it and all matters specially provided for in the Charter of the United Nations or in treaties and conventions in force.

The States parties to the Statute may at any time declare that they recognize as compulsory *ipso facto* and without special agreement, in relation to any other State accepting the same obligation, the jurisdiction of the Court in all legal disputes concerning:

(*a*) The interpretation of a treaty;

(*b*) Any question of international law;

(*c*) The existence of any fact which, if established, would constitute a breach of an international obligation;

(*d*) The nature or extent of the reparation to be made for the breach of an international obligation.

The declarations referred to above may be made unconditionally or on condition of reciprocity on the part of several or certain States, or for a certain time. Such declarations are to be deposited with the Secretary-General of the United Nations, who shall transmit copies thereof to the parties to the Statute and to the Registrar of the Court.

In the event of a dispute as to whether the Court has jurisdiction, the matter is to be settled by the decision of the Court (Article 36).

The Court, subject to and in conformity with its rules, may request of public international organizations information relevant to cases before it, and is to receive such information presented by such organizations on their own initiative.

Whenever the construction of the constituent instrument of a public international organization or of an international convention adopted thereunder is in question in a case before the Court, the Registrar must notify the public international organization concerned and must communicate to it copies of all the written proceedings (Article 34).

The Court, whose function is to decide in accordance with international law such disputes as are submitted to it, is to apply: (*a*) international conventions, whether general or particular, establishing rules expressly recognized by the contesting States; (*b*) international customs, as evidence of a general practice accepted as law; (*c*) the general principles of law recognized by civilized nations; (*d*) subject to the provisions of Article 59 (see below), judicial decisions and the teachings of the most highly qualified publicists of the various nations, as subsidiary means for the determination of rules of law.

This provision is not to prejudice the power of the Court to decide a case *ex aequo et bono*, if the parties agree thereto (Article 38).

*Procedure*

The parties to cases brought before the Court are represented by agents. They may have the assistance of counsel or advocates before the Court (Article 42, paragraphs 1 and 2).

The procedure consists of two parts: written and oral.

The written proceedings consist of the communication to the Court and to the parties of memorials, counter-memorials and, if necessary, replies; also all papers and documents in support.

These communications are to be made through the Registrar, in the order and within the time fixed by the Court.

A certified copy of every document produced by one party is to be communicated to the other party.

The oral proceedings consist of the hearing by the Court of witnesses, experts, agents, counsel, and advocates (Article 43).

The hearing in Court is public, unless the Court decides otherwise, or unless the parties demand that the public be not admitted (Article 46).

Minutes are made at each hearing and signed by the Registrar and the President (Article 47).

The deliberations of the Court take place in private and remain secret (Article 54, paragraph 3).

All questions are decided by a majority of the judges present. In the event of an equality of votes, the President or the judge who acts in his place shall have a casting vote (Article 55).

The judgement is to state the reasons on which it is based (Article 56, paragraph 1).

If the judgement does not represent in whole or in part the unanimous opinion of the judges, any judge is entitled to deliver a separate opinion (Article 57).

The decision of the Court has no binding force except between the parties and in respect of that particular case (Article 59).

The judgement of the Court is final and without appeal. In the event of dispute as to the meaning or scope of the judgement, the Court is to construe it upon the request of any party (Article 60).

An application for revision of a judgement may be made only when it is based upon the discovery of some fact of such a nature as to be a decisive factor, which fact was, when the judgement was given, unknown to the Court and also to the party claiming revision, always provided that such ignorance may not be due to negligence (Article 61, paragraph 1). The Court decides on the admissibility of proceedings in revision.

Should a State consider that it has an interest of a legal nature which may be affected by the decision in the case, it may submit a request to the Court to be permitted to intervene. It is for the Court to decide upon this request (Article 62).

Whenever the construction of a convention to which States other than those concerned in the case are parties is in question, the Registrar must notify all such States forthwith. Every State so notified has the right to intervene in the proceedings; but if it uses this right, the construction given by the judgement will be equally binding upon it (Article 63).

*Clauses in United Nations human rights conventions under which disputes may be referred to the International Court of Justice*

The following conventions in the field of human rights contain provisions according to which any dispute between the parties arising under such conventions can be referred to the International Court of Justice at the request of any of the parties to the dispute: Convention on the Prevention and Punishment of the Crime of Genocide (article IX); Convention relating to the Status of Refugees (article 38); Convention on the International Right of Correction (article V); Convention on the Political Rights of Women (article 9); Slavery Convention signed at Geneva on 25 September 1926 and amended by the Protocol signed at the Headquarters of the United Nations on 7 December 1953 (article 7); Supplementary Convention on the Abolition of Slavery, the Slave Trade, and Institutions and Practices Similar to Slavery (article 10); Convention on the Nationality of Married Women (article 10); Convention relating to the Status of Stateless Persons (article 34); Convention on the Reduction of Statelessness (article 14); International Convention on the Elimination of All Forms of Racial Discrimination (article 22).[57]

The Convention on Consent to Marriage, Minimum Age for Marriage and Registration of Marriages signed on 10 December 1962 provides that any dispute which may arise between two or more Contracting States concerning the interpretation or application of the Conventional shall, at the request of all the Parties to the dispute, be referred to the International Court of Justice for decision.

The International Covenants on Human Rights do not specifically provide for adjudication by the International Court of Justice.

*Advisory opinions*

The Court may give an advisory opinion on any legal question at the request of whatever body may be authorized by or in accordance with the Charter of the United Nations to make such a request.

Questions upon which the advisory opinion of the Court is asked are to be laid before the Court by means of a written request containing an exact statement of the question upon which an opinion is required, and accompanied by all documents likely to throw light upon the question (Article 65).

The Registrar must forthwith give notice of the request for an advisory opinion to all States entitled to appear before the Court.

The Registrar is also, by means of a special and direct communication, to notify any State entitled to appear before the Court or international organization considered by the Court, or, should it not be sitting, by the President, as likely to be able to furnish information on the question, that the Court will be prepared to receive, within a time-limit to be fixed by the President, written statements, or to hear, at a public sitting to be held for the purpose, oral statements relating to the question.

Should any such State entitled to appear before the Court have failed to receive the special communication referred to in paragraph 281 above, such State may express a desire to submit a written statement or to be heard; and the Court will decide.

States and organizations having presented written or oral statements or both are to be permitted to comment on the statements made by other States or organizations in the form, to the extent, and within the time-limits which the Court, or, should it not be sitting, the President, shall decide in each particular case. Accordingly, the Registrar

---

[57] Article 22 of the International Convention on the Elimination of All Forms of Racial Discrimination reads as follows : "Any dispute between two or more States Parties over the interpretation or application of this Convention, which is not settled by negotiation or by the procedures expressly provided for in this Convention, shall, at the request of any of the parties to the dispute, be referred to the International Court of Justice for decision, unless the disputants agree to another mode of settlement."

is to communicate in due time any such written statements to States and organizations having submitted similar statements (Article 66).

The Court is to deliver its advisory opinions in open court, notice having been given to the Secretary-General and to the representatives of Members of the United Nations, of other States and of international organizations immediately concerned (Article 67).

In the exercise of its advisory functions the Court is further to be guided by the provisions of its Statute which apply in contentious cases to the extent to which it recognizes them to be applicable (Article 68).

The advisory opinion rendered by the Court on the Legal Consequences for States of the Continued Presence of South Africa in Namibia (South West Africa) [58] which was referred to in chapter I of part one is of particular significance for the interpretation of the human rights provisions of the Charter.

### C. Conferences convened by United Nations organs to deal with matters of human rights

The General Assembly and the Economic and Social Council [59] have convened conferences to deal with matters of human rights, as follows:

(1) The United Nations Conference on Freedom of Information (1948);

(2) Four conferences of plenipotentiaries to deal with conventions in the field of human rights; [60]

(3) The International Conference on Human Rights, Teheran 1968;

(4) Two conferences of non-governmental organizations interested in the eradication of prejudice and discrimination. Each item is discussed separately below.

#### 1. *The United Nations Conference on Freedom of Information*

The General Assembly in resolution 59 (I) of 14 December 1946 instructed the Economic and Social Council to convoke a conference on freedom of information. In resolution 74 (V) of 15 August 1947, and more particularly in part I of the resolution, entitled "Organization of the United Nations Conference on Freedom of Information", the Economic and Social Council, taking note of the recommendations of the Sub-Commission on Freedom of Information and of the press regarding the organization of such a conference, decided on the time and place of the Conference. The Council also decided: (1) That voting rights at the Conference should be exercised only by Members of the United Nations. (2) That, in addition to States Members of the United Nations, 13 non-member States (mentioned by name in paragraph 3 of the resolution) should be invited to participate in the Conference. (3) That invitations to participate in preparations for the Conference and to attend it should be extended to such of the specialized agencies, intergovernmental organizations and non-governmental organizations listed by name in the resolution as would request such invitations. The list in question consisted of: specialized agencies which had or would conclude agreements with the United Nations; other intergovernmental organizations which would conclude agreements; non-governmental organizations in category A of consultative status with the Economic and Social Council; one non-governmental organization in category B.

Paragraph 4 (*b*) of part I of the resolution laid down in detail the basis on which the above specialized agencies, intergovernmental organizations and non-governmental organizations should "be invited to participate".

Other provisions of part I of the resolution concerned: governmental delegations to the Conference, including their composition and the number of delegations; the committees to be set up at the Conference, i.e., a general committee (bureau) with specified composition and functions, and four principal committees comprising representatives of each delegation, each committee to deal with specific items of the provisional agenda or other questions of a specified category.

In paragraph 5 of part I of the resolution the Secretary-General was requested to prepare draft rules of procedure for the Conference.

Paragraphs 8 and 9 of part I of the resolution recorded the decision of the Council:

"(*a*) To request the Secretary-General to send a request for information based upon the provisional agenda of the Conference to all States Members of the United Nations, and to all States not Members of the United Nations which will be invited to the International Conference on Freedom of Information; and

"(*b*) To request the Secretary-General to prepare a memorandum based upon the replies received, as documentation for the Conference;

"(*c*) To request UNESCO to submit the findings based upon its questionnaire concerning technical information needs in war devastated areas, together with other relevant material, to the Conference;

"(*d*) To request the Secretary-General to prepare the necessary documentation under each item of the proposed agenda for the Conference, and should he deem it necessary, to seek the co-operation of UNESCO and other international organizations working in this field;

"(*e*) To request that the documentation be organized under each item of the agenda and consist of a compilation and analysis of existing practices and problems."

Part III of resolution 74 (V) contained the provisional agenda which the Council at its fifth session decided to submit to the Conference. Any additional items recom-

[58] *Legal Consequences for States of the Continued Presence of South Africa in Namibia (South West Africa) notwithstanding Security Council Resolution 276 (1970), Advisory Opinion, I.C.J. Reports, 1971*, p. 16.

[59] Under Article 62 (4) of the United Nations Charter, the Economic and Social Council may call, in accordance with the rules prescribed by the United Nations, international conferences on matters falling within its competence.

[60] Concerning the conventions and draft conventions prepared by the Conferences listed under (1) and (2) above, see also part one.

mended by the Council at ist sixth session were to be submitted to the Conference as an additional list.

The Conference met at the United Nations Office at Geneva from 23 March to 21 April 1948.

The Conference was attended by: (*a*) delegations representing the Governments of 44 States Members of the United Nations; (*b*) delegations representing the Governments of 10 States which at that time were not Members of the United Nations; (*c*) observers representing the Governments of two States Members of the United Nations and one State non-Nember of the Organization; (*d*) observers and consultants from the International Labour Office, the International Telecommunication Union and the United Nations Educational, Scientific and Cultural Organization; and observers and consultants from five non-governmental organizations.

The Director of the Division of Human Rights of the United Nations Secretariat served as Executive Secretary to the Conference.

The Conference elected a President and seven Vice-Presidents from among the delegates representing Governments.

The Conference adopted as its agenda the provisional agenda proposed by the Economic and Social Council with the addition of two resolutions which had been referred to the Conference by the General Assembly, on Measures to be taken against Propaganda and the Inciters of a New War and on False or Distorted Reports; and two proposals made by the International Organization of Journalists.

On the basis of the deliberations of the Conference and its Committees, as recorded in the records and reports of the plenary meetings and the meetings of the respective Committees, the Conference prepared and forwarded to the Economic and Social Council three draft conventions: a Draft Convention on the Gathering and International Transmission of News; a Draft Convention Concerning the Institution of an International Right of Correction; and a Draft Convention on Freedom of Information.

At the request of the Economic and Social Council, the Conference also prepared draft articles for the Draft Declaration on Human Rights.

Furthermore, the Conference adopted 43 resolutions, most of them of a substantive nature, including one on possible modes of action by means of which the recommendations of the Conference could best be put into effect. Under this latter heading, the Conference, in resolution No. 43, resolved:

"1. That all documents passed by the Conference, resolutions or draft conventions, be referred to the Economic and Social Council for study at its next session;

"2. That all Governments invited to this Conference be requested to forward to the Secretary-General of the United Nations before 5 July 1948 their comments on the draft conventions proposed by the Conference and proposals for other draft conventions based on the recommendations of this Conference;

"3. That the Economic and Social Council be requested to examine at its seventh session the draft conventions referred to it by the Conference in the light of such comments and other proposed draft conventions as provided in paragraph 2, and to submit to the General Assembly at its third session draft conventions which may thereafter be opened at that session for signature or accession by those States entitled and willing to become parties thereto, and remain open subsequently for additional accessions."

The Final Act of the Conference may be found in United Nations publication, Sales No. 1948.XIV.2.[61]

### 2. *Conferences of plenipotentiaries convened by United Nations organs to deal with conventions in the field of human rights*

In accordance with Article 62, paragraph 4, of the Charter, rules for the calling of international conferences of States were approved and are contained in General Assembly resolution 366 (IV) of 3 December 1949. Four conferences of plenipotentiaries have so far been convened by the General Assembly or the Economic and Social Council to deal with conventions in the field of human rights concluded under the auspices of the United Nations.

Of the four conferences convened for the purpose of concluding international treaties in the human rights field, two were convened by the General Assembly and the other two by the Economic and Social Council. Two of the conferences were held at the United Nations Office at Geneva, one at United Nations Headquarters in New York, and one was held in two parts, with the first part meeting in Geneva and the second in New York.

The following two conferences were convened by the General Assembly:

#### (a) *The United Nations Conference of Plenipotentiaries on the Status of Refugees and Stateless Persons*

This conference was convened by General Assembly resolution 429 (V) of 14 December 1950 "to complete the drafting of and to sign both the Convention relating to the Status of Refugees and the Protocol [62] relating to the Status of Stateless Persons". The Conference met in Geneva commencing on 25 July 1951. It adopted and opened for signature the Convention relating to the Status of Refugees but decided not to take a decision with respect to the draft Protocol relating to the Status of Stateless Persons and to refer it back to the appropriate organs of the United Nations for further study.[63] The work of this Conference was continued by the United Nations Conference on the Status of Stateless Persons convened under Economic and Social Council resolution 526 A (XVII) of 26 April 1954.

---

[61] For two volumes of official material concerning freedom of information, including material connected with the action taken at the Conference, prepared by the United Nations Secretariat, see United Nations publication, Sales No. 1950.XVI.1, volumes I and II.

[62] See E/1850-E/AC.32/8.

[63] See *United Nations Conference of Plenipotentiaries on the Status of Refugees and Stateless Persons: Final Act and Convention Relating to the Status of Refugees*, United Nations publication, Sales No. 1951.IV.4, part III, p. 7.

(b) *The United Nations Conference on the Elimination or Reduction of Future Statelessness*

The General Assembly of the United Nations, by resolution 896 (IX) of 4 December 1954, expressed its desire that an international conference of plenipotentiaries be convened to conclude a convention for the reduction or elimination of future statelessness as soon as at least 20 States had communicated to the Secretary-General their willingness to co-operate in such a conference. The Secretary-General was requested to fix the exact time and place for the conference when that condition had been met. The General Assembly noted that the International Law Commission had submitted to it drafts of a Convention on the Elimination of Future Statelessness and a Convention on the Reduction of Future Statelessness in the Report of the International Law Commission covering its sixth session in 1954. The General Assembly requested the Governments of States invited to participate in the Conference to give early consideration to the merits of a multilateral convention on the elimination or reduction of future statelessness. Upon fulfilment of the condition envisaged in the resolution of the General Assembly, the Secretary-General convened a United Nations Conference on the Elimination or Reduction of Future Statelessness at the European Office of the United Nations in Geneva. The Conference met there from 24 March to 18 April 1959 but, being unable to terminate the work entrusted to it within the time provided, it adopted a resolution proposing to the competent organ of the United Nations to reconvene the Conference at the earliest possible time in order to continue and complete its work.[64] In pursuance of this resolution, the Secretary-General of the United Nations, after ascertaining the views of the participating States, decided that the Conference should be reconvened at the United Nations Headquarters in New York on 15 August 1961. It met there from 15 to 28 August 1961. The Conference prepared, adopted and opened for signature a Convention on the Reduction of Statelessness.

The following two conferences were convened by the Economic and Social Council:

(c) *The United Nations Conference on the Status of Stateless Persons* [65]

By resolution 526 A (XVII) of 26 April 1954, the Economic and Social Council, at its seventeenth session, having consulted the Secretary-General as prescribed in General Assembly resolution 366 (IV) approving the rules for the calling of international conferences of States, decided that a second conference of plenipotentiaries should be convened to revise, in the light of the provisions of the Convention Relating to the Status of Refugees of 28 July 1951 and of the observations made by Governments, the draft Protocol relating to the Status of Stateless Persons prepared by an *Ad Hoc* Committee of the Economic and Social Council in 1950 and to open the instrument for signature. The Conference, which met at the Headquarters of the United Nations in New York from 13 to 23 September 1954, decided to prepare a separate convention dealing with the status of stateless persons rather than a protocol to the the 1951 Convention Relating to the Status of Refugees. The Convention was adopted on 23 September 1954 and opened for signature.

(d) *The United Nations Conference of Plenipotentiaries on a Supplementary Convention on the Abolition of Slavery, the Slave Trade, and Institutions and Practices Similar to Slavery*

By resolution 608 (XXI) of 30 April 1956, the Economic and Social Council, at its twenty-first session, having consulted the Secretary-General as prescribed in General Assembly resolution 366 (IV) of 3 December 1949 approving the rules for the calling of international conferences of States, decided that a conference of plenipotentiaries should be convened in order to complete the drafting of the Supplementary Convention on the Abolition of Slavery, the Slave Trade, and Institutions and Practices Similar to Slavery and to open it for signature. The Conference met at the European Office of the United Nations in Geneva from 13 August to 4 September 1956. It adopted the Convention and opened it for signature.

*Participation in the Conferences*

In all cases the resolution convening any given conference has contained provisions specifying who should be invited to participate in it. Provisions concerning the representation of States not participating in the Conference by observers and of specialized agencies, intergovernmental organizations and non-governmental organizations in consultative status with the Economic and Social Council were included in the rules of procedure adopted by each conference.[66]

In the case of the United Nations Conference of Plenipotentiaries on the Status of Refugees and Stateless Persons, the General Assembly, in resolution 429 (V) of 14 December 1950, instructed the Secretary-General to invite the Governments of all States, both Members and non-Members of the United Nations, to attend the Conference, and called upon the United Nations High Commissioner for Refugees, in accordance with the provisions of the statute of his office, to participate in the work of the Conference. Actually, 26 States were represented at the Conference by plenipotentiaries and two States were represented by observers. Pursuant to the request of the General Assembly, the United Nations High Commissioner for Refugees participated, without the right to vote, in the deliberations of the Conference.

[64] See *Final Act of the United Nations Conference on the Elimination or Reduction of Future Statelessness*, document A/CONF.9/14, para. 5.

[65] In resolution 629 (VII), the General Assembly had requested the Council to take whatever action seemed useful in order that a text relating to the Status of Stateless Persons might be opened for signature after the Convention relating to the Status of Refugees had entered into force. The latter Convention having entered into force on 22 April 1954, the Council proceeded to call a conference of plenipotentiaries to deal with an instrument relating to the Status of Stateless Persons.

[66] The rules of procedure of some of the conferences contained provisions relating to the representation of the Office of the United Nations High Commissioner for Refugees.

The International Labour Organisation and the Council of Europe were represented at the Conference without the right to vote. At its second meeting, the Conference, acting on a proposal of one representative, unanimously decided to address an invitation to the Holy See to designate a plenipotentiary representative to participate in its work. A representative of the Holy See took his place at the Conference on 10 July 1951. In addition, representatives of 29 non-governmental organizations in consultative status with the Economic and Social Council (three from category A, 21 from category B and three from those on the register) were present as observers. Under the rules of procedure adopted by the Conference, representatives of non-governmental organizations in consultative status with the Economic and Social Council had the right to submit written or oral statements to the Conference.

In the case of the United Nations Conference on the Status of Stateless Persons, the Economic and Social Council, in resolution 526 (XVII) of 26 April 1954, decided that invitations to attend the Conference should be extended to all States which had been invited to attend the Conference of Plenipotentiaries on the Status of Refugees and Stateless Persons convened by General Assembly resolution 429 (V). Actually, 27 States were represented at the Conference by plenipotentiaries and five States were represented by observers. A representative of the United Nations High Commissioner for Refugees participated, without the right to vote, in the deliberations of the Conference. The Conference decided to invite interested specialized agencies to participate in the proceedings without the right to vote. The International Labour Organisation was accordingly represented. The Conference also decided to permit representatives of non-governmental organizations in consultative status with the Economic and Social Council to submit written or oral statements to the Conference. Representatives of 11 such organizations (two from category A, eight from category B and one from those on the register) were present as observers.

In the case of the United Nations Conference of Plenipotentiaries on a Supplementary Convention on the Abolition of Slavery, the Slave Trade, and Institutions and Practices Similar to Slavery, the Economic and Social Council, in resolution 608 (XXI) of 30 April 1956, decided that invitations to attend the Conference should be extended to all States which are Members of the United Nations and to those States non-Members of the United Nations which are members of any of the specialized agencies. Actually, 51 States were represented at the Conference by plenipotentiaries and eight States were represented by observers. The International Labour Organisation was represented at the Conference by three of its officers. Also represented were 12 non-governmental organizations in consultative status with the Economic and Social Council. These organizations were given the right to submit written or oral statements.

In the case of the United Nations Conference on the Elimination or Reduction of Future Statelessness, the General Assembly, in resolution 896 (IX) of 4 December 1954, requested the Secretary-General to issue invitations to Member States and to "each non-member State which is or hereafter becomes a member of one or more of the specialized agencies of the United Nations or which is or hereafter becomes a Party to the Statute of the International Court of Justice".[67] Actually, representation was as follows:

At the first part of the Conference, 35 States were represented by plenipotentiaries and two States were represented by observers. At the second part of the Conference, 30 States were represented by plenipotentiaries and two States were represented by observers. In addition, four intergovernmental organizations were represented by an observer at the first part of the Conference and one of them was so represented at the second part. At both parts of the Conference the Office of the United Nations High Commissioner for Refugees was represented by an observer.

*Executive Secretary to the Conference*

The Director of the Division of Human Rights of the United Nations Secretariat served as Representative of the Secretary-General and Executive Secretary to the first three (in chronological order) of the four conferences under consideration. The Director of the Codification Division of the Office of Legal Affairs of the United Nations Secretariat was appointed Executive Secretary to the fourth Conference, that on the elimination or reduction of future statelessness.

*Conference officers*

Each of the four conferences elected, in accordance with its rules of procedure, one President and two Vice-Presidents from among the participating plenipotentiaries. A separate election of officers was held in connexion with each of the two parts of the Conference on the Elimination or Reduction of Future Statelessness.

*Provisional agenda*

The provisional agenda for each of the four Conferences was prepared by the Secretary-General, taking into consideration any relevant provisions that might have been contained in the resolution convening the Conference.[68]

*Rules of procedure*

The Secretariat submitted provisional rules of procedure for the consideration of the Conferences. These rules were drafted on the basis of a pattern designed to facilitate the discharge of the functions of the Conferences to which they were intended to apply. They included provisions dealing with representation and verification of credentials; officers of the Conferences; secretariat, conduct of business; voting; languages and records of the Conferences; public and private sessions; committees of the Conferences; representation of States not participating in the Conferences; representation of specialized agencies and non-governmental organizations; and amendments to the rules. The rules of some other conferences [69] contained a provision dealing with representation of the

[67] See operative paragraph 3 (*a*) and (*b*) of the resolution.

[68] e.g., Economic and Social Council resolution 526 (XVII), paragraph 1 (*a*) concerning the provisional agenda of the Conference on the Status of Stateless Persons.

[69] e.g., Conference of Plenipotentiaries on the Status of Refugees.

United Nations High Commissioner for Refugees. Each of the four Conferences adopted the provisional rules of procedure drawn up by the Secretary-General, in some cases with certain additions, deletions or amendments made at the beginning or in the course of the session. For example, the Conference of Plenipotentiaries on the Status of Refugees and Stateless Persons decided to add to the provisional rules of procedure drawn up by the Secretary-General a provision authorizing a representative of the Council of Europe to be present at the Conference without the right to vote and to submit proposals.[70]

*Committees and working groups*

In connexion with the discharge of their functions, some of the Conferences set up one or more committees or working groups. For example, the United Nations Conference on the Status of Stateless Persons appointed (i) a Drafting Committee on the Definition of the Term "Stateless Person", which was composed of the President of the Conference and the representatives of seven participating States; (ii) an *Ad Hoc* Committee on the Question of the Travel Document for Stateless Persons composed of the President of the Conference and the representatives of six States; and (iii) a Style Committee composed of the President of the Conference and the representatives of four States. The United Nations Conference of Plenipotentiaries on the Status of Refugees and Stateless Persons established, prior to the second reading of the Convention relating to the Status of Refugees, a Style Committee [71] which redrafted the text which had been adopted by the Conference on first reading, particularly from the point of view of language and concordance between the English and French texts. At the second part of the Conference on the Reduction or Elimination of Future Statelessness, a Working Group was set up, consisting of the President of the Conference, who acted as Chairman, of representatives of eight designated States and of representatives of other States who desired to participate. The same Conference had set up a Committee of the Whole and a Drafting Committee.

*Conference resolutions*

In addition to the text of the Convention they had adopted, the Final Acts of some of the Conferences have contained decisions and resolutions; some of them amount to clarification or explanations as to the contents of the Convention in question while others recommended to United Nations organs or to States a course of action which might additionally contribute to the purpose of the Convention being served.[72]

[70] A/CONF.2/3/Rev.1. For other examples, see E/CONF.17/2/Add.1 and 2.

[71] Consisting of the President of the Conference and the representatives of six States together with the High Commissioner for Refugees.

[72] e.g., *United Nations Conference of Plenipotentiaries on a Supplementary Convention on the Abolition of Slavery, the Slave Trade and Institutions and Practices Similar to Slavery*, Final Act and Supplementary Convention (United Nations publication, Sales No. 1957.XIV.2), p. 6; *United Nations Conference on the Status of Stateless Persons*, Final Act and *Convention relating to the Status of Stateless Persons* (United Nations publication, Sales No. 1956.XIV.1), parts II, III, IV.

### 3. *The International Conference on Human Rights, Teheran, 1968*

By resolution 2081 (XX) of 20 December 1965, the General Assembly decided to convene an International Conference on Human Rights "to promote further the principles contained in the Universal Declaration of Human Rights, to develop and guarantee political, civil, economic, social and cultural rights and to end all discrimination and denial of human rights and fundamental freedoms on grounds of race, colour, sex, language or religion, and in particular, to permit the elimination of *apartheid*". The specific purposes of the Conference were (*a*) to review the progress which has been made in the field of human rights since the adoption of the Universal Declaration of Human Rights; (*b*) to evaluate the effectiveness of the methods used by the United Nations in the field of human rights, especially with respect to the elimination of all forms of racial discrimination and the practice of the policy of *apartheid*; (*c*) to formulate and prepare a programme of further measures to be taken subsequent to the celebration of the International Year for Human Rights. The General Assembly also set up a Preparatory Committee for the International Conference on Human Rights. It requested the Secretary-General to appoint an Executive Secretary for the Conference and the Secretary-General designated the Director of the Division of Human Rights to perform this task.

By General Assembly resolution 2217 G (XXI) of 19 December 1966 the General Assembly accepted the invitation by the Government of Iran for the International Conference to be held in Teheran. By the same resolution it invited States Members of the United Nations, States members of the specialized agencies, States parties to the Statute of the International Court of Justice and States that it might decide especially to invite to participate in the Conference. Eighty-four States were represented at the Conference as well as certain special United Nations organs and four specialized agencies (ILO, FAO, UNESCO and WHO). Observers of regional organizations also attended.

The substantive work of the Conference, which was held from 22 April to 13 May 1968, is described in *Final Act of the International Conference on Human Rights.* [73]

### 4. *Conferences of non-governmental organizations interested in the eradication of prejudice and discrimination*

Rules for the calling of non-governmental conferences by the Economic and Social Council were approved by the General Assembly in resolution 479 (V) of 12 December 1950.[74]

Two Conferences of non-governmental organizations interested in the eradication of prejudice and discrimination have been convened by the Council. Both of these Conferences were held in Geneva under the auspices of the United Nations, the first one in 1955 and the second in 1959.

[73] United Nations publication, Sales No. E.68.XIV.2.

[74] See also Economic and Social Council resolution 335 (XI) of 20 July 1950.

By resolution 546 (XVIII) of 3 August 1954, the Economic and Social Council authorized the Secretary-General to convene a conference in which non-governmental organizations in consultative status with the Council, interested in the eradication of prejudice and discrimination might: (*a*) exchange views concerning the most effective means of combating discrimination; (*b*) co-ordinate their endeavours in this way if they find it desirable and feasible; (*c*) consider the possibility of establishing common objectives and programmes. The Council also determined that each non-governmental organization in consultative status with the Council should be invited to send a representative to the conference.

By resolution 683 E (XXVI) of 21 July 1958, the Council decided, in accordance with General Assembly resolution 479 (V) of 12 December 1950, to authorize the Secretary-General to convene a second conference of non-governmental organizations interested in the eradication of prejudice and discrimination and determined that each non-governmental organization in consultative status with the Council should be invited to send to the conference not more than two authorized representatives, chosen on the basis of their statute and leadership, and such alternates as it may consider necessary, chosen on the basis of their technical competence to deal with questions on the agenda. The Council also requested the Secretary-General to invite interested specialized agencies to participate in the conference and further requested him to prepare, in consultation with the non-governmental organizations concerned, the provisional agenda of the conference, which was to include certain items specified by the Council. In both resolutions the Council requested the Secretary-General to invite interested specialized agencies: (*a*) to make available to the respective conference relevant studies; (*b*) to make such observations to the respective conference as they might deem appropriate; and requested the Commission on Human Rights to direct the Sub-Commission on Prevention of Discrimination and Protection of Minorities to include in its subsequent report to the Commission its observations on the proceedings of the respective conference.

The Secretary-General of the United Nations was represented at both Conferences. The Director of the Division of Human Rights of the United Nations Secretariat served as Executive Secretary to both Conferences and represented the Secretary-General at the second one. The first Conference was attended by representatives from 97 non-governmental organizations. The second Conference was attended by authorized representatives and alternates from 84 non-governmental organizations in consultative status with the Council, chosen in accordance with the relevant paragraphs of the Council resolution convening the Conference. In addition, observers from a number of international, national and local non-governmental organizations not having consultative status attended the Conference. In attendance were also representatives of the ILO, UNESCO, the Office of the High Commissioner for Refugees and the secretariat of the World Refugee Year. The secretariat of the Conference was provided by the United Nations.

A report on the proceedings of each Conference was brought to the attention of the Economic and Social Council and its competent subsidiary bodies (see E/NGO/CONF.1/8 and E/NGO/CONF.2/7).

## II. INTERNATIONAL INSTRUMENTS (RECOMMENDATIONS, DECLARATIONS, TREATIES)

The making of recommendations, the adoption of declarations and the preparation and adoption of international treaties (designated as conventions, agreements, covenants, protocols, etc.) represent methods employed by the United Nations for setting and urging the application of standards in human rights consistent with the Charter commitments of Member States.

In the case of the "International Bill of Rights" both a Declaration and treaties have been adopted, the Universal Declaration of Human Rights in 1948 and the International Covenants on Human Rights in 1966. The adoption in 1963 of the United Nations Declaration on the Elimination of All Forms of Racial Discrimination was followed in 1965 by the adoption and opening for signature and ratification of the International Convention on the Elimination of All Forms of Racial Discrimination. The adoption and opening for signature and ratification in 1962 of the Convention on Consent to Marriage, Minimum Age for Marriage and Registration of Marriages was followed by the adoption, in 1965, of the Recommendation on Consent to Marriage, Minimum Age for Marriage and Registration of Marriages. In this instance the term "Recommendation" has become part of the formal title of the instrument, the Recommendation of 1965 being somewhat comparable to a Recommendation of the International Labour Conference. Under the Constitution of the ILO a Recommendation of that Conference has, however, a special legal effect inolving the obligation for all States members to submit the instrument to the competent national legislative authorities and to report on national law and practice in regard to the instrument when requested.

The practice as to the use of the terms "Declaration" and "Recommendation" was described in the following terms in a memorandum prepared in 1962 by the Office of Legal Affairs and submitted to the Commission on Human Rights at its eighteenth session in 1962:

"3. In United Nations practice, a 'declaration' is a formal and solemn instrument, suitable for rare occasions when principles of great and lasting importance are being enunciated, such as the Declaration of Human Rights. A recommendation is less formal.

"4. Apart from the distinction just indicated, there is probably no difference between a 'recommendation' and a 'declaration' in United Nations practice as far as strict legal principle is concerned. A 'declaration' or 'recommendation' is adopted by resolution of a United Nations organ. As such it cannot be made binding upon Member States, in the sense that a treaty or convention is binding upon the parties to it, purely by the device of terming it a 'declaration' rather than a 'recommendation'. However, in view of the greater solemnity and significance of a 'declaration', it may be considered to impart, on behalf of the organ adopting it, a strong expectation that Members of the international community will abide by it. Consequently, in so far as the expectation is gradually justified by State practice, a declaration may by custom become recognized as laying down rules binding upon States.

"5. In conclusion, it may be said that in United Nations practice, a 'declaration' is a solemn instrument resorted to only in very rare cases relating to matters of major and lasting importance where maximum compliance is expected." [1]

### 1. *Declarations*

By the end of 1972 the following Declarations relating to human rights had been adopted by the General Assembly of the United Nations: [2]

Universal Declaration of Human Rights (1948);

Declaration of the Rights of the Child (1959);

Declaration on the Granting of Independence to Colonial Countries and Peoples (1960);

Declaration on Permanent Sovereignty over Natural Resources (1962);

United Nations Declaration on the Elimination of All Forms of Racial Discrimination (1963);

Declaration on the Promotion Among Youth of the Ideals of Peace, Mutual Respect and Understanding between Peoples (1965);

Declaration on the Elimination of Discrimination against Women (1967);

Declaration on Territorial Asylum (1967);

Declaration on Social Progress and Development (1969);

Declaration on the Occasion of the Twenty-fifth Anniversary of the United Nations (24 October 1970);

Declaration on Principles of International Law concerning Friendly Relations and Co-operation among States in accordance with the Charter of the United Nations (1970);

Declaration on the Strengthening of International Security (1970);

---

[1] *Official Records of the Economic and Social Council, Thirty-fourth Session, Supplement No. 8*, para. 105.

[2] The following draft Declarations are still under consideration by United Nations organs: draft Declaration on Freedom of Information; draft Declaration on the Elimination of All Forms of Religious Intolerance.

Declaration on the Rights of Mentally Retarded Persons (1971).

The Declaration of the United Nations Conference on the Human Environment was adopted by the Conference at Stockholm, in June 1972, taken note of with satisfaction by the General Assembly and drawn to the attention of Governments.

The Universal Declaration of Human Rights is, as already indicated, the first part of the International Bill of Rights. In regard to the status and impact of the Universal Declaration of Human Rights, see part one, chapter II B of this publication.

The Declaration of the Rights of the Child was adopted by the General Assembly on the original initiative of the Social Commission, and on the basis of work done by the Commission on Human Rights.

The idea of a Declaration on the Right of Peoples and Nations to Self-Determination was suggested to the General Assembly for the first time by the then Secretary-General in 1955.[3] The General Assembly was seized of a concrete proposal for such a Declaration by a letter dated 23 September 1960 from the Chairman of the Council of Ministers of the USSR to the President of the General Assembly.[4]

The Declaration on Permanent Sovereignty over Natural Wealth and Resources of 1962 is the outcome of studies and recommendations made by the Commission on Human Rights at the request of the General Assembly on the question of the right of peoples to self-determination and of the examination of the problem by a General Assembly commission.

The preparation and eventual adoption of the United Nations Declaration on the Elimination of All Forms of Racial Discrimination of 1963 was the outcome of the consideration by the General Assembly of the item, "Manifestations of racial prejudice and national and religious intolerance".

The Declaration on the Promotion Among Youth of the Ideals of Peace, Mutual Respect and Understanding between Peoples is due to the initiative of one member Government and the co-operative efforts between the United Nations and UNESCO.

The Declaration on the Elimination of Discrimination against Women is due to the initiative of the General Assembly.

The Declaration on Territorial Asylum is due to the initiative of the Commission on Human Rights.

### 2. *International treaties*

The following covenants, conventions and protocols in the human rights field were adopted and opened for signature and ratification or accession by the General Assembly or by international conferences convened by the General Assembly or the Economic and Social Council:

Convention on the Prevention and Punishment of the Crime of Genocide (General Assembly resolution 260 (III) of 9 December 1948). The Convention entered into force on 12 January 1951.

Convention for the Suppression of the Traffic in Persons and of the Exploitation of the Prostitution of Others (General Assembly resolution 317 (IV) of 2 December 1949). The Convention entered into force on 25 July 1951.

Convention relating to the Status of Refugees (adopted in 1951 by the United Nations Conference of Plenipotentiaries on the Status of Refugees and Stateless Persons convened by General Assembly resolution 429 (V) of 14 December 1950). The Convention entered into force on 22 April 1954.

Convention on the International Right of Correction (General Assembly resolution 630 (VII) of 16 December 1952). The Convention entered into force on 24 August 1962.

Convention on the Political Rights of Women (General Assembly resolution 640 (VII) of 20 December 1952). The Convention entered into force on 7 July 1954.

Protocol Amending the Slavery Convention signed at Geneva on 25 September 1926 (General Assembly resolution 794 (VIII) of 23 October 1953). The Protocol entered into force on 7 December 1953.

Convention relating to the Status of Stateless Persons (adopted in 1954 by a Conference of Plenipotentiaries convened by Economic and Social Council resolution 526 A (XVIII) of 26 April 1954). The Convention entered into force on 6 June 1960.

Supplementary Convention on the Abolition of Slavery, the Slave Trade, and Institutions and Practices Similar to Slavery (adopted in 1956 by a Conference of Plenipotentiaries convened by Economic and Social Council resolution 608 (XXI) of 30 April 1956). The Convention entered into force on 30 April 1957.

Convention on the Nationality of Married Women (General Assembly resolution 1040 (XI) of 29 January 1957). The Convention entered into force on 11 August 1958.

Convention on the Reduction of Statelessness (adopted in 1961 by a Conference of Plenipotentiaries which met in 1959 and reconvened in 1961 in pursuance of General Assembly resolution 896 (IX) of 4 December 1954). The Convention is not in force as of 31 December 1972.

Convention on Consent to Marriage, Minimum Age for Marriage and Registration of Marriages (General Assembly resolution 1763 A (XVII) of 7 November 1962). The Convention entered into force on 9 December 1964.

International Convention on the Elimination of All Forms of Racial Discrimination (General Assembly resolution 2106 A (XX) of 21 December 1965). The Convention entered into force on 4 January 1969.

International Covenant on Economic, Social and Cultural Rights; International Covenant on Civil and Politi-

---

[3] Report of the Third Committee, *Official Records of the General Assembly, Tenth Session, Annexes*, agenda item 28, document A/3077, para. 8.

[4] *Ibid., Fifteenth Session, Annexes*, agenda item 87, document A/4501.

cal Rights and the Optional Protocol to the International Covenant on Civil and Political Rights (General Assembly resolution 2200 (XXI) of 16 December 1966). These instruments are not in force as of 31 December 1972.

Protocol relating to the Status of Refugees, done at New York on 31 January 1967 (see Economic and Social Council resolution 1186 (XLI) of 18 December 1966 and General Assembly resolution 2198 (XXI) of 16 December 1966). The Protocol entered into force on 4 October 1967.

Convention on the Non-Applicability of Statutory Limitations to War Crimes and Crimes against Humanity (General Assembly resolution 2391 (XXIII) of 26 November 1968). The Convention entered into force on 11 November 1970.

The measures of implementation provided for in some of these instruments are described in chapter III below.

One of the instruments, the Supplementary Convention on Slavery of 1956, expressly prohibits the making of reservations. The Convention relating to the Status of Refugees, and the Protocol relating to the Status of Refugees, the Conventions relating to the Status of Stateless Persons, on the Reduction of Statelessness, on the Political Rights of Women, on the Nationality of Married Women and on the Elimination of All Forms of Racial Discrimination regulate the question of reservations by express provisions. The Convention on Consent to Marriage, Minimum Age for Marriage and Registration of Marriages of 1962, the International Covenants of 1966 and the Convention on the Non-Applicability of Statutory Limitations to War Crimes and Crimes against Humanity of 1968 do not contain provisions on the question of reservations.

With the exception of the Protocol of 1953 amending the Slavery Convention of 1926, all the treaties in the field of human rights concluded within or under the auspices of the United Nations provide that the consent of a State to be bound by them must be expressed by ratification, acceptance or accession. Some of the treaties provide that certain categories of States non-Members of the United Nations such as members of the specialized agencies or parties to the Statute of the International Court of Justice may become parties to them. In some cases the General Assembly or the Economic and Social Council is vested with the right to address invitations to become parties to the Conventions to non-Member States.

The General Assembly and the Economic and Social Council have repeatedly appealed to Member States and certain categories of non-Member States to become parties to the various Conventions. The General Assembly and the Economic and Social Council have also taken a great interest in Member States becoming parties to international treaties in the human rights field concluded not within the United Nations but under the auspices of the specialized agencies and have addressed appropriate appeals to these States.

### 3. *Methods of preparing international instruments*

The origins and detailed arrangements made for the drafting of the various international instruments in the human rights field have varied from case to case. Some examples of the methods employed are given below.

The idea of drafting an "International Bill of Rights", which eventually was to consist of the Universal Declaration on Human Rights of 1948 and the two Covenants and Optional Protocol of 1966, was implied in the outcome of the proceedings of the United Nations Conference on International Organization, San Francisco. The Executive Committee of the Preparatory Commission of the United Nations and the Preparatory Commission itself recommended that the "formulation of an International Bill of Rights be one of the first items of the work programme of the Commission on Human Rights". This recommendation was accepted by the principal organs of the United Nations concerned.

In preparing what eventually became the independent parts of the International Bill of Rights, the Commission on Human Rights had the assistance of the Secretariat, which prepared a draft outline, and of a Drafting Committee which was appointed by the Economic and Social Council. It had also at its disposal a comprehensive collection of documentation and drafts submitted by Member Governments. In the course of the preparation of both the Universal Declaration of Human Rights and the two Covenants, Member Governments were repeatedly consulted and their comments invited. At one stage the General Assembly was asked to make, and did make, policy decisions on certain controversial questions. The specialized agencies were also invited to participate in the process and suggestions were received from various non-governmental organizations in consultative status. The drafts prepared by the Commission on Human Rights were considered article by article by the Third Committee of the General Assembly, an activity which, in the case of the two Covenants, was pursued at all but one session of the General Assembly between 1954 and 1966.

The Convention on Genocide was initiated by the General Assembly and worked out on the basis of a Secretariat draft by a Committee of the Economic and Social Council. The drafting was completed by the Sixth Committee of the General Assembly at its third session in 1948.

The Conventions relating to the status of women all originated in the Commission on the Status of Women, a functional commission of the Economic and Social Council. In regard to what eventually became the Convention on Consent to Marriage, Minimum Age for Marriage and Registration of Marriages of 1962, the Economic and Social Council, on the suggestion of the Commission on the Status of Women, requested the Secretary-General to prepare a draft which was the basis of the Commission's first draft, subsequently revised in the light of Government comments and eventually approved by the General Assembly on the recommendation of its Third Committee. In this and in other instances drafts of the final clauses were, at the request of the Council, prepared by the Secretary-General.

The United Nations instruments in the field of slavery and related practices were recommended by a Committee of Experts appointed by the Economic and Social Council pursuant to action by the General Assembly. The actual draft of the Convention of 1956 was prepared by a Committee of the Economic and Social Council and completed by a Conference of Plenipotentiaries convened by that Council.

The decision to prepare a Convention on the Elimination of All Forms of Racial Discrimination was taken by the General Assembly when it considered the item "Manifestations of Racial Prejudice" at its seventeenth session in 1962. The first draft was prepared by the Sub-Commission on Prevention of Discrimination and Protection of Minorities; its draft was revised by the Commission on Human Rights and the final text was prepared by the Third Committee of the General Assembly. To this draft, the General Assembly in plenary meeting made one change only.

The Convention on the Non-Applicability of Statutory Limitations to War Crimes and Crimes against Humanity originated in the work of the Commission on Human Rights. The final text as adopted was drafted by a joint working group of the Third and Sixth Committees of the General Assembly.

## III. IMPLEMENTATION MACHINERY AND PROCEDURES

The effectiveness of United Nations instruments, be they international conventions or declarations and recommendations, is dependent on Member States acting upon them and implementing them. Some of the United Nations instruments also establish international machinery, the purpose of which is to assist in the application and supervision of the instruments.

### A. National measures of implementation

#### 1. *National measures for the implementation of treaties*

In becoming a party to an international agreement in the field of human rights, as in other fields, a State accepts the obligation to give effect to the agreement in good faith. The way in which a State gives effect to the provisions of an international agreement is, generally speaking, left to the discretion of its competent constitutional institutions and organs. However, in certain of the human rights international agreements specific means of national implementation are indicated in the text of the treaty.

Thus the States parties to the Convention on Genocide have undertaken to enact in accordance with their respective constitutions the necessary legislation to give effect to the provisions of the Convention.

In the International Convention on the Elimination of All Forms of Racial Discrimination the States parties undertake to ensure among other things that all public authorities act in conformity with the policies expressed in the Convention; pledge themselves to review domestic policies and to annul, rescind or nullify any laws or regulations which have the effect of creating or perpetuating the racial or discriminatory practices. The Convention imposes on States parties the obligation to prohibit and bring to an end by all appropriate means, including legislation as required by circumstances, racial discrimination by any person, group or organization.

In the International Covenant on Civil and Political Rights each State undertakes to adopt such legislative measures as may be necessary to give effect to the rights recognized in the Covenant.

In the Convention on the Non-Applicability of Statutory Limitations to War Crimes and Crimes Against Humanity, the States parties undertake to adopt all necessary domestic measures, legislative or otherwise with a view to making possible the extradition in accordance with international law of the persons who have committed war crimes or crimes against humanity. The States parties to that Convention also undertake to adopt, in accordance with their respective constitutional processes, any legislative or other measures to ensure that statutory or other limitations shall not apply to the prosecution or punishment of these crimes.

The International Convention on the Elimination of All Forms of Racial Discrimination and the International Covenant on Civil and Political Rights impose on States parties the obligation to assure to everyone within their jurisdiction effective protection and remedies (article 6 of the Convention) and to ensure that any person whose rights or freedoms are violated shall have an effective remedy (article 2, paragraph 3 (*a*) of the Covenant).

In the International Covenant on Economic, Social and Cultural Rights each State party undertakes to take steps to the maximum of its available resources with a view to achieving progressively the full realization of the rights recognized in the Covenant by all appropriate means including particularly the adoption of legislative measures.

In some of the treaties under consideration States parties undertake to make certain acts punishable offences under their domestic law. In the Genocide Convention the Contracting Parties undertake to provide effective penalties for persons guilty of genocide or related offences. Under the Supplementary Convention on Slavery and Institutions and Practices Similar to Slavery the act of conveying slaves from one country to another shall be a criminal offence under the laws of the States parties and persons convicted thereof shall be liable to very severe penalties. The act of enslaving another person shall also be a criminal offence under the laws of the States parties. The Convention on the Elimination of All Forms of Racial Discrimination provides, among other things, that States parties shall declare an offence punishable by law all dissemination of ideas based on racial superiority or hatred, incitement to racial discrimination, acts of violence, etc. Participation in organizations or activities which promote and incite racial discrimination shall also be made an offence punishable by law. Under the International Covenant on Civil and Political Rights propaganda for war and advocacy of national, racial or religious hatred that constitutes incitement to discrimination, hostility or violence shall be prohibited by law.

The Convention on the Elimination of All Forms of Racial Discrimination provides in article 14, subject to certain conditions, for the competence of the Committee on the Elimination of Racial Discrimination to receive and consider communications from individuals or groups of individuals claiming to be victims of a violation of any of the rights set forth in the Convention. The Convention further provides that any State party which accepts the competence of the Committee on the Elimination of Racial Discrimination may also establish or indicate a body within its national legal order which shall be competent to receive and consider petitions from individuals or groups of individuals within its jurisdiction who claim to be victims of a violation of any of the rights set forth in the Convention. The name of such a body shall be deposited with the Secretary-General of the United Nations. The body thus established or indicated shall keep a register of petitions. Certified copies of the register shall be filed annually with the Secretary-General of the United Nations (article 14, paragraphs 2 and 4).

### 2. *National measures under declarations and recommendations*

The Declaration on the Granting of Independence to Colonial Countries and Peoples provides that immediate steps shall be taken in non-independent Territories to transfer all power to the peoples of these Territories without any conditions or reservations in accordance with their freely expressed will and desire without any distinction as to race, creed or colour.

The Declaration on the Promotion among Youth of the Ideals of Peace, Mutual Respect and Understanding between Peoples calls upon Governments to ensure the observance of the principles set forth in the Declaration by means of appropriate measures.

The United Nations Declaration on the Elimination of All Forms of Racial Discrimination calls for the adoption of national and international measures to the end of speedily eliminating racial discrimination throughout the world. Under this Declaration everyone shall have the right to an effective remedy and protection against discrimination he may suffer on the grounds of race, colour or ethnic origin. All incitement to or acts of violence against any race or group of persons of another colour or ethnic origin shall be considered an offence against society and punishable under law.

In the Recommendation on Consent to Marriage, Minimum Age for Marriage and Registration of Marriages the General Assembly recommended that each Member State bring the Recommendation before the authorities competent to enact legislation or to take other action at the earliest practicable moment.

In resolution 842 (IX) of 17 December 1954 on the question of forced labour the General Assembly supported the appeal of the Economic and Social Council contained in the latter's resolution 524 (XVII) of 27 April 1954 to all Governments to re-examine their laws and administrative practices in the light of present conditions.[1]

The Declaration on the Elimination of Discrimination against Women provides for legislative and other action by States in regard to many aspects relating to women. Thus under its article 2 all appropriate measures shall be taken to abolish discriminatory laws; the principle of equality of the rights of men and women shall be embodied in the Constitution or otherwise guaranteed by law. Equal political rights shall be guaranteed by legislation. Provisions of penal codes which constitute discrimination against women shall be repealed and legislation covering all other problems of discrimination against women shall be enacted.

The Declaration of Social Progress and Development provides a detailed list of steps that are to be taken for national implementation. In its article 18 it provides that the achievement of the objectives of social progress and development requires the implementation of the following means and measures:

" (*a*) The adoption of appropriate legislative, administrative and other measures ensuring to everyone not only political and civil rights, but also the full realization of economic, social and cultural rights without any discrimination;

" (*b*) The promotion of democratically based social and institutional reforms and motivation for change basic to the elimination of all forms of discrimination and exploitation and conducive to high rates of economic and social progress, to include land reform, in which the ownership and use of land will be made to serve best the objectives of social justice and economic development;

" (*c*) The adoption of measures to boost and diversify agricultural production through, *inter alia*, the implementation of democratic agrarian reforms, to ensure an adequate and well-balanced supply of food, its equitable distribution among the whole population and the improvement of nutritional standards;

" (*d*) The adoption of measures to introduce, with the participation of the Government, low-cost housing programmes in both rural and urban areas;

" (*e*) Development and expansion of the system of transportation and communications, particularly in developing countries."

As early as in resolution 9 (II) of the Economic and Social Council of 21 June 1946, which laid down the amended terms of reference of the Commission on Human Rights, the Council invited Member States to consider the desirability of establishing information groups or local human rights committees within their respective countries to collaborate with them in furthering the work of the Commission on Human Rights. The question of national advisory committees on human rights was subsequently repeatedly considered by the Commission on Human Rights, by the Sub-Commission on Prevention of Discrimination and Protection of Minorities and by the Economic and Social Council. A series of resolutions on this question was adopted, including Economic and Social Council resolutions 772 B (XXX) of 25 July 1960 and 888 F (XXIV) of 24 July 1962, and in regard to proposals to establish national committees to assist in the development of information media in the less developed countries and to appoint national commissions on the status of women, Council resolutions 819 (XXXI) of 28 April 1961 and 961 (XXXVI) of 12 July 1963 respectively. The General Assembly considered the advisability of the proposals for the establishment of national commissions on human rights or the designation of other appropriate institutions in conjunction with the adoption of the International

---

[1] Requests addressed to Governments to give effect in their internal laws and practices to treaties, declarations and recommendations will be found also in General Assembly resolutions 1510 (XV) of 12 December 1960, 1778 (XVII) of 7 December 1962, 1779 (XVII) of 7 December 1962; 2017 (XX) of 1 November 1965, 2027 (XX) of 18 November 1965, 2142 (XXI) of 26 October 1966.

Covenants on Human Rights (General Assembly resolution 2200 C (XXI) of 16 December 1966).

## B. Procedures and machinery of implementation on the international level

### 1. *Reporting procedures established in pursuance of the provisions of the United Nations Charter*

The presentation of reports to an international authority is a procedure of long standing utilized even before the establishment of the United Nations.[2]

Article 64 of the Charter provides that the Economic and Social Council may make arrangements with the Members of the United Nations to obtain reports on the steps taken to give effect to its own recommendations and to recommendations on matters falling within the Council's competence made by the General Assembly.

In resolutions adopted at its eighth and tenth sessions in 1949 and 1950, the Economic and Social Council requested Governments to furnish reports with respect to a list of recommendations which included recommendations on matters of human rights.[3]

At its fourteenth session in 1952 the Economic and Social Council discontinued the general biennial reporting procedure on steps taken by members to give effect to recommendations in the economic and social, including the human rights, field which it had established at its tenth session and decided to include in its resolutions wherever practicable indications as to the timing of the reports expected from Governments in pursuance of the resolutions concerned.[4]

The following are examples of requests made by the Economic and Social Council for reports and, in some cases, of procedures for dealing with the reports: a resolution on the political rights of women adopted at the seventh session in 1948 in which the Council requested Member States where women did not have the same political rights as men to grant them such rights; the Council initiated an inquiry as to the plans of the Governments concerned to give effect to the affirmation by the Charter of equal rights for men and women in regard to the franchise and eligibility to public office;[5] a resolution of the General Assembly of 4 December 1950 inviting all States to adopt 10 December of each year as "Human Rights Day" and to report annually concerning the observance of Human Rights Day;[6] a resolution adopted by the General Assembly in 1962 concerning measures against racial prejudice and religious intolerance, inviting Governments to inform the Secretary-General of action taken by them in compliance with the resolution;[7] a resolution on the policies of *apartheid* of the Government of the Republic of South Africa adopted in 1962 in which the General Assembly requested Member States to take certain measures, separately or collectively, in conformity with the Charter to bring about the abandonment of those policies and at the same time invited Member States to inform the General Assembly regarding actions taken, separately or collectively, in dissuading the Government of South Africa from pursuing its policies of *apartheid*;[8] the Recommendation on Consent to Marriage, Minimum Age for Marriage and Registration of Marriages of 1965 by which it was recommended to Member States that they should report at the end of three years and thereafter at intervals of five years on their law and practice with regard to the matters dealt with in the Recommendation showing the "extent to which effect has been given to the provisions of the Recommendation and such modifications as have been found or may be found necessary in adapting or applying it"; the Commission on the Status of Women was invited to examine the reports thus received and to report thereon with such recommendations as it may deem fitting;[9] a resolution relating to the application of statutory limitation to war crimes and crimes against humanity adopted by the Economic and Social Council in 1966 which urged all States to take any measures necessary to prevent statutory limitation, to continue their efforts to ensure the punishment of persons responsible for such crimes, and which invited Governments to inform the United Nations of the measures they have adopted in pursuance of the resolution;[10] resolutions requesting Member States to report on the action taken by them in compliance with the principles of the Declaration on the Elimination of Discrimination against Women.[11]

#### *The system of periodic reports on human rights*

The question of establishing a system of periodic reports on human rights was suggested to the Commission on Human Rights by a delegation at its sixth session in 1950 and taken up with a concrete proposal by another delegation in 1953.[12]

After consideration of the proposal by the Economic and Social Council and by the General Assembly and after consultation with Governments, the Commission on Human Rights at its twelfth session in 1956 adopted resolution 1 (XII) on annual reports on human rights.[13]

---

[2] See article 22 of the Covenant of the League of Nations; articles 19 and 22 of the Constitution of the ILO; see also Articles 87 (*a*), 88, 83, 73 e of the Charter of the United Nations and article VIII of the Constitution of UNESCO.

[3] Economic and Social Council resolutions 210 (VIII) of 18 March 1949 and 283 (X) of 8 February 1950.

[4] Economic and Social Council resolution 450 (XIV) of 29 July 1952.

[5] Economic and Social Council resolution 154 A (VII) of 20 August 1948 based on General Assembly resolution 56 (I) of 11 December 1946; see also from among many other Council resolutions on the question of political rights of women resolutions 587 B (XX) of 3 August 1955 and 1132 (XLI) of 26 July 1966.

[6] General Assembly resolution 423 (V) of 4 December 1950.

[7] Resolution 1779 (XVII) of 7 December 1962.

[8] General Assembly resolution 1761 (XVII) of 6 November 1962.

[9] General Assembly resolution 2018 (XX) of 1 November 1965.

[10] Economic and Social Council resolution 1158 (XLI) of 5 August 1966.

[11] Economic and Social Council resolutions 1325 (XLIV) of 31 May 1968 and 1677 (LII) of 2 June 1972.

[12] Reports of the Commission on Human Rights on its sixth and ninth sessions in 1950 and 1953 respectively, *Official Records of the Economic and Social Council, Eleventh Session, Supplement No. 5*, para. 47; *ibid., Sixteenth Session, Supplement No. 8*, paras. 263-270.

[13] *Official Records of the Economic and Social Council, Eighteenth Session, Supplement No. 7*, paras. 336-351; *ibid., Twentieth Session, Supplement No. 6*, paras. 135-141; and *ibid., Twenty-second Session, Supplement No. 3*, para. 23.

On the basis of this recommendation, the Economic and Social Council, in resolution 624 B (XXII) of 1 August 1956, established a system of periodic reports on human rights. It requested States Members of the United Nations and of the specialized agencies to transmit to the Secretary-General, every three years, a report describing developments and the progress achieved during the preceding three years in the field of human rights, and measures taken to safeguard human liberty in their metropolitan area and Non-Self-Governing and Trust Territories, the reports to deal with rights enumerated in the Universal Declaration of Human Rights and with the right of peoples to self-determination. It invited the specialized agencies, in respect of rights coming within their purview, to transmit to the Secretary-General, every three years, a report on a topical basis, summarizing information which they had received from member States. Furthermore, it requested the Secretary-General to prepare and forward to Governments suggestions that might serve as a guide for the preparation of the reports by Governments on a topical basis, and to prepare a brief summary of the reports on the same basis for the Commission on Human Rights. It decided that the first reports to be submitted by Governments should cover the years 1954, 1955 and 1956. The Council also invited States Members of the United Nations or of the specialized agencies in preparing their reports every three years, to include a separate section on such right or group of rights as might from time to time be selected for special study by the Commission on Human Rights; and approved as the first subject for special study the right of everyone to be free from arbitrary arrest, detention and exile.

The Secretary-General's suggestions, prepared in consultation with the specialized agencies to assist Governments in preparing the triennial reports on human rights, were submitted by him to the Economic and Social Council, which approved them in 1959.[14]

At the thirty-ninth session of the Economic and Social Council in 1965 the system of reporting was revised so as to call for submission of information within a continuing three-year cycle scheduled as follows: (*a*) in the first year, on civil and political rights; (*b*) in the second year, on economic, social and cultural rights; and (*c*) in the third year, on freedom of information.[15] The same Council resolution, also effected changes in the form of presentation of the reports to the Commission on Human Rights. While under the original system as established in resolution 624 B (XXII) the Secretary-General had been requested to prepare a brief summary of the Governments' reports on a topical basis, the Council decided at its thirty-ninth session that he should be requested to forward the information received from States and specialized agencies in full together with a subject and country index to the Commission on Human Rights, to the Commission on the Status of Women and the Sub-Commission on Prevention of Discrimination and Protection of Minorities.

In its resolution 888 B (XXXIV) of 24 July 1962, the Economic and Social Council invited non-governmental organizations in consultative status to submit comments and observations of an objective character on the situation in the field of human rights to assist the Commission on Human Rights in its consideration of the summaries of periodic reports. In resolution 1074 C (XXXIX) of 28 July 1965 non-governmental organizations in consultative status were invited to continue to submit objective information in accordance with the earlier Council resolutions and in accordance with the subject and time schedule for submission of reports by Governments established by resolution 1074 C (XXXIX).

The Council decided that the comments received from non-governmental organizations in consultative status and any comments which might be made on them by the States concerned, are to be made available to the Commission on Human Rights, the Commission on the Status of Women and the Sub-Commission on Prevention of Discrimination and Protection of Minorities.

In resolution 1074 C (XXXIX) the Economic and Social Council also requested the Commission on Human Rights to establish an *ad hoc* committee[16] having as its mandate the study and evaluation of the periodic reports and other information received under the terms of the resolution and to submit to the Commission comments, conclusions and recommendations of an objective character.

The Council also requested the Sub-Commission on Prevention of Discrimination and Protection of Minorities to undertake the initial study of the materials received under the terms of the resolution governing the reporting procedure and to report thereon to the Commission on Human Rights and to submit comments and recommendations for consideration by the Commission.

In its resolution 1074 C (XXXIX) the Economic and Social Council also reiterated its belief that the reporting system was not only a source of information, but also a valuable incentive to Governments' efforts to protect human rights and fundamental freedoms and to the implementation of the Universal Declaration of Human Rights, the Declaration on the Granting of Independence to Colonial Countries and Peoples and the Declaration on the Elimination of All Forms of Racial Discrimination.

At its twenty-second and twenty-third sessions in 1966 and 1967 the Commission on Human Rights re-examined the whole question of periodic reports on human rights. It had before it a considerable amount of documentation,

---

[14] See *Official Records of the Economic and Social Council, Twenty-eighth Session, Supplement No. 8*, para. 96; and Economic and Social Council resolution 728 B (XXVIII) of 30 July 1959. See also Economic and Social Council resolutions 888 B (XXXIV) of 24 July 1962 and 1074 C (XXXIX) of 28 July 1965.

[15] Economic and Social Council resolution 1074 C (XXXIX) of 28 July 1965. It might also be noted that by resolution 718 II (XXVII) of 24 April 1959, the Council had requested the Secretary-General to prepare, in order to facilitate the Commission's regular reviews on this subject, an annual report on "developments affecting freedom of information, including the problems of providing technical assistance to under-developed countries in the field of information, on the basis of material furnished by the United Nations Educational, Scientific and Cultural Organization and other interested specialized agencies, as well as any other information available".

[16] On its own initiative, the Commission had previously established, at its seventeenth and twentieth sessions, an *ad hoc* committee to deal with periodic reports.

including reports on civil and political rights received from 44 States and reports on economic, social and cultural rights received from 26 States as well as reports by the ILO, UNESCO and WHO. In addition the Commission considered the problem in the light of comments and suggestions made by the Commission on the Status of Women at its twentieth session and by the Sub-Commission on Prevention of Discrimination and Protection of Minorities at its nineteenth session.

The *Ad Hoc* Committee on Periodic Reports submitted a report and study, prepared by its rapporteur, to the Commission at its 1967 session. The Commission concluded its consideration of the question by unanimously adopting resolution 16 (XXIII) in which it affirmed that early signature and ratification of the International Covenants on Human Rights were of primary importance and stated that the information collected by Governments in the preparation of periodic reports would be of direct value to their consideration of early signature and ratification of those instruments and their future implementation. The Commission expressed its belief that the reports on economic, social and cultural rights revealed the following trends as of special importance and common interest: (*a*) the concern of Member States to implement human rights according to standards established in United Nations instruments; (*b*) the constructive efforts in law and practice in States with varying systems of government and at different stages of development to promote the right to education, including the interest shown in the question of adult education, the right to social security, the rights of the child and the family, including the provision of special care and assistance for motherhood and childhood, the right to work and the right to an adequate standard of living; (*c*) the attempts by various States to overcome difficulties with respect to the implementation of economic, social and cultural rights, and, notably the concern to make available remedies for the violation of these rights.

In the same resolution, the Commission considered that the task of United Nations bodies concerned in identifying important trends in the periodic reports would be facilitated in future by concentrating on material of an objective character with the following characteristics: (*a*) the influence on Member States of United Nations instruments which contain principles and norms for the protection of human rights and fundamental freedoms and, in particular, measures adopted to implement such instruments; (*b*) the common interest of a number of States in particular aspects of the rights under consideration; (*c*) experience of difficulties in the field of human rights which may be of interest to other States; (*d*) new developments or methods which may be helpful in overcoming such difficulties; (*e*) the participation of increasing numbers of the population in the enjoyment of human rights.

The Economic and Social Council took note of the report of the Commission on Human Rights on its twenty-third session (resolution 1241 (XLII) of 6 June 1967).

At its forty-second session in 1967 by resolution 1230 (XLII) the Economic and Social Council decided on the recommendation of the Commission on Human Rights that the initial study of periodic reports by the Sub-Commission had become unnecessary as a consequence of arrangements made by resolution 16 (XXIII) of the Commission on Human Rights.

At its fiftieth session in 1971 the Economic and Social Council decided that, with effect from the date of its resolution (1596 (L) of 21 May 1971), Member States would be asked to submit periodic reports once every two years in a continuing cycle: the first, on civil and political rights, to be submitted in 1972; the second, on economic, social and cultural rights, in 1974; the third, on freedom of information, in 1976.

### 2. *Reports concerning the implementation of international agreements concluded within or under the auspices of the United Nations*

#### (a) *International agreements requiring the communication of information*

By the Conventions relating to the Status of Refugees of 1951, by the Protocol relating to the Status of Refugees of 1966 and by the Convention relating to the Status of Stateless Persons of 1954, States have undertaken to communicate to the Secretary-General of the United Nations the laws and regulations which they may adopt to ensure the application of the Convention concerned. Similarly, under the Supplementary Convention on the Abolition of Slavery, the Slave Trade, and Institutions and Practices Similar to Slavery, the parties undertake to communicate to the United Nations copies of any laws, regulations and administrative measures enacted or put into effect to implement the provisions of the Convention. Under the International Convention on the Elimination of All Forms of Racial Discrimination and under the two Covenants the reporting arrangements are more elaborate. Under the Racial Discrimination Convention a special organ of the States parties reporting to the General Assembly of the United Nations has been established, namely the Committee on the Elimination of Racial Discrimination, to receive reports on the legislative, judicial, administrative or other measures which they have adopted and which give effect to the provisions of the Convention. Similarly, under the International Covenant on Civil and Political Rights, States parties undertake to report on the measures they have adopted which give effect to the rights recognized in the Covenant and on the progress made in the enjoyment of those rights. These reports will be transmitted by the Secretary-General to an organ to be established under the Covenant, i.e. the Human Rights Committee. Under the Covenant on Economic, Social and Cultural Rights States parties also undertake to submit reports on the measures which they have adopted and the progress made in achieving the observance of the rights recognized in that Covenant. However, under that Covenant the reports are to be considered not by special bodies created by the Covenant but by the Economic and Social Council with the assistance, as appropriate, of the Commission on Human Rights and of the specialized agencies concerned.

(b) *Resolution requesting the submission of information on the implementation of conventions*

Some examples of international agreements providing for the submission of information by States parties have been given in the preceding section of the present study. In regard to these Conventions the General Assembly or the Economic and Social Council have occasionally addressed recommendations to States parties requesting those of them which have not already done so to co-operate fully and to submit the information concerned. An example is resolution 1841 (XVII) of the General Assembly of 19 December 1962, relating to the Supplementary Convention on the Abolition of Slavery, the Slave Trade and Institutions and Practices Similar to Slavery of 1956. In regard to one Convention which does not in its terms provide for the furnishing of information by States parties, namely the Convention on the Political Rights of Women of 1952, the Economic and Social Council in resolution 504 E (XVI) of 23 July 1953 requested States parties to that Convention to report on the measures taken by them to implement its provisions. In resolution 961 B of 12 July 1963 the Council addressed a similar request also to States not parties to the Convention.

3. *Reports concerning the implementation of declarations*

United Nations organs have at times called on States to submit information on action taken to implement the provisions of the Universal Declaration of Human Rights and of other Declarations on human rights. As regards Non-Self-Governing Territories, administering Powers have repeatedly been invited, in the context of the information required under Article 73 e of the Charter, to furnish information on the extent to which the Universal Declaration of Human Rights was implemented in the Non-Self-Governing Territories under their administration.[17]

The Special Committee on Information under Article 73 e of the Charter was requested to include in its report to the General Assembly such recommendations as it may deem desirable relating to the application in Non-Self-Governing Territories of the Principles contained in the Universal Declaration of Human Rights. The standard form under Article 73 e which had been adopted by the General Assembly in resolution 142 (II) of 3 November 1947 was revised in resolution 551 (VI) of 7 December 1951 to contain a request addressed to the Administering Authorities of Non-Self-Governing Territories to provide a description of the manner in which human rights were protected by law in accordance with the principles set forth in the Universal Declaration of Human Rights.[18]

After the adoption in 1960 of the Declaration on the Granting of Independence to Colonial Countries and Peoples and the establishment in 1961 of the Special Committee on the situation with regard to its implementation, questionnaires and requests for a reply to the Special Committee have regularly been addressed to Administering Authorities of the Territories concerned. States responsible for the administration of Non-Self-Governing Territories were requested to transmit or continue to transmit information as prescribed in Article 73 e of the Charter as well as the fullest possible information on political and constitutional developments for consideration by the Special Committee.[19]

As far as the United Nations Declaration on the Elimination of All Forms of Racial Discrimination of 1963 is concerned, a procedure of reporting based on the voluntary co-operation of Governments was also established.[20]

**C. Procedures other than reporting procedures and machinery under treaties in the field of human rights concluded within or under the auspices of the United Nations**

1. *Convention on the Prevention and Punishment of the Crime of Genocide of 1948*

Under the Convention any Contracting Party may call upon the competent organs of the United Nations to take such action under the Charter as they consider appropriate for the prevention and suppression of acts of genocide and related acts. While the Convention provides that persons charged with genocide or related acts shall be tried by a competent tribunal by the State in the territory of which the act was committed, the Convention also contemplates the trial of such persons by such international penal tribunal as may have jurisdiction with respect to those Contracting Parties which shall have accepted its jurisdiction. While attempts at establishing an international criminal jurisdiction have been made and the statute of such a tribunal was prepared by the Committee on International Criminal Jurisdiction in 1961 and 1953, no final action on this question has so far been taken by the United Nations.[21] At its twenty-third session in 1968 the General Assembly decided not to include the item relating to international criminal jurisdiction in the agenda of its twenty-third session but to defer it to a later session.[22]

---

[17] General Assembly resolution 446 (V) of 12 December 1950 on information on human rights in Non-Self-Governing Territories.

[18] *Official Records of the General Assembly, Sixth Session, Supplement No. 20*, chap. XV, p. 45; see also General Assembly resolution 1535 (XV) of 15 December 1960 on progress achieved in Non-Self-Governing Territories.

[19] General Assembly resolution 1970 (XVIII) of 16 December 1963, resolution 2109 (XX) of 21 December 1965 and resolution 2233 (XXI) of 20 December 1966.

[20] See resolutions of the Economic and Social Council: 1076 (XXXIX) of 28 July 1965 and 1146 (XVI) of 2 August 1966, and resolutions of the General Assembly: 1905 (XVIII) of 20 November 1963, 2017 (XX) of 1 November 1965 and 2142 (XXI) of 26 October 1966.

[21] See General Assembly resolutions 489 (V), 687 (VII), 898 (IX), 1186 and 1187 (XII).

[22] 1676th plenary meeting, 27 September 1968; see also General Assembly resolution 2392 (XXIII) of 26 November 1968 on the question of the punishment of war criminals and of persons who have committed crimes against humanity.

2. *Convention relating to the Status of Refugees of 1951*

In the Convention on the Status of Refugees States parties undertake to co-operate with the United Nations High Commissioner for Refugees or any other agency which may succeed his Office in regard to the application of the provisions of the Convention.

3. *Convention on the International Right of Correction of 1952*

The Convention on the International Right of Correction provides a series of remedies for a State complaining that another State has not complied with its obligation under the Convention. Among the remedies provided for in the Convention is the right to seek relief through the Secretary-General of the United Nations who shall give appropriate publicity through the information channels at its disposal to the statements of the Parties.

4. *Convention on the Reduction of Statelessness of 1961* [23]

The Convention on the Reduction of Statelessness provides that the Contracting States shall promote the establishment within the framework of the United Nations of a body to which a person claiming the benefit of the Convention may apply for the examination of his claim and for assistance in presenting it to the appropriate authorities.

5. *International Convention on the Elimination of All Forms of Racial Discrimination*

(a) *Committee on the Elimination of Racial Discrimination and the* ad hoc *Conciliation Commission*

*Establishment*

Article 8 of the International Convention on the Elimination of All Forms of Racial Discrimination provides for the establishment of an international body, a Committee on the Elimination of Racial Discrimination. Article 12 provides for the appointment of an *ad hoc* Conciliation Commission which is discussed below in the context of the procedures followed by the Committee on Racial Discrimination in the performance of its functions.

*Composition*

The Committee is to consist of 18 experts of high moral standing and acknowledged impartiality elected by States parties to the Convention from among their nationals who are to serve in their personal capacity, consideration being given to equitable geographical distribution and to the representation of the different forms of civilization as well as of the principal legal systems.

*Method of election and term of office*

The members of the Committee are to be elected by secret ballot from a list of persons nominated by the States parties. Each State party may nominate one person from among its own nationals. Elections of the members of the Committee are to be held at a meeting of States parties convened by the Secretary-General at the Headquarters of the United Nations. The members of the Committee are to be elected for a term of four years.

*Expenses*

States parties are to be responsible for the expenses of the members of the Committee while they are in performance of Committee duties. The secretariat of the Committee is to be provided by the Secretary-General of the United Nations and the costs are to be charged to United Nations funds. At the first meeting of the States parties to the Convention, held in 1969, the States parties decided that they all would share equally the expenses of the Committee for the first year, and thereafter until they met again to elect half of the members of the Committee, 50 per cent of the expenses of the members of the Committee would be borne equally among the States parties and 50 per cent on the basis of the scale of assessment of the regular budget of the United Nations. At the second meeting of the States parties in 1972 and at their seventh meeting in 1973 the reconsideration of the question of apportioning was discussed, but it was decided on 8 January 1973 that the present system of assessment would be continued on a provisional basis and as a compromise solution but that the States parties should take it up for further consideration at their next meeting in 1974.

*Rules of procedure*

At its first session in 1970 the Committee on the Elimination of Racial Discrimination adopted provisional rules of procedure, which were amended and supplemented at the fourth session in 1971 and at the fifth session in 1972.

(*b*) *Functions, competence and procedures of the Committee on the Elimination of Racial Discrimination*

The Committee, which is to report annually through the Secretary-General to the General Assembly on its activities, has the following tasks:

(i) To consider reports from States parties;

(ii) To deal with allegations which may be brought by one party that another party was not giving effect to the provisions of the Convention;

(iii) To deal with communications received from individuals or groups of individuals claiming to be victims of a violation of the rights set forth in the Convention;

(iv) To co-operate with competent United Nations organs in matters of petitions from and reports concerning non-independent territories;

(v) To report annually on its activities to the General Assembly.[24]

---

[23] Not in force as of 31 December 1972.

[24] Reports of the Committee on the Elimination of Racial Discrimination submitted to the General Assembly at its twenty-fifth, twenty-sixth and twenty-seventh sessions (*Official Records of the General Assembly, Twenty-fifth Session, Supplement No. 27*; *ibid., Twenty-sixth Session, Supplement No. 18*; *ibid., Twenty-seventh Session, Supplement No. 18*).

Of the four distinct functions listed under (i), (ii), (iii) and (iv) in the preceding paragraph, only two have so far been performed by the Committee on the Elimination of Racial Discrimination: the function listed under (i), the consideration of reports received from Governments and the making of suggestions and general recommendations based on their examination under article 9 of the Convention; and item (iv), the co-operation of the Committee with competent United Nations organs in regard to petitions addressed to these organs and in regard to reports received by them which are directly related to the principles and obligations of the Convention, and the submission of expressions and opinions and recommendations thereon to the United Nations bodies concerned (article 15 of the Convention).

During the years 1970, 1971 and 1972 no complaint under article 11 of the Convention (item (ii) above) was lodged by any State party against another State party. As of the beginning of 1973, therefore, the Committee had not been called upon to take any action on inter-State disputes, i.e. on complaints by a State party that another State party was not giving effect to the provisions of the Convention (articles 11-13 of the Convention).

The procedure listed under (iii) for receiving and considering communications from individuals or groups under article 14 is not yet operative. Under article 14 the Committee may receive and consider communications from individuals or groups of individuals within the jurisdiction of a State party which has recognized the competence of the Committee to this effect, and may forward suggestions and recommendations in regard to such communications. Article 14 will become operative when at least ten States parties are bound by declarations accepting this competence of the Committee. As of the end of 1972, only three States parties had made a declaration under article 14 of the Convention.

### (i) *The consideration of reports by the Committee*

In 1970 the Committee on the Elimination of Racial Discrimination addressed to the States parties a carefully prepared communication containing a detailed analysis of the provisions of the Convention on which reports were expected. In general, the efforts of the Committee in 1970 were mainly directed to receiving complete and comprehensive reports from all States parties and to inducing Governments which had delayed reporting to speed up the co-operation with the Committee. In 1970, and more comprehensively, in 1971 and 1972, the Committee considered one by one the reports which it had received from a great number of States parties.

In several instances the Committee requested from States parties additional information. In 1971 it also considered statements contained in reports by Member States to the effect that racial discrimination was practised on the territory of the reporting States which was under the authority of other States, non-parties to the Convention.

At its fifth session in February 1972, the Committee adopted two general recommendations dealing respectively with the obligation of States to report irrespective of whether or not racial discrimination exists in their respective territory and with the obligation of States to legislate, to make incitement of racial discrimination a punishable offence and to declare illegal and prohibit organizations which promote and incite racial discrimination.[25]

At its third session in 1971 the Committee rejected a request by a State party that it present its comments on the observations made in the Committee concerning the report presented by that State party under article 9 of the Convention. At its fifth session in 1972, however, the Committee adopted, at the suggestion of the General Assembly (resolution 2783 (XXVI) of 6 December 1971), a new rule of procedure (rule 64A) providing that the Committee should notify the States parties of the opening date, duration and the place of the session at which their respective reports will be examined. Representatives of the States parties may be present at the meetings. The Committee may also inform a State party from which it decides to seek further information that it may authorize its representative to be present at a specific meeting. Under the new rule such a representative should be able to answer questions which may be put to him by the Committee and make statements on the reports already submitted and he may also submit additional information from his State.

### (ii) *Inter-State proceedings*

If a State party considers that another State party is not giving effect to the provisions of this Convention, it may bring the matter to the attention of the Committee. The Committee must then transmit the communication to the State party concerned. Within three months, the receiving State must submit to the Committee written explanations or statements clarifying the matter and the remedy, if any, that may have been taken by that State.

If the matter is not adjusted to the satisfaction of both parties, either by bilateral negotiations or by any other procedure open to them, within six months after the receipt by the receiving State of the initial communication, either State is to have the right to refer the matter again to the Committee by notice given to the Committee and also to the other State.

The Committee is to deal with a matter thus referred to it after it has ascertained that all available domestic remedies have been invoked and exhausted in the case, in conformity with the generally recognized principles of international law. This is not to be the rule where the application of the remedies is unreasonably prolonged.

In any matter referred to it, the Committee may call upon the States parties concerned to supply any relevant information.

When any matter is being considered by the Committee under these provisions, the States parties concerned are entitled to be represented at and to take part in the proceedings of the Committee, without voting rights.

While, as already indicated, no case under articles 11-13 of the Convention had arisen by the end of 1972, the

---

[25] *Official Records of the General Assembly, Twenty-seventh Session, Supplement No. 18*, General recommendations I and II, resolutions 3 (V) and 4 (V).

Committee included in the provisional rules of procedure which it adopted at its first and second sessions in 1970, rules governing the handling of communications from States parties under article 11 of the Convention (rules 68-70).

After the Committee has obtained and collated all the information it thinks necessary, the Chairman is to appoint an *ad hoc* Conciliation Commission comprising five persons, who may or may not be members of the Committee. The members of the Commission are to be appointed with the unanimous consent of the parties to the dispute, and its good offices will be made available to the States concerned with a view to an amicable solution to the matter on the basis of respect for the Convention.

If the States parties to the dispute fail to reach agreement on all or part of the composition of the Commission within three months, the members of the Commission not agreed upon by the States parties to the dispute are to be elected by a two-thirds majority vote by secret ballot of the Committee from among its own members.[26]

The information obtained and collated by the Committee is to be made available to the Commission and the Commission may call upon the States concerned to supply any other relevant information. When the Commission has fully considered the matter, it is to prepare and submit to the Chairman of the Committee a report embodying its findings on all questions of fact relevant to the issue between the Parties and containing such recommendations as it may think proper for the amicable solution of the dispute.

The Chairman of the Committee is to communicate the report of the Commission to each of the States parties to the dispute. These States shall within three months inform the Chairman of the Committee whether or not they accept the recommendations contained in the report of the Commission.

Upon the expiry of that period, the Chairman of the Committee is to communicate the report of the Commission and the declarations of States parties concerned to the other States parties to the Convention.

When adopting its rules of procedure the Committee refrained from adopting any rules to give effect to those paragraphs of article 12 of the Convention that related to the procedures of an *ad hoc* Conciliation Commission or other cognate matters, inasmuch as paragraph 3 of article 12 of the Convention stipulated that the *ad hoc* Conciliation Commission itself should adopt its own rules of procedure. The Committee adopted, however, rules relating to the establishment of the *ad hoc* Conciliation Commission under articles 12 and 13 of the Convention (rules 71-78). Some of these rules deal with procedural matters not provided for in the Convention.[27]

[26] Paragraph 2 of article 8 provides that the members of the Commission are to serve in their personal capacity and they shall not be nationals of the States parties to the dispute or of a State not party to the Convention. Paragraphs 3-7 pertain to the procedure, meetings, secretariat and expenses of the Commission.

[27] *Official Records of the General Assembly, Twenty-fifth Session, Supplement No. 27*, annex II.

### (iii) *The task of the Committee in regard to communications received from individuals or groups*

As already indicated, a State party may at any time declare that it recognizes the competence of the Committee to receive and consider communications from individuals or groups of individuals within its jurisdiction claiming to be victims of a violation by that State party of any of the rights set forth in the Convention. No communication shall be received by the Committee if it concerns a State party which has not made such a Declaration nor may the function be exercised unless at least 10 States are bound by a declaration under article 14.

Any State party which makes such a declaration may establish or indicate a body within its national legal order which shall be competent to receive and consider petitions from individuals and groups of individuals within its jurisdiction who claim to be victims of a violation of any of the rights set forth in the Convention and who have exhausted other available local remedies.

In the event of failure to obtain satisfaction from the national body, the petitioner shall have the right to communicate the matter to the Committee within six months.

The Committee shall confidentially bring any communication referred to it to the attention of the State party alleged to be violating any provision of the Convention, but the identity of the individual or groups of individuals concerned shall not be revealed without his or their express consent.

Within three months, the receiving State is to submit to the Committee written explanations or statements clarifying the matter and the remedy, if any, that may have been taken by that State.

The Committee is to consider communications in the light of all information made available to it by the State party concerned and by the petitioner. The Committee is not to consider any communication from a petitioner unless it has ascertained that the petitioner has exhausted all available domestic remedies. However, this shall not be the rule where the application of the remedies is unreasonably prolonged.

The Committee is to forward its suggestions and recommendations, if any, to the State party concerned and to the petitioner.

The Committee is to include in its annual report a summary of such communications and, where appropriate, a summary of the explanations and statements of the States parties concerned and of its own suggestions and recommendations.

When the Committee in 1970 was preparing its provisional rules of procedure, no rules of procedure for the application of article 14 were considered, inasmuch as the prerequisites for the coming into force of the provisions of article 14 had not been met. As already stated, they had not yet been met at the time of the preparation of the present publication at the beginning of 1973.

(iv) *Co-operation of the Committee with United Nations organs in matters of petitions from and reports concerning non-independent Territories*

Article 15 of the Convention provides that the Committee on the Elimination of Racial Discrimination shall receive copies of the petitions from, and submit expressions of opinion and recommendations on these petitions to, the bodies of the United Nations which deal with matters directly related to the principles and objectives of the Convention in their consideration of petitions from the inhabitants of Trust and Non-Self-Governing Territories and all other territories to which General Assembly resolution 1514 (XV) applies, relating to matters covered by the Convention which are before these bodies. The Committee shall further receive from the competent bodies of the United Nations copies of the reports concerning the legislative, judicial, administrative or other measures directly related to the principles and objectives of the Convention applied by the administering Powers within the Territories, and shall express opinions and make recommendations to these bodies. In 1970 the Committee took some action in preparation of its activities under article 15. It appointed four working groups to examine the material it had received. On the basis of the examination of the material by these groups, the Committee adopted at its fourth, fifth and sixth sessions a series of detailed opinions and recommendations (resolutions 5(IV) and 4 (VI) in the 1971 and 1972 reports of the Committee) relating to the various territories.

### 6. *International Covenant on Economic, Social and Cultural Rights* [28]

Article 23 of the Covenant records the agreement of States parties that "international action for the achievement of the rights recognized in the present Covenant includes such methods as the conclusion of conventions, the adoption of recommendations, the furnishing of technical assistance and the holding of regional meetings and technical meetings for the purpose of consultation and study organized in conjunction with the Governments concerned".

### 7. *International Covenant on Civil and Political Rights and the Optional Protocol to the Covenant* [29]

#### *The Human Rights Committee and the* ad hoc *conciliation commission*

*Establishment*

Article 28 of the Covenant on Civil and Political Rights provides for the establishment of an international organ, a "Human Rights Committee" whose functions are described below. In connexion with the exercise of the Committee's functions, provisions are also made (see article 42) for the appointment of an *ad hoc* conciliation commission.

*Composition*

The Human Rights Committee is to be composed of nationals of the States parties to the Covenant who are persons of high moral character and recognized competence in the field of human rights, consideration being given to the usefulness of the participation of some persons having legal experience. The members of the Committee serve in their personal capacity. The Committee may not include more than one national of the same State.

*Election and term of office*

The members of the Committee are to be elected by secret ballot from a list of persons nominated by the States parties to the Covenant. Elections are to be held at a meeting of the States parties convened by the Secretary-General at the Headquarters of the United Nations. In the election of the Committee consideration shall be given to equitable geographical distribution of membership and to the representation of the different forms of civilization as well as of the principal legal system.

The members of the Committee are to be elected for a term of four years. They are to be eligible for re-election if renominated.

*Staff, meetings, reports*

The Secretary-General of the United Nations shall provide the necessary staff for the effective performance of the functions of the Committee under the Covenant.

After its initial meeting, the Committee is to meet at such time as shall be provided by its rules of procedure. The meetings of the Committee are normally to be held at the Headquarters of the United Nations or at the United Nations Office in Geneva.

The Committee is to submit to the General Assembly, through the Economic and Social Council, an annual report on its activities.

*Functions, competence, procedure*

The functions of the Committee are: (i) to consider and deal with, in accordance with a procedure described elsewhere in this study, reports from States parties on the measures they have adopted which give effect to the rights recognized in the Covenant; (ii) to receive and to deal with communications from States parties claiming that another State party is not fulfilling its obligations under the Covenant. The Committee is to receive and consider only communications submitted by, and con-

[28] The Covenant will enter into force three months after the date of the deposit with the Secretary-General of the United Nations of the thirty-fifth instrument of ratification or accession. As of 31 December 1972, 48 States had signed the International Covenant on Economic, Social and Cultural Rights; 18 States had ratified or acceded to it.

[29] The Covenant will enter into force three months after the date of the deposit with the Secretary-General of the United Nations of the thirty-fifth instrument of ratification or accession.

*(Foot-note 29 continued)*

As of 31 December 1972, 48 States had signed the International Covenant on Civil and Political Rights; 18 States had ratified or acceded to it.

Subject to the entry into force of the Covenant, the Optional Protocol will enter into force three months after the date of the deposit of the tenth instrument of ratification or accession. As of 31 December 1972, eight States had ratified or acceded to the Optional Protocol.

cerning, a State party to the Covenant which has made a declaration recognizing in regard to itself this competence of the Committee; (iii) to receive and consider communications from individuals, subject to the jurisdiction of a State party, claiming to be victims of a violation by that State party or any right set forth in the Covenant. This function is exercised under the Optional Protocol to the Covenant on Civil and Political Rights whose article 1 provides that a State Party to the Covenant who becomes a party to the said Optional Protocol recognizes the competence of the Human Rights Committee to receive and consider communications from individuals.

8. *Comparison of the respective competences of the Human Rights Committee and of the Committee on the Elimination of Racial Discrimination in regard to petitions from non-independent Territories. The Saving Clause in article 7 of the Optional Protocol relating to such petitions*

Both the Convention on the Elimination of All Forms of Racial Discrimination of 1965 and the Optional Protocol to the Covenant on Civil and Political Rights of 1966 contain provisions relating to petitions from Territories to which the Declaration on the Granting of Independence to Colonial Countries and Peoples applies pending the achievement of the objectives of that Declaration. Article 15 of the Convention of 1965 provides that the provisions of the Convention shall in no way limit the right of petition granted to these peoples by other international instruments or by the United Nations and its specialized agencies. In similar but not identical terms, article 7 of the Optional Protocol of 1966 stipulates that the provisions of the Protocol shall in no way limit the right of petition granted these peoples by the Charter of the United Nations and other international Conventions and instruments under the United Nations and its specialized agencies. The Convention of 1965 provides in addition that the Committee on the Elimination of Racial Discrimination shall receive copies of the petitions from, and submit expressions of opinion and recommendations on these petitions to, the bodies of the United Nations which deal with matters directly related to the principles and objectives of the 1965 Convention in their consideration of petitions from the inhabitants of Trust, Non-Self-Governing and other non-independent Territories. The Convention also provides that the Committee shall include in its report to the General Assembly a summary of the petitions and reports it has thus received and the expressions of opinion and recommendations of the Committee relating to the said petitions and reports. No corresponding provisions are contained in the Optional Protocol of 1966 as far as the Human Rights Committee under the International Covenant on Civil and Political Rights is concerned.

## D. Procedures for dealing with communications concerning human rights

At its first session in January-February 1947, the Commission on Human Rights established a Sub-Committee on the Handling of Communications, the function of which was to consider how communications concerning human rights, addressed to the Commission on Human Rights or to other organs of the United Nations, may be handled, and to make appropriate recommendations to that effect to the Commission on Human Rights.[30] The report of the Sub-Committee to the Commission (E/CN.4/14/Rev.2) contained, in paragraph 3, the statement that "The Commission has no power to take any action in regard to any complaints regarding human rights." Following the unanimous adoption by the Commission of that paragraph of the report of the Sub-Committee, one member of the Commission proposed that it be amended by adding the following: "The Commission draws the Economic and Social Council's attention to the serious gap which results from the absence of this power." The member of the Commission in question did not make any proposal for bridging the gap, but hoped that the Economic and Social Council would instruct the Commission to do so. The Chairman of the Commission suggested that no mention of the gap should be made in the Commission's report but that the Rapporteur should be asked to explain the situation orally to the Economic and Social Council. This suggestion was accepted by the member concerned, who withdrew his proposed amendment.

The Commission on the Status of Women also considered the problem of communications at its first session. It appointed a Sub-Committee with the task (*a*) to deal with communications concerning the status of women already received and to bring forward to the Commission such communications as might be of special interest; (*b*) to consider how the Commission should deal with such communications in the future. The Sub-Committee divided the communications into two categories; namely, those which express interest, give information or suggestions or offer co-operation and those which contain protests and requests for action. The Sub-Committee summarized the latter communications and drew the attention of the Commission thereto and assumed "that the subject matter therein contained would receive further discussion in the course of the development of the Commission's programme, since all of it is truly related to such a programme."

With respect to future communications the Sub-Committee recommended and the Commission subsequently approved a procedure for handling them. Unlike the corresponding recommendations of the Commission on Human Rights, the recommendations of the Commission on the Status of Women did not contain a statement to the effect that the Commission on the Status of Women has no power to take any action in regard to any complaints relating to matters within its competence. In other respects the recommendations of the Commission on the Status of Women did not substantially differ from the corresponding recommendations of the Commission on Human Rights.

The Economic and Social Council considered the reports of both Commissions at its fifth session. On the recommendation of its Social Committee the Economic

---

[30] E/CN.4/SR.4, p. 4 and E/CN.4/14/Rev.2, para. 1.

and Social Council on 5 August 1947 adopted resolutions 75 (V) and 76 (V) dealing respectively with communications concerning human rights and communications relating to the status of women. In resolution 75 (V) the Council approved the statement that the Commission on Human Rights "recognizes that it has no power to take any action in regard to any complaints concerning human rights". In resolution 76 (V) the Council stated that it recognizes that as in the case of the Commission on Human Rights, the Commission on the Status of Women has no power to take any action in regard to any complaints concerning the status of women.

The statement that the Commission on Human Rights has no power to take any action in regard to any complaints concerning human rights has, in subsequent years, repeatedly been the subject of consideration by the Commission and by principal organs. In 1949 the Secretary-General submitted to the Commission on Human Rights a comprehensive report "on the present situation with regard to communications concerning human rights" in which he made a series of technical observations including comments on the statement on the Commission's lack of power.[31]

At its seventh session in 1951 the Commission on Human Rights called the attention of the Economic and Social Council, in the Council's consideration of the question of petitions in connexion with the report of the seventh session of the Commission, to the fact that the Commission has been receiving communications concerning human rights since its establishment.[32]

At its sixth session in February 1952 the General Assembly "noting that the Economic and Social Council has taken no action with respect to the resolution of the Commission on Human Rights on communications concerning human rights, invited the Council to give instructions to the Commission with regard to communications and to request the Commission to formulate recommendations thereon".[33] At its eighth session in 1952 the Commission decided not to propose the reconsideration of Economic and Social Council resolution 75 (V) as amended.[34]

In resolution 441 (XIV) of 23 July 1952 the Economic and Social Council decided not to take action on the matter at that time in view of the action of the Commission on Human Rights that there should be no reconsideration of resolution 75 (V) and to inform the General Assembly of this decision.

At the eighth session of the General Assembly in 1953 one delegation proposed a draft resolution by which the General Assembly would have decided that pending the entry into force of the Covenants on Human Rights, the Commission on Human Rights should transmit to Governments concerned for their comments such communications as in the opinion of the Commission contain allegations of violations of human rights serious enough to justify such reference and should transmit to the Economic and Social Council such communications together with the replies or comments of Governments as the Commission considers should be brought to the attention of the Council. This draft resolution was rejected.[35]

At the eleventh session of the General Assembly in 1956-1957 one delegation proposed that, as interim measures pending entry into force of the Covenants on Human Rights, the proposal should be considered that the Commission on Human Rights instruct a committee to examine complaints of one Member State against another Member State concerning violations of human rights if, in the opinion of the Commission, the complaint should appear well founded. This proposal was not adopted; the General Assembly confined itself to transmitting the relevant documentation to the Commission on Human Rights.[36]

Another attempt to re-examine the rule contained in resolution 75 (V) of 1947 was made by the Commission on Human Rights in 1958 when, "desiring to recommend to the Economic and Social Council to re-examine its resolution 75 (V) with a view to establishing a procedure for handling communications which is better calcaluated to promote respect for and observance of fundamental human rights", it appointed a Committee to study the question.[37] The Committee's report was in the main in favour of a reaffirmation of the principle of resolution 75 (V), which in fact was maintained in what eventually became resolution 728 F (XXVIII) of 30 July 1959 of the Economic and Social Council, which contains the rules at present in force for the handling of communications.[38] The modification of this rule effected by resolutions 1235 (XLIII) and 1503 (XLVIII) of the Economic and Social Council is described later in the present chapter.

Recommendations to modify the rule of resolution 75 (V) were also made by the Sub-Commission on Prevention of Discrimination and Protection of Minorities at its second and third sessions in 1949 and 1950.[39] The Commission decided not to sanction any change in the procedure.[40]

The Sub-Commission on Freedom of Information and of the Press addressed itself at its third session in 1949 to the question of procedures for the handling of communications which were of concern to the Sub-Commission. It submitted to the Economic and Social Council a series of recommendations on this question,[41] and the Economic and Social Council laid down a series of rules

[31] E/CN.4/165.

[32] *Official Records of the Economic and Social Council, Thirteenth Session, Supplement No. 9*, chap. IV, para. 94.

[33] General Assembly resolution 542 (VI) of 4 February 1952.

[34] *Official Records of the Economic and Social Council, Fourteenth Session, Supplement No. 4*, chap. V, para. 295.

[35] *Official Records of the General Assembly, Eighth Session, Annexes*, agenda item 12, A/C.3/L.368.

[36] *Official Records of the General Assembly, Eleventh Session, Annexes*, agenda item 60, Report of the Third Committee, A/3524.

[37] *Official Records of the Economic and Social Council, Twenty-sixth Session, Supplement No. 8*, para. 194.

[38] Report of the Committee on Communications (E/CN.4/782); *Official Records of the Economic and Social Council, Twenty-eighth Session, Supplement No. 8*, chap. IX.

[39] E/CN.4/351, annex, draft resolution 6; and E/CN.4/358, paras. 19-21; see also E/CN.4/361.

[40] *Official Records of the Economic and Social Council, Eleventh Session, Supplement No. 5*, chap. IV, paras. 56 and 62.

[41] *Ibid., Ninth Session, Supplement No. 10A*, chap. V, para. 24.

on communications in this field.[42] One of the recommendations of the Sub-Commission related to communications containing specific criticism or complaints against Governments in the field of information. The Sub-Commission suggested that with respect to such communications the Secretary-General be requested to inform the Governments concerned and to request them to furnish any information they might wish to on the substance of the communication and its author. The Sub-Commission contemplated that it would examine in public or private session, as it might decide, the list of communications which the Secretary-General was requested to compile in order to determine which of those communications justified discussion and merited further consideration. In resolution 240 C (IX) of 28 July 1949 the Economic and Social Council requested the Secretary-General to compile and distribute twice a year to members of the Sub-Commission a list containing a brief summary of each communication received from any legally constituted national or international Press, information, broadcasting or newsreel enterprise or association relating to principles and practices in the field of information. This rule was, however, not to apply to communications which contained specific criticism or complaints against Governments in the field of freedom of information. These were to be dealt with according to whatever procedures and principles might be laid down in the Commission on Human Rights. The Commission on Human Rights, taking note of this Council resolution at its sixth session, was of the opinion that until it had decided upon measures of implementation of the International Covenants on Human Rights, it would be premature to sanction any procedure for dealing with complaints or petitions other than that which was then in force for dealing with communications concerning human rights.[43] The Sub-Commission on Freedom on Information and of the Press held its last session in 1952, and no special arrangements for communications concerning freedom of information are at present in force.

The rules laid down in resolution 75 (V) of 1947 were, as far as technical questions were concerned, repeatedly amended by subsequent resolutions of the Economic and Social Council. In resolution 728 F (XXVIII) of 30 July 1959 the Council consolidated the rules relating to communications. Resolution 728 F (XXVIII) is subject to the modifications described below, at present in force. It contains, as had resolution 75 (V), the approval of the statement repeatedly referred to that the Commission on Human Rights recognizes that it has no power to take any action in regard to any complaints concerning human rights. By virtue of the resolution, the Secretary-General is requested to compile two lists of communications: a non-confidential list containing a brief indication of the substance of each communication dealing with the principles involved in the promotion of universal respect for and observance of human rights, and a confidential list containing a brief indication of the substance of other communications concerning human rights, i.e. communications not restricted to dealing with the principles involved, and to furnish this list to the members of the Commission in private meeting.

The identity of the authors of communications included in the non-confidential list are divulged unless the authors indicate that they wish their names to remain confidential. In regard to communications not restricted to principles the opposite rule prevails, namely the identity of the authors is not divulged except in cases where the authors state that they have already divulged or intend to divulge their names or that they have no objection to their names being divulged.

The Secretary-General is further requested to enable the members of the Commission upon request to consult the originals of communications dealing with principles. He is to inform the writers of all communications that their communications will be handled in accordance with the resolution under consideration indicating that the Commission has no power to take any action with regard to any complaints concerning human rights. The Secretary-General is also requested to furnish each Member State concerned with a copy of any communication which refers explicitly to that State or to territories under its jurisdiction, without divulging the identity of its author except if the author indicates otherwise, and to ask Governments sending replies to communications brought to their attention whether they wish their replies to be brought to the attention of the Commission in summary form or in full. The members of the Sub-Commission on Prevention of Discrimination and Protection of Minorities have analogous facilities with respect to communications dealing with discrimination and minorities.

It may be noted that both resolution 75 (V) and resolution 728 F (XXVIII) of the Economic and Social Council suggested that the Commission on Human Rights set up at each session an *ad hoc* committee for the purpose of reviewing the confidential list of communications prepared by the Secretary-General. The Commission has followed this practice only at its third, fifth and sixth sessions.[44] It has been the practice of the Commission on Human Rights either to recall the fact that certain lists of communications had been submitted to it or to adopt a resolution by which it takes note of the distribution of the lists of communications. The Commission on the Status of Women, on the other hand, has at every session so far set up an *ad hoc* committee for the purpose of reviewing the confidential list of communications prepared by the Secretary-General under paragraph (*a*) of resolution 76 (V), as had been suggested by the Council in that resolution.

As far as communications concerning the status of women are concerned, Economic and Social Council resolution 76 (V) has remained the governing resolution. Its provisions are essentially similar to those of 728 F (XXVIII).

---

[42] Economic and Social Council resolution 240 C (IX) of 28 July 1949.

[43] *Official Records of the Economic and Social Council, Eleventh Session, Supplement No. 5*, chap. IV, para. 62.

[44] See *Official Records of the Economic and Social Council, Seventh Session, Supplement No. 2*, para. 20; *ibid., Ninth Session, Supplement No. 10*, para. 26; *ibid., Eleventh Session, Supplement No. 5*, para. 54. The reports of the respective Committees are contained in documents E/CN.4/96, E/CN.4/302 and E/CN.4/460/Rev.1.

On 4 March 1966, acting upon the initiative of the Special Committee on the Situation with regard to the Implementation of the Declaration on the Granting of Independence to Colonial Countries and Peoples, the Economic and Social Council invited the Commission on Human Rights to consider as a matter of importance and urgency the question of the violation of human rights and fundamental freedoms, including policies of racial discrimination and segregation and of *apartheid* in all countries with particular reference to colonial and other dependent countries and territories and to submit to the Council its recommendations on measures to halt these violations.[45] The Commission considered the question at its twenty-second session in 1966 and in its resolution 2 (XXII), part B,[46] the Commission informed the Council that, in order to deal completely with the question of violations of human rights in all countries, it would be necessary for the Commission to consider fully the means by which it might be more fully informed of violations of human rights with a view to devising recommendations for measures to halt them. The Economic and Social Council concurred in the Commission's view [47] and the General Assembly invited the Council and the Commission to give urgent consideration to ways and means of improving the capacity of the United Nations to put a stop to violations of human rights wherever they might occur.[48]

At its twenty-third session in 1967 the Commission on Human Rights undertook a comprehensive examination of the problems involved in giving effect to the directives it had received from the General Assembly and the Economic and Social Council.[49] By resolution 6 (XXIII) the Commission set up an *Ad Hoc* Study Group to study in all its aspects the proposal to establish regional commissions on human rights within the United Nations family. In operative paragraph 2 of resolution 9 (XXIII) it instructed the same Study Group to study in all its aspects the question of the ways and means by which the Commission might be enabled or assisted to discharge functions in relation to violations of human rights whilst maintaining and fulfilling its other functions. By resolution 7 (XXIII) the Commission decided to appoint a Special Rapporteur to survey United Nations past action in its efforts to eliminate *apartheid* and to study the legislation and practices in South Africa, South West Africa and Southern Rhodesia instituted to establish and maintain *apartheid*, racial discrimination and related phenomena.

In its resolution 8 (XXIII) the Commission requested the Economic and Social Council to authorize the Commission and the Sub-Commission on Prevention of Discrimination and Protection of Minorities to examine information relevant to gross violations of human rights contained in communications concerning human rights listed pursuant to Council resolution 728 F (XXVIII). In the same resolution the Commission further requested authority, in appropriate cases, and after careful consideration of the information thus made available to it, to make a thorough study and investigation of situations revealing a consistent pattern of violations of human rights. In operative paragraph I of resolution 9 (XXIII) the Commission recommended that the Council should confirm the inclusion in the terms of reference of the Commission of "the power to recommend and adopt general and specific measures to deal with violations o human rights".

At its forty-second session in May/June 1967 the Economic and Social Council took positive action on most of the recommendations of the Commission on Human Rights referred to in the preceding paragraph of this Supplement. In resolution 1235 (XLII) the Council noted resolution 8 (XXIII) of the Commission on Human Rights and granted to the Commission and the Sub-Commission the authority which it had requested in that resolution, i.e. to examine information relevant to gross violations of human rights and fundamental freedoms as exemplified by the policy of *apartheid* as practised in the Republic of South Africa and in the Territory of South West Africa under the direct responsibility of the United Nations and now illegally occupied by the Government of the Republic of South Africa, and to racial discrimination as practised notably in Southern Rhodesia, contained in the communications listed by the Secretary-General pursuant to Council resolution 728 F (XXVIII). The Council also decided that the Commission on Human Rights might, in appropriate cases, and after careful consideration of the information thus made available to it, make a thorough study of situations revealing a consistent pattern of violations of human rights as exemplified by the policies of *apartheid* and racial discrimination referred to in the preceding paragraph. The Economic and Social Council also decided to review these provisions after the entry into force of the International Covenants on Human Rights.[50] As far as the part of the Commission's resolution 9 (XXIII) is concerned in which the Commission recommended that the Council should confirm the inclusion in the terms of reference of the Commission of the power to recommend and adopt general and specific measures to deal with violations of human rights, the Council did not at that stage take action on this recommendation, apart from noting the resolution.

On the basis of the authorization granted to it by Council resolution 1235 (XLII) the Sub-Commission on Prevention of Discrimination and Protection of Minorities, in the report on its twentieth session (September-October 1967), noted that, despite the repeated appeals and condemnations voiced by the various organs of the United Nations, flagrant violations of human rights were still being committed in a number of cases.

The Sub-Commission also drew the attention of the Commission on Human Rights to some particularly

[45] Economic and Social Council resolution 1102 (XL) of 4 March 1966.

[46] *Official Records of the Economic and Social Council, Forty-first Session, Supplement No. 8*, para. 222.

[47] Economic and Social Council resolution 1164 (XLI) of 5 August 1966.

[48] General Assembly resolution 2144 (XXI) of 26 October 1966.

[49] *Official Records of the Economic and Social Council, Forty-second Session, Supplement No. 6*, chap. V, resolutions 5 (XXIII), 6 (XXIII) 7 (XXIII), 8 (XXIII) and 9 (XXIII).

[50] Economic and Social Council resolution 1235 (XLII) of 6 June 1967.

glaring examples of situations which revealed consistent patterns of violations of human rights, and regarding which the Sub-Commission had expressed its unanimous views in the course of its discussions. Two such examples were listed in the Sub-Commission's resolution.

The Sub-Commission recommended that the Commission on Human Rights establish a Special Committee of Experts similar to the Working Group established by resolution 2 (XXIII) of the Commission on Human Rights to investigate charges of torture and ill-treatment of prisoners, detainees or persons in police custody in South Africa, whose establishment and work are described in chapter V, section 10 below. The Sub-Commission further recommended that the Commission authorize the Special Committee of Experts: to consider the situations referred to in Sub-Commission resolution 3 (XX); to use such modalities of procedure as it might deem appropriate; to receive communications and hear witnesses as necessary; and to consider comments received from the Governments concerned.[51]

In its resolution 1235 (XLII), the Economic and Social Council had taken the decision of principle that in certain situations the Commission on Human Rights and the Sub-Commission on Prevention of Discrimination and Protection of Minorities might take action concerning complaints in the matter of human rights. This decision of principle has affected the earlier provisions of resolutions 75 (V) and 728 F (XXVIII). This decision of principle having been taken, what remained to be done was to regulate the procedure through which the Commission on Human Rights would perform the new tasks entrusted to it by Council resolution 1235 (XLII).

Work on this complex problem was undertaken first by the Sub-Commission on Prevention of Discrimination and Protection of Minorities at its twenty-first session in October 1968, when it prepared and submitted to the Commission for presentation to the Council, a draft resolution containing detailed provisions on this question.[52] On the basis of the draft submitted to it by the Sub-Commission, the Commission on Human Rights, at its twenty-fifth session in 1969, adopted and submitted to the Council for approval a draft resolution on "Procedures for dealing with communications relating to violations of human rights and fundamental freedoms".[53] The main provisions of the texts prepared by the Sub-Commission and the Commission were, as will be described presently, adopted by the Council in its resolution 1503 (XLVIII) of 27 May 1970.

When the Economic and Social Council at its forty-sixth session in 1969 received the draft resolution prepared by the Commission on Human Rights at its twenty-fifth session, it decided, out of regard for its particularly important nature, to transmit it and the relevant documents to States Members for consideration and comment, and referred the question back to the Commission on Human Rights.[54] At its twenty-sixth session, in 1970, the Commission on Human Rights, having received comments from a number of Governments, decided to reaffirm the recommendation which it had made in the previous year and which was contained in its resolution 17 (XXV), and decided to re-submit the recommendation to the Council.

At its forty-eighth session in 1970, the Economic and Social Council acted on the recommendation of the Commission on Human Rights. It made a number of changes in the Commission's original draft resolution 17 (XXVI) and took also into account recommendations which the Commission itself had made in its accompanying resolution of the twenty-sixth session. On 27 May 1970 the Economic and Social Council adopted its resolution entitled "Procedure for dealing with communications relating to violations of human rights and fundamental freedoms."[55]

### 1. *The principal provisions of Council resolution 1503 (XLVIII)*

In paragraph 1 of resolution 1503 (XLVIII), the Economic and Social Council authorized the Sub-Commission on Prevention of Discrimination and Protection of Minorities to appoint a working group consisting of not more than five members with due regard to geographical distribution, to meet once a year in private meetings for a period not exceeding 10 days immediately before the sessions of the Sub-Commission to consider all communications, including replies from Governments thereon, received by the Secretary-General under Council resolution 728 F (XXVIII) with a view to bringing to the attention of the Sub-Commission those communications, together with replies from Governments, if any, which appeared to reveal a consistent pattern of gross and reliably attested violations of human rights and fundamental freedoms within the terms of reference of the Sub-Commission.[56]

The terms of reference of the Sub-Commission contain the provision that the Sub-Commission shall "perform any other functions which may be entrusted to it by the Economic and Social Council or the Commission on Human Rights". Pursuant to this provision, both the Economic and Social Council and the Commission on Human Rights have added other functions to those set forth in 1949. Such an extension of the terms of reference of the Sub-Commission followed, therefore, in particular from resolution 1235 (XLII) of the Economic and Social Council.

[51] Report of the twentieth session of the Sub-Commission on Prevention of Discrimination and Protection of Minorities, E/CN.4/947, para. 95, resolution 3 (XX).

[52] Report of the twenty-first session of the Sub-Commission, October 1968, document E/CN.4/976, paras. 71-94; resolution 2 (XXI); and chapter XIII, draft resolution 2.

[53] Report of the Commission on Human Rights on its twenty-fifth session (1969), *Official Records of the Economic and Social Council, Forty-sixth Session*, paras. 407-435, resolution 17 (XXV); and chap. XIX, draft resolution 9.

[54] Economic and Social Council resolution 1422 (XLVI) of 6 June 1969.

[55] Economic and Social Council resolution 1503 (XLVIII) of 27 May 1970.

[56] For the terms of reference of the Sub-Commission on Prevention of Discrimination and Protection of Minorities, as defined in 1949, see chapter I of this part above.

In paragraph 2 of resolution 1503 (XLVIII) the Council decided that the Sub-Commission should, as the first stage in the implementation of the resolution, devise appropriate procedures for dealing with the question of admissibility of communications received under Council resolution 728 F (XXVIII) and in accordance with Council resolution 1235 (XXII). These provisional procedures will be described later in this chapter.[57]

### 2. *The various stages of the procedure under resolution 1503 (XLVIII)*

The first stage in the procedure contemplated in resolution 1503 (XLVIII) takes place in the working group to be appointed pursuant to operative paragraph 1 of the resolution. The working group is called upon to decide by majority vote which of the communications it has received it considers appropriate to bring to the attention of the Sub-Commission.

The second stage takes place in the full Sub-Commission. It is the Sub-Commission's task to consider in private meetings the communications brought before it, in accordance with the decision of a majority of the members of the working group, and any replies of Governments relating thereto and other relevant information, with a view to determining whether to refer to the Commission on Human Rights particular situations which appear to reveal a consistent pattern of gross and reliably attested violations of human rights requiring consideration by the Commission (resolution 1503 (XLVIII), paragraph 5).

The third stage of the proceedings consists in action by the Commission on Human Rights.

Under paragraph 6 of resolution 1503 (XLVIII), the Commission on Human Rights is requested, after it has examined any situation referred to it by the Sub-Commission to determine:

"(*a*) Whether it requires a thorough study by the Commission and a report and recommendations thereon to the Council in accordance with resolution 1235 (XLII);

"(*b*) Whether it may be a subject of investigation by an *ad hoc* committee to be appointed by the Commission which shall be undertaken only with the express consent of the State concerned and shall be conducted in constant co-operation with that State and under conditions determined by agreement with it."

If the Commission decides to appoint an *ad hoc* committee, then a series of provisions safeguarding the rights of States applies. These safeguards include the following:

(i) The investigation by an *ad hoc* committee shall be undertaken only with the express consent of the State concerned;

(ii) It shall be conducted in constant co-operation with that State;

(iii) Under conditions determined by agreement with it;

(iv) The composition of the *ad hoc* committee shall be determined by the Commission on Human Rights;

(v) The members of the *ad hoc* committee shall be independent persons whose competence and impartiality is beyond question;

(vi) Their appointment shall be subject to the consent of the Government concerned.

The admissibility of appointing an *ad hoc* committee is, pursuant to paragraph 6, further conditioned by the following:

(i) All available means at the national level must have been resorted to and exhausted;

(ii) The appointment of the *ad hoc* Committee is inadmissible as the situation relates to a matter which is being dealt with under other procedures prescribed in the constituent instruments of, or conventions adopted by, the United Nations and the specialized agencies, or in regional conventions, or which the State concerned wishes to submit to other procedures in accordance with general or special international agreements to which it is a party.

About the stage of proceedings by the *ad hoc* Committee, resolution 1503 (XLVIII) provides in paragraph 7 the following:

(i) The Committee shall establish its own rules of procedure;

(ii) It shall be subject to the quorum rule;

(iii) It shall have authority to receive communications and hear witnesses, as necessary;

(iv) The Committee's procedures shall be confidential, its proceedings shall be conducted in private meetings and its communications shall not be published in any way;

(v) The Committee shall strive for friendly solutions before, during and even after the investigation.

The work of the *ad hoc* Committee concludes with its reporting to the Commission on Human Rights with such observations and suggestions as it may deem necessary.

On the basis of the report of the *ad hoc* committee or, if it has not appointed an *ad hoc* committee, on the basis of its own thorough study under paragraph 6 (*a*), the Commission has then to decide whether to make recommendations to the Economic and Social Council.

Under paragraph 8 of resolution 1503 (XLVIII), all actions envisaged in the implementation of the resolution by the Sub-Commission or the Commission on Human Rights shall remain confidential until such time as the Commission may decide to make recommendations to the Economic and Social Council.

The proceedings before the Economic and Social Council are the last stage of the action under resolution 1503 (XLVIII). The question of which action the Economic and Social Council can take is regulated in Article 62 of the Charter, where it is provided that the Council may make recommendations with respect to international, economic, social, cultural, educational, health and related matters to the General Assembly, to the Members of the

[57] Report of the twenty-fourth session of the Sub-Commission (E/CN.4/1070) resolution 1 (XXIV), provisional procedures for dealing with the question of admissibility of communications pursuant to Council resolution 1503 (XLVIII), adopted by the Sub-Commission at its twenty-fourth session in 1971.

United Nations and to the specialized agencies concerned (Article 62, paragraph 1) and where it is further provided that the Council may make recommendations for the purpose of promoting respect for, and observance of, human rights and fundamental freedoms for all (Article 62, paragraph 2 of the Charter.)

### 3. *The provisional procedures for dealing with the question of admissibility of communications*

At its twenty-fourth session in 1971 the Sub-Commission completed the mandate entrusted to it in paragraph 2 of resolution 1503 (XLVIII) to devote appropriate procedures for dealing with the question of admissibility of communications.

The "provisional procedures" provide, under the heading "Standards and criteria", that the object of the communication must not be inconsistent with the relevant principles of the Charter, of the Universal Declaration of Human Rights and of the other applicable instruments in the field of human rights. The "provisional procedures" also paraphrase the provisions of Council resolutions 1235 (XLII) and 1503 (XLVIII) by providing that communications shall be admissible only if, after consideration thereof, together with the replies, if any, of the Governments concerned, there are reasonable grounds to believe that they may reveal a consistent pattern of gross and reliably attested violations of human rights and fundamental freedoms, including policies of racial discrimination or segregation or *apartheid*, of any country, including colonial and other dependent countries and peoples.

On the question of the source of communications the provisional procedures provide that admissible communications may originate from a person or group of persons who, it can be reasonably presumed, are victims of the violations and also from any person or group of persons who have direct and reliable knowledge of those violations. Communications from non-governmental organizations are admissible if the organization concerned acts in good faith in accordance with recognized principles of human rights, not resorting to politically motivated stands contrary to the provisions of the Charter and has direct and reliable knowledge of such violations. Communications shall not be inadmissible solely because the knowledge of the individual author is second hand, provided that they are accompanied by clear evidence. Anonymous communications shall be inadmissible.

The author of a communication, whether an individual, a group of individuals or an organization, must be clearly identified. This, however, is, pursuant to operative paragraph 4 (*b*) of resolution 1503 (XLVIII) and paragraph 2 (*b*) of the provisional procedures, subject to the provision of Council resolution 728 F (XXVIII), which provides that the identity of the authors must not be divulged except in cases where the authors state that they have already divulged or intend to divulge their names or that they have no objection to their names being divulged.

Under the heading "Contents of communications and nature of allegations", the provisional procedures provide for a series of further conditions of the admissibility of communications: the communication must contain a description of the facts and must indicate the purpose of the petition and the rights that have been violated. It is further provided that communications shall be inadmissible if their language is essentially abusive and in particular if they contain insulting references to the State against which the complaint is directed. It is provided, however, that such communications may be considered if they meet the other criteria for admissibility after deletion of the abusive language.

Elaborating upon the general requirement that the subject of the communication must not be inconsistent with the relevant principles of the Charter, the provisional procedures further provide that a communication shall be admissible if it has manifestly political motivations and its subject is contrary to the provisions of the Charter.

While as already indicated, communications are not inadmissible solely because the author's knowledge is second-hand, a communication is inadmissible if it appears to be based exclusively on reports disseminated by mass media.

Under the heading "Existence of other remedies", the provisional procedures make provision for the avoidance of the overlapping of the new procedures with other existing procedures, for the exhaustion of domestic remedies and for the exclusion of the repeated seizing of United Nations organs with communications already settled in accordance with human rights principles.

It is provided, in particular, that communications shall be inadmissible if their admission would prejudice the functions of the specialized agencies of the United Nations. Communications shall be inadmissible if domestic remedies have not been exhausted. In the latter regard it is provided that the exhaustion of domestic remedies is not required if it appears that such remedies would be ineffective or unreasonably prolonged and that any failure to exhaust remedies should be satisfactorily established.

The new procedure was applied for the first time by the Working Group meeting from 31 July to 11 August 1972 and by the Sub-Commission at its twenty-fifth session (August-September 1972). It is stated in the report of the Sub-Commission that the Working Group met from 31 July to 11 August 1972 and, after consideration of over 20,000 individual communications, submitted a confidential report to the Sub-Commission. The Sub-Commission discussed the report and certain communications drawn to its attention at meetings held in closed session.

In a unanimously adopted resolution (resolution 2 (XXV)), the Sub-Commission stated that it realized the importance of the work accomplished by the Working Group as referred to in the preceding paragraph. The Sub-Commission further realized the need for it to verify carefully the fulfillment of the requirements set forth in the relevant resolutions of the Economic and Social Council and of the Sub-Commission. It added that replies of Governments would clearly be useful for the verification of the fulfillment of these requirements. The Sub-Commission stated that it was convinced of the importance of continued work by the Working Group, as a necessary means of enabling the Sub-Commission and the Commission on Human Rights to perform the functions assigned to them under Council resolution 1503 (XLVIII). The Sub-Commission requested the Secretary-General to inform Governments of the importance the Sub-Commission attaches to such replies as Governments may wish to submit to communications transmitted to them. It decided that the Working Group should consider at its next session (in 1973) those communications it had not been able to examine at its 1972 session, as well as communications received thereafter and that it may re-examine the communications singled out in its report in the light of replies of Governments, if any.[58]

4. *Written statements by non-governmental organizations in consultative status*

Under the rules governing consultative arrangements with non-governmental organizations such organizations have certain rights to submit and circulate written statements.[59]

In 1952 some difficulty arose regarding the circulation of written statements submitted by non-governmental organizations in consultative status which constituted or contained complaints against Governments. For that reason the Secretariat consulted the Council Committee on Non-Governmental Organizations in the matter. The Secretariat asked for guidance from the Committee as to the procedure which should be followed in regard to written statements from non-governmental organizations containing complaints, including complaints against Governments. In its report, the Committee suggested that the Secretary-General handle communications which contain complaints of violation of human rights in accordance with resolution 75 (V) (now replaced by resolution 728 F (XXVIII). This recommendation was approved by the Economic and Social Council.[60]

**E. The creation of specialized agencies as a method to promote respect for certain human rights**

1. *The question of refugees and displaced persons*

One of the problems created and aggravated by the Second World War which the United Nations had to face immediately upon its establishment was the problem of refugees and displaced persons. In resolution 8 (I) adopted at the first part of the first session of the General Assembly in 1946 this problem was referred to the Economic and Social Council for examination and report. The relevant resolution foreshadowed the possibility of recognition or establishment of an international body concerned with the problem. After thorough consideration of the question by the Economic and Social Council and by a Special Committee on Refugees and Displaced Persons established by it the Economic and Social Council at its first session agreed on the necessity of establishing such a body and at its second session recommended to the General Assembly the establishment of a non-permanent organ as a specialized agency to be called the International Refugee Organization. Among many other preparatory steps in which the Council was assisted by the Special Committee on Refugees and Displaced Persons which it had established at its first session, a draft constitution for the International Refugee Organization was submitted to the General Assembly by the Economic and Social Council at the latter's third session.[61] The General Assembly approved the Constitution of the International Refugee Organization and related arrangements at the second part of its first session and opened the Constitution for signature.[62]

The method applied by the United Nations in the matter of refugees and displaced persons was thus the taking of the initiative towards the creation of a new specialized agency as contemplated in Article 59 of the Charter. Later, when the International Refugee Organization, a temporary organization, was dissolved, some of its functions were vested in the United Nations High Commissioner for Refugees whose office was established with effect from 1 January 1951.[63]

2. *The creation of the World Health Organization*

The right to a standard of living adequate for health and the right to medical care is one of the social rights proclaimed in article 25 of the Universal Declaration of Human Rights. In the International Covenant on Economic, Social and Cultural Rights the parties recognize the right of everyone to the enjoyment of the highest attainable standard of physical and mental health. It is appropriate therefore to mention in the present context that one of the earliest measures taken by the United Nations for the promotion of the right to health was the initiation of negotiation for the establishment of the World Health Organization (WHO) as a specialized agency of the United Nations. Negotiations for the creation of the WHO were initiated by the Economic and Social Council at its first session when the Council decided to call an International Conference to consider the scope of and the machinery for international action in the field of public health and proposals for the establishment of a single health organization of the United Nations. The Council established a Technical Preparatory Committee consisting of experts in the field to prepare documentation for the Conference.[64] The report of the Techni-

[58] Report of the Sub-Commission on Prevention of Discrimination and Protection of Minorities on its twenty-fifth session, August-September 1972, document E/CN.4/1101, paras. 107 to 112, and resolution 2 (XXV) adopted at the 655th meeting of the Sub-Commission on 28 August 1972 in chapter XIV of the report.

[59] Economic and Social Council resolution 1296 (XLIV) of 23 May 1968.

[60] Economic and Social Council resolution 454 (XIV) of 28 July 1952; report of the Committee. (*Official Records of the Economic and Social Council, Fourteenth Session, Annexes*, agenda item 48, document E/2270).

[61] Economic and Social Council resolutions 3 (I) of 16 February 1946, 2 (II) of 21 June 1946 and 18 (III) of 3 October 1946.

[62] General Assembly resolution 62 (I) of 12 February 1946.

[63] General Assembly resolution 428 (V) of 14 December 1950, to which the Statute of the United Nations High Commissioner for Refugees is annexed. See also General Assembly resolution 319 (IV) of 3 December 1949.

[64] Resolution 1 (I) of the Economic and Social Council of 15 February 1946.

cal Preparatory Committee was considered by the Council at its second session at which the Council transmitted to the International Health Conference the relevant recommendations, suggestions and observations. The International Health Conference met in New York in June-July 1946 and adopted, among other instruments, the WHO Constitution.[65]

### F. The question of regional commissions on human rights

At its twenty-third session in 1967 the Commission on Human Rights by its resolution 6 (XXIII) set up an *ad hoc* Study Group of 11 of its members to study in all its aspects the proposal to establish regional commissions on human rights within the United Nations family, in the light of the Commission's discussion of the subject. The Commission directed the Study Group to pay particular attention to certain questions specifically mentioned in the resolution and authorized it to consult the Chairman of the Commission on the Status of Women as well as the two existing Regional Commissions on Human Rights and/or the intergovernmental organizations from which they receive their powers.

The Commission took that decision, bearing in mind resolution 1164 (XLI) of the Economic and Social Council, in which the Council had concurred in the Commission's view that it would be necessary for the Commission to consider the means by which it might be more fully informed of violations of human rights, with a view to devising recommendations for measures to put a stop to them. The Commission acted having regard also to General Assembly resolution 2144 (XXI), in which the General Assembly invited the Council and the Commission to give urgent consideration to ways and means of improving the capacity of the United Nations to put a stop to violations of human rights wherever they may occur.

The *Ad Hoc* Study Group established at the twenty-third session of the Commission in 1967 submitted its report (E/CN.4/966 and Add.1) to the Commission on Human Rights at its twenty-fourth session in 1968. The views of the members of the *Ad Hoc* Study Group were sharply divided but there was agreement on one point, i.e., that if further regional commissions were to be created this should be done on the initiative of the States in the region and not be imposed by the United Nations. After a discussion of this report, the Commission in its resolution 7 (XXIV) of 1 March 1968 requested the Secretary-General to transmit the report to Member States and to regional intergovernmental organizations for their comments and further requested the Secretary-General to consider the possibility of arranging suitable regional seminars under the programme of advisory services in the field of human rights in those regions where no regional commission on human rights existed, for the purpose of discussing the usefulness and advisability of the establishment of such commissions (Commission resolution 7 (XXIV) of 1 March 1968).

[65] Final Act of the International Health Conference (E/155).

In September 1969, at the invitation of the Government of the United Arab Republic, a seminar on the establishment of regional commissions on human rights with special reference to Africa was held in Cairo. The Commission on Human Rights at its twenty-fifth session, in resolution 2 (XXV) of 21 February 1969, decided, in effect, to defer consideration of the question until the report (ST/TAO/HR.38) on the results of that seminar was available.

The participants at the seminar agreed unanimously to request the Secretary-General of the United Nations to communicate the report of the seminar to the Secretary-General of the Organization of African Unity and the Governments of its member States so that the Organization of African Unity might consider appropriate steps, including the convening of a preparatory committee representative of Organization of African Unity membership, with a view to establishing a regional commission on human rights. The participants appealed to all Governments of member States of the Organization of African Unity to give their support and co-operation in establishing a regional commission on human rights for Africa. They further requested the Secretary-General of the United Nations to offer all assistance under the programme of advisory services in the field of human rights in any effort towards establishing a regional commission on human rights for Africa and to draw the attention of the United Nations Commission on Human Rights to the report of the seminar and to arrange for full consideration and exchange of information between the Commission on Human Rights and the Organization of African Unity concerning the establishment of a regional commission on human rights for Africa. They also expressed the hope that the specialized agencies and regional organizations would, upon its request, offer their co-operation to the Organization of African Unity in connexion with the establishment of a regional commission on human rights for Africa.

At its twenty-sixth session in 1970 the Commission had before it the report of the *Ad Hoc* Study Group as well as comments by 29 member States and three regional intergovernmental organizations. The report of the Cairo seminar (ST/TAO/HR.38) was also made available to the Commission. In the resolution it adopted on the question (resolution 6 (XXVI)), the Commission on Human Rights noted the report and the conclusions of the Cairo seminar and in particular the request addressed by the seminar to the Secretary-General to draw the attention of the Commission to the report and to arrange for full consideration and exchange of information between the Commission and the Organization of African Unity concerning the question of the establishment of a regional commission on human rights for Africa.

### G. Methods applied in regard to forced labour

The joint United Nations-ILO *Ad Hoc* Committee on Forced Labour, the establishment of which is described in part one, chapter IX, section G, of the present publication, sought to obtain relevant information on a global basis by three principal means: (*a*) it transmitted to all Governments a questionnaire on forced labour to which forty-eight Governments replied and thirty-three did not reply: (*b*) it endeavoured to assemble all the documents and evidence which had been brought to the knowledge of the Economic and Social Council during its extensive debates on the subject, including allegations relating to forced labour and replies thereto; and (*c*) it invited non-governmental organizations and private individuals to submit relevant information.

As far as the third of these methods was concerned, the Committee decided that not only non-governmental organizations in consultative status but also other organizations and individuals, who on their own initiative, asked to do this should be permitted to submit documentary material and information and to be heard by the Committee. The Committee made special arrangements to this effect requiring the organizations and individuals concerned to submit memoranda not exceeding a certain size specifying the points on which they wished to be heard and questioned and indicating the precise matter of the documentary material and information which they intended to submit. Primarily on the basis of the memoranda thus submitted the Committee decided which organizations and individuals would be invited to be heard and questioned or invited to transmit material and information. The Committee reserved the right both to limit the time allowed for the hearing and questioning and to select from, or reject, as it deemed necessary, any documentary material or information submitted. Eventually, the Committe heard, in closed session, 15 non-governmental organizations, six of which had consultative status, and four individuals. The Committee decided to confine its detailed study to those countries or territories concerning which allegations regarding the existence of forced labour had been made. A summary of allegations and of the documentary material purporting to support them was transmitted to the twenty-four Governments concerned for their comments and observations. Ten of those Governments communicated their comments to the Committee. On the basis of the examination of the allegations, the documentary material and government comments, the Committee unanimously adopted its final report, document E/2341, for submission to the Economic and Social Council and to the Governing Body of the International Labour Office.

Subsequently, both the Economic and Social Council and the General Assembly, after considering the report of the *Ad Hoc* Committee, condemned forced labour and appealed to all Governments to re-examine their laws and administrative practices in the matter.[66]

In its resolution 524 (XVIII) of April 1954, the Council arranged for the continuation of part of the work of the *Ad Hoc* Committee by the Secretary-General and the Director-General of the International Labour Office who were invited to prepare jointly an additional report for consideration by the Council.[67]

At its 129th session in June 1955, the Governing Body of the International Labour Office set up an independent *Ad Hoc* Committee on Forced Labour. When advised of this measure,[68] i.e., of the setting-up of an ILO Committee, the Economic and Social Council recognized (resolution 607 (XXI) of 1 May 1956) that the ILO has special responsiblities in the field of combating forced labour and commended that specialized agency for the action it had taken and expressed its interest in further action to be taken.

The further action eventually taken included the adoption by the International Labour Conference of the Abolition of Forced Labour Convention of 1957 and the establishment of a new Committee on Forced Labour by the ILO, to which reference is made in part one, chapter IX, section F of the present publication.

### H. Methods applied in regard to allegations of infringements of trade union rights

In the years between 1947 and 1950 special procedures for the consideration of allegations concerning infringements of trade union rights were elaborated in co-operation between the Economic and Social Council and the Governing Body of the International Labour Office. Relevant information is given in part one, chapter IX, section Q, of the present publication. In the present context, some aspects of the methods applied in this matter will be described in greater detail.

As originally contemplated by the Council and the Governing Body in making arrangements for these procedures, the main organ for their operation was to be the Fact-Finding and Conciliation Commission on Freedom of Association established by the ILO on its own behalf and also on behalf of the United Nations. The arrangements were to the effect that allegations of infringements of trade union rights received from Governments or from employers' or workers' organizations might be referred to the Fact-Finding and Conciliation Commission with the consent of the Government concerned. Subsequently, the Governing Body established the Committee on Freedom of Association, which consists of nine of its members (three government representatives, three employers' members and three workers' members). It is entrusted with the preliminary examination of the complaints by Governments or by employers' or workers' organizations alleging the infringement of trade union rights. It is the task of the Freedom of Association Committee to consider for recommendation to the Governing Body whether cases brought before it are worthy of examination by the Governing Body and when so determined affirmatively by the Governing Body, to attempt to secure the consent of the Government concerned to the reference of such cases to the Fact-Finding and Conciliation Commission. The Committee is empowered to include in its report, in case of deliberate non-co-operation of the State concerned, recommendations on the "appropriate alternative action" which the Committee

[66] Economic and Social Council resolution 524 (XVIII) of 27 April 1954 and General Assembly resolutions 740 (VIII) of 7 December 1953 and 842 (IX) of 17 December 1954.

[67] The Secretary-General's and Director-General's joint report will be found in documents E/2815 and Add.1-6.

[68] *Official Records of the Economic and Social Council, Twenty-first Session, Annexes*, agenda item 11, document E/2807.

might believe the Governing Body might take. Both the Economic and Social Council in its resolution 277 (X) and the Governing Body in the relevant decision taken at its 117th session have contemplated the taking of such "appropriate alternative action".

Since its establishment in 1951 the Committee on Freedom of Association has examined hundreds of cases, details of which are described in the reports of the Committee published in the *Official Bulletin of the International Labour Office*. Three complaints have been referred with the consent of the Government concerned, to the Fact-Finding and Conciliation Commission, i.e., allegations relating to Japan in 1964, allegations relating to Greece in 1965 and allegations relating to Lesotho in 1972.[69]

In the course of the operation of this procedure special problems have arisen in regard to allegations which referred to States Members of the United Nations and not at the relevant time members of the ILO and also in regard to allegations relating to entities which at the time were neither Members of the United Nations nor of the ILO. By way of example reference may be made to allegations made by an international trade union organ ization concerning the situation in what was at the time the Free Territory of Trieste under Allied Military Government. The allegations were brought to the attention of the Allied Military Government, which in its reply observed that no question of trade union rights had been involved.[70] The Economic and Social Council dismissed the allegation as not meriting further examination (resolution 474 D (XV) of 9 April 1953).

At one stage the Council had also before it allegations of the violation of trade union rights in the Saar territory at a time before that territory became part of the Federal Republic of Germany.[71] Allegations relating to Trust Territories were also submitted to the Economic and Social Council. The communication in question had also been presented to the Trusteeship Council as a result of which the Economic and Social Council requested the Secretary-General to report to it on the action taken by the Trusteeship Council, which report was subsequently submitted.[72]

More recently, a problem arising out of the procedure relating to trade union rights was brought to the attention of the Commission on Human Rights by the Governing Body of the International Labour Office. In the course of the consideration of allegations of the infringement of trade union rights in a member country the Governing Body had come to the conclusion that the facts involved were not restricted to the question of trade union rights but touched upon the question of violation of human rights in general in the country concerned. The ILO therefore proposed the inclusion in the provisional agenda of the twenty-second session of the Commission on Human Rights of the question of violation of human rights in the country concerned.[73] The observer of that country stated that his Government was opposed to the inclusion of the item. In the course of the consideration of the question whether the item should be included in the agenda the observer of the member Government concerned stated that his Government was prepared to send a mission to the International Labour Office to establish the facts and hold discussions with that agency. The representative of the ILO, in the light of this statement, said that he did not press for the inclusion of the proposed item in the agenda of the twenty-second session of the Commission on Human Rights provided that the matter would be fully reported to the Economic and Social Council for its information and that of the General Assembly.[74]

At its forty-second session the Economic and Social Council decided to transmit a communication containing allegations concerning infringement of trade union rights in a Member State of the United Nations which had ceased to be a member of the International Labour Organization, and such comments thereon as might be received from the Government concerned, to the *Ad Hoc* Working Group of Experts, which the Commission on Human Rights had established by its resolution 2 (XXIII) to investigate charges of torture and ill-treatment of prisoners, detainees or persons in police custody in the Republic of South Africa (Council resolution 1216 (XLII) of 1 June 1967). The Council authorized the *Ad Hoc* Working Group to receive communications and hear witnesses as necessary in its examination of the allegations regarding infringements of trade union rights in South Africa. By resolution 1302 (XLIV) of 28 May 1968 the Economic and Social Council extended this assignment of the *Ad Hoc* Working Group to South West Africa (Namibia).

## I. Consideration of specific human rights situations by United Nations organs and procedures relevant thereto

In this section of the present publication some samples of methods followed by United Nations organs in considering specific human rights situations will be described, The methods applied in situations involving racial discrimination are discussed in chapter V of part one and in chapter V of part two.

### 1. *The violation of human rights in South Viet-Nam*

Under the item entitled "The violation of human rights in South Viet-Nam" the General Assembly considered at

---

[69] See report by the Director-General of the International Labour Office to the Economic and Social Council (*Official Records of the Economic and Social Council, Fortieth Session. Annexes*, agenda item 9, document E/4144) and E/5110.

[70] E/2154/Add.20 of 13 February 1952 and E/2335 of 29 October 1952.

[71] E/2154/Add.43 and Economic and Social Council resolution 444 (XIV) of 18 July 1952.

[72] E/2025/Add.1 of 9 August 1951 and Economic and Social Council resolution 351 (XII) of 28 February 1951.

[73] Under article III of the agreement between the United Nations and the ILO, approved by the General Assembly by resolution 50 (I) of 1946, the Economic and Social Council and its commissions are to include in their agenda items proposed by the ILO. See also rule 6 of the rules of procedure of the Functional Commissions.

[74] Report on the twenty-second session of the Commission on Human Rights, March-April 1966, *Official Records of the Economic and Social Council, Forty-First Session, Supplement No. 8*, paras. 13-15.

its eithteenth session in 1963 allegations by a number of Member States that the religious rights of Buddhists in that non-member country were being denied and violated by its Government. In connexion with this item the Government of South Viet-Nam extended an invitation to representatives of several Member States to visit Viet-Nam in order to find out for themselves the true situation regarding the relations between the Government and the Viet-Namese Buddhist community. Eventually the General Assembly, at its 1234th meeting, indicated that it had no objection to accepting the proposal of the Government of South Viet-Nam—that the President of the General Assembly should appoint a mission composed of representatives of Member States to visit South Viet-Nam in order to investigate the facts and to report to the General Assembly.[75] Subsequently, the President announced that in accordance with the authorization given him by the General Assembly, he had appointed a mission consisting of representatives of seven Member States, its purpose being to visit the Republic of Viet-Nam so as to ascertain the facts of the situation in that country as regards the relations between the Government and the Buddhist community. The Chairman at the time of the Commission on Human Rights became the Chairman of the mission and the Director of the Division of Human Rights its Principal Secretary. The mission adopted rules of procedure which included the following provisions:

"*Terms of reference of the Mission*

"12. The Mission is an *ad hoc* fact-finding body and has been established to ascertain the facts of the situation as regards the alleged violations of human rights by the Government of the Republic of Viet-Nam in its relations with the Buddhist community of that country.

"13. The Mission shall seek factual evidence. The Mission shall collect information, conduct on-the-spot investigations, receive petitions and hear witnesses. The impartiality of the Mission shall be demonstrated at all times.

"*Collection of information*

"14. The Mission in collecting information shall keep itself informed on:

"(*a*) The provisions of the law and regulations in force in the Republic of Viet-Nam;

"(*b*) Writings and articles in the press;

"(*c*) Activities of organizations interested in the observance of human rights.

"*On-the-spot investigations*

"15. The Mission shall carry out on-the-spot verifications or investigations.

"16. The itinerary for the visits shall be drawn up on the basis of a detailed study of the regions and the incidents in respect of which complaints are presented to the Mission.

"*Petitions*

"17. The Mission shall receive petitions from individuals, groups or associations.

"18. The Mission shall proceed in private session to examine petitions and subject their acceptance to a preliminary examination. The petitions should indicate the date, the place and the facts to which the precise allegations relate.

"*Hearing of witnesses*

"19. The Mission shall decide on the witnesses from whom it shall hear evidence. Such witnesses may include persons under restriction and the Mission shall make arrangements to hear such persons under conditions as it may deem necessary.

"20. Each witness before testifying shall take an oath."

In discharging its functions, the Mission held several meetings with officials of the Government of the Republic of Viet-Nam, including the then President of the Republic. At those meetings the position of the Government in the matter of its relations with the Buddhist Community was outlined to the Mission.

In examining witnesses, the Mission interviewed, among others, monks, nuns and Buddhist leaders in pagodas, one prison and one hospital.

All witnesses were asked to identify themselves. The purpose of the visit of the Mission was explained to them. They were told that they were considered to be under oath and were being interviewed in the absence of any government official and that anything they said would remain completely confidential.

The Mission received a total of 116 communications from individuals, groups of individuals and non-governmental organizations.

Three of the communications received in Viet-Nam contained requests by the petitioners to be allowed to appear before the Mission. All the petitioners were granted hearings. Three of the communications received in Viet-Nam alleged difficulties encountered in getting in touch with the Mission.

Of the 116 communications received, about 54 contained more or less detailed statements either alleging or denying discrimination against, or persecution of, the Buddhist community in Viet-Nam. The allegations of discrimination were brought to the attention of the Government of the Republic of Viet-Nam.

In the examination of petitions received, the Mission considered only the precise charges in relation to the Buddhist problem and not the more general expressions of political opinion not relevant to its terms of reference. It checked with the alleged author the authenticity of letters it had received indirectly from a religious leader.

By visiting places where incidents had occurred, primarily in order to interview witnesses, the Mission was able to form an idea of conditions at each spot visited.

The Mission reported that from its arrival in Viet-Nam on 20 October 1963 until the coup-d'état of 1 November of that year which overthrew the Government of President Diem that Government co-operated with the Mission. The authorities who took over the Government after

[75] A/PV.1232 and 1234 of 7 and 8 October 1963 and A/PV.1239 of 11 October 1963.

1 November 1963 spontaneously offered their assistance to the Mission.

All decisions of the Mission taken throughout the course of its work, including the adoption of its report, were taken unanimously. The report of the Mission was circulated to the General Assembly.[76]

As the Government against which the allegations of violations of human rights were directed had been overthrown on 1 November 1963, the General Assembly at its 1280th plenary meeting on 13 December 1963 decided not to continue the consideration of that item.

### 2. *Other situations*

The human rights provisions of the Charter have also been invoked and referred to when principal organs of the United Nations dealt with several other political problems.

In connexion with the question of Hungary, the General Assembly appointed a Special Committee,[77] which conducted an investigation and submitted reports to the General Assembly at its eleventh and thirteenth sessions.[78] The General Assembly [79] also requested the President of the eleventh session, Prince Wan Waithayakon, to take steps he deemed appropriate to achieve the objectives of the various General Assembly resolutions on the question. He reported to the General Assembly at its thirteenth session.[80]

The Universal Declaration of Human Rights, among other authorities, was invoked by the General Assembly at its fourteenth, sixteenth and twentieth sessions in resolutions that it adopted, in plenary meetings without reference to a Main Committee or any other organ, concerning a territory within a Member State.[81]

In connexion with the question of Cyprus and the relationship of the two communities on the island, the Security Council, by resolution 180 (1964) of 4 March 1964, appointed a mediator.

In 1969 Ireland requested an urgent meeting of the Security Council to consider the situation, including the human rights situation, in Northern Ireland.[82] At its 1503rd meeting, on 20 August 1969, the Council decided to adjourn before taking a decision on the adoption of the agenda.

Ireland also proposed the inscription on the agenda of the twenty-fourth session of the General Assembly of an item on the situation in the North of Ireland.[83] The General Committee, at its 180th meeting on 17 September 1969, decided to defer a decision on whether or not to recommend the inclusion in the agenda of the item.[84]

No action in the matter was subsequently taken either by the Security Council or by the General Committee.

## J. The Special Committee on the Situation with regard to the Implementation of the Declaration on the Granting of Independence to Colonial Countries and Peoples

The Special Committee on the Situation with regard to the Implementation of the Declaration on the Granting of Independence to Colonial Countries and Peoples is a subsidiary organ of the General Assembly which has played a very important role in the work of the United Nations undertaken for the implementation of the principle of equal rights and self-determination of peoples and the promotion of respect for human rights and fundamental freedoms. The establishment, composition and work of the Special Committee is described in part two, chapter I, above.

## K. The United Nations Council for South West Africa (Namibia)

Having assumed direct responsibility for the Territory of South West Africa (Namibia) by its resolution 2145 (XXI) of 27 October 1966, the General Assembly, by resolution 2248 (S-V) of 19 May 1967 established the United Nations Council for South West Africa, consisting of 11 Member States, to administer South West Africa until independence. The General Assembly also decided that the Council should entrust such executive and administrative tasks as it deemed necessary to a United Nations Commissioner for South West Africa. On the proposal of the Secretary-General several high officials of the Secretariat were, in succession, appointed acting United Nations Commissioners for South West Africa (Namibia).

## L. Methods of safeguarding human rights in the Middle East conflict

### 1. *The United Nations Relief and Works Agency for Palestine Refugees in the Near East*

The United Nations Relief and Works Agency for Palestine Refugees in the Near East (UNRWA) was estab-

[76] *Official Records of the General Assembly, Eighteenth Session, Annexes*, agenda item 77, document A/5630.

[77] General Assembly resolution 1132 (XI) of 10 January 1957 : for reports of the Committee see *Official Records of the General Assembly, Eleventh Session, Annexes*, agenda item 67, document A/3596; *ibid., Supplement No. 18*; *ibid., Thirteenth Session, Annexes*, agenda item 69, document A/3849.

[78] General Assembly resolutions 1133 (XI) of 14 September 1957 and 1312 (XIII) of 12 December 1958.

[79] General Assembly resolution 1133 (XI) of 14 September 1957.

[80] General Assembly resolution 1312 (XIII) of 12 December 1958; *Official Records of the General Assembly, Thirteenth session, Annexes*, agenda item 69, document A/3849.

[81] General Assembly resolutions 1353 (XIV) of 21 October 1959, 1723 (XVI) of 20 December 1963 and 2079 (XX) of 18 December 1965.

[82] *Official Records of the Security Council, Twenty-fourth Year, Supplement for July, August and September 1969*, document S/9394.

[83] *Official Records of the General Assembly, Twenty-fourth Session, Annexes*, agenda item 8, document A/7651.

[84] *Ibid.*, document A/7700, para. 11.

lished by General Assembly resolution 302 (IV) of 8 December 1949 to carry out the direct relief and works programmes for the Palestine refugees; it is the successor to the United Nations Relief for Palestine Refugees as established under General Assembly resolution 212 (III). In resolution 302 (IV) the General Assembly also directed UNRWA to consult with the United Nations Conciliation Commission for Palestine, with particular reference to paragraph 11 of General Assembly resolution 194 (III) of 11 December 1948. Paragraph 11 stated "that the refugees wishing to return to their homes and live at peace with their neighbours should be permitted to do so at the earliest practicable date, and that compensation should be paid for the property of those choosing not to return and for loss of or damage to property which, under principles of international law or in equity, should be made good by the Governments or authorities responsible" and instructed "the Conciliation Commission to facilitate the repatriation, resettlement and economic and social rehabilitation of the refugees and the payment of compensation, and to maintain close relations with the Director of the United Nations Relief for Palestine Refugees and, through him, with the appropriate organs and agencies of the United Nations".

The General Assembly, in resolution 1604 (XV) of 21 April 1961, requested the United Nations Conciliation Commission for Palestine to make further efforts to secure the implementation of paragraph 11 of Assembly resolution 194 (III) and report thereon not later than 15 October 1961. On 9 May 1961, the Conciliation Commission decided to explore by means of a Special Representative the precise views of the parties as to what action might usefully be undertaken in the implementation of paragraph 11 of resolution 194 (III). The report of the Special Representative, Mr. Joseph E. Johnson, is contained in an addendum to a report of the Conciliation Commission (A/4921/Add.1).[85] The General Assembly in its resolution 2052 (XX) of 15 December 1965 noted with deep regret that repatriation or compensation of the refugees, as provided for in paragraph 11 of General Assembly resolution 194 (III), had not been effected, and that, therefore, the situation of refugees continued to be matter of serious concern. The General Assembly has repeatedly expressed its concern, for example, in resolution 2963 A (XXVII) of 13 December 1972, in which it noted with regret that the "United Nations Conciliation Commission for Palestine was unable to find a means of achieving progress in the implementation of paragraph 11 of General Assembly resolution 194 (III)" and requested the Commission "to exert continued efforts towards the implementation thereof and to report thereon as appropriate, but no later than 1 October 1973".

In resolution 2963 D (XXVII) of 13 December 1972 the General Assembly, recalling previous resolutions "calling upon the Government of Israel to take effective and immediate steps for the return without delay of those inhabitants who had fled the areas since the outbreak of hostilities", called once more upon Israel "immediately to take steps for the return of the displaced inhabitants".

The Commission on Human Rights by its resolution 6 (XXV) of 4 March 1969, reaffirmed "the inalienable right of all the inhabitants who have left since the outbreak of hostilities to return, and calls upon the Government of Israel to immediately implement the United Nations resolutions to this effect".

2. *The situation of civilians in the territories occupied as a result of hostilities in the Middle East in June 1967*

Since the outbreak of hostilities in the Middle East in June 1967, United Nations organs have given consideration to the situation of the civilian population in the areas that came under military occupation by Israel.

On 14 June 1967 the Security Council, by resolution 237 (1967), called upon the Government of Israel "to ensure the safety, welfare and security of the inhabitants of the areas where military operations have taken place" and "to facilitate the return of those inhabitants who have fled the areas since the outbreak of hostilities". The Council recommended scrupulous respect of the humanitarian principles governing the treatment of prisoners of war and the protection of civilian persons in time of war contained in the Geneva Conventions of 12 August 1949. In accordance with the request of the Security Council to follow the "effective implementation of this resolution" the Secretary-General submitted a series of reports to the Council. These reports were based, at first, on information furnished by UNRWA. Subsequently, the Secretary-General informed the Security Council[86] that, given the burden and increased difficulties on UNRWA it was no longer justifiable to request the Commissioner-General of UNRWA to continue to fulfil the task required in implementing the Council's resolution. The Secretary-General, therefore, appointed as his Special Representative, Mr. Nils Göran Gussing who visited the area during July and August 1967. The Secretary-General reported to the Security Council on 2 October 1967 on Mr. Gussing's activities.[87] Towards the end of the mission of Mr. Gussing, difficulties developed in connexion with the interpretation of the mandate of the Special Representative under Security Council resolution 237 (1967). The Government of Israel maintained that resolution 237 (1967) also covered the situation of Jewish minorities in Arab countries in the area of conflict.

The Commission on Human Rights, on 27 February 1968, adopted resolution 6 (XXIV) on the question of human rights in the territories occupied as a result of hostilities in the Middle East. In this resolution the Commission requested the Secretary-General to keep the Commission informed of developments with respect to the resolutions adopted by the Security Council and the General Assembly "in accordance with the provisions of the Universal Declaration of Human Rights and the Geneva

---

[85] *Official Records of the General Assembly, Sixteenth Session, Annexes*, agenda item 25.

[86] *Official Records of the Security Council, Twenty-second Year, Supplement for April, May and June 1967*, document S/8021, para. 6.

[87] *Ibid., Supplement for October, November and December 1967*, document S/8158.

Conventions of 1949 regarding human rights in the territories occupied as a result of hostilities in the Middle East".

Following an exchange of correspondence between the Secretary-General and the Governments concerned on the terms of reference of a second mission, the Secretary-General announced on 31 July 1968 that there was no basis at that time on which a second mission could proceed.[88] On 27 September 1968 the Security Council adopted resolution 259 (1968) requesting the Secretary-General "urgently to dispatch a Special Representative to the Arab territories under military occupation by Israel following the hostilities of 5 June 1967, and to report on the implementation of resolution 237 (1967)". The Council requested the Government of Israel "to receive the Special Representative, to co-operate with him and to facilitate his work". The terms of reference of the Special Representative were the subject of further correspondence.

On 14 October 1968 the Secretary-General informed the Security Council that he had not been able to give effect to its decision. In his report[89] the Secretary-General reproduced the relevant exchange of correspondence with the Government of Israel.

On 19 December 1968 the General Assembly adopted resolution 2443 (XXIII) establishing a "Special Committee to Investigate Israeli Practices Affecting the Human Rights of the Population of the Occupied Territories" composed of three Member States. It requested the President of the General Assembly to appoint the members of the Special Committee, the Government of Israel to receive the Special Committee, co-operate with it and facilitate its work. Due to the death of the President of the Assembly, a special procedure for the appointment of the members of the Special Committee was approved by more than an absolute majority of Member States, following alternatives suggested by the Secretary-General.

On 12 September 1969 the Secretary-General announced that Sri Lanka (then Ceylon), Somalia and Yugoslavia had been appointed as members of the Special Committee by a Vice-President of the twenty-third session of the General Assembly, designated for that task by the other Vice-Presidents of the twenty-third session, in accordance with the approved procedure.

Meanwhile, at its twenty-fifth session, on 4 March 1969, the Commission on Human Rights adopted resolution 6 (XXV) whereby it established a Special Working Group of Experts, composed of the members of the *Ad hoc* Working Group of Experts established by it under resolutions 2 (XXIII) and 2 (XXIV), with the following mandate:

> "*(a)* To investigate allegations concerning Israel's violations of the Geneva Convention relative to the Protection of Civilian Persons in Time of War of 12 August 1949, in the territories occupied by Israel as a result of hostilities in the Middle East;
>
> "*(b)* To receive communications, to hear witnesses, and use such modalities of procedure as it may deem necessary;
>
> "*(c)* To report, with its conclusions and recommendations, to the Commission's twenty-sixth session;"

The Special Working Group of Experts was not able to enter the occupied territories to carry out its mandate. The Government of Israel gave its reasons for withholding its co-operation in a note verbale of 25 June 1969 (E/CN.4/1016, para. 9.). The Special Working Group of Experts heard testimony and received written evidence during a visit that it made to Cairo, Amman, Beirut and Damascus. Testimony was also heard in meetings held in Geneva and New York. The Special Working Group reported to the Commission at its twenty-sixth session in 1970.

The Special Committee on Israeli Practices Affecting the Human Rights of the Population of the Occupied Territories, which had been established in 1968 and formed in September 1969, was the subject of Generai Assembly resolution 2546 (XXIV), whereby the Assembly *inter alia,* reaffirmed its resolutions relating to the violations of human rights in the territories occupied by Israel and expressed "its grave concern at the continuing reports of violation of human rights in those territories". It requested the Special Committee to take cognizance of the provisions of that resolution. The Government of Israel communicated its objections to the manner in which the Special Committee had been established, stating that the Special Committee could not be impartial in the exercise of its mandate, and that for reasons stated, it was not prepared to extend co-operation or facilities to the Special Committee. On the basis of evidence received by the Special Committee from witnesses appearing before it in London, Geneva, Beirut, Damascus, Amman, Cairo and New York and on written communications received on the subject, the Special Committee submitted a report[90] to the Secretary-General on 5 October 1970. The report was considered by the General Assembly at its twenty-fifth session.

At subsequent sessions the mandate of the Special Committee was renewed by the General Assembly (resolutions 2727 (XXV), 2851 (XXVI), 3005 (XXVII)), and the Special Committee has continued to report to the Assembly on the basis of information received by it on the situation in the occupied territories.

---

[88] *Ibid., Twenty-third Year, Supplement for July, August and September 1968,* document S/8699, para. 15.

[89] *Ibid., Supplement for October, November and December 1968,* document S/8851.

[90] *Official Records of the General Assembly, Twenty-fifth Session,* agenda item 101, document A/8089.

# IV. PROMOTION OF HUMAN RIGHTS THROUGH THE PREPARATION OF STUDIES, THE EXCHANGE OF INFORMATION, DOCUMENTATION AND EXPERIENCE AND EDUCATIONAL AND RELATED METHODS

## A. Studies

The initiation and making of studies is one of the methods for the promotion of respect of human rights referred to in the Charter (Article 13, paragraph 1 (*b*) and Article 62, paragraphs 1 and 2).

### 1. *Purpose of studies*

Studies have been made and requested for the purpose of providing United Nations organs with information on the situation existing in law and in fact in respect of a variety of human rights questions. One of the main purposes of the studies is to obtain detailed information before the organ concerned decides on a course of action. Repeatedly the preparation of studies has been initiated as the preparatory work for drafting an international convention or other instrument. At its twelfth session in 1956 the Commission on Human Rights, when initiating the programme of studies of specific rights or groups of rights, emphasized that those studies were necessary for the purpose of ascertaining the existing conditions, the results obtained, and the difficulties encountered in the work for the wider observance of and respect for human rights and fundamental freedoms.[1]

When approving the studies on discrimination in various fields to be undertaken by and for the Sub Commission on Prevention of Discrimination and Protection of Minorities, the Commission on Human Rights specified that the studies were to be drawn up not only to serve as a basis for the Sub-Commission's recommendations "but also with a view to educating world opinion".[2]

While in some cases the studies were from the outset undertaken for the purpose of preparing an international instrument, in others the eventual drawing up of the instrument was a consequence of the study and its consideration by the principal organs concerned. The studies preceding the adoption of the Convention on the Prevention and Punishment of the Crime of Genocide of 1948 and those undertaken in preparation of what eventually became the International Bill of Rights (Universal Declaration of Human Rights, International Covenants on Human Rights, Optional Protocol of 1966) were undertaken for the express purpose of leading to the drafting of those instruments. The study undertaken by the *Ad Hoc* Committee on Slavery and subsequent studies on that subject[3] led to the adoption of the Protocol of 1953 transferring to the United Nations the functions exercised by the League of Nations under the Slavery Convention of 1926 and at a later stage also to the drafting and opening for signature of the Supplementary Convention on the Abolition of Slavery, the Slave Trade and Institutions and Practices Similar to Slavery, 1956. The study undertaken by the joint United Nations-ILO *Ad Hoc* Committee on Forced Labour was eventually followed by the adoption by the International Labour Conference of the Abolition of Forced Labour Convention, 1957. Similarly, the study of discrimination in education by the Sub-Commission on Prevention of Discrimination and Protection of Minorities resulted eventually in the adoption by the General Conference of UNESCO of the Convention against Discrimination in Education in 1960. The Convention of 1960 was followed in 1962 by the Protocol Instituting a Conciliation and Good Offices Commission to be responsible for seeking a settlement of any disputes which may arise between States Parties to the Convention against Discrimination in Education.

*Organs entrusted with preparation of studies*

A variety of organs have been charged with the preparation of studies. The study of the Commission on Human Rights of the right of everyone to be free from arbitrary arrest, detention and exile was entrusted to a Committee of four States Members represented on the Commission on Human Rights. On other occasions, e.g., in the field of slavery, in regard to the first United Nations study to be undertaken, a Committee of Experts serving in their personal capacities was charged with its preparation. Later studies in the same field and a study on freedom of information were entrusted to single rapporteurs.[4] The studies relating to discrimination in specific fields undertaken by the Sub-Commission on Prevention of Discrimination and Protection of Minorities were conducted by special rapporteurs elected from among the members of the Sub-Commission. The Division

[1] Report of the Commission on Human Rights on its twelfth session, *Official Records of the Economic and Social Council, Twenty-second Session, Supplement No. 3*, para. 49.

[2] *Official Records of the Economic and Social Council, Eighteenth Session, Supplement No. 7*, para. 377.

[3] E/1988, E/2357, E/2673 and Add.1-4.

[4] Economic and Social Council resolution 442 C (XIV) of 13 June 1952 (Freedom of Information); Economic and Social Council resolution 525 A (XVII) of 29 April 1954 (appointment of Mr. Engen as Special Rapporteur) and Economic and Social Council resolution 960 (XXXVI) of 13 July 1963.

of Human Rights furnished assistance in the preparation of all these studies.

In very many instances specialized agencies, particularly the ILO and UNESCO, were requested to prepare studies for the Economic and Social Council or its subsidiary bodies. Examples are requests addressed to the ILO to undertake a study on discrimination in the field of employment and occupation,[5] a series of requests addressed to the same specialized agency in regard to studies relating to the access of women to training and employment, on the age of retirement and pension rights; requests addressed to UNESCO in the matter of access of women to the teaching profession and of access of girls and women to education at different levels.

The United Nations Secretariat has played an important role in studies of all kinds. Among examples of comprehensive studies undertaken by the Secretary-General were the study of the question of the non-applicability of periods of limitation to war crimes and crimes against humanity prepared by the Secretary-General in accordance with the request by the Commission on Human Rights,[6] followed at the request of the Economic and Social Council by the preparation of a draft Convention on the same subject,[7] which Convention was adopted and opened for signature, ratification and accession by General Assembly resolution 2391 (XXIII) of 26 November 1968; and the analytical and technical study on the question concerning the implementation of human rights through a United Nations High Commissioner for Human Rights or some other appropriate international machinery prepared at the request of the Commission on Human Rights.[8]

Very frequently the Secretary-General was requested to co-operate in the preparation of the studies with the specialized agencies concerned. An example is the study of a unified long-term United Nations programme for the advancement of women authorized by resolution 1133 (XLI) of the Economic and Social Council on 26 July 1966.

*Sources of information*

The *Ad Hoc* Committee of Experts on the problem of slavery, appointed pursuant to resolution 238 (IX) of the Economic and Social Council, had before it information supplied by Governments in response to a questionnaire which the Committee had been authorized to transmit to Governments of Members and non-Members of the United Nations. The Committee also had before it statements by non-governmental organizations, research and similar institutions and information gathered by the members of the Committee.

The sources of information available to the *Ad Hoc* Committee on Forced Labour are described in chapter III of part two of the present publication.

The terms of reference and guidelines for the studies of discrimination in specific fields undertaken by the Sub-Commission on Prevention of Discrimination and Protection of Minorities are described in chapter I of part two of the present publication.

The two studies undertaken by the Commission on Human Rights through a four-member Committee, namely the study of the right of everyone to be free from arbitrary arrest, detention and exile and the study of the right of arrested persons to communicate with those whom it is necessary for them to consult, have under the terms set forth by the Commission, been based on the following sources: (i) Governments of States Members of the United Nations and of the specialized agencies, (ii) the Secretary-General, (iii) specialized agencies, (iv) non-governmental organizations in consultative status with the Economic and Social Council, and (v) writings of recognized scholars and scientists.[9]

A list of studies, other than those entrusted to the Secretary-General, undertaken by the Commission on Human Rights or by the Sub-Commission on Prevention of Discrimination and Protection of Minorities, follows. The list includes both completed studies and studies still in progress.

## 2. *Studies by the Commission on Human Rights*

Study of the right of everyone to be free from arbitrary arrest, detention and exile (Sales No. 65.XIV.2);

Study on the right of arrested persons to communicate with those whom it is necessary for them to consult in order to ensure their defence or to protect their essential interests (Document E/CN.4/966, submitted to the Commission at its twenty-fifth session in 1969);

Study of the realization of economic, social and cultural rights:

(*a*) Preliminary study of issues relating to the realization of economic and social rights contained in the Universal Declaration of Human Rights and in the International Covenant on Economic, Social and Cultural Rights (Document E/CN.4/938 and Add.1), submitted by the Secretary-General to the twenty-fifth session of the Commission in 1969;

(*b*) Study of the realization of economic, social and cultural rights. (Document E/CN.4/1108 and Add.1-9) submitted by the Special Rapporteur to the twenty-ninth session of the Commission in 1973;

Study of *apartheid* and racial discrimination in southern Africa. (Document E/CN.4/949 and addenda, submitted to the Commission at its twenty-fourth session in 1968 and document E/CN.4/979 and addenda, submitted to the Commission at its twenty-fifth session in 1969.)

[5] Resolution 545 C (XVIII).

[6] *Official Records of the Economic and Social Council, Thirty-ninth Session, Supplement No. 8*, para. 567, resolution 3 (XXI) of 9 April 1965.

[7] E/CN.4/928.

[8] E/CN.4/AC.21/L.1; Commission on Human Rights resolution 4 (XXII) 1966.

[9] Resolution II adopted at the twelfth session of the Commission, *Official Records of the Economic and Social Council, Twenty-second Session, Supplement No. 3*, para. 49; see also resolution of the Economic and Social Council 624 B (XXII) of 1 August 1956 in which the Council approved the study of arbitrary arrest, etc., as the first subject for special study.

### 3. *Studies by the Sub-Commission on Prevention of Discrimination and Protection of Minorities*

*Study of Discrimination in Education* (Sales No. 57. XIV.3);

*Study of Discrimination in the matter of Political Rights* (Sales No. 63.XIV.2);

*Study of Discrimination in the matter of Religious Rights and Practices* (Sales No. 60.XIV.2);

*Study of Discrimination in respect of the Right of Everyone to Leave any Country, Including his Own, and to Return to his Country* (Sales No. 64.XIV.2);

*Study of Discrimination against Persons Born out of Wedlock* (Sales No. 68.XIV.3);

*Study of Equality in the Administration of Justice* (Sales No. E.71.XIV.3);

*Special Study of Racial Discrimination in the Political, Economic, Social and Cultural Spheres* (Sales No. 71. XIV.2).

## B. United Nations Yearbook on Human Rights

Pursuant to a resolution of the Economic and Social Council adopted at its second session in 1946, the Secretary-General has annually compiled and published the *Yearbook on Human Rights*.[10] By the beginning of 1973, 24 volumes covering the years 1946-1969 had been published. The *Yearbook on Human Rights* is prepared by the Secretary-General with the co-operation of Governments of States Members of the United Nations and of the specialized agencies and with the assistance of Government-appointed correspondents. Under the provisions in force at the end of 1972, the *Yearbook* contains the texts or extracts from constitutions, constitutional amendments, legislation, delegated legislation and reports on important court decisions; analogous materials relating to Trust and Non-Self-Governing Territories and the texts of or extracts from international agreements bearing on human rights. The *Yearbook* also contains a table of ratifications of or accessions to such agreements and documentary references on United Nations action in relation to human rights.

## C. The programme of advisory services in human rights

During the period 1953-1954, the General Assembly, acting on relevant recommendations of the Economic and Social Council, authorized on several occasions the rendering, at the request of Member States, of services in certain human rights fields. These included the rights of women,[11] prevention of discrimination and protection of minorities [12] and freedom of information.[13] At its nineteenth session, the Economic and Social Council by its resolution 574 (XIX) of 26 May 1955 gave effect to the last decision of the General Assembly by requesting the Secretary-General to take steps, in close collaboration with UNESCO, to put into operation a programme to promote freedom of information by providing such services as experts, fellowships and seminars.

At its twentieth session the Council (resolution 586 (XX) of 29 July 1955) recommended to the General Assembly consolidation of the technical assistance programmes in the above-mentioned several fields with the broad programme of assistance in the field of human rights, the entire programme to be known as "Advisory services in the field of human rights". The General Assembly approved the proposal in resolution 926 (X) of 14 December 1955.

Under the advisory services programme, established by resolution 926 (X), the Secretary-General is authorized, subject to the directions of the Economic and Social Council, to make provision at the request of Governments, and with the co-operation of the specialized agencies where appropriate and without duplication of their existing activities, for the following forms of assistance with respect to human rights: (1) advisory services of experts; (2) seminars; (3) fellowships and scholarships. In 1967, the Commission on Human Rights requested an additional form of assistance namely (4) regional training courses. All of these activities are dealt with in detail below.

By resolution 926 (X) the Secretary-General is authorized to take the programme established by that resolution into account in preparing the budgetary estimates of the United Nations. This means that subject to the principle that each requesting Government is expected to assume responsiblity, as far as possible, for all or a considerable part of the expenses (described in subparagraph (*c*) of the following paragraph), the programme of advisory services in the field of human rights is financed from the regular budget of the United Nations. As a consequence the draft resolutions and resolutions of the various organs deciding upon or recommending details of the programme are always accompanied by statements of financial implications for the budget of the Organization.

The General Assembly requested the Secretary-General to undertake such assistance in agreement with the Governments concerned, on the basis of requests received from Governments and in accordance with the following policies:

(*a*) With respect to the provision of advisory services of experts, the kind of service to be rendered to each country shall be determined by the Governments concerned;

(*b*) The selection of the persons to be awarded fellowships and scholarships shall be made by the Secretary-General on the basis of proposals received from Governments;

---

[10] Economic and Social Council resolution 9 (II) of 21 June 1946, supplemented and amended by subsequent Council resolutions.

[11] Economic and Social Council resolution 504 II (XVI) of 25 July 1953 and General Assembly resolution 729 (VIII) of 23 October 1953.

[12] Economic and Social Council resolution 502 G (XVI) of 3 August 1953 and General Assembly resolution 730 (VIII) of 23 October 1953.

[13] Economic and Social Council resolution 522 J (XVII) of 29 April 1954 and General Assembly resolution 839 (IX) of 17 December 1954.

(*c*) The amount of assistance and the conditions under which it is to be rendered shall be decided by the Secretary-General, with due regard to the greater needs of the under-developed areas, and in conformity with the principle that each requesting Government shall be expected to assume responsiblity, as far as possible, for all or a considerable part of the expenses connected with the assistance furnished to it, either by making a contribution in cash, or by providing supporting staff, services and payment of local costs for the purpose of carrying out the programme.

Under resolution 926 (X) the Secretary-General is requested to report regularly to the Economic and Social Council, to the Commission on Human Rights and, as appropriate, to the Commission on the Status of Women, on the measures he has taken to carry out the advisory services programme. The provision of resolution 926 (X) was modified in 1969 when, at its forty-seventh session, the Economic and Social Council decided, at the 1637th plenary meeting on 8 August 1969, that the question of advisory services in the field of human rights should no longer be routinely included as an item on the Council's agenda, but that the Council should continue to be informed of developments through the reports of the Commission on Human Rights and the Commission on the Status of Women, unless in any given year special circumstances should lead the Council or the Secretary-General to believe that a separate item was required. Having considered the item relating to the report of the Economic and Social Council, the Third Committee of the General Assembly at its twenty-fourth session took note of that decision of the Council and in its report [14] on the item indicated that the relevant provisions of General Assembly resolution 926 (X) would thereafter be applied in conformity with the new procedure stipulated by the Council. At its 1834th plenary meeting on 15 December 1969, the General Assembly took note of the decision.

At its twenty-third session in 1967, the Commission on Human Rights requested the Secretary-General to consider the organization, from 1969 onwards, of an annual programme of advisory services in the field of human rights, consisting of at least two seminars on subjects of human rights—of which at least one should be on an international level—one or two seminars on the status of women and one or more regional training courses on human rights. The Commission also requested that the programme should include an award of an adequate number of human rights fellowships, taking into account the increasing interest expressed in the fellowships by Member States. The Commission further requested the Secretary-General to draw the attention of the Governing Council of the United Nations Development Programme to this resolution, and it invited the Governing Council to bear the resolution in mind in considering the recommendations to the Economic and Social Council relating to the level of appropriations for the relevant part of the United Nations budget. The Economic and Social Council in its resolution 1241 (XLII) of 6 June 1967 took note of the report of the Commission on Human Rights on its twenty-third session containing the Commission's resolution 17 (XXIII), parts of which have just been quoted.

At its fifty-second session in 1972 the Economic and Social Council, in resolution 1680 (LII) of 2 June 1972, noted resolution 17 (XXIII) of the Commission on Human Rights and invited the Secretary-General, in discharging his responsibility for the programme, to make every effort within the existing resources available to him to ensure so far as possible that two seminars on subjects relating to the status of women be held each year, especially in the years when the Commission on the Status of Women does not meet and that at least one of these seminars be an international seminar on a matter directly related to the work programme of the Commission on the Status of Women.

### 1. *Advisory services of experts*

A few Governments have availed themselves of the expert services provided for under the programme. Two Governments, for example, received advice concerning elections, electoral laws, procedures and techniques, while others have utilized assistance relating to the status of women. In 1970-1971 the Secretary-General, at the request of one Government, provided the services of an expert to advise on the promotion of the participation of women in national affairs and national development with particular emphasis on community development

### 2. *Human rights seminars*

By March 1973, 12 interregional or international and 32 regional human rights seminars had been organized. The subjects and the venue of these seminars are listed below.

Human rights seminars usually are scheduled for a two-week period, and the participants, who are nominated by Governments and confirmed by the Secretary-General, attend in their personal capacity at the invitation of the Secretary-General. They are highly qualified in their respective fields, and may include cabinet ministers and deputy ministers, attorneys-general, solicitors-general, judges of supreme courts and high courts, senior government officials, newspaper publishers, editors and writers, women leaders and persons of similar status.

United Nations bodies and specialized agencies of the United Nations system which have an interest in the subject-matter are invited to designate representatives. The Secretary-General also invites non-governmental organizations in consultative status with the Economic and Social Council, whose aims and purposes are closely related to the seminar topic, to nominate observers.

The seminar discussions are documented by background papers prepared by expert consultants and documentation prepared by the Secretariat. In addition, each participant submits a paper outlining the relevant experience in his own country, so that the seminar can proceed to discuss and compare experiences throughout the region. The participants exchange information and experience at

[14] *Official Records of the General Assembly, Twenty-fourth Session, Annexes*, agenda item 12, document A/7840, para. 45.

the working level under the guidance of a Chairman and other elected officers.

The seminar reports succinctly summarize the discussions and any conclusions which may have been reached by consensus. No voting takes place.

The following is a list of human rights seminars:

*Regional seminars*

1. Bangkok, Thailand, 5-16 August 1957—Seminar on the civic responsibilities and increased participation of Asian women in public life.
Report: ST/TAA/HR/1
2. Baguio City, Philippines, 17-28 February 1958—Seminar on the protection of human rights in criminal law and procedure.
Report: ST/TAA/HR/2
3. Santiago, Chile. 19-30 May 1958—Seminar on the protection of human rights in criminal law and procedure.
Report: ST/TAA/HR/3
4. Peradeniya (Kandy), Ceylon, 4-15 May 1959—Seminar on judicial and other remedies against the illegal exercise or abuse of administrative authority.
Report: ST/TAO/HR/4
5. Bogota, Colombia, 18-29 May 1959—Seminar on participation of women in public life.
Report: ST/TAO/HR/5
6. Buenos Aires, Argentina, 31 August-11 September 1959—Seminar on judicial and other remedies against the illegal exercise or abuse of administrative authority.
Report: ST/TAO/HR/6
7. Tokyo, Japan, 10-24 May 1960—Seminar on the role of substantive criminal law in the protection of human rights, and the purposes and legitimate limits of penal sacntions.
Report: ST/TAO/HR/7
8. Vienna, Austria, 20 June-4 July 1960—Seminar on the protection of human rights in criminal procedure.
Report: ST/TAO/HR/8
9. Addis Ababa, Ethiopia, 12-23 December 1960 Seminar on participation of women in public life.
Report: ST/TAO/HR/9
10. Wellington, New Zealand, 6-20 February 1961—Seminar on the protection of human rights in the administration of criminal justice.
Report: ST/TAO/HR/10
11. Bucharest, Romania, 19 June-2 July 1961—Seminar on the status of women in family law.
Report: ST/TAO/HR/11
12. Mexico City, Mexico, 15-28 August 1961—Seminar on *amparo*, *habeas corpus* and other similar remedies.
Report: ST/TAO/HR/12
13. New Delhi, India, 20 February-5 March 1962—Seminar on freedom of information.
Report: ST/TAO/HR/13
14. Tokyo, Japan, 8-21 May 1962—Seminar on the status of women in family law.
Report: ST/TAO/HR/14
15. Stockholm, Sweden, 12-25 June 1962—Seminar on judicial and other remedies against the abuse of administrative authority with special emphasis on the role of parliamentary institutions.
Report: ST/TAO/HR/15
16. Canberra, Australia, 30 April-14 May 1963—Seminar on the role of the police in the protection of human rights.
Report: ST/TAO/HR/16
17. Warsaw, Poland, 6-19 August 1963—Seminar on the rights of the child.
Report: ST/TAO/HR/17
18. Bogota, Colombia, 3-16 December 1963—Seminar on the status of women in family law.
Report: ST/TAO/HR/18
19. Rome, Italy, 7-20 April 1964—Seminar on freedom of information.
Report: ST/TAO/HR/20
20. Kabul, Afghanistan, 12-25 May 1964—Seminar on human rights in developing countries.
Report: ST/TAO/HR/21
21. Lomé, Togo, 18-31 August 1964—Seminar on the status of women in family law.
Report: ST/TAO/HR/22
22. Ulan Bator, Mongolia, 3-17 August 1965—Seminar on the participation of women in public life.
Report: ST/TAO/HR/24
23. Dakar, Senegal, 8-22 February 1966—Seminar on human rights in developing countries.
Report: ST/TAO/HR/25
24. Budapest, Hungary, 14-27 June 1966—Seminar on participation in local administration as a means of promoting human rights.
Report: ST/TAO/HR/26
25. Manila, Philippines, 6-19 December 1966—Seminar on measures required for the advancement of women with special reference to the establishment of a long-term programme.
Report: ST/TAO/HR/28
26. Kingston, Jamaica, 25 April-8 May 1967—Seminar on the effective realization of civil and political rights at the national level.[15]
Report: ST/TAO/HR/29
27. Warsaw, Poland, 15-28 August 1967—Seminar on the realization of economic and social rights contained in the Universal Declaration of Human Rights.
Report: ST/TAO/HR/31
28. Accra, Ghana, 19 November-2 December 1968—Seminar on the civic and political education of women.
Report: ST/TAO/HR/35
29. Iasi, Romania, 5-18 August 1969—Seminar on the effects of scientific and technological develop-

[15] In accordance with Economic and Social Council resolutions 1123 (XLI) of 26 July 1966 and 1125 (XLI) of 26 July 1966, the Secretary-General made arrangements for the attendance at this seminar of four participants from countries outside the western hemisphere.

ments on the status of women.

Report: ST/TAO/HR/37

30. Cairo, Egypt, 2-15 September 1969—Seminar on the establishment of regional commissions on human rights with special reference to Africa.

Report: ST/TAO/HR/38

31. Lusaka, Zambia, 23 June-4 July 1970—Seminar on the realization of economic and social rights with particular reference to developing countries.

Report: ST/TAO/HR/40

32. Libreville, Gabon, 27 July-9 August 1971—Seminar on the participation of women in economic life (with reference to the implementation of article 10 of the Declaration on the Elimination of Discrimination against Women and of General Assembly resolution 2716 (XXV)).

Report: ST/TAO/HR/43

*World-wide seminars*

1. Ljubljana, Yugoslavia, 8-22 June 1965—Seminar on the multinational society.

Report: ST/TAO/HR/23

2. Brasilia, Brazil, 23August-5 September 1966—Seminar on *apartheid*.[16]

Report: ST/TAO/HR/27

3. Helsinki, Finland, 1-14 August 1967—Seminar on the Civic and political education of women.

Report: ST/TAO/HR/30

4. London, United Kingdom, 18 June-1 July 1968—Seminar on freedom of association.

Report: ST/TAO/HR/32

5. New Delhi, India, 27 August-9 September 1968—Seminar on the question of the elimination of all forms of racial discrimination.

Report: ST/TAO/HR/34

6. Nicosia, Cyprus, 26 June-9 July 1969—Seminar on special problems relating to human rights in developing countries.

Report: ST/TAO/HR/36

7. Belgrade, Yugoslavia, 2-12 June 1970—Seminar on the role of youth in the promotion and protection of human rights.

Report: ST/TAO/HR/39

8. Moscow, USSR, 8-21 September 1970—Seminar on the participation of women in the economic life of their countries (with reference to the implementation of article 10 of the Declaration on the Elimination of Discrimination against Women).

Report: ST/TAO/HR/41

9. Yaoundé, Cameroon, 16-29 June 1971—Seminar on measures to be taken on the national level for the implementation of United Nations instruments aimed at combating and eliminating racial discrimination and for the promotion of harmonious race relations.

Report: ST/TAO/HR/42

10. Nice, France, 24 August-6 September 1971—Seminar on the dangers of a recrudescence of intolerance in all its forms and the search for means of preventing and combating it.

Report: ST/TAO/HR/44

11. Vienna, Austria, 19 June-1 July 1972—Seminar on human rights and scientific and technological developments.

Report: ST/TAO/HR/45

12. Istanbul, Turkey, 11-24 July 1972—Seminar on the status of women and family planning.

Report: ST/TAO/HR/46

### 3. *Fellowships and scholarships*

In the first years of the operation of the programme, only a few fellowships were awarded. The number of fellowships granted in 1962 was 21. Following a decision by the General Assembly (resolution 1782 (XVII) of 7 December 1962) that the advisory services programme should be further expanded with a view to increasing the resources for fellowships so as to permit the award of at least double the number of fellowships available in 1962, 39 fellowships were awarded in 1963, 44 in 1964, 54 in 1965, 19[17] in 1966, 43 in 1967, 47 in 1968, 46 in 1969, 46 in 1970, 63 in 1971 and 56 in 1972.

In the examination of each application received under this regular programme, consideration is given to geographical distribution and to the directive of the General Assembly in its resolution 926 (X) that due regard be paid to the "greater needs of the underdeveloped areas". In its resolution 1680 (LII) of 2 June 1972 the Economic and Social Council invited Governments of States Members of the United Nations to include the names of more women and of those involved in the work of eliminating discrimination on grounds of sex when forwarding nominations for human rights fellowships to the Secretary-General.

Human rights fellowships are available to qualified candidates nominated by Member States who are planning to study any subject in the field of human rights of concern to the United Nations (as defined in the International Covenants on Human Rights, declarations and resolutions with regard to universal respect for human rights and fundamental freedoms) provided, however, that the subject is one which does not fall within the scope of other existing technical assistance programmes and for which adequate advisory assistance is not available through a specialized agency. The Secretary-General, within the financial resources made available to him, has attempted, so far as it was possible, to ensure broad distribution among nationalities.

In the selection of candidates preference is given to persons having direct responsibilities in the field of implementation of human rights in their respective countries.

[16] See also chap. V of this study.

[17] The number was about half of what was originally planned. The reduction was a consequence of General Assembly resolution 2060 (XX) of 16 December 1965, which called for an international seminar on *apartheid* to be held in 1966 and authorized the Secretary-General to make readjustments within the budgetary allocations approved for the programme of advisory services in the field of human rights.

The Secretary-General has repeatedly reported that the candidates nominated by Governments continued to be of a high level as far as their qualifications were concerned. In 1972, the last year about which a report is available (E/CN.4/1122 - E/CN.6/569), the recipients of fellowship awards included in particular Government officials with responsiblity for the administration of justice and for legislative drafting, as well as officials of ministries of education, justice, interior, labour, and social affairs.

The following is a selected list of fields in which human rights fellowships have been awarded (annex to document E/CN.4/1087—E/CN.6/555 of 2 February 1972):

Protection of human rights in a multinational society

Measures to safeguard the human rights of refugees

Measures designed to advance the observance of the human rights of the indigenous population, with particular reference to matters concerning the sedentarization of nomads

Protection of the human rights of immigrants and resident aliens

Advancement of human rights in the formulation and implementation of economic and social legislation

Implementation of the economic and social rights contained in the Universal Declaration of Human Rights

Protection of human rights in the drafting and implementation of legislation, with special reference to methods of implementation at the national level of international conventions on human rights with regard to both law and practice

Judicial organization and administration in relation to the protection of human rights

Protection of human rights in the administration of justice

Protection of human rights in the administration of justice, with special reference to periods of emergency

Protection of human rights of juvenile delinquents in the administration of justice in children's courts and the role of the police in the protection of human rights of juvenile delinquents

Role of the police in the protection of human rights, with particular reference to the special needs of new immigrants and of groups of varying ethnic origins

Legal aid ad legal advice provisions in civil and criminal courts

Protection of human rights in preliminary investigations and pre-trial proceedings, with special emphasis on legal representation

Rights of the accused to a speedy trial

Protection of the human rights of convicted and released offenders and of their families

The use of the writ of *habeas corpus* in the protection of human rights

Judicial and other remedies against the abuse of administrative authority

Role of the ombusdman and related institutions in relation to the protection of the rights of the citizen

Protection of human rights in criminal procedure

Protection of human rights in criminal procedure, with particular emphasis on the treatment and rehabilitation of criminal offenders in need of psychiatric care

The role of the public prosecutor in the protection of human rights with reference to the protection of human rights in criminal procedure

Drafting and implementation of legislation related to the protection of the rights of the child and of the family

Protection of human rights in family law, with special reference to the administration of justice in family courts

Protection of human rights in family law, with particular reference to adoption and maintenance and to reconciliation of estranged spouses

Rights of the child, with particular reference to the protection of the rights of children placed for adoption and of children born out of wedlock

Protection of the rights of the child, with particular reference to the administration of justice in children's courts and to the implementation of legislation concerning minors

Judicial organization and administration in relation to the protection of human rights, with particular reference to the protection of human rights in the administration of justice in family courts

Protection of the rights of the child, with special reference to the responsibility of society for the welfare of children deprived of normal home life, juvenile delinquents and children of minority groups

Status of women in family law, with particular reference to the administration of justice in family courts

Status of women, with particular reference to civic activities of women

Participation of women in national development, with special reference to the community development in developing countries

Equal employment opportunities for women

Human environment and human rights

Protection of human rights in armed conflicts

This list was supplemented, in the annex to document E/CN.4/1122—E/CN.6/569 of 30 January 1973, by the following items:

Human rights and scientific and technological developments

Protection of human rights in the administration of justice with special reference to civil law and procedure

Participation of women in public life with special emphasis on the role of women's bureaux and similar offices in furthering the status of women

Drafting and implementation of legislation embodying the principles of equality between men and women and directed to the elimination of discrimination against women

The protection of human rights in developing countries

Education of youth in the respect for human rights

In resolution 1125 (XLI) of 26 July 1966 the Economic and Social Council requested the Secretary-General to consider the possiblity of using some fellowship funds for a pilot project in group, rather than individual, training. In accordance with this resolution the Secretary-General organized the first pilot project in group training in Fuchu, Japan with the co-operation of the Government of Japan and the collaboration of the United Nations Asia and Far East Institute for the Prevention of Crime and Treatment of Offenders. The specific topics selected for the project were: (*a*) human rights in the administration of justice; (*b*) human rights and penal sanctions. The group training took place for a period of six weeks between 15 June and 26 July 1967. (E/CN.4/964—E/CN.6/505 of 19 January 1968, paras. 18-19.) A second pilot project in group training for human rights fellows from French-speaking African countries was organized in co-operation with the Government of Poland in Warsaw, Poland between 8 July and 3 August 1968. The pilot project dealt with the realization of the rights of the child in the planning and administration at the national and local levels.

#### 4. *Regional training courses*

In resolution 959 (XXXVI) of 12 July 1963 the Economic and Social Council requested the Secretary-General to consider the organization—from savings available under part V of the United Nations budget, and on an experimental basis—of one or more regional courses in human rights. The holding of a training course was assigned to that category of the advisory services programme which could be put into operation only if funds became available through savings in the implementation of the operating programme. In the years from 1964 to 1971 no such funds were available. In its resolution 17 (XXIII) of 1967 the Commission on Human Rights requested the Secretary-General to consider the organization, from 1969 onwards, of one or more regional training courses in human rights. Eventually a training course in human rights was organized from 14 August to 13 September 1972 in Japan on the subject of human rights in the administration of criminal justice. The course was held at the United Nations Asia and Far East Institute for the Prevention of Crime and Treatment of Offenders, Fuchu, Tokyo, Japan, for participants from English-speaking countries in Africa which are members of the Economic Commission for Africa and from countries of the Asia-Far East region which are members of the Economic Commission for Asia and the Far East. In his report to the Commission on Human Rights at its twenty-ninth session, the Secretary-General reported that consultations were taking place with the Egyptian authorities concerning the organization of a human rights regional training course in June/July 1973 in Cairo, Egypt to study human rights in the administration of criminal justice.

### D. Informational and educational methods

The informational and educational methods employed by the United Nations in the performance of its task of the promotion of respect for human rights have been concerned primarily with: (1) use of information media aiming at the education of public opinion; (2) recommendations and suggestions concerning educational policies of Governments, the teaching in schools, including institutions of higher learning; and (3) suggestions and recommendations concerning educational activities of non-governmental organizations.

#### 1. *Public information*

When adopting an instrument in the field of human rights, the General Assembly has in many cases appealed to States to give to that instrument a wide circulation. Recommendations of that kind were made in connexion with the Universal Declaration of Human Rights,[18] the Convention on the Prevention and Punishment of the Crime of Genocide,[19] the Declaration of the Rights of the Child,[20] the Declaration on the Granting of Independence to Colonial Countries and Peoples,[21] the United Nations Declaration on the Elimination of All Forms of Racial Discrimination,[22] the International Convention on the Elimination of All Forms of Racial Discrimination and the International Covenants on Human Rights.

At its fifth session in 1950 the General Assembly invited all States and interested organizations to adopt the day on which it had approved the Universal Declaration o Human Rights, i.e., 10 December of each year, as Human Rights Day.

An analogous decision was taken later when the General Assembly at its twenty-first session in 1966 designated the anniversary of the Sharpeville incident (21 March) as International Day for the Elimination of Racial Discrimination.

For the commemoration of the tenth, fifteenth, twentieth and twenty-fifth anniversaries of the proclamation of the Universal Declaration of Human Rights see below.

At its twenty-fourth session (resolution 2544 (XXIV) of 11 December 1969) the General Assembly designated the year 1971 as International Year for Action to Combat Racism and Racial Discrimination.

By its resolution 2919 (XXVII) of 15 November 1972, the General Assembly decided to launch on 10 December 1973 the Decade for Action to Combat Racism and Racial Discrimination.

On 18 December 1972, by its resolution 3010 (XXVII), the General Assembly proclaimed the year 1975 International Women's Year.

Early in the history of the United Nations the General Assembly and the Economic and Social Council recommended that Member Governments take measures to encourage the teaching of the United Nations Charter

---

[18] General Assembly resolution 217 D (III) of 11 December 1948.

[19] General Assembly resolution 795 (VIII) of 3 November 1953.

[20] General Assembly resolution 1387 (XIV) of 20 November 1959.

[21] General Assembly resolution 1695 (XVI) of 19 December 1961; also resolution 1848 (XVII) of 19 December 1962.

[22] General Assembly resolution 1905 (XVIII) of 20 November 1963.

and the Purposes and Principles, the structure, background and activities of the United Nations in the schools and institutes of higher learning.[23] Appropriate recommendations were addressed to UNESCO. In one of the resolutions devoted to this problem the Economic and Social Council invited UNESCO to encourage and facilitate teaching about the Universal Declaration of Human Rights in schools and adult education programmes and through the press, radio and film services.[24] The United Nations repeatedly stressed educational measures and publicity also as means to improve the status of women, e.g., in regard to customs, ancient laws and practices affecting the human dignity of women,[25] and also in the matter of racial discrimination.[26]

In a resolution on further promotion and encouragement of respect for human rights and fundamental freedoms adopted in 1963, the Economic and Social Council invited universities, institutes, learned societies, trade unions and other organizations which are concerned with human rights to make available their contributions to wider knowledge and the advance of human rights, through education, research and discussion and also through publications, newspapers and periodicals. Member States were requested to give the widest possible dissemination to this invitation.[27]

2. *Educational activities of non-governmental organizations*

In many resolutions the General Assembly and the Economic and Social Council have called upon non-governmental organizations to assist in educational programmes and activities. Appeals were sometimes not restricted to those organizations which have been granted consultative status under Article 71 of the Charter but the relevant resolutions sometimes referred to non-governmental organizations or voluntary organizations in general. In 1954 the Economic and Social Council authorized the convening of a Conference of non-governmental organizations in consultative status interested in the eradication of prejudice and discrimination and in 1958 it authorized the convening of a second such conference. Details are given in part two, chapter I of the present publication.[28] Non-governmental organizations have also been expected to assist in the achievement of the objectives of the Declaration on the Granting of Independence to Colonial Countries and Peoples.[29]

3. *Publicity concerning violations of human rights*

United Nations organs have at times sought to expose and focus attention on violations or denials of human rights through publicity. For example, in a resolution adopted at its twenty-third session in 1967 the Commission on Human Rights requested the Secretary-General to give the widest possible publicity to documents containing depositions of political prisoners relating to the prisons of South Africa. The Commission also called upon all Member States to give the widest national publicity to the substance of the contents of those documents.

4. *Information and educational aspects of the commemoration of the tenth, fifteenth, twentieth and twenty-fifth anniversaries of the Universal Declaration of Human Rights and of the celebration of the International Year for Human Rights in 1968*

The United Nations organs have made extensive arrangements, including provisions for publicity and educational measures, for the observance and commemoration of the tenth, fifteenth, twentieth and twenty-fifth anniversaries of the adoption of the Universal Declaration of Human Rights. With regard to the tenth anniversary, the Economic and Social Council adopted a resolution by which it recommended that all States Members of the United Nations or Members of the specialized agencies consider the desirability of setting up national committees for the purpose of assisting in the observance of the anniversary and requested the Secretary-General, in co-operation with a committee consisting of representatives of Member States and in consultation with the Director-General of UNESCO and the executive heads of the other specialized agencies, to make the necessary arrangements to give effect to recommendations concerning the observations which had been made by the Commission on Human Rights.[30]

With regard to the fifteenth anniversary, the General Assembly established a special committee and charged it with the task of making preparations for the observance of the anniversary.[31]

The General Assembly designated 1968, the year in which the twentieth anniversary of the adoption of the Universal Declaration of Human Rights would fall, as the International Year for Human Rights.[32]

The programme of measures and activities envisaged for the International Year for Human Rights was set forth in General Assembly resolution 2217 (XXI) of 19 December 1966, sections A, B, C and D, and in an

[23] General Assembly resolution 137 (II) of 7 November 1947 and Economic and Social Council resolutions 203 (VIII) of 11 February 1949 and 609 (XXI) of 26 April 1956.

[24] Economic and Social Council resolution 314 (XI) of 24 July 1950.

[25] General Assembly resolution 843 (IX) of 17 December 1954.

[26] e.g., Economic and Social Council resolution 116 B (VII), 1948.

[27] Economic and Social Council resolution 958 D II (XXXVI) of 12 July 1963.

[28] For the proceedings of the two Conferences see E/NGO/CONF.1/8 and E/NGO/CONF.2/7.

[29] Economic and Social Council resolution 1651 (LI) of 29 October 1971 and General Assembly resolution 2907 (XXVII) of 2 November 1972.

[30] Economic and Social Council resolution 651 B (XXIV) of 24 July 1957; see also *Official Records of the Economic and Social Council, Twenty-second Session, Supplement No. 3,* E/2844, para. 113.

[31] See General Assembly resolution 1775 (XVII) of 7 December 1962 and also Economic and Social Council resolution 940 (XXXV) of 15 April 1963.

[32] General Assembly resolution 1961 (XVIII) of 12 December 1963; see also General Assembly resolution 2081 (XX) of 20 December 1965.

annex to resolution A. The very comprehensive and detailed programme recommended in resolution 2217 (XXI) for the International Year for Human Rights included the awarding of prizes to persons who had made outstanding contributions to the promotion and protection of the human rights and fundamental freedoms embodied in the Universal Declaration and in other United Nations instruments; the redoubling by States of their efforts to bring about the signature, ratification or acceptance of all the existing international treaties in the human rights field; the consideration of the possibility of commemorating the International Year by the establishment of public service or socially useful institutions, such as schools, hospitals, community centres, crêches and recreational parks; recommendations for activities by non-governmental organizations; co-ordination of the work nationally and internationally.

The winners of the human rights prizes awarded in 1968 were: Mr. Manuel Bianchi, Mr. René Cassin, Mr. Albert Luthuli (posthumously), Mrs. Mehranguiz Manoutchehrian, Mr. P. E. Nedbailo and Mrs. Eleanor Roosevelt (posthumously). They were selected by a special committee, composed of the President of the General Assembly, the President of the Economic and Social Council, the Chairman of the Commission on Human Rights, the Chairman of the Commission on the Status of Women and the Chairman of the Sub-Commission on Prevention of Discrimination and Protection of Minorities.

Further provisions for the International Year for Human Rights were made by resolution 2339 (XXII) of 18 December 1967. The International Conference on Human Rights was held in Teheran, Iran, from 22 April to 13 May 1968. The work of the Conference is described in various chapters of part one of this publication. In resolution 2441 (XXIII) of 19 December 1968 the General Assembly expressed its appreciation to the Member States, United Nations organs, specialized agencies, regional intergovernmental organizations and national and international organizations concerned for their efforts and undertakings in connexion with the International Year for Human Rights. In resolution 2442 (XXIII) of 19 December 1968, the General Assembly expressed its conviction that the Teheran Conference had made an important constructive contribution to the cause of human rights and that its results should be translated into effective action by States, the competent organs of the United Nations and its family of organizations, and other organizations concerned. The General Assembly expressed its gratitude to the Government and people of Iran and its appreciation to the Secretary-General, the Executive Secretary of the Conference and members of the Secretariat. The General Assembly endorsed the Proclamation of Teheran [33] and urged all States and organizations concerned to encourage and assist all media of mass communication in giving widespread publicity to the Proclamation of Teheran and the work of the Conference. In resolution 2588 A (XXIV) of 15 December 1969, the General Assembly noted with satisfaction the measures that had been taken and the progress that had been achieved in the implementation of the recommendations of the Teheran Conference. It expressed the hope that the measures and activities undertaken on the occasion of the International Year for Human Rights by Governments, United Nations organs, specialized agencies, regional intergovernmental organizations and non-governmental organizations genuinely concerned with human rights would be continued, developed and enlarged.

Arrangements for the celebration of the twenty-fifth anniversary of the Universal Declaration of Human Rights were initiated by General Assembly resolution 2860 (XXVI) of 20 December 1971, in which the General Assembly expressed its desire to mark, in 1973, the twenty-fifth anniversary of the Universal Declaration in a manner which would fit the occasion and serve the cause of human rights. It decided to consider this question at its twenty-seventh session and requested the Secretary-General to present, for consideration at that session, such suggestions as he might consider appropriate concerning suitable activities which could be undertaken in celebration of the twenty-fifth anniversary. As requested by this resolution, the Secretary-General submitted his report (A/8820 and Corr.1).

The Secretary-General's report made a number of suggestions concerning the commemoration of the Anniversary of the Proclamation of the Declaration on the national level and indicated the plans of the Office of Public Information to contribute to the wide and effective observance of the Anniversary. Recalling the awarding of prizes which had been initiated by General Assembly resolution 2217 (XXI) on the occasion of the Twentieth Anniversary in 1968, the Secretary-General expressed his assumption that the General Assembly would wish to continue awarding human rights prizes in 1973, a purpose for which he had made provision in the budget estimates for that year. In his report, the Secretary-General further recalled the two studies in the field of human rights prepared for the Teheran Conference, "Measures taken within the United Nations in the field of human rights" and "Methods used by the United Nations in the field of human rights", and the publication, "Human Rights: A Compilation of International Instruments of the United Nations". He suggested that revised versions of these documents be issued during 1973. The Secretary-General's report further suggested that the specialized agencies and other organizations be invited to proceed with the planning of individual programmes and that the regional organizations also be requested to co-operate in the Anniversary commemoration. He also favoured appeals and invitations to be addressed to international and national non-governmental organizations.

The Secretary-General suggested in particular four priorities for action to which the Twenty-fifth Anniversary should give strengthened impetus:

(*a*) The Twenty-fifth Anniversary should be an additional inducement to States to ratify the International Covenants on Human Rights, the Optional Protocol to the Convenant on Civil and Political Rights and the other human rights instruments emanating from the United Nations family of organizations;

[33] *Final Act of the International Conference on Human Rights* (United Nations publication, Sales No. E.68.XIV.2), p. 3.

(*b*) The elimination of racial discrimination has been rightly considered as a high priority area of United Nations action in the field of the protection of human rights. He referred to the implementation machinery provided by the Committee on the Elimination of Racial Discrimination under the International Convention on the Elimination of All Forms of Racial Discrimination and emphasized the great increase in the number of States parties to that Convention. He referred to the fact that the Commission on Human Rights and the Sub-Commission were engaged in the preparation of the programme for the Decade of Action to Combat Racism and Racial Discrimination;

(*c*) The Secretary-General's report indicated that the Twenty-fifth Anniversary would be celebrated with particular effectiveness and the cause of human rights well served if the Anniversary could be accompanied by a marked extension of the teaching of the international system of protection of human rights;

(*d*) The Secretary-General's report expressed the view that it might not be desirable or possible to hold an international conference on human rights in 1973, comparable to that of 1968. However, it would undoubtedly be useful if gatherings could be initiated by the United Nations or held under United Nations auspices at which, after adequate consideration of human rights problems of our time in the light of past and anticipated developments further areas of action and fresh priorities for United Nations work might prove to be the most appropriate.

The Secretary-General's report was considered by the Third Committee of the General Assembly at its 1909th to 1914th meetings from 28 September to 4 October 1972. On the recommendation of the Third Committee, the General Assembly adopted on 19 October 1972 its resolution 2906 (XXVII), in which it reaffirmed its adherence to the principles, values and ideals contained in the Universal Declaration of Human Rights. The General Assembly decided to hold a special meeting on 10 December 1973 at which the Decade for Action to Combat Racism and Racial Discrimination was to be launched. The General Assembly also took note with appreciation of the suggestions presented by the Secretary-General and requested him to take the necessary measures for the implementation of those suggestions falling within his area of responsiblity. The preparation of the present publication is one of the projects recommended by the Secretary-General and approved by the General Assembly in resolution 2906 (XXVII).

## V. METHODS AND PROCEDURES EMPLOYED BY THE UNITED NATIONS IN ITS STRUGGLE AGAINST RACIAL DISCRIMINATION AND *APARTHEID*

The principle of non-discrimination on the grounds of race, sex, language or religion is laid down in several provisions of the United Nations Charter. The Universal Declaration of Human Rights and the two International Covenants on Human Rights are also based on the idea of the proscription of discrimination on any ground. The various methods utilized by the Organization have been applied with particular emphasis on action against racial discrimination. The methods used in the struggle against discrimination, and racial discrimination in particular, included the following:

(*a*) The adoption of (in addition to the Universal Declaration of Human Rights and the International Covenants on Human Rights) the following instruments dealing particularly with racial discrimination: the United Nations Declaration on the Elimination of All Forms of Racial Discrimination (1963) and the International Convention on the Elimination of All Forms of Racial Discrimination (1965);

(*b*) The adoption by United Nations principal and subsidiary organs of a large number of substantive resolutions concerning racial discrimination, *apartheid* and similar practices;

(*c*) The establishment by the General Assembly and the Security Council of organs and institutions operating under a mandate aimed at eliminating policies and practices of racial discrimination and *apartheid* in accordance with the principles of the Charter and subsequent relevant pronouncements and instruments;

(*d*) Special responsiblities entrusted to the Secretary-General, including in one case a request to him to make adequate arrangements to uphold the principles and purposes of the Charter in connexion with racial discrimination and *apartheid*, and the establishment in the Secretariat of a special unit to deal with *apartheid*. These special arrangements have been supplemental to the normal activities of the Secretariat, of which the Division of Human Rights, its Section on Prevention of Discrimination and Protection of Minorities, the Department of Political and Security Council Affairs and the former Department of Trusteeship and Non-Self-Governing Territories (now Department of Political Affairs, Trusteeship and Decolonization) assist the various organs working in the field of human rights;

(*e*) The undertaking of studies by, among others, the Commission on Human Rights and its subsidiary body, the Sub-Commission on Prevention of Discrimination and Protection of Minorities, including studies assigned to special rapporteurs;

(*f*) The holding of seminars on the subject;

(*g*) The making of arrangements for the annual observance of the International Day for the Elimination of Racial Discrimination in addition to Human Rights Day;

(*h*) Other efforts to publicize, by international and national means, the evils of racial discrimination and *apartheid*.

### A. Resolutions of the United Nations organs on the problem of racial discrimination

#### 1. *Resolutions of a general character*

At its first session in 1946 the General Assembly adopted resolution 103 (I) of 19 November 1946 entitled "Persecution and Discrimination" in which it declared that it is in the higher interests of humanity to put an immediate end to religious and so-called racial persecution and discrimination, and called on the Governments and responsible authorities to conform both to the letter and to the spirit of the Charter of the United Nations, and to take the most prompt and energetic steps to that end.

In resolution 217 C (III) of 10 December 1948 on the fate of minorities, the General Assembly requested the Economic and Social Council to ask its competent subsidiary organs to make a thorough study of the problem of minorities in order that the United Nations may be able to take effective measures for the protection of racial, national, religious or linguistic minorities.

The General Assembly has adopted several resolutions on racial discrimination in Non-Self-Governing Territories. Their main provisions are set out below.

In resolution 328 (IV) of 2 December 1949, the General Assembly invited the Administering Members to take steps, where necessary, to establish equal treatment in matters related to education between inhabitants of the Non-Self-Governing Territories under their administration whether they be indigenous or not.

In resolution 644 (VII) of 10 December 1952, the General Assembly, having regard to the principles of the Charter and of the Universal Declaration of Human Rights emphasizing the necessity of promoting and encouraging respect for human rights and for fundamental freedoms for all without distinction as to race, sex, language, or religion recommended to the Members responsible for the administration of Non-Self-Governing Territories the abolition in those Territories of laws and practices contrary to the principles of the Charter and of the Universal Declaration of Human Rights. The General Assembly also recommended that the Administering

Members should examine all laws, statutes and ordinances in force in the Non-Self-Governing Territories under their administration as well as their application in the said Territories with a view to the abolition of any such discriminatory provisions or practices. The General Assembly further recommended that all public facilities should be open to all inhabitants of the Non-Self-Governing Territories without distinction as to race, and recognized that the establishment of improved race relations largely depends on the development of educational policies and commended all measures designed to improve among all pupils in all schools understanding of the needs and problems of the community as a whole.

In resolution 1328 (XIII) of 12 December 1958, the General Assembly, having regard to the fundamental importance of race relations, particularly under modern conditions, for the attainment of objectives of Chapter XI of the Charter of the United Nations and recognizing the necessity of intensifying the promotion and encouragement of respect for human rights and fundamental freedoms for all, regardless of race, sex, language or religion, reaffirmed its resolution 644 (VII). The General Assembly also invited the Administering Members to include in the annual reports submitted under Article 73 e of the Charter of the United Nations information on the measures taken by them for the implementation of resolutions calling for the elimination of discriminatory practices.

In resolution 1536 (XV) of 15 December 1960 the General Assembly endorsed the view of the Committee on Information from Non-Self-Governing Territories that not only is racial discrimination a violation of human rights, but it also constitutes a deterrent to progress in all fields of development in the Territories concerned. The General Assembly also urged the Administering Members to give full and immediate effect to the recommendation of the Committee that measures to solve the problem of race relations should include the extension to all inhabitants of the full exercise of basic political rights, in particular the right to vote, and the establishment of equality among the members of all races inhabiting the Non-Self-Governing Territories.

In resolution 1698 (XVI) of 19 December 1961 the General Assembly considered that racial discrimination and segregation in Non-Self-Governing Territories can be eradicated fully and with the greatest speed by the faithful implementation of the Declaration on the Granting of Independence to Colonial Countries and Peoples, and that, accordingly, efforts of the United Nations should be concentrated on that task. In the same resolution the General Assembly condemned resolutely the policy and practice of racial discrimination and segregation in Non-Self-Governing Territories and urged the Administering Members to include, among the measures that would contribute to the implementation of the Declaration steps to ensure the immediate rescinding or revocation of all laws and regulations which tend to encourage or sanction, directly or indirectly, discriminatory policies and practices based on racial considerations, the adoption of legislative measures making racial discrimination and segregation punishable by law, and the discouragement of such practices based on racial considerations by all other means possible, including administrative measures.

In resolution 1510 (XV) of 12 December 1960 on manifestations of racial and national hatred the General Assembly, expressing the principle that the United Nations was duty bound to combat those manifestations, to establish the facts and causes of their origin, and to recommend resolute and effective measures which could be taken against them, resolutely condemned all manifestations and practices of racial, religious and national hatred in the political, economic, social, educational and cultural spheres of the life of society as violations of the Charter of the United Nations and the Universal Declaration of Human Rights. The General Assembly called upon the Governments of all States to take all necessary measures to prevent all manifestations of racial, religious and national hatred.

In resolution 1779 (XVII) of 7 December 1962, the General Assembly, deeply disturbed by the continued existence and manifestations of racial prejudice and of national and religious intolerance in different parts of the world, and considering it essential to recommend further specific effective measures to eliminate those manifestations of prejudice and intolerance: (1) invited the Governments of all States, the specialized agencies and non-governmental and private organizations to continue to make sustained efforts to educate public opinion with a view to the eradication of racial prejudice and national and religious intolerance and the elimination of all undesirable influences promoting those and to take appropriate measures so that education might be directed with due regard to article 26 of the Universal Declaration of Human Rights and to principle 10 of the Declaration of the Rights of the Child adopted by the General Assembly on 20 November 1959; (2) called upon the Governments of all States to take all necessary steps to rescind discriminatory laws which have the effect of creating and perpetuating racial prejudice and national and religious intolerance wherever they still existed, to adopt legislation if necessary for prohibiting such discrimination, and to take such legislative or other appropriate measures to combat such prejudice and intolerance; (3) recommended the Governments of all States to discourage actively, through education and all media of information, the creation, propagation and dissemination of such prejudice and intolerance in any form whatever; (4) invited the specialized agencies and non-governmental organizations to co-operate fully with the Governments of States in their efforts to prevent and eradicate racial prejudice and national and religious intolerance; (5) invited the Governments of Member States, the specialized agencies and the non-governmental organizations concerned to inform the Secretary-General of action taken by them in compliance with the present resolution; (6) requested the Secretary-General to submit to the General Assembly at its eighteenth session a report on compliance with the resolution.

In resolution 2017 (XX) of 1 November 1965 concerning measures to implement the United Nations Declaration on the Elimination of All Forms of Racial Discrimination, the General Assembly, *inter alia*, called upon all States in which racial discrimination was practised to take urgent effective steps, including legislative measures, to implement that Declaration. The Assembly also requested the States where organizations were promoting, or inciting to, racial discrimination to take all necessary measures to prosecute and/or outlaw such organizations.

In resolution 2142 (XXI) of 26 October 1966 on the elimination of all forms of racial discrimination the General Assembly, *inter alia*, called again upon all States in which racial discrimination or *apartheid* is practised to comply speedily and faithfully with the United Nations Declaration on the Elimination of All Forms of Racial Discrimination, with the Universal Declaration of Human Rights and with the resolutions of the General Assembly concerning the elimination of racial discrimination and all other pertinent resolutions of that organ, and to take all necessary steps including legislative measures, for that purpose.

At its twenty-first session in 1966 the General Assembly also adopted resolution 2144 A (XXI) of 26 October 1966 on the question of the violation of human rights and fundamental freedoms, including policies of racial discrimination and segregation and of *apartheid*, in all countries, with particular reference to colonial and other dependent countries and territories. In that resolution the Assembly stated that gross violations of the rights and fundamental freedoms set forth in the Universal Declaration of Human Rights continued to occur in certain countries, especially in colonies and dependent territories, involving discrimination on grounds of race, colour, sex, language and religion, and the suppression of freedom of expression and opinion, the right to life, liberty and security of person and the right to protection by independent and impartial judicial organs and that these violations are designed to stifle the legitimate struggle of the people for independence and human dignity. The General Assembly, *inter alia*, reaffirmed its strong condemnation of the violations of human rights and fundamental freedoms wherever they occur, especially in all colonial and dependent territories, including the policies of *apartheid* in the Republic of South Africa, in the Territory of South West Africa and racial discrimination in the colonies of Southern Rhodesia, Angola, Mozambique, Portuguese Guinea, Cabinda, São Tomé and Príncipe. The General Assembly also urged Member States to take all necessary measures, in accordance with their domestic laws, against the operations of propaganda organizations of the Republic of South Africa and of private organizations which advocate policies of racial discrimination and domination.

At its twenty-third session the General Assembly adopted resolution 2446 (XXIII) of 19 December 1968, on measures to achieve the rapid and total elimination of all forms of racial discrimination in general and of the policy of *apartheid* in particular. In that resolution the General Assembly condemned the Governments of South Africa and Portugal for their persistent defiant stand towards the United Nations and world opinion in respect of their policies of *apartheid* and colonialism respectively. It also condemned the policy of racial discrimination of the illegal minority régime in Southern Rhodesia. It called upon all States to refrain scrupulously from giving any military or economic assistance to these régimes. It requested the Secretary-General to prepare a programme for the celebration in 1971 of the International Year for Action to Combat Racism and Racial Discrimination. The International Conference on Human Rights, Teheran, 1968, had already suggested preparations for the observance of such a year in its resolution XIV. At its twenty-fourth session in 1969 the General Assembly decided to designate the year 1971 as the International Year for Action to Combat Racism and Racial Discrimination. It approved the programme for the observance of this Year prepared by the Secretary-General and urgently appealed to all States and United Nations organs to co-operate and to participate (General Assembly resolution 2544 (XXIV) of 11 December 1969).

At its twenty-fifth, twenty-sixth and twenty-seventh sessions, the General Assembly again took action in the matter of the elimination of all forms of racial discrimination. In resolution 2646 (XXV) of 30 November 1970 the General Assembly called for increased and continued moral and material support to all peoples struggling for the realization of their right to self-determination and for the elimination of all forms of racial discrimination. In resolution 2784 (XXVI) of 6 December 1971 the General Assembly requested its President to forward the message annexed to the resolution directly to the Heads of State or Government of each State. The annex to resolution 2784 (XXVI) constitutes a comprehensive statement of United Nations policy against racial discrimination both in general and in the specific States and Territories where it is particularly rampant. At the twenty-seventh session the General Assembly by resolution 2919 (XXVII) of 15 November 1972 decided to launch the Decade for Action to Combat Racism and Racial Discrimination and to inaugurate the activities thereof on 10 December 1973. It noted that a detailed draft programme for this Decade for Action had been prepared by the Sub-Commission on Prevention of Discrimination and Protection of Minorities, and that the programme would be considered by the Commission on Human Rights at its twenty-ninth session in 1973, and submitted to the General Assembly at its twenty-eighth session for final consideration.

### 2. *Resolutions relating to particular countries and territories*

The General Assembly and its Special Committee on the Situation with Regard to the Implementation of the Declaration on the Granting of Independence to Colonial Countries and Peoples have adopted a number of resolutions relating to particular countries and territories which also contain provisions concerning the problem of racial discrimination in the territories concerned. Similar resolutions have also been adopted in some cases by the Security Council, particularly with reference to *apartheid*.[1]

[1] See, for example: Security Council resolutions of 4 December 1963 (1078th meeting) on the *apartheid* policies of the Government of South Africa; of 9 June 1964 (1128th meeting); and of 18 June 1964 (1135th meeting) on the same question; 163 (1961) of 9 June 1961 and 218 (1965) of 23 November 1965 on the

*(Continued on next page)*

These resolutions have been summarized elsewhere in the present publication.

## B. Organs and institutions established and procedures followed by the General Assembly and the Security Council

### 1. *Organs and procedures relating to the question of the treatment of people of Indian origin in South Africa*

Over the span of several years, the General Assembly resorted to a series of means of approaches in an effort to assist in the solution of the problem of the treatment of people of Indian origin in the Union of South Africa —a question which was raised at the first session of the General Assembly in 1946, and was further considered as a separate item on the agenda of the General Assembly until 1961.

In resolution 265 (III) of 14 May 1949, the General Assembly invited the Governments of India, Pakistan and the Union of South Africa to enter into discussion at a round-table conference, taking into consideration the purposes and principles of the Charter and the Universal Declaration of Human Rights. The recommendation for the holding of a round-table conference was repeated in resolution 395 (V) of 2 December 1950, in which the General Assembly further recommended that, in the event of failure to hold a conference or reach agreement thereat, a commission of three members be set up to assist the parties in carrying through appropriate negotiations.

In resolution 511 (VI) of 12 January 1952, the General Assembly reaffirmed the recommendation of resolution 395 (V) that a three-member Commission be established and further requested the Secretary-General, in the event of failure to establish such a commission, to lend his assistance to the Governments concerned and if necessary to appoint an individual who would render any additional assistance deemed advisable.

A three-member United Nations Good Offices Commission was established by General Assembly resolution 615 (VII) of 5 December 1952. Its task was to arrange and assist in negotiations between the Governments concerned in order that a satisfactory solution in accordance with the purposes and principles of the Charter and the Universal Declaration of Human Rights might be achieved.

The Commission having reported [2] that, in view of the response of the Government of the Union of South Africa, it had been unable to carry out its task, the General Assembly, in resolution 719 (VIII) of 11 November 1953, decided to continue the Commission and urged the Government of the Union of South Africa to co-operate with it.

In its report [3] the Commission stated that, in view of its past experience, it decided that an official, direct approach to the parties was not likely to be successful, owing to the refusal of South Africa to recognize the Commission, which it regarded as unconstitutional. The Commission resolved, therefore, to attempt to find some possible new approach through private, informal conversations between its members and officials of the countries concerned. However, the Commission had to report that it was not able by way of such conversations to discover any new procedure through which it could hope to fulfil its task to arrange and assist in negotiations between the three parties. The Commission stated that it was unable to submit any proposal likely to lead to a peaceful settlement of the problem on account of the unco-operative attitude of the Government of the Union of South Africa.

Having noted the report of the Commission, the General Assembly, in resolution 816 (IX) of 4 November 1954, suggested to the Governments concerned that they should seek a solution of the question by direct negotiations. The Assembly suggested, moreover, that the parties concerned should designate a Government, agency or person to facilitate contacts between them and assist them in settling the dispute. The Assembly also decided that, if within six months from the date of the adoption of resolution 816 (IX) the parties had not reached agreement on the procedures suggested by the Assembly, the Secretary-General should designate a person to facilitate contacts and assist in settling the dispute. On the expiration of the deadline set by resolution 816 (IX), a Brazilian diplomat was appointed. He concluded in his final letter [4] to the Secretary-General that, in view of the refusal of the Government of the Union of South Africa to co-operate, there was nothing he could do to facilitate negotiations between the parties.

On 14 December 1955, the General Assembly adopted resolution 919 (X) in which it urged the parties concerned to pursue negotiations with a view to bringing about a settlement of the question. The invitation to Member States to use their good offices to bring about the negotiations envisaged by the General Assembly was repeated several times in subsequent resolutions.

### 2. *The United Nations Commission on the Racial Situation in South Africa*

At its seventh session the General Assembly for the first time considered the general question of the racial situation in South Africa not confined to the treatment of persons of Indian and Pakistani origin. It did so under an agenda item entitled "The question of race conflict in South Africa resulting from the policies of *apartheid* of the Government of the Union of South Africa".

*(Foot-note 1 continued)*
situation in the Territories under Portuguese Administration; 202 (1965) of 6 May 1965, 216 (1965) of 12 November 1965 and 232 (1965) of 16 December 1965 on the situation in Southern Rhodesia; General Assembly resolutions 1819 (XVII) of 18 December 1962 on the situation in Angola, 1899 (XVIII) of 13 November 1963 on South West Africa, 2022 (XX) of 5 November 1965 on Southern Rhodesia; Committee of Twenty-Four resolutions of 17 June 1965 (372nd meeting) and of 9 June 1966 (439th meeting) on the question of South West Africa; of 31 May 1966 (427th meeting) on Southern Rhodesia.

[2] *Official Records of the General Assembly, Seventh Session, Annexes,* agenda item 20, document A/2473.

[3] *Ibid., Ninth Session, Annexes,* agenda item 22, document A/2723.

[4] *Official Records of the General Assembly, Tenth Session. Annexes,* agenda item 20, document A/3001, annex.

By resolution 616 A (VII) of 5 December 1952 the General Assembly established a Commission consisting of three members serving in their individual capacities to study the racial situation in the Union of South Africa. The General Assembly directed that the study was to be carried out in the light of the purposes and principles of the Charter, with due regard to the provisions of several Articles of the Charter specifically mentioned, and the resolutions of the United Nations on racial persecution and discrimination. Subsequently,[5] the Commission was requested by the General Assembly:

(*a*) To continue its study of the development of the racial situation in the Union of South Africa;

(i) With reference to the various implications of the situation for the population affected;

(ii) In relation to the provisions of the Charter, and in particular Article 14;

(*b*) To suggest measures to alleviate the situation and promote a peaceful settlement.

The Government of the Union of South Africa was invited by the General Assembly to extend its full co-operation to the Commission.

In the Commission's first report [6] it was stated that, in the absence of the co-operation of the Government of the Union of South Africa, the Commission was compelled to formulate methods of work which would enable it to study the problem referred to it by the General Assembly.

The Commission decided that, in the circumstances in which it had to work, it would have to try to make up for the lack of direct contact with the realities of the problem by examining the declarations of Union politicians, by studying thoroughly the principal legislative texts governing the life of individuals and groups in South Africa, and lastly, by studying whatever memoranda were submitted to it or by hearing witnesses in a position to inform it on the problem under study.

The Commission accordingly decided to hear representatives of non-governmental organizations or private individuals and to examine such written statements as they might submit. It also decided to hear representatives of the Governments of Member States and to receive such memoranda as those Governments might wish to transmit.

The Commission submitted three reports [7] to the General Assembly at the latter's eighth, ninth and tenth sessions respectively. In resolution 820 (IX) of 14 December 1954 the General Assembly noted the Commission's suggestions for facilitating a peaceful settlement of the problem contained in its second report [8] and invited the Government of the Union of South Africa to take those suggestions into consideration. In resolution 917 (X) of 6 December 1955, the General Assembly recommended the Government of South Africa to take note of the Commission's third report.

### 3. *Consultations of the Secretary-General with the Government of South Africa, 1960-1961*

The racial policies of the Union of South Africa came before the Security Council in 1960. After considering a complaint submitted by 29 Member States relating to "the situation arising out of the large-scale killings of unarmed and peaceful demonstrators against racial discrimination and segregation in the Union of South Africa", the Security Council adopted resolution 134 of 1 April 1960. In that resolution, the Council requested the Secretary-General, in consultation with the Government of the Union of South Africa, to make such arrangements as would adequately help in upholding the purposes and principles of the Charter and to report to the Security Council whenever necessary and appropriate.

In pursuance of that mandate, the Secretary-General engaged in consultations with representatives of the Government of the Union of South Africa on the basis of an agreement [9] that consent of that Government to discuss the Security Council's resolution with the Secretary-General would not require prior recognition of the United Nations authority by the Union Government. At the invitation of the Government the Secretary-General visited South Africa in January 1961. During his stay there, in addition to his meetings with high officials, he had unofficial contacts with members of various sections of the South African community.

Following the submission of two interim reports,[10] the Secretary-General submitted on 23 January 1961 his final report [11] to the Council. In it he stated that "during the discussions between the Secretary-General and the Prime Minister of the Union of South Africa so far no mutually acceptable arrangement has been found"[12] The Secretary-General added that in his view the lack of agreement was not conclusive and that he wished to give the matter his further consideration. "The Secretary-General", the report continued, "does not consider the consultations as having come to an end, and he looks forward to their continuation at an appropriate time with a view to further efforts from his side to find an adequate solution for the . . . problem." [13] Eventually, the matter was not pursued any further.

### 4. *The Special Committee on the Policies of* Apartheid *of the Government of the Republic of South Africa*

The organ that is at present (1973) specifically charged with dealing with the policies of *apartheid* started opera-

[5] See General Assembly resolution 721 (VIII) of 8 December 1953; also, General Assembly resolution 820 (IX) of 14 December 1954, para. 6.

[6] *Official Records of the General Assembly, Eighth Session, Supplement No. 16*, paras. 46-53.

[7] *Ibid., Ninth Session, Supplement No. 16*; *ibid., Tenth Session, Supplement No. 14*.

[8] Paras. 368-384.

[9] *Official Records of the Security Council, Fifteenth Year, Supplement for April, May and June 1960*, document S/4305, para. 5.

[10] *Ibid., Supplement for October, November and December 1960*, document S/4551.

[11] *Ibid., Supplement for January, February and March 1961*, document S/4635.

[12] *Ibid.*, para. 9.

[13] *Ibid.*, para. 10.

ting in 1962. It was established by General Assembly resolution 1761 (XVII) of 6 November 1962 as the Special Committee on the Policies of *Apartheid* of the Government of the Republic of South Africa with the mandate "to keep the racial policies of the Government of South Africa under review when the Assembly is not in session and to report either to the Assembly or to the Security Council or to both, as may be appropriate, from time to time". At its twenty-fifth session (1921st plenary meeting of 8 December 1970) the General Assembly decided to shorten the name of the Special Committee to read "Special Committee on *Apartheid*". In resolution 2671 A (XXV) of 8 December 1970 the General Assembly requested the Special Committee to review all aspects of the policies of *apartheid* in South Africa and its international repercussions, including:

(*a*) Legislative, administrative and other racially discriminatory measures in South Africa and their effects;

(*b*) Repression of opponents of *apartheid*;

(*c*) Efforts by the Government of South Africa to extend its inhuman policies of *apartheid* beyond the borders of South Africa;

(*d*) Ways and means of promoting concerted international action to secure the elimination of *apartheid.*

In respect of the composition of the *Apartheid* Committee, the General Assembly in resolution 1761 (XVII) provided that it should consist of Member States nominated by the President of the General Assembly, who proceeded to appoint 11 members, In paragraph 3 of General Assembly resolution 2054 (XX) of 15 December 1965, the Assembly decided to enlarge the Special Committee by the appointment of six additional members. However, these increases were not immediately effected. In paragraph 3 of resolution 2671 A (XXV) of 8 December 1970 the General Assembly decided to expand the membership of the Special Committee by not more than seven additional members. During the period under review in the Special Committee's report of August 1972 submitted to the General Assembly at its twenty-seventh session, [14] the Special Committee was composed of 16 members. Subsequent to resolution 2671 A (XXV) the President of the General Assembly appointed five members and indicated that no representative from the group of West European and other States had agreed to serve on the Special Committee.

At the start of its activities, the Special Committee announced that it would receive memoranda from organizations and individuals, and hear persons or representatives of organizations, who might be in a position to provide it with information pertinent to the exercise of its functions. The Special Committee also decided to invite the co-operation of several anti-*apartheid* movements and of non-governmental organizations accredited to the United Nations.[15]

[14] *Official Records of the General Assembly, Twenty-seventh Session, Supplement No. 22* (A/8722).

[15] See Report of the Special Committee. (*Official Records of the General Assembly, Eighteenth Session, Annexes*, agenda item 30, addendum, document A/5497-S/5426).

The screening of communications from organizations and individuals and of other requests for hearings has been entrusted by the Special Committee to a four-member Sub-Committee on Petitions.

In accordance with its terms of reference, the Special Committee reports, as and when necessary, to the General Assembly and the Security Council on the situation relating to the policies of *apartheid.* The Special Committee's reports usually contain conclusions and recommendations [16] most of which have been endorsed by the General Assembly.

The Special Committee has maintained contact with other United Nations organs, as well as specialized agencies and non-governmental organizations, in order to promote meaningful action at all levels.

As an instance of seeking assistance from a specialized agency, the request addressed by the Special Committee to UNESCO to prepare a report on the effects of the policies of *apartheid* in the fields of education, science, culture and information in South Africa may be mentioned.

Representatives of the Organization of African Unity have repeatedly at its invitation attended meetings of the Special Committee as Observers.

### *Co-operation of the Special Committee on* Apartheid *with the Commission on Human Rights*

In a communication dated 15 February 1967 from the Acting Chairman of the Special Committee, the Secretary-General was requested to draw the urgent attention of the Commission on Human Rights "to the continuing ill-treatment of prisoners, detainees and persons in police custody in the Republic of South Africa, particularly the numerous opponents of *apartheid* who have been imprisoned under arbitrary laws". The communication further stated that the Special Committee hoped "that the Commission on Human Rights will consider the matter urgently and take steps to secure an international investigation . . .". The Commission, at its twenty-third session, responded by establishing a working group.[17]

Acting on a recommendation of the Special Committee on the Policies of *Apartheid* of the Government of the Republic of South Africa, the General Assembly, in resolution 2060 (XX), requested the Secretary-General to organize in 1966, in consultation with the Special Committee and the Commission on Human Rights an international seminar on *apartheid.*[18] The Special Committee discussed the various aspects of the seminar and authorized its Chairman, in the light of the discussion and with the assistance of a four-member Sub-Committee to consult with the Chairman of the Commission on Human Rights and the representative of the host country. Proposals which were formulated during these consulta-

[16] *Official Records of the General Assembly, Twenty-first Session, Annexes*, agenda item 34, document A/6486-S/7565.

[17] Report of the twenty-third session of the Commission on Human Rights, *Official Records of the Economic and Social Council, Forty-Second Session, Supplement No. 6*, resolution 2 (XXIII) of 6 March 1967.

[18] At its 70th meeting on 17 March 1966.

tions [19] were discussed [20] by the Committee and the records of the discussions were sent to the Secretary-General so that he might take note of the views expressed by members of the Committee. The organization of the seminar held in Brasilia (Brazil) in 1966 was due to these initiatives.

5. *Resolution of the Security Council requesting the establishment by the Secretary-General of a group of experts*

By resolution 182 (1963) of 4 December 1963, the Security Council requested the Secretary-General to establish under his direction and reporting to him, a small group of experts to examine methods of resolving the present situation in South Africa through full, peaceful and orderly application of human rights and fundamental freedoms to all inhabitants of the territory as a whole, regardless of race, colour or creed, and to consider what part the United Nations might play in the achievement of that end. In paragraph 7 it invited the Government of the Republic of South Africa to avail itself of the assistance of that group in order to bring about such peaceful and orderly transformation.

The Group was duly appointed by the Secretary-General but was denied co-operation by the Government of South Africa which also rejected a request that it provide facilities for the Group to visit South Africa. One of the proposals and recommendations made by the Group in its report [21] was that the Security Council should invite the South African Government to take part in discussions under the auspices of the United Nations on the formation of a National Convention fully representative of all people of South Africa. The Group listed and commented upon some of the questions which the proposed Convention would discuss and decide. It suggested that the Security Council impose economic sanctions on South Africa should that Government refuse to co-operate with the calling of a national convention, and proposed that the interval pending the reply of the South African Government should be utilized by the Security Council for "the urgent examination of the logistics of sanctions". Another recommendation made by the Group concerned the establishment of a United Nations South African training programme.

6. *Resolution of the Security Council establishing an Expert Committee*

On 18 June 1964, the Security Council adopted a further resolution (191 (1964)) on the question of the race conflict resulting from *apartheid.* Following the relevant recommendation of the Group of Experts, the Security Council decided to establish an Expert Committee, composed of representatives of each member of the Security Council at that time, to undertake a technical and practical study and report to the Council as to the feasibility, effectiveness and implications of measures which could, as appropriate, be taken by the Council under the Charter of the United Nations. The Council also authorized the Expert Committee to request all States Members of the United Nations to co-operate with it and to submit to it their views on such measures.

The Expert Committee sought to obtain the views of Member States on issues relating to the subject of its deliberations. To this end it also circulated a questionnaire,[22] to which 34 replies were received. The report [23] of the Expert Committee contained conclusions approved by majority vote and also a dissenting vote submitted by two members of the Committee.

7. *Educational and training programme for southern Africa*

Following a recommendation of the Group of Experts which had been appointed pursuant to a Security Council resolution of 4 December 1963 and which reported in 1964, the Security Council arranged for the establishment of an educational and training programme abroad for South Africans.[24] The programme was established after consultations with the High Commissioner for Refugees and the specialized agencies and is financed by voluntary contributions from Member States.

At its twenty-first session in 1966 the General Assembly took the initiative with a view to consolidation and integration of the education and training programme for South Africa, the special educational and training programme for South West Africa and for Territories under Portuguese Administration.[25]

At its twenty-second session, the General Assembly decided to integrate the special educational and training programmes for South West Africa, the special training programme for Territories under Portuguese administration and the educational and training programme for South Africans. It further decided to include in the United Nations Training and Educational Programme assistance to persons from Southern Rhodesia. It decided that the programme should be financed from a trust fund made up of voluntary contributions (General Assembly resolution 2349 (XXII) of 19 December 1967). At its twenty-third session the General Assembly requested the Secretary-General to establish an Advisory Committee on the Programme composed of representatives of Member States to advise the Secretary-General. In that resolution and in a series of subsequent resolutions the General Assembly noted with concern that the voluntary contributions had been inadequate and decided that

---

[19] See A/AC.109/L.290.

[20] At its 71st meeting on 7 April 1966.

[21] *Official Records of the Security Council, Nineteenth Year, Supplement for April, May and June 1964,* document S/5658, annex.

[22] For the text of the questionnaire and the replies thereto, see *Official Records of the Security Council, Twentieth Year, Special Supplement No. 2.*

[23] *Ibid.*

[24] Security Council resolution 191 (1964) of 18 June 1964.

[25] General Assembly resolution 2235 (XXI) of 20 December 1966; see also resolution 1705 (XVI) of 19 December 1961 concerning South West Africa and General Assembly resolution 1808 (XVII) of 14 December 1962 relating to Territories under Portuguese Administration.

as a transitional measure provision should be made in the regular budget of a certain amount to ensure the continuity of the programme pending the receipt of adequate voluntary contributions. In its resolutions 2557 (XXIV) of 12 December 1969, 2706 (XXV) of 14 December 1970, 2875 (XXVI) of 20 December 1971 and 2981 (XXVII) of 14 December 1972, the General Assembly urgently appealed to all States, organizations and individuals to make generous contributions to the programme so that it might not only continue in operation but also be strengthened and expanded. In the earlier resolutions the General Assembly had also noted that the contributions had fallen far short of the original target, while in the resolution of 1972 it noted with satisfaction the increase in contributions.

### 8. *The United Nations Trust Funds for South Africa and Namibia*

By resolution 2054 B (XX) of 15 December 1965 the General Assembly requested the Secretary-General to establish a United Nations Trust Fund for South Africa, made up of voluntary contributions from States, organizations and individuals to be used for grants to voluntary organizations, Governments of host countries of refugees from South Africa and other appropriate bodies towards legal assistance, relief and education. The purposes of the fund were revised by General Assembly resolution 2397 (XXIII) of 2 December 1968, to the effect that the Fund shall provide:

(*a*) Legal assistance to persons persecuted under the repressive and discriminatory legislation of South Africa;

(*b*) Relief to such persons and their dependents;

(*c*) Education of such persons and their dependents;

(*d*) Relief for refugees from South Africa.

Resolution 2054 B (XX) requested the President of the General Assembly to nominate five Member States, each of which should appoint a person to serve on a Committee of Trustees of the Trust Fund which would decide on the uses of the Fund. In the same resolution the General Assembly appealed to Governments, organizations and individuals to contribute generously to the Fund. This appeal was repeated by resolution 2202 B (XXI) of 16 December 1966, by resolution 2397 (XXIII) of 2 December 1968, by resolution 2671 E (XXV) of 8 December 1970 and by resolution 2923 B (XXVII) of 15 November 1972. By resolution 2671 E (XXV) the General Assembly also authorized the Committee of Trustees to decide on grants from the Fund to voluntary organizations engaged in providing relief and assistance to persons persecuted under repressive and discriminatory legislation in Namibia and Southern Rhodesia.

In its resolution 283 (1970) of 29 July 1970 the Security Council requested the General Assembly to set up a United Nations Fund for Namibia to provide assistance to Namibians who had suffered from persecution and to finance the comprehensive educational and training programme for Namibians, with particular regard to their future administrative responsibilities in the Territory.

Having considered the request made by the Security Council, the General Assembly decided in resolution 2679 (XXV) of 9 December 1970 that a comprehensive United Nations Fund for Namibia should be established. In resolution 2872 (XXVI) of 20 December 1971 the General Assembly reaffirmed its previous decision (resolution 2679 (XXV)), and decided, as a transitional measure, to allocate to the Fund a certain sum from the regular budget of the United Nations for 1972. It authorized the Secretary-General to appeal to Governments for voluntary contributions to the Fund and requested the Secretary-General to make the necessary arrangements for the administration of the Fund. By resolution 3030 (XXVII) of 18 December 1972, the General Assembly decided to allocate to the Fund a certain sum from the regular budget of the United Nations for 1973 and authorized the Secretary-General to continue to appeal to Governments for voluntary contributions to the Fund. In the same resolution the General Assembly authorized the Secretary-General to implement the arrangements for the administration and supervision of the Fund, with the advice of the United Nations Council for Namibia and the *Ad Hoc* Sub-Committee on Namibia.[26]

### 9. *Establishment of a special unit in the Secretariat to deal with* apartheid

In resolution 2144 (XXI) of 26 October 1966 the General Assembly requested the Secretary-General to establish a unit within the Secretariat to deal exclusively with policies of *apartheid*, in consultation with the Special Committee on the Policies of *Apartheid* of the Government of the Republic of South Africa, in order that maximum publicity may be given to the evils of those policies. The unit has been established within the Department of Political and Security Council Affairs of the Secretariat.

### 10. *The* Ad Hoc *Working Group of Experts established by the Commission on Human Rights*

By resolution 2 (XXIII) of 1967, the Commission on Human Rights decided to establish an *Ad Hoc* Working Group of Experts to investigate the charges of torture and ill-treatment of prisoners, detainees or persons in police custody in South Africa. The Economic and Social Council welcomed this decision in its resolution 1236 (XLII) of 6 June 1967. By resolution 1216 (XLII) of 1 June 1967 the Economic and Social Council extended the terms of reference of the *Ad Hoc* Working Group to deal also with allegations regarding infringements of trade union rights in South Africa. At its twenty-fourth session in 1968 the Commission on Human Rights considered the first report of the *Ad Hoc* Working Group of Experts (E/CN.4/950) and deplored the evidence of inhuman practices of the Government of South Africa against the opponents of the evil policy of *apartheid*. Determined to protect human rights and fundamental freedoms in South Africa, the Commission condemned any and every practice of torture and ill-treatment, called upon the Government of South Africa to conform to

[26] Established by the Security Council under resolution 283 (1970).

the international standard minimum rules for the treatment of prisoners and listed 11 specific fields in which the standard rules were being violated and which had to be remedied. On the recommendation of the Commission and of those of the Economic and Social Council contained in resolution 1333 (XLIV) of 31 May 1968, the General Assembly expressed in its resolution 2440 (XXIII) of 19 December 1968 its grave concern at the evidence in the report of the *Ad Hoc* Working Group of Experts of the intensification of inhuman practices. It called upon the Government of South Africa to initiate investigations into the violations mentioned in the report of the *Ad Hoc* Working Group, with a view to establishing the degree of responsibility of persons listed in an appendix to the report of the Working Group and to afford the opportunity to all persons who had suffered damage to receive indemnification. It called for the repeal of various South African laws and for the immediate release of prisoners including one identified by name. In resolution 1302 (XLIV) of 28 May 1968 the Economic and Social Council noted with appreciation the work and the report of the *Ad Hoc* Working Group of Experts on allegations regarding infringements of trade union rights in South Africa and called upon the Government of South Africa for amendment of its laws and various other reforms. It further extended the task of the *Ad Hoc* Working Group to cover also violations of trade union rights in Namibia and in Southern Rhodesia.

At its twenty-fifth session in 1969 the Commission on Human Rights received a further report of the *Ad Hoc* Working Group of Experts (E/CN.4/984 and Add.1-19). It extended the mandate of the *Ad Hoc* Working Group to include an inquiry into the question of capital punishment in southern Africa, in accordance with General Assembly resolution 2394 (XXIII) of 26 November 1968, an inquiry into the treatment meted out to political prisoners as well as to captured freedom fighters in southern Africa and an investigation of grave manifestations of colonialism and racial discrimination present in the situation prevailing in Namibia, Southern Rhodesia, Angola, Mozambique and Guinea (Bissau) (resolution 21 (XXV) of the Commission).

At the forty-sixth session the Economic and Social Council adopted resolution 1412 (XLVI) of 6 June 1969, in which it noted that infringements of trade union rights continued unabated in South Africa, in Southern Rhodesia and in Namibia. The Council called upon the Government of South Africa to repeal certain legislation and to permit trade unionists of all races to benefit from the facilities offered by the major international trade unions as regards educational and other assistance in the trade union field. It requested the United Nations Council for Namibia to declare the international standards on trade union rights currently in force applicable to Namibia. It called for the intervention of the United Kingdom in Southern Rhodesia with a view to checking further infringements of trade union rights in Southern Rhodesia and to repeal various enactments being applied there. At its twenty-fourth session in 1969 the General Assembly again condemned the Government of South Africa for the inhuman and degrading treatment and torture meted out to political prisoners and detainees and made an analogous statement in regard to the Government of Portugal relating to political prisoners, detainees and captured freedom fighters in Angola, Mozambique, Guinea (Bissau) and São Tomé (General Assembly resolution 2547 A (XXIV) of 11 December 1969).

At its twenty-sixth session in 1970 the Commission on Human Rights continued the consideration of the report of the Working Group submitted at its twenty-fifth session (E/CN.4/984 and Add.1-19) and also considered a new report of the Group (E/CN.4/1020 and Add.1-3). It endorsed the Group's observations, conclusions and recommendations. It requested the Group to study, from the point of view of international penal law, the question of *apartheid*, which had been declared a crime against humanity (resolution 8 (XXVI)). On the recommendation of the Commission and of the Economic and Social Council (resolution 1501 (XLVIII) of 27 May 1970) the General Assembly, in resolution 2714 (XXV) of 15 December 1970, repeated its condemnation of any and every practice of torture and ill-treatment in the various territories, reaffirmed that the Standard Minimum Rules for the Treatment of Prisoners of 30 August 1955 apply to all political prisoners or detainees in prison or in police custody throughout South Africa, Namibia, Southern Rhodesia and the African territories under Portuguese domination. The General Assembly reaffirmed its earlier statements about the situation in South Africa and the other territories concerned and called upon the Government of South Africa to implement recommendations contained in the earlier reports of the Group, and also to take certain additional steps. Among the latter was the call upon the Government to disband immediately the Bureau of State Security, to discontinue the practice by which political detainees were compelled to testify against their former colleagues, and to permit a full and impartial investigation into the deaths of political prisoners and detainees in its jails. The General Assembly called upon the Government of Portugal to eradicate the practice of forced labour in its African colonies and to introduce a system in which the products of the African farmers could be freely bought and sold in normal market conditions.

At the twenty-seventh session of the Commission on Human Rights in 1971 the *Ad Hoc* Working Group of Experts submitted its report, prepared in accordance with resolution 21 (XXV) of the Commission (E/CN.4/1051 and Corr.1). The Commission was informed that the study on the question of *apartheid* from the point of view of international penal law would be submitted to the Commission in due course. In other respects the Commission endorsed the observations, conclusions and recommendations of the Group and requested its members to remain active and vigilant in their observation of colonial and racial discriminatory practices.

In 1972 the Commission on Human Rights receveid from the *Ad Hoc* Working Group of Experts two reports. One surveyed new developments in matters relating to human rights that had taken place in southern Africa during the year ending 4 February 1972 (E/CN.4/1076). The other report consisted of the study, from the point of view of international penal law, of the question of *apartheid*. The study dealt with the relevant doctrine, with international instruments relating to international penal law and with practices and manifestations of *apartheid* which could be considered as crimes under international law. The Commission on Human Rights in its resolution 2 (XXVIII) of 1972 requested the Economic and Social Council to transmit to Member States, the Special Committee on *Apartheid* and the International Law Commission the report of the Working Group concerning the question of *apartheid* from the point of view of international penal law, for their comments. The Economic and Social Council at its fifty-second session endorsed this request of the Commission and decided to transmit the report (E/CN.4/1075 and Corr.1) as recommended by the Commission (1818th meeting of the Economic and Social Council, 2 June 1972).

### C. Examinations, reports and studies specifically dealing with racial discrimination

#### 1. *Examinations and reports concerning racial discrimination in dependent Territories*

In the first years of the United Nations considerable effort had been devoted to the examination of questions of racial discrimination. At its fourth session, by resolution 332 (IV) of 2 December 1949, the General Assembly established the Special Committee on Information transmitted under Article 73 e of the Charter. By resolution 569 (VI) of 18 January 1952 the Committee was given the new title "Committee on Information from Non-Self-Governing Territories". By resolution 1970 (XXVIII) of 16 December 1963, the Committee on Information from Non-Self-Governing Territories was dissolved and the Special Committee on the Situation with regard to the Implementation of the Declaration of the Granting of Independence to Colonial Countries and Peoples was charged with the tasks which up to then had been performed by the Committee on Information from Non-Self-Governing Territories.

Both the Committee on Information from Non-Self-Governing Territories and the Special Committee have examined racial discrimination in Non-Self-Governing Territories in great detail. The results of these studies are recorded elsewhere in this publication. As early as 1952 the Committee on Information from Non-Self-Governing Territories included in its report a section describing its preliminary study of the subject which led to the proposal of a draft resolution subsequently adopted by the General Assembly as resolution 644 (VII) of 10 December 1952 on racial discrimination in Non-Self-Governing Territories. In it the General Assembly recommended to the Members responsible for the administration of Non-Self-Governing Territories the abolition in those territories of discriminatory laws and practices contrary to the principles of the Charter and of the Universal Declaration of Human Rights. The report prepared by the Committee on Information from Non-Self-Governing Territories [27] itself was approved by the General Assembly as a brief but considered indication of social conditions in Non-Self-Governing Territories and of the problems of social development.

In a second report [28] the Committee on Information dealt with various aspects of relations between "races"; education, working conditions, eligibility for responsible positions, freedom of domicile, etc. This second report was approved by the General Assembly in its resolution 929 (X) of 8 November 1955. A third study of racial discrimination in Non-Self-Governing Territories was prepared by the Committee on Information in 1958 [29] and approved by the General Assembly in resolution 1326 (XIII) of 12 December 1958. This third study contained a survey of measures taken to reduce racial discrimination wherever it existed and to promote racial harmony. It dealt with the participation of members of different groups in the activities of the public services, economic and cultural development, with anti-discrimination measures and methods of education.

While, in the period following the adoption of the Declaration on the Granting of Independence to Colonial Countries and Peoples of 1960 and at the stage when the functions of the Committee on Information had been taken over by the Special Committee (General Assembly resolution 1970 (XVIII) of 1963), the major emphasis had been laid on the elimination of the subjection of peoples to alien subjugation, domination and exploitation and the free determination by all peoples of their political status, the questions of the elimination of discrimination on the grounds of race, creed or colour nevertheless played a very great role in the work of both the Committee on Information and of the Special Committee and has, as stated in detail elsewhere, repeatedly been expressed in General Assembly resolutions adopted on the recommendation of the Special Committee. Thus to give a recent example, in resolution 2908 (XXVII) of 2 November 1972 the General Assembly again classified racism and *apartheid* as one of the forms and manifestations incompatible with the Charter, the Universal Declaration and the Declaration on the Granting of Independence.

#### 2. *Other studies devoted specifically to racial discrimination*

The two studies decribed below deal only with discrimination on the ground of race. Many of the studies listed above are devoted to discrimination in specific fields but include also the examination of discrimination on the grounds of sex, language or religion. They are, of course, also of great importance for a study of the over-all problem of discrimination on the grounds of race.

##### (a) *Special study on racial discrimination in the political economic, social and cultural spheres*

The special study on racial discrimination in the political, economic, social and cultural spheres, in short *Racial Discrimination* [30] by Mr. Hernán Santa Cruz, was published in connexion with the observance in 1971 of

[27] *Official Records of the General Assembly, Seventh Session, Supplement No. 18*, part II (A/2219).

[28] *Ibid., Tenth Session, Supplement No. 16* (A/2908).

[29] *Ibid., Thirteenth Session, Supplement No. 15* (A/3837).

[30] United Nations publication, Sales No. E.71.XIV.2.

the International Year for Action to Combat Racism and Racial Discrimination. The study was undertaken on the initiative taken at the seventeenth session in 1965 of the Sub-Commission on Prevention of Discrimination and Protection of Minorities and its undertaking was approved by the Commission on Human Rights, the Economic and Social Council and the General Assembly.[31]

### (b) *Study of* apartheid *and racial discrimination in southern Africa*

In resolution 7 (XXIII) of 16 March 1967, the Commission on Human Rights decided to appoint a Special Rapporteur to survey United Nations past actions in the effort to eliminate the policies and practices of *apartheid* in all its manifestations, to study the legislation and practices in South Africa, South West Africa and Southern Rhodesia including such matters as forced labour, inequality of opportunity in the economic, social and educational fields, arrest, detention and treatment of prisoners, right to counsel and fair trial. The Special Rapporteur was requested to make recommendations to the Commission on the appropriate measures which might be taken by the General Assembly effectively to combat racial discrimination and the policies of *apartheid* and segregation. The Commission on Human Rights authorized the Special Rapporteur to consult with the Sub-Commission on Prevention of Discrimination and Protection of Minorities and requested the specialized agencies, the Special Committee on the Policies of *Apartheid* of the Government of the Republic of South Africa, and the Special Committee on the Situation with regard to the Implementation of the Declaration on the Granting of Independence to Colonial Countries and Peoples to co-operate with the Special Rapporteur. At its twenty-fourth session in 1968 the Commission endorsed the conclusions and recommendations of the Special Rapporteur (E/CN.4/949/Add.4), requested the Secretary-General to transmit the report to the International Conference on Human Rights, and recommended that the Conference give consideration to certain concrete recommendations contained in the report (paragraph 1549). It also transmitted the report of the Special Rapporteur to the Special Committee on the Policies of *Apartheid* of the Republic of South Africa, the United Nations Council for South West Africa and the Special Committee on the Situation with regard to the Implementation of the Declaration on the Granting of Independence to Colonial Countries and Peoples (Commission on Human Rights resolutions 3 B, C and D (XXIV)). The Commission also requested the Special Rapporteur to continue his study and gave him additional instructions in that regard. At its twenty-fifth session in 1969, the Commission had before it a further report of the Special Rapporteur (E/CN.4/979 and Add.1 and Add.1/Corr.1 and Add.2-8). The Commission and, on its recommendation, the Economic and Social Council (resolution 1415 (XLVI) of 6 June 1969, and the General Assembly (in resolution 2547 B (XXIV) of 15 December 1969) endorsed those recommendations (E/CN.4/979/Add.5) of the Special Rapporteur, and called upon the Government of South Africa to take a series of steps to bring its policy into line with the Charter and the Universal Declaration of Human Rights. In its resolution 5 (XXV) the Commission also decided that the task of the Special Rapporteur to study *apartheid* and racial discrimination in southern Africa should be continued. However, at its forty-sixth session the Economic and Social Council decided (at its 1602nd meeting on 6 June 1969) that no immediate action should be taken on that recommendation until the Commission, at its twenty-sixth session, had had the opportunity to look at the matter again in the light of the following two alternatives: to abolish the Special Rapporteur's mandate altogether or to entrust the existing mandate to the *Ad Hoc* Working Group of Experts which had been reappointed under resolution 21 (XXV) of the Commission. At its twenty-sixth session in 1970 the Commission on Human Rights, at its 1078th meeting, agreed to terminate the mandate of the Special Rapporteur.

On the suggestion of the International Conference on Human Rights and after preliminary discussions at the twenty-third session of the General Assembly, the General Assembly decided at its twenty-fourth session in 1969 to designate the year 1971 as International Year for Action to Combat Racism and Racial Discrimination (General Assembly resolution 2544 (XXIV) of 11 December 1969). At its twenty-sixth[32] session the General Assembly recalled its resolutions 2446 (XXIII) of 19 December 1968, 2544 (XXIV) of 11 December 1969 in which it designated the year 1971 as International Year for Action to Combat Racism and Racial Discrimination and 2646 (XXV) of 30 November 1970 in which it welcomed the observance of 1971 as the International Year; and expressed its appreciation for their co-operation to Governments, United Nations organs, specialized agencies, regional intergovernmental organizations and non-governmental organizations which had contributed positively to the observance of the Year; and made a number of concrete recommendations on matters arising from the problems of racism and racial discrimination.

By resolution 2919 (XXVII) of 15 November 1972 the General Assembly, firmly convinced that racial discrimination in all its forms and manifestations was a total negation of the purposes and principles of the Charter and that it militated against human progress, peace and justice, and believing that the continuation of national, regional and international action against racial discrimination was a matter of vital importance if the world was to live in peace and justice, decided to launch the Decade for Action to Combat Racism and Racial Discrimination and to inaugurate the activities thereof on 10 December 1973 the twenty-fifth anniversary of the Universal Declaration of Human Rights.

---

[31] See report of the seventeenth session of the Sub-Commission (E/CN.4/882), resolution 6 (XVII); report of the twenty-first session of the Commission on Human Rights (*Official Records of the Economic and Social Council, Thirty-ninth Session, Supplement No. 8*), chap. VII; Economic and Social Council resolution 1076 (XXXIX) of 28 July 1965; General Assembly resolution 2017 (XX) of 1 November 1965.

[32] General Assembly resolution 2785 (XXVI).

### D. Seminars on racial discrimination and *apartheid*

The various seminars held under the programme of advisory services in human rights have been listed in chapter IV of part two of this publication. Of these the following were devoted to problems of racial discrimination, segregation and *apartheid.*

(i) Seminar on *apartheid,* Brasilia, Brazil, August-September 1966 (ST/TAO/HR/27).

(ii) Seminar on the question of the elimination of all forms of racial discrimination, New Delhi, India, August-September 1968 (ST/TAO/HR/34).

(iii) Seminar on measures to be taken on the national level for the implementation of United Nations instruments aimed at combating and eliminating racial discrimination and for the promotion of harmonious race relations: Symposium on the evils of racial discrimination, Yaoundé, Cameroon, 16-29 June 1971 (ST/TAO)/HR/42).

(iv) Seminar on the dangers of a recrudescence of intolerance in all its forms and the search for means of preventing and combating it, Nice, France, 24 August-6 September 1971 (ST/TAO/HR/44).

In resolution 2202 A (XXI) of 16 December 1966 the General Assembly requested the Secretary-General to organize as soon as possible an international conference or seminar on the problems of *apartheid,* racial discrimination and colonialism in southern Africa. This seminar was not part of the programme of advisory services in the field of human rights but, pursuant to the General Assembly resolution, was organized by the Secretary-General in consultation with the *Apartheid* Committee and the Special Committee. The International Seminar on *Apartheid,* Racial Discrimination and Colonialism in Southern Africa was held in 1967 at Kitwe, Zambia. At its twenty-second session, the General Assembly, by resolution 2307 (XXII) of 13 December 1967, took note with satisfaction of the report of the seminar (E/6818 and Corr.1). It requested the *Apartheid* Committee to intensify its co-operation with other special organs concerned with the problems of racial discrimination and colonialism in southern Africa, taking into account the conclusions and recommendations of the international seminar held at Kitwe. The General Assembly commended to the attention of all United Nations organs the report of the Kitwe seminar and also the report of the seminar on *apartheid* held at Brasilia, mentioned above.

### E. Educational methods and commemoration of events in the field of combating racial discrimination

When the United Nations Declaration on the Elimination of All Forms of Racial Discrimination, 1963, and the International Convention on the Elimination of All Forms of Racial Discrimination, 1965, were adopted, requests were addressed to the Governments of States and to non-governmental organizations to publicize the texts of those instruments in the same way as previously Governments had been requested to publicize the Universal Declaration of Human Rights and other instruments in this field.[33]

The States parties to the International Convention on the Elimination of All Forms of Racial Discrimination undertake the legal obligation to adopt immediate and effective measures particularly in the field of teaching, education, culture and information with a view to combating prejudices which lead to racial discrimination and to promoting understanding, tolerance and friendship among nations and racial or ethnic groups.

Corresponding to the decision of the General Assembly for an annual celebration of Human Rights Day on 10 December of each year is the decision taken by the General Assembly at its twenty-first session designating the anniversary of the Sharpeville Incident (21 March) to be observed each year as International Day for the Elimination of Racial Discrimination.[34] The Secretary-General was requested to submit to the General Assembly a report also on the implementation of that decision.

[33] General Assembly resolutions 1905 (XVIII) of 20 November 1963 and 2106 (XX) of 21 December 1965.

[34] General Assembly resolution 2142 (XXI) of 26 October 1966; see also Commission on Human Rights resolution 10 (XXIII) of 10 March 1967.

*CHAPTER 3*

# CURRENT STATUS OF COVENANTS

It is obviously not practicable to follow up in any ordered manner the vast range of topics dealt with in the foregoing analysis, but the present Chapter goes some way to supplementing the two preceding Chapters, in so far as UN document E/CN.A/1227 of 7 January 1977 brings some of the most important topics and proposals up to the end of 1976, while a later document, A/32/178 of 12 September 1977, looks further ahead and sketches the possibilities before the UN system and its component governments beyond 1977. This latter document was submitted to the UN's Thirty-Second General Assembly at the end of 1977, and summarises the views and actions of governments up to that date. It will be noted, too, that this document also includes the opinions presented by a large number of non-governmental organisations — a theme we shall pursue at greater length in Chapter 5 of Volume III in this Series.

UNITED NATIONS

# ECONOMIC AND SOCIAL COUNCIL

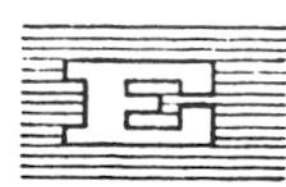

E/CN.4/1227
7 January 1977
Original: ENGLISH/
FRENCH/SPANISH

COMMISSION ON HUMAN RIGHTS

Thirty-third Session
Item 18 of the provisional agenda

## STATUS OF INTERNATIONAL COVENANTS ON HUMAN RIGHTS

*Note by the Secretary-General*

1. In its resolution 12 (XXXII) of 5 March 1976 concerning the status of the International Covenants on Human Rights, the Commission on Human Rights took note of the fact that the International Covenant on Economic, Social and Cultural Rights had entered into force on 3 January 1976 and that the International Covenant on Civil and Political Rights and the Optional Protocol thereto had already been ratified by the required number of States and would enter into force on 23 March 1976. The Commission invited all Member States to consider the question of the ratification of the International Covenants on Human Rights in the near future, and requested the Secretary-General to inform the Commission at each session of any new developments with regard to ratification and implementation of the International Covenants. The present note was prepared in response to that request.

2. For the purpose of gathering relevant data on the matter, the Secretary-General, in a note verbale dated 15 June 1976, invited all States Members of the United Nations or members of the specialized agencies or parties to the Statute of the International Court of Justice to send him before 30 November 1976 any information as to the steps they might have taken or envisaged with a view to ratifying or acceding to the International Covenants on Human Rights. As of 31 December 1976, the Secretary-General had received replies from the following Governments: *Austria*, Belgium, France, Guatemala, Italy, Liberia, Liechtenstein, Netherlands, New Zealand, Senegal, Trinidad and Tobago, United States of America and Venezuela. The relevant passages of substantive replies are reproduced in annex I.

3. Since the adoption of the Commission's resolution, the International Covenants on Human Rights were ratified by the United Kingdom of Great Britain and Northern Ireland on 20 May 1976 and signed by Panama on 27 July 1976, by Spain on 28 September 1976 and by Portugal on 7 October 1976.

In addition, Canada, on 19 May 1976, the United Republic of Tanzania, on 11 June 1976, Zaire, on 1 November 1976 and Surinam on 28 December 1976, acceded to the Covenants. As a result, on 31 December 1976, 42 States had become parties to the International Covenant on Economic, Social and Cultural Rights and 40 States parties to the International Covenant on Civil and Political Rights. The list of States that had signed, ratified or acceded to the Covenants, as well as the dates of their signature, ratification or accession, may be found in annexes II and III.

4. In addition, the United Kingdom of Great Britain and Northern Ireland made the declaration under article 41 of the International Covenant on Civil and Political Rights which recognizes the competence of the Human Rights Committee to receive and consider communications to the effect that a State party claims that another State party is not fulfilling its obligations under the said Covenant. The Governments of Denmark, Finland, the Federal Republic of Germany, Norway and Sweden had previously made such declarations. The Committee will become competent to exercise the functions provided for under article 41 when at least 10 States parties to the Covenant have made such a declaration.

5. Moreover, Canada on 19 May 1976, Zaire on 1 November 1976 and Surinam on 28 December 1976 acceded to the Optional Protocol to the International Covenant on Civil and Political Rights, which was also signed by Italy on 30 April 1976, by Panama on 22 July 1976, and by Venezuela on 15 November 1976. As of 31 December 1976, 15 States have become parties to the Optional Protocol, which entered into force on 23 March 1976. The list of States that had signed, ratified or acceded to the Optional Protocol, as well as the dates of their signature, ratification or accession, may be found in annex IV.

6. After the entry into force of the International Covenant on Economic, Social and Cultural Rights and in accordance with the provisions of part IV (Articles 16-25) thereof, the Economic and Social Council, at its sixtieth session, considered the procedures for the implementation of that Covenant. In its resolution 1988 (LX) of 11 May 1976 (see annex V), the Economic and Social Council expressed its appreciation to the Commission on Human Rights, the specialized agencies concerned and other organizations of the United Nations system for their readiness to co-operate in the implementation of the Covenant. In accordance with article 17 of the Covenant, the Council established the following programme under which the States parties to the Covenant would furnish in biennial stages the reports referred to in article 16 thereof: first stage, rights covered by articles 6-9; second stage, rights covered by articles 10-12; third stage, rights covered by articles 13-15. The Council requested the States parties to the Covenant, in reporting under this programme, to give full attention to the principles contained in parts I and II — articles 1-5 — of the Covenant.

7. The Council invited the States parties to the Covenant to submit to the Secretary-General reports on the rights included in the first stage of the programme by 1 September 1977, and reports on the subsequent stages

at biennial intervals thereafter. The Council called upon the specialized agencies to submit to it reports on the progress made in achieving the observance of the provisions of the Covenant falling within the scope of their activities. The reports on the rights included in the first stage of the programme should be transmitted by 1 December 1977, and the reports on the subsequent stages at biennial intervals thereafter.

8. The Council decided that: (a) a sessional working group of the Economic and Social Council, with appropriate representation of States parties to the Covenant, and with due regard to equitable geographical distribution, should be established by the Council whenever reports were due for consideration by the Council, for the purpose of assisting it in the consideration of such reports; (b) representatives of specialized agencies concerned might take part in the proceedings of the working group when matters falling within their respective fields of competence would be considered.

9. Upon entry into force of the International Covenant on Civil and Political Rights and in accordance with the provisions of articles 28 to 32 thereof, the Secretary-General, in a note dated 20 May 1976, drew the attention of the States parties to that Covenant to the provisions concerning the establishment of the Human Rights Committee, and invited them to submit their nominations for membership of the Committee within three months. The States parties to the Covenant held their first meeting at United Nations Headquarters on 20 September 1976 and, in accordance with the provisions of articles 28 to 32 of the Covenant, elected the following 18 members of the Human Rights Committee: Mr. Mohamed Ben-Fadhel (Tunisia), Mr. Ole Mogens Espersen (Denmark), Sir Vincent Evans (United Kingdom of Great Britain and Northern Ireland), Mr. Bernhard Graefrath (German Democratic Republic), Mr. Manouchehr Ganji (Iran), Mr. Vladimir Hanga (Romania), Mr. Haissam Kelani (Syrian Arab Republic), Mr. Luben G. Koulishev (Bulgaria), Mr. Rajsoomer Lallah (Mauritius), Mr. Andreas V. Mavrommatis (Cyprus), Mr. Fernando Mora Rojas (Costa Rica), Mr. Anatoly Petrovich Movchan (Union of Soviet Socialist Republics), Mr. Torkel Opsahl (Norway), Mr. Julio Prado Vallejo (Ecuador), Mr. Fulgence Seminega (Rwanda), Mr. Walter Surma Tarnopolsky (Canada), Mr. Christian Tomuschat (Germany, Federal Republic of) and Mr. Diego Uribe Vargas (Colombia).

10. The following members of the Committee were chosen by lot as those whose term would expire on 31 December 1978: Mr. Ole Mogens Espersen (Denmark), Mr. Mohamed Ben Fadhel (Tunisia), Mr. Bernhard Graefrath (German Democratic Republic), Mr. Rajsoomer Lallah (Mauritius), Mr. Fernando Mora Rojas (Costa Rica), Mr. Torkel Opsahl (Norway), Mr. Julio Prado Vallejo (Ecuador), Mr. Fulgence Seminega (Rwanda) and Mr. Christian Tomuschat (Federal Republic of Germany).

11. The Committee is scheduled to hold its first session from 21 March to 1 April 1977 at United Nations Headquarters, New York.

12. In its resolution 31/86 of 13 December 1976 (see annex VI) concerning the Status of the International Covenant on Economic, Social and

Cultural Rights, the International Covenant on Civil and Political Rights and the Optional Protocol to the International Covenant on Civil and Political Rights the General Assembly welcomed the entry into force of those instruments as a major step in the international efforts to promote universal respect for and observance of human rights and fundamental freedoms and invited once again all States to become parties to them. The Assembly, recognizing the important role of the Human Rights Committee in the implementation of the International Covenant on Civil and Political Rights, stated that appropriate arrangements should be made to enable the Human Rights Committee to hold sessions at such intervals and of such duration as may be necessary for it to carry out in an efficient manner the functions entrusted to it under that Protocol and the Optional Protocol thereto. The Assembly endorsed the appeal to States made by the Economic and Social Council in its resolution 1988 (LX) of 11 May 1976 that they include in their delegations to the sessions of the Council at which reports of States parties to the International Covenant on Economic, Social and Cultural Rights are examined experts competent in the subject matter of the relevant reports.

*Annex I*

## EXCERPTS FROM SUBSTANTIVE REPLIES OF GOVERNMENTS RELATING TO RATIFICATION OR ACCESSION

### AUSTRIA

[Original: English]
[15 November 1976]

'the Federal Government of Austria decided on 21 April 1976 to submit the International Covenant on Economic, Social and Cultural Rights and the International Covenant on Civil and Political Rights to the Austrian Parliament for parliamentary approval as required under the Austrian Constitution. Both aforementioned Covenants are presently being considered by the Austrian Parliament, with the view of their ratification."

### BELGIUM

[Original: French]
[24 November 1976]

"the procedure for approval of these international instruments by the Belgian parliament is now in progress."

### FRANCE

[Original: French]
[24 November 1976]

"studies are currently being made among the French administrations concerned with a view to France's accession to these Covenants."

### ITALY

[Original: French]
[28 October 1976]

"(1) The Italian Government approved on 7 September 1976 the bill for ratification and implementation of the Covenants;

(2) On 24 September, the bill was transmitted to the Senate of the Republic for consideration and approval."

## LIBERIA

[Original: English]
[October 1976]

"the question of the ratification of the International Covenant on Human Rights is claiming the urgent attention of the Government of Liberia."

## LIECHTENSTEIN

[Original: French]
[31 August 1976]

"the Government of the Principality has arranged to study the question of the possibility of the Principality's accession to the International Covenants..."

## NETHERLANDS

[Original: English]
[15 December 1976]

"The bill concerning the International Covenant on Economic, Social and Cultural Rights and the International Covenant on Civil and Political Rights and the Optional Protocol thereto has been presented to the Second Chamber of Parliament by Royal Message on 24 May 1976, accompanied by a detailed explanatory memorandum.

It is expected that discussion of the bill in the Second Chamber of Parliament will take place during the first half of 1977. Thereafter the First Chamber of Parliament will have to discuss the bill. Consequently it may be expected that the procedure of approval will only be accomplished by the end of 1977."

## NEW ZEALAND

[Original: English]
[9 November 1976]

"since the entry into force of the Covenants earlier this year the New Zealand Government has begun a closer examination of steps that will be required to implement the Covenants in New Zealand law. However, the fact that the Covenants cover the whole range of human rights means that extensive consultations must take place and may take some time to complete. No decisions have yet been taken on the steps which the New Zealand Government would need to take on this matter."

SENEGAL

[Original: French]
[2 December 1976]

"the procedure for ratification by Sénégal of the two International Covenants on Human Rights and of the Optional Protocol to the International Covenant on Civil and Political Rights is now in progress in accordance with the constitutional rules in force and the instruments of ratification will be transmitted [to the Secretary-General] upon completion of the procedure."

TRINIDAD AND TOBAGO

[Original: English]
[12 July 1976]

"consideration is presently being given to Trinidad and Tobago either ratifying or acceding to the two Covenants referred to therein."

VENEZUELA

[Original: Spanish]
[1 September 1976]

"extensive discussions are being held on the question of ratification of the Covenants prior to seeking the approval of the Congress of the Republic."

*Annex II*

## LIST OF STATES WHICH HAVE SIGNED, RATIFIED OR ACCEDED TO THE INTERNATIONAL COVENANT ON ECONOMIC, SOCIAL AND CULTURAL RIGHTS

| *States* | *Date of signature* | *Date of ratification or accession* |
|---|---|---|
| Algeria | 10 December 1968 | |
| Argentina | 19 February 1968 | |
| Australia | 18 December 1972 | 10 December 1975 |
| Austria | 10 December 1973 | |
| Barbados | | 5 January 1973[a] |
| Belgium | 10 December 1968 | |
| Bulgaria | 8 October 1968 | 21 September 1970 |
| Byelorussian Soviet Socialist Republic | 19 March 1968 | 12 November 1973 |
| Canada | | 19 May 1976[a] |
| Chile | 16 September 1969 | 10 February 1972 |
| China[b] | | |
| Colombia | 21 December 1966 | 29 October 1969 |
| Costa Rica | 19 December 1966 | 29 November 1968 |
| Cyprus | 9 January 1967 | 2 April 1969 |
| Czechoslovakia | 7 October 1968 | 23 December 1975 |
| Denmark | 20 March 1968 | 6 January 1972 |
| Ecuador | 29 September 1967 | 6 March 1969 |
| Egypt | 4 August 1967 | |
| El Salvador | 21 September 1967 | |

---

a Accession.

b Signed on behalf of the Republic of China on 5 October 1967. See note concerning signatures, ratifications, accessions, etc. on behalf of China in *Multilateral Treaties in respect of which the Secretary-General Performs Depositary Functions: List of Signatures, Ratifications, Accessions, etc. as at 31 December 1975* (United Nations publication, Sales No. E.76.V.7), preface, p. iii, and p. 95 note 2.

| *States* | *Date of signature* | *Date of ratification or accession* |
|---|---|---|
| Finland | 11 October 1967 | 19 August 1975 |
| German Democratic Republic | 27 March 1973 | 8 November 1973 |
| Germany, Federal Republic of | 9 October 1968 | 17 December 1973 |
| Guinea | 28 February 1967 | |
| Guyana | 22 August 1968 | |
| Honduras | 19 December 1966 | |
| Hungary | 25 March 1969 | 17 January 1974 |
| Iceland | 30 December 1968 | |
| Iran | 4 April 1968 | 24 June 1975 |
| Iraq | 18 February 1969 | 25 January 1971 |
| Ireland | 1 October 1973 | |
| Israel | 19 December 1966 | |
| Italy | 18 January 1967 | |
| Jamaica | 19 December 1966 | 3 October 1975 |
| Jordan | 30 June 1972 | 28 May 1975 |
| Kenya | | 1 May 1972[a] |
| Lebanon | | 3 November 1972[a] |
| Liberia | 18 April 1967 | |
| Libyan Arab Republic | | 15 May 1970[a] |
| Luxembourg | 26 November 1974 | |
| Madagascar | 14 April 1970 | 22 September 1971 |
| Mali | | 16 July 1974[a] |
| Malta | 22 October 1968 | |
| Mauritius | | 12 December 1973[a] |
| Mongolia | 5 June 1968 | 18 November 1974 |
| Netherlands | 25 June 1969 | |
| New Zealand | 12 November 1968 | |
| Norway | 20 March 1968 | 13 September 1972 |
| Panama | 27 July 1976 | |
| Philippines | 19 December 1966 | 7 June 1974 |
| Poland | 2 March 1967 | |
| Portugal | 7 October 1976 | |

| *States* | *Date of signature* | *Date of ratification or accession* |
|---|---|---|
| Romania | 27 June 1968 | 9 December 1974 |
| Rwanda | | 16 April 1975[a] |
| Senegal | 6 July 1970 | |
| Spain | 28 September 1976 | |
| Surinam | | 28 December 1976[a] |
| Sweden | 29 September 1967 | 6 December 1971 |
| Syrian Arab Republic | | 21 April 1969[a] |
| Tunisia | 30 April 1968 | 18 March 1969 |
| Ukrainian Soviet Socialist Republic | 20 March 1968 | 12 November 1973 |
| Union of Soviet Socialist Republics | 18 March 1968 | 16 October 1973 |
| United Kingdom of Great Britain and Northern Ireland | 16 September 1968 | 20 May 1976 |
| United Republic of Tanzania | | 11 June 1976[a] |
| Uruguay | 21 February 1967 | 1 April 1970 |
| Venezuela | 24 June 1969 | |
| Yugoslavia | 8 August 1967 | 2 June 1971 |
| Zaire | | 1 November 1976[a] |

E/CN.4/1227
Annex III

*Annex III*

LIST OF STATES WHICH HAVE SIGNED, RATIFIED OR ACCEDED TO THE INTERNATIONAL COVENANT ON CIVIL AND POLITICAL RIGHTS

| *States* | *Date of signature* | *Date of ratification or accession* |
| --- | --- | --- |
| Algeria | 10 December 1968 | |
| Argentina | 19 February 1968 | |
| Australia | 18 December 1972 | |
| Austria | 10 December 1973 | |
| Barbados | | 5 January 1973[a] |
| Belgium | 10 December 1968 | |
| Bulgaria | 8 October 1968 | 21 September 1970 |
| Byelorussian Soviet Socialist Republic | 19 March 1968 | 12 November 1973 |
| Canada | | 19 May 1976[a] |
| Chile | 16 September 1969 | 10 February 1972 |
| China[b] | | |
| Colombia | 21 December 1966 | 29 October 1969 |
| Costa Rica | 19 December 1966 | 29 November 1968 |
| Cyprus | 19 December 1966 | 2 April 1969 |
| Czechoslovakia | 7 October 1968 | 23 December 1975 |
| Denmark | 20 March 1968 | 6 January 1972 |
| Ecuador | 4 April 1968 | 6 March 1969 |
| Egypt | 4 August 1967 | |
| El Salvador | 21 September 1967 | |
| Finland | 11 October 1967 | 19 August 1975 |
| German Democratic Republic | 27 March 1973 | 8 November 1973 |
| Germany, Federal Republic of | 9 October 1968 | 17 December 1973 |

a Accession.

b See annex II, note b.

| States | Date of signature | Date of ratification or accession |
|---|---|---|
| Guinea | 28 February 1967 | |
| Guyana | 22 August 1968 | |
| Honduras | 19 December 1966 | |
| Hungary | 25 March 1969 | 17 January 1974 |
| Iceland | 30 December 1968 | |
| Iran | 4 April 1968 | 24 June 1975 |
| Iraq | 18 February 1969 | 25 January 1971 |
| Ireland | 1 October 1973 | |
| Israel | 19 December 1966 | |
| Italy | 18 January 1967 | |
| Jamaica | 19 December 1966 | 3 October 1975 |
| Jordan | 30 June 1972 | 28 May 1975 |
| Kenya | | 1 May 1972[a] |
| Lebanon | | 3 November 1972[a] |
| Liberia | 18 April 1967 | |
| Libyan Arab Republic | | 15 May 1970[a] |
| Luxembourg | 26 November 1974 | |
| Madagascar | 17 September 1969 | 21 June 1971 |
| Mali | | 16 July 1974[a] |
| Mauritius | | 12 December 1973[a] |
| Mongolia | 5 June 1968 | 18 November 1974 |
| Netherlands | 25 June 1969 | |
| New Zealand | 12 November 1968 | |
| Norway | 20 March 1968 | 13 September 1972 |
| Panama | 27 July 1976 | |
| Philippines | 19 December 1966 | |
| Poland | 2 March 1967 | |
| Portugal | 7 October 1976 | |
| Romania | 27 June 1968 | 9 December 1974 |
| Rwanda | | 16 April 1975[a] |
| Senegal | 6 July 1970 | |
| Spain | 28 September 1976 | |

| *States* | *Date of signature* | *Date of ratification or accession* |
|---|---|---|
| Surinam | | 28 December 1976[a] |
| Sweden | 29 September 1967 | 6 December 1971 |
| Syrian Arab Republic | | 21 April 1969[a] |
| Tunisia | 30 April 1968 | 18 March 1969 |
| Ukrainian Soviet Socialist Republic | 20 March 1968 | 12 November 1973 |
| Union of Soviet Socialist Republics | 18 March 1968 | 16 October 1973 |
| United Kingdom of Great Britain and Northern Ireland | 16 September 1968 | 20 May 1976 |
| United Republic of Tanzania | | 11 June 1976[a] |
| Uruguay | 21 February 1967 | 1 April 1970 |
| Venezuela | 24 June 1969 | |
| Yugoslavia | 8 August 1967 | 2 June 1971 |
| Zaire | | 1 November 1976[a] |

*Annex IV*

## LIST OF STATES WHICH HAVE SIGNED, RATIFIED OR ACCEDED TO THE OPTIONAL PROTOCOL TO THE INTERNATIONAL COVENANT ON CIVIL AND POLITICAL RIGHTS

| *States* | *Date of signature* | *Date of ratification or accession* |
|---|---|---|
| Austria | 10 December 1973 | |
| Barbados | | 5 January 1973[a] |
| Canada | | 19 May 1976[a] |
| China[b] | | |
| Colombia | 21 December 1966 | 29 October 1969 |
| Costa Rica | 19 December 1966 | 29 November 1968 |
| Cyprus | 19 December 1966 | |
| Denmark | 20 March 1968 | 6 January 1972 |
| Ecuador | 4 April 1968 | 6 March 1969 |
| El Salvador | 21 September 1967 | |
| Finland | 11 December 1967 | 19 August 1975 |
| Guinea | 19 March 1975 | |
| Honduras | 19 December 1966 | |
| Italy | 30 April 1976 | |
| Jamaica | 19 December 1966 | 3 October 1975 |
| Madagascar | 17 September 1969 | 21 June 1971 |
| Mauritius | | 12 December 1973[a] |
| Netherlands | 25 June 1969 | |
| Norway | 20 March 1968 | 13 September 1972 |
| Panama | 27 July 1976 | |
| Philippines | 19 December 1966 | |
| Senegal | 6 July 1970 | |

a Accession.

b See annex II, note b.

| *States* | *Date of signature* | *Date of ratification or accession* |
|---|---|---|
| Surinam | | 28 December 1976[a] |
| Sweden | 29 September 1967 | 6 December 1971 |
| Uruguay | 21 February 1967 | 1 April 1970 |
| Venezuela | 15 November 1976 | |
| Zaire | | 1 November 1976[a] |

*Annex V*

ECONOMIC AND SOCIAL COUNCIL RESOLUTION 1988 (LX) of 11 May 1976

1988 (LX). Procedures for the implementation of the International Covenant on Economic, Social and Cultural Rights

*The Economic and Social Council,*

*Welcoming* the entry into force on 3 January 1976 of the International Covenant on Economic, Social and Cultural Rights,[a]

*Expressing its appreciation* to those States which have become parties to the Covenant,

*Expressing the hope* that at the earliest practicable time other States will become parties to the Covenant, with a view to making its application universal,

*Noting* the important responsibilities placed on the Economic and Social Council by the Covenant and expressing its readiness to perform these responsibilities,

*Noting* in particular that international assistance and co-operation are among the methods envisaged in the Covenant for the guaranteeing of the rights enumerated therein,

*Having requested* the Secretary-General to conduct on its behalf consultations with the States parties to the Covenant and the specialized agencies concerned, as envisaged in article 17 of the Covenant, and having received with appreciation the report of the Secretary-General thereon,[b]

*Expressing its appreciation* to the Commission on Human Rights, the specialized agencies concerned and other organizations of the United Nations system for their readiness to co-operate in the implementation of the Covenant,

1. *Establishes* in accordance with article 17 of the International Covenant on Economic, Social and Cultural Rights, the following programme under which the States parties to the Covenant will furnish in biennial stages the reports referred to in article 16 thereof:

First stage: rights covered by articles 6-9;

---

a General Assembly resolution 2200 A (XXI) of 16 December 1966.
b E/5764.

Second stage: rights covered by articles 10-12;

Third stage: rights covered by articles 13-15;

2. *Requests* the States parties to the Covenant, in reporting under the programme established under paragraph 1 above, to give full attention to the principles contained in parts I and II — articles 1 to 5 — of the Covenant;

3. *Invites* the States parties to the Covenant to submit to the Secretary-General, in conformity with part IV of the Covenant, and in accordance with the programme established under paragraph 1 above, reports on the measures that they have adopted and the progress made in achieving the observance of the rights recognized in the Covenant, and to indicate, when necessary, factors and difficulties affecting the degree of fulfilment of their obligations under the Covenant;[c]

4. *Requests* the Secretary-General to transmit copies of the reports of the States parties to the Covenant to the Economic and Social Council for consideration in accordance with the provisions of the Covenant;

5. *Requests* the Secretary-General to transmit to the specialized agencies, in accordance with article 16, paragraph 2 (b), of the Covenant, copies of the reports, or any relevant parts thereof, from States parties to the Covenant which are also members of these specialized agencies, in so far as these reports, or parts thereof, relate to any matters which fall within the responsibilities of the said agencies in accordance with their constitutional instruments;

6. *Calls upon* the specialized agencies to submit to the Economic and Social Council, in accordance with the programme established under paragraph 1 above, and bearing in mind the provisions of article 16, paragraph 2, of the Covenant, reports on the progress made in achieving the observance of the provisions of the Covenant falling within the scope of their activities, as provided under article 18 of the Covenant, which reports may include particulars of decisions and recommendations on such implementation adopted by their competent organs;[d]

7. *Decides* that States parties to the Covenant which submit reports under the Covenant need not submit reports on similar questions under the reporting procedure established under Economic and Social Council resolution 1074 C (XXXIX) of 28 July 1965;

8. *Requests* the Secretary-General, in co-operation with the special-

---

c The reports of the rights included in the first stage of the programme should be transmitted by 1 September 1977, and the reports on the subsequent stages at biennial intervals thereafter.

d The reports on the rights included in the first stage of the programme should be transmitted by 1 December 1977, and the reports on the subsequent stages at biennial intervals thereafter.

ized agencies concerned, to draw general guidelines for the reports to be submitted by States parties to the Covenant and specialized agencies;

9. *Decides* that:

(a) A sessional working group of the Economic and Social Council with appropriate representation of States parties to the Covenant, and with due regard to equitable geographical distribution, shall be established by the Council whenever reports are due for consideration by the Council, for the purpose of assisting it in the consideration of such reports;

(b) Representatives of specialized agencies concerned may take part in the proceedings of the working group when matters falling within their respective fields of competence are considered;

10. *Appeals* to States to include, if possible, in their delegations to the relevant sessions of the Economic and Social Council, members competent in the subject-matters under consideration;

11. *Requests* the Secretary-General to take all steps to ensure the effective performance by the Economic and Social Council of its responsibilities under the Covenant.

*1999th plenary meeting*
*11 May 1976*

*Annex VI*

## GENERAL ASSEMBLY RESOLUTION 31/86 of 13 DECEMBER 1976

*Status of the International Covenant on Economic, Social and Cultural Rights, the International Covenant on Civil and Political Rights and the Optional Protocol to the International Covenant on Civil and Political Rights*

*The General Assembly,*

*Having noted* the report of the Secretary-General on the status of the International Covenant on Economic, Social and Cultural Rights, the International Covenant on Civil and Political Rights and the Optional Protocol to the International Covenant on Civil and Political Rights,[a]

*Recalling* its resolutions 2200 A (XXI) of 16 December 1966 and 3270 (XXIX) of 10 December 1974, and in particular its belief that the entry into force of the International Covenants on Human Rights will undoubtedly enhance the ability of the United Nations to promote and encourage respect for human rights and fundamental freedoms for all, and thus contribute greatly to the co-operation of States in the attainment of the purposes and principles of the Charter of the United Nations,

*Bearing in mind* the important responsibilities of the Economic and Social Council in the implementation of the International Covenant on Economic, Social and Cultural Rights,

*Recognizing* the important role of the Human Rights Committee in the implementation of the International Covenant on Civil and Political Rights,

*Convinced* that the International Covenants on Human Rights constitute the first all-embracing and legally binding international treaty in the field of human rights,

*Expressing its appreciation* to those States that have become parties to the above instruments,

1. *Welcomes with deep satisfaction* the entry into force of the International Covenant on Economic, Social and Cultural Rights, the International Covenant on Civil and Political Rights and the Optional Protocol to the International Covenant on Civil and Political Rights as a major step in the international efforts to promote universal respect for and observance of human rights and fundamental freedoms;

---

a A/31/202.

2. *Recognizes* that such resources as may be necessary should be allocated to enable the Secretary-General to provide the appropriate staff and facilities for the effective performance of the functions of the Human Rights Committee under the International Covenant on Civil and Political Rights and the Optional Protocol thereto;

3. *Recognizes* that appropriate arrangements should be made to enable the Human Rights Committee to hold sessions at such intervals and of such duration as may be necessary for it to carry out in an efficient manner the functions entrusted to it under the International Covenant on Civil and Political Rights and the Optional Protocol thereto;

4. *Endorses* the appeal to States made by the Economic and Social Council in its resolution 1988 (LX) of 11 May 1976 that they include in their delegations to the sessions of the Council at which reports of States parties to the International Covenant on Economic, Social and Cultural Rights are examined experts competent in the subject-matter of the relevant reports;

5. *Requests the Secretary-General* to submit to the General Assembly at its thirty-second session a report on the status of the International Covenant on Economic, Social and Cultural Rights, the International Covenant on Civil and Political Rights and the Optional Protocol to the International Covenant on Civil and Political Rights;

6. *Invites once again* all States to become parties to the International Covenant on Economic, Social and Cultural Rights and the International Covenant on Civil and Political Rights and the Optional Protocol thereto.

UNITED NATIONS

GENERAL
ASSEMBLY

A/32/178
12 September 1977
ENGLISH
Original: ENGLISH/
FRENCH

Thirty-second session
Item 76 of the provisional agenda*

# ALTERNATIVE APPROACHES AND WAYS AND MEANS WITHIN THE UNITED NATIONS SYSTEM FOR IMPROVING THE EFFECTIVE ENJOYMENT OF HUMAN RIGHTS AND FUNDAMENTAL FREEDOMS

*Report of the Secretary-General*

CONTENTS



* A/32/150.

## I. INTRODUCTION

1. The present report has been prepared in accordance with paragraph 3 of General Assembly resolution 3451 (XXX) of 9 December 1975, in which the Secretary-General was requested to submit to the Assembly at the thirty-second session an updated version of his report on alternative approaches and ways and means within the United Nations system for improving the effective enjoyment of human rights and fundamental freedoms (A/10235) in the light of further replies from Member States and non-governmental organizations in consultative status with the Economic and Social Council and of the views expressed on this subject at the thirtieth session of the General Assembly.

2. It may be recalled that the General Assembly, by resolution 3136 (XXVIII) of 14 December 1973, decided to keep under review the consideration of alternative approaches and ways and means within the United Nations system for improving the effective enjoyment of human rights and fundamental freedoms. By resolution 3221 (XXIX) of 6 November 1974, the Assembly requested the Secretary-General to solicit the views of Member States, the specialized agencies and regional intergovernmental organizations on alternative approaches and ways and means within the United Nations system for improving the effective enjoyment of human rights and fundamental freedoms. Non-governmental organizations in consultative status with the Economic and Social Council were invited to submit to the Secretary-General any relevant material on the subject, taking into account that such material should not be politically motivated contrary to the principles of the Charter of the United Nations. The Secretary-General was requested to prepare and submit to the General Assembly at its thirtieth session a concise analytical report based on the views and material submitted, taking into account the International Covenants on Human Rights,[1] the updated versions of the studies prepared for the International Conference on Human Rights, held at Teheran in 1968, on measures taken and methods utilized within the United Nations system in the field of human rights, which were published in 1974 under the title *United Nations Action in the Field of Human Rights*,[2] as well as any other relevant material. At its thirtieth session, the General Assembly, having considered the report of the Secretary-General, adopted resolution 3451 (XXX) in which it urged Member States that had not already done so to submit their views to the Secretary-General. The Secretary-General was requested, in the light of further replies from Member States and non-governmental organizations and of the views expressed during the proceedings of the thirtieth session of the Assembly, to submit an updated version of his report to the Assembly at its thirty-second session.

, annex.
IV.74.2.

The Assembly decided to consider the item with high priority at its thirty-second session.

3. As at 1 August 1977, in response to the Secretary-General's notes verbales sent in accordance with resolution 3451 (XXX), substantive replies had been received from the Governments of the following Member States: Austria, Belgium, Byelorussion Soviet Socialist Republic, Chile, Congo, Denmark, Finland, German Democratic Republic, Germany, Federal Republic of, Guatemala, India, Iraq, Italy, Japan, Libyan Arab Jamahiriya, Mauritius, Netherlands, Norway, Panama, Sweden, Ukrainian Soviet Socialist Republic, Union of Soviet Socialist Republics, United Kingdom of Great Britain and Northern Ireland and United States of America; and from the ILO. Replies were received from the following non-governmental organizations: Amnesty International, International Association for Social Progress, Baptist World Alliance, Christian Democratic World Union, International Federation of Resistance Movements, International Federation of Women in Legal Careers, Friends World Committee for Consultation, International Co-operative Alliance, International Council of Jewish Women, International Federation of Business and Professional Women, International Federation of Catholic Youth, International Federation of Women Lawyers, International Social Science Council, International Union of Judges, Inter-Parliamentary Union, Société de législation comparée, Soroptimist International, War Resisters International, Womens International League for Peace and Freedom, World Federation of Catholic Youth, World Federation of Trade Unions, World Fellowship of Buddhists, World Muslim Congress, World Young Women's Christian Association, World Union of Catholic Womens Organizations. A memorandum on the subject prepared under the aegis of the Non-Governmental Organizations Committee on Human Rights at United Nations Headquarters, and endorsed by 17 non-governmental organizations, was received by the Secretariat.

4. The views expressed during the discussion of the item at the thirtieth session of the General Assembly (A/3.C/SR.2168, 2169, 2171 and 2172; A/10404) and the additional replies received by the Secretary-General are summarized hereunder. The outline of this further report is essentially the same as that of the initial study contained in document A/10235. In each chapter, the debates at the General Assembly, the views of Governments, those of specialized agencies and the replies received from non-governmental organizations are summarized successively.

## II. GENERAL OBSERVATIONS

### A. *Debate at the thirtieth session of the General Assembly*

5. Some representatives stressed that, in their opinion, under Articles 55 and 56 of the Charter of the United Nations, all the activities of the United Nations in the field of human rights should be based on the voluntary co-operation of Member States (see, for instance, A/3.C/SR.2169, p. 16). The Charter was based on the assumption that the protection of human rights fell normally within the domestic jurisdiction of each State

and should take into account the various social systems and cultural traditions (*ibid.*, p. 5). However, the situation was clearly of international concern whenever gross and systematic violations of human rights were likely to impair friendly relations between States and to endanger international peace (*ibid.*, p. 6). Another general view was that, while the Charter of the United Nations, the Universal Declaration and the International Covenants on Human Rights had created a solid foundation upon which to base a universal approach to human rights issues, the United Nations must constantly review the suitability and effectiveness of the various policies and procedures adopted under its auspices (*ibid.*, p. 5).

6. Accoding to some representatives (*ibid.*, p. 2), an important distinction should be drawn between procedures which involved formal meetings and public debates, as in the Third Committee, the Economic and Social Council, the Commission on Human Rights and the Sub-Commission, and procedures of an informal character, which aimed at safeguarding human rights through good offices and conciliation. Both types of procedures could play a useful role in the international protection and promotion of human rights.

7. Several representatives stressed the need for the United Nations to concentrate on proposals which would be acceptable to all, since international action in matters of such a vital importance for mankind ought to be fully implemented in all parts of the world.

## B. *Views of Governments*

8. The replies of the Congo, the Federal Republic of Germany, Iraq, the Libyan Arab Jamahiriya, the United King om and the United States stressed in genera terms the importance and urgency of studying ways and means for a more effective protection of human rights, as recognized by General Assembly resolution 3451 (XXX).

9. The Government of the Congo felt that the problems raised by this resolution were closely related to that of strengthening the effectiveness of international law, in particular through according greater authority to United Nations resolutions.

10. The Federal Republic of Germany considered that the Secretary-General's report (A/10235) constituted a useful basis for the study called for in resolution 3451 (XXX). It felt that the task of standard-setting has largely been accomplished and that it was now increasingly important to use the existing instruments in order to achieve substantial improvements in the protection of human rights.

11. The Government of the United States referred in general terms to its views summarized in the report, which it considered to be still valid and timely.

12. In the view of the Government of India, the United Nations should further develop its programme of international economic and technical co-operation in order the eliminate poverty, which prevents millions of people from enjoying various human rights. The establishment of a new and more equitable world economic order could promote the effective enjoyment of human rights in the world. The Government of India also expressed support for the programme of the Decade for Action to Combat

Racism and Racial Discrimination, adopted by the General Assembly in its resolution 3057 (XXVIII) of 2 November 1973.

13. The Government of the Libyan Arab Jamahiriya emphasized the importance of United Nations action against racism and especially of the International Conference to be held in 1978. It called for an intensification of United Nations efforts to promote the self-determination of peoples still under foreign rule. It considered it necessary to organize special meetings to study further alternative ways and means of promoting human rights.

14. The Governments of the Byelorussian Soviet Socialist Republic, the German Democratic Republic, the Ukrainian Soviet Socialist Republic and the Union of Soviet Socialist Republics emphasized their views that, in accordance with the Charter, international action in the field of human rights should be based on the voluntary co-operation of Member States, in full respect for their sovereign equality, without intervention in their domestic affairs, and with due consideration for the various social systems and national and cultural traditions. International action was justified where gross and systematic violations of human rights occurred. The effectiveness of the work of the United Nations in the field of human rights depended above all on the development of their action to promote peace, understanding and disarmament, to struggle against aggression, colonialism and racism and to promote the rights and interests of the working masses.

15. In addition, the Byelorussian Soviet Socialist Republic considered that ways and means within the United Nations system for improving the effective enjoyment of human rights could be better identified if due attention were paid to various issues including: the right of individials to life, personal immunity and freedom in conditions of international peace and security, national legislative measures for the enjoyment of economic, social and cultural rights, utilization of the results of the scientific and technological revolution for the full enjoyment of economic, social and cultural rights, the rights and freedom of action of trade unions, the effectiveness of the procedures hitherto employed for examining individual complaints and the advisability of a change-over to the system provided for in the Covenants on Human Rights, the adverse consequences of the activities of multinational monopolies for human rights, and the favourable effects of the process of international détente upon the enjoyment of human rights.

16. The Government of the German Democratic Republic referred to the programme of the United Nations Decade for Women: Equality, Development and Peace, and to its proposals for the long-term programme of work of the Commission on Human Rights (E/CN.4/1168/Add.2). It considered that international implementation procedures expressly agreed to by States should be strictly applied and that any attempt to establish additional measures which were not recognized as binding by all States should not be pursued.

### C. *Views of the specialized agencies*

17. The ILO referred to the need for co-ordination and an appropriate division of responsibilities as regards both standard setting and implementation procedures in the field of human rights within the United Nations system. There already exist various arrangements between the ILO and the United Nations, FAO, UNESCO and WHO, and at the regional level more particularly with the Council of Europe, for collaboration in supervising the application of certain instruments of mutual interest. In the view of the ILO, a more developed system of co-ordination and collaboration among organizations in the United Nations system was called for in regard to the implementation of the International Covenants on Human Rights.

### D. *Replies of non-governmental organisations*

18. In a memorandum 17 non-governmental organizations expressed the view that the United Nations in its first 30 years had in many ways actively promoted human rights. Recently, however, the role of the United Nations in the field of human rights has been criticized. Some have alleged a "selective morality" of the United Nations in condemning violations of human rights only in certain political areas of the world, whereas such problems are virtually world-wide. Still another criticism of the United Nations was that emphasis had been given to promoting economic, social, and cultural rights while often, allegedly, neglecting civil and political rights. A fourth criticism was the lack of general standards of fair procedures for all situations. The United Nations system itself was currently engaged in several efforts to assess its own machinery in the field of human rights. Yet, where there was little or no political will, the best machinery would not enhance progress in the field of human rights. The non-governmental organizations underline the crucial importance for all nations individually and the world community to exert maximum political will to safeguard human rights in our time.

19. The World Federation of Trade Unions considered that it was important to prepare the report requested by resolution 3451 (XXX) since the number of Governments responding to demands for national and economic independence with continued and flagrant violations of human rights was growing throughout the world today and such violations often struck at progressive national movements and the working class.

## III. STRENGTHENING THE CAPACITY OF EXISTING UNITED NATIONS ORGANS TO PROMOTE THE EFFECTIVE ENJOYMENT OF HUMAN RIGHTS AND FUNDAMENTAL FREEDOMS

### A. *Debate at the thirtieth session of the General Assembly*

20. The view was expressed that the United Nations should pursue its efforts for improving and extending its machinery for the protection of

human rights, since even a development of great importance such as the coming into force of the Covenants would be far from solving the main problems in that field (A/C.3/SR.2168, p. 6). Some other representatives, however, were of the opinion that, rather than adopting new systems, the United Nations should concentrate its efforts towards ensuring the effectiveness of the newly established covenant machinery and of the United Nations organs already in existence (A/C.3/SR.2171, p. 12).

21. The central role in the United Nations system of the Commission on Human Rights and the Sub-Commission for the protection and promotion of human rights was emphasized. The suggestion that the Economic and Social Council should submit reports of the Commission on Human Rights directly to the General Assembly without debate was noted with interest by some representatives (A/C.3/SR.2168, p. 17). It was further suggested that consideration might be given to the possibility of transforming the Trusteeship Council into a Human Rights Council (*ibid.*). However, some representatives felt that the Trusteeship Council should be maintained, since it had been expressly entrusted by the Charter with the very important functions of implementing the right of the peoples of Trust Territories to self-determination (A/C.3/SR.2169, p. 17).

## B. *Views of Governments*

22. The Government of Finland expressed the view that the working methods of the Commission on Human Rights and the Sub-Commission on Prevention of Discrimination and Protection of Minorities should be rationalized in order to enable them to accomplish their task more effectively. In particular, the procedures for dealing with communications concerning human rights under Economic and Social Council resolution 1503 (XLVIII) should be fully utilized, including the appointment of *ad hoc* working groups of inquiry. Other fact-finding procedures might also be developed with the co-operation of the Governments directly concerned.

23. The Government of the Netherlands considered it desirable that the working methods of the Commission on Human Rights and of its suborgans, notably the Sub-Commission on Prevention of Discrimination and Protection of Minorities, be adapted in such a manner as to enable those bodies to act more systematically, speedily and effectively with regard to human rights emergencies. This could be effected by having more frequent regular sessions of those organs or by convening emergency sessions.

24. The Government of the German Democratic Republic considered that the three member groups of the Commission on Human Rights to be appointed under article IX of the Convention on the Suppression of *Apartheid* should start work as early as possible and that the Commission on Human Rights should fully carry out the mandate given to it under article X of the Convention.

25. The Government of India, although not opposed in principle to the establishment of new organs for the protection of human rights, felt that the whole of the existing machinery for dealing with alleged violations of human rights should first be tested, and, if necessary, improved upon before any additional organ is created.

26. The Byelorussian SSR felt that the entry into force of the Covenants on Human Rights has rendered superfluous the activities of a number of subsidiary United Nations bodies. The Human Rights Committee set up under the International Covenant on Civil and Political Rights would be dealing, *inter alia*, with the adoption of measures to guarantee the rights of ethnic, religious and national minorities, a matter at present dealt with by the Sub-Commission on Prevention of Discrimination and Protection of Minorities. Eliminating this Sub-Commission would consequently contribute to the rationalization of the work of the United Nations. It was also felt that the setting up of the Human Rights Committee made superfluous the activities of the *Ad Hoc* Committee on Periodic Reports established under Economic and Social Council resolution 1596 (L). The Government further considered that, after the entry into force of the Covenants, the procedure provided for in resolution 1503 (XLVIII), envisaged as a temporary measure, should lapse.

27. The Governments of the USSR and the Ukrainian SSR similarly express the view that the work of the Human Rights Committee and the Economic and Social Council's consideration of reports under the International Covenant on Economic, Social and Cultural Rights will clarify the areas in which duplication and overlapping must be eliminated and will enable outdated procedures to be changed.

## C. *Replies of non-governmental organisations*

28. The memorandum from 17 non-governmental organizations contains various views and suggestions on strengthening the United Nations Human Rights organs. As the general debate in the plenary meetings of the General Assembly often reflects the concern for human rights by Member States, the publication of a summary of observations made during the plenary, produced by the Secretariat immediately at its conclusion, would be a valuable service to States, intergovernmental organizations, and non-governmental organizations.

29. Efforts should be made to rationalize the work of the Third Committee to increase its effectiveness in dealing with human rights issues, particularly those involving civil and political rights. Economic, social and cultural rights could be considered jointly by the Second and Third committees. The detailed consideration of conventions relating to human rights should be referred to the Sixth Committee.

30. The Social Committee of the Economic and Social Council deals with too many diverse issues, including narcotics, human rights and women. This Committee should more properly be referred to as "the Humanitarian

Committee" and consider only reports of the Commission on Women and the Commission on Human Rights. The report of the Commission on Narcotics would be more properly considered by another committee of the Council.

31. The Commission on Human Rights was considering ways to improve its methods of work. Separating economic, social and cultural rights from civil and political rights would be counter-productive, as many questions involve a combination of both. From the global United Nations viewpoint, care should be taken not to duplicate efforts in other organs devoted to economic and social rights, particularly the Commission for Social Development.

32. It was also suggested that the items on the Commission's agenda should be cycled over a three, four or even five year programme of work, to permit the delegations and the Secretariat to concentrate on fewer documents and thereby improve the quality of the work. To avoid unnecessary delay from duplicate cycling, it would be advisable to await the results of the Sub-Commission cycle which will *de facto* result in a cycling of the Commission items which originate from, or relate to, the Sub-Commission items.

33. The Commission should consider giving its subordinate bodies - the Sub-Commission, *ad hoc* groups, and its own Bureau - more responsibility between sessions to resolve time-consuming issues and make proposals to facilitate the Commission's decision-making process. At the beginning of each session of the Commission, a representative of each of the various organs or agencies involved with human rights issues (e.g. Economic and Social Council, Commission for Social Development, Commission on the Status of Women, and the ILO) should provide information on recent developments and projects that call for co-ordination.

34. In recent years, the Commission, it was felt, had become less successful in drafting conventions, declarations and codes. The drafting of such instruments should be referred to intersessional working groups of experts so as not to detract from the other work of the Commission. Although the Sub-Commission, as the permanent body of experts in the human rights field, is the most competent to undertake this normative task, care should be taken not to overtax its agenda with projects requiring concentrated efforts which would best be performed between sessions.

35. In 1976 the Economic and Social Council authorized the outgoing Bureau of the Commission on Human Rights to meet for one week prior to the next session to review not only the work programme but the proposals to improve the Commission's work. Such a practice might become permanent not only on the question of the organization of work, but on discussing possible solutions for the various issues under review. The Bureau could also be given the mandate to meet between sessions at the discretion of the Chairman or on petition of 10 members of the Commission to consider questions of an urgent nature requiring the action of the Commission. Although the Bureau might not be authorised to take positions on urgent situations, it could certainly express its concern and make

inquiries with the Governments involved, collect data and present recommendations to the Commission for emergency action.

36. The decision to hold all Commission and Sub-Commission sessions at Geneva, it was felt, reversed a long-standing practice of alternating sessions between Headquarters and Geneva. Holding sessions only at Geneva may work to the disadvantage of smaller States, since some do not have missions at Geneva and therefore cannot give office support to their members. The 17 non-governmental organizations suggested that the earlier practice should be reconsidered of alternating sessions of the Commission and Sub-Commission between Headquarters and Geneva, and even that consideration should be given to holding these sessions occasionally in various world capitals.

37. The Sub-Commission had difficulty completing its agenda each year. The special studies required several years to complete, while other United Nations organs were requesting that more studies be undertaken. The result was a very inadequate discussion both of reports during their preparation and little consideration of the final report or action flowing from it. In order to lighten its burden, the Sub-Commission recently created a five-year programme of work, rotating its agenda items. This will, of course, also slow down the productivity of the Commission and all other organs in the field of human rights. The Commission on Human Rights, at its thirty-second session in 1976, considered a proposal to create two new sub-commissions of five members each - one on the promotion of human rights and the other on its protection. Perhaps a membership of 13 experts on each would facilitate a more even distribution of the work. Until such time as two subsidiary organs are created, the Sub-Commission should be scheduled to meet between the conclusion of the annual session of the General Assembly and the beginning of the annual session of the Commission. The latter could possibly meet later each year. Thus a human rights project could flow from the most subordinate body to the most superior body more quickly, and ideally within one year.

38. The proposed creation of a Council on Human Rights to replace the Trusteeship Council would seem to necessitate an amendment to the Charter. Alternatively, the General Assembly could, under Article 7, paragraph 2, of the Charter create a new human rights body - with a status equivalent to that of UNICEF or UNCTAD. Such a United Nations agency for human rights could be given the powers in the field of human rights now residing in both the Economic and Social Council and the Commission on Human Rights.

39. The 17 non-governmental organizations felt that the Division of Human Rights could be both more creative and more effective and that it should be given more adequate financing. The distance of the Division from Headquarters and the Secretary-General remains a serious one. The geographical distance of the Division from United Nations missions, especially of smaller States which have no offices in Geneva, works to a disadvantage for these States. There should be simultaneous release of documents in Geneva and New York using modern transmission methods.

Both at Geneva and New York, a staff member should be assigned in the Human Rights Division to work with non-governmental organizations.

40. The Christian Democratic World Union suggested that the Trusteeship Council should be merged with the Commission on Human Rights to create a United Nations Council on Human Rights responsible directly to the General Assembly. The Council on Human Rights should be subdivided into commissions for: (a) civil and political rights; (b) socio-economic rights; and (c) cultural rights. The Council should have regional offices. The competence of the Council would be: to review the situation in the field of human rights on the world level and to formulate general recommendations to develop the international human rights law; to assist Governments in the promotion of human rights; to consider complaints and carry out inquiries, directly or through non-governmental organizations; and to make specific recommendations to interested Governments.

41. The Baptist World Alliance expressed the wish that the practice of alternating the meetings of Human Rights Commission between Europe and North America be restored.

42. Soroptimist International suggests that the United Nations Commission on Human Rights should hold special sessions wherever urgent situations arise involving a pattern of violations of human rights.

43. The International Union of Judges, in the belief that it was essential that the representatives of Governments on the Commission on Human Rights should be particularly qualified and independent, expressed support for the proposal that the selection of members of the Commission should be entrusted to the International Court of Justice.

44. In the view of Amnesty International, the General Assembly should ensure that, pursuant to resolution 3 (XXIX) of the Sub-Commission on Prevention of Discrimination and Protection of Minorities, a working group of the Sub-Commission is established to analyse the materials received in connexion with the Sub-Commission's annual review of developments relating to the question of the human rights of persons subjected to any form of detention or imprisonment.

## IV. RATIFICATION OF THE INTERNATIONAL COVENANTS ON HUMAN RIGHTS AND OTHER HUMAN RIGHTS CONVENTIONS

### A. *Debate at the thirtieth session of the General Assembly*

45. At the thirtieth session of the General Assembly, it was felt that attention should be paid to measures designed to increase the number of parties to basic international conventions on human rights, particularly the International Covenants on Human Rights and the International Convention on the Elimination of Racial Discrimination, with the aim of making their geographical scope universal (A/C.3/SR.2169, p. 11).

46. The great significance of the coming into force of the Covenants was hailed by a large number of representatives. It was said, in particular, that the United Nations should concentrate on making the implementation machinery of the Covenants fully effective (A/C.3/SR.2171, p. 12; see also sect. B above). One view, however, was that the Covenants, important as they were, were not an end in themselves: reference was made to the qualifications contained in several of their articles, and to limitations on the effectiveness of the reporting system of the Covenants stemming from the fact that States were being asked to report on their own practices (A/C.3/SR.2168, p. 6; see also sect. B above).

### B. *Views of Governments*

47. All Governments which commented on this matter - the Federal Republic of Germany, Finland, the German Democratic Republic, India, the Ukrainian SSR, the United Kingdom, the USSR - stressed the importance of promoting the widest ratification of United Nations Human Rights Conventions, especially the Covenants, with the aim of making their acceptance universal.

48. The Government of Finland suggested that States parties to the International Covenant on Civil and Political Rights be encouraged to make declarations under article 41 thereof.

49. This view was also expressed by the Government of the Netherlands which felt that States should be invited to accept all optional clauses and instruments relating to inter-State complaints and communications from individuals.

50. It was emphasized by the Governments of the Ukrainian SSR and the USSR that the entry into force of the Covenants marked the beginning of a qualitatively new stage in international co-operation for the protection of human rights, since these instruments provided an international legal basis for such co-operation.

### C. *Replies of non-governmental organisations*

51. The Friends World Committee expressed the hope that the coming into force of the International Covenants would in no way blunt the drive to secure further ratifications and accessions, in particular, to the Optional Protocol.

## V. SUGGESTIONS CONCERNING THE ADOPTION OF NEW SUBSTANTIVE INSTRUMENTS

### A. *Debate at the thirtieth session of the General Assembly*

52. The view was expressed that, although the standard-setting achieve-

ments of the United Nations had been impressive, its work was by no means complete. Attention was drawn in particular to the need for a declaration and, in due course, a convention on the elimination of all forms of religious intolerance, and a convention on the elimination of discrimination against women (A/C.3/SR.2168, p. 16).

53. In the view of some representatives (A/C.3/SR.2169, p. 12), the effectiveness of United Nations activities would depend largely on the extent to which new efforts at codification in the field of human rights were in harmony with the interests and aspirations of progressive forces in the world, concerning in particular: the right of everyone to live in conditions of international peace and security, the need for legal guarantees aimed at ensuring the enjoyment of economic, social and cultural rights, the study of the negative consequences of the activities of trasnational corporations on the enjoyment of human rights, and the need to strengthen the rights and freedoms of trade union organizations.

## B. *Views of Governments*

54. The Government of India supported the proposal for an international convention on the elimination of all forms of religious intolerance. The Government also placed high value on work currently in progress on the preparation of a convention on the elimination of discrimination against women.

55. The Ukrainian SSR suggested that the activities of the United Nations should be directed towards the preparation and adoption of new international legal instruments to protect human rights such as, in particular, the draft Convention on the Elimination of Discrimination against Women. The proposal put forward by the Soviet Union in the Commision on Human Rights concerning the right to live in conditions of international peace and security, and the proposals on legal guarantees and international measures to promote economic, social and cultural rights, on protecting the activities of professional workers' organizations and on the unfavourable consequences of activities of multinational monopolies for the enjoyment of human rights also hold promise.

## C. *Views of the specialised agencies*

56. The ILO observed that the framing of international standards constituted part of the regular activity of the International Labour Conference, which was conducted according to an established procedure, based on provisions of the Organisation's Constitution. The practice of the ILO has been to deal item by item with distinct aspects of social policy. In this way a comprehensive body of instruments has been built up. The ILO suggested that consideration might be given to a similar process of standard-setting by the United Nations to define in greater detail the guarantees necessary to ensure the enjoyment of civil and political rights falling within its competence. Various studies carried

out within the United Nations, for example, in regard to the administration of justice, suggested that more detailed standards of this kind could perform a most useful function.

57. The ILO further stated that, with an increasing amount of standard-setting within the United Nations system, there should be appropriate co-ordination and division of work according to the specific responsibilities of each organization.

### D. *Replies of non-governmental organisations*

58. Soroptimist International suggested that: (a) a covenant should be prepared based on the Declaration on the Protection of All Persons from Torture and other Cruel, Inhuman, Degrading Treatment or Punishment; (b) work should be completed on the Declaration and Convention on the Elimination of all Forms of Religious Intolerance; (c) the United Nations should be urged to complete work on a declaration and convention on the elimination of terrorism; (d) the United Nations should adopt a declaration and covenant to eliminate threats to human rights posed by scientific and technological developments: (e) the United Nations should prepare a declaration and convention on the rights of indigenous people; (f) the United Nations should support the Protocols to the Geneva Conventions on Humanitarian Laws Applicable to Armed Conflicts; and (g) the United Nations should adopt a convention on the elimination of discrimination against women.

59. In the opinion of Amnesty International, the General Assembly should ensure the rapid preparation of a body of principles for the protection of all persons subject to any form of detention or imprisonment, based on the Draft Principles on Freedom from Arbitrary Arrest and Detention and the principles contained in the second preambular paragraph of resolution 7 (XXVII) of the Sub-Commission on Prevention of Discrimination and Protection of Minorities. The General Assembly should then elaborate a convention on the suppression of torture and the protection of all prisoners, confirming torture to be a crime under international law and incorporating the principles contained in the declaration against torture as well as the body of principles referred to above. The test of a code of conduct for law enforcement officials, containing at least the principles enunciated in the draft code prepared by the Committee on Crime Prevention and Control at its fourth session, should be adopted. The General Assembly should also continue its co-operation with the World Health Organisation, with a view to approving a code of ethics for medical personnel relevant to the prevention of torture and other cruel, inhuman or degrading treatment or punishment.

60. The Baptist World Alliance suggests that the adoption of a declaration on the elimination of religious discrimination and intolerance should be expedited and that a draft instrument should be prepared by the Commission on Human Rights to provide some form of judicial settlement for grievances pertaining to violations of human rights and fundamental freedoms.

61. The International Federation of Resistance Movements expressed the hope that the United Nations would soon take up the study of a draft convention against torture and other cruel, inhuman or degrading treatment or punishment.

62. The Friends World Committee for Consultation suggested that a full week should be added to the duration of a forthcoming session of the Commission exclusively for the purpose of completing the draft Declaration on the Elimination of all forms of Religious Intolerance requested by the General Assembly in 1962. It also suggests the drafting of a convention on the treatment of offenders based on the standard minimum rules.

## VI. SYSTEMS OF PERIODIC REPORTS ON HUMAN RIGHTS

### A. *Debate at the thirtieth session of the General Assembly*

63. It was generally considered that a careful study was called for of the various systems of periodic reports on human rights mentioned in the report of the Secretary-General (A/10235) with a view to avoiding duplication of work (A/C.3/SR.2169, p. 13). It was felt that a more careful evaluation could be made of the numerous reports submitted by Member States, in particular the voluminous material available concerning economic, social and cultural rights (A/C.3.SR.2169, p. 8).

### B. *Views of Governments*

64. The Government of India considered that periodic reporting systems were useful for the protection of human rights.

65. The German Democratic Republic felt that the reports of the States parties on the implementation of the International Covenant on Economic, Social and Cultural Rights should be examined within the Economic and Social Council in the same way as the reports submitted to the Committee on the Elimination of Racial Discrimination (CERD). The periodic reports submitted pursuant to Council resolution 1074 C (XXXIX) by States which are not yet parties to the International Convention on the Elimination of All Forms of Racial Discrimination and to the two human rights covenants of 1966 should be examined by the Commission on Human Rights in similar depth, with like thoroughness and at the same intervals as those provided for in the CERD procedure. The Council should include in its report under article 21 of the Covenant on Economic, Social and Cultural Rights the results emerging from the examination of reports pursuant to its resolution 1074 C (XXXIX) and it should submit that report, if possible annually, together with the report of the Human Rights Committee (article 45 of the Convention on Civil and Political Rights) to the General Assembly for simultaneous consideration.

### C. *Replies of non-governmental organizations*

66. The Christian Democratic World Union stated that as one of their priority tasks to ensure the full enjoyment of human rights, Governments should submit fuller reports explaining what they have done to implement the articles of the Universal Declaration on human rights and the Covenants.

67. The International Union of Judges, noting that it would be a long time before the Covenants were ratified by a large number of States, expressed the view that it would be advisable for the Commission on Human Rights to implement a procedure providing for the possibility of the study of full reports on the various problems relating to human rights and the formulation of recommendations which could deal with specific situations. The task of studying such reports should be entrusted to persons of the highest competence appointed in their personal capacity.

## VII. PROCEDURES APPLICABLE TO ALLEGATIONS OF VIOLATIONS OF HUMAN RIGHTS

### A. *Debate at the thirtieth session of the General Assembly*

68. The view was expressed by several representatives that the communications procedure under Economic and Social Council resolution 1503 (XLVIII) was very valuable but had so far been imperfectly developed (A/C.3/SR.2168, pp. 16-17). It was felt, in particular, that procedures should be worked out to enable the various organs concerned to examine the communications on a more regular and timely basis (A/C.3/SR.2169, p. 3). A further suggestion was that amendments to the system should be made to provide for the notification to the senders of communications and the Governments concerned of any decisions taken with respect to the communications (*ibid.*).

### B. *Views of Governments*

69. The Federal Republic of Germany felt that the opportunities opened by Council resolution 1503 (XLVIII) for dealing with communications relating to violations of human rights continued to be of great importance for progress towards a universal guarantee of human rights.

70. Regarding the application of Council resolution 728 F (XXVIII), the Government of Chile considered that a system should be devised to prevent the repetitious transmittal of the same allegations to Governments when those Governments had already replied to them and no further information was required. With respect to Council resolution 1503 (XLVIII) and resolution 1 (XXIV) of the Sub-Commission, the Government of Chile felt that the concept of "consistent pattern of gross and reliably attested violations" should be clarified. The Government concerned should be informed of what was said about it in the confidential report

of the Working Group, so that it had an opportunity to reply. The entire discussion ofmatters concerning the Government in question should be caried on in its presence. The report of the Sub-Commission to the Commission on Human Rights should be brought to the attention of the Government concerned before being submitted to the Commission on Human Rights together with the Government's reply, if any. The full discussion in the Commission on Human Rights should be held in the presence of the Government concerned. The Government of Chile further considered that the provisions of resolution 1 (XXIV) of the Sub-Commission on Prevention of Discrimination and Protection of Minorities should be applied strictly and in their entirety, particularly paragraphs 2, 3, 4 and 5. The Government claimed that, as regards its own situation in particular, the provisions of that resolution had either not been applied or had been applied under an extraordinarily broad interpretation.

71. The Byelorussian SSR considered that attention should be concentrated chiefly upon measures to eliminate massive and gross violations of human rights that were a matter of grave concern to the majority of States Members of the United Nations. Among the questions which should be included in this category were: violations of human rights in territories occupied as a result of hostilities in the Near East; gross and massive violations of human rights consequent upon policies of racial discrimination and *apartheid*; and violations of human rights by the military junta in Chile. Effective measures should be taken to eliminate the gross and massive violations of human rights which were continuing as a result of the policy and practice of racism, *apartheid*, colonialism and neo-colonialism and in consequence of the suppression of national liberation struggles and of imperialist aggression and foreign occupation. The Byelorussian SSR further expressed the view that practice had demonstrated the futility of the machinery set up for examining individual communications under Economic and Social Council resolution 1503 (XLVIII). Attempts to give an international body such functions inevitably led to interference in the domestic affairs of States and tended to complicate relations between them. After the entry into force of the Covenants the procedure provided for in resolution 1503 (XLVIII) should lapse.

72. Recalling paragraph 4 of Council resolution 1235 (XLII) and paragraph 10 of Council resolution 1503 (XLVIII), the German Democratic Republic considered that it was necessary to review the procedures prescribed in the two resolutions, which had been established as an interim system pending the entry into force of specific treaty arrangements. Since separate mechanisms of enforcement had entered into force for the States parties to the International Convention on the Elimination of All Forms of Racial Discrimination and to the International Covenant on Civil and Political Rights, these States should be released from the procedures provided for in Council resolution 1235 (XLII) and 1503 (XLVIII). The German Democratic Republic felt that the United Nations should promote measures to mobilize democratic world opinion against massive and brutal violations of human rights, such as those manifested in aggressions, *apartheid*, other forms of racial discrimination, colonialism and

neo-colonialism, and the suppression of national liberation organizations and of other progressive movements fighting against exploitation.

### C. *Replies of non-governmental organizations*

73. The memorandum from 17 non-governmental organizations stated that the procedures created by Council resolution 1503 (XLVIII) had not been fully applied. The following suggestions were submitted. The Sub-Commission should be requested to present in its report to the Commission a more analytical summary of the communications forwarded to identify issues and propose recommendations. That would facilitate the Commission's decision-making process and eliminate duplication of effort. A rapporteur should be appointed from the Sub-Commission Working Group to report to the Sub-Commission as well as to the Commission on the findings of the former bodies. Members of the Sub-Commission and the Commission should be permitted to read on request any communication that was before the Sub-Commission's Working Group in order to review the basis of its decision on admissibility. The Secretary-General should forward to the Commission members any communication referring to a situation under review which had been received too late for the Sub-Commission Working Group to consider. The author of a communication under review should be invited to present oral or written testimony in closed meetings under these procedures in order to supplement the information or respond to questions.

74. The Secretariat should be authorized to convey a governmental reply to the author of the communication or, where necessary, to an intermediary organization in cases where the reply of the Government either explicitly or implicitly envisaged that its response should in fact be so transmitted. The author should be informed forthwith of any decision, negative or positive, as regards a particular communication and of the basis for such decision.

75. The memorandum from 17 non-governmental organizations further claimed that the confidentiality rule of resolution 1503 (XLVIII) was interpreted too broadly, rendering the whole procedure ineffective. The rule was based on a desire to prevent possible retaliation during consideration of the case and to encourage friendly settlements without undue embarrassment to the Government concerned. But where it precluded all public oversight of the progress of the procedures, it insulated the States Members from ever having to take action against a fellow State Member.

76. The memorandum referred to the expeditious *ad hoc* procedures set up by the Commission, which had maintained a balance between the need for confidentiality and for public disclosure during their investigations and preparation of reports. Those procedures should never, however, be considered a substitute for the resolution 1503 (XLVIII) procedures which protect the individual right of redress.

77. Under existing practices, the consideration of communications by the Commission on the Status of Women does not preclude action by the Commission on Human Rights. According to the 17 non-governmental organizations, the separate procedures should be preserved. The Economic and Social Council could, moreover, authorize the Commission on the Status of Women to take action on such communications by creating procedures parallel to, but not necessarily similar with, those of the Commission on Human Rights under the procedures in resolution 1503 (XLVIII).

78. The International Federation of Women in Legal Careers suggested that support of all kinds, in particular financial support, should be given to the legal aid which lawyers and judges endeavoured to provide to the victims of violations of human rights.

79. The Friends World Committee for Consultation suggested that representatives of non-governmental organizations should be permitted to attend sessions of the Commission devoted to situations which reveal a consistent pattern of gross violations of human rights, when they had furnished evidence relating to the situations under discussion.

80. The International Union of Judges suggested the establishment of a standing committee of the Commission on Human Rights, composed of highly competent independent individuals of unquestionable morality, within the framework of resolution 1503 (XLVIII). It would be useful if each of the parties were in a position to hear the arguments of the other in accordance with the systems generally adopted in international proceedings.

81. The World Union of Catholic Women's Organizations expressed the view that other procedures, more closely associated with non-governmental organizations, should be established for the submission of individual communications concerning violations of human rights.

## VIII. FACT-FINDING AND INVESTIGATION PROCEDURES

### A. *Debate at the thirtieth session of the General Assembly*

82. Special arrangements such as the *Ad Hoc* Working Group of Experts on southern Africa and the *Ad Hoc* Working Group on Chile were said to have proved their usefulness. It was noted, however, that at present there were no pre-established general principles and criteria that could be applied to future investigations. The suggestion was made that the Third Committee should study ways and means of ensuring that commissions of inquiry were established, perhaps automatically, whenever needed, and that it should elaborate in advance general criteria to govern their composition and methods of work (A/C.3/SR.2168, pp. 8-9; A/C.3/SR.2171, p. 14). One view was, however, that under the Charter no State could be subjected to an international investigation procedure by a majority decision of an international organ without its express consent (A/C.3/SR. 2169, p. 7).

83. A proposal was made by Chile (A/C.3/SR.2169, p. 16) according to which the General Assembly would have instructed the Secretary-General "to appoint a group of 10 experts of recognized integrity and proven knowledge in the field of human rights, in which the different geographical areas are represented and the different legal systems taken into account, for the purpose of preparing a study on the establishment of a system for investigating allegations of violations of human rights". Such a system, according to this proposal, "should allow for appropriate participation by regional organizations, should be universal in scope and automatic and compulsory for all Member States, should avoid duplication, should ensure adequate machinery for co-operation between the Organization and the States investigated and should confer upon such States appropriate guarantees regarding discretion and fairness".

84. It was argued in favour of this proposal that the system for investigating alleged violations of human rights should be universal and automatic, so that it would come into effect whenever violations of human rights occurred (A/C.3/SR.2168, p. 14). It was also said that the proposal represented a step forward in efforts to provide adequate machinery not only for investigations of alleged violations of human rights but also for the prevention of such violations (A/C.3/SR.2169, p. 15).

85. Against the proposal, it was argued that it contradicted the United Nations Charter and had been motivated by political considerations (A/C.3/SR.2169, p. 18); A/C.3/SR.2171, p. 8; A/C.3/SR.2171, p. 13). It was said that it would seriously threaten the Charter system of peaceful co-operation between sovereign States through encouraging interference in the domestic affairs of States (A/C.3/SR.2169, p. 6).

86. Another view was that, although the proposal was interesting, it would be premature to discuss it, especially in view of lack of time at the thirtieth session. It was suggested that it might be made part of the replies to the request by the Secretary-General for views on the question, which would enable Members to give it proper consideration (A/C.3/SR.2171, p. 15; see also A/C.3/SR.2168, p. 18; A/C.3/SR.2169, p.23; A/C.3/SR.2171, pp. 4,10,15; A/C.3/SR.2171, p.15).

## B. *Views of Governments*

87. The Government of Belgium drew attention to paragraph 6 (b) of Council resolution 1503 (XLVIII), whereby a particular situation which appeared to reveal a pattern of flagrant and systematic violations of human rights could lead the Commission on Human Rights to determine whether that situation should be the subject of an investigation by a committee appointed for that purpose. Under that paragraph, the investigation decided on by the Commission on Human Rights could be undertaken only with the express consent of the State concerned. The Government of Belgium suggested that States should consider voluntarily renouncing their right under paragraph 6 (b) of resolution 1503 (XLVIII) not to agree to an investigation in matters of human rights.

88. The Government of the Netherlands considered that fact-finding procedures were an important means for helping to secure compliance with basic human rights standards, and felt that more recourse should be had to such procedures. The establishment of a permanent panel of independent experts for this purpose, instead of appointing working groups or special committees on an *ad hoc* basis, would constitute considerable progress in this field. It submitted that such a permanent fact-finding panel could be utilized for dealing with situations revealing a consistent pattern of gross violations of human rights in accordance with Human Rights Commission resolution 8 (XXIII) and Economic and Social Council resolutions 1235 (XLII) and 1503 (XLVIII).

89. The Government of Chile recalled its proposal at the thirtieth session of the General Assembly quoted in section A above. It was of the opinion that the lack of a pre-established procedure had been one of the main problems with the *ad hoc* Working Group appointed by the Commission on Human Rights to inquire into the present situation of human rights in that country. The Government felt that the alleged practice of selectivity in human rights investigations should be abolished and a general and universally applicable system should be established.

## IX. QUESTIONS REGARDING THE ESTABLISHMENT OF AN INTERNATIONAL COURT ON HUMAN RIGHTS

90. The Government of the Federal Republic of Germany considered that there was need for an independent international authority passing objective judgements to ensure that human rights were safeguarded in all parts of the world. Its belief was strengthened by its experience with the protective system of the European Convention on Human Rights which had proved its value for more than two decades and which would not lose anything of its importance if the United Nations established an institution along its lines.

91. On the other hand, the Government of India felt that, in the present state of international law, proposals for the establishment of an international court of human rights and similar institutions were not practical.

## X. QUESTIONS RELATING TO INTERNATIONAL SANCTIONS IN CASE OF GROSS VIOLATIONS OF HUMAN RIGHTS

### A. *Views of Governments*

92. The Government of the Byelorussian SSR felt that there was need for a maximum mobilization of forces and strong measures at the international level to eradicate the policies and practices of racism, *apartheid*, colonialism and neo-colonialism, imperialist aggression, foreign occupation and the suppression of national liberation struggles.

93. In the opinion of the Government of the Libyan Arab Jamahiriya, strong political and economic sanctions should be imposed by the United Nations against racist régimes in southern Africa and those States which extended financial or moral assistance to such régimes. Policital and economic sanctions should likewise be inflicted to countries which assist zionism.

### B. *Replies of non-governmental organizations*

94. The World Federation of Trade Unions suggested that consideration should be given to sanctions against Governments which violated conventions and recommendations relating to human rights. Consideration might be given to the possibility, for example, of denying Governments which constantly violated fundamental human rights the right to vote or to speak, or at least, of establishing, by a decision of the General Assembly, a rule whereby countries accused of such violations could not be elected members of the various United Nations bodies dealing with human rights.

## XI. QUESTION OF THE ESTABLISHMENT OF A UNITED NATIONS HIGH COMMISSIONER FOR HUMAN RIGHTS OR SIMILAR MACHINERY

### A. *Debate at the thirtieth session of the General Assembly*

95. Some representatives stressed that, in their opinion, the authority of existing United Nations bodies could be most effectively strengthened by the establishment of a United Nations High Commissioner for Human Rights. As an independent authority, a High Commissioner could approach Governments directly with a view in particular to facilitating the settlement of disputes and encouraging the ratification of human rights conventions. In the view of these representatives, the activities of a High Commissioner for Human Rights would not constitute interference in domestic affairs, since violations of human rights were now considered a fully legitimate concern of the international community (see, for instance, A/C.3/SR.2169, p. 19).

96. Opposition to the proposal was restated by other representatives, on the grounds, *inter alia*, that it was based on the erroneous view according to which existing United Nations organs were not able to solve the problems concerning the international protection of human rights, and that the institution of a High Commissioner would lead to open or covert intervention in the domestic affairs of States. The representatives opposed to the proposal considered that the establishment of such a post would be contradictory to some of the basic principles of the Charter regarding international co-operation in promoting the observance of human rights (A/C.3/SR.2169, p. 17).

97. Different views were also expressed on the question of the establishment of regional commissioners for human rights. One representative

suggested the establishment of a board of five human rights commissioners - one from each regional group in the United Nations - composed of independent experts which might come under the authority of the General Assembly and whose primary functions would be to use their good offices for the settlement of problems in the field of human rights at the regional level and to work in close contact with the Commission on Human Rights and the Sub-Commission on Prevention of Discrimination and Protection of Minorities (A/C.3/SR.2168, p. 7). Another representative felt that a single High Commissioner for Human Rights could more appropriately be responsible for links between regional bodies and the United Nations (A/C.3/SR.2169, p. 22).

## B. *Views of Governments*

98. In the view of the Government of the Netherlands, there was a need for the United Nations to further develop effective contacts with Governments on human rights matters, without such contacts being prejudiced by political considerations. In this sense, the proposal transmitted by the Economic and Social Council in its resolution 1237 (XLII) concerning the establishment of an independent United Nations High Commissioner for Human Rights deserved positive attention and renewed active consideration. Alternatively, or in addition, the establishment of regional commissioners for human rights needed close consideration.

99. The Governments of the Federal Republic of Germany and the United Kingdom considered that the proposal to establish a High Commissioner's Office which, in their view, would constitute an important advance, should be given further consideration.

100. The Government of India stated that it was not in favour of the creation of a post of High Commissioner for Human Rights as it might pave the way for interference in the internal affairs of States. It reiterated its stand that the functions contemplated for the High Commissioner should rather be entrusted to the Secretary-General.

101. The Governments of the Ukrainian SSR and the USSR reiterated their strong opposition to the proposal to establish a High Commissioner's Office, an institution which, in their view, would be contrary to the United Nations Charter as it would openly or covertly interfere in the internal affairs of States.

102. In the opinion of the Government of Finland, the relevant General Assembly resolutions might be interpreted in such a way that, for the time being, there were no realistic possibilities of having a post of United Nations High Commissioner for Human Rights or any other new organ having similar legal functions established within the framework of the United Nations, no matter how useful such an organ might be. Thus, other workable solutions should be found to meet such a need.

### C. *Replies of non-governmental organizations*

103. The Baptist World Alliance suggested the creation of the proposed post of High Commissioner for Human Rights, with rank and status equivalent to that of the High Commissioner for Refugees. The creation of the post of High Commissioner for Human Rights was also supported by the International Union of Judges.

104. The Christian Democratic World Union suggested that the most practical way of carrying this proposal into effect would be to extend the competence of the existing Office of the High Commissioner for Refugees to human rights matters, having particularly in mind the fact that refugees were victims of the violation of human rights.

105. The World Union of Catholic Women's Organizations considered that if the appointment of a High Commissioner for Human Rights met with a certain degree of opposition, the establishment, within the framework of a High Commissioner's Office, of a small standing group of independent experts, with due regard for equitable geographical distribution, might perhaps gain more votes.

106. In the memorandum from 17 non-governmental organizations, the view was expressed that the proposal for a High Commissioner filled the need for an executive to deal with human rights violations independently of political considerations. This proposal would not be a threat to the sovereignty of States, but could be consistent with their own enlightened self-interest.

## XII. QUESTION OF THE ESTABLISHMENT OF REGIONAL ORGANS IN THE FIELD OF HUMAN RIGHTS

### A. *Debate at the thirtieth session of the General Assembly*

107. The view was expressed that it would be desirable for regional commissions on human rights based on regional conventions to be established on all continents, as had been the case in the Americas and Western Europe (A/C.3/SR.2168, pp. 7-8). Alternatively, it was suggested that the General Assembly could recommend the establishment within the United Nations system of regional human rights commissions similar to the regional economic commissions. In order to ensure the necessary harmonization of regional efforts under broad universal guidelines, appropriate links would have to be established between regional institutions and the competent United Nations bodies, in particular the Commission on Human Rights (A/C.3/SR.2168, p. 10). Reference was made to the recommendation of the United Nations seminar, held at Dar es Salaam in 1973, calling for the establishment of African regional machinery in the field of human rights.

### B. *Views of Governments*

108. The Government of Chile considered that regional systems for the protection of human rights should be established in geographical areas where there were none at present, or machinery should be set up for purposes of co-ordination between the United Nations and regional organizations where these existed. In the absence of regional machinery, there was a risk that certain aspects, which could be properly appreciated only be persons living in the same region, would not be taken into account. Moreover, the lack of co-ordinating machinery between the United Nations and regional bodies may result in contradictory decisions being taken by the two bodies. The Government of Chile claimed that such problems occurred, to its detriment, as regards the situation of human rights in its country. In its view, the General Assembly at its thirty-first session wrongly disregarded previous action taken by the competent regional organization, the Organization of American States.

109. The Government of the United Kingdom would particularly like to stress the value of developing regional machinery in areas where no such organs existed.

### C. *Replies of non-governmental organizations*

110. The World Union of Catholic Women's Organizations suggested that the establishment of complementary regional systems for the protection of human rights which would permit the particular conditions in each region to be taken into account could be beneficial provided that such regional systems were based on the principles in force within the United Nations and provided that relations were established between the regional institutions and the competent United Nations bodies, in particular, the Commission on Human Rights. Non-governmental organizations should have the right to be heard within those regional organs.

111. The International Union of Judges supported the proposal regarding the establishment of regional human rights commissions similar to the regional economic commissions.

## XIII. GOOD OFFICES OF THE SECRETARY-GENERAL

### A. *Debate at the thirtieth session of the General Assembly*

112. Great importance was attached to the role of the Secretary-General in promoting human rights through his good offices. His achievements in this field were appreciated and the hope was expressed that the Secretary-General, assisted in particular by the Division of Human Rights of the Secretariat, would continue to give high priority to such efforts (A/C.3/SR.2168, p. 6).

### B. *Views of Governments*

113. The Government of the Netherlands suggested that the good offices functions of the Secretary-General of the United Nations should be further developed and strengthened with a view to assisting in the resolutions of human rights problems and in the alleviation of human suffering. The Netherlands had this objective in mind when submitting at the twenty-seventh session of the General Assembly the draft resolution contained in document A/C.3/L.1932, to which attention was again drawn.

## XIV. STUDIES ON HUMAN RIGHTS

### A. *Debate at the thirtieth session of the General Assembly*

114. It was noted with interest that some non-governmental organizations in consultative status had suggested that the Sub-Commission on Prevention of Discrimination and Protection of Minorities should consider, as a subject for study, the existing relationship between the human rights provisions and Article 2, paragraph 7, of the Charter, with a view to establishing criteria under which violations of human rights could be considered as matters for legitimate international concern, and to ensuring that Member States did not, in any way, use that provision to avoid their responsibility to protect human rights (A/C.3/SR.2169, pp. 19-200).

### B. *Views of Governments*

115. The Government of India expressed support for the suggestion of the International Commission of Jurists regarding the establishment of an advisory body of experts to study the relationship between human rights and Article 2, paragraph 7, of the Charter of the United Nations, with a view to establishing criteria under which violations of human rights could be considered as matters for legitimate international concern.

116. The Governments of the Ukrainian SSR and the USSR suggested that greater prominence should be given by United Nations bodies to studying the positive influence on the promotion of human rights of measures adopted by States to strengthen international peace and security. At the same time, the negative consequences which arose for human rights when peace was violated, international tensions were created and policies of aggression, colonialism and racism were pursued should also be studied. In addition, consideration should be given to the influence on human rights of the continuation of the arms race and the development of new weapons of mass destruction and measures to limit and halt such trends. The positive significance of the measures adopted by States to check the arms race and bring out disarmament for the establishment of a situation in the world which would promote enjoyment of human rights and, above all, the right to live in peace and security, should be studied. Research should also be done on the relationship between the slowing down of the arms race and disarmament measures, on the one hand and human rights, on the other, from the standpoint of using the resources released

to promote the social and economic rights of the broad mass of workers. Another important task of United Nations bodies concerned with human rights was to study the existing relationship between active international economic co-operation among States on an equitable, equal and mutually advantageous basis, on the one hand, and increasing the efficiency of international co-operation in the sphere of human rights, on the other.

### C. *Replies of non-governmental organizations*

117. The International Federation of Resistance Movements suggested that the Sub-Commission should examine in depth the problem of the resurgence of nazism and fascism in a special study.

## XV. INFORMATION AND EDUCATION IN THE FIELD OF HUMAN RIGHTS

### A. *Debate at the thirtieth session of the General Assembly*

118. The view was expressed that efforts should be made to bring to the attention of a larger number of people the basic human rights instruments adopted by the United Nations, in particular by translating into all the major languages of the world the compilation of international instruments in the field of human rights.[1] Governments should be urged to ensure the dissemination of information on human rights and the United Nations should continue to promote exchange of experience and views on various important human rights issues, particularly through seminars under the advisory services programme (A/C.3/SR.2168, p. 11).

### B. *Views of Governments*

119. The Government of Finland believed that alerting public opinion against Governments hostile to human rights might bring about speedy results. Therefore, it suggested that a careful study should be made to determine how world public opinion could be most effectively mobilized in concrete cases.

120. In the opinion of the Government of the Netherlands, Governments and non-governmental organizations had an important role to play by means of information and education to make people aware of their human rights at all levels, in particular at the grass-roots level. The United Nations and the relevant specialized agencies should assist Governments and non-governmental organizations in carrying out this task by providing on a large scale basic and easily accessible information on internationally recognized human rights.

121. The Government of India felt that more emphasis should be placed

---

[1] *Human Rights: A Compilation of International Instruments*, (United Nations publication, Sales No. E.73.XIV.2); see also A/C.3/SR.2168, p. 11.

in schools and through the mass media on human rights matters. Student workshops should be organized for the teaching of international law with particular reference to human rights. Further studies, research and publications dealing with human rights should be encouraged.

### *C. Replies of non-governmental organizations*

122. The International Social Science Council believed that adequate teaching of the subject of human rights, based on an analysis of all available documents and international agreements, was likely to promote a better understanding of human rights and their implementation.

123. The International Federation of Women in Legal Careers suggested that it was essential to publicize, in particular through the mass media, the situation of victims of violations of human rights. Such publicity would tend to create world-wide solidarity with those victims, place obstacles in the way of financial assistance being provided to oppressive régimes and thus help to restore the effective enjoyment of human rights.

## XVI. CO-OPERATION WITH NON-GOVERNMENTAL ORGANIZATIONS

### *A. Debate at the thirtieth session of the General Assembly*

124. The view was expressed that the co-operation of non-governmental organizations was essential, in particular as regards the dissemination of information concerning human rights (A/C.3/SR.2169, p. 3).

### *B. Views of Governments*

125. The Government of Chile considered it important that the Economic and Social Council should take steps to ensure that certain non-governmental organizations in consultative status with it did not depart from the spirit, purposes and principles of the United Nations Charter, whose observance was a prerequisite for granting them consultative status in accordance with Council resolution 1296 (XLIV).

### *C. Replies of non-governmental organizations*

126. The International Federation of Resistance Movements suggested that still closer contacts should be established between the Commission on Human Rights and non-governmental organizations.

127. The World Federation of Trade Unions suggested in connexion with the procedures followed in the Economic and Social Council and in its various bodies (the Commission, the Sub-Commission and working groups dealing with human rights), that it would be necessary to adopt amendments to ensure the full participation of non-governmental organizations.

In particular, meetings should be public and documents reproducing the discussions on communications and recommendations should be published in full.

128. The Christian Democratic World Union suggested that specialized non-governmental organizations of an international character should be authorized by the competent United Nations organ to carry out missions of inquiry into alleged violations of human rights.

129. The memorandum from 17 non-governmental organizations stated that at every stage in the work of the United Nations in the field of human rights, non-governmental organizations have played an innovative, catalytic, and implementory role. Since the whole consultative relationship of non-governmental organizations with the Economic and Social Council was being reviewed, attention was called to the recommendations made by the Conference of Non-Governmental Organizations in Consultative Status with the United Nations Economic and Social Council.

## XVII. PROMOTION OF HUMAN RIGHTS THROUGH ADVISORY SERVICES

### *Replies of non-governmental organizations*

130. The Friends World Committee for Consultation recommended the strengthening and extension of the Programme of Advisory Services in the field of human rights, notably by the organization of more regional — and, where appropriate, international — seminars, to deal with such subjects as the rights of minorities, the treatment of offenders of all kinds and methods of combating terrorist activities.

## XVIII. ACTION OF SPECIALIZED AGENCIES

### A. *Debate at the thirtieth session of the General Assembly*

131. The opinion was expressed by several representatives that, in view of various factors, including the intensified work of the specialized agencies in the field of human rights, co-ordination of all relevant activities within the United Nations system was of increasing importance.

### B. *Reply from the International Labour Organisation*

132. The ILO drew attention to the means available to it for monitoring the observance of international standards in the field of human rights, investigating alleged violations and assisting in the elimination of problems. It referred to reports which it had previously presented to the United Nations.[2] The ILO stressed that, although special procedures

---

[2] Report on the organizational and procedural arrangements for the implementation of ILO Conventions and Recommendations (E.4144). Supplement to

have been established to deal with questions arising in certain fields, its arrangements for supervising the implementation of the Organisation's standards were of comprehensive scope. Thus, the obligation to submit Conventions and Recommendations to the competent national authorities for the enactment of legislation or other action applied to all such instruments adopted by the Conference. The systems of reporting on ratified Conventions, on unratified Conventions and on Recommendations were similarly of general application. So were the arrangements for checking compliance with the various obligations existing under or in relation to ILO instruments through the Committee of Experts on the Application of Conventions and Recommendations and the Conference Committee on the Application of Conventions and Recommendations. The procedure of direct contacts between member States and the Organisation made possible consideration, as desired by the Government concerned, of all questions relating to ILO Conventions and Recommendations. The constitutional procedures of representations and complaints of non-observance of ratified Conventions likewise applied to all such instruments. There was also close co-ordination between those different procedures.

133. All ILO implementation procedures had certain features in common: (a) the procedures were subject to safeguards of a quasi-judicial character: thus at certain levels, the examination of the situation was entrusted to bodies composed of independent members appointed on the proposal of the Director-General of the International Labour Office; (b) States were given every opportunity to make statements on the situation existing in their countries and to reply to any complaints which concerned them; (c) employers' and workers' organizations were closely associated in the procedures in question, both by their participation in the policy-making bodies of the ILO (Governing Body, Conference) and by the possibility afforded to them to make complaints or representations; and (d) the quasi-judicial stage and the political stage of the examination of cases formed a whole but were nevertheless clearly distinct one from the other.

134. There was a close interrelationship between the Organisation's standard-setting and technical co-operation activities. Technical co-operation was viewed as the means for working towards the attainment of ILO standards. It was in this spirit that the ILO had over the past six years developed the procedure of direct contacts with member States concerning the implementation of Conventions and Recommendations. This procedure made it possible to review, through discussions with Governments and consultation with employers' and workers' organizations,

---

the above report (A/6699/Add.1). Note on the effectiveness of ILO Conventions and Recommendations and the machinery for supervising their implementation (E/CN.4/1023/Add.1). Memoranda concerning ILO action against discrimination presented to the Sub-Commission on Prevention of Discrimination and Protection of Minorities (E/CN.4/Sub.2/239, para. 6, and E/CN.4/Sub.2/346, para. 9 — indications concerning the ILO procedure for special surveys on situations connected with the elimination of discrimination in employment).

problems which had arisen in the application of ratified Conventions or in regard to compliance with constitutional obligations relating to ILO instruments. The actual nature of the direct contacts may vary from a form of technical assistance provided by ILO officials in reviewing legislation or administrative practices to a form of fact finding and conciliation. At the final stage, the results of such contacts were evaluated by the competent supervisory bodies.

---

*CHAPTER 4*

# SOME SPECIAL CATEGORIES

The present Volume can best be completed by drawing attention to several related areas of human rights which might appear, amidst so many substantial issues, to have escaped general notice: such as the rights of youth in general and of 'conscientious objectors' in particular, as well as so-called 'religious' rights.

The two documents on "The Role of Youth" reproduced here complement each other in so far as the Report of the UN Advisory Group composed of younger people, held in July-August 1975 (E/CN.4/1241), is supplemented by the second document (E/CN.4/1223), containing an interesting variety of views submitted by governments outlining their national programmes, up to the end of 1976. The strong nationalistic emphasis reflected in some of these programmes will not go unnoticed by those who would themselves put most stress on the international character of human rights.

Nor can it be claimed that the related objectives of religious freedom and of conscientious objection, which, in separate ways, have been before the Human Rights Commission for some years, have made much progress in terms of global acceptance. A "draft declaration on the elimination of all forms of religious intolerance" (E/CN.4/1145), which is still under consideration by the Commission, is carried up to the end of 1975 by a General Assembly note (A/10148).

A short paper concludes this Chapter, relating the role of youth with the question of conscientious objection to military service (E/CN.4/NGO/

181), which was submitted to the Commission in 1974 on behalf of a number of NGO's.

UNITED NATIONS

# ECONOMIC AND SOCIAL COUNCIL

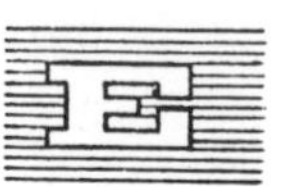

E/CN.4/1241
8 December 1976
Original: ENGLISH

COMMISSION ON HUMAN RIGHTS
Thirty-third session

## THE ROLE OF YOUTH IN THE PROMOTION AND PROTECTION OF HUMAN RIGHTS

## CHANNELS OF COMMUNICATION WITH YOUTH AND INTERNATIONAL YOUTH ORGANIZATIONS

*Report of the Ad Hoc Advisory Group on Youth on its third meeting at United Nations Headquarters from 21 July - 1 August 1975*

CONTENTS

D. Financing the Forum and its Administrative Secretariat

E. Intermediate Measures

V. DEVELOPMENT OF A COMPREHENSIVE UNITED NATIONS POLICY AND CO-ORDINATED PROGRAMMES TO MEET THE NEEDS AND ASPIRATIONS OF YOUTH

A. Principles for Meaningful and Substantial Participation of Young People

B. Need for a Comprehensive and Co-ordinated Policy throughout the United Nations System on the Needs and Aspirations of Youth

C. Organized Service by Youth, and United Nations Volunteers Programme

D. UNDP and National Channels of Communication

E. Regional Economic Commissions

F. Co-operative Arrangement among Youth Research and Information Centres

G. United Nations University

H. The International Youth Year

I. Unemployment and Underemployment of Youth

J. Health

VI. ADDITIONAL RECOMMENDATIONS

## LETTER OF TRANSMITTAL

Dear Mr. Secretary-General,

Herein we present you the report of the 1975 meeting of the *Ad Hoc* Advisory Group on Youth which was mandated, in the terms of General Assembly resolution 3022 (XXVII) and Economic and Social Council resolution 1842 (LVI):

> "to advise (you) on activities that should be undertaken by the United Nations to meet the needs and aspirations of youth."

We realize that we have come to the close of the three-year testing process of identifying and testing measures to *establish effective channels of communication* between the United Nations system, and youth and international youth organizations. Consequently, we recognise that our meeting marks the close of one major channel of communication with you.

Therefore, we have envisioned our present task as basically one of methodology and implementation formulation for previous *Ad Hoc* recommendations, particularly:

1. The establishment of a firmer and more representative structure that speaks with a confident mandate from young people themselves to carry on a two-way co-operative communication with you and the United Nations system.

2. The realization of the necessary prerequisite to adequate representation of youth, namely the promotion of conscious awareness of their human rights and responsibilities, the obvious lack of which in many countries has denied youth the benefits of participation and major channels of communication.

3. The achievement of substantial and meaningful participation by ensuring youth partnership in all the programming, implementation and evaluation stages of United Nations policies and programmes. Our point of departure from existing attitudes in the United Nations system is our call for programmes *with* youth as opposed to programmes for youth.

To ensure the commitment of the future generation it is necessary that the United Nations sincerely attempt to overcome the difficulties in actively implementing its principles, policies and programmes with member nations. We therefore hope that our report along with the previous two reports of your Ad Hoc Advisory Groups on Youth will be of assistance in this task and that you shall seriously consider all our previous and present recommendations when formulating your comments and recommendations.

We further realize that youth globally and you on behalf of the United Nations have been aspiring towards establishing adequate opportunities for a meaningful and representative youth participation, and we urge, at the close of our transitional mission, that you will find the ways and means for youth to substantially co-operate with the United Nations in developing a progressively better world for both old and young to share.

Yours sincerely,

Jon Alexander
Horacio Arguello
Nadia Atif
Marlo V. Buaron
Golie Jansen
Uzo Nwala
Patrick Ojong
Mihail Stoica
Uffe Torm

# I. INTRODUCTION

## A. *Background and Terms of Reference*

1. The General Assembly in resolution 2497 adopted on 28 October 1969, during its twenty-fourth session, asked the Secretary-General to report on "measures to be taken to establish channels of communication with youth and international youth organizations." Accordingly, the Secretary-General submitted his report (A/8743) to the General Assembly for consideration at its twenty-seventh session (1972). The report contained a review of the existing situation and suggestions on measures to improve channels of communication with youth and international youth organizations.

2. The General Assembly, on 18 December 1972, adopted resolution 3022 (XXVII) on channels of communication with youth and international youth organizations. It approved the recommendations of the Secretary-General to convene an *Ad Hoc* Advisory Group on Youth (henceforth referred to in this report as the "Advisory Group") and defined the functions of the Advisory Group as follows: "to advise him (the Secretary-General) on activities that should be undertaken by the United Nations to meet the needs and aspirations of youth."

3. The Advisory Group was to be part of a multi-faceted approach towards the establishment of effective channels of communication between the United Nations and youth and international youth organizations. The Advisory Group and other methods of communication referred to in General Assembly resolution 3022 (XXVII) are being tested during a three-year period ending in 1975. The General Assembly, at its thirtieth session in 1975, will consider proposals for longer term action in this area.

4. General Assembly resolution 3022 (XXVII) further requested the Secretary-General to transmit the conclusions and recommendations of the Advisory Group together with his comments, to the Economic and Social Council at its fifty-sixth session (Spring 1974), which was to consider, among other things, the continuation of the Group.

5. The Advisory Group held its first meeting at the United Nations Headquarters in New York from 20-28 August 1973. The ten members of the Group were: Nadia I. Atif (Egypt); Ovidiu Badina (Romania); Mamadou Diop (Mali); Richard J. Harmston (Canada); Anwar Ibrahim (Malaysia); Golie Jansen (Netherlands); Mnyeti Sinkutu Kabuaye (Tanzania); Janet McKoy (Jamaica); Ernesto Ottone (Chile) and Newton Perara (Sri Lanka). Representatives were present from the Food and Agriculture Organization of the United Nations, the International Labour Organisation, the United Nations Development Programme, the United Nations Educational, Scientific and Cultural Organization, the United Nations Fund for Population Activities, the United Nations Children's Fund, the World Health Organization, as well as from the Centre for Social Development and Humanitarian Affairs, the Division of Social Affairs in Geneva and the Division of Human Rights.

6. The report of the Advisory Group's first meeting (ESA/SDHA/AC.4/2)[1] was forwarded to the Secretary-General who then submitted his comments and recommendations (E/5427) to the fifty-sixth session of the Economic and Social Council (Spring 1974).

7. On 15 May 1974 the Economic and Social Council adopted resolution 1842 (LVI) in which it requested the Secretary-General:

(a) To transmit his report (E/5427) to Member States and interested international youth organizations in consultative status with the Economic and Social Council;

(b) To communicate the report of the Advisory Group along with his comments and recommendations to the Commission for Social Development, the Commission on Human Rights, the Commission on the Status of Women and the Population Commission for their consideration;

(c) To initiate consultation with research and information centres on youth at the national and regional levels regarding the feasibility of sharing their experience through a co-operative arrangement, and to report to its fifty-eighth session (Spring 1975).

8. In the same resolution the Council also

(a) recommended to the Commission for Social Development, the Commission on Human Rights and the Commission on the Status of Women the holding of international and regional meetings on youth issues and programmes ensuring youth participation;

(b) invited the Secretary-General to consider the feasibility of voluntary contributions to assist United Nations youth programmes, and to report to its fifty-eighth session (Spring 1975).

9. The Economic and Social Council further decided by resolution 1842 (LVI) to approve the recommendation of the Secretary-General that two additional meetings of the Advisory Group be convened in 1974 and in 1975, "in order to study further the problems mentioned in General Assembly resolution 3022 (XXVII) and in the report of the Secretary-General (E/5427)."

10. The Advisory Group, composed entirely of new members, held its second meeting at the United Nations Headquarters in New York from 16-25 September 1974. The ten members of the Group were: Jon Alexander (United Kingdom); David Asante (Ghana); Charles Fremes (Canada); Elham O. Khalil (Egypt); Patrick Ojong (Sierra Leone); Phouangphanh Sananikone (Laos); Mihail Stoica (Romania); Uffe Torm (Denmark); Gonzalo Torrico (Bolivia) and Ingrid Williams (St. Vincent).

---

[1] Which later became E/CN.5/508.

11. In attendance at different times were representatives from the Centre for Social Development and Humanitarian Affairs, from the Food and Agriculture Organization of the United Nations, the International Labour Organisation, the United Nations Development Programme, the United Nations Environment Programme, the United Nations Educational, Scientific and Cultural Organization, the United Nations Fund for Population Activities, the United Nations Children's Fund, the United Nations Volunteers, the World Health Organization, as well as the Disarmament Division and the Division of Human Rights. Each regional economic commission had been invited to send a representative, but none had been able to attend, primarily for financial reasons.

12. In January 1975 the Commission for Social Development, at its twenty-fourth session, referred to the work of the Advisory Group during its consideration of the item entitled "Youth Policies and Programmes". On the basis of the Commission's recommendations, the Economic and Social Council subsequently adopted at its fifty-eighth session resolution 1922 (LVIII) on the feasibility of voluntary contributions in support of United Nations youth programmes, and resolution 1923 (LVIII) on an international youth policy and on the feasibility of establishing a co-operative arrangement among youth research and information centres. The Governing Council of the United Nations Development Programme at its twentieth session in June 1975 endorsed Council resolution 1922 (LVIII).

13. The Advisory Group, composed of various members from its first and second meetings together with some new participants, held its third meeting at the United Nations Headquarters in New York from 21 July to 1 August 1975. In attendance were: Jon Alexander (United Kingdom); Horacio Arguello (Nicaragua); Nadia Atif (Egypt); Marlo V. Buaron (Philippines); Golie Jansen (Netherlands); Uzo Nwala (Nigeria); Patrick Ojong (Sierra Leone); Mihail Stoica (Romania) and Uffe Torm (Denmark). Two members were unable to attend: David Asante (Ghana) and Phousang Phanh Sananikone (Laos).

14. At various times representatives attended from the Centre for Social Development and Humanitarian Affairs, the Food and Agriculture Organization of the United Nations, the International Labour Organisation, the United Nations Development Programme, the United Nations Educational, Scientific and Cultural Organization, the United Nations Volunteers, the World Health Organization, the Division of Human Rights, the Liaison Office for the United Nations University, the Liaison Office for the regional economic commissions and the Economic Commission for Africa and the Economic and Social Commission for Asia and the Pacific.

## B. *Adoption of Agenda, and Methods of Work*

15. The following agenda was adopted unanimously:

A. Welcome

B. Election of Officers

C. Adoption of the Agenda

D. Review of the youth policies and programmes of the United Nations and its specialized agencies.

E. (1) Implementative progress following the reports of the 1973 and 1974 meetings of the *Ad Hoc* Advisory Group on Youth

(2) Purpose and functions of the 1975 meeting of the *Ad Hoc* Advisory Group on Youth.

F. Development of a comprehensive United Nations policy to meet needs and aspirations of youth.

G. Activities of the United Nations to promote *meaningful and substantial participation* of youth in national development.

H. Development of a representative forum for consultation between the United Nations and youth and international youth organizations.

I. Consideration and adoption of the report.

J. Miscellaneous issues

16. To ensure the greatest representation of the Group, a rotating moderator was elected daily, and three of its members to act as co-rapporteurs who were assisted by a technical secretary from the United Nations Secretariat.

17. A number of background documents prepared by the United Nations relating to the items of the agenda were made available to the Group, who sought additional information from the representatives of the United Nations and the specialized agencies.

18. The meeting was officially opened, on behalf of the Secretary-General, by Mr. Emmanuel Keukjian (Assistant Director for Planning and Evaluation, Social Development Division).

19. At our request, the Advisory Group was officially received by Mr. Rafeeuddin Ahmed, Executive Assistant to the Secretary-General, on behalf of the Secretary-General in pursuance of our objective to exchange views on youth through a two-way communication channel.

### C. *Status and Distribution of Advisory Group Reports*

20. The report of the first meeting of the Advisory Group had been communicated to the functional commissions of the Economic and Social Council, in accordance with Economic and Social Council resolution 1842 at its fifty-sixth session, and was also available in three languages for wider distribution.

21. However, the report of the second meeting was only available in English, and had not been circulated to either functional commissions or to Member States. In view of the wide range of substantive recommendations contained in the report of the 1974 meeting in the areas of competence of many parts of the United Nations, we cannot over-emphasize the importance of making the report available to the functional commissions and Member States. We would also stress the need to involve the widest range of youth organizations in the on-going dialogue on these issues, at the national, regional and global levels. It is therefore essential that the report of the second meeting of the Advisory Group be made available in at least three languages.

22. Similar considerations would also apply to the report of the third meeting of the Advisory Group, particularly the wide distribution of the report prior to the deliberations of the coming General Assembly meeting.

## II. ASSESSMENT OF CURRENT REVIEW OF CHANNELS OF COMMUNICATION BETWEEN THE UNITED NATIONS, YOUTH AND YOUTH ORGANIZATIONS

23. We considered in detail the current three-year review within the United Nations on channels of communication between the United Nations and youth and youth organizations, of which our Group is a part. In so doing we paid attention to developments relating to existing channels such as the increase in number of youth organizations in consultative status with the Economic and Social Council, and the activities of informal groupings of youth organizations. Attention was also given to the relative cost and representativeness of the different existing channels and their respective potentials, such as their ability and willingness to make contacts, and their capacity to substantially develop their process of consultation.

24. We noted a number of positive developments, particularly on the part of youth organizations in substantially increasing their relations with major parts of the United Nations system, the expansion of participation and programmes under the auspices of the Geneva Informal Meetings of International Youth Non-governmental Organizations, the activities of the United Nations Headquarters Non-governmental Organizations Youth Caucus, and the wider and more substantive use of consultative status with the Economic and Social Council (paras. 59-60).

25. We also noted, from the Group's collective experience over three years, that the complexity of the United Nations system in its present form makes it extraordinarily difficult for any youth organization, even one that is international and has considerable resources at its disposal, to conduct any kind of meaningful and substantive dialogue with the United Nations system as a whole, or even any specific part of it. This is partially a question of structure and procedure, but in our view it is usually a matter of institutional and individual attitudes.

26. On the basis of concrete experiences, we are therefore compelled to reiterate the conclusion arrived at by members of the second meeting that:

> "no part of the United Nations system enables young people or youth organizations to participate meaningfully and substantially in the formulation and implementation of policy, or the planning, execution and evaluation of projects relevant to young people to the extent which their potential contribution warrants." (para. 60).

27. In fact, in two areas where substantive issues related to the question of greater youth participation have been under discussion within the Secretariat during the past year, we have to conclude that the concept of effective consultation has often been ignored by the Secretariat. This has led to an increased sense of alienation among those youth organizations which have the greatest interest in identifying concrete

ways in which they can work with the United Nations at a substantive policy and programme level.

28. The first of these areas was the question of "the feasibility of voluntary contributions in support of United Nations youth programmes" (E/CN.5/502). This is a matter of central importance to the channels of communication issue because progress in this area depends largely on the amount of funding available. Furthermore, it was specifically linked by the Secretary-General to "the long-term actions that the General Assembly may decide upon at its thirtieth session for strengthening channels of communication with youth and international youth organizations" (para. 16)

29. Undoubtedly, adequate timing is a prerequisite for enabling substantial consultation to take place. Yet the first indication which youth organizations received, primarily those in consultative status with the Economic and Social Council, that such funds should be provided from the United Nations Volunteers programme's Special Voluntary Fund and that the issue should be linked to the widening of the United Nations Volunteers mandate to include domestic voluntary service and other pilot projects, was in November 1974. Shortly afterwards in January 1975 a draft resolution to that effect emerged at the twenty-fourth session of the Commission for Social Development. Obviously meaningful and substantial consultation could not have taken place in such a short period between November 1974 and January 1975. In addition, the resolution was subsequently adopted by the Economic and Social Council (E/RES/1922 (LVIII) and endorsed by the Governing Council of the United Nations Development Programme without adequate prior consultations with youth.

30. In our view therefore the process of consultation with youth organizations, let alone collective groupings of youth organizations, was perfunctory and did not permit a co-operative in-depth examination of the issues involved. Nor is there a simple reference to the participation of youth or youth organizations in the planning, implementation or evaluation of programmes as envisioned in the resolution. Furthermore, and rather importantly, the designation of the United Nations Volunteers as the "*principal** operational unit of the United Nations for the execution of youth programmes" implies, in practice since the United Nations Volunteers' mandate mainly concerns development, an exclusion of programmes with youth in other areas of concern, including the needed dissemination of information about the United Nations and its ideals.

31. On such an important issue consultation was crucial and sadly neglected. The decision offered as a *fait accompli* undoubtedly resulted in a marked disappointment particularly by 15 major youth organi tions of varied interests and orientations (see para. 99). We fear that it appears evident that the only provision for youth participation is as cheap labour to implement projects previously designed, supervized and evaluated without their further participation.

---

* Our emphasis.

32. We therefore conclude, should this be typical of the results which follow our three-year testing period, that we undoubtedly have been utilizing valuable resources that could have been more functionally channelled into assuring, for at least eight years more at current cost level, the continued financing of a major channel such as the Geneva Informal Meetings of International Youth Non-governmental Organizations in order that they become more representative and substantially involved in meaningful communication with the United Nations.

33. The second area is in programmes regarding youth and population. This is an area in which not only is there a crucial necessity to involve young people effectively because of the relation between the average period of maximum fertility and population growth, but it is also an area in which many youth organizations have been very active at the national, regional and international levels, both in co-operation with the United Nations system and in other ways.

34. It was therefore with considerable disappointment that we learned that the joint project of the United Nations Social Development Division and the United Nations Fund for Population Activities to define guidelines for future assistance to activities of national and international youth organizations did not invite youth participation in suggesting the guidelines for such an important project.

35. We consider the participation of youth, presently envisioned in the execution of the project, as being too narrow and restrictive by mainly involving youth in the completion of questionnaires about projects undertaken by organizations and routine bilateral discussions either at the field level about specific projects or at the headquarters of individual organizations, as well as visits to established field projects.

36. We therefore strongly RECOMMEND that national and international youth organizations be enabled a more active participation in the development of the suggested guidelines to ensure its relevance to realities faced by young people globally as they see and experience them. Particularly involvement should be encouraged in the evaluation of the information collected at the field level during the initial one-year stage of the project to assure the implementative success of the second three-year stage of the project.

## III. REVIEW ON IMPLEMENTATION OF PREVIOUS ADVISORY GROUP RECOMMENDATIONS ON UNITED NATIONS YOUTH POLICIES AND PROGRAMMES

37. We reviewed in detail all the recommendations made by the previous Advisory Group meetings in order to assess the degree of implementation, especially where they referred to United Nations youth policies and programmes.

38. It should be noted that we clearly differentiated between recommendations endorsing previous United Nations considerations and resolutions, and those recommendations that were unique and hence specific to the Advisory Groups themselves.

39. In the case of recommendations endorsing previous United Nations policies and programmes we realized that progress could not be measured in terms of implementation as youth understand meaningful progress to be, but rather in terms of further references and resolutions within the United Nations system.

40. For example, regarding recommendations of Advisory Groups endorsing previous United Nations considerations and resolutions, we noted that a number of them had been commended by the Secretary-General to the Economic and Social Council and to the Commission for Social Development. Furthermore, only some pertaining to the first Advisory Group were referred by the Economic and Social Council to appropriate functional commissions. However, too few of the functional commissions had reached a decision on issues referred to them from the first Advisory Group. Furthermore, in the case of many concrete recommendations of the second Advisory Group, none have been referred to appropriate organs for further decisions .

41. Regarding the specific recommendations unique to the Advisory Groups, we noted that although some had been taken into consideration the major thrust of our recommendations to meaningfully and substantially involve youth at all levels had not been taken into account. In short, we observed that no deliberate effort had been made by the United Nations system to involve youth in the planning, programming, implementation, review and evaluation of its policies and programmes as specifically recommended by the Advisory Groups. Consequently, where there had been discussion of a recommendation within the Secretariat, for example on the future role of the United Nations Volunteers programme, the process of meaningful consultation and involvement of young people and youth organizations, the main objective throughout all our work, had been conspicuously absent. In addition, many of our recommendations have not received adequate or any attention until this date. These recommendations are contained in paragraphs 25, 66c, 67a and b, 76 and 92 of the first report, and paragraphs 104, 105, 114c and 142 of the second report and deal with such issues as dissemination of information, disarmament, human rights, women, health and adequate youth representation at United Nations meetings.

42. In short, our review of implementative progress of our earlier recommendations on United Nations policies and programmes reaffirms the crucial necessity for the United Nations to develop procedures and mechanisms for the meaningful and substantial participation of youth in programme planning, implementation and evaluation on youth-related issues at all levels. Anything short of that connotes a paternalistic tokenism, *on* or *for* youth, which merely serves to further alienate young people from the United Nations system and maintain their current marginal status in the world community of which they are an integral part.

43. We therefore strongly restate our previous RECOMMENDATION that United Nations youth policies and programmes be developed *with* youth at *all* stages of their formulation, implementation and evaluation.

44. Furthermore, we RECOMMEND that every effort should be made to evolve *procedures* and *mechanisms* which facilitate joint programme planning, joint implementation and joint evaluation, so that the substantive potential of meaningful and substantial participation by youth may be achieved.

45. To facilitate the above necessary United Nations procedures and mechanisms we would wish to RECOMMEND as a first stage the following areas for immediate action:

(a) The establishment of co-production between the Centre for Economic and Social Information and youth and youth organizations, particularly at the national and local levels.

(b) That International Youth Non-governmental Organizations and all other interested youth groups be enabled a close consultation and collaboration on United Nations youth employment policies and procedures.

(c) That the United Nations and its specialized agencies encourage Member States to include at least one young person from a representative national youth non-governmental organization in their national delegations to United Nations governing bodies meetings.

(d) That the United Nations include youth participants at meetings dealing with co-ordination of United Nations policies and programmes.

(e) That there be close collaboration with youth and youth non-governmental organizations on the preparation of regional meetings, with special emphasis on the composition of delegations, selection of participants, agenda and conference management to assure their resulting in action plans, as well as close collaboration on the preparation, implementation and evaluation of regional and national trainers programmes and workshops.

(f) That a separate Voluntary Youth Fund, other than that of the United Nations Volunteers, be seriously investigated to enable the establishment of all the varied youth activities and representation of youth concerns on all levels in areas other than development. Youth NGOs could play a major role in the raising of such a Fund as was the case with the International Youth Population Conference.

46. The above conclusions underline the need for permanent channels of communication of a representative nature between the United Nations and youth organizations at all levels so that the views of youth on United Nations policies and programmes can be obtained and the modalities of *meaningful and substantial participation* by youth can be developed on a long-term basis. There is some evidence that those members of the United Nations system who have worked most closely with youth organizations and young people have some, even if limited, understanding of the potential and means of effectively involving young people in this way, but this is often not the case with member Governments of the United Nations and the decision-making bodies of the United Nations system. Considerable efforts and resources will be required before that potential is realized to any significant degree.

47. One clear and concrete example of the failure to realize this potential is the United Nations University. Despite the close involvement of a number of youth organizations throughout the preparatory work before it was established by General Assembly resolution 2951 (XXVII), despite the fact that its Charter (Article IV 1) stipulates that its Council should include "appropriate representation of young scholars", despite the fact that nominations for young scholars be considered for appointment to the Council were sought and received from youth organizations and others, despite representations by our earlier meetings and other groupings of youth organizations, the Council was appointed without a single young scholar.

48. Keeping in mind the Charter stipulation that "the University shall devote its work to research into the pressing global problems of human survival, development and welfare that are the concern of the United Nations and its agencies" and undoubtedly the concern of any integral member of society be they old, young, male or female; and keeping in mind that this can only be achieved by "the generation of new ideas" which constitutes one of the central functions of the University as stated by the Secretary-General in his address to the United Nations University Council in May 1974; and further recalling that all the above is in pursuance to one of the major rationale given for the establishment of the University as quoted from Sir Robert Jackson in a United Nations University summary prepared for the United States Committee for the United Nations University, August 1973, the rationale being to create a Brains Trust for "launching new ideas and methods, challenging established practices, and provoking thought inside and outside the system", we fail to understand how such creative and youthful objectives could be achieved by the election of 24 predominantly elderly male members (only one female) whose top-ranking occupational positions represent the traditional status quo and often obsolete systems which the

University purports to change, and whose educational backgrounds are seeped in traditional systems predating the fifties when it is commonly believed that innovative cognative orientation as well as contributive involvement in the new economic and social order is evident in the educational systems which emerged in the sixties.

49. It is our firm belief that one can hardly expect the infusion of catalytic policies and innovative programmes, the very target of such a University, to emanate from such a make-up of Council members, not to mention that the fears, initially expressed by many member Governments, of creating yet another traditional bureaucracy is imminent.

50. We agree that sex and age are not major criteria for membership to the Council but surely invigorating and creative youthful attitudes should be. Specifically when Universities world-wide have recognized the urgent need to involve the younger sectors of their academic community in the management of that community, and where there is, as in the case of the United Nations University, explicit Charter provisions for such representation to achieve objective alluded to above, we cannot but totally fail to understand the inability and unwillingness to implement that provision.

51. This is further underscored by the fact that the agenda for the next Council meeting to be held in Caracas, Venezuela in January 1976 includes an item on "The Association of Young Scholars with the Work of the United Nations University", and yet no attempt has been made to secure the representative participation of youth at such a crucial decision-making meeting.

52. In addition, since the full number of Council members has already been elected and will not undergo any major change until 1977, this can only imply a secondary status for youth which does not conform to the Charter stipulation. Nor is there any clear indication that young scholars will be involved in the substantial process of developing innovative research projects on issues of global concern, which is the University's *raison d'être* among the dozen or so other research centres attached to the United Nations system. Furthermore, no attempt has been made to have young people participate in the meetings of the working groups scheduled in Tokyo in October 1975. We therefore wish to draw attention to our substantive recommendations relating to the United Nations University contained elsewhere in this report.

# IV. DEVELOPMENT OF A REPRESENTATIVE FORUM FOR CONSULTATION BETWEEN THE UNITED NATIONS AND YOUTH AND INTERNATIONAL YOUTH ORGANIZATIONS

## A. *Introduction*

53. Throughout the three-year review of channels of communication one of our recurrent concerns has been the development of existing machinery to include the Geneva Informal Meetings of IYNGOs, the United Nations Headquarters NGO Youth Caucus, youth organizations in consultative status with ECOSOC, and regional and national youth on a more permanent and representative basis. In particular the second meeting of the Advisory Group devoted considerable attention to this question (see paragraphs 165-173 of the report). We therefore endorse its conclusion and strongly RECOMMEND that there is no need for any new machinery. However, wider participation should be promoted within the existing machinery, especially from the less-developed regions and youth on the local level.

54. The primary basis for the Advisory Group's concern was that the best means be found for continuing and developing the substantive contributions which young people can make to the development process, through their involvement in programmes at the national, regional and international levels.

55. As a continuation of the role of the Advisory Group we fully recognized the need to entrust the on-going and important task of maintaining and improving the dialogue with the United Nations system on all matters of relevance to youth to a more permanent and representative machinery involving youth organizations.

56. This is in keeping with the views expressed by the Secretary-General in his report on the second meeting of the Advisory Group (E/CN.5/520). In his report the Secretary-General, having referred to the proposals made by the second Advisory Group, went on to recommend that at its third meeting "the Advisory Group concentrate its attention on possible long-term channels of communication with youth" (para. 16). The Commission for Social Development at its twenty-fourth session also recognized the useful role the Advisory Group could play in this respect.

## B. *Need for, and functions of, representative international youth forum*

57. Governments and young people globally have become increasingly aware that real progress can only be achieved when meaningful and substantial participation of youth in development and other issues such as disarmament, security and *apartheid* is assured. However, the crucial prerequisite to such a representative participation is the establishment of the much needed *two-way channels of communication* at the national, regional and international levels.

58. We have worked to identify the simplest, most effective and least expensive mechanism at the global level through which a substantive dialogue between the United Nations and young people can be channelled, as a development of existing experience and structures.

59. We have noted, for example, that the Geneva Informal Meeting of International Youth Non-governmental Organizations has recently widened its participation to include the six most representative regional youth non-governmental organizations from Africa, Asia and Latin America, and has been in contact with the newly-formed Arab Youth Federation. Following the International Youth Population Conference, its programme activities have also been extended, and it has funded in developing countries 20 projects in the field of development and population, ranging from regional training workshops to rural health education programmes carried out by young people, and is planning a Working Party on Youth and Environment.

60. Similarly we noted the work of the United Nations Headquarters Non-governmental Organizations Youth Caucus in the field of environment where a workshop on Human Settlements was held following its survey of youth activities in the environmental field. Also noted was their continued publication of a Directory of Youth Internships within the United Nations, its specialized agencies and non-governmental organizations, and their consultation with United Nations University Council members and Rector regarding youth participation in the work of the University.

61. We have also noted that useful work was being undertaken by other "ad hoc" groupings of young people or youth organizations such as UNESCO's Youth Advisory Group, and that progress was being made towards the establishment of a Youth Advisory Group to the Executive Secretary of ESCAP.

62. Furthermore, in accordance with the recommendation made by the Advisory Group at its second meeting (paragraph 127c) we recognized the desire and ability of youth to follow up and act upon recommendations made by youth groups, as evidenced by the United Nations Headquarters Non-governmental Organizations Youth Caucus and the Geneva Informal Meetings who had initiated discussions continuing to this day on recommended youth issues. However, it should be noted that the task for the participants of the Geneval Informal Meetings was not facilitated by the fact that the second report was available only in the English language.

63. On the basis of all these developments, we concluded:

(a) That it was now paramount to facilitate the substantial involvement of young people in United Nations youth programmes by developing the existing mechanisms (see para. 53) into a more representative global youth forum on all United Nations youth related issues with officially recognized links to the General Assembly and the United Nations Secretariat.

(b) That unless and until a permanent and representative channel of communication at a level of substance was provided, which would include a minimal administrative secretariat, little would be achieved in significantly furthering the development of programmes of many youth organizations, national, regional and international, in areas of concern to the United Nations and to youth.

(c) That there had been considerable progress in the Geneva Informal Meeting of International Youth Non-governmental Organizations, both in extending its representativeness expecially in developing regions, and in enlarging its programme of activities especially in the area of development.

(d) That the ideas formulated by the Advisory Group should be the basis of wide-ranging consultations among all interested youth organizations, and within the United Nations Secretariat.

64. In detailing the functions of such a forum, we felt that they might include the following:

(a) To provide a major but not exclusive two-way channel for information on United Nations youth programmes and United Nations affairs generally, and for the views of youth on such programmes and on the needs and aspirations of youth.

(b) To review continuously the meaningful participation of youth in all areas of concern to the United Nations, with a view to updating policy and improving programme implementation.

(c) To mobilize human and material resources for development.

(d) To initiate/co-ordinate studies by youth organizations on issues/needs specifically related to youth.

(e) To disseminate documentation and information on United Nations issues and events to youth organizations.

(f) To organize occasional regional and international meetings and workshops of young people on issues of major concern to them.

(g) To co-ordinate the work of forum representatives attached to different parts of the United Nations system.

(h) To direct the work of the forum's administrative secretariat.

65. The composition of such a global forum should be based on organizations of youth, and should develop out of existing machinery as envisioned in paragraph 53 with priority given to participation by representative organizations from the developing regions. It should represent the widest spectrum of interests and orientations and consideration should be given to the most effective means of involving national youth organizations and 'ad hoc' youth action groups.

66. It therefore was RECOMMENDED that a Register of all interested national youth organizations be developed, all of whom would receive information about the work of the forum and be entitled to attend its meetings.

67. We felt that although the forum might usually meet three times per year in a place which facilitated contact with the United Nations system at the least cost, the possibility of holding occasional meetings in the different regions of the world should be investigated.

68. In addition, we strongly RECOMMEND that any representative global channel of communication between the United Nations and youth have both an officially recognized status with the Secretary-General's office and the right to relate directly (through brief written statements on youth issues) to the General Assembly which as the United Nations' sovereign organ is the only one which deals with all matters relevant to youth. The urgent implementation of our recommendation is essential to ensure that the potential of meaningful youth participation in the work of the United Nations be fully realized.

69. We would emphasize that we regard the recommended global youth forum as a necessary development of existing mechanisms, and supplementary to bilateral channels of communication between the United Nations and individual international and regional youth organizations (through consultative status with the Economic and Social Council). However, the establishment of such a forum should not preclude, but rather promote, other means of consulting unorganized youth.

70. In this respect, we noted that there was a growing interest among international youth organizations in developing a substantial involvement with issues of concern to the United Nations system, but that the details of the provision for non-governmental organizations to obtain consultative status with the Economic and Social Council and the procedures connected to it are relatively unknown.

71. We therefore RECOMMEND that the United Nations Secretariat produce a simple leaflet outlining the basis of the consultative relationship with non-governmental organizations and the procedure for intervening before the Economic and Social Council and its subsidiary organs, and give it the widest distribution.

### C. *Need for, and functions of, forum's administrative secretariat*

72. Experience has shown that with the Geneva Informal Meetings and the New York Headquarters Youth Caucus that it is not possible to undertake all the tasks effectively and to maintain the necessary degree of continuity, when this has to be combined with the normal workloads of the representatives of the participating organizations, which inevitably demand an element of priority. This would be even more the case, if the expanded functions of the forum are to be realized at the substantial level which is desired.

73. Urgent need therefore instigates us to strongly RECOMMEND the establishment of a minimal administrative secretariat, under the direction of the forum, at a location to be determined by the forum, perhaps com-

posed of five people initially, drawn on a rotating basis from organizations participating in the forum, with due attention paid to geographical, political and sex representation.

74. We further RECOMMEND that there be the closest co-operation between such a secretariat and all youth groups and organizations, especially those linked to different parts of the United Nations system, including United Nations Headquarters, the specialized agencies, and the regional economic commissions.

75. We felt that the functions of such an administrative secretariat of the forum might include:

(a) Maintaining regular contact with the United Nations Secretariat at a substantive level on programmes and issues related to youth.

(b) Facilitating contact between the United Nations and youth organizations especially at the national level.

(c) Preparing for meetings organized by the forum.

(d) Disseminating information on innovative projects executed by young people.

(e) Fulfilling mandates of forum in respect of studies on issues and needs related to youth, documentation and information on United Nations issues and events, co-ordination, etc.

## D. *Financing the forum and its administrative secretariat*

76. Initial estimates for the forum and its administrative secretariat, based on three meetings annually of the forum, and a five-person secretariat, total $90,000 per year. This sum was drawn up after a thorough study of a detailed budget by the Advisory Group and includes $60,000 for personnel costs, $20,000 for travel of participants, $10,000 for office administration. In addition to the estimated $90,000 there will be a need for an initial amount of $10,000 to cover capital expenditures on office machinery. Our estimated budget may be placed in a clearer perspective when compared with the $1 million cost of the World Youth Assembly in 1970, and the current level of $4,500 per annum provided from the World Youth Assembly surplus funds to cover travel of representatives of international youth non-governmental organizations not based in Geneva to attend the sessions of the Geneva Informal Meetings.

77. In the light of the very limited funds available to most youth organizations, and the difficulties in arranging financing for the forum directly from Governments, it is clear to us that we must RECOMMEND that the major portion of the funds, at least in the initial stages, should come from the United Nations, though we would anticipate that each participating organization make a financial contribution to the forum, and that all other sources would be investigated.

78. We are aware that the provision of funds for such a forum and secretariat from the regular budget may not easily fit existing regulations and financial procedures within the United Nations. But we do not consider this to be the fundamental question - it is more a matter of determining whether the need for such machinery is justified. If the substantive case for such a forum and secretariat is accepted, we are confident that the means to fund it, at least for an experimental period, will be found. We therefore RECOMMEND that this question be examined in detail jointly by the United Nations Secretariat and all interested youth organizations.

E. *Intermediate measures*

79. In view of the need for further discussion and consultation, both within the United Nations and among youth organizations, on the functions and structure of the proposed forum and its secretariat, as a means of continuing the two-way traffic of information and ideas between the United Nations and youth and to realize the full potential of youth participation in United Nations youth policies and programmes on a long-term and representative basis, and in view of the need to secure the continuation of the dialogue in the interim, we make the following RECOMMENDATIONS:

(a) That the Secretary-General be invited to conduct a feasibility study on the functions, structure and costs of the proposed forum and its administrative secretariat including the officially recognized links with the Secretariat and the General Assembly in the closest consultation with interested youth organizations presenting it to the Commission for Social Development at its twenty-fifth session and to the Economic and Social Council at its sixty-second session.

(b) That in the meantime the Geneva Informal Meeting of International Youth Non-Governmental Organizations be recognized as one of the major channels of communication between the United Nations, youth and international youth organizations, and be consulted on all questions relating to United Nations youth policies and programmes.

(c) That sufficient funding be continued by the United Nations through 1976-1977 to maintain assistance for the travel of representatives attending the Geneva Informal Meeting from organizations based outside Geneva, especially those from developing countries and including the United Nations Headquarters NGO Youth Caucus. The estimated sum involved, based on previous experiences, would be $10,000 per year for three meetings.

(d) That the Secretariat promote the involvement of regional youth organizations from the developing regions in all questions relating to United Nations youth policies and programmes, including the development of consultative relations with the Economic and Social Council and regional economic commissions.

(e) That the Secretariat continue to facilitate the work of the United Nations Headquarters NGO Youth Caucus, as a New York focus for youth participation related to United Nations Headquarters, with special attention to increasing the representativeness of its participation and the co-ordination of its activities with those of the Geneva Informal Meetings.

## V. DEVELOPMENT OF A COMPREHENSIVE UNITED NATIONS POLICY AND CO-ORDINATED PROGRAMMES TO MEET THE NEEDS AND ASPIRATIONS OF YOUTH

### A. *Principles for Meaningful and Substantial Participation of Young People*

80. As was emphasized in our previous reports, the key to any effective mobilization of young people for development, or on any other issue related to them, is the opportunity to *participate meaningfully and substantially* in all stages of the process, namely in the definition of needs, in the planning and implementation of projects, and in the evaluation of progress.

81. We have observed that very often United Nations and governmental programming *on* or *for* youth regards youth as an object, the passive recipient of the results of development programmes. However, we believe that contemporary issues demand the practice of a more constructive and imaginative approach since youth is an integral sector of society and as such can be an *active agent* of development. We therefore RECOMMEND that maximum opportunity for substantial and direct participation in all aspects of development in their community be offered to youth.

82. We further RECOMMEND that it is vital, as a part of this process, that the following principles be observed:

(a) the right to self-determination;

(b) the right to organize in associations of young people;

(c) the right for all, including young people, to participate meaningfully and substantially in their community's policies and programmes.

83. We also feel that in a world characterized by injustice and exploitation, participation must not be limited to remedial work on current situations or the endorsement of existing systems. A critical approach to the status quo can be a healthy and positive feature of youth activity. Consequently, in order that conditions for social justice be created, we RECOMMEND that young people be fully involved in the process of revising policies and updating programmes.

84. We attach priority to the development of effective opportunities for participation by young people at the national and regional levels and we RECOMMEND that the primary area for such participation should be economic, social and cultural development but that this should not lead to a neglect of other global issues of concern to young people, such as disarmament, security, *apartheid* and colonialism.

B. *Need for a Comprehensive and Co-ordinated Policy throughout the United Nations System on the Needs and Aspirations of Youth*

85. We have noted that the General Assembly in resolution 3140 (XXVIII) of 14 December 1973 requested the Economic and Social Council "to invite the Commission for Social Development to study the possibility of re-defining an international policy concerning the involvement of youth at the national and international levels, including the advisability of an international document on youth, taking into consideration, *inter alia*, relevant provisions contained in existing documents and the views expressed by the Governments of Member States and by interested non-governmental organizations in consultative status with the Council." (para. 4)

86. At its twenty-fourth session the Commission for Social Development considered this matter on the basis of a note by the Secretary-General (E/CN.5/501), which reported that, following consultations with Governments and non-governmental organizations in consultative status with the Council:

(a) "A clear preference emerged in the replies* for activities in which young people are the agents of change and development rather than being simply the beneficiaries of development." (para. 15)

(b) "Most replies (on the advisability of an international document on youth) expressed doubts as to the value and usefulness of a general document on youth and stated that implementation of existing instruments and declarations concerning youth involvement would be more important than the formulation of a new general document on the subject." (para. 18)

87. The Secretary-General concluded that "any new document on this subject should deal with the creation of specific opportunities for youth participation in development rather than with broad principles."

88. A number of divergent views were expressed on this matter during the twenty-fourth session of the Commission for Social Development that proposed a resolution subsequently adopted by the Economic and Social Council in which the Council "requests the Secretary-General to study the feasibility of incorporating the principle contained in the preceding paragraph ('the principle of creating specific opportunities for youth to participate in development at the national and international levels') in a possible international document, setting out practical modalities for involving youth in development activities." (E/RES/1923 (LVIII), para. 2). The Secretary-General's study will be considered by the Commission for Social Development at its twenty-fifth session in November 1976 and then submitted to the Economic and Social Council at its sixty-second session (Spring 1977).

---

* Replies on the subject were received from 21 Governments and 11 non-governmental organizations.

89. We have doubts as to the valid need for the document as envisioned in the Secretary-General's note (E/CN.5/501), to deal with general principles of youth involvement, rights and responsibilities and guidelines for practical modalities. We feel strongly that various principles have already been stated, some experiences already exist in many countries, and therefore it is now essential that the United Nations and Governments *implement* their declarations in their country level programmes.

90. However, we strongly RECOMMEND the drawing up of a comprehensive and co-ordinated policy stating the needs and aspirations of youth which would bring together, amplify and update the various separate elements of existing policies and principles, and which would include the recommendations of the three Advisory Groups especially on issues other than development.

91. Furthermore, this task should not be restricted to the United Nations alone, but should be prepared in the closest collaboration with the specialized agencies and youth organizations. It is essential that interested youth organizations be involved in any such process, and it should be based on the principle of the fullest participation of youth at all levels.

92. In addition we strongly RECOMMEND that the document be envisioned as a device for drawing attention to member Governments to issues concerning youth and more importantly as a device for action by specifically spelling out modes for the implementation of the stated broad principles. We cannot overemphasize our unanimous opinion that an international document would remain meaninglessly ineffective unless implemented at the local level.

93. We would therefore RECOMMEND that an *action-oriented pamphlet* be drawn up, based on the content of the international document. We envision the need for the Centre for Economic and Social Information to be actively involved in the formulation and distribution of such a pamphlet to field personnel and interested indigenous groups and organizations to assure the implementation of an international youth document on the local level.

94. We would further RECOMMEND the crucial necessity for co-ordination within the United Nations system in the area of youth policies and programmes, in accordance with General Assembly resolution 3022 (XXVII) in order that the benefits gained by each part of the system may be shared, and the maximum may be achieved with available resources by avoiding unnecessary duplication. We further RECOMMEND that a useful opportunity for initiating this process would be the expansion of the present regulations of the *Ad Hoc* ACC Meeting on youth issues early in 1976 to enable the full participation of youth non-governmental organizations, as well as prior and later consultations with youth non-governmental organizations at a substantive level.

C. *Organized Service by Youth, and United Nations Volunteers Programme*

95. As a means of involving young people in the national development process, we attach particular importance to the promotion of organized forms of developmental service by youth, in which a wide range of youth organizations (national, regional, international) have broad experience.

96. The precise form and substance of the service will depend on the situation and needs of each country. In some it will be voluntary, in others obligatory, in others there may be both. Whatever approach is utilized, we RECOMMEND that it is vital for the participants to be fully involved in the planning and implementation of the programmes, and that there should be no exploitation of such schemes as cheap forms of labour, and that furthermore such schemes should be developed with all sectors of youth. We also recognize that when a scheme is non-compulsory it provides a useful yardstick for the relevance of the programme to the needs of society as the participating young people see them.

97. We therefore would like to stress the necessity for the fullest preparation of such schemes. Their success will very largely depend on the efficiency of such preparation, and the degree to which young people in the areas concerned are involved in the planning, implementation and evaluation of such schemes.

98. We therefore welcome the expansion of the United Nations Volunteers programme from its original concept to include domestic volunteer services, especially in view of the limited impact of the export volunteer programme, which has now become an Associate Expert Scheme.

99. It is regrettable, however, that the process of designating the United Nations Volunteers programme as the "*principal*"* operational unit of the United Nations for the execution of youth programmes" (see paras. 28-31, and E/RES/1922 (LVIII)) was undertaken without any consultation among youth organizations, and that no involvement of youth in the implementation of the resolution is indicated explicitly. In this sense we support the reservations on the above lines, as expressed in the statement issued by 15 international youth non-governmental organizations dated 20 June 1975 who also requested a postponement of a decision on this resolution, but we RECOMMEND that the United Nations Secretariat and the United Nations Volunteers remove the need for such a postponement by rapidly engaging in a substantive dialogue on the implementation of the resolution with interested youth organizations, and by appointing to their staff personnel with direct experience of domestic "volunteer programmes.

100. We therefore RECOMMEND:

(a) That the General Assembly adopt E/RES/1922 (LVIII) with the clear provision that the United Nations Volunteers programme be "a *major* operational unit within the United Nations for

---

* Our emphasis.

the execution of youth programmes" and that "the meaningful and substantial participation of youth and youth organizations in the planning, implementation and evaluation of United Nations Volunteers projects related to youth" be explicitly included in the resolution.

(b) That the United Nations Secretariat and the United Nations Volunteers with interested youth non-governmental organizations organize in the near future a consultation on the implementation of United Nations Volunteers' extended mandate, to be followed by a continued process of consultation, in order to ensure the most effective forms of youth participation in United Nations Volunteers projects, particularly the inclusion of global issues other than development that are of concern to young people.

101. In addition, we RECOMMEND that every effort be made to experiment with pilot schemes for innovative work-study programmes involving young people especially the young unemployed in the rural and urban areas. We here wish to draw attention to the need for *relevant* education programmes replacing or amplifying the established formal education systems, such as:

(a) Non-formal education programmes particularly for the rural sectors where the emphasis would rightly be placed on training cum production aiming at a certain amount of economic independence for young people.

(b) Study programmes in the urban centres geared more closely to a preparatory training for gainful employment.

(c) Life-long learning programmes for both rural and urban youth.

(d) Greater emphasis on vocationally-oriented study programmes.

102. All these recommendations presuppose the necessity to promote conscious awareness of human rights and responsibilities among youth to assure their meaningful participation and adequate representation in community development.

## D. *UNDP and National Channels of Communication*

103. We reaffirm the recommendations made in our earlier reports concerning effective two-way channels of communication between national youth organizations and the UNDP Resident Representative in each country. In this connexion we welcome the progress made by UNDP in continuing its efforts through guidelines issued to Resident Representatives in January 1975 to increase the involvement of competent non-governmental organizations in their country programmes.

104. We RECOMMEND:

(a) That at least one of the pilot projects shortly to be undertaken be specifically youth-oriented in its objectives and participation.

(b) That, in consultation with the Government, a Youth Advisory Group, composed of young representatives of national youth organizations, be established as a link with the office of each UNDP Resident Representative to serve as a channel of communication through which concrete opportunities for youth participation in development can be identified and information on United Nations policies and programmes disseminated.

(c) That UNDP with the United Nations Volunteers experiment with the placing of young internes from the country in the offices of UNDP Resident Representatives with responsibility for liaising with youth and youth organizations, in order to realize the above objective.

(d) That special attention be given to the development of trainers programmes as opposed to trainees for local leaders, and workshop planning and implementation on the community level.

## E. *Regional Economic Commissions*

105. We have noted the expansion of regional programming through the regional economic commissions, and we welcome the growing interest shown at the regional level in involving young people substantively in the development process, particularly the appointment by the Economic and Social Commission for Asia and the Pacific of a Youth Liaison Officer with supportive staff and the progress towards the establishment of a Regional Youth Advisory Group composed of young people drawn primarily from national and regional youth organizations.

106. In order to facilitate further progress in this area, and to ensure the fullest participation of young people from each region in the process of communication and co-operation with the United Nations at the global level, we make the following RECOMMENDATIONS:

(a) That each regional economic commission appoint a Youth Liaison Officer and establish a Regional Youth Advisory Group composed of young representatives from youth organizations.

(b) That facilitation of more youth groups' registration with the Economic and Social Council is pursued to enable a wider representation of youth at regional commissions. However, we strongly recommend that unorganized youth be recognized and allowed to participate in national and regional affairs.

(c) That a clearing house for United Nations programmes and information be established whereby youth can acquire relevant literature and more importantly be offered a forum for presenting their local needs.

(d) That a youth information kit be drawn up with adequate youth participation in its formulation and dissemination.

(e) That the United Nations pursue with more vigour the subcontracting of United Nations programmes to youth groups and organizations.

(f) That existing United Nations programmes be expanded to include youth-related issues. Emphasis should be on action-oriented programmes involving representative youth participation.

(g) That where political conditions in the country where the regional economic commission is situated restrict substantive access to the commission, every effort should be made to provide channels of communication through an office elsewhere in the region.

107. In addition, we see the role of UNDP and the United Nations Volunteers in this context to be the stepping up of action programmes on the national and local levels. Special attention therefore needs to be drawn to:

(a) interneship programmes for local youth leaders;

(b) workshop formulation and implementation with adequate youth participation in both stages.

108. We therefore urge that UNDP Resident Representatives' responsibilities and duties include concrete developments in those areas recommended in paragraph 104 as well as co-operating in the implementation of those recommendations contained in paragraph 106 where appropriate to the national and local levels. For that purpose we strongly RECOMMEND that the UNDP Administrator communicate all our above recommendations in a policy directive to all of the Resident Representatives asking them to report annually on the progress they make in implementing these recommendations.

### F. *Co-operative Arrangement among Youth Research and Information Centres*

109. We acknowledge the Secretary-General's recommendations concerning the establishment of a co-operative arrangement among youth research and information centres (E/CN.5/503) and express our support for the initial action in this respect as approved by the Economic and Social Council at its fifty-eighth session (E/RES/1923 (LVIII)).

110. We welcome the progress made thus far; however, we would wish to point out that unless the United Nations actively pursues with member Governments the establishment of youth research and information centres, particularly in the developing countries which often markedly lack them, that further attempts at co-operation would undoubtedly be unfeasible.

111. We therefore strongly RECOMMEND that the United Nations pursue such an initiative as an important prerequisite for the establishment of co-operative arrangements particularly in the area of sharing experiences between research centres in developed and developing countries.

112. In addition, we wish to draw attention to our concern with meaningful and substantial participation of youth in *all* spheres of activity and as such we RECOMMEND that young people be involved in the programming, implementation and evaluation of such research relating to youth.

113. Concurrently we are concerned that the content of research should not deal with youth out of the socio-cultural context but rather incorporate youth as an integral member of any issue under study. We therefore RECOMMEND that the selection of research topics encourage proposals to be made by youth groups and student youth bodies.

114. We further RECOMMEND that task forces be initially established among students youth bodies to investigate and propose topics for research, as well as encouragement be made for the participation of youth as member researchers not simply formulators.

115. We would here like to reiterate the recommendations made in the section dealing with the United Nations University on the issue of co-operative research work. We urge that, following the establishment of a co-operative arrangement under the auspices of the United Nations, due attention should be given to youth organizations already engaged in youth research work. As such we RECOMMEND that co-operation not be limited to arrangements between nations but that it should include co-operative arrangements within each country among national research bodies to assure the widest representative and co-ordinated base at the primary level, and to assure that the results of such research lead to practical action-oriented programmes involving young people.

## G. *United Nations University*

116. In view of our conviction that the United Nations University should provide concrete opportunities for the substantial participation of youth, and in spite of our considerable disappointment with its failure to implement the Charter provision for "appropriate representation of young scholars" on the Council (see para. 47), we make the following RECOMMENDATIONS:

(a) that the Charter provision for "appropriate representation of young scholars" on the Council be implemented at the Council meeting in January 1976;

(b) that young scholars be involved substantially in the meetings of the working groups on the three priority areas for research work, at the sessions scheduled for Tokyo in October 1975;

(c) that all efforts be made to establish meaningful links with national youth research centres to co-ordinate existing research work and together develop, in close consultation with the global youth forum, task forces to select appropriate research topics related to youth (this is in keeping with paragraph 8 of General Assembly resolution 3022 (XXVII));

(d) that the United Nations University Council establish an interdisciplinary group of young scholars as part of its research efforts within at least one of the three priority areas with adequate resources to complete a meaningful study, such as in the area of hunger;

(e) that concerned non-governmental organizations in consultative status be invited to observe the meeting of the Council in Caracas (January 1976), and subsequent meetings, and be provided with reasonable notice and full documentation for such meetings;

(f) that the Secretary-General of the United Nations and the Director-General of UNESCO ensure the proper representation of women along with youth on the Council at the time of the appointment of new members in 1977;

(g) that a definition of the United Nations University relationship with government and intergovernmental processes be spelt out early to assure the implementation of its action-oriented research proposals;

(h) that considerable attention be re-channelled to the issue of developing an international character among its participants as initially envisioned and desired by the former Secretary-General, even if this should ultimately imply the future establishment of undergraduate programmes.

## H. *The International Youth Year*

117. In the context of United Nations long-term policy on youth, we have considered the advisability of declaring an International Youth Year. In approaching this matter we have in mind the increasing positive role of the youth in the national and international struggle for development as well as the establishment of a new economic and social order.

118. We recognize and appreciate the measures adopted by the United Nations to encourage programmes that would integrate the youth into the national and international society.

119. We have come to the conclusion, after having analysed and evaluated the effects of a World Population Year and an International Women's Year, that both have contributed positively to the awareness and increasing interest of public opinion on these problems, leading to the implementation of concrete programmes to help solve these problems in the international scope, especially at the national level.

120. We are convinced that these positive effects could be obtained similarly by focusing public awareness and interest in the recognition and acceptance of the youth as an agent of development, a resource for development, and a fully integrated and responsible participant in development.

121. We, therefore, propose that the United Nations declare a year within the near future, as an INTERNATIONAL YOUTH YEAR.

122. In pursuance to such a year, the following RECOMMENDATIONS should be observed:

(a) That the global youth forum play an important role in facilitating such a process at all its various stages, particularly in the necessary follow-up and evaluation of the International Youth Year.

(b) The Year should aim at increasing concrete action in the field of youth, both at the national and international levels. Such concrete actions should aim at developing co-operation among national, regional and international youth organizations, as well as improving channels of communication between these organizations and the United Nations.

(c) Since action is the primary goal of an International Youth Year, we would urge, should a World Youth Conference be held, that it take place at the start of the year as opposed to other International Years, the objective being the formulation of a global plan of action that would be immediately effective in nature.

(d) Undoubtedly this requires that the World Youth Conference be preceded by meetings on major issues relevant to youth at the national and regional levels leading to the design and plan of the Conference itself to assure an action-oriented year. Again, special effort must be made to involve non-organized and rural youth.

## I. *Unemployment and Underemployment of Youth*

123. We noted the convening in June 1976 of a "Tripartite World Conference on Employment, Income Distribution, Social Progress and the International Division of Labour".

124. Recognizing the importance of the problem as it concerns millions of young people, we would RECOMMEND:

(a) That the ILO invite each Government to arrange for the inclusion of young people on a tripartite basis in its national delegation.

(b) That the Geneva Informal Meeting be invited to consider the convening of an International Youth Conference on Unemployment of Youth prior to the Tripartite World Conference.

(c) That priority should be given to the participation of unemployed youth from rural and urban areas, together with young members of national delegations and participants nominated by youth organizations.

(d) That the International Youth Conference be organized with an emphasis on identifying areas in which concrete programmes involving young people will be developed as a follow-up to the Conference.

(e) That the ILO be invited to facilitate the presentation of the conclusion of the International Youth Conference to the Tripartite World Conference.

J. *Health*

125. We believe that the right to health precedes any consideration to the right to participate generally.

126. We observed that the report of the second Advisory Group considered ill-health as a major problem in many developing countries especially among youth. For example, recent health problems such as drug abuse, venereal diseases, alcoholism and suicide require immediate attention, particularly during the reproductive period of a woman where often it constitutes a risk to her health especially when involving clandestine abortion, unwanted pregnancies or over-abundant childbirths. For mothers this generally implies a complete deterioration of health due to malnutrition and insufficient health care.

127. In analysing these issues we realize the interrelationship of health issues with the encompassing socio-cultural environment of the individuals involved, and therefore RECOMMEND the need for a more interdisciplinary approach to health problems.

128. We further RECOMMEND that the United Nations call upon member Governments to involve youth organizations in analysing these youth related health problems and to reach a comprehensive youth diagnosis on and with youth. Consequently, youth organizations should be involved in the planning and implementation of actions aimed at solving health problems, particularly youth participation in health education in the rural and urban areas and in paramedical services.

## VI. ADDITIONAL RECOMMENDATIONS

129. We realize that we have come to the close of the three-year testing period concerning channels of communication and meaningful participation. As such we are concerned with the *implementation* of all our past and present recommendations to ensure substantial youth participation and communication with the United Nations system.

130. First and foremost, we wish to endorse our recurring opinion throughout the past three years by RECOMMENDING that the United Nations system redefine its policies and field operations so as to permit the participation of youth in the formulation, implementation and evaluation of national, regional and international policies and programmes. This recommendation is of utmost importance since it stands as a *prerequisite* to any further action taken to substantially communicate and participate with youth.

131. In addition, we have made concrete recommendations, many of which demand immediate action, that are crucial to ensuring *intermediary and long-term* substantial youth participation and communication with the United Nations system. These include:

(i) developing procedures and mechanisms for youth involvement in United Nations youth policies and programmes (paras. 43-45);

(ii) development of a representative forum for consultation between the United Nations and youth and international youth organizations (paras. 53, 66, 68, 71, 74, 77);

(iii) intermediary measures (paras. 79);

(iv) development of a comprehensive United Nations policy and co-ordinated programmes to meet youth needs and aspirations (paras. 81-84, 90, 92-94);

(v) organized service by youth and United Nations Volunteers programme (paras. 96, 100, 101);

(vi) UNDP and national channels of communication (para. 104);

(vii) regional economic commissions (paras. 106, 108);

(viii) co-operative arrangement among youth research and information centres (paras. 111, 113-115);

(ix) United Nations University (para. 116);

(x) International Youth Year (para. 122);

(xi) unemployment and underemployment of youth (para. 124);

(xii) health (paras. 127, 128);

(xiii) United Nations/UNFPA joint project on youth and population (para. 36).

132. In this respect we wish to point out our belief in the necessity for our present and previous recommendations becoming the basis for wide-range consultations among youth and between the United Nations, youth and youth organizations. We therefore strongly RECOMMEND that the United Nations Secretariat make a comprehensive list of all our Advisory Group's recommendations and avail it to youth organizations, particularly the Geneva Informal Meeting and the United Nations Headquarters NGO Youth Caucus, for further reproduction and distribution.

133. Finally, we strongly RECOMMEND that this report as well as the second report of the *Ad Hoc* Advisory Group on Youth be referred to functional commissions, specialized agencies, and regional economic commissions for further consideration. Special effort should be made by the United Nations and non-governmental youth organizations to circulate these reports among members of the General Assembly prior to their coming deliberations, as well as pursue together close consultation on the contents of the reports.

UNITED NATIONS

# ECONOMIC AND SOCIAL COUNCIL

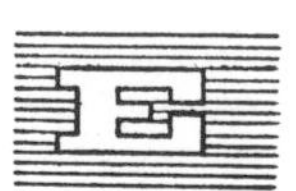

E/CN.4/1223
17 January 1977
Original: ENGLISH

COMMISSION ON HUMAN RIGHTS
Thirty-Third Session
Item 14 of the provisional agenda

## THE ROLE OF YOUTH IN THE PROMOTION AND PROTECTION OF HUMAN RIGHTS

*Report of the Secretary-General*

### INTRODUCTION

1. The present document is issued in pursuance of paragraph 4 of resolution 1 B (XXXII), adopted by the Commission on Human Rights at its 1348th meeting, on 11 February 1976.

2. In that provision of resolution 1 B (XXXII), the Commission decided to consider at its thirty-third session the question of the role of youth in the promotion and protection of human rights on the basis, *inter alia*, of a report by the Secretary-General summarizing information submitted by the Governments of Member States, the appropriate United Nations organs, the specialized agencies and the non-governmental organizations in consultative status concerned on steps taken, in pursuance of paragraph 1 of the resolution, regarding the promotion within their respective spheres of competence of the following measures for the involvement of youth in human rights:

"(a) Active participation of young people in the implementation of the Programme for the Decade for Action to Combat Racism and Racial Discrimination, including the organization of youth meetings on the national and regional levels and youth workshops in order to examine racial prejudice and to identify and evaluate manifestations or symptoms of racial prejudice, in particular as contained in textbooks and other publications and the mass communications media;

"(b) Active promotion of the participation of young people, in particular young women and girls, in the development of society, in particular by ensuring to them equal rights and opportunities in education, in employment and in the other areas of economic, social and cultural life;

"(c) Development of a special curriculum on human rights for use in the various educational systems, whether at the primary, secondary or technical level, and through the United Nations University, and study of the possibility of the introduction of a special curriculum on human rights in universities, in accordance with Commission resolution 17 (XXIX);

"(d) The use of mass media, particularly television, to propagate among youth respect for human rights in accordance with the principles of the Universal Declaration of Human Rights, the International Covenants on Human Rights, the Declaration on the Promotion among Youth of the Ideals of Peace, Mutual Respect and Understanding between Peoples and other relevant United Nations instruments;

"(e) Development of youth projects with the purpose of identifying and examining situations where the human rights of young people are being seriously restricted or violated;

"(f) Study of the possibility of the appointment by youth organizations in each country of a youth correspondent with the United Nations for issues related to human rights".

3. The present summary is based on information provided to the Secretary-General in accordance with paragraph 2 of the resolution. Replies were received from the following Governments of Member States: Australia, Austria, Chile, Egypt, Finland, German Democratic Republic, Ireland, Jamaica, Madagascar, Netherlands, New Zealand, Norway, Pakistan, Philippines, Rwanda, Sweden, United Republic of Cameroon. Information was also transmitted by the World Food Programme (WFP), the International Labour Organization (ILO) and the United Nations Educational, Scientific and Cultural Organization (UNESCO). In addition, the following non-governmental organizations in consultative status sent information: *category I*: League of Red Cross Societies, Planned Parenthood Federation, World Federation of Trade Unions; *category II*: Friends World Committee for Consultation, Pax Romana (International Movement of Catholic Students), World Association of Girl Guides and Girl Scouts, World University Service; *Roster*: The Population Council.

4. As regards the United Nations organs concerned, Commission resolution 1 B (XXXII) was brought to the attention of the Commission for Social Development at its twenty-fifth session (11 January - 4 February 1977) under the item of its agenda concerning youth policies and programmes. The Commission on Human Rights will be informed in the course of its thirty-third session of the results of the consideration of this question by the Commission for Social Development.

5. The General Assembly at its thirty-first session adopted four resolutions in connexion with its consideration of the item on its agenda entitled "Policies and programmes relating to youth: reports of the Secretary-General". They are resolution 31/129, entitled "Policies and programmes relating to youth"; resolution 31/130, entitled "Role of youth"; resolution 31/131, entitled "United Nations Volunteers programme"; and resolution 31/132, entitled "Channels of communication with youth and youth organizations". The text of these resolutions will be made available to the members of the Commission.

# I. PARTICIPATION OF YOUNG PEOPLE IN THE IMPLEMENTATION OF THE PROGRAMME FOR THE DECADE FOR ACTION TO COMBAT RACISM AND RACIAL DISCRIMINATION

## A. *Information submitted by Governments*

*Australia*

Although no specific action has so far been taken at the Commonwealth Government level to promote youth meetings or other yough programmes to address this subject, Australia, as a country which has had high immigration for most of the post-war years, has had several initiatives aimed at minimizing racism and social discrimination and facilitating the integration of migrants into the Australian culture. While generally aimed at the whole community, they obviously relate to young people also. These initiatives include the Racial Discrimination Act 1975, which established a Commissioner for Community Relations and a Community Relations Council, and the setting up of Good Neighbour Councils in most states with significant state government assistance. The Councils address themselves to the needs of migrant residents. For the most part, youth workers are employed, who are actively attempting to motivate youth in order to minimize social discrimination.

*Austria*

To supplement schooling, Austrian schools are continually advised to take part in parascholastic programmes (European pupils competition; participation in other international competitions and in the UNESCO schools projects of the Associated Schools; pupils' correspondence and exchange schemes) that appear suitable to promote understanding between nations and to check any discriminatory trends and eliminate stereotypes incompatible with human rights and fundamental freedoms.

*Chile*

There are two small ethnic groups in Chile whose human rights are equal to those of other citizens but which are living in distinct settlements with their special characteristics and cultures: the Mapuche Indians and the Easter Islanders. Both include large numbers of young people. The Government has been particularly concerned to integrate them into society, while fully respecting their culture and traditions. In particular, schools have been opened with instruction in their language, in addition to Spanish, a dictionary of their language has been produced, and courses are given on television.

The endeavours being made to help the people of Easter Island, with their age-old traditions, merit special mention. A development plan is being put into effect, covering the social, cultural and economis fields, its twofold aim being the preservation of the group and its active participation in the economic and social development of the country. The younger generation is the chief beneficiary of this national endeavour.

*German Democratic Republic*

The German Democratic Republic encourages the active participation of youth in the struggle for peace, détente and international security, against colonialism, *apartheid* and racism in all its forms, and against the massive and systematic violation of human rights.

In this context mention must be made of the "Friendship work teams" formed by young people of the German Democratic Republic who are working in a number of African countries, including Algeria, Guinea, Guinea-Bissau, Mali and Somalia, and are making a major contribution to strengthening the national independence of these countries and to deepening the friendship between the peoples.

In the German Democratic Republic in general, encouragement is given to all aspirations of the United Nations that are designed to educate youth in a spirit of peaceful coexistence and mutual understanding of peoples and States, respect for the right to self-determination, social progress in the world and observance of human rights.

*Madagascar*

Young people in Madagascar are playing an important role in the promotion and protection of human rights, since this is the objective of the present Malagasy Revolution aimed at the establishment of a society from which discrimination, domination and the exploitation of man by man will be banished forever.

The Charter of the Malagasy Socialist Revolution advocates the support of the Malagasy people for the unconditional liberation of peoples oppressed, *inter alia*, by racism. In order to create an awareness of this issue among the masses, the Ministry of Youth is organizing ideological seminars in accordance with the common ideology of egalitarian socialism, and the formation of a Young People's Revolutionary Front is envisaged.

*Netherlands*

Concerning the participation of young people in the fight against racial discrimination, the Netherlands Government, in co-operation with non-governmental organizations, provides information, both inside and outside schools, on youth education with regard to racial equality in general and in particular concerning people with different social and cultural backgrounds, such as immigrants from the Netherlands Antilles, Moluccans and caravan dwellers in the Netherlands. The information is given in the form of leaflets, magazines, films, radio and television programmes and discussion evenings. The Dutch Centre for Foreigners, a national organization subsidized by the Ministry of Cultural Affairs, Recreation and Social Work, plays an important role in this field.

*New Zealand*

Young New Zealanders are involved in action to combat racism, both internationally and within the country.

The elimination of *apartheid* constitutes a major goal at the international level. New Zealand has, in proportion to its population, the largest anti-*apartheid* movement in the western world, and young people provide most of the leadership and membership of this movement. A National Anti-*Apartheid* Committee stresses economic action against *apartheid* and has produced a kit for use in secondary schools to inform pupils about life in South Africa. In 1969 university students set up an organization ("Halt All Racist Tours") to campaign against sporting contacts with South Africa.

Domestically there is a growing awareness that the absence of racial problems in the past has been partly due to the assimilation of a European life style by the Maori people. It is now recognized that, while the Maori has had to make considerable adaptations, there has been little cultural exchange between the two groups, and that Europeans must now make greater efforts to understand Maori culture. To this end, young non-Maoris are becoming involved in the study of the Maori language and culture at school and in community activities designed to promote understanding and good relations between different ethnic groups. Examples are: workshops being organized to sensitize community leaders to the situation of ethnic minorities; the distribution by the Vocational Training Council of a series of booklets to help New Zealanders understand people from different cultures and races, and the establishment of Pacific Islands Advisory Groups to serve as a forum for Island immigrants to voice their opinions on decisions affecting them.

## B. *Information submitted by non-governmental organizations in consultative status*

*Friends World Committee for Consultation*

Many past and present activities of the Society of Friends (Quakers) represent an attempt to involve young people in a practical expression of their concern to promote mutual understanding between those of different national and racial backgrounds. These youth activities, which include international seminars and work camps, promoted by bodies such as the American Friends Service Committee (Philadelphia, United States of America) and the Friends Service Council (London, United Kingdom), reflect their determination to combat racial and other forms of discrimination.

*League of Red Cross Societies*

The Council of Delegates at the International Conference of the Red Cross which took place in Teheran in 1973 reaffirmed that it was necessary to "engage still more actively in the struggle for the elimination of racism and racial discrimination, thus joining in the struggle in the world and so contributing to the implementation of the programmes of the Decade for Action to Combat Racial Discrimination....". Furthermore, it invited all National Societies to devote special attention to youth in this programme of action, in particular, to establish close co-operation between young people and adult members in carrying out certain activities, to provide for more intensive training of youth and for their increased participation in programmes which may contribute to the elimination of racism and the promotion of a spirit of racial tolerance, and to support the organization of study centres and meetings for young people.

All National Societies promote as part of their Red Cross youth programme a special component known as International Friendship and Understanding. The basic aim of this programme, which has existed for well over 50 years, is to teach young people to get to know the values and customs of other groups, to combat prejudice and to promote solidarity.

The activities of young Red Cross members include exchanges of arts and crafts, albums depicting national culture and so forth. A large number of international camps are organized and friendship activities play an important role in them.

## II. PROMOTION OF THE PARTICIPATION OF YOUNG PEOPLE, IN PARTICULAR YOUNG WOMEN AND GIRLS, IN THE DEVELOPMENT OF SOCIETY

### A. *Information submitted by Governments of Member States*

*Australia*

The Government's educational policies are based on the principle of equality of educational opportunity. The Government is committed to encouraging schools to remove bias in educational curricula, providing wider opportunities for students of both sexes to make significant choices affecting their lives, promoting initiatives for the provision of educational programmes for women, and ensuring that vocational guidance is given without bias on grounds of sex.

In recent years the increase in school retention rates has been greater among girls than boys, and the difference between the sexes in this respect has been considerably reduced.

There is in law no discrimination on grounds of sex as regards access to education at any level in Australia. However, social and economic factors, such as lower educational and career expectations for young women than for young men, have resulted in fewer women than men continuing with their education beyond the school leaving age. In recent years, however, more women have been completing the final two years of secondary school and continuing on to post-secondary education.

There is no discrimination as regards access to the teaching profession at any level.

During 1975, most State Education Departments undertook initiatives as part of their International Women's Year programme to assist schools to counteract sexual bias. Three states established committees to look at the effect on girls of existing syllabus materials and teaching practices, and two others began in-service development programmes to encourage teachers to eliminate sexual bias in school programmes and activities. At the national level, the Curriculum Development Centre has recently issued guidelines for teachers and schools to avoid stereotyping of curriculum materials. The Schools Commission has reported that socio-economic factors are now the main cause of the educational disadvantage of girls and is giving financial support to schools for schemes that reduce curricular distinctions between boys and girls and for actions that promote consideration in schools of the social roles of the sexes and the assumptions underlying them. The Australian Department of Education is at present establishing a Women's Unit to assist in the development and review of policies of equality of opportunity.

The Australian Government and the state governments provide a wide range of scholarships and study grants at all levels of education with no discrimination on grounds of sex.

With regard to equal rights and opportunities in employment, the Australian Government is committed to the following goals which are of concern to young people: removing any remaining legal discrimination in employment; ensuring the abolition of male and female categories of work in legislative and industrial awards establishing equal opportunity for recruitment, training, retraining and advancement of all groups in the community. The Government has also established a special bureau, the Equal Employment Opportunities Section, to advise the Public Service Board and other public authorities on employment practices which deny equal opportunity.

*Austria*

Austria considers that particular importance must be attached to youth education promoting the observance of human rights. Therefore, observance of the principle of equality as recognized in the Austrian Federal Constitution plays a fundamental role in the curricula of Austrian schools. An example is the following extract from the curriculum on "History and Sociology - Geography and Economics" established by Federal Law No. 275/1970 for the eighth grades of general secondary schools from the school year 1971/72 onwards: "8th grade: Working Group (two weekly lessons, in conjunction with geography and economics): influence of science and technology; emancipation of women; social, national and racial prejudices".

The School Education Act, effective as of 1 September 1974 regulates the pupils' co-management: beginning in the 9th grade, class, division and school spokesmen are elected to promote the interests of pupils. In the Joint School Committees, composed of three representatives each of teachers, parents and pupils, the pupils' representatives have a right of co-determination on all matters concerning the internal operation of the schools.

The establishment of a system of pupils' advisory boards is not yet regulated by law. These advisory boards are to be heard in advance on all measures to be taken by school authorities and on all legislative initiatives and they have a right to submit suggestions and thus to cooperate in the organization of school life as a whole.

*Chile*

In order to provide a suitable channel for youth participation, the Government of Chile, on 28 October 1973, set up the National Youth Secretariat, which is an organization aimed at giving young people in Chile an appropriate role within the Government. This organization has now become a nationwide institution that has regional, provincial, district and local branches and answers the social, cultural, sporting, recreative and educational needs of young people.

Similarly, on 10 July 1975 another body was established in Chile which is independent of the Government, namely, the Youth Front for

National Unity, which strives for national unity among young people and which is guided by the ideals of the Universal Declaration of Human Rights, the International Covenants on Human Rights and the Declaration on the Promotion among Youth of the Ideals of Peace, Mutual Respect and Understanding between Peoples.

In addition to the institutions mentioned, Chile has a large number of youth organizations, covering the whole range of matters of concern to young people. These bodies are totally independent from the Government. The principles of equal rights and opportunities for men and women is recognized in the country's Political Constitution.

With a view to ensuring that equality of educational opportunity is not diminished by financial handicaps, the Minister of Education has recently announced a plan to introduce a system of grants for higher education which will favour the most economically disadvantaged among the young.

*Egypt*

The Ministry of Social Affairs of Egypt has taken a number of steps to promote the participation of young people, especially young women and girls, in the development of society towards a strengthening of human rights.

Law No. 76 (1973), concerning public service for young people who have completed the various stages of their education, makes the Ministry of Social Affairs responsible for assigning such persons to public service for a period of one year under its supervision so that they may participate in efforts to achieve comprehensive development and eliminate backwardness in all its forms. They have been given tasks in various parts of the country and in various fields, such as literacy, environmental improvement, family planning, local community development, agricultural guidance, educational services, nursing and health care, consumer guidance and child care services.

In pursuance of the agreement entered into between the Ministry of Social Affairs and UNICEF in 1965, and in harmony with the Ministry's policy of encouraging the participation of women in social development programmes in local communities with a view to providing a broader base for popular activities, the Girl Leader Project has been implemented. A number of young women and girls have been trained with a view to the creation of female voluntary social leadership groups capable of assuming the task of local community promotion and improvement. These volunteers have been studying the local community and its needs, providing the population with guidance and assistance so as to bring its tendencies and ideas into line with those of the modern developing society. The number of these girl leaders trained up to 1975 was 1,007.

The women's clubs, currently numbering about 200, provide the framework within which young leaders carry out their activities which aim at arousing social awareness, developing the community and guiding its endeavours along sound, profitable and productive lines in a number of fields, thereby helping to bring women out of their isolation. This is in addition to the setting-up of various centres and facilities in which Egyptian women can develop their new aptitudes by taking part in up-to-date social and cultural activities.

The Ministry has created workshops and training centres where boys, girls and women from educationally backward groups are trained in various occupations, including knitting, needlework and handicrafts in general, so as to enable them to rely on their own efforts in earning a living. Up to the end of 1975, 2,050 of these workshops and centres had been established in various parts of Egypt and were responsible for the training of more than 6,848 young people of both sexes. This was in addition to the existing vocational training sections in the social foundations controlled by the Ministry, in which approximately 3,160 young people of both sexes were enrolled during 1974.

Vocational training centres are attended by groups that have failed to complete their education, who are thus given an opportunity to receive up-to-date training in various trades and attain adequate competence in them, thereby ensuring that those trained are equipped with the necessary know-how to enable them to participate in the country's progress both socially and economically.

By the end of 1975, the number of these centres had reached 54, and the number of students being trained in them was approximately 4,430.

*Finland*

By the year 1977, the comprehensive school system will have been adopted throughout Finland. Under this system basic education is guaranteed to all young people on an equal basis, irrespective of social, economic and regional differences. At present, the education at the intermediate level is under reform, with the purpose of creating equal possibilities for people with vocational training to proceed to studies at institutes of higher education. The entire educational system is being developed with a view to guaranteeing unobstructed opportunities for continued studies.

In 1972, a special body, the Council for Equality, was established within the Council of State. Its functions include, *inter alia*, the promotion of equality between the sexes and the examination of issues relative to its implementation.

In the early 1970s, special legislation concerning youth was developed in Finland. Its objective is to encourage young people to engage in free civic activities of their own.

The system of government subsidies is applied in respect of 65 national youth organizations. An average of 40 per cent of their expenditure is covered by financial aid from the Governments. Approximately 50 per cent of the country's young people are members of these organizations. Society endeavours, mainly by means of municipal youth services, to support the cultural and other activities of even those young people who are not members of youth organizations and to offer them facilities for leisure activities.

*German Democratic Republic*

Young people in the German Democratic Republic (GDR) enjoy special attention and care on the part of the State. The Constitution, the Youth Act of 28 February 1974 and various regulations provide for the responsible participation of youth in building the socialist system of society.

Thus, as a result of the 1974 local elections, the percentage of representatives in the age bracket from 18 to 25 elected to community and municipal assemblies rose from 10.6 to 14.6 and to district and municipal borough assemblies from 16 to 21.7. Since the German Democratic Republic was founded, its citizens have had the right to vote from the age of 18. In 1970 the age at which they can stand for election was lowered to 18 years for local representative bodies, and in 1974 this provision was extended to include the country's Parliament, the People's Chamber, where youth is represented by a 40-member group of its own.

As regards education, school textbooks and lessons in the German Democratic Republic are designed to stress the concern of society to educate youth to be patriotic and internationalist and to work consciously for the strengthening of peace and friendship among peoples.

*Ireland*

Measures taken in Ireland to ensure to young people equal rights and opportunities in employment include the adoption of the Anti-Discrimination (Pay) Act, 1974, which came into force on 31 December 1975 and establishes the legal right to equal pay for men and women employed in similar work. The Anti-Discrimination (Employment) Bill, which was introduced in the Dâil in October 1975, will make it unlawful to discriminate on grounds of sex or marriage status as regards access to employment, including apprenticeship, training and promotion.

Equal rights in education are guaranteed to young women and girls in Ireland, and free education is available to all at primary and secondary levels.

*Jamaica*

The Government of Jamaica is committed to the principle of equality between the sexes and to the integration of women in development, and appropriate machinery has been set up to accelerate progress in these areas.

In October 1974 a Women's Desk was established in the Ministry of Youth and Community Development, and in June 1975 this was upgraded to a Women's Bureau and transferred to the Office of the Prime Minister. The functions of the Bureau are: information, data collection and research; education; co-ordination; social welfare; liaison; and advice. The focus is on the low-income women and on programmes aimed at providing more opportunities for training and employment for women. The age group 14-25 is a special target group, since females in this age range experience the highest levels of unemployment.

The Government of Jamaica has also established machinery through the Ministry of Youth and Community Development for effective dialogue with youth groups and youth leaders at all levels, national, regional and parish, in order to secure the participation of youth in the formulation of development plans and programmes.

Most of the programmes providing training, employment and cultural activities for young people are operated by the Social Development Commission and Vocational Training Division of the Ministry of Youth and Community Development. The most significant are the following.

The Youth Community Training Centres offer a comprehensive programme of remedial education, vocational training and Family Life Education, together with cultural and recreational programmes for youth with primary level education. These centres are co-educational and in 1976 a total of 350 girls were enrolled.

Industrial Training Centres, operated by the Vocational Training Division of the Ministry of Youth and Community Development, provide vocational training at a higher level. These Centres are also open to boys and girls on an equal basis, but as 80 per cent of the training offered is in traditional male skills, only a few girls need to opt for such training. However, since the launching of the programmes conducted by the Women's Bureau during International Women's Year, their number has increased significantly.

The Pioneer Corps programme was launched in 1973 to deal with the problem of unemployment among youth. Young people are given the opportunity to learn skills in agriculture, forestry, and community projects. Less than 10 per cent of the young people who have benefited from this programme are female. The Women's Bureau is working towards increasing this percentage in the future, especially as the number of unemployed females in the age group for which the programme is designed is more than double that of unemployed males.

*Madagascar*

In Madagascar, in general, action relating to youth in the economic field tends to enable young people to participate effectively in building a truly independent economy.

In connexion with the agrarian reform being carried out in the Alaotra region the Ministry of Youth intends to involve the efforts of young people in the socialization of the means of production. Thus, youth work camps are being organized to help those poor peasants who have been given a few acres of paddy fields by the State but lack the necessary means of production.

The Ministry of Youth will endeavour to maintain the existing social and sports infrastructure and to carry out a number of new projects, such as the creation of new youth centres and the establishment of youth villages or "co-operative villages", together with the construction of sports grounds and swimming pools in the provinces.

The Malagasy Government endeavours to eliminate discrimination against young women and girls, in employment and other areas. The seminar on the International Women's Year, held at Majunga in 1975, was considered to be an important event under this programme to achieve equal rights for men and women. The National Women's Service plays an important role in this field.

Concerning action in the cultural field relating to young people, the library service of the Ministry of Revolutionary Art and Culture has distributed books and documents describing Malagasy culture and civilization which are particularly intended for youth. Young people are also playing an important role in protecting cultural assets and the environment.

In education, new structures based on the principles of decentralization and democratization, will be established at all three levels: primary, secondary and technical, and higher. As regards basic education, planning estimates indicate that all Malagasy children of school age will be attending school by 1980.

*Netherlands*

The youth policy of the Government of the Netherlands is based on the principle of encouraging young people to take an active part in the development of society. The policy hinges on the Memorandum on Youth Policy (1969) and the Memorandum on New Trends in Work on behalf of Youth and Young Adults (1971) and involves as a rule all ministries. The Minister of Cultural Affairs, Recreation and Social Work is responsible for co-ordinating youth policy. There is an Interministerial Steering Committee on Youth Affairs to act as liaison between the ministries most involved in youth matters. In principle, this Steering Committee deals with all important issues concerning youth policy before they are decided upon by the Government. There is also the Council for Youth Education, an independent government advisory body. The Council is concerned with a variety of current issues affecting young people, such as: young working people and questions relating to unemployment amongst them, the human environment, political education of young people, the role of young people in the armed forces, scientific research on youth policy and the future educational system.

The youth policy, which is based on encouraging young people to participate in the development of society, is implemented to a large extent through work on behalf of youth and young adults and through club and neighbourhood centre work. The Government's socio-cultural and educational policy is striving for maximum co-operation between clubs, neighbourhood centres and centres for young people and other similar facilities such as libraries and creativity centres, activities connected with education and development work, and club and neighbourhood community work.

The employment policy aims at improving opportunities for young people on the labour market. Measures will be taken to provide young people with further skills and additional jobs will be created for them. All these measures apply equally to young men and young women. The participation of girls in employment is being promoted by providing career advice and by introducing statutory measures.

Finally, it can be stated that the Dutch education system offers equal rights to boys and girls. Within its competence the Netherlands Government promotes equal opportunity in education for all members of society.

*New Zealand*

In New Zealand the Commonwealth Youth Programme, which aims at actively involving young people in the process of national development, is administered by the Ministry of Recreation and Sport in association with the Ministry of Foreign Affairs, the Departments of Education and Maori Affairs and the National Youth Council. The Programme provides: Regional Youth Development Centres, whose principal purpose is to provide opportunities for training in youth work for key personnel from Commonwealth countries; study fellowships and bursaries to enable people to travel to Commonwealth countries to study various aspects of youth work; applied research aimed at monitoring developments relevant to youth in the education, employment, economic, social and cultural fields; a Youth Information Service, the function of which is to facilitate the exchange of information concerning youth matters amongst Commonwealth countries; Youth Projects, a scheme aimed at encouraging young people to initiate community projects; and support for operating youth programmes, in particular programmes in developing countries within the Commonwealth.

Regarding opportunities for young people to participate in cultural life, there are sponsored award schemes for young writers and artists; youth orchestras and youth bands in the four major centres; and specialist schools in both drama and music.

There has been a shift of emphasis from the mere protection of young people against exploitation towards ensuring them equal rights. The purpose is to enable young people, both male and female, to achieve their full potential by removing barriers to their participation in employment. The existing job information system and career guidance systems are being broadened and further developed. Some special measures are being undertaken to reinstate unemployed young people.

It is in the area of women's employment that progress in the promotion of equal rights and opportunities has been most rapid. The Equal Pay Act 1972 was introduced so as to eliminate the traditional disparity in earnings between men and women by the end of the implementation period in 1977. In addition, the introduction of anti-discrimination legislation and other human rights legislation is being considered. The aim of this proposed legislation is to prohibit discrimination in, among other areas, employment on the grounds of sex, marital status, or national origin. Although the legislation as presently envisaged does not specifically cover discrimination on the grounds of age, it should alleviate existing discrimination against young women workers who, in 1971, made up 40.72 per cent of New Zealand's female work force.

Special measures to promote the participation of Maori youth in social and cultural life include the setting up of groups for ethnic cultural activities, while in the city with the highest Maori population special teams offer guidance and advice to young people on finding employment and accommodation. To further equality of opportunity in employment for rural Maori and Polynesian school leavers, pre-apprenticeship courses in 12 trades are conducted at technical institutes in main centres to better equip participants to compete for places in apprenticeship trades.

New Zealand policy also allows for young persons from developing countries (particularly those of South East Asia and the Pacific) to undertake training in New Zealand which will equip them to contribute to the economic and social development of their home countries, where facilities for higher and specialized education are often not yet available.

*Pakistan*

In Pakistan the society recognizes the potential of youth and endeavours to channel this potential towards constructive activity. This effort is being led by the Department of Social Welfare and Education, working through its Community Development Programmes (rural and urban), the Pakistan Girl Guides Movement and the Pakistan Boy Scouts Movement.

The Community Development Programmes aim at organizing the young people and helping them to assess community needs and to mobilize community resources in order to improve the quality of life and ultimately remove the social imbalance which is an obstacle to the promotion of human rights. With this objective in view, interest groups are formed and leadership is developed from the grass-roots level.

There are at present 178 urban and rural community development projects in operation all over Pakistan, where young people are enabled to develop qualities of leadership and discipline and to appreciate the dignity of labour.

The guidance programme of the Pakistan Girl Guide Movement offers an opportunity for girls to get proper training and to equip themselves for their future role as responsible citizens and also provides them with the opportunity to attain positions of leadership in the community. The principle of this guidance and the spirit which it engenders is meant to cut across all classes, creeds and geographical divisions.

As members of the Boy Scouts Movement, boys learn and practise group behaviour, conduct literacy and sanitation campaigns and render help, relief and protection to people in need. They themselves learn the dignity and worth of the human persons and develop the quality of compassion.

*Philippines*

Being largely a nation of young people, the Philippines today seeks the full development and mobilization of youth in the tasks of social, economic, cultural and political development of the nation, as a pre-requisite to success. Special emphasis has thus been placed on the total development of young people - physical as well as intellectual, professional, cultural and social.

In acknowledging the importance of youth development in the process of nation-building, the Government recognizes and upholds the human rights of young people, clearly stated in the New Constitution of the Philippines, the Child and Youth Welfare Code and Presidential Decree No. 684. The constitutional provisions and the provisions in the Child and Youth Welfare Code have been further specified in Presidential Decree No. 604 and concretized with the creation of the Department of Youth and Sports Development (DYSD) on 10 December 1974.

As clearly stated in decree No. 604, the rationale for the creation of the new department is "to integrate nationwide youth development, physical fitness and amateur sports development programmes". In support of this rationale, the specific objectives are, *inter alia*, to encourage, initiate and establish organizations to promote and develop youth activities; to carry out applied and basic research on youth development; and co-ordinate with other government agencies, such as the Department of Education and Culture, the Department of National Defence, the Department of Labour and the Department of Social Welfare regarding youth activities. The DYSD has formulated programmes which include directing youth participation in agricultural activities tapping the services of medical and paramedical students who will serve as assistants to health personnel, and directing youth energy in infrastructure rehabilitation and construction programmes of the Government.

Furthermore, the Philippine Government in Presidential Decree No. 684, recognized the role of youth in restructuring society by encouraging participation in legislative affairs and membership in the legislative units of the government through the youth *barangay*. The decree strengthens and defines the role of the youth *barangay* and the recognition is extended also to the development of members of the youth *barangay* through leadership, training and sports management activities.

*Rwanda*

In Rwanda there are at present 10 youth movements and all young people of the three Rwandese groups (Hutu, Twa and Tsi) are welcomed without distinction as to race, sex or social status, with a view to their integration into the national development process.

The social development centres were originally set up in order to further the emancipation of women, who appeared to have been left on the fringes of society in relation to men. At present, efforts are being made to integrate men, including young men, into these centres. In 1975 there were 390 centres, reaching a population of 942,189 women and girls.

In employment policy, the Rwandese Government is attentive to ethnic proportions and regional balance. It offers all the Rwandese groups the same employment opportunities and seeks to avoid discrimination in the regrading of posts occupied by young people.

With respect to education, the Rwandese Government has found it necessary to adapt Rwandese instruction to the social and economic conditions of the country, since 90 per cent of the children who had completed their primary education had difficulty in settling down in the society. In order to establish a link between education and the economy, the Government decided, through the Ministry of National Education, to set up supplementary education centres for young people leaving primary school who are unable to go on to the secondary level. These are the Domestic Science Centres for girls and the Rwandese Rural and Craft Education Centres for boys. There are at present 20 of the latter centres throughout the country.

An experiment in rural development is being conducted in the Rural and Craft Development Centres. The method used in these centres is the continuing training of team-leaders, fathers, mothers and young men and women from the same commune who will in turn pass on the knowledge they acquire to other members of their teams. The over-all objective is the integration of the whole population in the development process.

The Government aims at achieving the objective of a 100 per cent school enrolment. Article 4 of the Education Act of 27 August 1976 provides that "primary schooling shall be free and compulsory for all children domiciled in Rwandese territory, without distinction as to race, clan, colour, sex or religion". The free and compulsory nature of primary education is emphasized by the Presidential Decree of 28 April 1967 establishing the general regulations for education. Since that date, the Government has steadily increased school enrolment, in compliance with the strongly expressed desire of the people.

*Sweden*

Swedish citizens who have attained the age of 18 years, who are legally competent and residing in Sweden or have been residing there during the previous seven years, are entitled to vote in the elections for the Parliament (Rikstag) or for the county and municipal councils. A person who fulfils the requirements for the right to vote and who is legally competent can be a member of the Parliament or of the county or municipal councils. The number of young people in the popularly elected organs has been increasing in recent elections.

The basic principle of Swedish youth policy is that the young people's own organizations should constitute an important link in the democratic process. The members of these organizations decide themselves on the goals and the contents of their activities. Many organizations perform a valuable function in focusing public opinion on serious problems. They are often engaged in international activities, which are in many cases co-ordinated through the National Council of Swedish Youth Organizations.

There are, on both the national and the local level, regular contacts between the public and youth organizations for the discussion of matters of mutual concern. On the national level, at least part of these contacts are channelled through the National Swedish Youth Council. Youth organizations may receive financial grants from the State and from county and municipal councils.

## B. *Information submitted by specialized and related agencies*

### *World Food Programme*

The World Food Programme provides food assistance to government-sponsored schemes and therefore can do very little directly to ensure the involvement of youth in the projects it assists. However, the Programme is very much concerned that as far as possible young people are reached by its assistance not only in the field of development of human resources, but also in that of economic and social development activities which foresee the employment of labour and the creation of jobs.

With regard to the active promotion of the participation of young women and girls in the development of society, WFP has taken positive steps since thedeclaration of International Women's Year to improve the status of women and foster their integration in development.

Thus, in 1975, the Programme adopted a set of guidelines for headquarters and field officers to follow when they are developing and implementing projects. These guidelines were fully endorsed by the WFP governing body, which "gave broad agreement to the guidelines established by the Executive Director for project planners to ensure that conscious efforts were made to involve the participation of women in the development process".

Moreover, in May 1976, the Executive Director *ad interim* established in WFP an Interdivisional Working Group on Women in Development, whose main tasks are, *inter alia*, to advise the Executive Director on policies and programmes for the use of food-aided projects for the purpose of integrating women into development, especially agricultural and rural development, as called for by various United Nations General Assembly and Economic and Social Council resolutions; and to ensure the application of the guidelines referred to above.

The Working Group has already started its activities and endeavours to ensure that the Programme continue its efforts to help improve, through its projects, women's conditions and to involve them more fully in the development process of their countries.

*International Labour Organisation*

In the first place, an important part of the work being done under the World Employment Programme, whose purpose is to assist countries in achieving full, productive and freely chosen employment, is inspired by the need to prepare young people for employment and integrate them into the employment market. The comprehensive employment strategy missions which have so far been sent to Colombia, Ceylon, the Dominican Republic, Kenya, Iran, the Philippines and the Sudan have emphasized the relationship between education and employment as an essential element for the integration of young people into the employment market.

In June 1976, the World Employment Conference, which was convened to examine the dimensions of the world employment problem and the work done so far and to draw up policy conclusions for the future, endorsed the following basic principle as an element in national development policies to create full employment and meet basic needs: "In the implementation of basic needs strategies, there should be no discrimination against the young, the aged or the handicapped. Every effort should be made to provide the young with productive employment, equal opportunities and equal pay for work of equal value, vocational training and working conditions suited to their age. Exploitation of child labour should be prohibited in accordance with the relevant ILO standards" (World Conference Declaration of Principles, point 17).

The promotion of training and employment for young people is also the subject of standards laid down in several instruments adopted by the International Labour Conference. Thus the Employment Service Convention, 1948 (No. 88) provides in article 8 that "special arrangements for juveniles shall be initiated and developed within the framework of the employment and vocational guidance services", the essential duty of the employment service being laid down in article 1 as "to ensure ... the best possible organization of the employment market as an integral part of the national programme for the achievement and maintenance of full employment and the development and use of productive resources". The Special Youth Schemes Recommendation, 1970 (No. 136) lays down guidelines for special schemes designed to enable young persons to take part in activities directed to the economic and social development of their country and to acquire education, skills and experience facilitating their subsequent economic activity on a lasting bases and promoting their participation in society. The Human Resources Development Convention, 1975 (No. 142) and Recommendation, 1975 (No. 150) lay down standards for the adoption and development of comprehensive and co-ordinated policies and programmes of vocational guidance and vocational training for both young persons and adults, detailed provisions more particularly relevant to young persons being found in paragraphs 8 (1) (a) - (c), 9 (a) and (b), 11 (a) and 18-20 of the Recommendation. For certain occupations, specialized Recommendations have been adopted, namely, the Vocational Training (Fishermen) Recommendation, 1966 (No. 126) and the Vocational Training (Seafarers) Recommendation, 1970 (No. 137)

The ILO has from the outset been concerned to ensure that children and young persons are not admitted to employment likely to be harmful to their health or development. To this end it has adopted a series of Conventions on the minimum age for admission to employment, the most recent and comprehensive instrument being the Minimum Age Convention, 1973 (No. 138), which requires ratifying States to "pursue a national policy designed to ensure the effective abolition of child labour and to raise progressively the minimum age for admission to employment or work to a level consistent with the fullest physical and mental development of young persons". More detailed guidelines for the implementation of this national policy, in relation to plans and programmes for the promotion of full employment, the raising of family living standards, the development of social security and family welfare measures, the provision of education, vocational guidance and training and school attendance requirements, are contained in part 1 of the Minimum Age Recommendation, 1973 (No. 146).

In the field of technical co-operation, training activities represent the major part of ILO assistance to developing countries, with the largest number of projects covering some aspect of vocational training. Thus on 1 September 1976, 105 projects were operative in 59 countries, with 239 experts in the field. Most of these projects cater directly or indirectly to young people. Other projects have assisted in the development of special youth training schemes aimed in particular at vocational preparation or pre-vocational training.

*United Nations Educational, Scientific and Cultural Organization*

The United Nations Educational, Scientific and Cultural Organization has been assisting non-governmental organizations for various activities in this domain of human rights. For instance, UNESCO helped the International Confederation of Free Trade Unions to organize two seminars on youth and unemployment during the second half of 1976 and contributed towards the training of young women leaders in the rural areas of Peru in co-operation with the World Association of Girl Guides and Girl Scouts.

## C. *Information submitted by non-governmental organizations*

### *Friends World Committee for Consultation*

A basic element in the youth projects undertaken by the Friends World Committee for Consultation is the Quaker emphasis on the equal participation and rights of young men and women. An important ongoing example of Friends' work in the promotion of equal rights for girls and young women is provided by the Quaker schools in Kenya.

### *International Movement of Catholic Students*

Participation in the tasks called for by the defence of human rights is a major concern of the International Movement of Catholic Students (IMCS). Primary goals of the IMCS are, *inter alia*: to create and sustain a viable Catholic Student Movement possessing an awareness of, and a commitment to, the task of constructing a just world order and to undertake concerted action in order to strive for social justice among the poor and the underprivileged.

### *International Planned Parenthood Federation*

The International Planned Parenthood Federation (IPPF) believes that young people, who comprise a large proportion of the world's population, have an important part to play in the achievement of social and economic development goals in the future. There is a growing recognition in IPPF that young people should have a right to basic information and education on population questions and a right to discuss, influence and participate in the formulation of policies and programmes in fields which will affect their lives. It has also been recognized that through such participation young people could better contribute to the socio-economic development efforts of their countries.

In recent years the IPPF has expanded its youth education programmes and has encouraged member associations to develop programmes of responsible parenthood and of population and family life education. Activities undertaken by member associations have included the establishment of curriculum advisory committees, the provision and preparation of teaching resources, the organization of teachers' seminars and the implementation of pilot projects in schools. More recent developments have focused on the development of population and family life education for out-of-school youth, who comprise a majority of the young population of many countries.

A corner-stone of the policies and programmes of IPPF since its inception has been a commitment to the emancipation of women and their acceptance as equal partners with men in all socio-economic development activities including family life improvements.

International Women's Year (1975) provided a good opportunity for IPPF to focus on the needs of young women. With assistance and guidance from IPPF, the Family Planning Associations started many projects aimed at improving the health and status of women and the delivery of services and also in removing legal barriers which inhibit the improvement of women's status. A stronger thrust has been given in 1976 by IPPF through supporting grass-roots projects which have a practical effect on the lives of women, preferably with a strong element of self-help.

*The Population Council*

The Population Council is in the process of recruiting persons who will be principally involved with the development of programmes on the status and role of women of all ages and the means of integrating those programmes into the regional programmes of the Council.

*World Association of Girl Guides and Girl Scouts*

As an educational youth movement with a large membership, the World Association, through its national organizations, develops projects promoting equality of access of girls and women to education, employment and other areas of economic, social and cultural life. Recognizing the need for greater participation of women in public life, the World Association puts a special stress on literacy programmes, leadership training and vocational training schemes. Member organizations also continue to develop their career orientation and guidance programmes for girls.

*World Federation of Trade Unions*

The World Federation of Trade Unions (WFTU) is concerned with the promotion of the rights of young workers so that they may play an effective part in political, economic, social and cultural life, in accordance with their aspirations. In 1958 and again in 1970, WFTU therefore held World Trade Union Conferences on this subject which, among other things, resulted in the drafting of a Charter setting out the demands of young workers. Also, a World Trade Union Conference to discuss vocational training was organized by the WFTU at Turin, Italy, in 1968 and a Charter on vocational training was adopted by that Conference.

*World University Service*

The World University Service (WUS) is involved basically in two types of programme, both of which seek to put the expertise of the university at the service of mankind, particularly those who are being exploited or discriminated against.

The Social Action Programmes involve students and university personnel in working with villagers with a view to overcoming development problems for communities near to university campuses. By this method, village communities profit from the learning of a university, while university personnel benefit from the practical experience of the villagers. Examples of projects of this nature are the programmes being run by the Indonesian, Rwandese and Tanzanian committees of WUS.

The Anti-discrimination Programmes are mostly concerned with the award of scholarships for students who are prevented, in one way or another, from continuing their education past the primary level. WUS is therefore carrying out large-scale programmes designed to assist blacks in South Africa, Southern Rhodesia and Namibia and for Chileans who can no longer continue their studies in their own country but who wish to complete their work in other countries of Latin America. Where it is impossible for a person to continue his studies in his own country, then it is a fundamental precept in a WUS Anti-discrimination Programme that that person should be encouraged to continue his studies in a country which is culturally close to his own. This is to prevent, as far as is possible, the occurrence of brain drain to industrialized countries.

Development education is perhaps the major feature underlying all WUS programmes, in both developed and developing countries. Practical programmes are organized to help students understand the extent to which they are part of a system which perpetuates discrimination and the ways in which they can overcome inequality and injustice. This work involves participation by students in university organization, the planning of changes in the curriculum, studies of the effects that higher education is having on students, and the involvement of students and university personnel in community development and anti-discrimination programmes.

## III. DEVELOPMENT OF A SPECIAL CURRICULUM ON HUMAN RIGHTS FOR USE IN THE VARIOUS EDUCATIONAL SYSTEMS

### A. *Information submitted by Governments*

*Australia*

Schools throughout Australia strive to develop in pupils suitable attitudes to citizenship, such as respect for the rights of the individual and for democratic processes, international understanding and an appreciation of the need for law and order.

Australian institutions that are participating in the UNESCO Associated Schools Project (eight primary schools, five secondary schools and one teachers' college) have adopted as the main subject themes those in the fields of human rights and the study of the lifestyles of children in other countries. Studies of race attitudes are also discussed at all levels.

*Austria*

Attention is drawn to the "Order of Principle" (*Grundsatzerlass*) drawn up by the Austrian Federal Ministry of Education and the Arts which is expected to come into force in 1977 and which stipulates that "political education" is a principle governing all instruction. Human rights concepts are dealt with in the draft Order, in particular in paragraph 5, which includes the following: "The educational principle of 'political education' within the framework of curricula contents is aimed at creating the basis for: ... the capacity and the readiness to champion inviolable fundamental values such as freedom and the dignity of man, to eliminate prejudices and, if occasion arises, to stand up for the interests of those discriminated against; the realization that bringing about just peace and order is essential for the survival of mankind and that the achievement of this objective requires a commitment on the part of all the forces in the world, and beyond this, involves the personal responsibility of every individual".

In recent years, the educational authorities took several measures for the promotion of human rights and fundamental freedoms. In 1970, they published a booklet entitled "The protection of the fundamental rights of the individual in Austria", issued in the series "Political Education" for the information of teachers of upper primary schools and all intermediate and secondary schools. In 1972, they issued a pamphlet entitled "Materials on world politics" for the Working Group on "History and Sociology, Geography and Economics" in the eighth grade of general secondary schools, including a comprehensive chapter on "Human rights" in conformity with the curriculum. In 1973, the topic "Twenty-fifth anniversary of the Universal Declaration on Human Rights" was included as an educational theme on the occasion of the National Day.

In higher education in Austria, the promotion and protection of human rights is a paramount guiding principle, particularly for teaching and research on all levels of the theological faculties and at the law faculties, where human rights are the subject of special courses, and human rights provide the frame of reference for work in family law, labour law, penal law, criminology, administrative law and the law of nations. They figure importantly also in teaching and research at the medical faculties, in political science, sociology, philosophy and the educational sciences.

*Chile*

In the curricula for social science studies and in elementary, secondary and higher education, Chile is now placing special emphasis on matters relating to human rights.

*Finland*

In the educational system of Finland, special attention is attached to education towards internationalism. The comprehensive school curriculum emphasizes the importance of regarding the Universal Declaration of Human Rights as the guiding principle in teaching. The working group on education for the promotion of peace, appointed by the Ministry of Education in 1973, issued directives on how human rights and education towards the understanding of the significance of peace should be emphasized in the educational programmes of schools.

*Ireland*

The development of human rights in the educational curricula of Ireland is secured by the inclusion of programmes on "Civics" at the primary and secondary levels.

At the primary level "Civics" is that part of school activity which helps the child to become a better member of society and to appreciate his rights and obligations towards it. The main concern is with the development of acceptable social and moral attitudes which take into account the rights of other members of society.

The main object of the "Civics" course at the secondary level is training for citizenship. Education is concerned with the inculcation of virtues and of right moral principles, with the formation of correct habits and attitudes towards oneself, one's family, one's fellow men, one's own country and the world community.

*Jamaica*

The development of the special curriculum on human rights for use in the various educational institutions would come within the purview of the Ministry of Education of Jamaica. Through the Ministry's implementing agency, the Social Development Commission, a "Life Skills Programme" is being developed, which is being used in the Youth Community Training Centres and Youth Clubs and which is designed to achieve, *inter alia*, the following broad objectives: to lead people to a greater readiness to assess their strengths and weaknesses as individuals, to assess themselves in realistic terms and to modify their behaviour in order to become more effective human beings; to encourage individuals to examine their roles and responsibilities in family living and to improve interpersonal relationships, both in their families and in the broader society; to encourage informal discussions of social, political and economic institutions and behaviour in the Caribbean; to stimulate a consciousness of individual and community rights and responsibilities, thereby enabling people to define the needs of their communities and how they can mobilize resources to meet those needs.

*Netherlands*

Increasing attention is being given in education in the Netherlands to problems of racial discrimination and other forms of discrimination and such subjects as international economic and political relations, war and peace, development co-operation and human rights. Numerous teachers deal with these topics in their lessons; others work together in teams and often adopt a project-type approach to these issues.

In many cases the teachers have inadequate or insufficient materials at their disposal to deal satisfactorily with these complex issues. They then seek outside advice and guidance from organizations such as School and the World or from school advisory services. Educational project groups are seeking co-operation with other groups concerned with the same problems.

The law faculty of the University of Amsterdam offers a special optional human rights course for bachelors of law and post-graduate students. The course concentrates on the promotion and protection of human rights at the international level.

In all the law faculties of Netherlands universities, human rights issues are dealt with in the context of the various courses on constitutional law, administrative law, European law and international law. The issue of human rights is in some instances also a part of the curriculum of other faculties, notably theology. The Technical University of Twente has created a special section on human rights and international organizations within its programme of social sciences.

For some years now, a remarkable project entitled "Young people and the United Nations" has been carried out by the Political Youth Council, which is a national non-governmental organization. The project, subsidized by the Ministry of Cultural Affairs, Recreation and Social Work, seeks to promote the participation of young people, both in school and outside (in education centres), in United Nations affairs, focusing particularly on the annual sessions of the United Nations General Assembly and on subjects of world significance with which the Assembly deals, such as human rights, co-operation, development for decolonization, and youth policy. During the three-month session of the General Assembly, the Political Youth Council publishes a series of "educational newspapers". A special youth member of the Netherlands delegation to the United Nations General Assembly reports on the sessions. When he returns to the Netherlands, the youth delegate spends three months visiting various schools. At present, 81 schools are taking part in the project.

*New Zealand*

Human rights issues are included in social studies courses at both the primary and secondary school levels. A majority of secondary schools in Auckland, New Zealand's largest and most polyglot city, study multiracial societies and their inherent problems. Most schools use resource material such as newspaper editorials to obtain several points of view, in order to identify bias either for or against a situation. Some schools have active programmes on values in New Zealand society to show that different values are determined by cultural positions. Sex-stereotyping is also studied as an integral part of social studies programmes.

*Norway*

The greater part of the work being undertaken today in Norway in order to encourage the involvement and interest of youth in the promotion of human rights is carried out under the Norwegian school administration. For the schools it is a central aim to further the pupils' understanding of intrinsic human equality, as well as of such values as equality of status, intellectual liberty and tolerance. Human rights are also included in the formal teaching curriculum of several different subjects (e.g., history, social science and Norwegian).

In recent years the United Nations Association has regarded it as one of its most important missions to provide the students enrolled in Norwegian teaching colleges with information and orientation courses on the work of the United Nations, the idea being that this information will then be disseminated in the schools in Norway. Teaching on the subject of human rights represents the core of this work.

Besides this, attention may be drawn to the work designed to promote human rights which is now being done by humanitarian associations and organizations, to which young people make a very substantial contribution.

*Sweden*

One of the aims of education in Sweden is to impart general democratic values and to prepare students for the exercise of their rights and obligations in a democratic society. Thus the curricula established by the Government and Parliament include instruction on the fundamental democratic values, such as human rights in general.

The instruction in human rights is meant to lay the foundation for international understanding and international co-operation. The curriculum for the nine-year compulsory schooling (not including upper secondary school) stipulates, for instance, that "one should endeavour, in teaching, to get away from any strictly national or West European perspective. Instead, one should try to comprehend the views and values of other cultures in order to achieve a more all-round understanding".

Also, the curriculum for the upper secondary education has as one of its aims to promote international understanding and to provide a broad view of religions and cultures in other parts of the world. Various United Nations instruments in the field of human rights are included in the teaching material.

At the university level, the question of human rights is dealt with in the context of political science as well as of the study of law. The latter curriculum includes a one-month course in public international law, during which existing international instruments (declarations, conventions, etc.) are studied.

Mention should also be made of two one-term interdisciplinary courses, established on an experimental basis, which deals *inter alia* with the subject of human rights, *viz*, peace and conflict studies of international relations.

### B. *Information submitted by non-governmental organizations in consultative status*

*Friends World Committee for Consultation*

The Friends World Committee for Consultation is making an informal review of the question of establishing a special curriculum on human rights for use in educational systems.

*League of Red Cross Societies*

The programme Red Cross Youth, whose objective is mainly educational, has for many years stressed the dissemination of the Principles of the Red Cross and the Geneva Conventions of 1949, as a contribution to the civic education of young people. Moreover, international friendship and understanding have always had a place in this programme.

## IV. THE USE OF MASS MEDIA, PARTICULARLY TELEVISION, TO PROPAGATE AMONG YOUTH RESPECT FOR HUMAN RIGHTS

### A. *Information submitted by Governments*

*Austria*

As regards the use of the mass media for the dissemination among young people of respect for human rights, reference must be made to the legal responsibilities of the Austrian Broadcasting System. Article 2, paragraph 1, subparagraph 2, of the Federal Act concerning the Responsibilities and the Institution of the Austrian Broadcasting System (Fed. Law Gaz. No. 397, 1974) provides that the Broadcasting System shall arrange for the "dissemination of public and youth education, having particular regard to the promotion of school and adult education and the understanding of all the problems of democratic community existence". Human rights naturally have a prominent place among these "problems of democratic community existence".

*Finland*

Human rights and related matters are dealt with frequently in the Finnish radio and television programmes, particularly in connexion with programmes relating to the United Nations and the specialized agencies. These questions are also dealt with in the various broadcasting programmes for schools.

*German Democratic Republic*

The mass media of the German Democratic Republic (GDR) give active support to youth in its solidarity endeavours. Special radio and television serials and youth magazines and newspapers give prominent coverage to the concern of the young people in the GDR to work resolutely for peace, international understanding and the elimination of all forms of racial discrimination, *apartheid* and human rights violations.

*Jamaica*

Several Jamaican Ministries and agencies are involved as regards the utilization of the mass media to propagate among youth respect for human rights, notably the Ministry of Education, working through the Agency for Public Information, which falls under the ambit of the Office of the Prime Minister.

*Netherlands*

The Netherlands Government, in co-operation with non-governmental organizations, gives information concerning racial equality in the form of leaflets, magazines, films, radio and television programmes and discussion evenings. In general, ample attention is given in radio and television programmes to the promotion among young people of a belief in human rights. One actual instance of a film being used to bring the human rights position of cultural minorities to the attention of large sectors of the population, including young people is the discussion film entitled: "Ahmed or Bertus" (or "How the Dutch react to foreign workers"). This film is shown and discussed in schools, youth clubs and neighbourhood centres to try to promote greater awareness of the problems faced by young foreign workers.

*New Zealand*

Although there has not, to date, been any organized use of the media to publicize human rights issues in general, documentaries often treat individual examples of infringement of particular human rights, for example, the right to work, to social services, or to adequate housing.

*Sweden*

Both radio and television in Sweden devote much time to subjects relating to human rights.

### B. *Information submitted by specialized and related agencies*

*United Nations Educational, Scientific and Cultural Organization*

In May 1976 UNESCO organized at Headquarters a symposium of young workers from various regions of the world on "The quality of work and work prospects", to discuss the rights and responsibilities of young workers, as well as their contribution to the promotion of human rights. A film entitled "Young People and Work" was produced by UNESCO and is available in English, French and Spanish. Participants were mostly from the least privileged group of the working class and they had the opportunity of exposing their problems, their frustrations and what they think should be the remedy.

Every year UNESCO's Human Rights Division organizes at Headquarters a Youth Day in connexion with the anniversary of the proclamation of the Universal Declaration of Human Rights by the United Nations General Assembly. At the 1976 Youth Day the topics centred on problems of the environment and human habitat.

## V. DEVELOPMENT OF YOUTH PROJECTS WITH THE PURPOSE OF IDENTIFYING AND EXAMINING SITUATIONS WHERE THE HUMAN RIGHTS OF YOUNG PEOPLE ARE BEING SERIOUSLY RESTRICTED OR VIOLATED

*Information submitted by Governments*

*Australia*

Various programmes have been conducted in Australia over a period of time which have sought to involve young people in activities of a community development nature. The effective result of many of these programmes has been to identify and examine situations where the human rights of young people are being restricted or violated.

The extent of these programmes has varied, for example, from major state-wide conferences of youth, sponsored by the Victorian State Government, to local initiatives by young people to form co-operative food buying and growing groups. Underlying this whole issue is an inherent need to provide suitably trained and experienced youth workers in strategic locations throughout the community; for this reason the Commonwealth Government has provided significant financial support in the area of youth workers and education for several years now.

*Chile*

The development of youth projects for examining situations where human rights are being violated or restricted was the Chilean Government's aim in forming the National Youth Secretariat. One of its tasks is to act as a channel of communication between young people and the government authorities, for the latter must be kept informed of matters causing concern at the human level and of any possible excesses, so that corrective action may be applied.

*Finland*

The youth organizations have organized numerous seminars and other meetings dealing with the violations of human rights that have taken place in various countries, especially in the light of recent concrete cases occurring in these countries.

## VI. STUDY OF THE POSSIBILITY OF THE APPOINTMENT BY YOUTH ORGANIZATIONS IN EACH COUNTRY OF A YOUTH CORRESPONDENT WITH THE UNITED NATIONS FOR ISSUES RELATED TO HUMAN RIGHTS

*Information submitted by Governments*

*Chile*

Owing to the active role of young people in Chile and throughout the world, it is considered by Chile that it would be extremely useful to study the possibility of appointing a youth correspondent with the United Nations, in the belief that youth has much to contribute to the solution of the far-reaching problems that affect the world in general and their own generation in particular.

*Finland*

The functions of the proposed liaison officer are exercised by the Finnish United Nations Association, which maintains contacts between the various United Nations organs and authorities and Finnish civic organizations.

*Ireland*

The National Youth Council of Ireland, a voluntary youth organization, is a member of the Council of European National Youth Committees, which in turn has liaison with the United Nations. The Council is responsible for the representation of Irish youth organizations at youth activities abroad and assists the participation of Irish young people in many international events.

*New Zealand*

New Zealand supports the establishment of such a post and the Government authorities concerned with youth programmes have recommended that the National Youth Council should serve as youth correspondent with the United Nations. The Council has itself expressed strong support for this proposal and indicated its willingness to serve as correspondent.

The Council has affiliated to it 34 youth organizations in New Zealand, and its functions include liaison with the Government on all matters directly affecting youth. It is affiliated to the World Assembly of Youth.

*Rwanda*

The Rwandese Republic supports the proposal concerning the possible appointment in each country of a youth correspondent with the United Nations for issues related to human rights.

*United Republic of Cameroon*

The Director of Youth in the United Republic of Cameroon has been appointed as the youth correspondent for issues concerning human rights.

---

UNITED NATIONS

ECONOMIC AND SOCIAL COUNCIL

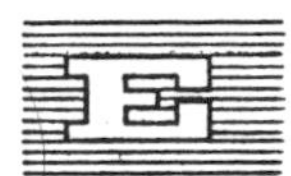

E/CN.4/1223/Add.1
15 February 1977
Original: ENGLISH/RUSSIAN

COMMISSION ON HUMAN RIGHTS
Thirty-third session
Item 14 of the agenda

# THE ROLE OF YOUTH IN THE PROMOTION AND PROTECTION OF HUMAN RIGHTS

*Addendum*

## I. PARTICIPATION OF YOUNG PEOPLE IN THE IMPLEMENTATION OF THE PROGRAMME FOR THE DECADE FOR ACTION TO COMBAT RACISM AND RACIAL DISCRIMINATION

### A. *Information submitted by Governments of Member States*

*USSR*

1. In contributing to the implementation of the Decade for Action to Combat Racism and Racial Discrimination and other important United Nations decisions on decolonization, racism and *apartheid*, Soviet youth has consistently given and is giving wholehearted support and assistance to peoples fighting against racism in South Africa. Soviet youth organizations have submitted a series of proposals to various bodies, including UNESCO, on various aspects of racial discrimination and racism. They call for the recognition of the right to self-determination and independence for the people of Zimbabwe, Namibia and the indigenous inhabitants of the Republic of South Africa, for the exposure of projects for the creation of "Bantu States".

2. The youth organizations of the USSR maintain contacts with the youth sections of the national liberation movements of Namibia, Zimbabwe and South Africa. The most important forms of co-operation and solidarity with these movements are as follows: (a) On the occasion of the International Youth Solidarity Day (25 April), the Central Committee of the All-Union Lenin Young Communist League and the Committee of Youth Organizations of the USSR issued a declaration expressing wholehearted solidarity with the peoples and youth of colonial and dependent countries and

territories. Speakers at the mass meetings of Soviet youth held that day in Moscow and in a number of other towns of the USSR expressed support for the legitimate struggle of the peoples of Asia, Africa and Latin America against imperialism, colonialism and neo-colonialism, reaction, fascism, racism and *apartheid*. (b) A joint declaration concerning events in Soweto (Republic of South Africa) appeared on 22 June 1976 in the newspaper "Komsomolskaya Pravda", which regularly publishes articles, commentaries and sets of photographs relating to the struggle of the peoples and youth of South Africa for freedom and independence. Similar materials are published in the central and local youth press and broadcast as part of the special youth radio programmes and the television programmes.

3. Training and scholarships are offered by Soviet higher and intermediate specialized educational establishments to representatives of the youth of Zimbabwe, Namibia and the Republic of South Africa and other peoples which are fighting for their independence or which recently achieved their independence. Assistance, at the request of officials of various movements, was also given in organizing in the USSR major manifestations for youth fighting against racism and racial discrimination in the African countries.

4. Contributions to the Youth Solidarity Fund, created at the initiative of the Lenin Komsomol, are made on a voluntary basis both individually and collectively by schoolchildren, students, young workers and young members of collective farms. The resources of this fund are used in particular to provide financial assistance to youth organizations in countries which have recently achieved independence or which are struggling for independence.

5. There is also a Soviet volunteer doctor movement. A team of young medical workers was sent out to Guinea-Bissau at the time of the war of liberation; a similar group spent more than six months in Mozambique.

6. Many delegations have visited the USSR to discuss matters connected with the struggle against racism and racial discrimination since 1971 at the invitation of the Central Committee of the All-Union Lenin Young Communist League and the Committee of Youth Organizations of the USSR.

7. Millions of Soviet boys and girls are taking an active part in the world-wide campaign "Youth stands for anti-imperialistic solidarity, peace and progress", launched in anticipation of the eleventh Universal Youth and Student Festival (Cuba 1978). The activities being carried out are an expression of solidarity with the peoples and youth fighting against fascist and dictatorial regimes, against racisn and *apartheid*, for national liberation, democracy and social progress.

## D. *Information submitted by United Nations Organs*

*United Nations Secretariat (Office of Public Information)*

8. Most of the United Nations Information Centres, in order to ensure the active participation of young people in the implementation of the programme for the Decade for Action to Combat Racism and Racial Discrimination, initiated and offered substantive assistance for many student programmes on human rights.

9. Many Centres, on occasions like the International Day for the Elimination of Racial Discrimination and the Week of Solidarity with the Colonial Peoples of Southern Africa, put special emphasis on the role of youth in achieving basic human rights.

## II. PROMOTION OF THE PARTICIPATION OF YOUNG PEOPLE, IN PARTICULAR YOUNG WOMEN AND GIRLS, IN THE DEVELOPMENT OF SOCIETY

### A. *Information submitted by Governments of Member States*

*USSR*

10. Soviet youth is making a worthy contribution to international efforts aimed at affirming the ideals of peace and mutual understanding between peoples and of respect for human rights and dignity. A leading role in this respect is played by Soviet youth organizations, and particularly the All-Union Lenin Young Communist League and the Committee of Youth Organizations of the USSR. They are contributing to the achievement of mutual understanding between youth associations of various political, philosophical and religious leanings mainly through their activities and joint efforts aimed at the strengthening of peace, security and co-operation, and at promoting respect for human rights and fundamental freedoms. Soviet youth organizations are actively participating in the democratic international youth associations such as the World Federation of Democratic Youth and the International Union of Students. Great importance is attached to the results of the European Meeting of Youth and Students (Polish People's Republic, June 1976), where questions relating to the practical participation by youth in the struggle for a durable peace, security, co-operation and social progress were discussed. Recent activities include the organization of a number of international and regional seminars devoted to questions of the establishment and protection of the rights of specific categories of young persons.

### D. *Information submitted by United Nations Organs*

*United Nations Secretariat (Office of Public Information)*

11. Many United Nations Information Centres have initiated special discussions with the departments of the ministries and other government departments of Member States responsible for youth in order to assure its active involvement in the promotion and protection of human rights.

12. The Education Information Programmes Unit of the United Nations Office of Public Information (OPI) has worked on the subject mainly throught teachers' organizations and United Nations Associations. The Special Projects Unit of the OPI, as well, in the organization and conducting of its annual Summer Student Interne Programme, schedules its work in such a way as to cover as many subjects relating to human rights as possible. In 1976, emphasis was placed on inviting to the Programme more young people from developing countries than had previously been the case.

## III. DEVELOPMENT OF A SPECIAL CURRICULUM ON HUMAN RIGHTS FOR USE IN THE VARIOUS EDUCATIONAL SYSTEMS

### D. *Information submitted by United Nations Organs*

*United Nations Secretariat (Office of Public Information)*

13. United Nations Information Centres have endeavoured in their contacts with the educational authorities and institutions and through their information activities to encourage the development of a special curriculum on human rights for use in the various levels of the educational systems and the introduction of a special curriculum on human rights in universities. Another important aspect in the campaign by the Centres in this regard was the growing interest of the students in most countries in the inclusion of human rights in their formal curricula.

## IV. THE USE OF MASS MEDIA, PARTICULARLY TELEVISION, TO PROPAGATE AMONG YOUTH RESPECT FOR HUMAN RIGHTS

### A. *Information submitted by Governments*

*USSR*

14. The Soviet youth press attaches great importance to the dissemination of ideas of humanism and respect for human rights and freedoms. Articles on this subject are published regularly in the "Komsomolskaya Pravda" and "Moskovsky Komsomolets" newspapers, in the journals "Molodoy Kommunist", "Selskaya Molodezh", "Rovesnik", "Studenchesky Meridian", "Novosti" press agency's daily "Molodezh Segodnya", etc.. They devote a great deal of space to questions of the protection of the rights of youth in various countries. Information is also published on the struggle of youth against racist regimes, for freedom, self-determination and national independence. These questions also receive considerable coverage in youth radio and television programmes.

15. Soviet youth has expressed its solidarity with the struggle of the Arab peoples for the recognition of the lawful national rights of the Arab people of Palestine, and for the achievement of a just and durable peace in the Near East. Activities of many kinds are being organized as an expression of solidarity with Chilean patriots and democrats against the violation of fundamental human rights and freedoms in that country and against flagrant violations, *inter alia* of the International Covenants on human rights, of which Chile is a signatory.

### D. *Information submitted by United Nations Organs*

*United Nations Secretariat (Office of Public Information)*

16. Youth organizations and youth in general have consistently been a major target of the United Nations Information Centres and efforts in publicizing human rights issues have been extensive and successful. In the light of resolution 1 B (XXXII), additional efforts were undertaken by all United Nations Information Centres to encourage and stimulate the involvement of youth in the promotion and protection of human rights.

17. The United Nations Information Centres helped educational institutions, non-governmental organizations, student organizations, United Nations clubs, UNESCO clubs, and trade unions to organize meetings, workshops, seminars, debates and exhibitions, thus encouraging and stimulating the involvement of youth in the promotion and protection of human rights. The Non-Governmental Organizations Section of the United Nations Office of Public Information (OPI) organized a special briefing for non-governmental organizations representatives which was devoted to the role of youth in promoting and protecting human rights. The Centres, also provided relevant pamphlets, brochures and other publications produced by

OPI, as well as United Nations films. Furthermore, whenever international meetings on youth took place, the United Nations Information Centre in the country concerned involved itself in joint actions with youth organizations to mount United Nations book exhibitions with particular stress on human rights and related subjects. The Directors of Information Centres frequently addressed youth meetings and lectured on various subjects related to human rights during 1976.

18. All the Information Centres have used the mass media, and in particular television, in their intensive efforts to propagate among youth the awareness of and respect for human rights in accordance with the principles of the Universal Declaration of Human Rights, the Declaration on the Promotion among Youth of the Ideals of Peace, Mutual Respect and Understanding between Peoples and other United Nations instruments. It is worth mentioning among the United Nations television series, "International Zone", ten half-hour colour films which are devoted to the problems of youth, including two on the First World Youth Assembly held at United Nations Headquarters.

19. The discussions by the Commission on Human Rights at its thirty-second session on the role of youth in the promotion and protection of human rights were fully covered by the United Nations in its relevant OPI press releases. Publicity has also been given to the Declaration on the Promotion among Youth of the Ideals of Peace, Mutual Respect and Understanding among People, the text of which is kept in print in a variety of languages for permanent distribution through the United Nations Information Centres and by the non-governmental organizations concerned.

20. Most Centre Directors maintained close contact with the organizers of youth programmes for the television and radio, and a steady flow of documentation, tapes and films on human rights was supplied for this purpose by the Centres. All the news media, radio stations and television networks have been regularly supplied with background information, photos and other appropriate information material on human rights.

UNITED NATIONS

# ECONOMIC AND SOCIAL COUNCIL

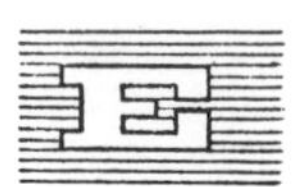

E/CN.4/1223/Add.2
18 March 1977
Original: ENGLISH

COMMISSION ON HUMAN RIGHTS
Thirty-third session
Agenda item 14

## THE ROLE OF YOUTH IN THE PROMOTION AND PROTECTION OF HUMAN RIGHTS

*Report of the Secretary-General*

*Addendum*

*Information submitted by Governments of Member States (continued)*

### CYPRUS

[23 February 1977]

I. *Participation of young people in the implementation of the Programme for the Decade for Action to Combat Racism and Racial Discrimination*

Efforts are in progress for the establishment of a National Human Rights Committee in all free parts of the island, which will promote a 10-year Programme of Action. Youth organizations will be represented on the Committee and the programme will include the active participation of youth.

II. *Promotion of the participation of young people, in particular young women and girls, in the development of society*

In general, young people enjoy equal rights in this sphere. So far as education is concerned, the authorities are promoting free education in order to offer equal opportunity. At present free education is provided at the primary level and for the first three years of secondary schooling, including technical schools.

III. *Development of a special curriculum on human rights for use in the various educational systems.*

Some aspects of human rights are included in the current school curricula of the Ministry of Education. The Ministry is to study the possibility of adopting a special curriculum at all educational levels.

IV. *The use of mass media, particularly television, to propagate among youth respect for human rights*

Mass media, particularly radio and television, are being used from time to time to project and propagate respect for human rights. Relevant youth activities are being prepared for television programmes.

V. *Development of youth projects with the purpose of identifying and examining situations where the human rights of young people are being seriously restricted or violated*

Youth gatherings and other youth activities are planned in connexion with the situation of youth in the occupied parts of the island.

VI. *Study of the possibility of the appointment by youth organizations in each country of a youth correspondent with the United Nations for issues related to human rights*

The appointment of a Youth Correspondent with the United Nations for issues related to human rights is being pursued in co-operation with youth organizations.

UNITED NATIONS

ECONOMIC AND SOCIAL COUNCIL

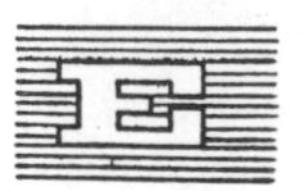

E/CN.4/1223/Add.3
14 November 1977
Original: ARABIC/ENGLISH FRENCH/RUSSIAN

COMMISSION ON HUMAN RIGHTS
Thirty-fourth session
Item 15 of the provisional agenda

# THE ROLE OF YOUTH IN THE PROMOTION AND PROTECTION OF HUMAN RIGHTS

*Report of the Secretary-General*

*Addendum*

## I. PARTICIPATION OF YOUNG PEOPLE IN THE IMPLEMENTATION OF THE PROGRAMME FOR THE DECADE FOR ACTION TO COMBAT RACISM AND RACIAL DISCRIMINATION

*Information submitted by Governments of Member States*

*Byelorussian Soviet Socialist Republic*

The young people of the Byelorussian Soviet Socialist Republic, by developing co-operation with foreign youth organizations and participating in international events, are expressing their fraternal solidarity with young people struggling against racism and *apartheid* and for national liberation, democracy and social progress. Examples of the active participation of Byelorussian youth in the struggle against racism, racial discrimination and all forms of oppression and exploitation, have been the campaign "Youth Stands for Anti-Imperialistic Solidarity, Peace and Progress" conducted on a wide scale in the Republic, and solidarity activities with nations and young people struggling against racism and for national independence which have taken place in connexion with the preparations for the eleventh World Universal Youth and Student Festival.

Byelorussian youth have adopted the "Programme of further struggle for peace and international co-operation and for the freedom and independence of peoples", launched by the twenty-fifth Congress of the Communist Party of the Soviet Union, as the basis for their international activity.

*Federal Republic of Germany*

The Government of the Federal Republic of Germany attaches considerable importance to the promotion of programmes which serve to further international understanding and remove prejudices of a racial character, especially programmes in association with developing countries. Such programmes include projects for out-of-school education undertaken by young people's organizations and public youth institutions. In this context, the Federal Government's Youth Plan is designed to support programmes developed and implemented by the aforementioned bodies themselves.

*Socialist Republic of Romania*

The Socialist Republic of Romania has adopted a whole series of laws reflecting its concern to guarantee the fundamental rights and freedoms of its citizens, including young people, and to adopt a firm stand in the struggle against discrimination based on race, nationality, sex or religion. Furthermore, the principles of respect for human rights and fundamental freedoms set forth in the Constitution of the Socialist Republic of Romania for all its citizens are guaranteed and defended through the legal procedure constituted by the indictment of offences against peace and humanity, such as genocide, the fanning of racial hatred, obstacles to the freedom of religious practices, slavery and other acts which interfere with human freedom and dignity.

The Union of Communist Youth, the Union of Associations of Communist Students of Romania and the Association of Youth and Students of Romania for the United Nations takes an active part in all action designed to promote human rights, including action initiated by the United Nations such as International Day for the Elimination of Racial Discrimination.

## II. PROMOTION OF THE PARTICIPATION OF YOUNG PEOPLE, IN PARTICULAR YOUNG WOMEN AND GIRLS, IN THE DEVELOPMENT OF SOCIETY

*Federal Republic of Germany*

Young people participate in programmes under the Federal Youth Plan, governed by the General Guidelines for the Federal Youth Plan of 3 November 1970 and the (annual) implementing ordinance, on the basis of full equality of rights regardless of sex. Women enjoy equal rights in the fields of general, higher and vocational education, in the employment market, and in economic, social and cultural life.

*Kuwait*

Kuwait's approach to youth falls within the context of its respect for the principles of Islam and for human rights and freedoms in general. To celebrate the anniversary of the Universal Declaration of Human Rights, for instance: information media are used to explain the contents of the Declaration, to discuss its relation to religious education, sociology and languages; symposia are held on human rights, with competitions to encourage young people to submit their own studies on the subject; theatrical and similar displays illustrate themes connected with human rights; United Nations publications and pamphlets are distributed; and the basic role of Islam in honouring human dignity and the rights of oppressed peoples is stressed.

*Socialist Republic of Romania*

An essential feature of the policy furthered by the Socialist Republic of Romania with regard to youth is the application of a series of measures of an economic, educational and legislative nature ensuring all-round training of youth for work and for life, and for an active role in society.

The right to education is guaranteed by article 21 of the Constitution and article 4 of the Education Law of 13 May 1968, which stipulate that the citizens of the Socialist Republic of Romania have the right to education, irrespective of nationality, race or religion, and without any other restrictions which could constitute discrimination.

Young people employed in productive work have access to a wide range of opportunities provided by the appropriate legislative and economic measures, so that they can be employed according to their skills and training and adequately remunerated, without any discrimination. Under the law on the Organization and Direction of the Socialist units of the State (Law No. 11/1971), representative elected youth bodies and some members of youth organizations take part in the activities of the workers' councils — agencies for the collective management of enterprises and institutions. The right of young people to take part in the management, organization and control of the units in which they work has been sanctioned by the Labour Code adopted by the supreme legislative body in Romania, the Grand National Assembly (Law No. 10 of 23 November 1972).

Young people are also elected and hold office in local and central State organs. In the central organs, representatives of youth organizations participate, *inter alia*, in the administrative councils of the Ministry of Labour, in the Culture Council and in the Socialist Education Council of the Ministry of Education. A number of representatives of youth organizations in the Socialist Republic of Romania are also full members of Departmental Councils and the Central Council of Worker Control of Economic and Social Activity.

## III. DEVELOPMENT OF A SPECIAL CURRICULUM ON HUMAN RIGHTS FOR USE IN THE VARIOUS EDUCATIONAL SYSTEMS

*Federal Republic of Germany*

In their educational aims, curricula and teaching directives, the Schools of the Länder of the Federal Republic of Germany take into account the Recommendation adopted by UNESCO in 1975, concerning the education in international understanding and co-operation and world peace and in human rights and fundamental freedoms. In addition, the Federal Centre for Civic Education has developed a number of activities in the field of human rights for the benefit of young people in particular.

*Socialist Republic of Romania*

The civic education of young Romanian people is based on the principles promoted by Romania in its aims of peace, international co-operation between all countries, respect for independence and national sovereignty, non-interference in internal affairs, in complete equality of rights.

Young people are taught the fundamental obligations and rights of citizens in the compulsory general schools, in a subject area entitled "Notions of law and the constitution". University education is designed fundamentally to inculcate in young people deep humanistic convictions, develop in them positive civic and personality traits and train them as defenders of human rights and fundamental freedoms. In the law faculties, each subject area includes the relevant aspects of respect for human rights and freedoms; topics such as the Declaration of Human Rights and the Covenants on Human Rights are included, and the course on penal law covers the subject of indictment for offences against peace and humanity.

## IV. THE USE OF MASS MEDIA, PARTICULARLY TELEVISION, TO PROPAGATE AMONG YOUTH RESPECT FOR HUMAN RIGHTS

*Byelorussian Soviet Socialist Republic*

The press, radio and television in Byelorussia are actively engaged in spreading respect for human rights among young people in accordance with the principles of the Universal Declaration of Human Rights, the International Covenants on Human Rights and the Declaration on the Promotion Among Youth of the Ideals of Peace, Mutual Respect and Understanding Between Peoples. The youth newspapers "Chyrvana Zmena" and "Snamya Yunosti", in their sections entitled respectively "From every parallel and meridian" and "The world on the axis of events and facts", regularly publish information about the situation of youth in other countries. The weekly radio programme "PLanet 76" regularly includes broadcasts about popular struggles against colonial régimes in southern Africa, which also expose the creation of Bantustan States and condemn the support of racist régimes. In a programme entitled "Your coeval abroad", the "Byelorusskaya Molodezhnaya" radio station regularly informs listeners about progressive youth organizations throughout the world and their struggle for human rights.

As regards the use of television to propagate respect for human rights among young people, the Byelorussian television Youth Service has prepared a number of interesting programmes, among which mention should be made of programmes on International Youth Day and the Week of Solidarity with the Struggle of the Chilean People.

*Federal Republic of Germany*

The Federal Government encourages programmes organized by associations or groups of the pupils' and students' press or editors of youth magazines, etc., broadcast by radio and television corporations, as well as programmes by young film directors designed to promote international co-operation.

*Socialist Republic of Romania*

Television and radio broadcasts and press publications include items for young people and children to promote their education in a spirit of mutual understanding among peoples and the respect for fundamental human rights and freedoms.

## V. DEVELOPMENT OF YOUTH PROJECTS WITH THE PURPOSE OF IDENTIFYING AND EXAMINING SITUATIONS WHERE THE HUMAN RIGHTS OF YOUNG PEOPLE ARE BEING SERIOUSLY RESTRICTED OR VIOLATED

*Federal Republic of Germany*

In the Federal Republic of Germany youth associations and youth workshops in particular concentrate an appreciable part of their work on programmes with peripheral groups of young people in danger of social isolation or discrimination; these efforts are supported by the Federal Government.

## VI. STUDY OF THE POSSIBILITY OF THE APPOINTMENT BY YOUTH ORGANIZATIONS IN EACH COUNTRY OF A YOUTH CORRESPONDENT WITH THE UNITED NATIONS FOR ISSUES RELATED TO HUMAN RIGHTS

*Federal Republic of Germany*

The Government of the Federal Republic of Germany endorses the idea of nominating youth correspondents to deal with human rights questions; for this purpose contact has been made with the German National Committee for International Youth Questions.

UNITED NATIONS

# ECONOMIC AND SOCIAL COUNCIL

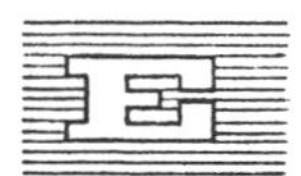

E/CN.4/1145
5 December 1973
Original: ENGLISH

COMMISSION ON HUMAN RIGHTS
Thirtieth session
Item 6 of the provisional agenda

## DRAFT DECLARATION ON THE ELIMINATION OF ALL FORMS OF RELIGIOUS INTOLERANCE

*Working paper prepared by the Secretariat*

CONTENTS

*Paragraphs*

CONTENTS (continued)

ANNEXES

## INTRODUCTION

1. The General Assembly, at its twenty-eighth session, adopted on 30 November 1973, resolution 3069 (XXVIII), in which the Assembly,

> "*Considering* that the draft articles prepared by the Working Group set up by the Commission on Human Rights at its twentieth session, and suggestions, comments and amendments thereto presented by Member States, constituted a suitable orientation for the preparation of a draft Declaration on the Elimination of All Forms of Religious Intolerance,
>
> "1. *Invites* the Economic and Social Council to request the Commission on Human Rights at its next session to consider with priority the elaboration of a draft Declaration on the Elimination of All Forms of Religious Intolerance taking into account observations presented by Governments as well as the opinions expressed, the suggestions put forward and the amendments submitted in the course of the discussion of this question at the twenty-eighth session of the General Assembly, and to submit, if possible, a single draft Declaration to the twenty-ninth session of the General Assembly, through the Economic and Social Council;
>
> "2. *Invites* Governments to transmit to the Secretary-General their additional comments and suggestions on the said articles and amendments in time for consideration at the next session of the Commission on Human Rights;
>
> "3. *Requests* the Secretary-General to transmit all the documentation on the subject that was before the General Assembly at its twenty-eighth session to the Commission on Human Rights;
>
> "4. *Decides* to inscribe this item on the agenda of the twenty-ninth session with a view to consider, complete and adopt, if possible, a Declaration on the Elimination of All Forms of Religious Intolerance."

2. The present document was prepared in compliance with paragraph 3 of the resolution and in order to indicate clearly the present state of consideration of the texts which the General Assembly took as a basis for discussion of the draft Declaration on the Elimination of All Forms of Religious Intolerance.

3. In this connexion, it may be useful to recall that the following action was previously taken by United Nations organs on the matter:

(a) In resolution 1781 (XVII) of 7 December 1962, the General Assembly requested the Economic and Social Council to ask the Commission on Human Rights, bearing in mind the views of the Sub-Commission on Prevention of Discrimination and the Protection of Minorities, the debates at the seventeenth session of the General Assembly, any proposals on the matter that might be submitted by Governments and any international instruments already adopted in this field by the specialized agencies, to prepare: (i) a draft declaration on the elimination of all forms of religious intolerance, to be submitted to the Assembly for consideration at its eighteenth session; and (ii) a draft international convention on the elimination of all forms of religious intolerance, to be submitted to the Assembly if possible at its nineteenth session and, in any case, not later than at its twentieth session. The Assembly invited Member States to submit their comments and proposals concerning the draft convention by 15 January 1964;

(b) At its resumed thirty-fourth session, the Economic and Social Council, on 19 December 1962 (1238th meeting), decided to transmit the resolution of the General Assembly to the Commission on Human Rights and to the Sub-Commission on Prevention of Discrimination and the Protection of Minorities;

(c) At its nineteenth session, in 1963, the Commission held a preliminary debate on resolution 1781 (XVII) and decided[1] to give priority at its twentieth session to the preparation of a draft declaration on the elimination of all forms of religious intolerance. The Commission requested the Sub-Commission to prepare and submit to the Commission at its twentieth session a preliminary draft of such a declaration, taking into account the views expressed during the debate on the subject at the nineteenth session of the Commission, and requested the Secretary-General to invite the Governments of Member States to submit any proposals which they might wish to make as to the provisions which such a declaration should contain in time for consideration by the Commission at its twentieth session;

(d) The Sub-Commission on Prevention of Discrimination and Protection of Minorities at its sixteenth session, in 1964, prepared and submitted to the Commission a preliminary draft of a United Nations Declaration on the Elimination of All Forms of Religious Intolerance,[2] together with other relevant documentation;

(e) The Commission, at its twentieth session in 1964,[3] set up a working group to prepare, on the basis of the preliminary draft of the Sub-Commission and all other relevant documentation, a draft declaration on the elimination of all forms of religious intolerance. The working group, however, was able to consider only the first six articles of the text submitted by the Sub-Commission, in relation to which it prepared a provisional text consisting of six articles. It also submitted to the Commission certain alternative texts and proposals. Owing to lack of time, the Commission was unable to adopt a draft declaration on the elim-

---

[1] *Official Records of the Economic and Social Council, Thirty-sixth Session, Supplement No. 8* (E/3873), chap. X, resolution 10 (XIX).

[2] E/CN.4/873, para. 142.

[3] See *Official Records of the Economic and Social Council, Thirty-seventh Session, Supplement No. 8* (E/3873), chap. III.

ation of all forms or religious intolerance. In resolution 2 (XX), the Commission requested the Secretary-General to transmit to Member Governments for comments the report of the working group[4] and the preliminary draft of a Declaration on the Elimination of All Forms of Religious Intolerance submitted by the Sub-Commission,[5] and to submit to the Economic and Social Council at its thirty-seventh session the comments of Governments as well as the working group's report and the Sub-Commission's draft of a Declaration. The Commission recommended to the Council:

> "To give such further consideration as it may deem practicable to the drafting of a Declaration on the Elimination of All Forms of Religious Intolerance, in the light of the comments of Governments, and that it transmit the appropriate documents to the General Assembly for consideration at its nineteenth session."

(f) The Council, in resolution 1015 C (XXXVII) of 30 July 1964, decided to refer to the General Assembly resolution 2 (XX) of the Commission, together with the documents mentioned therein, as well as the records of the debate held on the subject at the Countil's thirty-ninth session,[6] and suggested to the Assembly that it take a decision on the further course to be followed in the matter. The General Assembly was unable to consider the draft Declaration at its nineteenth session;

(g) The General Assembly, in resolution 2020 (XX) of 1 November 1965, requested the Council to invite the Commission on Human Rights to make every effort to complete, at its twenty-second session, the preparation of the draft Declaration and the draft Convention, in order that they might be submitted to the Assembly at its twenty-first session. The Commission on Human Rights, however, has not considered the preparation of a draft Declaration since its twentieth session;

(h) The General Assembly did not consider the question of the preparation of a draft Declaration from its twenty-first to twenty-sixth sessions, but at its twenty-seventh session, the Assembly adopted resolution 3027 (XXVII) of 18 December 1972 in which it decided to accord priority to the completion of the Declaration on the Elimination of All Forms of Religious Intolerance before resuming consideration of the draft International Convention on this subject; requested the Secretary-General to transmit to States Members of the United Nations or members of specialized agencies the preliminary draft of a United Nations Declaration on the Elimination of All Forms of Religious Intolerance prepared by the Sub-Commision on Prevention of Discrimination and Protection of Minorities and the report of the Working Group set up by the Commission on Human Rights at its twentieth session to prepare a draft Declaration on the

---

[4] *Ibid.*, para. 296.

[5] *Ibid.*, para. 294.

[6] Documents E/SR.1314 and 1338, and E/AC.7/SR.490-496. See also the report of the Economic and Social Council to the General Assembly, *Official Records of the General Assembly, Nineteenth Session, Supplement No. 3* (A/5803), chap. IX, sect. II.

Elimination of All Forms of Religious Intolerance; invited Governments to transmit to the Secretary-General their observations on the above-mentioned documents; requested the Secretary-General to submit the observations received, together with an analytical presentation, to the General Assembly at its twenty-eighth session and decided to give priority at that session to the elaboration of a Declaration on the Elimination of All Forms of Religious Intolerance with a view to the adoption, if possible, of such a declaration as part of the observance of the twenty-fifth anniversary of the Universal Declaration of Human Rights;

(i) At its twenty-eighth session, the General Assembly considered the question and allocated it to the Third Committee. In connexion with the item, the Third Committee had before it a report containing the observations received from Governments (A/9134 and addenda 1 and 2) and an analytical presentation of the observations received up to 15 August 1973 prepared in accordance with General Assembly resolution 3027 (XXVII). The Committee focused its discussion on the text of the preamble of the draft Declaration prepared by the Sub-Commission and on the text of draft articles prepared by the Working Group as well as amendments thereto. In this connexion, it may be recalled that at the twentieth session of the Commission on Human Rights, the Vice-Chairman of the Working Group, in introducing the report of the Group, stated that the report did not deal with the preamble, in accordance with the practice of the United Nations bodies to deal first with the substantive provisions before drafting the preamble;[7]

(j) While it was considered during the debate in the Third Committee that the draft articles prepared by the Working Group and the suggestions, comments and amendments thereto presented by Member States, constituted a suitable orientation for the preparation of a draft Declaration on the Elimination of All Forms of Religious Intolerance, the belief was expressed that the matter required additional study. On the unanimous recommendation of the Committee, the General Assembly adopted resolution 3069 (XXVIII).

4. This working paper contains two sections dealing respectively with the present state of consideration of the preamble of the draft Declaration prepared by the Sub-Commission and of the draft articles prepared by the Working Group. Therefore, after reproducing each provision and the amendments thereto which were submitted by representatives of Member States in the course of the debate in the Third Committee of the General Assembly, references are made immediately thereafter (a) to the suggestions and observations transmitted by Governments under resolution 3027 (XXVII) of the General Assembly; (b) to the views expressed by representatives of Member States during the discussion on the matter in the Third Committee; and (c) to the relevant proposals, if any, contained in the report of the Working Group set up by the Commission at its twentieth

[7] *Official Records of the Economic and Social Council, Thirty-seventh Session, Supplement No. 8* (E/3873), chap. III, para. 297.

session.

5. The texts of the preliminary draft of a Declaration prepared by the Sub-Commission and the relevant parts of the report of the Working Group not reproduced in other parts of this document are set forth in annex I and annex II of the present document, respectively.

6. The observations received from Governements pursuant to the request contained in paragraph 2 of General Assembly resolution 3069 (XXVIII) will be distributed in document E/CN.4/1146.

7. In accordance with paragraph 3 of the resolution, the following documents, which were before the General Assembly at its twenty-eighth session, will be made available to the Commission:

(a) Document A/9134 and Add.1 and 2, containing the substantive observations of the following 25 Governments on the Sub-Commission's preliminary draft of a Declaration and on the report of the Commission's Working Group: Austria, Brazil, Byelorussian Soviet Socialist Republic, Canada, Egypt, Finland, Greece, Holy See, India, Iraq, Italy, Netherlands, Nigeria, Pakistan, Philippines, Rwanda, Singapore, Sweden, Syrian Arab Republic, Togo, Ukrainian Soviet Socialist Republic, Union of Soviet Socialist Republics, United Kingdom of Great Britain and Northern Ireland, United States of America and Zambia.

(b) Document A/9135, containing an analytical presentation of the observations contained in document A/9134. The document is divided into two sections: in section II A, observations of a general character are summarized; in section II B, observations concerning the texts prepared by the Sub-Commission and by the Working Group are set out provision by provision. In this connexion, it will be recalled that the Working Group used as a basis for its discussion the preliminary draft submitted by the Sub-Commission, but was able to take into consideration only six articles of that draft. Moreover, as a result of modifications made by the Working Group, the articles which it prepared did not in all cases correspond to those contained in the Sub-Commission's preliminary draft. For purposes of clarity, the Secretary-General in document A/9135 used the Sub-Commission's draft as a basis for the analytical presentation; before summarizing the comments on each provision, the text prepared by the Sub-Commission was reproduced first and the corresponding text submitted by the Working Group, if any, is reproduced immediately thereafter.

(c) A document containing the summary records of the discussion at the 2006th, 2009th to 2014th meetings of the Third Committee during the twenty-eighth session of the General Assembly.

## I. AMENDMENTS, OBSERVATIONS AND SUGGESTIONS RELATING TO THE PREAMBLE OF THE TEXT PREPARED BY THE SUB-COMMISSION

8. As indicated in paragraph 3 (i) above, the Third Committee of the General Assembly used the text prepared by the Sub-Commission as a basis for its consideration of the preamble of a draft Declaration on the Elimination of All Forms of Religious Intolerance.

### *Title*

9. The title of the draft Declaration, as it appears in the texts prepared by the Sub-Commission and by the Working Group reads as follows: "United Nations Declaration on the Elimination of All Forms of Religious Intolerance".

10. The following amendment was submitted: *Morocco* proposed (A/C.3/L. 2029) that the title of the draft Declaration should read as follows: "Draft International Declaration on the Elimination of All Forms of Intolerance and of Discrimination based on Religion or Belief".

11. Suggestions and observation relating to the title were made by *Austria* (A/9134 and A/9135, paragraph 6), *Brazil* and *Morocco* (A/C.3/SR. 2010); *Morocco* (A/C.3/SR.2012).

### *Preamble*

12. In the text submitted by the Sub-Commission, the preamble reads as follows:

> "*The General Assembly*
>
> "*Considering* that the Charter of the United Nations is based on the principles of the dignity and equality of all human beings and seeks, among other basic objectives, to achieve international co-operation in promoting and encouraging respect for human rights and fundamental freedoms for all without distinction as to race, sex, language or religion,
>
> "*Considering* that the Universal Declaration of Human Rights proclaims that all human beings are born free and equal in dignity and rights and that everyone is entitled to all the rights and freedoms set forth in the Declaration, without distinction of any kind, in particular as to race, colour, religion or national origin,
>
> "*Considering* that the Universal Declaration of Human Rights proclaims further that all are equal before the law and are entitled without any discrimination to equal protection of the law and that all are entitled to equal protection against any discrimination and against any incitement to such discrimination,

"*Considering further* that the right of everyone to freedom of thought, conscience and religion has been proclaimed in the Universal Declaration of Human Rights, which right includes freedom to change one's religion or belief, and freedom, either alone or in community with others and in public or private to manifest one's religion or belief in teaching, practice, worship or observance,

"*Noting* that the disregard of human rights and fundamental freedoms through discrimination because of religion and the denial of the right to freedom of thought, conscience and religion has brought in the past untold sorrow to mankind by inflicting grievous suffering on those who were its victims and in injuring those responsible for them,

"*Considering* that in order to eliminate and prevent all such forms of religious intolerance it is vital for Governments to take legislative, educational and other measures to that end, and for organizations and private persons to lend their fullest support to the achievement of this objective,

"*Convinced* that the building of a world society free from all forms of religious intolerance is one of the fundamental objectives of the United Nations,

"*Solemnly affirms* the necessity of adopting national and international measures to that end and in order to secure the universal and effective recognition and observance of the principles set forth below,

"*Proclaims* this declaration:"

13. The following amendment was submitted: *Canada* proposed (A/C.3/L.2031) to amend the end of the second preambular paragraph to read: "without distinction of any kind, in particular as to race, colour, sex, religion or national origin".

14. Suggestions and observations relating to the fourth preambular paragraph were made by the *Byelorussian Soviet Socialist Republic* (A/C.3/SR. 2012).

15. Suggestions and observations relating to the fifth preambular paragraph were made by *Austria* and the *Ukrainian Soviet Socialist Republic* (A/9134 and A/9135, paragraph 8), the *Union of Soviet Socialist Republics*, the *German Democratic Republic*, the *Philippines*, *Italy* and *Morocco* (A/C. 3/SR.2012).

16. Suggestions and observations relating to the sixth preambular paragraph were made by *Austria* (A/9134 and A/9135, paragraph 8) and the *Union of Soviet Socialist Republics* (A/C.3/SR.2012).

17. Suggestions and observations relating to the seventh preambular paragraph were made by *Austria* (A/9134 and A/9135, paragraph 8), the *Ukrainian Soviet Socialist Republic*, the *Union of Soviet Socialist Republics*, *Ghana*,

*Iraq*, the *Byelorussian Soviet Socialist Republic*, *Morocco* (A/C.3/SR.2012).

18. Suggestions and observations relating to the eighth and ninth preambular paragraphs were made by the *Union of Soviet Socialist Republics* (A/C.3/SR.2012).

19. Suggestions and observations relating to additional preambular paragraphs were made by the *Union of Soviet Socialist Republics* (A/9135, paragraph 9) and by the *Holy See* (A/9134/Add.2).

## II. AMENDMENTS, OBSERVATIONS AND SUGGESTIONS RELATING TO THE DRAFT ARTICLES PREPARED BY THE WORKING GROUP SET UP BY THE COMMISSION ON HUMAN RIGHTS AT ITS TWENTIETH SESSION

20. As indicated in paragraph 3 (i) above, the Third Committee used the text prepared by the Working Group as a basis for its consideration of the substantive provisions of a draft Declaration on the Elimination of All Forms of Religious Intolerance.

### *Article I*

21. Article I of the text submitted by the Working Group reads as follows:

> "Everyone has the right to freedom of thought, conscience and religion. This right shall include freedom to adhere or not to adhere to any religion or [to any religious or non-religious] belief and to change his religion or belief in accordance with the dictates of his conscience, without being subjected to any coercion likely to impair his freedom of choice or decision in the matter."[8]

22. The following amendments to the above-mentioned text were submitted:

(a) *Netherlands* proposed (A/C.3/L.2027) to delete the words in square brackets, "to any religious or non-religious', and to add the following sentence at the end of the article: The expression 'religion or belief' shall include theistic, non-theistic and atheistic beliefs."

(b) *Morocco* submitted a subamendment (A/C.3/L.2041) whereby the second sentence of the amendments to article I submitted by the Netherlands in document A/C.3/L.2027 would read as follows: "The expression 'belief' shall include non-theistic and atheistic beliefs."

(c) The *German Democratic Republic* and *Poland* proposed (A/C.3/L.2033): (i) to replace the words "to adhere or not to adhere to any religion or belief" by "to have or to adopt a religion or belief of his choice"; (ii) to add the following sentence at the end of the article: "The expression 'religion or belief' shall include theistic or non-theistic beliefs and atheistic convictions, it shall exclude racism, nazism, *apartheid* and all similar ideologies which are based on racial intolerance and terror as a gross violation of human rights and fundamental freedoms."

(d) *New Zealand* proposed (A/C.3/L.2034) to add the following sentence at the end of article I: "The expression 'religion or belief' shall include theistic, agnostic and atheistic beliefs or convictions."

---

[8] The words in square brackets are those on which no agreement was reached in the Working Group.

(e) *Morocco* proposed (A/C.3/L.2042) that the amendment submitted by New Zealand in document A/C.3/L.2034 should read as follows: "The expression 'belief' shall include agnostic and atheistic beliefs."

(f) *Morocco* proposed (A/C.3/L.2040) to add after the words "any religion or" in article I the words "religious belief" and to delete the words between square brackets.

(g) *Brazil* proposed (A/C.3/L.2043) (i) to replace the words "to any religion or to any religious or non-religious belief" by the words "to any theistic, non-theistic or agnostic beliefs"; (ii) to replace the words "change his religion or belief" by the words "change his or her teaching"; (iii) to add the words "or her" after the words "dictates of his" and after the words "impair his"; (iv) to replace in this and all subsequent articles the words "of religion or belief" by the words "theistic, non-theistic or agnostic beliefs"; and (v) to add in this and all subsequent articles, wherever the word "his" occurs, the words "or her".[9]

23. Suggestions and observations relating to article I were made by *Austria*, the *Netherlands* and the *Ukrainian Soviet Socialist Republic* (A/9134 and A/9135, paragraphs 23 and 24); *Italy*, *United Kingdom*, *United States of America* (A/9134/Add.1); the *Holy See* (A/9134/Add.2); the *German Democratic Republic*, *Morocco*, the *Netherlands*, the *United States of America* and *Egypt* (A/C.3/SR.2012).

### *Article II*

24. Article II of the text submitted by the Working Group reads as follows:

> "Discrimination between human beings on the ground of religion or belief is an offence to human dignity and shall be condemned as a denial of the principles of the Charter of the United Nations, as a violation of the human rights and fundamental freedoms proclaimed in the Universal Declaration of Human Rights and as an obstacle to friendly and peaceful relations among nations."

25. The following amendments to the above-mentioned text were submitted:

(a) The *Netherlands* proposed (A/C.3/L.2027) to insert after the words "the Universal Declaration of Human Rights" the following words: "and elaborated in the International Covenants on Human Rights."

(b) The *Ukranian SSR* proposed (A/C.3/L.2037) to replace article II by an article reading as follows:

> "In order that freedom of conscience may be fully guaranteed,

---

[9] Brazil proposed that the last two amendments should apply also to all subsequent articles (A/C.3/L.2043).

the Church shall be separated from the State and the School from the Church. All churches and religious creeds and tendencies shall be equal before the law. No single church, religion or religious organization shall or may be accorded privileges of any kind or be subject to restrictions of any kind in its activities. No church or religion shall have a position of *de jure* or *de facto* domination."

26. Suggestions and observations relating to article II were made by *Austria*, *Canada*, the *Netherlands*, the *Philippines*, *Sweden* (A/9134 and A/9135, paragraph 12). *Austria*, the *Ukrainian Soviet Socialist Republic* and the *United Kingdom of Great Britain and Northern Ireland* (A/9135, paragraph 13); the *United Kingdom*, the *United States of America* (A/9134/Add.1); the *Holy See* (A/9134/Add.2), the *Ukrainian Soviet Socialist Republic*, the *Netherlands*, the *United States of America*, the *Byelorussian Soviet Socialist Republic*, the *Federal Republic of Germany* and the *Netherlands* (A/C.3/SR.2013).

### *Article III*

27. Article III of the text submitted by the Working Group reads as follows:

"1. No individual or group shall be subjected by any State, institution, group or individual on the ground of religion or belief to any discrimination in the recognition, exercise and enjoyment of human rights and fundamental freedoms.

"2. Everyone has the right to effective remedial relief by the competent national tribunals against any acts violating the rights set forth in this Declaration or any acts of discrimination he may suffer on the grounds of religion or belief [with respect to his fundamental rights and freedoms] [as defined by the constitution or law]."

28. The following amendments to the above mentioned text were submitted:

(a) The *Netherlands* proposed (A/C.3/L.2027) to remove in the second paragraph the first pair of brackets and to delete the following words in the second pair of brackets: "as defined by the constitution or by law".

(b) *New Zealand* proposed (A/C.3/L.2034) to replace in paragraph 2 the words "by the competent national tribunals" by the words "by whatever means may be appropriate".

(c) *Zambia* proposed (A/C.3/L.2038) to add at the end of paragraph 1 the words "subject to the interests of society as a whole".

(d) *Brazil* proposed (A/C.3/L.2043) to add the following new subparagraph 3:

"No individual, group or institution shall practice or disseminate its teachings considered to be detrimental to the nationalistic, cultural, civil, economic, political and social development of the State, nor to use its teachings to interfere in the electoral processes of the State, as defined by the Constitutoin or law of the State."

29. Suggestions and observations relating to article III were made by *India* and *Austria* (A/9134 and A/9135, paragraphs 17 and 21); the *United Kingdom*, the *United States* (A/9134/Add.1); the *Holy See* (A/9134/Add.2); *New Zealand*, *Zambia*, the *Federal Republic of Germany*, the *United States of America*, *Sweden*, the *Byelorussian Soviet Socialist Republic*, the *German Democratic Republic*, the *Philippines* and *Denmark* (A/C.3/SR.2013).

*Article IV*

30. Article IV of the text submitted by the Working Group reads as follows:

"[1.] All States shall take effective measures to prevent and eliminate discrimination based on religion or belief, in the recognition, exercise and enjoyment of human rights and fundamental freedoms in all fields of civil, political, economic, social and cultural life. They should enact or rescind legislation where necessary to prohibit such discrimination and take all appropriate measures to combat those prejudices which lead to religious intolerance."

"[2. Particular efforts shall be made to prevent discrimination based on religion or belief, especially in the fields of civil rights [access to] citizenship and the enjoyment of political rights, such as the right to participate in elections, to hold public office, or in other ways to take part in the government of the country as well as in the field of labour and employment.]"

31. The following amendments to the above mentioned text were submitted:

(a) The *Netherlands* proposed (A/C.3/L.2027) to replace in the second sentence of paragraph 1 the word "should" by "shall" and to delete the second paragraph.

(b) *Morocco* proposed (A/C.3/L.2029) to replace, in paragraph 1 of article IV, the words "religious intolerance" by "intolerance in the matter of religion or belief".

(c) The *Ukrainian SSR* proposed (A/C.3/L.2037) (i) to include the following new paragraph 2 in article IV:

All persons shall be guaranteed equality in all spheres of economic, governmental, cultural, social and political life, irrespective of their religion or other beliefs."

(ii) In the original paragraph 2, which becomes paragraph 3, to replace the words "belief, especially in the fields of civil rights" by "other beliefs in the matter of".

(d) *Zambia* proposed (A/C.3/L.2038) to add at the end of paragraph 2 of article IV the words "so long as the interests of society as a whole are not compromised".

32. Suggestions and observations relating to article IV were made by *Austria* and *Canada* (A/9134 and A/9135, paragraph 21); *Italy*, the *United Kingdom* and the *United States* (A/9134/Add.1); *Bolivia* (A/C.3/SR.2011); *Sweden*, *New Zealand*, the *Byelorussian Soviet Socialist Republic*, *Canada*, *Morocco*, the *United States of America*, *Italy*, *Liberia* and *Venezuela* (A/C.3/SR.2013).

*Article V*

33. Article V of the text submitted by the Working Group reads as follows:

> "[1.] Parents or legal guardians have the right to decide upon the religion or belief in which a child should be brought up. In the case of a child who has been deprived of his parents, their expressed [or presumed] wish shall be duly taken into account, the best interests of the child being the guiding principle. [If the child has reached a sufficient degree of understanding, his wish shall be taken into account.]
>
> "[2. The decision concerning the religion or belief in which a child should be brought up must not be injurious to its interest or health, and must not do him physical or moral harm. The child must be guarded against practices which might inculcate in him any discrimination on account of religion or belief.]

34. The following amendments to the above mentioned text have been submitted:

(a) The *Netherlands* proposed (A/C.3/L.2027) (i) to delete the second sentence of the first paragraph; (ii) to remove the square brackets from the last sentence of the first paragraph; and (iii) to delete paragraph 2.

(b) *Morocco* proposed (A/C.3/L.2029): (i) to replace in the first sentence of paragraph 1 (French version) the word "doit" by "devrait"; (ii) to delete in paragraph 1 everything after the words "duly taken into account".

(c) The *Ukrainian SSR*/proposed (A/C.3/L.2037) to insert the words "until he becomes of full age" after the words "brought up" in the first sentence of article V, paragraph 2.

(d) *Zambia* proposed (A/C.3/L.2038): (i) to delete in paragraph 1 of article V after the word "parent" the word "or" and to insert the following words: "traditional and other social institutions and"; (ii) to delete the second sentence of paragraph 1.

(e) *Brazil* proposed (A/C.3/L.2043): (i) to delete in paragraph 1 everything after the words "duly taken into account"; (ii) to delete the second sentence of paragraph 2.

35. Suggestions and observations concerning article V were made by *Austria*, *Canada*, the *Netherlands*, *Sweden* and the *Ukrainian Soviet Socialist Republic* (A/9134 and A/9135, paras, 26 and 27); *Italy*, the *United Kingdom* and the *United States of America* (A/9134/Add.1); the *Holy See* (A/9134/Add.2); *Morocco* (A/C.3/SR.2010); *Zambia*, the *Ukrainian Soviet Socialist Republic*, *New Zealand*, *Spain*, the *Netherlands*, *Sweden*, the *Federal Republic of Germany*, *Canada*, the *Byelorussian Soviet Socialist Republic*, the *United States of America*, *Italy* and *Morocco* (A/C.3/SR.2013).

### *Article VI*

36. Article VI of the text submitted by the Working Group reads as follows:

> "Every person and every group or community has the right to manifest their religion or belief in public or in private, without being subjected to any discrimination on the grounds of religion or belief; this right includes in particular:
>
> "(a) freedom to worship, to assemble and to establish and maintain places of worship or assembly;
>
> "(b) freedom to teach, to disseminate [at home and abroad], and to learn their religion or belief, and also its sacred languages or traditions;
>
> "(c) freedom to practise their religion or belief by establishing and maintaining charitable and educational institutions and by expressing the implications of religion or belief in public life;
>
> "(d) freedom to observe the rites or customs of their religion or belief."

37. The following amendments to the above-mentioned text were submitted:

(a) The *Netherlands* proposed (A/C.3/L.2027) to delete in subparagraph (b) the words in square brackets "at home and abroad".

(b) *Morocco* proposed (A/C.3/L.2029): (i) to replace subparagraph (a) of article VI by the following: "freedom to practise their religion alone or in a group and to express the implications of their religion or belief in public life"; and (ii) to replace subparagraph (c) by the following: "the freedom of nationals of a country to establish and maintain places of worship or assembly and educational institutions and establishments in the basis of their religion or belief".

(c) The *German Democratic Republic* and *Poland* proposed (A/C.3/L. 2033) to and in article VI, after the words "every person and every group or community has the right" the words "in accordance with domestic law".

(d) *Poland* proposed (A/C.3/L.2036) to delete subparagraph (c) of article VI.

(e) The *Ukrainian Soviet Socialist Republic* proposed (A/C.3/L.2037) to delete article VI.

(f) *Zambia* proposed (A/C.3/L.2038) to insert in article VI, between the words "right" and "includes" the following words: "which is subject to the interests of society as a whole".

(g) *Brazil* proposed (A/C.3/L.2043): (i) in subparagraph (a) to replace the words "freedom to worship" by the words "freedom to practise their beliefs or teachings"; (ii) in subparagraph (b) to delete the words "at home and abroad" in square brackets.

(h) The *Federal Republic of Germany* and the *Philippines* (A/C.3/L. 2044) proposed to add a second paragraph to article VI as follows:

> "Freedom to manifest one's religion or beliefs may be subject only to such limitations as are prescribed by law and are necessary to protect public safety, order, health, or morals or the fundamental rights and freedoms of others."

38. Suggestions and observations concerning article VI were made by *Austria, India,* the *Netherlands,* the *Philippines* and *Sweden* (A/9134 and A/9135, para. 30); the *United Kingdom,* the *United States of America* (A/9134/Add.1); the *Holy See* (A/9134/Add.2); *Brazil* and *Morocco* (A/C.3/ SR.2010); the *Ukrainian Soviet Socialist Republic, Pakistan, Zambia, Morocco, New Zealand, Sweden,* the *German Democratic Republic,* the *Federal Republic of Germany,* and the *United States of America* (A/C.3/SR.2013).

*Additional articles*

39. The following additional articles to the text prepared by the Working Group were proposed:

(a) The *Netherlands* Proposed (A/C.3/L.2027) to add the following articles to the text prepared by the Working Group:

"*Article VII*

"Religious congregations have the right to train ministers and teachers and to have contacts with communities and institutions belonging to the same religion or belief both within the country and abroad.

"*Article VIII*

"Neither the establishment of a religion or belief nor the recognition of a religion or belief by a State nor the separation of religion or belief from the State shall by itself be considerd discrimination on the ground of religion or belief.

"*Article IX*

"Governments, organizations and private persons shall strive to promote through education, as well as by other means, understanding, tolerance and respect in matters relating to freedom of religion and belief. Freedom of religious and non-religious belief shall not be used for purposes of kindling hatred between peoples and different religious and national groups."

(b) The *German Democratic Republic* and *Poland* proposed (A/C.3/L. 2032) to add the words "in accordance with domestic law" after the words "Religious congregations" in article VII of the amendments submitted by the Netherlands in document A/C.3/L.2027.

(c) *Morocco* proposed (A/C.3/L.2028) to add the following new paragraph to article IX of the amendments submitted by the Netherlands in document A/C.3/L.2027:

"No Government, organization or individual shall be entitled to use religion or belief as a pretext for interfering in the internal affairs of a State."

(d) The *Philippines* proposed (A/C.3/L.2039) to add a new article X to the text submitted by the Netherlands in document A/C.3/L.2027 as follows:

"The rights granted to individuals and groups to the full exercise of their religions or beliefs impose upon them the correlative duty to exercise these rights with due regard for the rights of other individuals and groups and the peace and security of the State."

(e) *Morocco* proposed (A/C.3/L.2046) as amendments to the amendment submitted by the Philippines in document A/C.3/L.2039: (i) to replace the word "granted" by the words "that the State shall guarantee"; (ii) to replace the words "impose upon them the correlative" by the words "shall impose upon them the"; (iii) to delete the last part of the sentence starting with the words "with due regard for ..." and replace it by the following: "in a spirit of tolerance towards the religions or beliefs of other individuals and groups".

(f) The *Union of Soviet Socialist Republics* proposed (A/C.3/L.2035) to include the following provisions in the text prepared by the Working Group:

> "States shall be required to respect and guarantee freedom of atheistic beliefs, including the right to express such beliefs;
>
> "It is forbidden to make use of freedom of religious belief for purposes which threaten the security of society or to engage, under the guise of presenting religious teachings or conducting religious services, in activities which cause injury to health or other impairment of the personality or rights of citizens, which cause citizens to refuse to perform public activities or civic duties, and which cause the involvement of minors in the aforesaid activities;
>
> "It is recognized that, if complete freedom of conscience is to be ensured, all churches and religious teachings and movements must be equal before the law, no single church, teaching or religious organization being accorded privileges of any kind and no single church or teaching having a dominant position;
>
> "It is forbidden to make use of religious creeds or beliefs in order to prejudice the interests of strengthening universal peace and security or friendship and co-operation between peoples and States;
>
> "All acts whose purpose or intention is to interfere with the exercise of freedom of religion or worship in conformity with the law are prohibited;
>
> "Freedom of religion or atheistic beliefs shall not be used for purposes of political or electoral campaigns or the kindling of hatred between peoples and different religious and national groups."

40. Suggestions and observations relating to the addition articles proposed by the Netherlands were made by *Sweden* and *Morocco* (A/C.3/SR.2014).

41. Suggestions and observations relating to the addition of other provisions to the text prepared by the Working Group were made by the *Ukrainian Soviet Socialist Republic* (A/9135. para. 31), the *Union of Soviet Socialist Republics* (A/9135. para. 32), the *United States of America* (A/9134/Add.1 and A/9135, para. 33), the *Netherlands* and the *Philippines* (A/9135, para. 51).

*Annex I*

PRELIMINARY DRAFT OF A UNITED NATIONS DECLARATION ON THE ELIMINATION OF ALL FORMS OF RELIGIOUS INTOLERANCE, PREPARED BY THE SUB-COMMISSION ON PREVENTION OF DISCRIMINATION AND PROTECTION OF MINORITIES[a]

[The text of the preamble is reproduced in paragraph 12 of the present working paper]

*Article I*

Discrimination between human beings on the grounds of religion or belief is an offence to human dignity and shall be condemned as a denial of the principles of the Charter of the United Nations, as a violation of the human rights and fundamental freedoms proclaimed in the Universal Declaration of Human Rights and as an obstacle to friendly and peaceful relations among nations.

*Article II*

No States, institution, group or individual shall make any discrimination in matters of human rights and fundamental freedoms in the treatment of persons on the grounds of their religion or their belief.

*Article III*

1. Particular efforts shall be made to prevent discrimination based on religion, especially in the fields of civil rights, access to citizenship and the enjoyment of political rights, such as the right to participate in elections, to hold public office, or in other ways to take part in the Government of his country.

2. Everyone has the right to effective remedial relief by the competent national tribunals against any discrimination he may suffer on the grounds of religion or belief, through acts violating fundamental rights granted him by the constitution or by law.

*Article IV*

Everyone has the right to adhere, or not to adhere, to a religion or belief and to change in accordance with the dictates of his conscience —

---

a *Official Records of the Economic and Social Council, Thirty-seventh Session, Supplement No. 8* (E/3873), para. 294.

without being subjected to any pressure, inducement or undue influence likely to impair his freedom of choice or decision in this matter.

*Article V*

Parents or legal guardians have the right to decide upon the religion or belief in which a child should be brought up. In the case of a child who has been deprived of its parents, the best interests of the child being the guiding principle, their expressed or presumed wish shall be duly taken into account.

*Article VI*

Everyone has the right to comply with what is prescribed by his religion or belief and shall be free to worship, and profess, in public or in private, without suffering any discrimination on account of his religion or belief and specifically:

1. Every person and every group has the right to worship, either alone or together with others, in public or in private, and to maintain houses of worship in accordance with the prescription of their belief.

2. (i) Every individual has the right in association with others, without any limitation based on the number of members, to form and maintain religious communities and institutions.

(ii) Every religious community and institution has the right, in association with similar religious communities and institutions, to form territorial federations on a national, regional or local basis.

3. Everyone has the right to teach and to learn his religion or belief, his sacred language and religious traditions, either in public or in private. No one shall be compelled to receive instruction in a religion or belief contrary to his convictions or, in the case of children, contrary to the wishes of their parents, or legal guardians. All education shall be directed to promote understanding, tolerance and friendship among all religions and beliefs.

4. Every religious group or community has the right to write, to print and to publish religious books and texts and shall be permitted to train the personnel required for the performance of its practices or rites. No religious group or community shall be prevented from bringing teachers from abroad for this purpose. Every religious group or community shall be enabled to have contacts with communities and institutions belonging to the same religion abroad.

5. (i) Everyone has the right to observe the dietary practices prescribed by his religion or belief. Any individual or any religious community shall be permitted to acquire and produce all materials and

objects necessary for the observance of prescribed ritual or practices, including dietary practices.

(ii) Where the State controls the means of production and distribution, it shall help to provide the above-mentioned materials, or the materials and means necessary for their production, to religious communities of the religions concerned and to its members, and if necessary allow them to be imported.

6. Everyone has the right to make pilgrimage to sites held in veneration, whether inside or outside his country, and every State shall grant freedom of access to these places.

7. Equal legal protection shall be accorded to all forms of worship, places of worship and institutions. Similar guarantees shall be accorded to ritual objects, language of worship and sacred books.

8. Due account shall be taken of the prescriptions of each religion or belief relating to holy days and days of rest, and all discrimination in this regard between persons of different religions or beliefs shall be prohibited.

*Article VII*

Everyone shall have the right to have marriage rites performed in accordance with the prescriptions of his religion or belief, and no one shall be compelled to undergo a religious marriage ceremony not in conformity with his convictions. Nothing in this Article shall, however, dispense anyone from the obligations to observe other requirements and formalities laid down by the law regarding marriage.

*Article VIII*

The prescriptions of the religion of a deceased person shall be followed in all matters affecting burial customs, subject to the wishes, if any, expressed by the deceased during his lifetime, or failing that those of his family.

*Article IX*

Equal legal protection shall be afforded to all cemeteries or other burial place and also to the funeral or memorial rites of all religions or beliefs.

*Article X*

[Religious communities shall have the right to receive the funds necessary for the carrying out of their functions.]

*Article XI*

No one shall be compelled to take an oath of a religious nature contrary to his convictions.

*Article XII*

No State shall discriminate in the granting of subsidies, in taxation or in exemptions from taxation, between different religions or beliefs or their adherents. However, public authorities shall not be precluded from levying general taxes or from contributing funds for the preservation of religious structures recognized as monuments of historic or artistic value.

*Article XIII*

1. The freedoms and rights set out in articles I, II, III, IV, V and XI shall not be subject to any restrictions.

2. The freedoms and rights set out elsewhere in this Declaration shall be subject only to the restrictions prescribed by law solely for the purpose of securing due recognition and respect for the rights and freedoms of others and of meeting the legitimate requirements of morality, health, public order and the general welfare in a democratic society. Any restrictions which may be imposed shall be consistent with the purposes and principles of the United Nations and with the rights and freedoms stated in the Universal Declaration of Human Rights. These freedoms and rights may in no case be exercised contrary to the purposes and principles of the United Nations.

*Article XIV*

1. All acts directed or intended to prevent or to restrict the freedom of religion or cult shall be prohibited.

2. All incitements to hatred or acts of violence, whether by individuals or organizations against any religious group of persons belonging to a religious community, shall be considered an offence against society and punishable by law and all propaganda designed to foster or justify it, shall be condemned.

3. In order to put into effect the purposes and principles of the present declaration, all States shall take immediate and positive measures, including legislative and other measures, to prosecute and/or declare illegal organizations which promote and incite to religious discrimination

or incite to, or use violence for purposes of discrimination based on religion.

4. The United Nations, the specialized agencies, Member States and non-governmental organizations shall do all in their power to promote energetic action, through research, education, information and appropriate legislation, with a view to hastening the elimination of all forms of religious discrimination and intolerance.

*Annex II*

## REPORT OF THE WORKING GROUP SET UP BY THE COMMISSION ON HUMAN RIGHTS AT ITS TWENTIETH SESSION TO PREPARE A DRAFT DECLARATION ON THE ELIMINATION OF ALL FORMS OF RELIGIOUS INTOLERANCE[a]

... The Working Group was instructed by the Commission to prepare a draft declaration on the elimination of all forms of religious intolerance, using as a basis for its discussion the text submitted by the Sub-Commission on Prevention of Discrimination and Protection of Minorities (E/CN.4/873, para. 142).

There was no disagreement in the Working Group that the declaration should protect equally the right to adhere to any religion and the right to maintain any non-religious belief. Certain members felt, however, that the text of the draft declaration submitted by the Sub-Commission (E/CN.4/873, para. 142), which used the words "religion or belief", did not adequately cover the notion of non-religious beliefs, particularly "atheism". They would like to have the draft declaration spell out clearly and categorically the right to non-religious beliefs, including "atheism" and to this end proposed that a definition along those lines should be inserted before article I. On the other hand, several members felt that it was unnecessary to define the terms "religion" and "belief" since they were terms whose meanings were well understood in United Nations usage. However, a number of members were prepared to co-operate in drafting a definition if one was deemed essential. The Working Group [agreed to leave the question of a definition to the Commission and decided to transmit to the Commission the following suggested definitions:

(*a*) *Austria*: ["For the purpose of this Declaration the term 'belief' is understood as expression for the various theistic creeds or such other beliefs as agnosticism, free thought, atheism and rationalism."]

(*b*) *Ukrainian SSR*: ["In this Declaration the term 'religion or belief' means both religious beliefs and atheistic convictions."]

(*c*) *United Kingdom*: ["In this Declaration the term 'belief' includes both religious and non-religious beliefs."]]

The Working Group was not able to take into consideration more than the first six articles of the text submitted by the Sub-Commission (E/CN. 4/873, para. 142) in relation to which it prepared the draft provisions set forth below. The words in square brackets are those on which no agreement was reached in the Working Group. The words "religion or belief" which appear throughout the Working Group's text are provisional

---

a *Official Records of the Economic and Social Council, Thirty-seventh Session, Supplement No. 8* (E/3873), para. 296.

only, and their final form will depend on the Commission's decision on the question of a definition mentioned above.

*Text of the articles as prepared by the working group*

[For texts of articles I to V see paragraphs 21, 24, 27, 30 and 33 of this working paper]

*Article VI*[b]

Every person and every group or community has the right to manifest their religion or belief in public or in private, without being subjected to any discrimination on the grounds of religion or belief; this right includes in particular:

(*a*) Freedom to worship, to assemble and to establish and maintain places of worship or assembly;

(*b*) Freedom to teach, to disseminate [at home and abroad], and to learn their religion or belief, and also its sacred languages or traditions;

(*c*) Freedom to practise their religion or belief by establishing and maintaining charitable and educational institutions and by expressing the implications of religion or belief in public life;

(*d*) Freedom to observe the rites or customs of their religion or belief.

*Annex*

The following proposals submitted to the working group could not be discussed because of lack of time:

1. *Ukrainian SSR* – proposal for a new article:

"1. In order to ensure full freedom of conscience, the Church is [shall be] separated from the State and the School from the Church.

---

b The inclusion of this article was agreed upon by all members of the Working Group. The representative of the United States of America felt, however, that the text failed to reflect all of the points covered in the original text of article VI, as transmitted by the Sub-Commission, and that it needed completing with the further provisions proposed by his delegation and appearing in the annex.

"2. All churches, religious creeds and movements are equal before the law. No church, creed or religious organization is or may be the object of any privileges or restrictions in their activities. The domination, whether in name or in fact, of a particular church or creed shall be eliminated.

2. *Union of Soviet Socialist Republics*

(*a*) Proposal for a new preambular paragraph as follows:

"*Considering* that freedom of atheistic beliefs is of the utmost importance to those who profess them, and that freedom of those beliefs, including the right to express them, should therefore be respected and guaranteed.

(*b*) Proposal for a new article:

"Freedom of religious and non-religious belief, and the rights and duties of persons of different beliefs, shall not be used for purposes of political or electoral campaigns or the kindling of hatred between peoples and different religious and national groups."

(*c*) Proposal for a new article:

"No religious creed or belief of any kind shall in any circumstances be used in order to prejudice the interests of strengthening universal peace and security or friendship and co-operation between peoples and States.

3. *United States of America* — proposal for new articles to follow after article VI:

"*I*

"Everyone, alone or in association with others, shall be free to comply with the tenets of his religion or belief, to observe its rituals, dietary and other practices, and to produce the objects, foods and other articles and facilities customarily used in its observances and practices, with freedom to import such articles from abroad if necessary. Where the State controls the means of production and distribution, it shall make these articles and foods available or provide the means for their purchase or production.

"*II*

"Everyone shall be free to observe the Holy Days associated with his religion or belief. Everyone shall have the right to make pilgrimages and other journeys in connexion with his religion or belief, whether inside or outside his country, and free access shall be granted to all Holy Places.

"*III*

"Every individual and religious group has the right to legal protection for its places of worship, for its rites, ceremonies, and activities, and for the burial places associated with its religion or belief.

"*IV*

"Every person and every group, in accordance with his religion or belief, shall have the right to organize and maintain local, regional, national and international associations in connexion with their activities. Everyone shall have the right to communicate with and visit his co-religionists and believers, whether individuals or organizations at home and abroad."

---

UNITED NATIONS

GENERAL ASSEMBLY

A/10148
25 July 1975
Original: ENGLISH

Thirtieth session
Item 80 of the provisional agenda*

ELIMINATION OF ALL FORMS OF RELIGIOUS INTOLERANCE

*Note by the Secretary-General*

## I. DRAFT DECLARATION ON THE ELIMINATION OF ALL FORMS OF RELIGIOUS INTOLERANCE

### A. *Action by the General Assembly*

1. In resolution 3267 (XXIX) of 10 December 1974, the General Assembly requested the Secretary-General to transmit to the Commission on Human Rights all the opinions expressed and suggestions put forward in the course of the discussion of the question at the twenty-ninth session of the General Assembly; also requested the Commission on Human Rights to submit, through the Economic and Social Council, to the General Assembly at its thirtieth session a single draft Declaration on the Elimination of All Forms of Intolerance and of Discrimination Based on Religion or Belief; and decided to include in the provisional agenda of its thirtieth session the item entitled "Elimination of all forms of religious intolerance" with a view to assessing progress on the elaboration of a Declaration on the Elimination of All Forms of Intolerance and of Discrimination Based on Religion or Belief and to considering, completing and adopting, if possible, the Declaration, provided a single draft was completed by the Commission on Human Rights.

### B. *Action by the Commission on Human Rights*

2. The Commission on Human Rights considered the question at its thirty-first session, held at Geneva from 5 February to 5 March 1975. The Commission had before it: (a) a report of the Secretary-General (A/9134 and Add.1 and 2) containing the observations submitted by Governments pursu-

* A/10150.

ant to General Assembly resolution 3027 (XXVII) of 18 December 1972; (*b*) a note by the Secretary-General (A/9135) containing an analytical presentation of the observations in document A/9134; (*c*) the summary records of the 2006th and 2009th to 2014th meetings of the Third Committee of the General Assembly at its twenty-eighth session; (*d*) the summary records of the 2091st to 2096th meetings of the Third Committee of the General Assembly at its twenty-ninth session (A/C.3/SR.2091-2096) and the record of the 2311th meeting of the General Assembly (A/PV.2311); (*e*) the report of the Third Committee on the question to the General Assembly at its twenty-ninth session (A/9893); (*f*) a working paper prepared by the Secretariat (E/CN.4/1145) indicating the present state of consideration of the texts which the General Assembly, at its twenty-eighth session, took as a basis for discussion of a draft Declaration on the Elimination of All Forms of Religious Intolerance; and (*g*) a report of the Secretary-General (E/CN.4/1146 and Add.1-3) containing the replies received from Governments in compliance with General Assembly resolution 3069 (XXVIII).

3. At its 1293rd meeting, the Commission set up an informal Working Group open to all members of the Commission to continue the consideration of a draft Declaration on the Elimination of All Forms of Intolerance and Discrimination based on Religion and Belief. The informal Working Group considered paragraphs 2 to 9 of the preamble of a draft declaration based on the text submitted by the representative of the Byelorussian Soviet Socialist Republic to the Commission at its thirtieth session (E/5464, para. 57) and a text proposed by the Netherlands (E/CN.4/L.1289/Add.1). The Working Group adopted provisionally the second, third, fourth, sixth, seventh and eighth paragraphs of the preamble of a draft declaration (E/5635, paras. 169-176). The Commission decided to request the Economic and Social Council to inform the General Assembly that, although the Commission had made some progress, it had not completed its work on the draft declaration and that it intended to accord priority to the drafting of the declaration at its next session.

### C. *Action by the Economic and Social Council*

4. The Economic and Social Council considered the matter at its fifty-eighth session. At its 1948th plenary meeting, held on 6 May 1975, the Council decided to transmit to the General Assembly the above-mentioned information furnished by the Commission on Human Rights.

## II. DRAFT INTERNATIONAL CONVENTION ON THE ELIMINATION OF ALL FORMS OF INTOLERANCE AND OF DISCRIMINATION BASED ON RELIGION OR BELIEF

5. In resolution 3027 (XXVII) of 18 December 1972, the General Assembly decided to accord priority to the completion of the Declaration on the Elimination of All Forms of Religious Intolerance before resuming consideration of the draft International Convention on this subject.

6. In a note submitted to the General Assembly at its twenty-sixth session (A/8330),[1] the Secretary-General gave an account of previous consideration of the question by United Nations organs. The note contains in paragraphs 16 to 21 details of the action taken by the Assembly when it last considered this item at its twenty-second session, and, as annexes, the following texts relating to a draft international convention on the subject:

> Preamble and 12 articles of the draft Internation Convention on the Elimination of All Forms of Religious Intolerance, adopted by the Commission on Human Rights at its twenty-first, twenty-second and twenty-third sessions (annex III);
>
> Additional draft article submitted by Jamaica to the Commission on Human Rights (annex IV);
>
> Draft article XIII submitted by the Sub-Commission on Prevention of Discrimination and Protection of Minorities to the Commission on Human Rights (annex V);
>
> Preliminary draft on additional measures of implementation transmitted to the Commission on Human Rights by the Sub-Commission on Prevention of Discrimination and Protection of Minorities (annex VI).

---

[1] In compliance with General Assembly resolution 2836 (XXVI) of 17 December 1971 on publications and documentation of the United Nations, the material contained in document A/8330 is not reproduced in the present report. Copies of that document will be available upon request.

UNITED NATIONS

ECONOMIC
AND
SOCIAL COUNCIL

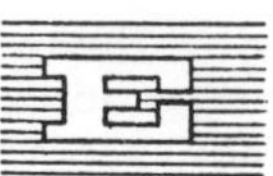

E/CN.4/NGO/181
27 February 1974
Original: ENGLISH

COMMISSION ON HUMAN RIGHTS
Thirtieth session

## THE ROLE OF YOUTH AND THE QUESTION OF CONSCIENTIOUS OBJECTION TO MILITARY SERVICE

*Statement dated 26 February 1974 submitted by Amnesty International, Commission of the Churches on International Affairs, Co-ordinating Board of Jewish Organizations, Friends World Committee for Consultation, International Catholic Child Bureau, International Commission of Jurists, International Confederation of Catholic Charities, International Movement for Fraternal Union among Races and Peoples, Pax Romana—International Movement of Catholic Students and Graduates, Women's International League for Peace and Freedom and World Conference of Religion for Peace, non-governmental organizations in category II consultative status*[1]

The non-governmental organizations listed above, representing various tendencies, unite in supporting further study and eventual acceptance of conscientious objection to military service in the context of a basic human right.

While, in general, it is young people who are most directly concerned with the question, their elders have an over-arching concern since it is their decisions which institute compulsory conscription during peacetime and wartime. It is the obedience of youth that is abused in carrying out the anti-human excesses that accompany modern wars.

Again and again, international youth organizations have raised their voices at United Nations bodies for the implementation of the Universal Declaration of Human Rights and for the recognition of the rights of conscience that flow from Article 18 of the Declaration. During the Seminar on Youth in the Promotion and Protection of Human Rights held in Belgrade in June 1970, some participants vigorously advocated the recognition of the right of conscientious objection.

[1] Circulated in accordance with paragraphs 29 and 30 of Economic and Social Council resolution 1296 (XLIV).

These young people see their rejection of militarism and war as their action towards the disarmament so needed by the world community. They see this rejection as a positive step allowing their energies and resources (and hopefully the energies and resources of the world's nations) to be utilized in works of peace, of development, of combating poverty and of saving the environment.

This Commission hardly needs to be reminded that besides the statements made by youth organizations, bodies representing large segments of the human community have made declarations in favour of recognizing objection to military service as a human right and the need for alternative civilian service. Recent declarations include: the 1965 declaration of the Catholic Bishops of the world at the Second Vatican Council in Rome; the 1968 declaration of the World Council of Churches at Uppsala; the 1970 declaration of the ten major living world religions at the World Conference of Religion for Peace in Kyoto.

In 1968, a humanist group marked United Nations International Human Rights Year by conducting a World Appeal for the Recognition of Conscientious Objection as a Human Right. The 40,000 signatures collected in 27 countries by this organization, War Resisters International, are lodged in the storage facilities of the United Nations.

The question did receive attention at the General Assembly on 11 November 1970, when through the Economic and Social Council, document A/C.3/L.1766/Rev.3 was transmitted to this Commission. Among its recommendations for the fulfilling of youth's "hope and aspirations for bringing about universal peace" was the following:

> "Not to conscript arbitrarily any youth to join the armed forces of his country if such youth conscientiously objects to being involved in war."

The question of conscientious objection was given consideration in the context of human rights at the World Congress of Peace forces held in Moscow in October 1973. The report issued by the Social Progress and Human Rights Commission stated, "Consideration was given to the right of conscientious objection especially with respect to a particular war which is considered unjust by a person subject to conscription." The subsequent document on the entire Congress declared, "The right to life is equally tied to the right to refuse to kill."

Certain considerations regarding conscientious objection are of special concern within the purview of a United Nations body.

1. It is encouraging to NGO's that many member States which do not have compulsory military service have *not* opted out of this discussion because they see the importance of the human rights aspect of the matter. There is the added concern that compulsory military service could be instituted almost instantaneously in the case of hostilities and the experience of other member States in this matter would be valuable.

2. The constitutions of many nations assert a duty on the part of citizens to defend the nation especially in time of national danger. Study of these constitutions reveals that the clauses in which this duty is expressed are of an exhorting rather than a formally binding nature. In fact, five countries whose constitutions enjoin compulsory conscription do not have it at all. The phrases exhorting citizens to defend the nation rarely make explicit the means to be used. The person who cannot in conscience kill or injure another human being can answer the call of his country by other than military means. The representative of the International Commission of Jurists* who spoke before the twenty-ninth session of this Commission made the point that "A constitutional provision requiring *all citizens* to defend the country should prove no barrier to the legal recognition of conscientious objection any more than it requires universal conscription or that women and children be placed on a battle front in war."

3. Many developing nations requiring military service deploy recruits in national service tasks of civic betterment. One of the countries replying to the Secretary-General's Report on this subject (E/CN.4/1118) defined its national defence in terms of "combating underdevelopment" and has introduced "a new form of national service known as 'national service outside the armed forces'" to provide for conscientious objectors. Thus developing countries can allow objectors to perform tasks of national importance without military insignia or weaponry.

4. In urging national communities and the international community to respect and recognize the conscience of those who object to military service, there is no intention to impugn the consciences of those who hold that military service is a sacred duty, nor to belittle the immense sacrifices made by soldiers in defence of their countries.

5. The urging of recognition of conscientious objection as a human right and an invitation by the international community to individual states to take steps towards this recognition cannot be construed as a denial of national sovereignty—any more than the Universal Declaration of Human Rights can be so construed.

6. The suffering borne by some conscientious objectors is now honoured as military heroism has heretofore been honoured. Examples include Franz Jägerstätter, Austrian peasant beheaded for refusing to take any part in Hitler's war; the young Europeans who resisted service in Algeria; the young people who claimed their right of conscience under the law in refusing participation in what they considered an unjust conflict in Viet-Nam, and the young Europeans who

---

* *THE REVIEW*, International Commission of Jurists for December 1972 contains an updated study entitled "Conscientious Objection to Military Service as a Human Right".

are choosing exile by the tens of thousands rather than be recruited for colonial actions in two parts of Africa. It has been pointed out that conscientious objectors make real contributions to liberation movements by their refusal to serve in colonial forces. In other cases, young people who opt out of all modern war because of the possibility of the nuclear cremation of millions of human beings, are often treated punitively. The willingness to recognize the objector to colonial wars and wars of aggression harks back to the ancient tradition of the just war. It is a tenable assumption, however, that no war can be just in the nuclear age when a just cause can be vitiated by anti-human and genocidal weaponry. In just war thinking, it is the nation that decides if its cause is just, and no nation, according to its own account, ever conscripts soldiers to fight anything but a just war. Thus the decision to serve or object can only rest with the human being called upon to take part in military service or war.

7. Some have expressed the view that exempting the conscientious objector from military service creates a privilege entailing discriminatory treatment of others. All that any nation can require is a person's service and commitment. Both the military recruit and the objector performing other national service give equally of their time and energy. Whatever discrimination may seem to exist in comparative hazards or hardships would have its counterpart in society and in the military itself, where frontline service is more hazardous than necessary support services. In certain cases, where objectors are involved in medical terms and anti-epidemic service, the hazards they face are no less than those of the military recruit and are possibly more acute.

8. The twenty-fifth Anniversary of the Universal Declaration of Human Rights was an occasion for the reiteration of the importance of this epochal document in human history. Many people, especially the young who form by far the largest constituency of the United Nations, are unwilling to accept the triumphal proclamation of ideals unless there is concrete activity to realize and implement these ideals. One humble, concrete step to realize and implement the Declaration of Human Rights would be the recognition of conscientious objection to military service as a human right.

*Note* — A recent report by War Resisters International (publishers of *CONSCRIPTION: A WORLD SURVEY*) indicates that among the 85 countries where there is compulsory military service, 25 guarantee the right to conscientious objection and 12 others have administrative regulations relating to this question. *In 49 countries which do not recognize conscientious objection, recent cases have caused the question to be raised.* Sixty-seven countries do not have conscription.

---

# HUMAN RIGHTS
# INTERNATIONAL INSTRUMENTS

## Signatures, Ratifications, Accessions, etc.
## 1 January 1978

**UNITED NATIONS**
**New York, 1978**

# HUMAN RIGHTS
# INTERNATIONAL INSTRUMENTS

## Signatures, Ratifications, Accessions, etc.
## 1 January 1978

### NOTE

The information in the present chart has been extracted from the publication *Multilateral Treaties in respect of which the Secretary-General Performs Depositary Functions, List of Signatures, Ratifications, Accessions, etc., as at 31 December 1976* (ST/LEG/SER.D/10; United Nations publication, Sales No. E.77.V.7) prepared by the Office of Legal Affairs of the Secretariat and brought up to date as at 1 January 1978.

ST/HR/4

| States | (1) International Covenant on Economic, Social and Cultural Rights | (2) International Covenant on Civil and Political Rights | (3) Optional Protocol to the International Covenant on Civil and Political Rights | (4) Convention on the Prevention and Punishment of the Crime of Genocide | (5) Convention on the Non-Applicability of Statutory Limitations to War Crimes and Crimes against Humanity | (6) International Convention on the Elimination of All Forms of Racial Discrimination | (7) Convention relating to the Status of Refugees | (8) Protocol relating to the Status of Refugees | (9) Convention relating to the Status of Stateless Persons | (10) Convention on the Reduction of Statelessness | (11) Convention on the Political Rights of Women | (12) Convention on the Nationality of Married Women | (13) Convention on Consent to Marriage, Minimum Age for Marriage and Registration of Marriages | (14) Convention on the International Right of Correction | Slavery Convention of 25 September 1926: (15) Protocol amending Slavery Convention | Slavery Convention of 25 September 1926: (16) Slavery Convention as amended | (17) Supplementary Convention on the Abolition of Slavery, the Slave Trade, and Institutions and Practices Similar to Slavery | (18) Convention for the Suppression of the Traffic in Persons and of the Exploitation of the Prostitution of Others | (19) International Convention on the Suppression and Punishment of the Crime of Apartheid | States |
|---|---|---|---|---|---|---|---|---|---|---|---|---|---|---|---|---|---|---|---|---|
| Entry into force | 3 January 1976 | 23 March 1976 | 23 March 1976 | 12 January 1951 | 11 November 1970 | 4 January 1969 | 22 April 1954 | 4 October 1967 | 6 June 1960 | 13 December 1975 | 7 July 1954 | 11 August 1958 | 9 December 1964 | 24 August 1962 | 7 December 1953 | 7 July 1955 | 30 April 1957 | 25 July 1951 | 18 July 1976 | Entry into force |
| Afghanistan | | | | x | | | | | | | x | | | | x | x | x | | | Afghanistan |
| Albania | | | | x | x | | | | | | x | x | | | | x | x | x | | Albania |
| Algeria | s | s | | x | | x | x | x | x | | | | | | | x | x | x | s | Algeria |
| Angola | | | | | | | | | | | | | | | | | | | | Angola |
| Argentina | s | s | | x | | x | x | x | x | | x | x | x | s | | | x | x | s | Argentina |
| Australia | x | s | | x | | x | x | x | x | x | x | x | | | x | x | x | | | Australia |
| Austria | s | s | s | x | | x | x | x | | x | x | x | x | | x | x | x | | | Austria |
| Bahamas | | | | x | | x | | | | | x | x | | | x | x | x | | | Bahamas |
| Bahrain | | | | | | | | | | | | | | | | | | | | Bahrain |
| Bangladesh | | | | | | | | | | | | | | | | | | | | Bangladesh |
| Barbados | x | x | x | | | x | | | x | | x | | | | x | x | x | | | Barbados |
| Belgium | s | s | | x | | x | x | x | x | | x | s | | | x | x | x | x | | Belgium |
| Benin | | | | | | s | x | x | | | | | x | | | | | | x | Benin |
| Bhutan | | | | | | s | | | | | | | | | | | | | | Bhutan |
| Bolivia | | | | s | | x | | | | | x | | | | | | | | | Bolivia |
| Botswana | | | | | | x | x | x | x | | | | | | | | | | | Botswana |
| Brazil | | | | x | | x | x | x | s | | x | x | x | | | x | x | x | | Brazil |
| Bulgaria | x | x | | x | x | x | | | | | x | x | | | | | x | x | x | Bulgaria |
| Burma | | | | x | | | | | | | s | | | | x | x | | s | | Burma |
| Burundi | | | | | | x | x | x | | | | | | | | | | | | Burundi |
| Byelorussian SSR | x | x | | x | x | x | | | | | x | x | | | | x | x | x | x | Byelorussian SSR |
| Canada | x | x | x | x | | x | x | x | | | x | x | | | x | x | x | | | Canada |
| Cape Verde | | | | | | | | | | | | | | | | | | | | Cape Verde |
| Central African Empire | | | | | | x | x | x | | | x | | | | | | x | | | Central African Empire |
| Chad | | | | | | x | | | | | | | | | | | | | x | Chad |

| States | (1) International Covenant on Economic, Social and Cultural Rights | (2) International Covenant on Civil and Political Rights | (3) Optional Protocol to the International Covenant on Civil and Political Rights | (4) Convention on the Prevention and Punishment of the Crime of Genocide | (5) Convention on the Non-Applicability of Statutory Limitations to War Crimes and Crimes against Humanity | (6) International Convention on the Elimination of All Forms of Racial Discrimination | (7) Convention relating to the Status of Refugees | (8) Protocol relating to the Status of Refugees | (9) Convention relating to the Status of Stateless Persons | (10) Convention on the Reduction of Statelessness | (11) Convention on the Political Rights of Women | (12) Convention on the Nationality of Married Women | (13) Convention on Consent to Marriage, Minimum Age for Marriage and Registration of Marriages | (14) Convention on the International Right of Correction | Slavery Convention of 25 September 1926: (15) Protocol amending Slavery Convention | Slavery Convention of 25 September 1926: (16) Slavery Convention as amended | (17) Supplementary Convention on the Abolition of Slavery, the Slave Trade, and Institutions and Practices Similar to Slavery | (18) Convention for the Suppression of the Traffic in Persons and of the Exploitation of the Prostitution of Others | (19) International Convention on the Suppression and Punishment of the Crime of Apartheid | States |
|---|---|---|---|---|---|---|---|---|---|---|---|---|---|---|---|---|---|---|---|---|
| Chile | x | x | | x | | x | x | x | | | x | s | s | s | | | | | | Chile |
| China[a] | | | | | | | | | | | | | | | | | | | | China[a] |
| Colombia | x | x | x | x | | s | x | | s | | | s | | | | | | | | Colombia |
| Comoros | | | | | | | | | | | | | | | | | | | | Comoros |
| Congo | | | | | | | x | x | | | x | | | | | | x̲ | x̲ | | Congo |
| Costa Rica | x | x | x | x | | x | | | x̲ | x̲ | x | | | | | | | | | Costa Rica |
| Cuba | | | | x | x | x | | | | | x | x | x | x | x | x | x | x | x̲ | Cuba |
| Cyprus | x | x | s | | | x | x | x | | | x | x | | x | | | x | | | Cyprus |
| Czechoslovakia | x | x | | x | x | x | | | | | x | x | x | | | | x | x | x | Czechoslovakia |
| Democratic Kampuchea | | | | x | | s | | | | | | | | | | | x | | | Democratic Kampuchea |
| Democratic People's Republic of Korea | | | | | | | | | | | | | | | | | | | | Democratic People's Republic of Korea |
| [Democratic Republic of Viet-Nam][b] | | | | | | | | | | | | | | | | | | | | [Democratic Republic of Viet Nam][b] |
| Democratic Yemen | | | | | | x | | | | | | | | | | | | | s | Democratic Yemen |
| Denmark | x | xd | x | x | | x | x̲ | x | x | x̲ | x | x | x | | x | x | x | s | | Denmark |
| Djibouti | | | | | | | x̲ | x̲ | | | | | | | | | | | | Djibouti |
| Dominican Republic | | | | s | | | | | | s | x | x | x | | | | x | | | Dominican Republic |
| Ecuador | x | x | x | x | | x | x | x | x | | x | x | | s | x | x | x | s | x | Ecuador |
| Egypt | s | s | | x | | x | | | | | | | | x | x | x | x | x | x̲ | Egypt |
| El Salvador | s | s | s | x | | | | | s | | s | | | x | · | | s | | | El Salvador |
| Equatorial Guinea | | | | | | | | | | | | | | | | | | | | Equatorial Guinea |
| Ethiopia | | | | x | | x | x | x | | | x | | | x | | x | x | | | Ethiopia |
| Fiji | | | | x | | x | x | x | x | | x | x | x | | x | x | x | | | Fiji |
| Finland | x | xd | x | x | | x | x | x | x | | x | x | x | | x | x | x | x | | Finland |
| France | | | | x | | x | x | x | x | s | x | | s | x | x | x | x | x | | France |
| Gabon | | | | | | s | x | x | | | x | | | | | | | | | Gabon |
| Gambia | | | | | | | x | x | | | | | | | | | | | | Gambia |
| German Democratic Republic | x | x | | x | x | x | | | | | x | x | x | | x | x | x | x | x | German Democratic Republic |
| Germany, Federal Republic of | x | xd | | x | | x | x | x | x | x̲ | x | x | x | | x | x | x | | | Germany, Federal Republic of |
| Ghana | | | | x | | x | x | x | | | x | x | | | | | x | | | Ghana |
| Greece | | | | x | | x | x | x | x | | x | | s | | x | x | x | | | Greece |
| Grenada | | | | | | | | | | | | | | | | | | | | Grenada |
| Guatemala | | | | x | | s | | | s | | x | x | | x | | | s | | | Guatemala |
| Guinea | s | s | s | | x | x̲ | x | x | x | | s | s | s | s | x | x | x̲ | x | x | Guinea |
| Guinea-Bissau | | | | | | | x | x | | | | | | | | | | | | Guinea-Bissau |

| States | (1) International Covenant on Economic, Social and Cultural Rights | (2) International Covenant on Civil and Political Rights | (3) Optional Protocol to the International Covenant on Civil and Political Rights | (4) Convention on the Prevention and Punishment of the Crime of Genocide | (5) Convention on the Non-Applicability of Statutory Limitations to War Crimes and Crimes against Humanity | (6) International Convention on the Elimination of All Forms of Racial Discrimination | (7) Convention relating to the Status of Refugees | (8) Protocol relating to the Status of Refugees | (9) Convention relating to the Status of Stateless Persons | (10) Convention on the Reduction of Statelessness | (11) Convention on the Political Rights of Women | (12) Convention on the Nationality of Married Women | (13) Convention on Consent to Marriage, Minimum Age for Marriage and Registration of Marriages | (14) Convention on the International Right of Correction | Slavery Convention of 25 September 1926: (15) Protocol amending Slavery Convention | (16) Slavery Convention as amended | (17) Supplementary Convention on the Abolition of Slavery, the Slave Trade, and Institutions and Practices Similar to Slavery | (18) Convention for the Suppression of the Traffic in Persons and of the Exploitation of the Prostitution of Others | (19) International Convention on the Suppression and Punishment of the Crime of Apartheid | States |
|---|---|---|---|---|---|---|---|---|---|---|---|---|---|---|---|---|---|---|---|---|
| Guyana | <u>x</u> | <u>x</u> | | | | <u>x</u> | | | | | | | | | | | | | <u>x</u> | Guyana |
| Haiti | | | | x | | x | | | | | x | | | | | | x | x | <u>x</u> | Haiti |
| Holy See | | | | | | x | x | x | s | | | | | | | | | | | Holy See |
| Honduras | s | s | s | x | | | | | s | | | | | | | | | s | | Honduras |
| Hungary | x | x | | x | x | x | | | | | x | x | x | | x | x | x | x | x | Hungary |
| Iceland | s | s | | x | | x | x | x | | | x | <u>x</u> | <u>x</u> | | | | x | | | Iceland |
| India | | | | x | x | x | | | | | x | s | | | x | x | x | x | <u>x</u> | India |
| Indonesia | | | | | | | | | | | x | | | | | | | | | Indonesia |
| Iran | x | x | | x | | x | x | x | | | | | | | | | x | s | | Iran |
| Iraq | x | x | | x | | x | | | | | | | | | x | x | x | x | x | Iraq |
| Ireland | s | s | | x | | s | x | x | x | x | x | x | | | x | x | x | | | Ireland |
| Israel | s | s | | x | | s | x | x | x | s | x | x | s | | x | x | x | x | | Israel |
| Italy | s | s | s | x | | x | x | x | x | | x | | s | | x | x | x | | | Italy |
| Ivory Coast | | | | | | x | x | x | | | | | | | | | x | | | Ivory Coast |
| Jamaica | x | x | x | x | | x | x | | | | x | x | | x | | x | x | | <u>x</u> | Jamaica |
| Japan | | | | | | | | | | | x | | | | | | | x | | Japan |
| Jordan | x | x | | x | | x | | | | | | | | | | x | x | x | s | Jordan |
| Kenya | x | x | | | x | | x | | | | | | | | | | | | s | Kenya |
| Kuwait | | | | | | x | | | | | | | | | | x | x | x | <u>x</u> | Kuwait |
| Lao People's Democratic Republic | | | | x | | x | | | | | x | | | | | | x | | | Lao People's Democratic Republic |
| Lebanon | x | x | | x | | x | | | | | x | | | | | | | | | Lebanon |
| Lesotho | | | | x | | x | | | x | | x | x | | | | x | x | | | Lesotho |
| Liberia | s | s | | x | | x | x | | x | | s | | | | x | x | s | s | x | Liberia |
| Libyan Arab Jamahiriya | x | x | | | | x | | | | | | | | | | x | | x | x | Libyan Arab Jamahiriya |
| Liechtenstein | | | | | | | x | x | s | | | | | | | | | | | Liechtenstein |
| Luxembourg | s | s | | | | s | x | x | x | | x | <u>x</u> | | | | | x | s | | Luxembourg |
| Madagascar | x | x | x | | | x | x | | | | x | | | | | x | x | | <u>x</u> | Madagascar |
| Malawi | | | | | | | | | | | x | x | | | | x | x | x | | Malawi |
| Malaysia | | | | | | | | | | | | x | | | | | x | | | Malaysia |
| Maldives | | | | | | | | | | | | | | | | | | | | Maldives |
| Mali | x | x | | x | | x | x | x | | | x | x | x | | x | x | x | x | <u>x</u> | Mali |
| Malta | s | | | | | x | x | x | | | x | x | | | | x | x | | | Malta |
| Mauritania | | | | | | s | | | | | x | | | | | | | | | Mauritania |
| Mauritius | x | x | x | | | x | | | | | x | x | | | | x | x | | | Mauritius |

| States | International Covenant on Economic, Social and Cultural Rights (1) | International Covenant on Civil and Political Rights (2) | Optional Protocol to the International Covenant on Civil and Political Rights (3) | Convention on the Prevention and Punishment of the Crime of Genocide (4) | Convention on the Non-Applicability of Statutory Limitations to War Crimes and Crimes against Humanity (5) | International Convention on the Elimination of All Forms of Racial Discrimination (6) | Convention relating to the Status of Refugees (7) | Protocol relating to the Status of Refugees (8) | Convention relating to the Status of Stateless Persons (9) | Convention on the Reduction of Statelessness (10) | Convention on the Political Rights of Women (11) | Convention on the Nationality of Married Women (12) | Convention on Consent to Marriage, Minimum Age for Marriage and Registration of Marriages (13) | Convention on the International Right of Correction (14) | Slavery Convention of 25 September 1926: Protocol amending Slavery Convention (15) | Slavery Convention of 25 September 1926: Slavery Convention as amended (16) | Supplementary Convention on the Abolition of Slavery, the Slave Trade, and Institutions and Practices Similar to Slavery (17) | Convention for the Suppression of the Traffic in Persons and of the Exploitation of the Prostitution of Others (18) | International Convention on the Suppression and Punishment of the Crime of Apartheid (19) | States |
|---|---|---|---|---|---|---|---|---|---|---|---|---|---|---|---|---|---|---|---|---|
| Mexico | | | | x | s | x | | | | | s | | | | x | x | x | x | | Mexico |
| Monaco | | | | x | | | x | | | | | | | | x | x | | | | Monaco |
| Mongolia | x | x | | x | x | x | | | | | x | | | | | x | x | | x | Mongolia |
| Morocco | s̲ | s̲ | | x | | x | x | x | | | x | | | | x | x | x | x | | Morocco |
| Mozambique | | | | | | | | | | | | | | | | | | | | Mozambique |
| Nauru | | | | | | | | | | | | | | | | | | | | Nauru |
| Nepal | | | | x | | x | | | | | x | | | | | x | x | | x̲ | Nepal |
| Netherlands | s | s | s | x | | x | x | x | x | s | x | x | x | | x | x | x | | | Netherlands |
| New Zealand | s | s | | s | | x | x | x | | | x | x | x | | x | x | x | | | New Zealand |
| Nicaragua | | | | x | | | | | | | x | | | | | | | | | Nicaragua |
| Niger | | | | | | x | x | x | | | x | | x | | x | x | x | x̲ | | Niger |
| Nigeria | | | | | x | x | x | x | | | | | | | | x | x | | x̲ | Nigeria |
| Norway | x | xd | x | x | | x | x | x | x | x | x | x | x | | x | x | x | x | | Norway |
| Oman | | | | | | | | | | | | | | | | | | | s | Oman |
| Pakistan | | | | x | | x | | | | | x | s | | | | x | x | x | | Pakistan |
| Panama | x̲ | x̲ | x̲ | x | | x | | | | | | | | | | | | | x̲ | Panama |
| Papua New Guinea | | | | | | | | | | | | | | | | | | | | Papua New Guinea |
| Paraguay | | | | s | | | x | x | | | s | | | s | | | | | | Paraguay |
| Peru | s̲ | s̲ | s̲ | x | | x | x | | | | x | | | s | | | s | | | Peru |
| Philippines | x | s | s | x | x | x | | | s | | x | | x | | | x | x | x | s | Philippines |
| Poland | x̲ | x̲ | | x | x | x | | | | | x | x | x | | | | x | x | x | Poland |
| Portugal | s | s | | | | | x | x | | | | s | | | | | x | | | Portugal |
| Qatar | | | | | | x | | | | | | | | | | | | | x | Qatar |
| Republic of Korea | | | | x | | | | | x | | x | | | | | | | x | | Republic of Korea |
| [Republic of South Viet-Nam][b] | | | | x | | | | | | | | | | | | x | s | | | [Republic of South Viet-Nam][b] |
| Romania | x | x | | x | x | x | | | | | x | x | s | | x | x | x | x | s | Romania |
| Rwanda | x | x | | x | x | x | | | | | | | | | | | | | s | Rwanda |
| Samoa | | | | | | | | | | | | | x | | | | | | | Samoa |
| San Marino | | | | | | | | | | | | | | | | | x | | | San Marino |
| Sao Tome and Principe | | | | | | | | | | | | | | | | | | | | Sao Tome and Principe |
| Saudi Arabia | | | | x | | | | | | | | | | | | x | x | | | Saudi Arabia |
| Senegal | s | s | s | | | x | x | x | | | x | | | | | | | | x̲ | Senegal |
| Seychelles | | | | | | | | | | | | | | | | | | | | Seychelles |
| Sierra Leone | | | | | | x | | | | | x | x | | x | | x | x | | | Sierra Leone |

| States | (1) International Covenant on Economic, Social and Cultural Rights | (2) International Covenant on Civil and Political Rights | (3) Optional Protocol to the International Covenant on Civil and Political Rights | (4) Convention on the Prevention and Punishment of the Crime of Genocide | (5) Convention on the Non-Applicability of Statutory Limitations to War Crimes and Crimes against Humanity | (6) International Convention on the Elimination of All Forms of Racial Discrimination | (7) Convention relating to the Status of Refugees | (8) Protocol relating to the Status of Refugees | (9) Convention relating to the Status of Stateless Persons | (10) Convention on the Reduction of Statelessness | (11) Convention on the Political Rights of Women | (12) Convention on the Nationality of Married Women | (13) Convention on Consent to Marriage, Minimum Age for Marriage and Registration of Marriages | (14) Convention on the International Right of Correction | Slavery Convention of 25 September 1926: (15) Protocol amending Slavery Convention | Slavery Convention of 25 September 1926: (16) Slavery Convention as amended | (17) Supplementary Convention on the Abolition of Slavery, the Slave Trade, and Institutions and Practices Similar to Slavery | (18) Convention for the Suppression of the Traffic in Persons and of the Exploitation of the Prostitution of Others | (19) International Convention on the Suppression and Punishment of the Crime of Apartheid | States |
|---|---|---|---|---|---|---|---|---|---|---|---|---|---|---|---|---|---|---|---|---|
| Singapore | | | | | | | | | | | | x | | | | | x | x | | Singapore |
| Somalia | | | | | | x | | | | | | | | | | | | | x | Somalia |
| South Africa | | | | | | | | | | | | | | | x | x | | x | | South Africa |
| Spain | x̲ | x̲ | | x | | x | | | | | x | | x | | x | x | x | x | | Spain |
| Sri Lanka | | | | x | | | | | | | | x | s | | | x | x | x | | Sri Lanka |
| Sudan | | | | | | x̲ | x | x | | | | | | | | x | x | | x̲ | Sudan |
| Surinam | x | x | x | | | | | | | | | | | | | | | | | Surinam |
| Swaziland | | | | | | x | | x | | | x | x | | | | | | | | Swaziland |
| Sweden | x | xd | x | x | | x | x | x | x | x | x | x | x | | x | x | x | | | Sweden |
| Switzerland | | | | | | | x | x | x | | | | | | x | x | x | | | Switzerland |
| Syrian Arab Republic | x | x | | x | | x | | | | | | | | | x | x | x | x | x | Syrian Arab Republic |
| Thailand | | | | | | | | | | | x | | | | | | | | | Thailand |
| Togo | | | | | | x | x | x | | | | | | | | | | | | Togo |
| Tonga | | | | x | | x | | | | | | | | | | | | | | Tonga |
| Trinidad and Tobago | | | | | | x | | | x | | x | x | x | | | x | x | | s | Trinidad and Tobago |
| Tunisia | x | x | | x | x | x | x | x | x | | x | x | x | | | x | x | | x̲ | Tunisia |
| Turkey | | | | x | | s | x | x | | | x | | | | x | x | x | | | Turkey |
| Uganda | | | | | | | x | x | x | | | x | | | | x | x | | s | Uganda |
| Ukrainian SSR | x | x | | x | x | x | | | | | x | x | | | | x | x | x | x | Ukrainian SSR |
| Union of Soviet Socialist Republics | x | x | | x | x | x | | | | | x | x | | | | x | x | x | x | Union of Soviet Socialist Republics |
| United Arab Emirates | | | | | | x | | | | | | | | | | | | | x | United Arab Emirates |
| United Kingdom of Great Britain and Northern Ireland | x | xd | | x | | x | x | x | x | x | x | x | x | | x | x | x | | | United Kingdom of Great Britain and Northern Ireland |
| United Republic of Cameroon | | | | | x | x | x | x | | | | | | | | | | | x | United Republic of Cameroon |
| United Republic of Tanzania | x | x | | | | x | x | x | | | x | x | | | | x | x | | x | United Republic of Tanzania |
| United States of America | s̲ | s̲ | | s | | s | | x | | | x | | s | | x | x | x | | | United States of America |
| Upper Volta | | | | x | | x | | | | | | | x | | | | | x | s | Upper Volta |
| Uruguay | x | x | x | x | | x | x | x | | | s | s | | | | | | | | Uruguay |
| Venezuela | s | s | s | x | | x | | | | | | | | | | | | x | | Venezuela |
| Viet Nam[b] | | | | | | | | | | | | | | | | | | | | Viet Nam[b] |
| Yemen | | | | | | | | | | | | | | | | | | | | Yemen |
| Yugoslavia | x | x | | x | x | x | x | x | x | | x | x | x | x | x | x | x | x | x | Yugoslavia |
| Zaire | x | x | x | x | | x | x | x | | | x̲ | | | | | | x | | | Zaire |
| Zambia | | | | | | x | x | x | x | | x | x | | | | x | x | | | Zambia |

| States | (1) International Covenant on Economic, Social and Cultural Rights | (2) International Covenant on Civil and Political Rights | (3) Optional Protocol to the International Covenant on Civil and Political Rights | (4) Convention on the Prevention and Punishment of the Crime of Genocide | (5) Convention on the Non-Applicability of Statutory Limitations to War Crimes and Crimes against Humanity | (6) International Convention on the Elimination of All Forms of Racial Discrimination | (7) Convention relating to the Status of Refugees | (8) Protocol relating to the Status of Refugees | (9) Convention relating to the Status of Stateless Persons | (10) Convention on the Reduction of Statelessness | (11) Convention on the Political Rights of Women | (12) Convention on the Nationality of Married Women | (13) Convention on Consent to Marriage, Minimum Age for Marriage and Registration of Marriages | (14) Convention on the International Right of Correction | Slavery Convention of 25 September 1926: (15) Protocol amending Slavery Convention | Slavery Convention of 25 September 1926: (16) Slavery Convention as amended | (17) Supplementary Convention on the Abolition of Slavery, the Slave Trade, and Institutions and Practices Similar to Slavery | (18) Convention for the Suppression of the Traffic in Persons and of the Exploitation of the Prostitution of Others | (19) International Convention on the Suppression and Punishment of the Crime of Apartheid | States |
|---|---|---|---|---|---|---|---|---|---|---|---|---|---|---|---|---|---|---|---|---|
| TOTAL NUMBER OF STATES PARTIES | 46 | 44 | 16 | 82 | 21 | 97 | 69 | 64 | 32 | 9 | 84 | 52 | 29 | 10 | 44 | 75 | 90 | 45 | 38 | TOTAL NUMBER OF STATES PARTIES |
| Signatures not followed by ratification | 23 | 24 | 11 | 5 | 1 | 12 | 0 | 0 | 8 | 4 | 7 | 8 | 9 | 6 | 0 | 0 | 5 | 7 | 12 | Signatures not followed by ratification |

x Ratification, accession, notification of succession, acceptance or definitive signature.

s Signature not yet followed by ratification.

s x Action taken in 1977.

d Declaration recognizing the competence of the Human Rights Committee under article 41 of the International Covenant on Civil and Political Rights.

a Following on the adoption of resolution 2758 (XXVI) of 25 October 1971 on the lawful rights of the People's Republic of China in the United Nations by the General Assembly, the Minister for Foreign Affairs of the People's Republic of China, by a note addressed to the Secretary-General, received on 29 September 1972, stated:

"1. With regard to the multilateral treaties signed, ratified or acceded to by the defunct Chinese government before the establishment of the People's Republic of China, my Government will examine their contents before making a decision in the light of the circumstances as to whether or not they should be recognized.

"2. As from 1 October, 1949, the day of the founding of the People's Republic of China, the Chiang Kai-shek clique has no right at all to represent China. Its signature and ratification of, or accession to, any multilateral treaties by usurping the name of 'China' are all illegal and null and void. My Government will study these multilateral treaties before making a decision in the light of the circumstances as to whether or not they should be acceded to."

Subsequent to 1 October 1949, and prior to 25 October 1971, the Republic of China: (a) ratified, acceded to or accepted the conventions listed above under the numbers (6), (11), (12), (15), (16) and (17), and (b) signed, but did not ratify the conventions listed under numbers (1), (2), (3) and (13). The convention listed under number (4) was signed on behalf of the Republic of China on 20 July 1949 and an instrument of ratification by the Republic of China was deposited on 19 July 1951. (For further information, see United Nations publication, Sales No. E.77.V.7, note on pages iii and iv and under the conventions concerned.)

b The Democratic Republic of Viet-Nam and the Republic of South Viet-Nam (the latter of which replaced the Republic of Viet-Nam) united on 2 July 1976 to constitute the Socialist Republic of Viet Nam; as at 1 January 1978 the Government of the Socialist Republic of Viet Nam had not indicated its position on the question of succession.

*APPENDIX B*

# PERIODICAL BULLETINS (CONTENTS)

Since early in 1969 a record has been presented by the Division of Human Rights of all the major current United Nations documents relating to human rights. These have been published *in extenso* in a Bulletin issued twice a year. The Contents pages of these Bulletins, up to the end of 1976, are reproduced below. They form a convenient guide to the titles of official documents, as deposited during the last ten years in the United Nations records.

# HUMAN RIGHTS BULLETIN

Issued by the Division of Human Rights

United Nations, New York

Number 1 July 1969

CONTENTS

Page

# HUMAN RIGHTS BULLETIN

Issued by the Division of Human Rights

United Nations, New York

---

Number 2 January 1970

CONTENTS

# HUMAN RIGHTS BULLETIN

**Issued by the Division of Human Rights**

**United Nations, New York**

Number 3 July 1970

[The current issue of the bulletin contains information covering the period from 1 January to 30 June 1970. Meetings of United Nations organs dealing with human rights questions are listed in chronological order].

CONTENTS

Page

HUMAN RIGHTS BULLETIN

**Issued by the Division of Human Rights**

**United Nations, New York**

Number 4 January 1971

[The current issue of the bulletin contains information covering the period from 1 July to 31 December 1970. Meetings of United Nations organs dealing with human rights questions are listed in chronological order].

CONTENTS

# HUMAN RIGHTS BULLETIN

**Issued by the Division of Human Rights**

**United Nations, New York**

Number 5 July 1971

[The current issue of the bulletin contains information covering the period from 1 January to 30 June 1971. Meetings of United Nations organs dealing with human rights questions are listed in chronological order].

CONTENTS

# HUMAN RIGHTS BULLETIN

**Issued by the Division of Human Rights**

**United Nations, New York**

Number 6 January 1972


[The current issue of the bulletin contains information covering the period from 1 July to 31 December 1971. Meetings of United Nations organs dealing with human rights questions are listed in chronological order.]

CONTENTS

# HUMAN RIGHTS BULLETIN

Issued by the **Division of Human Rights**

United Nations, **New York**

Number 7 July 1972


[The current issue of the bulletin contains information covering the period from 1 January to 30 June 1972. Meetings of United Nations organs dealing with human rights questions are listed in chronological order.]

CONTENTS

# HUMAN RIGHTS BULLETIN

Issued by the Division of Human Rights
United Nations, New York

Number 8 January 1973

[The current issue of the bulletin contains information covering the period from 1 July to 31 December 1972. Meetings of United Nations organs dealing with human rights questions are listed in chronological order.]

CONTENTS

# HUMAN RIGHTS BULLETIN

**Issued by the Division of Human Rights**
**United Nations, New York**

Number 9 January - June 1973

[Meetings of United Nations organs dealing with human rights questions are listed in chronological order.]

CONTENTS

**HUMAN RIGHTS BULLETIN**

**Issued by the Division of Human Rights**

**United Nations, New York**

Number 10 July - December 1973

[Meetings of United Nations organs dealing with human rights questions are listed in chronological order.]

CONTENTS

# HUMAN RIGHTS BULLETIN

**Issued by the Division of Human Rights**

**United Nations, New York**

Number 11 January - June 1974


[Meetings of United Nations organs dealing with human rights questions are listed in chronological order.]

CONTENTS

*Page*



* In accordance with decisions taken by the General Assembly at its twenty-seventh (1972) and twenty-eighth (1973) sessions the Division of Human Rights was transferred from United Nations Headquarters to the United Nations Office at Geneva with effect from 15 June 1974. Consequently, the Human Rights Bulletin is now published and distributed at the United Nations Office at Geneva.

Page

# HUMAN RIGHTS BULLETIN

Issued by the Division of Human Rights
United Nations, New York

Number 12 July - December 1974

[Meetings of United Nations organs dealing with human rights questions are listed in chronological order.]

CONTENTS

[1] See Section IV - B.

# HUMAN RIGHTS BULLETIN

**Issued by the Division of Human Rights**
**United Nations, New York**

Number 13 January - June 1975

CONTENTS



---

* Meetings are listed in chronological order.

# HUMAN RIGHTS BULLETIN

**Issued by the Division of Human Rights**

**United Nations, New York**

Number 14 June - December 1975

[Meetings of United Nations organs dealing with human rights questions are listed in chronological order.]

CONTENTS

Page

# HUMAN RIGHTS BULLETIN

**Issued by the Division of Human Rights**

**United Nations, New York**

Number 15 January - June 1976


CONTENTS



* Meetings are listed in chronological order.

*Page*

# HUMAN RIGHTS BULLETIN

Issued by the Division of Human Rights

United Nations, New York

Number 16 July - December 1976


[Meetings of United Nations organs dealing with human rights questions are listed in chronological order.]

CONTENTS